Outlook from Purdue Mountain in the Midstate Alleghenies across Bald Eagle Valley (Courtesy of Dick Brown).

A HISTORY
OF PENNSYLVANIA

Philip S. Klein
Pennsylvania State University

Ari Hoogenboom
Brooklyn College

McGraw-Hill Book Company

New York St. Louis San Francisco Düsseldorf Johannesburg Kuala Lumpur London
Mexico Montreal New Delhi Panama Rio de Janeiro Singapore Sydney Toronto

Library of Congress Cataloging in Publication Data

Klein, Philip Shriver, 1909–
    A history of Pennsylvania.

    Includes bibliographies.
    1. Pennsylvania—History.   I. Hoogenboom, Ari
Arthur, 1927–   II. Title.
F149.K55   917.48′03   72-3991
ISBN 0-07-035037-X
        0-07-035039-6 (text ed.)

A HISTORY
OF PENNSYLVANIA

1234567890KPKP798765432

This book was set in English by University
Graphics, Inc. The editors were Robert P.
Rainier and David Dunham; the designer was
Rolando Morales; and the production super-
visor was Ted Agrillo.
The printer and binder was Kingsport Press,
Inc.

FOR

DOUG

&

LYNN

ARI, JR.

JAN

WHO GREW UP IN PENNSYLVANIA

CONTENTS

PART 2 LABORATORY OF DEMOCRACY: 1763–1861

PART 3 LABORATORY OF INDUSTRIAL SOCIETY: 1861–1900

PART 4 AN AGE OF TRANSPORTATION: 1900 TO THE PRESENT

PREFACE

The need for community is one of the primal forces among living creatures. Community life appears to be a universal phenomenon characterizing all forms of life. The lower forms achieve community life by environmental necessity and by instinct. Man, whose instinct seems to recede as his powers of reason grow and who can in some ways alter his environment, uses history as a substitute for the forces which draw other life forms together. It is our awareness of the unique history of any group which changes that group into what we call a community.

The modern age has in many ways weakened the sense of community life and of regional identity which men once knew. Technology, standardization, and centralization press us into a mold of harrassed uniformity, captives of sameness in our education, our work, our play, our material goods, and our values. As a consequence, modern man has lost some of his former sense of individuality and unique identity.

One antidote to the poison of standardization is a refreshed awareness of one's regional heritage. In the United States, this identity is most easily discovered by the study of one's native or adopted state. Even our national identity can be perceived most clearly by observing national ideals and objectives as they are carried out in a particular state setting, for local responses to any broad national policy normally differ from one place to another. In short, national history is played out on regional, state, and local fields. State history brings national generalities down to the level of particular acts of particular people in their state setting.

As the United States faces its two-hundredth anniversary, and as Pennsylvania, birthplace of the nation, approaches the tricentennial of its founding, people will inevitably pause to look back over the path they have traveled and compare past performance with future expectations. Such an overview will help them wisely to reconsider their objectives and to reframe their values. This book has been written in part to fill these needs. But beyond such general objectives, this book has been planned for those who find familiarity with their own state a quest which brings its own rewards. And it has been designed with special attention to the requirements of teachers of Pennsylvania history.

The book provides selective rather than encyclopedic coverage. Pennsylvania has been so diversified and productive of ideas, leaders, and material goods that a survey of the entire regional experience would necessarily result in a catalog. We have chosen to concentrate upon major themes at the cost of many deliberate omissions. We have built the factual narrative around a chronological sequence of concepts. Part I, The Peaceable Kingdom, examines the attempt of the Quakers to create their special form of a Utopian society; Part

II, Laboratory of Democracy, stresses the experimentation with popular government from the 1760s until the Civil War; Part III, Laboratory of Industrial Society, emphasizes the efforts of a largely agricultural and commercial society to adjust to the sudden emergence of big industry based on iron, coal, timber, and oil; and Part IV, An Age of Transition, looks at changes wrought in the urban twentieth century by new technological, social, and economic experiences.

During the past generation, scholars have produced over five hundred doctoral dissertations on Pennsylvania topics. These specialized studies have produced many revisions of the traditional Pennsylvania story. Much of this new scholarly output has been incorporated into this book, and we have tried to emphasize the unique quality of the Pennsylvania experience at the same time that we have paid more attention than our predecessors to the relationship between Pennsylvania and the developing nation. We hope that our efforts may stimulate interest and continuing inquiry into the unique and ever-changing society which grew out of William Penn's dream of a "Peaceable Kingdom."

We acknowledge with deep appreciation work on this project by Dorothy Klein and Olive Hoogenboom. We are also grateful for the counsel, the critical suggestions, and many kinds of assistance given by numerous colleagues, notably Harold W. Aurand, Robert L. Bloom, Ira V. Brown, Harold E. Dickson, John B. Frantz, Jr., Howard Harris, Donald H. Kent, Theodore Lauer, M. Nelson McGeary, Harold L. Myers, Peter Parker, Irwin Richman, Merritt Roe Smith, Sylvester K. Stevens, Nicholas B. Wainwright, and Winston Weisman.

Philip S. Klein
Ari Hoogenboom

PART

1

The Peaceable Kingdom: 1609–1763

CHAPTER ONE

Settlement of the Delaware Valley

For nearly three centuries travelers of the wooded hills and rocky streams which lie between the valley of the Delaware and the Forks of the Ohio have commented on the remarkable natural beauty of the region. Once an expanse of nearly unbroken forest, Pennsylvania's outward appearance has been changed, sometimes for the better under the influence of the ax and the plow; sometimes for the worse under the impact of the dragline and the bulldozer. But all the years of chopping, digging, cultivating, building, and leveling down and piling up of the earth have not very much changed the natural features which have, since time immemorial, given zest and interest to life in Pennsylvania. If industry has at some places scarred the terrain, it has at others rendered it more exciting; if agriculture has destroyed some of the woodland, it has substituted the contoured fields.

THE LAND

The physical form of the landscape has had more effect on the people than the people have had on it. The whole geography is a kind of compromise. The rivers neither rush in torrents nor rest sluggishly in placid slack water, but flow rapidly. The mountains are neither towering and rugged, nor mere rises in a plain, but form a substantial barrier which challenges man's ingenuity but does not wholly bar his way. The annual mean temperature is about 50 degrees Fahrenheit, but occasionally the weather brings a reminder of the polar circles or of the equatorial zone. Because of an annual average rainfall of about 40 inches, Pennsylvania has no deserts and few swamps. Waterfalls abound, but none so gigantic as

Victoria or Kaieteur or Niagara. The highlands provide long vistas, but not so limitless as on the prairie nor so restricted as in the Alps. The winds play in a range between gusts and zephyrs, but do not blow day and night in a steady gale nor settle into sleepy calm. Fog and icy rain come in their turn, as do clear dry days and starry nights. Nature has set a pattern of variety for Pennsylvania, and man in this region has responded by developing a similar life pattern. Thus, diversity, the dominant theme of Pennsylvania history, emerges first from the soil itself.

Pennsylvania forms a rectangle upon which three small triangles have been superimposed, two of them in the east, outlining the course of the Delaware River, and the third in the northwest, known as the Erie Triangle. The average length of the state from east to west is 285 miles, and its average breadth from north to south is 156 miles. It occupies an area of 45,045 square miles lying approximately between the 40th and the 42nd parallels of north latitude, and the 74th and the 81st lines of west longitude. On a 16-inch world globe this remarkable region takes up a space about the size of a grain of corn or an orange pip.

Neither Charles II who granted it nor William Penn who became its Proprietor had any conception of the incredible riches that were centered in this small spot or any idea how strategic its location was. Under the soil lay coal, iron ore, petroleum, limestone, and clay; on the fertile surface grew hardwoods and conifers. It had four outlets by water: to the Atlantic Ocean through Delaware Bay; to the Chesapeake Bay via the Susquehanna River; to the Great Lakes and the Gulf of St. Lawrence through Lake Erie; and to the Gulf of Mexico by way of the Ohio and Mississippi Rivers.

Almost as if to counterbalance the gift of such a concentration of resources, nature set the Appalachian Mountains diagonally across the state, from northeast to southwest in two distinct sets of ridges. In the southeast running from Easton to Chambersburg are the low ranges, which seldom rise above 1,000 feet and which are known as the Blue or South Mountains. Further west, in a curving line through Wilkes-Barre, Williamsport, Altoona, and Bedford, lie the main ridges of the Appalachians, known in Pennsylvania as the Allegheny Mountains. Rising from 2,000 to 3,000 feet above sea level, these mountains separate the rivers flowing into the Atlantic Ocean and into the Gulf of Mexico. From the Allegheny front, or eastern escarpment, the mountains form a barrier 50 miles wide, beginning with a series of parallel ridges and valleys, developing into a broad plateau, and terminating in the confusion of humps, mounds, and ravines which characterize the western part of the state.

Of all the physical features of Pennsylvania, the mountains have most influenced the course of its history. Dividing the Piedmont region of the southeast from the foothills in the west, they have played an important role in the growth of Pennsylvania's major characteristics: a diversified economy, a heterogeneous society, and sectional politics. Pennsylvania's two greatest cities, Philadelphia and Pittsburgh, developed different economic and political interests. Through most of its history, the government of Pennsylvania has had to make a continual effort to ease passage across the mountains by wagon road, by canal, by railroad, and more recently by turnpike and by air. The mountain barrier led western Pennsylvanians several times into efforts to form themselves into a separate state.

While the mountains interrupted the free flow of men, goods, and ideas, the rivers and valleys aided such movement, especially in the early days. Each of the three geographic sections of the state has access to a major river system. The Delaware and its major branches, the Lehigh and the Schuylkill, serve the eastern area. The Susquehanna and its tributaries

Shaded relief map of Pennsylvania. (From Joseph R. Bien: *Atlas of the State of Pennsylvania,* 1901)

penetrate successive ranges of the Alleghenies, offering a watercourse route into and out of the central mountains. The Allegheny and the Monongahela Rivers, joining to form the Ohio, provided the easiest paths of travel among the formidable hills of the west until modern times.

THE INDIANS

The Pennsylvanian interested in his own locality who asks the common question: "What Indians used to live here?" exposes one of the original barriers to understanding between the races. Indian tribes maintained no settled habitat; they moved about from one place to another and bore the names of their languages or bloodlines, not of their habitats.

When the first Europeans appeared in the Middle Atlantic area, Indians of the Algonquian language stock occupied the Delaware River valley. They called themselves *Lenni-Lenape,* signifying "the real people" or "the original people," with a connotation of superiority and special destiny. The English later gave these Indians the name "Delawares." According to Delaware legend, they had migrated eastward from the Pacific Coast and, in alliance with the Iroquois, had driven out the earlier inhabitants of the New York–Pennsylvania region, the Eries and the Monongahela people. The Iroquois then settled around the Finger Lakes and the Lenni-Lenape made their home from the Allegheny Mountains to the Atlantic Ocean. The Lenni-Lenape divided into the Wolf tribe, or Minsi, who lived along the eastern ridges of the mountains; the Turtle tribe, or Unamis, who hunted and farmed in the lower Delaware valley; and the Turkey tribe, or Unalachtigos, who occupied the area between Delaware

Bay and the Atlantic Ocean. Other Algonquian tribes related to the Delawares included the Mohicans along the Hudson River, the Nanticokes and Conoys south of the Potomac, and the Shawnees along the Ohio.

The Iroquois lived as a tribal confederation known as the Five Nations consisting of the Mohawks, the Oneidas, the Onondagas, the Cayugas, and the Senecas. These tribes, in the order named, settled from the Mohawk Valley westward to Lake Erie, and held their League council at Onondaga, which was later to become Syracuse, New York. The Tuscaroras, who would become the sixth Iroquois nation, at first lived in the Carolinas, but migrated northward and in the early 1700s made their way up the Susquehanna Valley and into New York. Another tribe, the Susquehannocks, held sway along the shores of Chesapeake Bay and the Susquehanna River valley. They were enemies of the Five Nations until conquered by them about 1680.

European explorers and settlers often described the aborigines of America as barbarians and savages, but the Iroquois and Delawares possessed a civilization worthy of comparison with that of their white conquerors. They had developed concepts and procedures of government, religion, education, social responsibility, morality, and personal honor quite as functional as and in some ways more idealistic than those of their European counterparts. But in material culture they lagged far behind.

Although Indian chiefs or "kings," as the Europeans called them, nominally ruled the tribes, they governed more by consensus than by edict. The whole tribe often met in council, the chief in the center, surrounded by elders, young warriors, women, and in the outermost circle, children. Penn remarked "how powerful the Kings are, yet how they move by the breath of their people." The Indians had the rudiments of representative government, for the chiefs skillfully ascertained the will of the tribe. They had developed formal procedures for policy making, diplomacy, declaring war, making peace, and handling personal misconduct. The Delawares, among the most independent and liberty loving of the eastern Indians, had simpler governing procedures than the Iroquois.

Although the Delawares had no religion in the European sense of a contrived theology, they based their lives on certain beliefs about their Creator and the expectancy of judgment in an afterlife. The Indians had phrased the ideal of the Golden Rule long before they ever heard of the Bible, and found no difficulty in accepting many Christian concepts. But they did have trouble with the Europeans because, as one Indian said, the whites "did not act according to the *good words* which they told us." Conrad Weiser, who had studied both Christian theology and Indian life, wrote that "if by the word religion we understand the knitting of the soul to God, and the intimate relation to, and hunger after the highest Being arising therefrom, then we must certainly allow this apparently barbarous people a religion."

The Indian ranked pride high in the list of personal values. He defined this not as vanity of prowess or esteem for possessions, but rather as good conscience, resulting from honorable action. A man should be proud of right action. The tribe would share the benefits of it and willingly grant an extra measure of respect for it. Indians also had a keen sense of justice. They readily forgave injury whenever it arose from accident; but when wronged by intent they sought blood revenge. In respect for their elders, consideration for their womenfolk, and love for their children, the Indians maintained standards comparable to the Europeans.

These primitive people contributed much to the early colonists. They shared their knowledge of agriculture and introduced Europeans to such crops as potatoes, corn, beans, squash, tomatoes, and tobacco. They provided the pelts for colonial ventures in the fur trade.

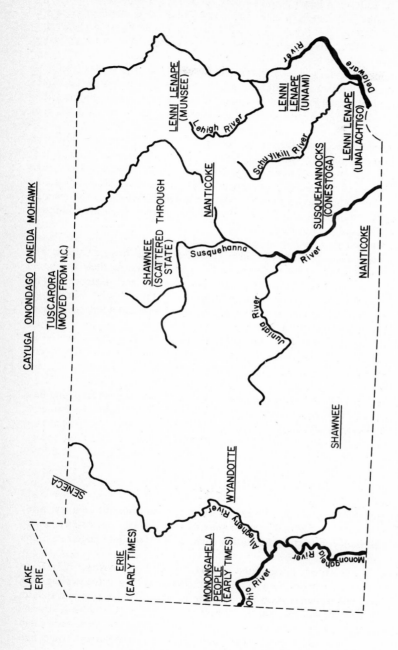

Location of major Indian tribes which inhabited the Pennsylvania region prior to the Walking Purchase of 1737.

They eased access to the interior of Pennsylvania not only by their canoes but by a network of well-defined Indian paths, so numerous and well placed that many of the routes still serve their original purpose, traversed by modern vehicles rather than deerskin moccasins. Their language, though unwritten, lives on in hundreds of picturesque names for counties, towns, mountains, and rivers.

The Indians played an important role in intercolonial affairs in the earliest days of European exploration and settlement. The friendship of local Indian tribes gave the whites added security from assaults by rival European powers. The relationship of the Indian tribes to each other thus became a matter of importance in the international competition for land in eastern North America.

The advance agents of three great European powers, seeking a foothold along the Atlantic seaboard, raised the flags of their respective countries within several hundred miles of each other at almost the same time. In the summer of 1608, Captain John Smith from Britain's Virginia colony explored the Chesapeake Bay. Grounding his ketch at the head of tidewater, near Conowingo, he held parley with the Susquehannocks of the vicinity, presented gifts, and impressed on their minds that the banner he carried signified friendship and power. In time, the Iroquois would learn of this.

In July of 1609, the Marquis de Champlain, exploring for France in company with some Hurons, unexpectedly met a party of Mohawks near Ticonderoga and fired on them. The Mohawks, facing firearms for the first time, fled in terror and reported to their Iroquoian allies that the men who carried the French flag came as enemies and destroyers. This incident not only contributed to later war between the Iroquois and the Hurons, but inaugurated a hatred of France by the Iroquois which persisted for a century and a half and played its part in the British conquest of New France in the 1750s.

Also in 1609, Henry Hudson, employed by the Dutch East India Company, briefly put into Delaware Bay, sailed on to discover the river we call the Hudson, and met with Indians of Algonquian stock who accepted presents from him and worshipped him as an emissary from the Great Spirit.

Thus, within thirteen months, in a region between Lake Champlain and Chesapeake Bay, the English had befriended the Susquehannocks, the French had outraged the Iroquois, and the Dutch had filled the cousins of the Delawares with superstitious awe. When these European nations expanded their settlements, they would bring the Indians into their rivalry.

FIRST DUTCH CLAIM

The Dutch and Swedish settlements along the Delaware in the seventeenth century, prior to the chartering of Pennsylvania, formed a small part of the gigantic power struggle in Europe which began with the Protestant Reformation early in the 1500s and lasted until the defeat of Napoleon in 1815.

The Dutch claims in North America originated with Henry Hudson's voyage of 1609. In 1613 two Dutchmen, Hendrick Christiansen and Adrian Block, set up a fur-trading post on Manhattan Island, but the Virginians soon forced them to acknowledge England's claim on the region and to pay tribute. Thereupon, the Dutch States General in 1614, to thwart the English, offered a trade monopoly to citizens who might make new discoveries and settlements in America. A very brief taste of the profits of the American fur trade had aroused the interest of merchants. Cornelis Jacobsen May sailed around the southern tip of New Jersey, named Cape May for him, and carefully examined Delaware Bay, hoping to get the fur-trade monopoly there. Meanwhile, in 1615, Adrian Block induced the States General to charter the United New Netherlands Company, with a three-year trading monopoly in the region from Maryland to Maine.

The company had accomplished nothing when its charter expired in 1618. The British London Company then invited a band of English dissenters living in Holland to occupy the Delaware Bay area in their name; but the Pilgrims, as we call them, lost their way and landed at Plymouth Rock in 1620. The *Mayflower's* error proved a good fortune for the Dutch who in 1621 chartered the West India Company. The company proclaimed possession of the regions explored by the defunct United New Netherlands Company, and several years later set up posts at New Amsterdam on Manhattan Island and at Fort Nassau on the east shore of Delaware Bay, nearly opposite the future site of Philadelphia.

To stimulate settlement, the company offered a "patroonship," or a land grant of 16 miles of river front, to anyone who would plant fifty settlers in four years. Samuel Blommaert and Samuel Godyn elected to take up tracts along the east and west shores of Delaware Bay. These two, in 1629, became the first European landowners in the lower Delaware Bay.

Godyn persuaded Captain David Pieter de Vries to lead a party of settlers to the Delaware to fulfill the terms of the land grant. De Vries in December 1630 sent out the first ship, *Walvis,* with a cargo of building materials and cattle, and also carrying several dozen colonists. The expedition reached Lewes Creek, on Delaware Bay, in the spring of 1631. The settlers built a little village called Swanendael, "the valley of swans," protected it by a stockade, cleared some fields and planted them, and prepared for winter. Thirty-three men decided to stay at Swanendael. The *Walvis* then set sail to pick up a second contingent of settlers.

Pieter de Vries himself came out on the next trip, landing at Swanendael on December 6, 1632. The men found nothing but charred ruins of the crude settlement. Eventually some Indians related a story of the massacre of the little Dutch community. Upon hearing this narrative, the new immigrants had little enthusiasm for remaining. De Vries, after further explorations, concluded that Swanendael could not become a financial success. The expedition returned home in the spring of 1633, and in February 1635, the patroons resold their land to the company. Thus ended the first formal effort at European settlement along the Delaware Bay.

NEW SWEDEN

By 1630, the Protestant cause in the Thirty Years' War seemed nearly hopeless. At this critical moment, young Gustavus Adolphus, King of Sweden, joined the conflict, swept the enemy from the field, and brought Sweden to the forefront as one of the great powers of Europe. The possession of colonies by a nation in the seventeenth century not only promised increased riches and power, but served as a symbol of prestige. The government created a New Sweden Company which would occupy the area of Blommaert's former patroonship along Delaware Bay and seek to develop trade in furs with the Susquehannocks. In February 1637 the New Sweden Company began preparations for planting a colony on the

Delaware under the direction of Peter Minuit, former governor of the Dutch settlements who had made the famous purchase of Manhattan from the Indians.

The managers obtained two ships, the *Kalmar Nyckel* ("key of Kalmar") and the *Vogel Grip* ("bird griffin"), outfitted them, hired crewmen, and recruited two dozen soldiers as colonists. The ships set sail in November 1637 and after a troublesome and dangerous passage reached Delaware Bay in March 1638. Minuit bought land from local Indians and began the construction of Fort Christina, on the location which is now Wilmington, Delaware. In these activities he followed confidential instructions ordering him to sail secretly to the Delaware River in order not to raise the suspicions of the Dutch. But in this he failed, for very shortly he received vigorous protests from William Kieft, Director-General of New Netherlands, and from William Berkeley, Governor of Virginia, each asserting the right of his country to Delaware Bay and warning Minuit not to assume possession. However, the Swedes continued their work without interference.

Minuit, on the return voyage of *Kalmar Nyckel,* lost his life when a ship which he was visiting in St. Christopher was blown out of the harbor by a hurricane and destroyed. The company named another Dutchman, Peter Hollandaer Ridder, as governor of the little colony and sent a second shipload of settlers who arrived in April 1640. Life in New Sweden during the first years was quiet, except for occasional alarms of encroachment by the Dutch or English. But when Governor Johan Printz arrived in New Sweden on February 15, 1643, the colony took on new life.

Lieutenant Colonel Johan Printz of the West Gotha cavalry, the third Governor of New Sweden, looms large among the picturesque personalities of American colonial history. He dominated events in his colony as did John Smith in early Virginia and Peter Stuyvesant in New Netherlands. This man-mountain made the welcoming Swedes gasp in amazement as he strode majestically down the creaking gangplank. "A man of brave size, who weighed over four hundred pounds," wrote Pieter de Vries; yet he was not fat, but all bone and muscle. He had strength of mind and will comparable to his Gargantuan physique.

Printz immediately set about making the struggling settlement into a profitable and defensible establishment. He stopped the planting of corn, which could be cheaply bought from the Indians, and began growing tobacco, which yielded a much greater income. After a brief tour of his domain, he determined to establish his headquarters not at Fort Christina, but further up-river on Tinicum Island. Here, near the later site of Philadelphia, he built the Printzhof, an imposing two-story structure of logs, to serve as the governor's mansion. He ordered the construction of a gristmill, a storehouse, and a church. The latter particularly gratified Rev. Roerus Torkillus, the first Lutheran minister in America, who occupied a position of leadership among the settlers.

Printz quickly sized up the military requirements of the colony. Faced by hostile Englishmen and Dutch, he would have to join one to protect himself against the other. He reached an agreement with mild-mannered Director-General Kieft of New Netherlands to join forces against English intruders, and the two of them ousted a colony of Massachusetts people on the Delaware planted by William Aspinwall. With the English out of the way, Printz now had to eliminate the Dutch, who still claimed the Delaware Valley. For years, the Dutch had maintained a trading post called Fort Nassau, which stood on the east or Jersey shore of the Delaware, immediately opposite Printz's headquarters on Tinicum Island. Here, the Dutch had been accustomed to receive furs from the Minqua or Susquehannock Indians. Printz now planted Fort Elfsburgh, south of Fort Nassau, in order to control traffic moving

Delaware Chief Tishcohan, signer of the Walking Purchase Treaty of 1737. Painting by Hesselius. (Historical Society of Pennsylvania)

Johan Printz, Governor of New Sweden, 1643–1653. (Pennsylvania Historical and Museum Commission)

William Penn at the age of twenty-two. (Pennsylvania Historical and Museum Commission)

William Penn's second wife, Hannah Callowhill Penn. (Historical Society of Pennsylvania)

in or out of Delaware Bay. Next he built three more forts westward along the Schuylkill to intercept the furs of the Minquas before they could reach the Dutch.

When Peter Stuyvesant replaced Kieft as Director-General for New Netherlands in 1647, Printz discovered he had a more formidable adversary. Stuyvesant in the spring of 1648 sent an expedition to build a fort on the Schuylkill further inland than any of the Swedish posts. This he called Fort Beversreede—"beaver road"—for its purpose was to be the first point of contact with the Minqua traders. But before the summer had passed, Printz built a Swedish fort, "right in front of our Fort Beversreede," wrote an indignant Dutchman. This building stood between the water's edge and the Dutch blockhouse, its back wall standing just 12 feet from the palisade gate of Fort Beversreede. The Indians thus found Swedes at the anchoring place, and could not even see the Dutch post from the water.

The Dutch, outflanked by the Swedes on both the Schuylkill and the Delaware, faced the choice of abandoning their Indian trade in this area or of taking some decisive action. Stuyvesant chose the latter course. He built a new and larger post called Fort Casimir on the west bank of Delaware Bay, some miles south of the Swedish Fort Christina. Instead of Printz holding the river "locked up for himself," the Dutch held the key, and no ship could pass into or out of the bay without the consent of Andreas Hudde, commandant in charge of Fort Casimir, who had cannon and two warships to enforce his demands.

At this moment, when Printz needed encouragement and reinforcements from home, Christina, aged eighteen, became Queen of Sweden, and her government forgot its colony on the Delaware. For four years no company ship came from Sweden, although Printz wrote voluminous reports explaining his need for settlers, troops, and supplies. Printz eventually concluded that he had better return to Sweden himself to get supplies. In October 1653 he set sail for home with his wife, his daughters, and two dozen discouraged settlers.

In the meantime, Queen Christina, momentarily concerned, had appointed Johan Classon Rising as commander of a new colonizing expedition. Rising landed at Fort Elfsborg where he learned of Governor Printz's departure the previous fall. Hearing that only a handful of Dutch occupied Fort Casimir, Rising captured the fort and renamed it Trinity. He would have done well to act less hastily. Since Printz had left, Rising held the rank of Director of New Sweden and the responsibility for its safety. That meant dealing with Peter Stuyvesant who took summary action. On September 1, 1655, seven Dutch ships entered Delaware Bay and discharged 600 soldiers. Half of them took a position between Fort Trinity and Fort Christina to prevent communication, and the rest sealed off Fort Trinity by land while the ships blocked exit by sea. The fort surrendered without firing a shot. A little later Fort Christina capitulated, and then all New Sweden.

Stuyvesant and Rising personally worked out the terms of peace which, like the little war which preceded it, seemed more like a stage play than real life. In the whole conflict the only person to be hurt was a Swede who, while climbing over a palisade to escape, had been shot in the leg by a comrade. On October 11, 1655, Rising and the soldiers embarked for home, but most of the settlers remained to continue life as before.

New Sweden at its largest comprised no more than several hundred families. Nonetheless, these Scandinavian people, half Swedes and half Finns, proved among the most durable of all the early European immigrants. Their adaptation of the log buildings of their homeland into the log cabin and the blockhouse fort of colonial America provided one of the most practically significant European contributions to American frontier life. Though few in number, the Swedes provided a foundation on which Penn could build. They cleared and stocked the first farms, introduced Lutheranism and built the first churches, established good relations with the Lenni-Lenape and the Susquehannock Indians, explored and charted the Delaware Bay and its surroundings, provided an ideal solution of the housing problem, set the bench marks for future land surveys, started the practice of European government with its legal forms and sanctions, and gave a historical base to Penn's later venture.

The Dutch, in command of the entire area from Delaware Bay to the Connecticut River after 1655, did little to develop their southern domain. Few Dutch came into the Delaware Bay sector of New Netherlands, and the Swedes continued to set the pattern of life there.

DELAWARE BAY AS A PART OF NEW YORK

The one-time collaboration between England and Holland had degenerated into bitter commercial rivalry by the mid-seventeenth century. While English Cavaliers and Roundheads fought their bloody civil war, and while Oliver Cromwell tried vainly to stabilize the new Puritan Commonwealth, the Dutch expanded their commerce and became the world's chief overseas carrier. Cromwell, partly to distract his people from troubles at home and partly to recoup England's commercial prestige, initiated the Navigation Acts in 1650 and 1651 to bring colonial trade back to British ships and exclude the Dutch. The trade war soon grew into full-scale military war which, though it lasted only two years, set a precedent for continuing hostility between these rival neighbors.

After the Restoration, Charles II continued to harass the Dutch. In 1664 he granted to his brother James, Duke of York, "all the land from the west side of Connecticutte River to the East Side of De la Ware Bay," and gave him "power and Authority of Government" over all the people. Having made a present of New Netherland to James, the King dispatched an English fleet to conquer the gift. On August 18, 1664, Col. Richard Nicolls arrived in the harbor at New Amsterdam and invited Peter Stuyvesant to yield up his control over territory claimed by England. Stuyvesant raged, blustered, and stamped his wooden leg, but could not persuade the civilian Dutchmen to fight. He had no recourse but to surrender on August 29, 1664. New Netherland now became the British colony, New York.

Reduction of the southern part of New Netherland, on Delaware Bay, caused more difficulty than the seizure of Manhattan. Nicolls sent Sir Robert Carr to receive the surrender of New Amstel, the southern capital. The grant to the Duke of York applied only to the eastern shore of Delaware Bay, but Nicolls wanted to unseat the Dutch whether they were within the grant or not. The Dutch vice-Director, Alexander d'Hinoyossa, preferred fighting to surrendering. In a very brief contest he lost, and the colonial venture of the Dutch along the eastern seaboard ended. In 1664 King Charles gave the land east of the Delaware River, now New Jersey, to Lord John Berkeley and Sir George Carteret.

By 1680, when William Penn began seriously considering the planting of an ideal commonwealth along the Delaware Bay, the region contained perhaps 2,000 people, half of them Swedes and Finns on the west shore and the rest mostly Dutch and English who spread out on both sides of the river and bay. Some 500 people lived in the lower reaches of the Schuylkill Valley, around the site of Philadelphia, and at the new government headquarters of Upland, now Chester. It was a small beginning; yet some of these families had occupied this soil for nearly fifty years. Their houses had become homes, and their homes had roots and a heritage before the word "Pennsylvania" had been coined.

BIBLIOGRAPHY

The essential starting point for further study is Norman B. Wilkinson: *Bibliography of Pennsylvania History* (1957), an annotated list of nearly 10,000 books and articles grouped topically and indexed thoroughly by subject and author. The handiest general collection of sources is Asa E. Martin and Hiram Shenk: *Pennsylvania History as Told by Contemporaries* (1925). Of the many historical society publications, three are of special importance: the *Pennsylvania Magazine of History and Biography*, with articles relating mainly to southeastern Pennsylvania; the *Western Pennsylvania Historical Magazine*, stressing the history of that region; and *Pennsylvania History*, dealing with the history of the entire state. All these journals have been comprehensively indexed. Finally, Roland M. Baumann has compiled a listing of over 700 Ph.D. theses on Pennsylvania history, most of them unpublished, in "Dissertations on Pennsylvania History, 1866-1971: A Bibliography," *Pennsylvania History*, vol. 39 (1972), pp. 72-114.

Well-balanced general histories of Pennsylvania include H. M. Jenkins (ed.): *Pennsylvania, Colonial and Federal*, 3 vols. (1903), a cooperative work covering political, economic, and social aspects; and Sylvester K. Stevens: *Pennsylvania, the Heritage of a Commonwealth*, 4 vols. (1968), providing broad coverage and biographies of modern Pennsylvanians. Shorter general works by highly qualified scholars include Wayland F. Dunaway: *A History of Pennsylvania*, 3d ed. (1948), a factual treastise; Paul A. W. Wallace: *Pennsylvania: Seed of a Nation* (1962), a brief interpretive work; and S. K. Stevens: *Pennsylvania: Birthplace of a Nation* (1964), an excellent volume for the general reader.

The best single volume on Indians is Paul A. W. Wallace: *Indians in Pennsylvania* (1961), which treats the natives with sympathy and understanding. Randolph C. Downes: *Council Fires on the Upper Ohio* (1940); and two volumes by C. Hale Sipe: *The Indian Chiefs of Pennsylvania* (1927) and *The Indian Wars of Pennsylvania* (1929), also emphasize the Indian viewpoint. Howard H. Peckham: *Pontiac and the Indian Uprising* (1947), has largely supplanted the nineteenth-century classic *The Conspiracy of Pontiac* by Francis Parkman.

For an early account of the Lenni-Lenape, see John G. E. Heckewelder: *History, Manners and Customs of the Indian Nations Who Once Inhabited Pennsylvania and the Neighboring States* (1876), a book supplemented by Paul A. W. Wallace (ed.): *Thirty Thousand Miles with John Heckewelder* (1958). Also consult Daniel G. Brinton: *Lenapé and Their Legends* (1885); and many books and articles by Frank G. Speck.

The difficulties of Indian adaptation to European culture are exposed in Anthony W. Wallace: *Teedyuscung, King of the Delawares* (1949). On the same problem, see Roy H. Pearce: *The Savages of America: A Study of the Indian and the Idea of Civilization* (1953); and Francis Jennings: "Incident at Tulpehocken," *Pennsylvania History*, vol. 35 (1968), pp. 335-355. Relations of European settlers with the Indians can be traced in Elma E. Gray: *Wilderness Christians, the Moravian Mission to the Delaware Indians* (1955); Paul A. W. Wallace: *Conrad Weiser: Friend of Colonist and Mohawk* (1945); and Nicholas B. Wainwright: *George Croghan: Wilderness Diplomat* (1959).

Indian travel routes are covered in Paul A. W. Wallace: *Indian Paths of Pennsylvania* (1965). The legacy of Indian names throughout Pennsylvania has been studied by A. Howry Espenshade: *Pennsylvania Place Names* (1925); and George P. Donehoo: *A History of the Indian Villages and Place Names in Pennsylvania* (1928).

There are several useful source collections on early Delaware Valley settlements by Europeans, notably Samuel Hazard (ed.): *Annals of Pennsylvania from the Discovery of the Delaware, 1609-1682* (1850); and Albert Cook Meyers (ed.): *Narratives of Early Pennsylvania, West Jersey and Delaware, 1630-1707* (1912). Israel Acrelius: *A History of New Sweden* (1874) is an indispensable source. Secondary works include the old but still standard study by Amandus Johnson: *Swedish Settlements on the Delaware*, 2 vols. (1911); E. A. Louhi: *The Delaware Finns* (1925); Christopher Ward: *The Dutch and the Swedes on the Delaware, 1609–1664* (1930) and his more specialized *New Sweden on the Delaware* (1938); and John H. Wuorinen: *The Finns on the Delaware, 1638–1655* (1938).

Books by Charles A. Weslager: *The Dutch Explorers, Traders and Settlers in the Delaware Valley, 1609–1664* (1961), and *The English on the Delaware, 1610–1692* (1967), round out the story of international rivalry for control of the Delaware River valley.

CHAPTER TWO

Founding of Pennsylvania

The life span of the two William Penns, father and son, very nearly coincides with the period of the Stuart dynasty in England. James I took the throne in 1603 and his house ruled, except for the Interregnum of eleven years, until the death of Queen Anne in 1714. Admiral William Penn, the father, was born in 1621; his son, William, the founder of Pennsylvania, lived until 1718. During the turbulent seventeenth century, England was wracked by religious persecution and civil conflict at home, and distracted by incessant foreign wars—the Thirty Years' War, three wars with Holland, and four with France. In this era of intrigue, suspicion, and tumult of arms, the father became a fighter in Britain's navy under Charles I, Oliver Cromwell, and Charles II, ending his career as an admiral and a knight; the son became a pacifist and an outspoken member of a little group hated by most Englishmen of that day as subversive and traitorous—the Society of Friends.

ADMIRAL WILLIAM PENN

The elder Penn became an officer in Cromwell's navy after the civil war broke out between the king and Parliament in 1642. He proved able and, with the help of influential friends, rose rapidly in the service. In 1645 he became a fleet commander and in 1652 vice-admiral of England, next to the senior command post in the nation. In the first war with the Dutch, Admiral Penn won such a decisive victory over the enemy fleet at the island of Texel that he brought the war suddenly to an end. In 1653, a week after this battle, Cromwell elevated him to the highest naval command, general of the sea.

Penn, no Puritan himself, believed with many others that the day would come when exiled Prince Charles, heir to the throne, would return to power. He secretly sent word to Charles, in France, that he would welcome his return to power.

Cromwell's death in 1658 and the restoration of Charles II two years later opened the final chapter of Admiral Penn's public career. In the spring of 1660 he was elected to Parliament, and King Charles knighted him on board the ship that returned the new monarch to England. At the age of thirty-nine he was Sir William Penn, M.P. His son, William, aged sixteen, was preparing to enter college at Oxford. Before the year had ended, King Charles II heaped additional honors on the admiral, naming him commissioner of the admiralty and commissioner of the navy.

But family troubles arose. Writing in March 1662, the diarist Samuel Pepys noted that "His son William is at home, not well. But all things, I fear, do not go well with them—they look discontentedly, but I know not what ails them." A month later he knew. Young Penn had taken up with the Quakers at Oxford.

The elder Penn sent his son off to Paris and applied himself hard to navy work, eager to please his new supervisor, James, Duke of York and Lord High Admiral. Penn had advanced out of his own pocket some £12,000 to outfit the fleet of Col. Richard Nicolls for the conquest of New Netherland in 1664 when King Charles found it awkward to use treasury funds for this purpose.

When Admiral Penn died in 1670 he left his son more than estates in Ireland and England and a balance due from the Crown. He left the name Penn surrounded by an aura of prestige and naval glory matched in its day only by Robert Blake. When his son had persisted in his adherence to Quakerism and had begun to suffer periodic imprisonment, the admiral had written both to King Charles and to James, begging their intercession should even more serious punishments threaten. Both gave him their promise of interest and fatherly concern for William, and both kept the promises with remarkable good faith.

THE QUAKERS

English Protestants reacted with some misgiving to the accession of James I, for they feared that he and his Stuart descendants might try to unite the kingdom with the Roman Catholic Church, but James promised to enforce conformity to the Established Church of England. He did this harshly. When he proclaimed: "I shall make them conform themselves or I will harry them out of the land," he affronted the whole Puritan movement and gave impetus to English nonconformity on a large scale. Separatists like the Pilgrims fled to Holland or to America. Catholics, with whom the Stuarts sympathized, found a haven in Maryland.

During the reign of Charles I, starting in 1625, the English people became irreconcilably divided. On one side stood the Crown, the Established Church, and the landed aristocracy; on the other, the Parliament, the Puritans, and the merchants. Under Charles I, the cruelty of religious persecution by Archbishop Laud, and especially his savage punishment of Puritans by whipping, nose slitting, ear cutting, cheek branding, and summary imprisonment, raised the spirit of anticlericalism, or hatred of established churches, to a fever pitch. Laud's repressive policy aroused the moral indignation necessary to civil war.

Many people roamed the land expressing their dissatisfaction with all formal churches, so many that they became known collectively as the "Seekers" or "Seekers after Truth." One of these was George Fox, who founded the Society of Friends. Born in 1624, Fox experienced in his impressionable youth the full impact of the arrogance, vindictiveness, and hollow formality that passed as religion in the England of his day. In 1647, when he was twenty-three, he experienced a kind of revelation that made his heart "leap for joy." God could speak directly to all; man had but to listen quietly, to believe, and to obey. "No need of water baptism, of elaborate church ceremonies, of human intermediaries, of exacting and incredible creeds. Each man was in a direct relation with his Maker who would, if allowed to do so, direct his life." Fox spoke of his sense of "inner light" to others and soon achieved a following of Seekers. Together they formed the Society of Friends. These people created no church; they provided no hierarchy, sacraments, or formalized creed. They did form "a Society of people who were disgusted with . . . hypocrisy, insincerity, and worldliness . . . and who were eager for spiritual reality and power in simple lives." The society, soon to become known derisively as "Quakers," numbered around 60,000 in England by the time Pennsylvania was chartered in 1681.

The average Londoner of the 1670s, with little knowledge of Quaker thought, misunderstood Quaker actions. He considered them rude and insubordinate when they failed to remove their hats in the presence of superiors. In a society based on a rigid class system, in which distinctive garb differentiated the social levels, such failure to acknowledge special rank seemed more than mere boorishness; it constituted a thumbing of the nose at authority, an insult to the whole system of a titled aristocracy. But the Quakers believed that the Deity recognized no such distinctions among men.

Many of the Friends refused to pay tithes and wrote against them. They would not join any military organization and urged others to be practicing pacifists. By refusing to take oaths in court, they obstructed the accepted legal procedure. They addressed people by the familiar "thee" and "thou," with brotherly intent but disastrous consequences when the nobility insisted upon being addressed by the proper title. Quakers did not keep the Sabbath as English law and custom decreed, nor observe fast days. They opposed sports, amusements, singing, and dancing; they denied the validity of church rites, of the sacraments, of dogmas such as original sin and the Trinity, and of the need for a professional clergy or for church buildings.

Most Englishmen viewed such ideas as subversive and dangerous to society: If they spread, they would undermine the system of nobility, upset the theory of the divine right of kings, threaten the existence of the Established Church, wreck the national treasury, destroy the military might of the kingdom, and at length bring England to ruin. With such fears in mind, the English government persecuted the Quakers more harshly than any of the recusant sects. In two decades before the founding of Pennyslvania, over 10,000 Quakers had been imprisoned in England, and 250 of them had died for their faith. This was the sect which attracted the interest of young William Penn, son of Britain's naval hero, the General of the Sea.

WILLIAM PENN, THE QUAKER

William Penn was born in London on October 24, 1644 (date adjusted to present calendar), in the midst of the civil war and just a few weeks before his father sailed off on his first cruise for the Roundheads. In a few years the Penns moved from London to nearby

Chigwell, in Essex, to be close to the famous school there. Young Penn attended Chigwell School from the age of four until he was twelve. The family then went to live at the admiral's recently acquired estate at Macroom, west of Cork in Ireland, where William continued his education under private tutors. During these years of schooling, from 1648 to 1660, Penn saw on every side the ugly manifestations of religious intolerance and hypocrisy. If Puritan dogmatism and harsh repression in England seemed a disturbing everyday reality, the condition of the Irish even more affected the young Penn. A sensitive youth with an inquiring mind, who had been much protected and had spent most of his time with his mother and a younger sister, Margaret, he worried about the inconsistencies between the preachings and the practices of his time.

In 1660, the year of the Restoration and of the knighting of Admiral Penn, sixteen-year-old William entered Christ Church College, Oxford, as a freshman. The youth's recent religious experiences combined with the sudden return of England to worldliness and gaiety after years of restraint by the Puritans produced a combination that foretold trouble for the boy. As the son of a famous father who was currently high in the favor of the new King, William might have been expected to celebrate his first escape from home by trying the pleasures and sampling the temptations which Oxford could provide. Rather, he rebelled. At Christ Church College he encountered freethinkers among both students and faculty who fired his indignation against religious conformity. He did not yet understand the difference between the provocative but sober observations of the Dean of the College, Dr. John Owen, a pronounced independent in religion, and the practical application of such doctrines by tearing gowns from the backs of fellow students as a demonstration of his own independency. Penn consorted with Quakers at Oxford and became so involved in the war on campus regalia that the college dismissed him.

Penn described the first encounter with his irate father as "bitter usage . . . whipping, beating, and turning out of doors." The father eventually concluded that the best occupation for the boy would be a season of travel on the Continent. There he could practice the French, Dutch, and German languages that he had studied at Oxford and perhaps be turned to interests more useful in the future than heresy. William set out for Paris in the summer of 1662 in company with the sons of several British nobles. At the French Court he learned the manners and address of a courtier, including swordplay, an art at which he became sufficiently adept to save his own life during an assault on him one night. From Paris he went to Saumur where he studied for some months under Moses Aymrault, an eminent Protestant theologian noted for the incisiveness of his logic and his unshakable commitment to religious toleration. At length, in the summer of 1664, he returned home much altered. At twenty he had become a lithe, athletic, and remarkably handsome young man, wide awake to the latest fashions, well informed, and a lively conversationalist. He seemed a man of the world, and women found him fascinating.

For a year he studied law in Lincoln's Inn, London, and then served under his father briefly at the battle of Lowestoft, carrying the news of that victory directly to King Charles. The black plague came to London in the summer of 1665, bringing such a dreadful toll of agony and death that the Penns left the city and William became troubled at this apparent evidence of God's anger at a sinful people. His father also worried, but chiefly about William's relapse into unorthodox religious ideas. He sent him off to Ireland to serve in the army under the Duke of Ormonde at Dublin. As a volunteer on the expedition to quell a mutiny at Carrickfergus castle he conducted himself coolly and with valor. Hearing that a former acquaintance, Thomas Loe, would hold a Quaker meeting at Cork, Penn determined to attend. Loe, on seeing Penn, directed his remarks primarily to him, and took as his text: "There is a faith which overcometh the world, and a faith which is overcome by the world." On the instant the doubts and wonderings of earlier days came to certainty and decision in Penn's mind. He would become a Quaker and follow this humble and dedicated way regardless of family, king, or future prospects. Before the year had ended, Penn lay in jail at Cork for attending a Quaker meeting.

The admiral heard quickly of these events and ordered William to be released and sent home. Their meeting proved agonizing. The father said he would pray God to destroy his son on the instant rather than see him become a Quaker; William said he would respond to such a prayer by committing suicide. Sobered by their own violence, they talked of terms. The admiral would accept William as a Quaker if he would but promise, for the sake of the family honor, to remove his hat before the Duke of York and the king. William refused. He left home to make a life with his Quaker friends, and within a year was back in jail, this time in the Tower of London.

Just before this imprisonment he wrote two books, *Truth Exalted* and *The Sandy Foundation Shaken.* These two polemic theological tracts were not distinguished by tolerance; the *Sandy Foundation* became the basis of the charges against him, incited by his father's enemies at court. While in the Tower, Penn wrote one of the best known of the hundred-odd books and pamphlets that he would produce: *No Cross, No Crown,* a historical treatise on the development of religious ideas, leading to his definition of man's duty. Admiral Penn stood the unhappy publicity of his son's imprisonment as long as he could, and then appealed to the Duke of York for help. The Duke sent a chaplain to try to bend young Penn's will, but when William remained adamant the Duke released him anyway. In August 1670, Penn again landed in jail, charged with preaching and speaking in Grace Church Street, London, and thereby causing a riot. The authorities began his trial on September 1, 1670, and in the course of it made a martyr of the younger William Penn.

The Hat Trial derived its name from a provocative incident at the very start of the proceedings. Penn, anticipating harassment, removed his hat on entering court, but the judge ordered an officer to replace it on Penn's head. The bench then badgered him for having his hat on and fined him for contempt. The episode set the tone for the trial and gained Penn sympathy from the spectators in the crowded courtroom. Penn conducted his own defense with devastating effect, and soon put the court itself on trial for callous disregard of the rights of Englishmen. The jury found Penn "not guilty," to the immense satisfaction of the spectators, but the judge then fined and imprisoned the jury for contempt, and sent Penn back to jail on the same complaint. The Hat Trial advertised the tyranny of the court throughout all England and made Penn appear not a subversive but a champion of freedoms cherished by all his countrymen. Perhaps most important, it impressed Penn himself so deeply that he later took special pains to provide judicial procedures in Pennsylvania that would carefully protect the rights of the accused in court.

Father Penn at last could be proud of his son. Two weeks after the trial had ended, he died in peace, having reunited his family and made William his executor and heir to his entire estate. The door of opportunity now stood wide open to William Penn the Quaker. Independent, wealthy, a friend of the Stuarts, respected as a man of high conscience and widely acclaimed as a defender of tolerance and freedom, William Penn pondered how to serve mankind.

THE FOUNDING OF PENNSYLVANIA

For ten years after the death of his father, Penn lived as a missionary for Quakerism and a famous witness to its ideals. He was arrested again in 1671, but after being freed of the charge against him had to serve six months in Newgate prison because he refused to take an oath at the hearing. During this interlude he wrote *The Great Case of Liberty of Conscience,* a book expounding the theme that moved him most deeply—religious toleration. Upon his release he embarked on a preaching tour in Holland and Germany where he found many who inclined to a religion of simplicity and pietism, and who listened eagerly to him. He returned to England to marry Gulielma Maria Springett on April 4, 1672. He had met her four years before at the home of her Quaker stepfather, and had instantly fallen in love. Guli possessed both inner and outward beauty, and in addition a considerable fortune.

Events in England in 1673 brought a renewal of violent persecution of religious nonconformers. The attempt of Charles II to free Catholics of restriction by his Declaration of Indulgence brought a storm of reprisal. Parliament passed a Test Act which barred from public service everyone not a communicant of the Church of England, and peace officers all over the kingdom used the public outcry as an excuse for renewed persecution which fell with extreme severity on the Quakers. George Fox went to prison and Penn had to intercede at court for him. Fox had earlier spent some time in America visiting refugee Quakers and investigating the prospects of establishing a colony for the English Friends. Partly as an outgrowth of his visit, Quaker John Fenwick bought West Jersey from Lord Berkeley in 1675, pledging payment from funds he held in trust for Edward Byllynge. When Byllynge protested, the Quakers selected Penn to arbitrate their dispute.

Penn's serious interest in planning an ideal commonwealth in America began with his energetic efforts to untangle the Jersey snarl. He achieved a financial agreement, encouraged settlement, and in 1677 helped prepare the first Jersey constitution, called the Concessions and Agreement. His experience of laying the groundwork for a colonial enterprise in New Jersey prepared him to bring Pennsylvania into being.

Penn applied to King Charles II for a grant of land west of the river Delaware in June 1680. His petition went to the Privy Council, which referred it to the Lords of Trade, who heard arguments on boundaries from agents of the Duke of York and Lord Baltimore, the two proprietors whose land might be involved in a grant of the region Penn wanted. After Penn obtained a release from James, the Lords of Trade reached a boundary agreement with the Maryland agents and drew up a proprietary charter. The charter took effect on March 4 and was announced by royal proclamation on April 2, 1681. The Great Charter described the land grant, the governing powers of the proprietor, and the rights reserved by the Crown. Penn had proposed to call his colony New Wales, or Sylvania, but the king, "having regard to the memory and merits of his late father," insisted on Pennsylvania.

Exactly what had Penn in mind at the time he sought the colony? The recently intensified attacks on English Quakers certainly sharpened and gave a sense of urgency to his thinking about a haven of refuge from persecution. Other American colonies provided ample precedent, and the repression of Seekers along the Rhine promised plenty of potential settlers. The creation of a utopian society where tolerance and freedom of conscience should reign appealed strongly to him. Penn hoped that in his province "an example may be set up to the nations" and foresaw "a free colony for all mankind," a kind of holy experiment.

In addition to his hopes of utopia, Penn had some shrewdly practical motives. As the struggle between the Crown and Parliament intensified, Penn's prospects for a cash payment of the debt owing to his father diminished. Furthermore, his expenses for missionary work had been growing, and his income decreasing. Penn could write with truth that he sought Pennsylvania "for the Lord's sake," but he was not unmindful of the financial security promised by the sale of American land and the income from quitrents in perpetuity. His proposal of a land grant to defray the King's debt worked to mutual advantage: it would rid the King both of the debt and of the troublesome Quakers and would provide Penn a permanent income for his family and for his personal mission.

For a year after receiving his charter, Penn devoted all his energies to working out the complex details of inaugurating the administration of Pennsylvania. He had to create a preliminary government, clarify his intentions to the Indians and European inhabitants, provide for land distribution and the founding of towns, initiate a campaign to promote immigration, draw up a formal constitution, and plan his own private affairs prior to moving to America.

Penn immediately sent his cousin, Captain William Markham, to inform the authorities in New York and the settlers along the Delaware of the new dispensation. Leaving England in April, Markham arrived in June 1681 and read to an assembly of Swedes and Dutchmen assembled at Upland (Chester) Penn's letter explaining that "it hath pleased God . . . to cast you in my lot and care. . . . You are now fixed at the mercy of no Governor who comes to make his fortune great; you shall be governed by laws of your own making." Markham, in compliance with instructions, created a temporary governing council of nine, set up local courts, conferred briefly with Maryland authorities about the southern boundary line, and began the sale of land.

Penn had expected to sail for America in the fall of 1681, but planning work in England required so much time that he had to postpone his removal for a year. He wrote prodigiously, publishing nearly a dozen publicity pamphlets to circulate in England and on the Continent for the information of prospective settlers. The first, entitled *Some Account of the Province of Pennsylvania,* expounded the arguments in favor of colonies, described briefly the geography, the economic opportunities and the government, commented on the types of people most fitted to succeed in the new land, and advised them on preparations for the journey, the prices of Pennsylvania land, and what they would need to survive the first year.

Preparing prospectuses was a work of joy, for these mainly put into words Penn's future hopes; but devising explicit plans to solve immediate practical problems proved a more arduous task. On July 11, 1681, Penn completed his *Conditions or Concessions* which gave instructions for laying out "a large town" on the Delaware River, for the purchase and occupation of land, and for the relations between the settlers and the Indians. To prevent speculators from monopolizing the most desirable tracts, Penn ordered that purchasers of 1,000-acre plots could not own these adjacent to each other unless they planted a family on each plot within three years. Anyone who failed to "plant or man" a tract within three years after it had been surveyed might lose it to newcomers. Indentured servants would receive 50 acres at the end of their service, and if these came from the master's land, the master would receive 100 additional acres from Penn. The Proprietor also ordered that settlers should preserve 1 acre of trees for every 5 acres cleared—the first conservation law in Pennsylvania history.

The definition of relations between Indians and whites in the *Concessions* was the most farsighted and remarkable part of that document. Penn decreed "that the Indians shall have liberty to do all things . . . that any of the planters shall enjoy." Differences between them should be "ended by twelve men, that is, by six planters and six natives." Any planter who affronted an Indian in word or deed would be punished "as if he had committed it against his fellow-planter," but if any Indian injured a planter, the latter should not "be his own judge against the Indian" but should report to a provincial magistrate who would deal with the Indian's chief to obtain satisfaction. Penn expressed the hope that "so we may live friendly together."

Ships clearing from Ireland and England that summer showed that Penn's promotion had stirred wide interest. Companies formed in London, Liverpool, and Bristol to organize emigration. Welsh, Dutch, and German adventurers planned similar enterprises. A Free Society of Traders bought 20,000 acres. And a Maryland enterpriser offered to buy a monopoly of the fur trade for £6,000 and an annual royalty, a proposal which, though tempting, Penn declined. The rapid influx of settlers prompted Penn to send three commissioners with more explicit instructions to Markham for the sale of land, and also with instructions to choose a site for the "great town" and to plan for its streets, statehouses, markets, and private dwellings. Provincial Surveyor Thomas Holme took charge of the city-planning project and, following Penn's carefully thought out instructions for his "green country town" with gridiron streets, began the surveys for Philadelphia.

Almost ready to leave for his new home, Penn began to fear trouble unless he acquired title to the shore of Delaware Bay south of Chester. Both Lord Baltimore and the Duke of York had claims to this region. With some difficulty Penn persuaded the Duke of York to make him a grant of the Lower Counties, later to become Delaware, by a deed of August 24, 1682. He set sail for Pennsylvania aboard the *Welcome* six days later, with a shipload of new settlers, and landed at New Castle on October 27 (date adjusted to present calendar). Because Penn had entered Delaware Bay on October 24, his birthday, Pennsylvanians have habitually used the latter date for celebrations commemorating both events.

PENN'S FIRST VISIT

After the arrival of the Proprietor, all matters which had been managed on an interim basis had to be formalized and rendered permanent. The institutions of government had to be translated from paper to practice, town sites built from hopes into houses, real estate transactions clarified by precise surveys, relations with the Indians developed from kind words to specific understandings, boundaries defined for adjacent colonies, the general platform of English law made locally explicit by provincial statutes; these and dozens of other immediate needs pressed on Penn for attention.

He wasted no time. Two days after landing at New Castle he sailed north to the site Thomas Holme had picked for Philadelphia, where he approved and authorized laying out the streets and plots according to the plan Holme had drawn. From his headquarters at Upland he called for elections to create the first Council and Assembly which should meet on December 6, and supervised the preparation of a provincial code which he desired these bodies to enact into law.

The laws enacted in December 1682 provided the foundation for human relations in Pennsylvania. One group of some sixty statutes, known collectively as the Great Law, wove Quaker principles into the fabric of Pennsylvania government so tightly that the threads dominated the pattern of colonial living, and many of them remain clearly visible to this day. The preamble defined freedom of conscience and provided strong safeguards for religious liberty. Only professed anarchists and atheists were explicitly excluded from protection. While members of all religions enjoyed protection and equal rights of ballot, only Christians held the right to serve in public office. The Great Law abolished oaths and established the system of affirmation in court, eliminated the death penalty for all offenses except murder and treason, erected safeguards for an accused by providing jury trials in both civil and criminal proceedings, and eliminated savage and brutal punishments. In addition, it defined many routine matters, setting standards of weights and measures; creating record-keeping agencies to handle wills, births, and court records; and describing election procedures. Other early statutes incorporated the Lower Counties (Delaware) into the province of Pennsylvania, and conferred English citizenship on the local Dutch, Finns, and Swedes.

Sixty ships docked at Philadelphia in 1683, bringing thousands of settlers to swell this rapidly growing town and to take up land in the interior. Among the "First Purchasers," 392 colonists took up tracts of less than 675 acres, 196 bought plots from 750 to 3,000 acres, and 69 bought 5,000 acres or more—a total of more than three-quarters of a million acres. Penn sold land at 40 shillings per 100 acres, with an annual quitrent forever of a shilling per 100 acres. In modern terms, this meant the sale price was 10 cents per acre, and the annual quitrent ¼ cent per acre. Penn hoped that the purchase price would finance the early years of colonial management, and that the quitrent would support his family in years to come.

The rapid sale and occupation of Pennsylvania land required Penn to acquire the release of it by the Indians promptly, and to clarify with Lord Baltimore any uncertainties about the boundary between the two provinces. No conclusive written record exists of the conference now famous in legend, Penn's treaty with the Indians under the Treaty Elm at Shackamaxon (Kensington) late in 1682, but all the indirect evidence supports the reality of the event. Although not everything occurred there that the fancy of artists and literary men later created, yet some of the romanticized versions may not have strayed far from the truth. Penn's reputation preceded him, by report from earlier Quaker settlers, by the provisions of the *Concessions,* and by several letters he sent to the Indians. From records of his other Indian parleys, better authenticated, we can be sure that he came to Shackamaxon unarmed, with dignity but without show; that he stood not aloof but joined in games and dances; that he spoke partly in the Indian tongue, and when speaking in English conveyed sincerity in his countenance as well as in his words; and finally that he made good his earlier promise "to live justly, peaceably, and friendly with you." Delaware Chief Tamanend (Tammany) responded. "We will live in peace with Onas (Penn) and his children as long as the sun and moon shall endure." It should not be forgotten that the Dutch, Swedes, and Finns had for fifty years lived peacefully among the Indians, so that Penn had some good feelings to build on.

Penn made several land purchases from the Indians and traveled inland with natives as guides to explore his "quiet land" as far west as the Susquehanna Valley. He visited New York and proposed to buy the Susquehanna country from the Iroquois, but the Board of Trade blocked his effort. He laid out Pennsbury Manor, a 6,000-acre tract along the Delaware in southern Bucks County, and began the construction of a mansion for his family. He visited Lord Baltimore to discuss conflicts of view about the boundaries of southern Pennsylvania and of Delaware, but the two found no way to resolve their differences. Lord Baltimore sent his claims to England for review and judgment by the Privy Council. Penn felt that he needed to act personally to protect his property. Hence, in August 1684, after two of the busiest and happiest years in his life, he set sail for England on the ship *Endeavor.*

BIBLIOGRAPHY

Elbert Russell: *History of Quakerism* (1942) is the best one-volume treatment. William S. Comfort: *The Quakers* (1948) and Howard Brinton: *Friends for Three Hundred Years* (1952) both take a philosophical approach. For more localized accounts see A. C. Applegarth: *Quakers in Pennsylvania* (1890); Sydney George Fisher: *The Making of Pennsylvania* (1896); Rufus M. Jones: *Quakers in the American Colonies* (1911); and Isaac Sharpless: *A History of Quaker Government in Pennsylvania*, 2 vols. (1900). The deferential view of some of these books is countered by the more realistic work of Edwin B. Bronner: *William Penn's Holy Experiment, The Founding of Pennsylvania, 1681–1701* (1962); and Gary B. Nash: *Quakers and Politics: Pennsylvania, 1681–1726* (1968).

Special features of Quakerism are examined in Sydney V. James: *A People among Peoples: Quaker Benevolence in Eighteenth Century America* (1963); Caroline N. Jacob: *Builders of the Quaker Road* (1953), presenting several dozen biographies, mostly of Pennsylvanians; Frederick B. Tolles: *Meeting House and Counting House: The Quaker Merchants of Colonial Philadelphia, 1682–1763* (1948) and also his *Quakers and the Atlantic Culture* (1960); and Edwin B. Bronner: "The Quakers and Non-violence in Pennsylvania," *Pennsylvania History*, vol. 35 (1968), pp. 1–22.

Of many biographies, the following will prove most useful: Vernon Noble: *The Man in Leather Breeches, The Life and Times of George Fox* (1953); Frederick B. Tolles: *James B. Logan and the Culture of Provincial America* (1957); George S. Brooks: *Friend Anthony Benezet* (1937); Marion D. Learned: *Life of Francis Daniel Pastorius* (1908); and Theodore Thayer: *Israel Pemberton, King of the Quakers* (1943).

Scores of people have written biographies of William Penn. Catherine O. Peare: *William Penn: A Biography* (1957) is the best narrative account. Others worthy of attention are Edward C. O. Beatty: *William Penn as a Social Philosopher* (1939); William W. Comfort: *William Penn, 1644–1718* (1944); Sydney George Fisher: *The True William Penn* (1900); William I. Hull: *William Penn, A Topical Biography* (1937); and C. E. Vulliamy: *William Penn* (1934). Specialized studies of Penn include John W. Graham: *William Penn, Founder of Pennsylvania* (1917), which emphasizes his writings; Joseph Illick: *William Penn the Politician: His Relations with the English Government* (1965); and Mary Maples Dunn: *William Penn, Politics and Conscience* (1967), which shows Penn as more realistic than idealistic. Arthur Pound: *The Penns of Pennsylvania and England* (1932), gives a story of the entire family, following the heirs down to modern times. Frederick B. Tolles and Gordon E. Alderfer (eds.): *The Witness of William Penn* (1957) have printed selections of Penn's writings. An extensive listing of materials on Penn will be found in the previously cited work by Wilkinson: *Bibliography of Pennsylvania History*, pp. 42–53.

CHAPTER THREE

The Trials of a Proprietor

History affords few more unlikely collaborations than that between King James II and William Penn following Penn's return to England in 1684 to defend his interests against the claims of Lord Baltimore. After Charles II died in February 1685, his brother James ascended the English throne and shortly thereafter made William Penn his intimate confidential adviser. Historians have never quite satisfactorily explained this implausible association which had important consequences for William Penn and his American colony.

A FRIEND AT COURT

Early in his reign, King James pursued a course which convinced English Protestants that he intended to reestablish Catholicism in the realm at whatever cost, and that he proposed to crush Parliament in the process. William Penn's growing intimacy with James and his support of the king's unpopular policies must be viewed against this background.

Penn's best claim to the area south of Philadelphia rested upon the king's good will, for the original dispute lay between Lord Baltimore and James. That Baltimore was a Catholic did not ease Penn's mind. The future of Pennsylvania depended on a decision favorable to Penn, for so long as the populated area of his colony remained in contest, land titles could not be guaranteed. Penn actively pressed his case and, on October 17, 1685, was rewarded by an order of the king in Council confirming his title to the Lower Counties and postponing settlement of the boundary dispute with Maryland.

Penn might have returned now to America, but James by this time had decided to make use of his Quaker friend. No one seems quite sure whether James deceived Penn, whether Penn succumbed to the temptations of wealth and power, or whether Penn thought that he could actually guide the crafty James into paths of righteousness. Whatever the causes, the facts emerged that James bestowed personal and official favors on his protégé and that Penn established himself in London as the king's adviser.

James's position had already grown desperate when, on June 10, 1688, the birth of a Catholic son and heir apparent brought affairs to a crisis. England could no longer look to an early day of deliverance from a Catholic monarch and, in a matter of months, the Glorious Revolution took place. The powerful Protestants of England invited William, King of the Netherlands, and his wife Mary, Protestant daughter of James II, to accept the crown of England. James fled without a struggle and by December 1688 the reign of William and Mary had begun. The Church of England, established by Elizabeth in 1570, remained as a strong support of the monarchy.

YEARS OF MISFORTUNE

When King William came to power in 1688, he had Penn arrested for treason and held in £6,000 bail. Penn cleared himself but he was soon arrested again on the same charge. His name became one for Englishmen to revile and curse: "Penn the Traitor" or "Penn the Jacobite."

Condemned in England as an agent of James, Penn was blamed in Pennsylvania for political conflicts which embittered that colony. During his absence, the Council and Assembly not only fell to fighting for power between themselves, but neglected to carry out such basic responsibilities as submitting laws to England for approval and enforcing the imperial trade acts. On September 16, 1688, Penn named John Blackwell, former officer in Cromwell's army and lately a New England businessman, to the position of deputy governor of Pennsylvania.

When they received this news, the Quakers of Pennsylvania quit fighting among themselves and joined ranks to fight against Blackwell. When he arrived, government officers ignored him. Thomas Lloyd hid the Great Seal of the province and refused to authenticate any paper he did not approve. The Governor could not make appointments or sign bills into law except with Lloyd's consent. Blackwell wrote Penn scorching letters about the obstructive tactics of the Quakers and brought Thomas Lloyd before Council for impeachment. The Council so confused the issue that no one could be quite sure what action it had taken, except that Lloyd remained in good standing. Blackwell, in April 1689, sent his resignation to William Penn and from that day until the king deprived Penn of his charter in 1692, the Pennsylvania Quakers ran the government as they pleased.

Their effort at self-rule brought political turmoil before the first year had passed. The people of the Lower Counties refused to be governed by the Pennsylvania representatives, but the latter imposed their power. They appointed their own deputy governor, Thomas Lloyd, thus confirming what John Blackwell had earlier told Penn—that Lloyd had laid out his whole course to gain this position. Markham, who also wanted the job, was sidetracked by the Quakers into the post of deputy governor of Delaware. As if the political infighting were not enough to shake Penn's confidence in his "holy experiment," the Quakers fell into discord over their own beliefs. In 1690 George Keith split the Society of Friends by insisting that Quakers ought to stay out of politics. By 1692 the Keithian Schism had come to a climax of bad feeling, name calling, and libel suits.

Penn, writing letters from England, tried vainly to bring peace to his troubled land. He sincerely wished for a better example than this of his statecraft, but he also had a strong financial motive for desiring a more effective government. He poured his wealth into Pennsylvania until little remained; he wished quitrents to be collected and sent to him. But instead of receiving money due him, he received only abuse and demands for further outlays of the proprietary funds. The War of the League of Augsburg had begun between England and France, and King William wished the colonies to prepare for their defense. Pennsylvania's Assembly refused to defend its own ports or to provide any assistance to neighbors. Penn would either have to finance the defense of his land personally or return to Pennsylvania and try to mobilize men and money among the non-Quakers there.

He prepared to undertake this mission early in 1691, but just before his departure George Fox died and Penn stayed in England to deliver the funeral oration. When he had concluded, officers arrested him on another charge of treason and conspiracy. Though the charge eventually was dismissed, Penn had to remain for a year under house arrest at his home at Worminghurst. In the meantime, on March 10, 1692, King William, partly as a defense measure, canceled Penn's charter and reannexed Pennsylvania to New York, whose governor, Benjamin Fletcher, would provide for its security against the French.

Penn at this moment perhaps recalled his father's last words: "Be not troubled at disappointments, for afflictions make wise." Suspected of treason, execrated, stripped of honors and of property, oppressed by debt, and condemned by the Quakers of Pennsylvania, Penn had cause enough for bitterness and despair. Instead of complaining, he wrote two remarkable books. The first, *Fruits of Solitude*, contained maxims of wit, wisdom, and human understanding; the other, *An Essay toward the Present and Future Peace of Europe*, proposed a confederation of European nations prophetic of the hopes of later centuries.

Penn's wife had died in 1694, and his son Springett Penn two years later, leaving of his seven children only his daughter Letitia and young William. The latter had become a wild, unruly, and headstrong youth who brought his father little but grief. Anyone who seeks an example of courageous response to personal misfortune can find one in William Penn during the years 1689 to 1696. In *Fruits of Solitude* he wrote: "Nor can we fall below the *Arms* of God, how low soever it be we fall." An acquaintance observed: "The more he is pressed, the more he rises."

Rumors of a plan to unite the northern colonies of British America into a single unit for easier administration and defense prodded Penn into an effort to regain his charter. Appealing to Queen Mary while William was at war on the Continent, Penn promised to take responsibility for proper defense of his domain. On August 9, 1694, William Penn regained possession of his proprietorship. In 1696 he married Hannah Callowhill, aged twenty-six, the daughter of a Bristol merchant. Hannah proved as fruitful a wife as Guli, bearing seven children to William Penn. In her later years she ably managed the province.

SECOND VISIT TO PENNSYLVANIA

In the autumn of 1699 Penn set sail for Pennsylvania accompanied by his wife, his daughter Letitia, and James Logan, his private secretary. Much had happened since 1684. William Markham, whom Governor Fletcher of New York had appointed his deputy in charge of

Pennsylvania in 1692, remained in this post after Penn regained the colony. By this time the Assembly had so far seized the lawmaking power that a return to its status under the constitution of 1683 seemed impossible. Penn had instructed Markham to provide adequate defense for the province, but the Assembly refused to approve any funds for this purpose unless it obtained the right to initiate legislation. As a result, the Pennsylvanians drafted a new constitution, known as Markham's Frame or the Third Frame of 1696, granting the lawmaking power and other privileges to the Assembly. The Assembly then passed a defense bill, and Markham approved the new constitution. Penn never sanctioned this instrument because it weakened his political control, but permitted it to function until he should arrive in America to observe the government at first hand.

Markham's Frame had dubious legal status, for it had been adopted merely as a legislative act. Some Quakers called it an "unwarrantable, illegal & arbitrary Act," refused to acknowledge its legitimacy, and caused trouble by holding elections under the old 1683 constitution. Penn himself asserted that any change in the government "is my own peculiar prerogative." He withheld approval of the new document partly for this reason and partly because he feared that, if he made it official, he would have to submit it to the Crown which would very likely reject it.

Penn knew when he left England in 1699 that the task of making a constitution awaited him. He knew also from the many letters he had received that his utopian dream of a "holy experiment" had vanished. Complaints seemed to come from every quarter. Officials in adjacent colonies said that Pennsylvania disrupted their fur trade, stole their commerce, and lured away their settlers.

Royal officers stationed in Pennsylvania reported that Delaware Bay and even the port of Philadelphia had become headquarters for smugglers and pirates. The merchants shipped tobacco illegally to Europe in casks with a little flour at each end. Pirates freely used the bay with the cooperation of local citizens. Governor Markham could get no money to hire an armed force, and failed in his attempts to muster volunteers because he refused them the right to keep pirate booty. A Philadelphia magistrate forced officers of the admiralty court to return goods to a captured smuggler. Admiralty Judge Robert Quary called the Pennsylvanians "a perverse, obstenant and turbulent people, that will not submit to any power or Lawes but their owne," and charged them with encouraging piracy. The Anglicans, too, raised protest. Members of Christ Church alleged that the Quakers excluded them from participation in the government, and imposed "misseries and hardships" upon them. Such were the distractions and disorders Penn would have to face when he resumed the governorship of the colony.

A joyous welcome greeted the Penn family when the Proprietor reached Philadelphia in November 1699. The city had grown impressively in fifteen years from a few score houses to a population of 5,000. It already rivaled New York in wealth and trade. Although no one had kept account of the immigrants, Penn recorded that new settlers had been coming in at the rate of about 1,500 a year. Though the government always pleaded poverty and Penn could collect little rent money, the population seemed prosperous and the economy flourishing.

The Penns lived for a short time in Philadelphia and then moved to Pennsbury Manor, where the Proprietor enjoyed the life of an English gentleman amid furnishings and finery not entirely in keeping with Quaker simplicity. Familiar with the ways of a royal court, Penn conducted official activities with a good deal of pomp, but otherwise retained his old informality and friendliness. His aristocratic tendencies, however, underlay a contest soon to arise with stricter Quakers led by Attorney General David Lloyd under the banner of the Popular party.

Pennsylvania's government was in disorder. Some people claimed that the constitution of 1683 still remained in effect; others said that Markham's Frame had superseded it. Penn tried to resolve the difficulty by ordering an election under the provisions of the Second Frame in the expectation that the Council and Assembly would revise and amend the older constitution. But the Assembly balked in protest against its inferiority to the Council under the 1683 Frame. Penn then proposed that he rule the colony without regard to either constitution until a new one could be prepared, and the Legislature approved. From June 7, 1700, until October 28, 1701, Penn governed the colony without any constitution.

Penn's interim government brought increasing order to Pennsylvania, though not without raising resentments and disagreements which would later create party warfare. At the insistence of the British Board of Trade, he removed William Markham and David Lloyd from office and appointed an advisory council of nine. These two acts laid out the lines of two political groups; one known as the Proprietary party, composed of Penn's wealthy Philadelphia counselors headed by James Logan; the other called the Popular party, led by David Lloyd and composed mostly of the poorer back-country Quakers.

Penn devoted most of his time to consultations with the governors of colonies bordering Pennsylvania, trying to devise some effective solutions for land disputes and to solve the riddle of Delaware's legal status. He kept in close touch with the Earl of Bellomont, Governor of New York; Sir Francis Nicholson, Governor of Virginia; and Governor Andrew Hamilton of New Jersey, on such matters as the suppression of piracy, the extradition of criminals, boundaries, colonial defense, and uniform laws on marriage, naturalization, and coinage. The granting of deeds to land in Pennsylvania had created conflicting claims almost beyond human ingenuity to resolve. Not only had grants been assigned without precise definition, but the records themselves were in disorder and full of erasures, blots, and interlineations. Penn put the Assembly to work on the problem and in 1701 signed a lengthy document known as the Bill of Property which was intended to settle the main problem of faulty first surveys. Finally, there was the problem of the Lower Counties, whose inhabitants denied the right of Pennsylvania's government to rule and protested by noncooperation. Penn concluded that Delaware would have to be separated, somehow, from Pennsylvania.

All these weighty matters stood in the form of unfinished business when word came that the English government was planning a unification of American colonies for defense and might bring them all under the Crown. Penn arranged to leave for England in the fall of 1701 to resist this proposal, but some government would have to be created for Pennsylvania to serve in his absence. The Assembly had discussed a new constitution, but had shown no hurry to reach a decision. Now the time for action had come. After a brief debate, the Assembly agreed to a constitution which essentially placed the governing power in its own hands, and asked Penn for approval. He hurriedly agreed, and on October 28, 1701, Pennsylvania's fourth constitution, known as the Charter of Privileges, became law.

LAST YEARS

King William's death in 1702 brought Queen Anne to the throne and temporarily ended the movement to unite the American colonies. Penn could now have returned to his province, but the marriage of his daughter, Letitia, the birth of more children, and his growing financial difficulties induced him to remain in England. Penn's estate had become entangled by encumbrances of a description that nearly passed belief. This sad and incredible chapter of Penn's life had been carefully plotted for twenty years by the Proprietor's trusted but thoroughly dishonest steward, Philip Ford.

Penn had hired the Quaker Ford as manager of his father's Irish estates in 1669. Ford collected rents and kept account of the expenses of Penn's properties, charging his master from time to time for funds Ford claimed to have spent in performing his job. Unable to pay debts to Ford which had accumulated over many years, Penn gave Ford a mortgage on the entire province of Pennsylvania, and periodically signed further certificates of indebtedness until he had obligated himself to pay Ford £20,000 to redeem the mortgage.

After Philip Ford died, his widow pressed Penn for payment and, as he had no funds, had him thrown in prison for debt. Penn remained in debtor's prison through most of the year 1708. He had by this time come to doubt whether he could much longer carry the responsibility of the proprietorship. He estimated that, including the original £16.000 he had exchanged for Pennsylvania, the province in twenty-five years had cost him £75,000. He lay in debtor's prison with scarce a shilling in quitrents to feed his family. "A melancholy scene enough," he wrote to James Logan. "Expense, disappointment, ingratitude, poverty. . . . I must perish with gold in my view but not in my power."

At length he decided that Pennsylvania ought to be returned to the Crown. By this change, the costs of administration and of a defense establishment could be borne by the Queen's treasury, and the Quakers could be relieved of the responsibility for military appropriations. Papers for the transfer had been drawn up ready for Penn's signature when, in the spring of 1712, he suffered a paralytic stroke. Penn never signed the documents that would have made Pennsylvania a royal colony. Hannah Penn, with a firm and competent administrative hand, took up her husband's duties. On July 30, 1718, in his seventy-fourth year, William Penn died.

THE MANY-SIDED WILLIAM PENN

In summarizing the life of the founder of Pennsylvania, we may apply to him a phrase usually reserved to Benjamin Franklin, and speak of "the many-sided William Penn." William Penn had distinctive talents and exercised lasting influence as a religious leader, a political philosopher, a social reformer, a founder of states, a writer, a promoter, a city planner, and a conservationist.

Penn's conversion to the ideals of the Society of Friends at the cost of sacrificing a career in English public life and of suffering banishment from home, proved the depth and sincerity of his religious conviction. The later persecutions he endured for the sake of conscience marked him as a religious martyr. He had no relish for such a role, however, and took no pride in suffering for a cause; rather, he had the spirit to turn successive imprisonments to good account by studying, writing, and optimistically planning for later good works. He remained a preacher from first to last, in youth and in old age, in wealth and in poverty, in high public position and in political disgrace. His continuing eagerness to bear witness to the religious truths that filled his mind constituted the most vigorous and compelling aspect of his character. He talked to the mighty with as much frankness as to peasants. His contemporaries ranked him as a notable religious leader, as have succeeding generations.

Penn's belief in the close relation between the Deity and the political state led him into the realm of political philosophy. He opposed the imposition of any one formal religious creed by the state, but nonetheless held that "government, in itself, is a venerable ordinance of God." Thus, he laid the groundwork for the separation of church and state, but insisted at the same time that the state be rooted in a belief in divine order. For this reason he excluded atheists and anarchists from civil privileges and protection in Pennsylvania's constitutions.

He pondered the failure of governments to bring benefits to their people, read the classic studies of ideal or utopian societies, and tried to plan a commonwealth in which a simple and committed people could try, in real life, a "holy experiment." In his planning he not only read widely but consulted directly with such thinkers as John Locke, Benjamin Furly, and Algernon Sidney. His letter to the people of Delaware Bay in April 1681 had a new and dramatic ring: "You are now fixed at the mercy of no governor who comes to make his fortune great. . . . I shall not usurp the right of any, or oppress his person."

Penn tried hard to achieve a workable balance between the claims of people to rights of property, rights of political control, and rights of equality of treatment. He did not solve this tangle, but unraveled a few of the knots in it. At his behest the Pennsylvania colonial courts granted more procedural protection for defendants, and restrained arbitrary acts of public officials against citizens according to more clearly defined rules and fairer concepts than prevailed in most colonies. The specific proposals in his *Concessions* of July 1681 aimed at nothing less than the complete integration of the Indians into the legal and commercial life of the Europeans. The grant of power to the Assembly in 1701, though Penn doubted its wisdom at the moment, demonstrated that he trusted the capacity of human beings to govern themselves through elected representatives three-quarters of a century before the American Revolution.

Penn's political philosophy rested on the concepts of a God-ordered universe, of toleration for different modes of acknowledging the Deity, of justice, and of political equality. He added mercy and piety to these ideas as a basis for introducing numerous social reforms. Penn's "holy experiment" would provide public schooling not for a select few but for "all children within the province"; courts would impose not the savage penalties commonly ordered in Europe but mild and humane punishments; legal fees would be moderate, and all offenses but murder and treason bailable; prisons would not charge inmates for board and room, but would function as workhouses; gambling, lotteries, riotous and bloody sports, and other public excitements would be outlawed; the number of taverns would be limited to the clear needs of a locality; human slavery would be forbidden. While not all these reforms achieved immediate application, they illustrate Penn's view of an ideal government.

As a writer, Penn produced prodigiously, and he merits a larger measure of attention than modern anthologists have accorded him. His knowledge of foreign languages and his familiarity with theology, social philosophy, history, and political economy gave him a scholarly background and enriched his productions with illustrative data. While he was no stylist, he spoke loudly and clearly to people of his own time. He wrote theological works, polemic tracts in support of his ideas, promotional literature, travel accounts, political studies, philosophic observations, and innumerable letters.

It would be too much to expect that a man of such a variety of interests as Penn would have had the mentality and habits of a man of business. He had high regard for property and hoped to profit from it, but paid little attention to details of management and gave extensions instead of pressing for the settlement of debts. Yet he proved energetic and successful in promoting the settlement of his colony and in defending its boundaries. His province rapidly achieved financial stability, but Penn never managed to gain the anticipated return from his investment. He showed foresight and originality in planning the city of Philadelphia, in setting up regulations to distribute land among many small holders, in providing for the conservation of timber resources, and in creating from the outset standards of fair practice in the marketplace. In such matters he showed good business sense. But in terms of forecasting and providing for his own financial needs he failed.

As a husband and parent, Penn experienced both more grief and more happiness than most people know. His marriage to Gulielma Springett was nearly idyllic, but their children brought them mostly sorrow. Five of them died young. Letitia married a man who became thoroughly obnoxious and hounded Penn in later years for some money he had loaned his father-in-law. William broke with the Quakers, became a wastrel, and humiliated his parents. Penn also had seven children by his second wife, Hannah, of whom four survived to maturity. The three boys, John, Thomas, and Richard, all shared in the proprietorship of Pennsylvania after their mother's death in 1727, and played an important role in the later history of the province.

BIBLIOGRAPHY

Pennsylvania's history during Penn's lifetime is most dependably treated by Edwin B. Bronner: *Penn's Holy Experiment* and Gary B. Nash: *Quakers and Politics,* both previously cited. For the British relationship, see Vincent Buranelli: *The King and The Quaker: A Study of William Penn and James II* (1962); Joseph E. Illick: *William Penn the Politician, His Relations with the English Government* (1965); and M. G. Hall, L. H. Leder, and M. G. Kammen: *The Glorious Revolution in America* (1964).

General histories of colonial Pennsylvania give detailed coverage to this period. Written from the Quaker viewpoint are Robert Proud: *History of Pennsylvania,* 2 vols. (1797–1798); and Isaac Sharpless: *A History of Quaker Government in Pennsylvania,* 2 vols. (1900). The best books on the provincial era are William R. Shepherd: *History of Proprietary Government in Pennsylvania* (1896); Albert S. Bolles: *Pennsylvania, Province and State, 1609–1790,* 2 vols. (1899); and Charles P. Keith: *Chronicles of Pennsylvania from the English Revolution to the Peace of Aix-la-Chappelle, 1688–1748,* 2 vols. (1917).

Much source material has been printed in Samuel Hazard (ed.): *Hazard's Register of Pennsylvania,* 16 vols. (1828–1836). Hazard also edited the *Colonial Records,* 16 vols. (1838–1853), in which vols. 1–10 give the "Minutes of the Provincial Council, 1682–1776." The *Pennsylvania Archives,* first series, 12 vols. (1852–1856), prints the "Papers of the Secretary of the Commonwealth, 1664–1790," a record which parallels and supplements the *Colonial Records.* The *Pennsylvania Archives,* eighth series, 8 vols. (1931–1935), prints the "Votes and Proceedings of the House of Representatives" from the beginning until 1776.

Biographies bearing on this period, in addition to those previously cited, include Roy N. Lokken: *David Lloyd, Colonial Lawmaker* (1959); Isaac Sharpless: *Political Leaders of Provincial Pennsylvania* (1919); and William S. Armor: *Lives of the Governors* (1872). The latter, though old and uncritical, provides the best extant summary of the lives of all Pennsylvania governors from 1624 to 1872, and is useful for this politically turbulent period. William H. Lloyd: *Early Courts of Pennsylvania* (1910), provides much valuable information on the administration of Pennsylvania government during Penn's lifetime.

CHAPTER FOUR

The Seed of a Nation

Few societies have made the transition from autocratic to popular government as swiftly or peacefully as the Pennsylvania Quakers. Within twenty years, between 1681 and 1701, these people moved steadily from a system of monarchical power vested in William Penn by his proprietary charter to control of the province by a popularly elected assembly. The successive stages of this extraordinary swing from one-man rule to representative government can be explicitly marked in five basic documents: the Charter of 1681 and the four colonial constitutions of Pennsylvania.

THE COLONIAL CONSTITUTIONS

The Pennsylvania Charter of 1681 All the English proprietary charters except that of Pennsylvania gave the proprietors the powers of the Bishop of Durham—a grant equivalent to independent sovereignty, limited only by loyalty to the King. In Penn's charter, the King somewhat modified the traditional powers of the proprietor. Penn received no right to grant titles of nobility and he had to submit provincial laws to the King for approval, to acknowledge the right of Parliament to tax the colony, to maintain a provincial agent in London, and to present all Pennsylvania laws to "the freemen" or to "their delegates" for approval.

But except for these restrictions, the charter granted Penn "absolute power" over his principality. He had the sole authority to make laws, levy taxes, coin money, regulate commerce, appoint provincial officials, administer justice, grant pardons, make war, erect manors, sell land, and perform all other acts pertaining to sovereignty. The charter gave

Penn the broadest latitude in planning the details of the political structure and administration of his province.

The first two frames of government: 1682 and 1683 The First Frame took longer to make than it lasted, for it became effective on April 25, 1682, and was abandoned a year later. Penn prepared more than a score of preliminary drafts. He approached the task more as a scholar than as a statesman, wrestling with the philosophic problem of the nature of man and the ultimate purpose of government. He summarized his conclusions on these matters in a moralistic preface to the First Frame.

Government, Penn wrote, was a mechanism of God to terrify evildoers and to aid those who do good. Most thinkers agreed that government ought to promote happiness, but no two agreed on the means to this end. "I do not find a model in the world," Penn observed, "that time, place, and some singular emergencies have not necessarily altered, nor is it easy to frame a civil government that shall serve all places alike." He declined to choose among monarchy, aristocracy, and democracy, but would adopt the idea that "any government is free to the people under it where the laws rule and the people are a party to those laws." No mere scheme or system of government would, of itself, bring good results. "Governments, like clocks, go from the motion men give them. Let men be good, and the government cannot be bad; if it be ill, they will cure it. But if men be bad, let the government be ever so good, they will endeavour to warp and spoil it."

The First Frame provided that a governor and a provincial Council of seventy-two over which the governor presided would perform all the major functions of government—executive, legislative, and judicial. A General Assembly of 200 would give or withhold its assent to bills proposed by the Council, and could suggest amendments. All freemen had the right to participate in elections for council members and assemblymen. A freeman was defined as anyone who owned 50 acres of land or had £50 in property. Under pressure from large purchasers of land, Penn had contrived a system that kept his power intact, for he appointed all the first officers and exercised strong influence in naming the candidates for council.

The first trial of the constitution of 1682 showed that the Council and Assembly were too large, and that insufficient time had been permitted for consideration of bills by the Assembly. On April 2, 1683, Penn approved the Second Frame in which he adopted the idea of geographical representation by creating a council of eighteen and an assembly of thirty-six members, who would be apportioned equally among the original counties, Philadelphia, Chester, and Bucks. Bills should be published twenty days before the date set by council for the convening of the assembly. The Proprietor lost his triple vote in council, and agreed never to "perform any public act of State whatever . . . but by and with the advice and consent of the Provincial Council."

These seemingly minor changes contained a major transfer of power from Penn to the Council. The Proprietor in the First Frame had given up his exclusive power to make or veto laws. In the Second Frame he gave up the triple vote, which would have weighed heavily in a council of eighteen. Finally, he agreed not to act in any public capacity except with the consent of the Council. Taken together, these three items constituted the assignment of Penn's legislative and executive powers to council, and made him subordinate to it. The Assembly gained additional time to consider bills, and changed from a group of voters having the veto power to a deliberative and consultative body of representatives. In fact, the

Assembly from the start had declared its right to propose bills. The first day it met under the Second Frame, a member introduced a resolution that the Assembly ought to make legislative proposals. Under the first two constitutions the Assembly had not been granted power to initiate legislation, but in practice it usurped this power. When Governor Fletcher of New York took charge of Pennsylvania in 1692, he ordered the election of a special Assembly and charged it with the task of passing defense bills despite protests from the Council. Thus, by the time Penn's colony had been restored in 1694, the Assembly had in fact been acting as a legislature. When it refused to approve any bills until it received constitutional sanction for its legislative functions, Deputy Governor Markham felt he had no alternative except to create a new constitution which would give a basis in law to existing practice.

Markham's Frame and the Charter of Privileges   In 1696 the Assembly drafted a constitution known as Markham's Frame. Under it the Council would consist of two members from each county, and the Assembly of four from each; all would hold office for one year and receive pay for their services. The Assembly would have the right to initiate legislation equally with the Council, and the right to determine the times of its own adjournment. Otherwise, Markham's Frame was much like the Second Frame. But an important development had occurred, for Pennsylvania now had a bicameral legislature. The Council still held the more powerful position, as it exercised administrative and judicial as well as legislative functions, but the Assembly had carved out a major place for itself as a lawmaking body. Penn did not approve of this change, nor did a number of the old councilmen who resisted their loss of status and denied the legitimacy of the new constitution. Nonetheless, Pennsylvania operated under Markham's Frame until Penn returned to America in 1699.

On October 28, 1701, Penn signed the constitution of 1701, or Charter of Privileges, which the Assembly had hurriedly drafted before his departure for England. The new constitution made several substantial alterations in the governmental structure and created a political blueprint that is recognizably modern. Under it, an Assembly of four men (later increased to eight) from each county, elected annually by the freemen, became the single lawmaking body. The Council ceased to be an elective body and lost its legislative powers. It now comprised men appointed by the governor to serve him in an advisory capacity. The governor no longer needed to obtain the consent of the Council to act, but reassumed independent executive authority. The constitution explicitly recognized the power of the Proprietor and the Crown to veto provincial laws.

For the first time, this constitution clearly erected an executive branch comprising the governor and his advisory Council; a legislative branch, comprising the unicameral Assembly; and a judicial branch, composed of the appointed judges and the elected county judicial officers. Step by step, a paternalistic government controlled by William Penn had grown into a constitutional republic with the power tied closely to the freemen, or £50 freeholders. This swing of the pendulum from authoritarian to popular rule had occurred peacefully in the brief period of twenty years. The rapidity of the democratization of Pennsylvania can be attributed to three factors: the willingness of Penn to relinquish power, the equalitarian spirit of the Quakers, and the invitation to experiment afforded them by a new, sparsely settled country. Many of the framers of the Charter of Privileges conceived of their work as a temporary or standby government; Penn certainly numbered among these. But this constitution was destined to remain in force for seventy-five years and to create a strong tradition of popular government in Pennsylvania.

THE PEOPLE

The simplest way to describe the populating of colonial Pennsylvania is to picture a stake driven into the ground at the waterfront of Philadelphia. A 25-mile radius from this peg would encompass the area of Pennsylvania settled mainly by English immigrants between 1680 and 1710. Extend the radius to the length of 75 miles, and the outer 50 miles of the circle would correspond roughly to the "Dutch" country from Northampton to York Counties. Here, from 1710 to 1750, the German-speaking immigrants to colonial Pennsylvania made their homes. Again extend the radius to 150 miles, and in the outermost circumference, corresponding roughly to the arc of the Allegheny Mountains and valleys, the Scotch-Irish settled from 1717 to the Revolutionary War. These three—the English, the Germans, and the Scotch-Irish—immigrated one after the other, occupied regions successively further west, and together constituted the largest part of the colonial population. This image conveys the essential truth of Pennsylvania settlement, but is much oversimplified. The major groups were concentrated in the regions described, but were by no means confined to them; they came in a distinct sequence of waves, but with minor inflow throughout the colonial era; and while the English, Germans, and Scotch-Irish constituted the largest numerical groups, they were joined by a larger variety of other immigrants than could be found in any other American province.

The English era: 1680–1710 Pennsylvania drew most of its first settlers from the English Quakers, for the colony had been created as a haven for this persecuted sect. But while English Quakers outnumbered all others during the first thirty years, they were joined by many other Quaker groups, especially the Welsh and the Dutch, who created a diverse base for the province from the outset. The glowing reports they sent to Europe gave substantive proof to the descriptions and promises contained in Penn's advertising booklets, and encouraged many sectarians, who would never have thought of removing to Massachusetts or Virginia because of the religious conformity required there, to dream of making a new home in Penn's colony. The news that others of their own sort had found opportunity for peace and a good life spread widely through Europe and attracted the attention of persecuted sects and of poor families who believed they might improve their lot in Pennsylvania.

Before Penn ever set foot in his province, he had sold 875,000 acres of land, most of it to English Quakers. Several hundred of these came to settle in the summer of 1681 aboard the ships *John and Sarah, Amity,* and *Bristol Factor.* Penn brought more in the *Welcome* in 1682, and a year later reported that fifty or sixty ships had put into Philadelphia and discharged some 4,000 new settlers. The rapid pace of English Quaker migration in the two decades after 1681 arose from many causes. Penn's popularity and his liberal distribution of land had much to do with it. The increasing severity of English attacks on Quakers by local magistrates during the reign of King William played a part. The Toleration Act of 1689 required an oath of allegiance to the Crown which Quakers would not take, and King William exercised toleration only within the strict letter of the act. The outbreak of war with France in 1689 gave the peaceful Quakers additional reason to leave. There was the dramatic appeal of Penn's "holy experiment," for many Quakers had a sincere wish to participate in such a novel effort at creating the ideal society. And finally, the hope of making money stimulated many; Quaker thought placed no restraint on efforts to make an ample living. Quakers in joint stock companies bought large tracts in the expectation of a profit and promoted settlement as a part of the business enterprise. London, Liverpool, and Bristol merchants bought into colonization companies.

While Quakers were the most numerous of the English settlers, many other Englishmen also came. For example, by 1700 some 200 Anglicans had become communicants at Christ Church, Philadelphia. At least three Baptist congregations had been organized in Pennsylvania by the turn of the century, composed of English and Welsh immigrants. A group of English Presbyterians from Barbados came to Pennsylvania in 1698 and established the first of their churches in Penn's land.

Welshmen composed the second most numerous class of immigrants up to 1710. These fiercely independent inhabitants of western Britain had a language and culture of their own which they zealously tried to protect against encroachment by English civilization. As the Society of Friends had achieved a large following in Wales, a group of leading Welsh Quakers conferred with Penn in London in 1681 about the creation of an American colony for their countrymen. It will be recalled that Penn first planned to call his domain New Wales. The Welsh agreed to purchase 40,000 acres of land, known as the Welsh Tract or the Welsh Barony, west of the Schuylkill River in Chester County.

The Welshmen who negotiated to buy this 62-square-mile manor hoped to establish there a duplicate of the old country, revitalize their unique language and their ancient folkways, and create a separate, autonomous, miniature state within the larger Pennsylvania. Several thousand Welsh farmers soon moved into the Welsh Tract and established Quaker meetings which became, in fact, assemblies for the political management of the area. But trouble arose in obtaining money to pay for the Welsh Tract, from conflicting land grants within it, and from the determination of the Philadelphia government to exercise political control. Upon the failure of the Welsh to pay for the entire tract, Penn terminated the agreement and began to sell portions of the original Welsh Barony to others. By 1690 the patriotic enthusiasm for an American "New Wales" had waned, and this project came to an end.

Welsh immigration, however, continued. Individuals and groups with less ambitious plans bought smaller plots and began settlements at places named after their homes—St. Davids, Gwynedd, Bryn Mawr, and Cynwyd. The nearby hills became the Welsh Mountains. These people continued to come until about 1720, when perhaps 6,000 had made their way to southeastern Pennsylvania.

Third in importance among the first adventurers were the Dutch Quakers, a group much more influential than its small number might suggest. Two companies, the Krefeld Economy and the Frankfort Company, bought large tracts of land in 1682 and 1683. The subscribers were Dutch Quakers who, before coming to Pennsylvania in 1683, had been living in the Rhenish provinces of Germany. Coming from the towns of Krefeld and Krisheim in the Rhine Valley, they established the community of Germantown. Penn had visited them on his continental tours of 1671 and 1677, and these early evangelical efforts bore fruit. While the Krisheim and Krefeld settlers established the village of Germantown, many of them living in riverbank caves until they could erect suitable houses, a young German scholar, Francis Daniel Pastorius, waited anxiously in Philadelphia for the arrival of immigrants to be sent by the Frankfort Company. He was its agent, and had purchased land for the company on his way to America in 1683. But the company failed to recruit settlers and eventually forfeited its 25,000-acre tract. Pastorius moved to Germantown in 1685, and became the leading spiritual and political leader there and an effective promoter of colonization.

The German immigration: 1708–1750 It is one of the oddities of Pennsylvania history that the settlers of Germantown were Dutchmen, whereas the people commonly called the Pennsylvania Dutch were Germans. The Germans came mainly in two waves, first the *sect people,* from about 1708 to 1720, and second the *church people,* that is, the Reformed, the Lutherans, and the Moravians, between 1720 and 1750. The dates indicate not precise limits but eras in which peaks of activity took place.

In 1708 a heavy migration began to pour into Pennsylvania from Alsace, Lorraine, Swabia, Baden, and Württemburg, and especially from the Rhenish Palatinate and Switzerland. These settlers, mostly Mennonites and Dunkers (Dunkards or German Baptist Brethren), came to be called Palatines. They left their homes at this particular moment because the armies of England and France, fighting the War of the Spanish Succession, had utterly devastated their country between 1704 and 1708. If this was the immediate cause, it was also the culmination of a century of misery for farmers of the Rhineland. The Thirty Years' War, from 1618 to 1648, raged so fiercely in this valley that its original population all but disappeared. French King Louis XIV invaded the Palatinate and laid waste its fields in 1674, 1680, and 1689. When England began to contest the French, these two countries fought their battles in Germany. The armies wiped out towns, obliterated villages, and repeatedly stole or destroyed the crops of the surviving peasants. Thus the great German trek to Pennsylvania was a flight of war refugees.

But other pressures also existed. The revocation of the Edict of Nantes in 1685 denied Protestants the right to worship in regions controlled by Louis XIV. Where Protestants ruled, they persecuted the Anabaptists and Pietists. Local German princes, in straitened circumstances because of the wars, imposed heavier tax levies on their already impoverished subjects. And as if enough wretchedness had not fallen upon the Palatinate, the winter of 1708–1709 brought storms and cold of unprecedented severity.

In 1709 a group of Mennonites from Switzerland settled along Pequea Creek in Lancaster County. Delighted with their new home, they sent one of their number back to Switzerland to persuade others to migrate. Hundreds of Swiss Mennonites responded and soon established a thriving community along the Conestoga and Pequea Creeks.

In 1714 that branch of the Mennonites known as the Amish began settlements in Berks County. Five years later Peter Becker, a Dunker preacher from Krefeld, led his people to Lancaster County. Other Dunkers followed and located near the Mennonites along the Conestoga, at Oley in Berks County, and at Falckner's Swamp in Montgomery County. After the first Mennonite, Amish, and Dunker colonies had been successfully established, the influx of these people steadily continued as news of their life in Pennsylvania circulated among the brethren in Europe.

In the summer of 1708, while war was raging in the Rhine Valley, many Palatines fled to England. Queen Anne sympathized and formulated a plan to send these refugees to her New York colony. The German émigré settlement at Schoharie, southwest of Albany, soon moved to Berks County, entering Pennsylvania by the north branch of the Susquehanna. Although the European war ended in 1713, the Palatine migration continued. By 1717, Pennsylvania's Governor William Keith complained that ships came to Philadelphia discharging hundreds of Germans who had sailed from England without the government's knowledge. In 1719, some 7,000 Palatines entered the port of Philadelphia.

Religious groups, persecuted by orthodox Protestant churches as well as by Catholics in Europe, sought safety in Pennsylvania. In 1720 Conrad Beissel, a German mystic, brought a body of "perfectionists" to Germantown in hopes of joining the Wissahickon community of Johann Kelpius. As that had already broken up, Beissel moved to Cocalico Creek in Lancaster County and founded a society of Seventh Day Baptists which he named Ephrata. The Schwenkfelders arrived from Silesia in 1734, making their settlement along Perkiomen Creek from Pennsburg to Skippack.

Members of the Moravian Church in Poland, Hungary, and Moravia removed to Georgia in 1735. In 1740 some of the Moravians from Georgia moved to Pennsylvania, and the following year they purchased land along the Lehigh River, which became the site of their major town, Bethlehem. Others came from Europe to set up the new communities of Nazareth and Lititz.

By the middle of the eighteenth century the Germanic immigration had become a steady flow. The German Reformed people had grown so numerous by the 1740s that the Synod of Holland assigned a special agent, Michael Schlatter, to work in Pennsylvania with the nearly fifty congregations there. The Lutherans, who had a local history going back to the days of Swedish dominion, migrated in larger numbers than the Reformed people.

Moravian Bishop August G. Spangenberg estimated that 100,000 German-speaking people lived in Pennsylvania by 1750. In 1749 alone the new German arrivals at Philadelphia numbered 8,778. As the German communities became settled and the prospects of a newcomer finding familiar churches and fellow countrymen increased, the type of immigration changed. It was no longer necessary, for safety and companionship, that a whole congregation move at once. After 1730 more and more Germans signed for passage privately as indentured servants, in the expectation of finding a place among their own people in the Pennsylvania Dutch country. The Assembly often considered ways to check this immigration, but Thomas Penn wrote:

> This province has for some years been the asylum of the distressed Protestants of the Palatinate, and other parts of Germany, and I believe it may with truth be said that the present flourishing condition of it is in a great measure owing to the industry of these people; and should any discouragement divert them from coming hither, it may well be apprehended that the value of your lands will fall, and your advances to wealth be much slower; for it is not altogether the goodness of the soil, but the number and industry of the people that make a flourishing country.

The Scotch-Irish immigration: 1717–1776 The third great migration to Pennsylvania brought the Scotch-Irish, or lowland Scots, who for some generations had lived in northern Ireland. During the seventeenth century they rejuvenated the run-down farms of the dispossessed Irish, built substantial houses and barns, and developed a flourishing agriculture which raised their economic condition and made them fiercely loyal to Ulster. But the Ulster Scots encountered troubles in the early 1700s which started the migration to America. The Test Act of 1689 threatened their Kirk, and depression in the linen industry, curtailment of the wool trade, rising rents, and periodic famines made life in Ulster intolerable. Between 1717 and 1776, 250,000 Ulstermen migrated overseas. Even before the major migrations began, many Scotch-Irish Presbyterians had come to Pennsylvania for religious freedom. The first American Presbytery had been established at Philadelphia, and the city had thirteen Presbyterian churches by 1717. But the later migrations grew from economic distress in Ulster.

There were five great waves of Scotch-Irish immigration. The migration of 1717–1718 grew directly out of rack renting, or the practice by a landlord of raising the rent on expiration of the lease. Such a practice in Scotland had brought these people to Ulster, and during the early years long-term leases had given them protection. Now the short-term leases had returned and landlords often rerented to the highest bidder. Thousands of dispossessed and angry Scotch-Irish fled to America. During the second period, 1725–1729, so many left Ulster that Parliament feared a loss of the entire Protestant population in Ireland. In Philadelphia, Secretary Logan wrote in 1729, "It looks as if Ireland is to send all its inhabitants hither. . . .The Indians themselves are alarmed at the swarms of strangers, and we are afraid of a breach between them—for the Irish are very rough with them." Continued rack renting and increased taxes caused this wave.

So far, most of the Scotch-Irish coming to Pennsylvania had settled near the Germans. Until increasing numbers brought both groups to the eastern edge of the Alleghenies, their settlements proceeded in an "alternating and parallel movement," so that concentrations of both could be found in Chester, Lancaster, and Berks Counties, and in the later counties of Dauphin, Lebanon, York, and Adams. They did not mingle, but lived apart from each other, though nearby. The third Scotch-Irish wave changed this pattern. An Irish famine in 1740, which brought death to perhaps 400,000 people there, set off another race for America. By this time the eastern lands of Pennsylvania had become so heavily settled that the newcomers for the first time entered the valleys of the Alleghenies. In 1754–1755 a drought in Ulster brought another mass migration which converged on the valleys west of the Susquehanna. The movement of the Scotch-Irish southward through these valleys gave Pennsylvania a new reputation as the "distributing center of the Scotch-Irish population." Between 1771 and 1775, the final influx of Scotch-Irish occurred. So many Scots had already abandoned Ulster that the remainder, living in a kind of economic vacuum, grew poorer each year. When one of the largest landowners, the Marquis of Donegal, raised rents on all his holdings in 1771, some 25,000 enraged farmers and linen workers left for America.

Throughout the period of migration, more than three-fourths of the Ulstermen entered America through the ports of Philadelphia, Chester, or New Castle. Of these, about the same proportion had authorized their ship master to obtain the passage money by selling them as indentured servants in America. Large landowners who needed to populate their holdings in order to confirm their titles bought the indentures of many of the Scotch-Irish. They also received free an extra hundred acres for each family planted. Few of the Scotch-Irish came in groups as church congregations, or as stock holders in land companies. In contrast to the Germans, who brought several dozen different religious sects into Pennsylvania, the Scotch-Irish were almost all Presbyterians. They arrived as families in the hope of finding as soon as possible a piece of land deep enough in the wilderness that they could appropriate it without any dealings with the provincial land office. In so doing they invaded regions not yet purchased from the Indians, and quickly raised trouble with the natives.

After the 1730s few of the Scotch-Irish settled in unoccupied parts of the "Dutch country"; the newcomers now moved into the frontier, sitting down, as Logan wrote, "Any where with or without leave, and on any spott that they think will turn out grain." Their Pennsylvania habitat lay between the Maryland line and the west branch of the Susquehanna. They moved into the Conococheague Valley, founded Chambersburg, and moved west into Bedford. Further north some occupied the Juniata Valley, while others pushed slowly up the Susquehanna to Northumberland and then west toward Clearfield. Their progress came to a halt during the French and Indian War, but after the defeat of the Indians in Pontiac's uprising of 1763, the Scotch-Irish made the western branches of the Susquehanna their own.

The first-generation Scotch-Irish settlers had little alternative but to farm for a living, but as a group they never achieved the reputation the Germans had of being careful husbandmen. In part the land may have been to blame, and in part the remoteness of their settlements from market. But also, the Scots seemed less devoted to farm work than the Germans, and unlike some of the German Plain Sects, did not view tilling the soil as the fulfillment of an ordinance of God. Impetuous, imaginative, ambitious for wealth and power, full of zest for a fight, impatient, and easily distracted, they viewed farming as a means to other ways of life rather than as an end in itself.

The composite population No reliable population statistics exist for colonial Pennsylvania. Estimates list the population at about 500 in 1681, 20,000 in 1700, 50,000 in 1720, 100,000 in 1740, 200,000 in 1760, and 300,000 in 1776. After 1740, each of the major groups—English, German, and Scotch-Irish—constituted about one-third of the total.

Initially, all these immigrants began settlements between the Delaware and the Susquehanna Rivers, but as time went on each group tended to establish a numerical predominance in a separate section: the English around Philadelphia, the Germans in a circle beyond them, and the Scotch-Irish west and north of the Germans. Though Pennsylvania received many people from many lands and of diverse language and traditions, the settlers did not tend to merge in the colonial era. Historians have noted that the English, Germans, and Scotch-Irish in Pennsylvania remained "remarkably unmixed" and retained their original character. Pennsylvania became the receptacle for an extremely heterogeneous population, but it did not serve as a melting pot. The tolerance which attracted people served also to permit them to retain their several cultures, languages, and traditions.

By the end of the colonial period, the Indians ceased to be a factor in the population. Many early missionaries had made efforts to train these people in Christianity and the European languages, arts, and crafts. The Quakers and the Moravians were particularly active as missionaries. But pressure for land, the hatreds which developed on the frontier, and the massacres by both Indians and whites brought the experiment to an end. By the 1790s the Indians of Pennsylvania, except for small, isolated bands, had been killed or driven from the area.

The early Dutch, Swedes, and Finns intermarried with the newcomers and gradually lost their national customs and identity. The later immigrants from Holland, mainly Dutch Quakers, also slowly amalgamated with the English around Philadelphia. The Welsh long gave their peculiar flavor to the region of the Welsh Tract where they had concentrated, but became so outnumbered that by the end of the Revolution they could no longer maintain a unique character.

A good many French Huguenots came to Pennsylvania, but spread so widely that they never created a self-conscious community. Many of these French Protestants, persecuted by Louis XIV, first fled to the Rhine Valley, and from there came to America along with the Germans. They first settled in the early 1700s in Lancaster and Berks Counties, and moved on to the present York and Adams Counties. While perhaps not more than 8,000 Huguenots entered Pennsylvania, they became an influential part of the population, for they were people of substance. At home they had been intellectual and economic leaders, and in

Pennsylvania they quickly became active townbuilders and promoters of enterprise. But they ultimately merged into the larger population and can be traced only with difficulty by their family names.

About 10,000 Scots, directly from their own land, and a similar number of Catholic Irish came to Penn's colony during its first century. There was some immigration of Jews, perhaps a thousand by the time of the adoption of the Federal Constitution. Negro slaves had been brought in by the Dutch in considerable numbers in the early days. The Assembly in 1712 placed a tax of £20 on the importation of a slave, but the Privy Council disallowed the bill. Despite the Quaker opposition to slavery, some 4,000 slaves had been brought to Pennsylvania by 1730, most of them owned by the English, Welsh, and Scotch-Irish. The Federal census of 1790 showed that the number of blacks had by that time increased to about 10,000.

BIBLIOGRAPHY

Students will find the texts of the several colonial constitutions in Francis N. Thorpe (comp.): *The Federal and State Constitutions, Colonial Charters, and other Organic Laws of the States, Territories and Colonies now or heretofore forming the United States of America,* 7 vols. (1909). The colonial constitutions of Pennsylvania are covered in the general histories by Charles P. Keith: *Chronicles of Pennsylvania,* 2 vols. (1917); and William R. Shepherd: *History of Proprietary Government in Pennsylvania* (1896). They are covered more briefly in the previously cited works by Bolles, Sharpless, Bronner, and Nash. Sydney G. Fisher: "The Fundamentale Constitutions of Pennsylvania," *Pennsylvania Magazine of History and Biography,* vol. 20 (1896), pp. 283–301, is useful.

The standard general work on settlement is S. H. Sutherland: *Population Distribution in Colonial America* (1936). On Pennsylvania, see Isaac D. Rupp: *Foreign Immigrants to Pennsylvania, 1717–1776* (1898); and Bertha Hamilton: "The Colonization of Pennsylvania" (doctoral dissertation, University of Wisconsin, Madison, 1932).

References on Quaker immigration are listed at the end of Chapter 2.

The Pennsylvania Germans are placed in national perspective in Carl Wittke: *We Who Built America* (1937); and Thomas J. Wertenbaker: *The Founding of American Civilization: The Middle Colonies* (1938), chaps. 8, 9. Albert B. Faust: *The German Element in the United States,* 2 vols. (1909), is the standard treatise. Dependable brief introductions to the subject may be found in Russell W. Gilbert: *A Picture of the Pennsylvania Germans* (1948); and Ralph Wood (ed.): *The Pennsylvania Germans* (1942). Other sound volumes on the topic include: Frederick Klees: *The Pennsylvania Dutch* (1950); James O. Knauss: *Social Conditions among the Pennsylvania Germans in the Eighteenth Century* (1922); Frederick Krebs and Milton Rubicam: *Emigrants from the Palatinate to the American Colonies in the Eighteenth Century* (1953); Levi Oscar Kuhns; *The German and Swiss Settlements of Colonial Pennsylvania, a Study of the So-called Pennsylvania Dutch* (1901); and Jesse L. Rosenberger: *The Pennsylvania Germans* (1923).

On the Scotch-Irish, the best books are Wayland F. Dunaway: *The Scotch-Irish of Colonial Pennsylvania* (1944); Charles A. Hanna: *The Wilderness Trail or the Ventures and Adventures of the Pennsylvania Traders on the Allegheny Path,* 2 vols. (1911); and Guy S. Klett: *Presbyterians in Colonial Pennsylvania* (1937) and *The Scotch-Irish in Pennsylvania* (1948).

For the Welsh, the standard history is Charles H. Browning: *Welsh Settlement of Pennsylvania* (1912). T. Mardy Rees: *A History of the Quakers in Wales and Their Emigration to North America* (1924) contains material on the Welsh Tract; and Edward G. Hartmann: *Americans from Wales* (1967) is helpful. Two articles that provide excellent summaries are Wayland F. Dunaway: "Early Welsh Settlers of Pennsylvania," *Pennsylvania History,* vol. 12 (1945), pp. 251–269; and James J. Levick: "The

Early Welsh Quakers and their Emigration to Pennsylvania," in *Pennsylvania Magazine of History and Biography,* vol. 17 (1893), pp. 385–413.

On the French Huguenots, see Amon Stapleton: *Memorials of the Huguenots in America, with Special Reference to their Emigration to Pennsylvania* (1901); James B. Laux; *The Huguenot Element in Pennsylvania* (1896); and Wayland F. Dunaway: "The French Racial Strain in Colonial Pennsylvania," *Pennsylvania Magazine of History and Biography,* vol. 53 (1929), pp. 322–342.

The Irish are studied with meticulous care by Albert Cook Myers: *Immigration of the Irish Quakers into Pennsylvania, 1682–1750* (1902).

Blacks in early Pennsylvania history have been the subject of studies by Edward R. Turner: *The Negro in Pennsylvania: Slavery—Servitude—Freedom, 1639–1861* (1911); and Ira V. Brown: *The Negro in Pennsylvania History* (1970). Articles of special importance are Frank J. Klingberg: "The African Immigrant in Colonial Pennsylvania and Delaware," *Protestant Episcopal Church History Magazine,* vol. 11 (1942), pp. 126–153; Edward R. Turner: "Slavery in Colonial Pennsylvania," *Pennsylvania Magazine of History and Biography,* vol. 35 (1911), pp. 141–151; and Joseph E. Walker: "Negro Labor in the Charcoal Iron Industry of Southeastern Pennsylvania, *Pennsylvania Magazine of History and Biography,* vol. 93 (1969), pp. 466–486. Andrew E. Murray: *Presbyterians and the Negro—A History* (1966); and Arthur Zilversmit: *The First Emancipation: The Abolition of Slavery in the North* (1967) both contain Pennsylvania material. Darold D. Wax has written two important articles in *Pennsylvania History:* "Negro Imports into Pennsylvania," vol. 32 (1965), pp. 254–287, and "The Demand for Slave Labor in Colonial Pennsylvania," vol. 34 (1967), pp. 331–345.

On the Jews, see Henry S. Morais: *The Jews of Philadelphia: Their History from the Earliest Settlement to the Present Time* (1894); Hyman P. Rosenbach; *The Jews in Philadelphia Prior to 1800* (1883); and Edwin Wolf and Maxwell Whiteman: *The History of the Jews of Philadelphia from Colonial Times to the Age of Jackson* (1956).

English settlers, apart from the Quakers, are treated by Wayland F. Dunaway: "English Settlers in Colonial Pennsylvania," *Pennsylvania Magazine of History and Biography,* vol. 52 (1928), pp. 317–341. Colonial immigrants from Italy have been studied by Howard R. Marraro; "Italo-Americans in Pennsylvania during the Eighteenth Century," *Pennsylvania History,* vol. 7 (1940), pp. 159–166.

Wayland F. Dunaway has analyzed the movement of population beyond the province in his article, "Pennsylvania as an Early Distributing Center of Population," *Pennsylvania Magazine of History and Biography,* vol. 55 (1931), pp. 134–169. On population movement inside the state, see John Florin: "The Advance of Frontier Settlement in Pennsylvania, 1638–1850," (master's thesis, Pennsylvania State University, University Park, 1966).

CHAPTER FIVE

Provincial Politics: 1701–1754

The Pennsylvania constitution of 1701 proved a splendid example of Penn's maxim that "Governments, like clocks, go from the motion men give them." From the very start, people disagreed on whether the Charter of Privileges of 1701 gave control of the province to the popularly elected Assembly or to the Proprietor, for its phraseology invited wide differences of opinion about the center of power. This fact, observed immediately by the men of Penn's day, led to a political contest among them for control. James Logan, Penn's loyal secretary, believed the Proprietor to be the fountainhead of power, and mobilized those who agreed with him into the Proprietary party. David Lloyd, who believed the Assembly to be the center of provincial authority, became the leader of the Popular party and fought for thirty years to make his viewpoint a political reality. Thus began the long struggle between the friends of the Proprietor and the friends of the Assembly, a contest in which each side interpreted the Charter of Privileges in the way that would best promote its own interests.

COLONIAL POLITICAL PARTIES

James Logan had been raised as a Scotch-Irish Quaker. In 1699, Penn brought him to Pennsylvania as provincial secretary. The Penn family appointed him its legal agent, and Pennsylvania chose him as secretary of the Council, mayor of Philadelphia, chief justice, and, for a time, acting-Governor. From the day of his arrival until his death in 1751, Logan exercised great influence. In choosing this young man, William Penn made one of his wisest appointments, for Logan devoted his life to the interests of the Penn family. He had the audacity to win advantage for the Proprietary party, the courage to defy David Lloyd, and the intelligence to give continuity to affairs of state during the terms of Governors Evans, Gookin, Keith, Gordon, Thomas, and Hamilton.

David Lloyd, a Welsh Quaker born in 1656, came to Pennsylvania in 1686 as Penn's attorney general. Contentious, cantankerous, and—toward William Penn—treacherous, Lloyd spent his life in Pennsylvania breaking down the power of the Proprietor and the King and building up the power and prestige of the popular Assembly, which he controlled. After Penn, at royal request, removed him from the attorney generalship, Lloyd soured and became one of the Proprietor's bitterest enemies. He took command of the Popular party, became perennial speaker of the Assembly, and served as chief justice of Pennsylvania from 1718 until his death in 1731. Lloyd was admittedly the best lawyer in the province; even Logan acknowledged and praised his technical skill in drafting most of the laws passed by the Assembly. He professed to be a great champion of democracy, but his suspicion of outside authority became nearly an obsession, and he saw the threat of tyranny in every little act of government that he did not himself control. Once he brought Assembly business to a halt rather than permit a member to rise when speaking to the governor. He defied court orders he disliked, and publicly ridiculed and vilified the king.

Political parties of these early days had little similarity to the later organizations. They constituted, rather, the local friends of some important man who stood openly on one side or other of the contest between the Assembly and the Proprietor. The leaders devised strategy and tactics informally at meetings in homes or taverns. Even the Assembly, which had only twenty-six members (eight from each of the three original counties and two from the city of Philadelphia) had no regular meeting place, but moved about the homes which had "a great front Room." Not until 1736 would it find a permanent location in the State House, now Independence Hall, which Andrew Hamilton had designed. The sheriff conducted the annual elections of assemblymen at the county courthouse, assisted by an inspector from each township who could recognize and qualify the voters from his locality. As no nominating procedure existed, voters knew the names of candidates only by hearsay; yet little confusion resulted for the same candidates ran year after year. Shortly after the polls had closed, the sheriff would announce the result from the courthouse steps. Few people voted, for in the city not many owned 50 acres or had property valued at £50, and in the country most people lived far from the polling places.

Until the late 1730s, the party contests occurred primarily between rival groups of Quakers. The country Quakers, concerned about their land titles, their religious scruples, and their political rights, followed the brilliant, forceful Lloyd, and constituted the majority of the Popular party. The best-educated wealthiest Quakers, most of them Philadelphians, composed the main strength of the Proprietary party. Many of its leaders had served at one time or another on the Governor's Council. The governors generally appointed men of this group to administrative positions and looked to them for advice and support. James Logan acted as their main spokesman.

For several years after 1701 a third party existed called the Churchmen or the Non-Quaker Church party, composed of Anglicans and Crown officials led by Admiralty Court Judge Robert Quary. This party tried to discredit Penn by sending tales of mismanagement back to England in the hope of persuading the Privy Council to recall the charter and make Pennsylvania a royal province. After Penn's death most of these people joined Logan's Proprietary party.

Throughout most of the colonial era the basic political question remained the same: whether the elected Assembly or the proprietary establishment should rule the province. Backers of the Assembly formed the Popular party of the early 1700s, the Country party in the 1740s, and the Antiproprietary party in the 1750s. Supporters of the Penns called themselves the Proprietary party in the early days, the Gentlemen's party in the 1740s, and again the Proprietary party in the 1750s. The Quakers and Plain Sect Germans who dominated the Assembly parties advocated three policies: resistance to provincial appropriations for defense, exclusion of western counties from a proportional voice in the Assembly, and taxation of the proprietary lands. For leadership they looked to David Lloyd, Isaac Norris II, James Pemberton and his sons, and Benjamin Franklin.

The Anglicans and the Scotch-Irish who united in support of the Penns in the 1740s had as their political objectives: providing adequate military defense for the province, breaking Quaker control of the Assembly by extending representation to settlers on the frontier, and defending the political and property rights of the proprietorship. Leadership of this group rested first with James Logan but in the 1740s passed into the hands of William Allen.

THE GOVERNORS VERSUS THE ASSEMBLY

After William Penn discovered that he could not quickly return to Pennsylvania, he replaced the temporary executive Council he had set up in 1701 by appointing John Evans as deputy governor in 1704. Evans, a twenty-six-year-old Welshman and not a Quaker, had initiative and some administrative ability; he preferred action to talk, and lived zestfully without much concern for morality or the opinion of others. He might have served well as a governor of a military people. Penn needed him as a soldier and instructed him to make preparations for defense of the colony during Queen Anne's War, for the Crown had been complaining that the Quakers had done nothing. With Evans came Penn's dissolute son, William. This pair soon gave the straitlaced Assembly Quakers occasion for righteous resistance.

Governor Evans asked the Assembly for military defense funds, promising that New Yorkers would do the fighting, but the Quakers declined to act. Evans then called up provincial militia by executive proclamation. Though this act lay within the proprietary powers and followed the Queen's wishes, it outraged the Quakers and recruited so few volunteers that one French man-of-war could have captured Delaware Bay. Evans determined to shock the defenseless province into action by staging a mock enemy attack. He arranged with some friends in Wilmington to have a disheveled messenger ride madly into Philadelphia on the day of the annual fair, announcing the approach of the French fleet. The masquerade threw the population into hysteria. People hurriedly bundled their valuables into wells and fled the city, some receiving injuries in their headlong flight. This madcap episode terminated the usefulness of Governor Evans.

In 1709 Penn appointed Col. Charles Gookin as Governor. The leaders of the Assembly greeted Governor Gookin with a demand that he institute criminal proceedings against ex-Governor Evans for high crimes and misdemeanors. When Gookin refused, the Assembly tried to prosecute the members of Council for conspiring with Evans. Gookin would have nothing to do with this petty local war, but took seriously his instructions to achieve Pennsylvania's participation in the Anglo-French war. He asked for 150 militiamen and a grant of £4,000 to aid the expedition against Canada, but the Assembly refused to vote either.

To convey an appearance of cooperation it appropriated £500 for defense, hedged with so many restrictions as to make the grant useless.

Because the Assembly had earlier denied the right of the Council to discuss bills, Penn particularly instructed Governor Gookin to approve no bill unless the Council had first given its assent. Encouraged by this evidence of the determination of the Proprietor to assert his power, Logan brought impeachment charges against his rival, Lloyd, who was again serving as Speaker of the Assembly. In the course of the proceedings, Logan made violent statements and the Assembly ordered him imprisoned. Governor Gookin forbade it. Logan sailed for England in 1710 to explain to Penn the whole course of political events since 1701. Public knowledge of the Proprietor's financial difficulties, a growing apprehension that he might soon return his province to the Crown, and perhaps a popular weariness with the incessant bickering which emanated from Lloyd's Assembly brought a sudden change in the political atmosphere. Not a single assemblyman of 1710 was returned to sit in the session of 1711. Shortly after this election a letter arrived from Penn reminding the Quakers of his early hopes for the "holy experiment" and warning them sharply that unless they awoke to duty he would retire and they would then have a new and harder master. The letter contained both appeal and threat, and achieved political results. For a few years Logan's party controlled the Assembly, and as the Governor, Council, and Assembly were now all of the same party, the government ran harmoniously.

But the Popular party regained strength. In 1715 the old conflict between the Governor and the Assembly reappeared because the latter neglected to pay Gookin's salary. The Governor, who had earlier shown signs of mental unbalance, eventually became so unreasonable and unpredictable that the Council in 1717, fearing his complete mental breakdown, unanimously called for his removal.

Gookin's term produced little permanent change except in the matter of oaths. For years the Quakers had quietly gone about their business without the oath-taking procedure, assuming office and conducting court business by simple affirmation. But in 1715 a new British law excluded from office all people who would not swear according to a prescribed oath. Gookin applied this rule to Pennsylvania. It put the provincial courts out of action, and for a time criminals either went unpunished or were punished by groups with no legal status. Governor William Keith solved the impasse by persuading David Lloyd's partisans to accept the harsh English penal code as part of an agreement that affirmations could be used in Pennsylvania. The British authorities approved this in 1725.

PARTISAN INTERLUDE

Hannah Penn appointed Sir William Keith to succeed Gookin. Keith had been a Crown officer in Delaware prior to his appointment as Governor of Pennsylvania in 1717, and consequently knew something of local politics. From the beginning he treated the Assembly with marked consideration, altering its usual meeting dates to accommodate the pressing demands of harvest and seeding time. The Assembly, unaccustomed to such a mark of thoughtfulness in a governor, voted his salary without a murmur, authorized him to mobilize a militia force, and created a provincial court of equity composed of the Governor and several of the Council. The Quaker lawmakers had repeatedly defeated such proposals when made by earlier governors. Keith also proposed and the Assembly passed in 1723 a currency bill authorizing the emission of paper money by the province, backed by silver plate and land. The new Pennsylvania paper currency, in bills ranging from a shilling to a pound, proved a boon to the whole population, for little metal money existed and barter proved a poor substitute.

Governor Keith ruled without relying on Council, in contrast to his predecessor who, on William Penn's orders, had deferred to the Council's decision on whether to approve or reject laws. By his independent procedure, Keith threw his lot with the Popular party and aroused the bitter antagonism of Logan, the members of Council, and the followers of the Proprietary party. In consequence of Logan's hostility, Keith dismissed him from his post as provincial secretary, whereupon Logan visited Hannah Penn in England to regain his position. When Keith firmly refused to reinstate Logan, Hannah Penn relieved Keith of the governorship on July 9, 1726. Keith remained in Pennsylvania and tried to work out a future for himself as leader of the Popular party in the Assembly. He won a seat in that body, but aroused the suspicions of David Lloyd. When Keith sought election as speaker of the Assembly, Lloyd put his well-disciplined forces to work, won the speakership for himself, and made Keith a laughingstock.

Patrick Gordon served as Governor from 1726 to 1736. A retired professional soldier, he was sixty-two years old when he took office. Gordon frankly told all parties that he knew nothing of politics and proposed to meet issues as they arose with blunt frankness. Although former Governor Keith caused some trouble, Gordon managed to bring more harmony to the administration of the province than had existed since Penn's second visit. Gordon carefully honored every right of the Assembly, he met with and listened to advice from his Council, and he managed to keep on good terms with Logan and out of trouble with Lloyd. During his administration Hannah Penn died, and the proprietorship, after brief litigation, descended to her three sons, John, Thomas, and Richard.

After Gordon took office, a new political force took shape in the west. As the Scotch-Irish Presbyterians began to occupy the Cumberland Valley, the Quakers, to preserve their control of the Assembly, planned to resist the erection of counties in the west. Lancaster County, the fourth to be created, came into existence in 1729. The Assembly alloted it only four delegates, or one-half as many as each of the original three counties. No more counties were created for twenty years; and when the Asssmbly did yield to pressure for new counties it again cut the representation. York (1749) and Cumberland (1750) were given two assembly-men each; Berks (1752) and Northampton (1752) only one each. After this no more counties were created until 1771. By such means the eastern Quakers kept the Assembly in their own hands.

Governor Gordon died in 1736. His ten-year term had proved the most harmonious and prosperous that the province had known for many years or would know for many years to come. The Governor himself deserved much credit for this happy state of affairs. His fine personal qualities and his advanced age removed suspicions that he acted from private ambition; his consideration of others and his ability to achieve the respect both of the Assembly and of the Proprietors gained for him a unique place in the roll of governors.

Other factors eased his administration. As England remained at peace, he did not need to face the problem of a military budget. The period of "salutary neglect" still continued in imperial policy, permitting greater colonial freedom of trade. The increase in domestic wealth made it less painful for the thrifty assemblymen to appropriate funds for salaries of officials. And finally, the proprietorship itself had entered a new and still tentative phase with the death of Hannah Penn in 1727. John and Thomas Penn visited the colony in 1723, the latter remaining to serve actively in the government for nine years. With their brother, Richard, they succeeded to the proprietorship, but none of them held the Quaker ideals of their father. Thus Gordon's administration marked the end of an era, for subsequent governors would be serving the interests of Proprietors who were not Friends. Their partisans, too, would be different—the non-Quakers of Philadelphia and the Scotch-Irish frontiersmen. The Quakers, on their part, would hold on to the Germans, and would find in Benjamin Franklin a leader just as politically ambitious as David Lloyd. The year Gordon died, Franklin became clerk of the Assembly.

THE MILITARY DEFENSE ISSUE

James Logan, as President of the Council, was acting-Governor from August 1736 until the appointment of Governor George Thomas in June 1738. The War of Jenkins' Ear between England and Spain in 1739 and the ensuing Anglo-French War from 1744 to 1748 created new problems of defense.

Governor Thomas, a planter from Antigua, received instructions from the king, via the Proprietors, to raise troops for imperial defense, to exempt from service those conscientiously opposed to war, but to collect from the latter a money payment. Thomas sent a copy of these instructions to the Assembly, which declined to make any appropriation for defense. The Governor then mobilized seven militia companies by enrolling indentured servants who, on enlistment, became free of their obligation to the master. This action spurred the Assembly to pass a defense money bill, with the proviso that no funds should be released until all enlisted servants had been returned to their masters, and until recruiting officers gave guarantees that no more servants would be enrolled. The Assembly then began prosecution of the recruiting officers for depriving masters of their property—the servants—without due process of law. Thus the Assembly had managed to provide money but no troops, or troops and no money, and either way to embarrass the Governor.

Governor Thomas lost patience with such trifling in the midst of a war; he wrote a violent letter to the British Board of Trade saying that Pennsylvania could never be defended unless Quakers were excluded from office. When a report of this reached Philadelphia, the Assembly denounced Thomas as an enemy of the people. The breach between the Governor and the Assembly widened and effective government ceased. These events created the Gentlemen's party, led by the Governor, and the Country party of Assembly Quakers. The election of 1741 brought fistfights at the polls, and the election of 1742 touched off a large-scale riot in Philadelphia. In both elections the voters gave overwhelming approval to the stand of the Assembly.

The Crown officers in England suggested that Pennsylvania enact a defense appropriation to pay masters for the loss to the militia of their indentured servants. This the assemblymen promptly did, and to blunt the growing anger in Parliament against Quakers, they also appropriated £3,000 more for the King's use. In the end, the Assembly provided more money than had been asked for defense, and by devious procedure and insistence on its prerogatives, emerged in triumph from its contest with Thomas. The Governor, convinced that he could not rule without the Assembly, became more conciliatory. In May 1744, when the Governor promised more regard for the wishes of the Assembly, the assemblymen paid his back salary and agreed to vote money for defense so far as their Quaker consciences would allow.

The reconciliation came just in time, for in June 1744 King George's War with France began. The Assembly voted £4,000 for beef, pork, flour, wheat, and "other grain," which Governor Thomas, at Franklin's suggestion, interpreted to mean grains of gunpowder. No one complained when Thomas used the money to buy munitions for the expedition against Louisburg. When the British undertook the conquest of Canada in 1746, the Assembly voted money to equip four Pennsylvania companies, but after they had been sent out, the Assembly refused further funds to feed or pay them. Nor would the lawmakers agree to arm any Pennsylvania ships against enemy privateers which had been roving the Delaware Bay. One French ship spent nearly a week off New Castle, cannonading the town without receiving so much as a musket shot in return.

The term of Governor Thomas, from 1738 to 1747, created a new party division in Pennsylvania and brought to the forefront new leaders who would exercise growing influence in the future. The Gentlemen's party of Governor Thomas consisted mostly of wealthy Anglicans and Scotch Presbyterian frontiersmen. James Logan, torn between his duty to the Penns and his Quaker conscience, gradually withdrew from active politics.

William Allen, a well-educated Scotch-Irish Presbyterian who had made a fortune in trade and land speculation, became the leader of the Gentlemen's party. Physically huge, and known as "the Giant," Allen had a commanding presence, urbane manners, and a genial wit. He had the ability to perceive human quality, and became the patron of such talented young men as Dr. John Morgan, the painters Benjamin West and Charles Willson Peale, and Benjamin Franklin, who surpassed Allen's expectations by becoming his most powerful political rival. Allen served in the Assembly, in Council, as mayor of Philadelphia, as recorder, and from 1751 until 1774 as chief justice of Pennsylvania. For thirty years Allen was probably the most influential figure in Pennsylvania politics.

Benjamin Franklin assumed virtual command of the Country party. The ambitious young freethinker, after serving as a printer's apprentice, became the publisher of the *Pennsylvania Gazette* from 1729 to 1748, the editor of *Poor Richard's Almanac,* clerk of the Assembly, printer of the provincial laws, founder of the Junto and of the American Philosophical Society, and by midcentury deputy postmaster general of the American colonies and a scientist of world renown. His publication in 1729 of the *Modest Enquiry into the Nature and Necessity of a Paper Currency* marked him as a clever political propagandist as well as an astute businessman, for he obtained the contract to print £40,000 of the new money. The tone of his journal and his tact, shrewd wit, and practical good sense had by 1738 already made him a champion of the common people.

In 1747 Franklin proposed a solution to the defense problem which, though attacked by the strict Quakers on the one hand and the leaders of the Gentlemen's party on the other, achieved the warm support of nearly everyone else. He established a public lottery of £20,000, from the proceeds of which he earmarked £3,000 to be spent on building defenses along the Delaware River by a group called the Association. The members of this organization, called Associators, would form themselves into militia companies who would choose their own officers and set up an internal government to create rules and regulations for their military units. The first lottery proved so great a success that a second was soon announced. By May 1748, Philadelphia had formed ten military companies and the rest of the province reported ninety others. Many Quakers contributed to the Association, for Franklin had published a pamphlet, *Plain Truth or Serious Considerations,* in which he quoted some of their own preachers in support of self-defense.

When the election of militia officers took place, not the gentlemen but the popular leaders received the highest military ranks. It thus became immediately obvious that the Associators could act as a political phalanx, and that Franklin had created a political machine for himself as well as an army for the colony. The leaders of the Gentlemen's party called the whole plan illegal. Allen presumed that Franklin would use the Associators as a voting machine in the 1748 Assembly election, but the end of the war in that year altered conditions and Franklin decided against such use of his army. He had, however, demonstrated how a little ingenuity and determination could overcome the traditional stalemate between military-minded governors and the stubbornly pacifist Assembly.

THE CURRENCY ISSUE

To replace Governor Thomas, the Penns in 1748 appointed James Hamilton, Pennsylvania-born son of the famous lawyer Andrew Hamilton. The new Governor faced two problems, each of which continued throughout his term: the problem of paper currency and relations with the Indians. In the 1720s Pennsylvanians had imported goods costing far beyond the value of their exports. This meant such a rapid flight of gold and silver out of the colony that economic depression threatened. Some demanded that the exportation of metal money should be forbidden, but most called for the creation of a paper currency.

The Assembly in 1723 had passed two laws providing for the printing of a total of £45,000 in currency, to be loaned to citizens in exchange for property mortgages or silver plate at a rate of 5 percent interest, and to be retired in eight years. A loan office received the collateral and put the money into circulation, reporting periodically to a committee of the Assembly. The currency was legal tender for everything, including repayment of the loans, and strict penalties were enacted against counterfeiting. Although the paper circulated at only about 70 percent of the value of an equivalent unit of sterling, it nonetheless greatly improved the economic condition of Pennsylvania and became a favorite panacea for everyone who owed or wanted to borrow money—groups which constituted a vast majority of the citizens. In 1729 the Assembly authorized £30,000 more in Pennsylvania currency to be loaned at 5 percent and retired in sixteen years. The British Board of Trade, in order to exert some control against inflation, had asked that no new bills of credit (i.e., paper money) be issued without the prior consent of the King; and the Proprietors wished to have quitrents paid only in sterling, but the 1729 measure remained in force in disregard of the wishes both of the Privy Council and the Penns.

Thereafter, Pennsylvania periodically retired its currency and reissued new notes until, in 1739, it had £80,000 in circulation. In that year the British Parliament discussed colonial paper currency at length and passed an act ordering that no provincial law for issuing currency should be valid unless approved by the king prior to release of the notes. The Pennsylvania Assembly tested this in 1744 by voting £5,000 to the king for military use in new Pennsylvania currency, without obtaining prior approval. The Crown took the money.

In 1751 Parliament enacted a currency law forbidding the New England colonies to reissue bills of credit. Thomas Penn had worked hard to persuade Parliament to exempt Pennsylvania from the restrictions of the Currency Act of 1751. In this he had succeeded, but he had been warned that unless the Pennsylvanians always obtained prior approval from the ministry for new currency issues, they might be brought under the same restrictions as New England. Penn therefore instructed Governor Hamilton to veto any money bill that lacked a "suspending clause," that is, a provision suspending the issue of new currency until approval had been given by the ministry in London; but he also instructed Governor Hamilton never to reveal these instructions.

By 1753 the province had boiled into violent rage against the Governor and the Proprietors on the paper money question. When Hamilton tried to justify his vetoes on the ground of compliance with a royal order requiring a "suspending clause," the Assembly argued that the order had no force in Pennsylvania, for the king had given up his rights in the 1681 Charter; and the Proprietors had no rights in this matter, having given them up in the constitution of 1701. The Assembly claimed power to carry out its will. This approximated a declaration of independence. Hamilton said he would resign in 1754, despairing of accomplishing anything unless his instructions were changed, because the Assembly would do nothing, he wrote, "until they have their beloved paper money."

INDIAN POLICY

The relations between the province of Pennsylvania and the Indians fall into two periods, before 1732 and after 1732. In the earlier era, William Penn's ideas, focusing primarily on the Delaware tribes, dominated provincial policy. In the later era, James Logan's ideas, focusing primarily on the Iroquois Confederation, controlled policy.

Penn's insistence upon fair treatment of the Indians soon raised a host of practical problems arising from trading and possession of land. In the Concessions of 1681, Penn had rather unrealistically applied the same rules of trade to both Indians and whites, but private traders carried rum to the interior, got the Indians drunk, and cheated them of their furs. The Assembly barred nonresidents from the Indian trade, forbade anyone to carry rum to an Indian village, required all Indian traders to be licensed, and ordered that no Indian trade should take place except in a settled village or at the residence of a licensed trader. These laws could not be enforced. The Indian kings had continuing cause for dissatisfaction, but at the same time they acknowledged that Penn's government had acted on their behalf.

Penn's plan to purchase Indian land before selling to European settlers introduced a different set of problems. The whites, with their law of private property, took exclusive possession and barred Indians from the land. The Indians, accustomed to a communal, migrant life, initially thought of a land-purchase treaty as an invitation to the whites to share the hunting lands with them. The Indians eventually learned the full import of selling land to Europeans.

Furthermore, the Delawares from whom most of the early purchases were made had so loose a government that no one could be sure which chief or group of them possessed the authority to grant a tract of land and receive the payment. Penn, because he wished to be sure that all possible Indian claimants had been satisfied, often paid several different chiefs for the same region. The Indians considered this fair insofar as several tribes frequently utilized the same hunting lands. Some chiefs later took advantage of this practice and freely sold the same area several times over to different European buyers. The Delawares achieved a reputation for proposing a land sale whenever they ran short of rum. But other tribes did the same thing.

Despite irritations arising from the fur trade, the rum trade, and land disputes, William and Hannah Penn's policy of maintaining peace and friendship with the Delaware Indians, by treating them as prior owners of the land and entitled to the same legal consideration as Europeans in trade, proved successful. The Delaware Indians and their white neighbors remained on good terms through the first half century of Pennsylvania's history. That happy relation changed after 1732.

Penn's old policy of dealing with Delaware chiefs in the vicinity of Philadelphia without much regard for the interior began to break down when the increasing population spilled beyond the three original counties. The movement of whites created sensitive spots in Indian relations in the lower Susquehanna Valley and the upper Delaware Valley. Pennsylvania's traditional Indian policy provided no sure way to avert the dangers that threatened in these trouble spots.

Three men became the chief architects of a new Indian policy, initiated in 1732, which would last until the Revolutionary War: James Logan, who represented the proprietary interests; John Shickellamy, who spoke for the Iroquois Confederacy; and Conrad Weiser, who served as interpreter and trusted adviser for both. Logan first recognized the problem and tentatively suggested the answer. He foresaw that the Scotch-Irish would penetrate the Indian country, kill the natives, and turn them from friends into enemies; he knew that the Quaker Assembly would provide no military defense for the province; and he suspected that the French would try to extend their power south and east of Lake Erie into western Pennsylvania. As early as 1731 he expressed doubt that the English could defend this region against the French and wrote that a close understanding with the Six Nations would be "our only security agst the french in case of a Rupture." He framed a new policy to strengthen the hands of the Six Nations by acknowledging their dominion over all the tribes resident in Pennsylvania. Such a policy would establish a single power with which to treat for the Pennsylvania lands currently in dispute, and would bind the Iroquois to the English against the French.

John Shickellamy, born a Cayuga, had been raised by the Oneidas and gained respect among the Iroquois as a man of strength and vision. In 1728 the Six Nations appointed him as principal chief in charge of the cousin tribes in Pennsylvania, with headquarters at Shamokin (Sunbury), where the north and west branches of the Susquehanna joined. Shickellamy, with an eye to his own position, saw nothing but advantage in a policy of treating Pennsylvania tribes as subjects of the Iroquois. This would broaden his responsibility while at the same time it enhanced the power of the Six Nations.

Conrad Weiser, one of the Palatines who had lived at Schoharie in New York before the migration to the Tulpehocken Valley, lived among the Mohawks as a boy, learned their language and customs, and became an adopted member of the tribe. Many Iroquois chiefs knew and trusted him. When James Logan, in 1731, invited Shickellamy to attend a conference at Philadelphia to discuss the new Indian policy, Shickellamy asked Weiser to come as his interpreter. In later years, after Weiser had become the paid interpreter for Pennsylvania, he still was regarded by the Six Nations as one who represented their interests. At the conference in the fall of 1732, attended by Thomas Penn who had just arrived from England, the new Indian policy took shape. The Penns would negotiate only with the Iroquois for land in Pennsylvania.

Four years later, in 1736, after Governor Gordon had died, James Logan, who now was acting-Governor, received from the Onondaga Council of Iroquois a request for a conference at Philadelphia to settle the question of the Susquehanna lands. The Iroquois proposed to sell the lower Susquehanna Valley to the Penns as a precedent for claims they later would make to land in Maryland and Virginia. Weiser and Shickellamy met the chiefs at Shamokin and escorted them to Philadelphia that fall where a treaty of sale was drawn and ratified. It was an occasion of unprecedented interest, for never before had the whole Iroquois Council of Chiefs, accompanied by warriors and families, visited the province. The Penns paid little for the land, because the Iroquois sought primarily the recognition by Pennsylvania of their right to sell the southern region. The Treaty of 1736 settled the problem of the lower Susquehanna, leaving only the land around the Forks of the Delaware in contest.

Before the Onondaga chiefs returned home, Logan asked them to state that the Penns, by prior purchase, already had obtained good title to the land along the Delaware River up the Lehigh Fork. This they did in one letter asserting that the Iroquois released all their rights to this region, and in a second that their Delaware cousins, having already sold this land, had "no Land remaining to them."

With such backing, James Logan proposed that in the autumn of 1737 the area of the Delaware lands which had first been marked for sale in 1686 should be defined. According to the original agreement, the Delaware Indians had promised to grant a tract between the Delaware River and a line starting at Wrightstown, Bucks County, and running northwest parallel to the river as far as a man could walk in a day and a half. By Indian custom, the terms of the 1686 agreement were very clear. A day's walk meant a walk as Indians traveled, with time to hunt, prepare meals, make up a campsite, and rest. It would cover about 20 miles; a walk of a day and a half would extend 30 miles. No evidence suggests that the provincial authorities lacked knowledge of this Indian mode of reckoning distance.

Prior to the walk, Logan had the line surveyed and a path cleared, advertised for fast walkers, and promised a prize of £25 and 50 acres of land to the winner among three walkers. He arranged not a walk but a race. Soon after the walk started at dawn on September 19, 1737, the Indian observers who intended to accompany the Pennsylvania walkers quit in disgust at what they now labeled a swindle. After traveling 60 miles, one walker reached the foot of the Kittatinny Mountains, where the surveyors projected a line not eastward to the river but northeast toward the Delaware Water Gap, encompassing a tract much larger than that which the Indians had initially envisioned; it comprised nearly the entire homeland of the Delawares. The outraged Indians protested vigorously and found an ally in the Quaker Assembly, which discovered in this episode a useful political weapon with which to attack Logan and the Proprietary party. When the Assembly championed the Delawares' cause against the Proprietors, Logan called his new friends, the Iroquois, into conference at Philadelphia in 1742 to hear and judge their cousins, the Delawares.

It was at this point that the new Indian policy received its first serious test. The Iroquois did not come to Philadelphia to do Logan's bidding. They opened the meeting by stating that they had sold the Susquehanna lands too cheaply. The Proprietaries took the hint and made a substantial additional payment for the lands they had bought in 1736. After this the Iroquois spokesman, Canasatego, faced the Delawares of the Forks and harshly denounced them. They were women, they had no right to sell land, nor any land to sell if they had the right. They should leave the Delaware region and move to Shamokin or to the Wyoming Valley where the Iroquois "shall see how 'they' behave." The Shawnees, who had recently come from Ohio to live near the Delaware Water Gap, should also move. The Philadelphia conference of 1742 appeared to confirm the alliance of the Iroquois with the Proprietary leaders and to prove the wisdom of Logan's policy.

The new relation with the Iroquois, however, brought its own dangers. The Delawares, after the Walking Purchase and the insults heaped on them at Philadelphia in 1742, stored bitterness in their hearts against the Pennsylvania Proprietors and the Iroquois. Most of them, except for a remnant led by the Moravian-trained Teedyuscung, spurned living under Iroquois domination and moved to the Ohio country where the French welcomed them

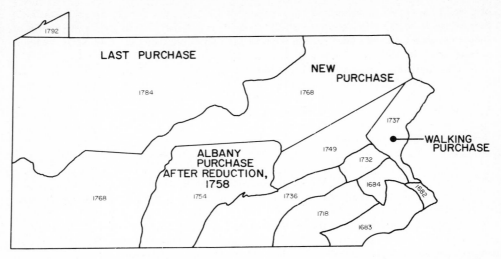

Major purchases of land by the Pennsylvania authorities from the Indians. The Purchase of 1754 originally included most of the land west of the Susquehanna, but this huge grant was reduced in 1758 as part of a peace agreement between the British Crown and the Indians.

and promised them a chance for future revenge. The Shawnees, too, went west to join the French.

Nearly everyone recognized that the Treaty of Aix-la-Chapelle in 1748 did not mean peace between England and France, but merely a truce. That very year Conrad Weiser learned from a French agent in the Ohio Valley that France intended to occupy that whole river valley and to use the Indians against any English resistance. When the French began to mark their claims by burying metal plates south of Lake Erie, Pennsylvania took more seriously the danger which James Logan had foretold twenty years before. Logan died in 1751, but his outlook and policy were ably continued by Richard Peters, secretary of the land office. Peters became so disturbed by the damage to Indian relations wrought by illegal squatters on Indian land that in 1750 he gathered a force of deputies to drive these people out of closed areas of newly formed Cumberland County. By the time he had finished his mission, the region of the Juniata Valley, Path Valley, and the Big Cove had come to be known as the "burnt cabins." Such drastic action was a measure of the concern he felt for keeping good faith with the Indians to prevent them from allying with the French. The Assembly between 1748 and 1754 still refused to appropriate any money for a Pennsylvania militia or for frontier forts, but it did prove generous in granting funds to purchase the continuing friendship of the local Indians. It paid out over £5,000 for Indian gifts, and at a conference in Carlisle in 1753 gave an additional £800 to western Indians for a promise of loyalty to the English.

After the French and Indian War actually began in the spring of 1754, the English colonies held a conference at Albany to prepare unified plans for defense and to strengthen their alliance with the Six Nations. Weiser had warned as early as 1750 that many of the Iroquois had "turned Frenchmen." Two of the Pennsylvania agents at Albany, John Penn and Richard Peters, used the meeting to conclude a land-purchase treaty with the Six Nations covering all the territory west of the Susquehanna and south of a line between the present towns of Sunbury and Warren—in short, the western two-thirds of the province. In this region lived not only Shawnees, Delawares, and Wyandots, but many of the Iroquois of the Seneca tribe. They protested that the purchase was void because not approved by the whole Iroquois Council at Onondaga, but the Proprietors ignored their complaint. This land transaction proved the last of the series of indignities which forced the western Pennsylvania Indians into the open arms of the French.

BIBLIOGRAPHY

The previously cited general histories by Robert Proud, Issac Sharpless, Charles P. Keith, A. S. Bolles, and William Shepherd provide material on the period 1701–1754. In addition, Thomas F. Gordon: *The History of Pennsylvania, from Its Discovery by Europeans, to the Declaration of Independence* (1829) is an excellent political history. Three monographs that are indispensable are Theodore Thayer: *Pennsylvania Politics and the Growth of Democracy, 1740–1776* (1953); Gary B. Nash: *Quakers and Politics, Pennsylvania, 1681–1726* (1968); and William S. Hanna: *Benjamin Franklin and Pennsylvania Politics* (1964).

Other important political studies are Wayne C. Keller: "Pennsylvania Government, 1701–1740," (doctoral dissertation, University of Washington, Seattle, 1967); Chester R. Young: "The Evolution of the Pennsylvania Assembly, 1682–1754," *Pennsylvania History,* vol. 35 (1968), pp. 147–167; Sister Joan de Lourdes Leonard: "The Organization of the Pennsylvania Assembly, 1682–1776," *Pennsylvania Magazine of History and Biography,* vol. 72 (1948), pp. 215–239, 376–412; William T. Johnson: "Some Aspects of the Relations of the Government and German Settlers in Colonial Pennsylvania, 1683–1754," *Pennsylvania History,* vol. 11 (1944), pp. 81–102, 200–207; and Thomas Wendel: "The Keith-Lloyd Alliance: Factional and Coalition Politics in Colonial Pennsylvania," *Pennsylvania Magazine of History and Biography,* vol. 92 (1968), pp. 289–305.

On the currency problem, see C. W. MacFarlane: *Pennsylvania Paper Currency* (1896); William R. Riddell: "Benjamin Franklin and Colonial Money," *Pennsylvania Magazine of History and Biography,* vol. 54 (1930), pp. 52–64; Richard A. Lester: "Currency Issues to Overcome Depressions in Pennsylvania, 1723 and 1729," *Journal of Political Economy,* vol. 46 (1938), pp. 324–375; and Harrold E. Gillingham: *Counterfeiting in Colonial Pennsylvania* (1939).

On Indian policy, the major works are George A. Cribbs: *The Frontier Policy of Pennsylvania* (1919); Robert L. D. Davidson: *War Comes to Quaker Pennsylvania, 1682–1756* (1957); Joseph S. Walton: *Conrad Weiser and the Indian Policy of Colonial Pennsylvania* (1900); Paul A. W. Wallace: "Conrad Weiser and the Delawares," *Pennsylvania History,* vol. 4 (1937), pp. 139–152; and William J. Buck: *History of the Indian Walk Performed for the Proprietaries of Pennsylvania in 1737* (1886). Sherman P. Uhler: "Pennsylvania's Indian Relations to 1754" (doctoral dissertation, Temple University, Philadelphia, 1950); and Francis P. Jennings: "Miquon's Passing: Indian European Relations in Colonial Pennsylvania, 1674–1755" (doctoral dissertation, University of Pennsylvania, Philadelphia, 1965), are both important, the latter showing how Penn's policy was ruined by deceitful associates.

Other topical studies concentrating on early-eighteenth-century Pennsylvania history are Winifred T. Root: *The Relations of Pennsylvania with the British Government, 1696–1765* (1912); Frederick B. Tolles: *Meeting House and Counting House,* previously cited; and Mabel P. Wolff: *The Colonial Agency of Pennsylvania, 1712–1757* (1933).

The pertinent biographical studies are: Charles P. Keith: *Provincial Councillors of Pennsylvania, 1733–1766* (1882); Roy N. Lokken: *David Lloyd, Colonial Lawmaker* (1959); Frederick B. Tolles: *James Logan* (1957); Norman S. Cohen: "William Allen: Chief Justice of Pennsylvania, 1704–1780" (doctoral dissertation, University of California, Berkeley, 1966); Hubertis M. Cummings: *Richard Peters, Provincial Secretary and Cleric* (1944); Theodore Thayer: *Israel Pemberton, King of the Quakers* (1943); Sewell E. Slick: *William Trent and the West* (1947); Anthony F. C. Wallace: *King of the Delawares: Teedyuscung, 1700–1763* (1949); and the previously cited biographies of George Croghan and of Conrad Weiser. For Benjamin Franklin, see Carl Van Doren: *Benjamin Franklin* (1938).

CHAPTER SIX

The French and Indian War: 1753–1763

Few settlers of colonial Pennsylvania concerned themselves about the activities of the French in far-off Canada, or about the developing imperial rivalry between France and England. Having left behind them the religious persecutions and dynastic wars of Europe, and never having experienced in Pennsylvania any serious threat from Indians or foreign invaders, these people for several generations had grown accustomed to a quiet life in the "peaceable Kingdom." Their vision became narrow and provincial, limited to the personal war with nature on their farms and the parochial contest for power between the governors and the Assembly. They did not discern the interconnectedness of human affairs and failed to perceive how their simple existence might trigger events of worldwide import. Yet, as Voltaire commented, such was the complication of international politics in 1753 that a shot fired in the remote wilderness of western Pennsylvania "could give the signal that set Europe in a blaze."

While many Pennsylvanians of the 1750s viewed the French and Indian War as an isolated event, modern students can see it as one link in a long chain of events in the contest for imperial power between France and England, a contest which generated six wars between 1689 and 1815.

BACKGROUND OF THE WAR

In 1750, French North America comprised essentially the two great river systems, the St. Lawrence anchored at Quebec and the Mississippi anchored at New Orleans. The security of this vast region depended upon safe communication between the extremities, and this, in turn, depended upon the friendship of Indian tribes and the maintenance of forts at strategic points along the inland waterways. As English settlements expanded, fur traders and land speculators moved westward beyond the mountains. The great Ohio Company claimed land along the Monongahela and Ohio Rivers, while an observer in Philadelphia reported that "Every great fortune made here within these fifty years has been by land." The English fur traders and land buyers paid the Indians more than the French, and by 1750, commanders of French forts were complaining that all the Ohio Indians were siding with the English.

This threat to the safety of New France caused the French to erect forts on Lake Erie and at the headwaters of the Ohio River. Marquis Duquesne de Menneville, Governor of New France, sent expeditions to build Fort Presqu'isle (Erie), Fort Le Boeuf (Waterford), and Fort Machault (Franklin) some miles to the south. These tied Lake Erie to the Allegheny River which provided direct water access to the Forks of the Ohio, where another fort would be built later. By the spring of 1753, the strength of the new Lake Erie forts so impressed the nearby Indians that many chiefs abandoned the English and pledged their friendship to the French.

The failure of the Pennsylvania government to resist French occupation of the trans-Allegheny lands grew from the bitter, uncompromising fight for power which the Quaker Assembly waged against the Penns. If the proprietary governors achieved control of defense policy and war should later break out, they would then as a matter of course take financial control under pressure of military necessity. But if the Assembly Quakers kept a firm grip on defense and financial policy, then if war came they could keep their power and exact further privileges such as the issuance of paper money or the taxation of proprietary lands as the price of cooperation. It has often been stated that the Quakers stayed aloof from the French and Indian War because of their pacifism, but more likely the preservation of their political power was their main interest.

Thomas Penn, in England, had a clearer view of the French menace than did the Pennsylvania Assembly. As early as 1749 he had instructed Governor Hamilton to establish forts east of the mountains and had pledged to pay more than half of the cost himself, but the Assembly refused to vote the remainder. Penn then urged officers of the Ohio Company to undertake defense of the region, but Quaker stockholders delayed action by the company. In 1753, when some western Indians appealed for English help against the French, the Assembly supported the conference at Carlisle called by the efforts of George Croghan, a redoubtable Irish fur trader and land speculator who became the major contact between the western Indians and the provincial government. The Assembly provided gifts to strengthen Indian loyalty, but would appropriate no funds to enable the Governor to undertake practical defense measures. Some Quakers openly stated that they would prefer to live under French rule than to give in to the Proprietors. The determination of the Assembly not to defend the proprietary lands so long as this real estate remained tax-free, and to reject defense appropriations unless the Governor approved paper money bills left Pennsylvania without forts and without troops to resist the French.

OUTBREAK OF THE WAR: 1753–1754

Virginia, which also claimed the Forks of the Ohio, took the initiative in challenging French intrusion. Governor Robert Dinwiddie, whose zeal to protect the Virginia domain was heightened by his private investment in the Ohio Company lands, demanded French withdrawal. To carry his letter to Fort LeBoeuf he chose twenty-one-year-old Major George Washington of the Virginia militia. With Christopher Gist, an explorer for the Ohio Company, Washington made his way to Wills Creek (Cumberland, Maryland), and proceeded down the Monongahela. At John Fraser's trading post on Turtle Creek he learned that the French had planned to build a new fort at the Forks of the Ohio but supplies had not arrived in time. The main force had left Presqu'isle to spend the winter in Montreal, and would return to the Forks in the spring of 1754. On December 7, 1753, Washington reached the French outpost at Fort Machault and from there was escorted by four Frenchmen to Fort LeBoeuf where he arrived on December 11.

The commander of Fort LeBoeuf, Legardeur de Saint-Pierre, who had been in charge for only a week, appealed to his senior commander at Fort Presqu'isle, Legardeur de Repentigny, for aid in drafting a reply to Dinwiddie's letter. On December 15 the two French commanders told Washington that they would communicate with the Marquis Dusquesne, and until hearing from him would maintain French authority in the Ohio Valley. Washington returned to Venango on December 23 and with Gist set out for home. Near the Forks they found the Allegheny full of ice, tried to cross on a hastily built raft, upset, and considered themselves lucky to make a landing on an island in the middle of the river. The Allegheny froze enough that night that they could cross it next day and reach the cabin of trader Fraser, frostbitten and nearly dead from cold. On January 16, 1754, Washington delivered the French reply to Governor Dinwiddie at Williamsburg.

Fully informed about the continuing political deadlock in Pennsylvania, Governor Dinwiddie determined to act. In January 1754 he sent a company of Virginia militia under Captain William Trent to anticipate the French by placing a fort at the Forks. This work progressed during February and March when Trent returned to Wills Creek, leaving the half-finished fort in charge of Ensign Edward Ward. The French, spurred by Washington's visit, hurriedly organized their expedition to plant a fort at the same place. On April 17, a force of 500 French and their Indian allies set out from Fort LeBoeuf, came down the Allegheny in a flotilla of canoes, and quickly dislodged the few Virginians. The French dismantled the British stockade and began the construction of the formidable structure which they called Fort Duquesne.

Governor Dinwiddie appealed to the governors of nearby colonies for troops, and mobilized a force of 300 Virginia militiamen who started west under the command of Col. Joshua Fry, with Washington as second in command, to reinforce Captain Trent. These men soon learned that the French had seized their objective. Assuming that the French had initiated war, Colonel Fry ordered Washington to reconnoiter. By May 24, Washington had cut a road and moved his men as far as Great Meadows, where he learned from Half King, a friendly Indian chief, that a French force was moving east from Fort Duquesne. On May 27, Washington learned from the Indians that the French had been sighted nearby. Leaving half his men to guard his camp, he took the rest to Half King's Rocks, held a council with the Indians, and before dawn followed Indian scouts to a ravine in which a small French detachment had made camp. Washington soon captured the entire French party except one who escaped to carry the tale to Captain Pierre de Contrecoseur, commandant of Fort Duquesne. In the brief engagement, the Virginians killed nine, wounded one, and captured twenty-one; but among the dead was Ensign Joseph Coulon de Villiers, Sieur de Jumonville, the French commander for whom this spot has been named.

For a month after the engagement at Jumonville Hollow, both sides prepared for more decisive combat. The French strengthened their posts in western Pennsylvania and sent a brother of Jumonville to lead the attack against the English. Washington built a stockade at Great Meadows which he called Fort Necessity. When Colonel Fry's sudden death placed command in Washington's hands, he ordered all troops into the new fort.

On July 3, 1754, about 600 Frenchmen and 100 Indians moved into the wooded hills facing Fort Necessity from the south. All day long the two forces exchanged fire, neither attempting to cross the open field separating them, but it seemed clear that Washington's small force could not hold out very long. Early that night the French invited a parley to which Washington sent his interpreter, Jacob Van Braam. He brought back a document, written in French, proposing that the Virginians should return home, that the English should not fortify any point west of the mountains for a year, and that Washington should admit his unprovoked attack on the French. The young Virginian signed these articles and on July 4 began his retreat. Only later did he learn that because Van Braam had mistranslated, he had signed a document declaring that he had "assassinated" Jumonville and took responsibility for starting a war. Of this brief conflict William Makepeace Thackeray wrote:

> It was strange that in a savage forest of Pennsylvania, a young Virginia officer should fire a shot and waken up a war which was to last for sixty years, to cost France her American colonies, to sever ours from us, to create a great Western Republic, to rage over the Old World when extinguished in the New, and of all the myriads engaged in the vast contest, to leave the prize of greatest fame with him who struck the first blow.

FRENCH ASCENDANCY

Although the expansion of New France threatened the western frontiers of nearly every English colony, none came to the aid of Virginia. Iroquois complaints that New York gave them no protection against the French led the Board of Trade to call an intercolonial meeting, the Albany Conference, on June 19, 1754, to consider Indian relations and frontier defense. Only Pennsylvania, New York, Maryland, and the New England colonies participated, and their delegates spent as much time trying to buy land from the Indians as they did in considering the French threat. While they deliberated, the French captured Fort Necessity. Benjamin Franklin proposed an intercolonial union centering in an American Parliament, but neither England nor the provinces showed interest.

The British government now took charge of defense. It placed Major General Edward Braddock of the Coldstream Guards in command of all British troops in America, with orders to oust the French from the major forts intruding on British-claimed territory: Forts Duquesne and Niagara in the west, and Crown Point and Beausejour in the northeast.

Braddock landed at Hampton, Virginia, on February 20, 1755, with two regiments, the Forty-fourth commanded by Sir Peter Halkett and the Forty-eighth under Col. Thomas Dunbar. He chose Virginia, rather than Pennsylvania, as his operating base because Governor Dinwiddie wished it and because Pennsylvania showed no interest in military activity. At a series of conferences with provincial governors in Alexandria, Braddock outlined his plans. He assigned operations against Fort Beausejour to Col. Robert Monckton, Crown Point to Sir William Johnson of New York, Niagara to Governor William Shirley of Massachusetts, and Fort Duquesne to himself. He called for militia from Virginia, New York, North Carolina, South Carolina, and Maryland to join the Fort Duquesne expedition. Franklin, who attended this meeting, suggested that since Pennsylvania had no troops, it might provide transport and supplies. Braddock ordered Franklin to see to it that Pennsylvania bestir itself to provide horses, wagons, and provisions for the army which he hoped to move early in May.

Since his entry into politics as leader of the Associators in the late 1740s, Franklin had played an ambiguous role. His personal talents and his solid popularity in Philadelphia established him as a minor power in provincial politics, but no one could be sure which side he favored, and both the Proprietary and Antiproprietary parties sought his support. Thomas Penn had promoted his appointment to deputy postmaster general in 1753, thinking Franklin would become a voice for Proprietary policy in the Assembly. The Quakers, too, courted him. Both sides were eager to use him, but neither entirely trusted him.

With local politics still at a deadlock, Braddock's call for the delivery of supplies to the army arrived. The Assembly would take no action unless Penn relinquished his right to instruct the governors, and approved paper money bills without a suspending clause. Penn faced trouble, for leaders of the British government held him accountable for supporting the war effort and had grown impatient of explanations and excuses. At length, Braddock's commissary general, John St. Clair, angrily warned Pennsylvanians that if they did not forward supplies, he would use the army to seize them. Franklin saw that Quaker intransigence might backfire. If Braddock should win without Pennsylvania help, it would utterly discredit the Assembly, and if he lost under these conditions the result would be catastrophic. Some members of Parliament already talked of banning Quakers from office in the province. Franklin, acting as agent of the Governor, went to work in the counties west of Philadelphia with a propaganda program to persuade farmers to forward wagons, horses, and foodstuff to army agents, explaining that the British would pay for the goods if promptly sent, but otherwise might seize them. Then, with keen insight into human nature, he persuaded the Assembly to send special delicacies to Braddock and the British officers. Soon letters were on their way to England from Braddock's command, praising Pennsylvania for supplying the army and providing the officers with horses, wines, and gourmet foods that made the wilderness seem less harsh.

With about 2,000 men, nearly half of them colonials, Braddock marched slowly to Cumberland, Maryland, and then to Great Meadows where he left Col. Thomas Dunbar with the supplies and half the troops. The rest became a task force to capture Fort Duquesne. By July 9 they had reached Fraser's cabin at the junction of the Monongahela and Turtle Creek, about 7 miles from the fort. Shortly after noon, an advance guard of light infantry left the plain where the army had rested and entered the wooded hills to the west. They shortly encountered the French who, with their Indian allies, already occupied the woods from the bank of Turtle Creek to the Monongahela. The British were trapped. They fought bravely in an exposed position, but could find few targets, while the enemy, protected by natural cover, did fearful execution. Braddock lost his life and most of his army, and the remainder fled in disorder.

The command now devolved upon Colonel Dunbar. He still had 1,000 reserves and several hundred survivors of the battle, and might have initiated another attack, but despite the pleas of colonial officers that he maintain a force in the west to protect the frontier, he destroyed the supplies and ordered the army east to Philadelphia. This decision exposed Pennsylvania, for the first time in its history, to the horrors of Indian war on its soil.

The Delawares and Shawnees, encouraged by the French, eagerly avenged the loss of their homeland. In early fall, two groups of war parties began to harass the frontier. One moved east along Penn's Creek to the Susquehanna, and from there southeast to the Tulpe-hocken settlements; the other followed the southern border through Bedford and Cove Gap toward Carlisle. The war parties were small but there were many of them, and they struck isolated farms, murdering the inhabitants, taking captives, killing livestock, and burning the crops and buildings. By the end of October the whole frontier was in flight and eventually scarcely any white population remained west of the Susquehanna.

THE DEFENSE OF PENNSYLVANIA

Governor Robert Hunter Morris, responding to letters and petitions which poured into his office demanding action, called the Assembly into session on November 3, 1755. This Assembly had been elected in early October before the raids began, and the Quakers had maintained their hold.

For three weeks the Assembly leadership continued to act out its traditional ritual, abusing the Proprietary leaders, rejecting all defense measures except in exchange for paper money issues and taxation of Penn's lands, and protesting all the while that they acted as defenders of the liberties of the people. But the temper of the times had changed, and people being scalped and massacred did not respond calmly to pious talk and threadbare excuses while Indian war parties roamed at will except in the immediate vicinity of Philadelphia. Even many of the Mennonites took up arms in defense of their families and prayed the Governor to raise troops. Governor Morris, in desperation, wrote to neighboring provinces for help and received predictable replies. New York responded that Pennsylvania's helpless plight "may be all for the better" as it might "open the eyes of your Province." New Jersey expressed amazement that so large and wealthy a colony should seek protection from so small a neighbor. Maryland sent token aid. The friendly Indians could not believe that Pennsylvania would take no action in the face of destruction. Chief Scaryoudy appeared before the Assembly with tears in his eyes to state that since he could not defeat the enemy with only 300 braves and since the Assembly would offer no hope of support, he had no alternative but to join with the French.

The week of November 20, a mob of enraged Germans gathered at the home of Conrad Weiser in Womelsdorf, demanding at gun point that he lead them to Philadelphia where they would force the Assembly to act. Governor Morris met them and showed them an order he had just received from Penn to apply £5,000 of the Proprietor's quitrents to defense measures, a sum larger than the much debated proprietary estate tax would have brought into the treasury. The timely receipt of this letter convinced the overwrought Germans that the Quakers in the Assembly had been playing the back country false. On the evening of November 25, a delegation from the "Dutch mob" entered the Assembly hall to demand immediate passage of a defense bill.

The Quakers in the Assembly knew long in advance that they faced serious trouble, but until the last minute thought that they could weather it. But Franklin, who had thrown his lot with the War Quakers after a bitter personal dispute with Thomas Penn during the summer, knew the full measure of the crisis. His gamble in having the Assembly send gifts to Braddock had quieted the outcry in England against the Quaker government. A victory by Braddock would have solved the Pennsylvania political struggle and more firmly entrenched the Quakers in power, but Braddock's defeat proved fatal to their hopes. All the old allegations in London about Quaker incapacity to govern revived, and reports of the Indian raids amplified them a hundredfold.

The Quakers now split. Franklin put it to them very clearly. If they wished to retain political power, they would have to swallow their scruples and pass a militia bill; or if they wished to obey their consciences, they would have to retire from the Assembly or be ejected forcibly by angry frontiersmen. Israel Pemberton, leader of the "principled" Quakers, was willing to withdraw, but Isaac Norris believed it wiser to bend under the storm, to provide money for defense, and to preserve the Quaker power. Franklin strongly supported the Norrisite Quakers and through them achieved a temporary solution. A defense bill that had been drawn beforehand was introduced and passed while the German delegation watched. The "principled" Quakers refrained from voting, while the Norrisite "War Quakers" and the ten western assemblymen provided the needed majority.

The militia bill of November 26, 1755, did not markedly affect the military situation; in fact the Privy Council later vetoed it. But it proved perhaps the most important measure, politically, since the constitution of 1701. By splitting the Friends into Pemberton's "Old Party" and Norris's War Quakers, it ended the Quaker monopoly of power in Pennsylvania government. After the October elections of 1756, only twelve Quakers remained in the Assembly. The Quaker oligarchy did not cease to exert influence, but it ceased to exercise control. The bill fractured the traditional subservience of the Germans to the Quakers, and marked the beginning of a new political alliance between Germans and Scotch-Irish.

The militia bill, weakly phrased, devoted most of its verbiage to exempting conscientious objectors from military service, but it did create a militia, and it did appropriate £60,000 for defense. As Indian massacres continued all through December, especially in Berks and Northampton Counties where all the Moravian settlements were destroyed, the Governor sought to establish a defense perimeter along the eastern or Blue Mountains by a chain of forts from Easton to Mercersburg. Militia companies, rapidly recruited, began work on them immediately. At 20-mile intervals they built sizable stockades to hold a militia company and several dozen families during a period of alarm. At 5-mile intervals between these main forts, they built small blockhouses where families could flee for temporary shelter. Periodically the militia marched between forts to collect refugees in the blockhouses. The line of forts not only followed the arc of the mountains from Easton to Mercersburg, but stretched up the Susquehanna from Fort Hunter near Harrisburg to Fort Augusta (Sunbury), and up the Juniata to Fort Patterson (Mexico) and Fort Granville (Lewistown). Many Pennsylvania towns had their origin in these forts. By February 1756 the chain had been essentially completed. The forts did not prevent Indian raids, but they give a sense of security and satisfied the frontier people that the government was taking some action. In April, Governor Morris offered a bounty of $150 for Delaware scalps.

BRITISH ASCENDANCY: 1756–1758

As sporadic Indian massacres continued through the summer, Col. John Armstrong proposed an attack upon the main Delaware headquarters at Kittanning, which served as supply base and starting point for Indian war parties. His military purpose acquired a personal motivation when Armstrong learned that his brother, Lieutenant Edward Armstrong, had been killed at Fort Granville which the Delaware chief, Captain Jacobs, seized and

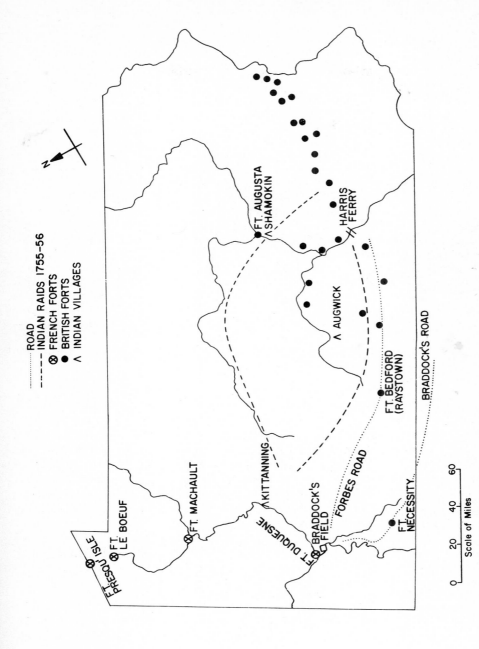

The French and Indian War in Pennsylvania. Symbols for British Forts between the Delaware River and Fort Bedford show the major defense posts built by Pennsylvania after the Indian raids of 1755–1756.

burned. Jacobs and his braves lived at Kittanning. Armstrong, with a force of 300 volunteers, set out from Carlisle and at daybreak on September 8, 1756, surprised the Kittanning settlement, burned the town, killed about forty Indians including Captain Jacobs, and dispersed the rest. Armstrong's rangers destroyed what the Indians said was "a sufficient stock of ammunition for a ten Year War with the English." After the Kittanning raid, the Delawares moved to Logstown (Ambridge) to be within protection of Fort Duquesne. Armstrong's raid, apart from its sobering effect on the Delawares, marked the first move by Pennsylvania to carry war to the enemy. It brought to an end the purely defensive period of the war.

Great Britain formally declared war on France on May 18, 1756. As the conflict now assumed worldwide dimensions, the British government determined to take full charge of the colonial war effort. Parliament appropriated £81,000 to create four battalions of Pennsylvania volunteers, which were mobilized into a British regiment called the "Royal Americans." Recruiters sought Scotch-Irish, German, and Swiss troops and provided officers who could speak German. From 1756 until the end of the war, these battalions fought in every important engagement: at Cape Breton Island, at the capture of Louisburg, at Fort William Henry, at Fort Ticonderoga, at Fort Frontenac, at Fort Duquesne, at Fort Niagara, at Fort Oswego, and finally at the capture of Quebec where General James Wolfe gave the Royal Americans their regimental motto—Celer et Audax. Swiss-born Col. Henry Bouquet led the First Battalion of the Royal Americans.

When King George II placed William Pitt, Earl of Chatham, in charge of the war effort in 1757, Pitt sent a new commander, Brigadier General John Forbes, to Philadelphia in April 1758, with 1,600 Highlanders, for an attack on Fort Duquesne through Pennsylvania. He mobilized an army of 6,000, including his Highlanders, the First Battalion of Royal Americans under Colonel Bouquet, and some 2,700 militiamen. The Assembly aided by offering a bounty to volunteers and appropriating £100,000 for supplies. Forbes ordered wagons and equipment to be gathered at Carlisle, troops to assemble at Raystown (Bedford), and directed a new road to be constructed from Carlisle through Raystown to Fort Duquesne.

By midsummer of 1758 most of the preparation had been completed and the army began to move west, though Forbes had become ill and remained in Philadelphia until early fall. In the meantime, Colonel Bouquet took charge of the field campaign, assembled his troops at Raystown, and then moved over Forbes' Road to Fort Ligonier within about 50 miles of Fort Duquesne. Washington, with Virginia's militia, used Braddock's Road to join him.

For a year before the Forbes expedition the British had been trying to pacify the Delaware and Shawnee Indians and take them out of the war. Sir William Johnson, superintendent of Indian affairs in the colonies, joined with the Proprietary party leaders of Pennsylvania to call a conference with the Delawares at Easton in July 1757, with Croghan and Conrad Weiser as their deputies. Most of the western Indians were ready for peace, but Quaker leaders of the Antiproprietary party seriously impeded the negotiations, insisting that Pennsylvania should admit it had defrauded the Delawares in the land purchases of 1737 and 1754 and should return this land before anyone talked of peace. Their course obstructed the road to peace and put the Quakers in alliance with the enemies of their government. Croghan and Weiser could not permit the conference to discuss the land sales, for these had been contracted with the Iroquois and could not be called fraudulent or rescinded in their absence without insult.

Both Croghan and Weiser recognized that the Iroquois needed to be restored to their former suzerainty over the Delawares which the war had all but destroyed. The English needed the friendship of the Iroquois more than they needed peace with the Delawares. To this end, Johnson arranged another conference at Easton in October 1758, which was attended by a large delegation from the Six Nations and a number of Delaware chiefs. The latter by this time had learned that the English were ready to revoke the Albany land purchase of 1754, and that Colonel Bouquet was advancing on Fort Duquesne with an army large enough to overpower the French. At the grand council at Easton, Croghan and Weiser, acting as agents of the British Crown and of the Penns, dealt directly with the Iroquois and surrendered back to them the lands which the Penns had purchased at Albany. This treaty recognized the Iroquois as the legitimate original owners of the land and thus sustained their position as ruler of the Delawares; and it protected the Delawares and Shawnees, lately allies of the French, from the consequences of the anticipated British capture of Fort Duquesne. The Delaware chiefs at Kuskusky raised the British flag on November 20.

Four days later the British troops approaching Fort Duquesne heard a muffled explosion in the distance. Hurrying forward, they discovered that the French garrison had blown up Fort Duquesne and retired, and the British marched into the ruins without firing a shot. General Forbes renamed the site Fort Pitt, placed Colonel Bouquet in command of the Forks, and returned to Philadelphia to report that French control of western Pennsylvania had been ended.

Forbes died in March 1759, to be succeeded by General John Stanwix who began the construction of the massive new British bastion which occupied the site of the modern "Triangle" at Pittsburgh. The following year General Robert Monckton became commandant at Fort Pitt and with the aid of Col. Hugh Mercer took possession of the three French forts to the north, Machault, LeBoeuf, and Presqu'isle. War on Pennsylvania soil had come to an end, though Pennsylvania troops continued to serve elsewhere, from Cuba to Quebec, until the final French surrender at Montreal on September 8, 1760.

PONTIAC'S WAR: 1763

Three years elapsed between the end of the fighting in America and the signing of the Treaty of Paris on February 10, 1763, which formally concluded hostilities between England and France. During these critical years the Pennsylvania frontier settlers and many footloose adventurers from the militia began the rapid settlement of homesteads west of the mountains, in brash disregard of the pledges made to the Indians in the Easton Treaty of 1758. Furthermore, the English continued building and strengthening the western forts, though Forbes, Monckton, Mercer, and others had repeatedly assured the Indians that upon defeating the French, the British would abandon the forts and withdraw east of the Alleghenies. By 1763 it became evident to the Indians that neither Pennsylvania nor the British government had any intention of keeping its word. The transfer of French possessions in North America to the English in February 1763 brought the Indians face to face with the certainty that their hunting lands would soon be appropriated by English farmers, despite any promises to the contrary.

Angered by the breach of faith and foreseeing that the English and Indian ways of life could not exist side by side, Chief Pontiac of the Ottawas created a military confederation of Indian tribes designed to destroy the entire British colonial establishment and repossess by force the Indian homeland on both sides of the Alleghenies. Pontiac brought into his plan the Indians of Pennsylvania, the Ohio Valley, and the lakes, and even the Seneca tribe of Iroquois whose hunting grounds lay south of Lake Erie. In a coordinated surprise attack, war parties would simultaneously strike all the major frontier forts, and then carry the hatchet to the farm settlements and eastern villages. The attack had been astutely planned, for many forts contained only a few dozen militiamen as garrison. Rumors of the impending attack leaked, but even with forewarning the colonists were unprepared for the intensity of the assault. In Pennsylvania the Indians quickly captured all the western forts except Pitt, Ligonier, and Bedford, and to these they laid seige. During June and July war parties ranged through the Juniata, Tuscarora, and Cumberland Valleys, repeating the scenes that had followed Braddock's defeat. Again the population fled east of the Susquehanna and appealed to the Assembly for help.

At the time Pontiac's warriors struck, Colonel Bouquet was in Philadelphia. To relieve Fort Pitt, Bouquet set out for the west with a few companies and such militia as he could assemble. He reached Fort Bedford in late July, Fort Ligonier early in August, and Bushy Run, about 20 miles from Fort Pitt, on August 5. Here the Indians surrounded and attacked him. The battle raged all day, and the following morning the Indians resumed fighting with uncommon persistence. Outnumbered, surrounded, and nearly exhausted, Bouquet's force seemed doomed. In a last desperate expedient, Bouquet ordered several companies to draw off as if in retreat to lure the Indians out of the woods in pursuit. The Indians sensing victory ran out to capture an apparently retreating force, and Bouquet's men poured fire into them from front and flank. Within a few minutes the attackers fled, and Bouquet continued on to Fort Pitt. The battle of Bushy Run has properly been called the most important Indian conflict in Pennsylvania history, not only because it stopped the momentum of Indian success in Pontiac's War, but because it provided convincing evidence that in sustained and organized warfare, the Indians could not successfully resist the Europeans.

Bouquet's victory broke the hopes of the Indians of driving the white man into the sea, but added hatred and bitterness to their spirit, which was heightened by Pennsylvania's renewal of a bounty for Indian scalps. Isolated raids continued all over the province until December 1764, when Governor John Penn announced that peace had been reestablished with the Delawares, the Shawnees, and the hostile western tribes.

This whole chain of events, from broken pledges to calculated revenge to impassioned counter revenge, led to one of the most savage consequences of the Pontiac War: the Conestoga Massacre. Christian Indians trained by the Moravians were brought to Philadelphia for protection against wild frontiersmen who would kill any Indian they saw. A small tribe of farming Indians, the Conestogas, lived in Lancaster County. On December 14, 1763, fifty Scotch-Irish living near Harrisburg, known as the "Paxton Boys," rode to Conestoga Town, outside Lancaster, and killed and scalped two Indian women, three old men, and a young boy. The fourteen remaining inhabitants of the town begged for protection, and were placed in the Lancaster jail. Two days after Christmas the Paxton Boys, now numbering a hundred, returned to Lancaster, broke into the jail, and hacked to pieces and scalped all the remaining members of the tribe—three old men, three women, five small boys, and three young girls. Mounting their horses, they announced that they would next exterminate the Moravian Indians.

The Christian Indians at the Moravian settlements, in fear for their lives, set out in January for New York where they had been promised protection by the British army. When the Governor of New York denied them entry, they proceeded through New Jersey to Philadelphia under military escort. In February the Paxton Boys advanced as far as Germantown in search of their quarry, but the local population, with fixed bayonets and artillery, persuaded them to retire.

The Moravian Indians later moved to the Wyalusing Valley in northeastern Pennsylvania; migrated into western Pennsylvania and then to Muskingum, Ohio, as a result of the Treaty of Greenville in 1795; were driven to Detroit by Ohio settlers; and during the war of 1812 were nearly annihilated by the Americans under General William Hull. The remnants of the Lenni-Lenape who in William Penn's day had made their home in Pennsylvania are now on reservations in Oklahoma, or live in Canada at Moraviantown, at Muncey Town, or in the Six Nations Reserve at Oshweken.

RESULTS OF THE FRENCH AND INDIAN WAR

The French and Indian War brought many changes to life in Pennsylvania. Politically it terminated the control of Pennsylvania government by the Quaker oligarchy. It broke the old alliance between Germans and Quakers, and began the coalition between Germans and Scotch-Irish. The war did not end the ancient contest between the governors and the Assembly, nor the continuing struggle between the Proprietary and the Antiproprietary parties, but it did serve to alter the issues, the constituency, and the leadership of these rivals. The experience of Pennsylvanians in the army gave them more confidence in their own prowess and less respect for the British troops than they had before the war began. At the same time, the conduct of British commanders who ignored, snubbed, or degraded colonial troops and officers aroused resentments which weakened loyalty to England and aggravated the protests against the new British colonial policy inaugurated in 1763.

The war also had significant economic effects in Pennsylvania. The two military roads, Braddock's and Forbes's, made commercial traffic possible across the mountains. Thousands of men for the first time saw the transmontane country and set up homesteads there. Land speculators and Indian traders foresaw fortunes to be made in this region. But at the very moment that old homes had been made secure and new ones planned, all hopes were summarily dashed by the Proclamation of 1763, which banned settlement west of the mountains and forbade Indian trading except for persons licensed by England.

Social results also grew from the war. The population had engaged in many quasi-governmental activities requiring meetings, leadership, and action. The traditional ideas of Europe—that one class should govern and the other be governed—weakened when the common folk learned that they could conduct government locally and achieve results. The militia elections, the marches on the Assembly, the evidence that leadership existed in the backwoods as well as in the manor houses stirred thoughts that very shortly would lead to the outright challenge of the whole system of hereditary privilege.

The French and Indian War ended one set of problems—those involving the Indians and the French. It inaugurated a new set of problems—those involving the compatibility of British imperial policy with the way of life of the North American colonials.

BIBLIOGRAPHY

Of many histories of the French and Indian War, two stand out as major classics: Francis Parkman: *France and England in North America,* 7 vols. (1865–1892), of which vol. 6, *A Half Century of Conflict,* deals with Pennsylvania; and Lawrence H. Gipson: *The British Empire before the American Revolution,* 13 vols. (1961–1967), of which vols. 4–7 relate to Pennsylvania history. Briefer general histories are Harrison Bird: *Battle for a Continent: The French and Indian War, 1754–1763* (1965); Hugh Cleland: *George Washington in the Ohio Valley* (1955); Mary C. Darlington: *History of Col. Henry Bouquet and the Western Frontiers of Pennsylvania, 1747–1764* (1920); and Randolph C. Downes: *Council Fires on the Upper Ohio* (1940).

The beginnings of the war are treated in Frank H. Severance: *An Old Frontier of France: the Niagara Region and Adjacent Lakes under French Control,* 2 vols. (1917), a scholarly and standard treatise; and the dependable but briefer work by Donald H. Kent: *The French Invasion of Western Pennsylvania, 1753* (1954).

Braddock's expedition is covered in Lee McCardell: *Ill-starred General: Braddock of the Coldstream Guards* (1958); Douglas S. Freeman: *George Washington, A Biography,* 7 vols. (1948–1957); Julius F. Sachse: *The Braddock Expedition: Conditions of Pennsylvania during the Year 1755* (1917); Stanley Pargellis: "Braddock's Defeat," in *American History Review,* vol. 41 (1936), pp. 253–269; and Franklin T. Nichols: "The Braddock Expedition" (doctoral dissertation, Harvard University, Cambridge, Mass., 1947).

The frontier forts have been treated most accurately by William A. Hunter: *Forts on the Pennsylvania Frontier, 1753–1758* (1960). Other volumes stressing the forts are Walter O'Meara: *Guns at the Forks* (1965); Alfred P. James and Charles Stotz: *Drums in the Forest* (1958), both dealing with Forts Duquesne and Pitt; and C. Hale Sipe: *Fort Ligonier and Its Times: A History of the First English Fort West of the Allegheny Mountains* (1923).

For special aspects of the war, see William A. Hunter: "First Line of Defense, 1755–1756: Beginnings of the Frontier Forts," in *Pennsylvania History,* vol. 22 (1955), pp. 229–255; and "Victory at Kittanning," in *Pennsylvania History,* vol. 23 (1956), pp. 376–407; J. W. King: "Colonel John Armstrong: His Place in the History of Southwestern Pennsylvania," *Western Pennsylvania Historical Magazine,* vol. 10 (1927), pp. 129–145; Charles F. Snyder: "The Penn's Creek Massacre," *Northumberland County Historical Society Proceedings,* vol. 11 (1939), pp. 147–173; and William H. Rice: "The Gnaddenhutten Massacres: A Brief History of Two Historic Tragedies," *Pennsylvania German,* vol. 7 (1906), pp. 26–31, 71–79.

Pontiac's Rebellion has been best examined by Howard H Peckham: *Pontiac and the Indian Uprising* (1947). On the Paxton Boys, see Lottie M. Bausman: "Massacre of the Conestoga Indians, 1763," in *Lancaster County Historical Society Papers,* vol. 18 (1914), pp. 169–185; and Brooke Hindle: "The March of the Paxton Boys," in *William and Mary Quarterly,* vol. 3 (1946), pp. 461–486.

Biographies of Conrad Weiser and George Croghan, previously cited, are important, as are Lily Lee Nixon: *James Burd, Frontier Defender* (1941); Sewell Slick: *William Trent and the West* (1947); and William T. Parsons: "Isaac Norris II, The Speaker" (doctoral dissertation, University of Pennsylvania, Philadelphia, 1955).

PART

2

Laboratory of Democracy: 1763–1861

CHAPTER SEVEN

The Movement toward Independence

At the end of the French and Indian War, Great Britain found herself responsible for the cost of administering a vast new empire while at the same time trying to fund an unprecedented national debt. To protect this empire and to ease the financial burden, the British ministry created a new colonial policy. As applied to America, this new policy took two forms. First, it attempted to maintain peace and security as cheaply as possible by such devices as the Proclamation of 1763 and the Quartering Acts. Second, it sought financial aid from the colonials by stiffening old trade and currency laws, and by inventing new tax or revenue laws. One part of the financial policy aimed to prevent smuggling and actually to collect customs duties which had been levied but evaded for years. The writs of assistance and an increase in the number of enforcement officers illustrated the government's seriousness of purpose. Britain modified some of the old trade laws and tried to channel goods, duties, and profits to her own shores by the Sugar Act of 1764 and the Townshend Acts of 1767. The ministry also experimented with direct taxation in the Stamp Act of 1765. These regulations aroused resistance in all the colonies, but each responded in its own way to the new imperial policy. Our interest lies in the reaction of Pennsylvania.

THE PROCLAMATION OF 1763

In Penn's land, the Proclamation of 1763 damaged relations with the mother country perhaps more than any subsequent regulation. Of all the colonies, only Pennsylvania had begun substantial settlement west of the Appalachians. In the eyes of Pennsylvania frontiersmen, the recent war had been fought to protect and preserve their homes, and after the war they returned west, accompanied by thousands of newcomers. But they forgot or ignored what the British ministry remembered—that at Easton in 1758, as the price of stopping Indian massacres, the provincial authorities had returned to the Indians the land lying west of the Susquehanna. The King ratified this treaty so that it had become a British as well as a Pennsylvania obligation. Because the settlers broke the Easton Treaty, and the British commanders broke their promises to withdraw garrisons from the western forts when the French surrendered, Pontiac's War had ensued. To avert further fighting and expense, the King issued a proclamation on October 7, 1763, forbidding colonial settlement west of the mountains and placing trade with the Indians under royal control.

The Proclamation of 1763, intended by the British to conciliate the Indians, infuriated the Scotch-Irish who, after serving and suffering in the war, were ordered off the western land so that their late enemy, the Indians, could have it. The Scotch-Irish never fully recovered from their shock at this order, which filled them with hatred for the home government. The impossibility of maintaining the Proclamation Line of settlement soon became so obvious that the Pennsylvania government, in 1768, negotiated a new Indian treaty at Fort Stanwix to purchase land south of a line crossing the province diagonally from the northeast corner to the southwest corner. This legitimized most of the then-existing settlements west of the mountains, but it did not ease the resentment of western Pennsylvanians against the recent effort to dispossess them of their farms.

THE STAMP ACT IN PENNSYLVANIA POLITICS

As the Proclamation of 1763 excited western Pennsylvania, so the Stamp Act affected the east. The political ramifications of Pennsylvania's response to this revenue law and of Franklin's equivocal course regarding it in London need to be understood to comprehend Pennsylvania's role in the revolutionary movement.

Recall that Braddock's defeat in 1755 broke the power of the pacifist or "stiff" Quakers in Pennsylvania government. Members of this faction voluntarily withdrew from the Assembly. Franklin managed to have many of their places filled with his own friends, chief among them Joseph Galloway. For the next ten years, from 1756 to 1766, Franklin tried to destroy the proprietorship of the Penns and to make Pennsylvania a royal colony.

The Antiproprietary party under Franklin's leadership grudgingly supported the war against the French, but avidly pursued its private war against Thomas Penn and his friends of the Proprietary party. The Assembly in 1757 sent Franklin to London as colonial agent with instructions to persuade Penn to agree to taxation of the proprietary estates. Penn met this appeal by telling Franklin that it verged on the ridiculous to award tenants the power to tax the property of their landlord. The Assembly responded by tying to every money bill a clause taxing proprietary land, knowing that no governor could sign such a law.

On the tax controversy, time worked against Thomas Penn. The old concept of feudal landholding had ceased to exist in America, where taxable freeholds had replaced the privileged real estate of a lord. By the end of the French and Indian War, the Antiproprietary party had successfully overcome the temporary unpopularity resulting from its negligence and obstructionism in the Assembly during the first years of the war. The Assembly of 1761 had most of the population on its side on the three key issues of the moment: taxation of

Penn's lands, paper money, and a voluntary militia controlled by the lawmakers, not the governor.

In England, Franklin's efforts to have the proprietary charter revoked failed. After a fruitless interview with Thomas Penn in 1759, Franklin wrote home denouncing the Proprietor in the most scathing language. A copy leaked out and seriously injured the Assembly's cause, for even the Quakers did not condone the venom of Franklin's attack and refused to petition formally for an end to the proprietorship.

Franklin returned to Pennsylvania in 1762 and in October 1763 was elected again to the Assembly. The Proclamation of 1763 had just been issued, Pontiac's War was still in progress, and within a short time everyone would be talking about the bloody work of the Paxton Boys. These events intensified the contest between the Proprietary and the Antiproprietary parties. John Penn, the Proprietor's nephew, had recently succeeded James Hamilton as Governor. When the Paxton Boys threatened Philadelphia, the Assembly eagerly cooperated with Governor Penn by passing local defense bills instantly. Franklin, condemning the westerners as "white savages," worked closely with the Governor to protect the city, and several hundred Quakers laid down their conscientious scruples and picked up guns. Once the threat of the Scotch-Irish invasion had ended, the Antiproprietary leaders tried to extract political advantage from the crisis.

Franklin blamed the Penns for the raids by the Paxton Boys, and for the failure of local sheriffs to make any arrests or bring anyone to trial. The Antiproprietary leaders charged that the Proprietary party had entered an alliance with the western Presbyterians who would soon reduce the province to anarchy. The proprietorship had failed; only royal government could restore public order and private safety to Pennsylvania.

The Proprietary party leaders had no alternative but to face the issue thus thrust upon them. While they disliked bringing the terrorist exploits of the Paxton Boys into politics, they had to rebut the Assembly charges, and attributed the Conestoga Massacre to the Assembly's blind disregard of western appeals for protection and for representation. They pointed out how little the Quakers had permitted their alleged scruples to interfere with the quick passage of defense bills when Quaker rather than Presbyterian lives had been threatened. The Assembly attack thus served to weld together more tightly the interests of the western frontiersmen and the eastern supporters of the Proprietary party.

The 1764 campaign to elect assemblymen proved one of the most exciting in Pennsylvania colonial history. In the Antiproprietary party Franklin based his own campaign for reelection upon having the Assembly petition for royal government of Pennsylvania. The Antiproprietary writings urged royal government to check lawlessness, to give the Assembly power over distribution of public land, to place responsibility for defense upon the Crown, and to prevent the Presbyterians from gaining political control of the province. The Proprietary party leaders argued that Franklin's personal ambition lay at the root of the matter. They pointed to his hatred of the Penns, his hope of controlling the distribution of political jobs in a reorganized colony, his interest in vast land speculation schemes in the Ohio Valley, and his desire to be named royal Governor of Pennsylvania.

The Proprietary party in 1764 achieved a significant victory by defeating both Franklin and Galloway in Philadelphia. Franklin, however, continued to dominate the Assembly even after being voted out of it. He brought in his petition for royal government, with 3,500 signatures, and persuaded the Assembly first to adopt it and then to appoint him as the agent to carry it to London. He chose John Hughes as his spokesman in the Assembly to replace

Isaac Norris who had by this time repudiated Franklin's leadership. Benjamin Franklin arrived in London early in 1765, just before the passage of the Stamp Act.

When the Grenville ministry called colonial agents into conference to inform them that a stamp duty would be proposed, Franklin expressed doubts, but he considered the overthrow of the proprietorship as his main task and saw the stamp tax as a possible aid. The ministry had embarked on a new colonial policy which required more centralized control. To convert proprietary into Crown colonies would be a move in this direction. Franklin therefore gave Grenville his pledge to support the stamp tax, in return for Grenville's promise to support Pennsylvania's application for royal government. After Parliament passed the Stamp Act in March 1765, Franklin named the collector of stamp duties in New Jersey, and appointed his personal lieutenant, John Hughes, for Pennsylvania. In doing so he intentionally bypassed Thomas Penn, who shrewdly expressed his pleasure that he did not have to make such unpleasant appointments. Franklin advised the editor of his Philadelphia newspaper to explain the Stamp Act calmly and to bring people to recognize their obligation to the Crown and the empire.

News of the passage of the Stamp Act quickly raised colonial tempers to the explosion point. Proprietary party leaders, fully acquainted with Franklin's course in London, grasped the opportunity to lead the protest against the act, and to place responsibility for it on Franklin's party. They publicized Franklin's support of the hated stamp tax as a lever to gain the ministry's approval of his petition for royal government. This charge seemed undeniable when Franklin's two chief Pennsylvania spokesmen, John Hughes and Joseph Galloway, firmly backed the new law. Opposition to the stamp tax became so strong that many of the Antiproprietary people, especially the Quaker merchants, joined the protest. When the Assembly met in September, it sent a delegation of Franklin's enemies to attend the Stamp Act Congress in New York.

Shortly thereafter, Philadelphia mobs went into action. A mass meeting at the State House decided that Hughes should resign as collector. Led by men of the Proprietary party, this meeting marched to the collector's house where Hughes, with a loaded gun in his hand, said he had not yet received his commission and so could not resign it. Despite the mounting pressure, Franklin's party maintained its control of the Assembly in the October elections. But when the ship carrying the stamps arrived a few days later, rioting broke out in Philadelphia. A shouting mob visited Hughes again but found him adamant.

The law which went into effect on November 1 required stamps on legal documents, business papers, newspapers, and almanacs. Printers issued the 1766 almanacs in August 1765, newspapers planned to suspend publication, shipowners hurriedly sent out their vessels, and lawyers pondered what to do. The stamp tax raised so much disturbance partly because it affected exactly those portions of the population which controlled public opinion: editors, lawyers, and businessmen. Philadelphia, America's largest city, was a center of all these professions. Legal activity for a time came to a halt. Galloway wrote: "No business can be legally transacted, no lawsuits prosecuted, no vessels sail, no securities for money taken." The lawyers ultimately agreed to undertake business without stamps, saying prophetically that a law they considered unconstitutional need not be obeyed.

Meanwhile, the Stamp Act Congress in New York had recommended the "Association," a semivoluntary agreement among merchants not to deal in any British goods. Local committees undertook to enforce this boycott. As opposition to the Stamp Act spread throughout the colonies, the party contests about it in Pennsylvania declined, for even the Antiproprietary leaders could not swim against such a current.

The colonial response to the Stamp Act so disrupted British business that the law had to be repealed. The Grenville ministry also fell, to be replaced by that of Rockingham. Before retiring, Grenville gave Franklin an opportunity to repair the damage to his reputation in Pennsylvania, a favor he owed since he had not delivered his part of the bargain to end the proprietorship. Grenville arranged to have Franklin participate in the repeal of the Stamp Act. The ministry carefully staged Franklin's appearance before Parliament in February 1766 to quiet colonial fears by placing a colonial agent in the role of a respected consultant in the repeal, and to quiet English apprehensions by making Parliament seem to respond to colonial arguments, and not to colonial mobs and threats. The interview quickly reestablished Franklin's prestige, but it did not remove suspicion from all quarters and it did not influence Parliament to repeal the Stamp Act, for that decision had been reached beforehand.

The end of the Stamp Act brought an end to political excitement for several years. The Antiproprietary party quietly carried the elections in 1766 and 1767, and the political scene, in Chief Justice William Allen's words, remained "in a profound calm."

THE TOWNSHEND ACTS

The Townshend Acts went into effect in November 1767. They sought to obtain revenue by a tax on imported glass, lead, painters' colors, paper, and tea. The income would be used to pay for the administration of justice and support of government in America. This meant an increase in the size of the British staff in the colonies charged with enforcement of all the navigation and trade acts. This feature of the Townshend Acts seemed to cause more concern than the import tax itself. If British merchants could no longer accept colonial paper money as legal tender, and the government actually succeeded in forcing all trade into British ports, which would cut off the specie supply, the colonies faced bankruptcy.

John Dickinson urged opposition to the Townshend Acts and proposed a union of the colonies for mutual protection. He published a series of tracts entitled *Letters from a Farmer in Pennsylvania* which explored the whole problem of taxation within the empire and provided many of the arguments which became the polemical currency of the rising resistance movement. Massachusetts, in a "circular letter," invited other colonies to renew the boycott of England which had proved effective in upsetting the Stamp Act, but Pennsylvania merchants believed that a boycott would damage them more than the import duties. The Pennsylvania Assembly declined to endorse the proposed boycott.

A harsh British response to the Massachusetts circular letter, sharply condemning the colonials for protesting, reignited a flame which until then had been dying. William Allen, who was far from being a Son of Liberty, reported that even moderates had been passionately aroused by the British assumption that a formal statement of grievances verged on treason. Allen called a meeting at the State House in Philadelphia at which the main speakers represented leadership of the two opposing parties: John Dickinson of the Proprietary party, and Charles Thomson of the Antiproprietary party. The meeting demanded that the Assembly forward a petition against the Townshend Acts to the king. Galloway fought against it, but the Assembly obeyed the decision of the town meeting. Public pressure forced the Philadelphia merchants to adopt a nonimportation agreement in February 1769.

After a year, the determination of the merchants began to weaken, for they suffered almost the entire brunt of the boycott policy. Britain, in April 1770, repealed all Townshend duties except the tax on tea. In the summer of 1770, New York lifted her boycott on British wares and the Philadelphia merchants then decided to handle all British goods except tea.

THE PHILADELPHIA TEA PARTY

For several more years Pennsylvania enjoyed comparative political quiet as the recent storms over imperial policy died away. Then, quite suddenly, the Parliamentary Act of May 1773, to aid the British East India Company dispose of excess tea, generated another colonial hurricane. Parliament rescinded the export tax on tea, while the East India Company planned to sell its tea at cost to liquidate an oversupply; as a result, tea, still bearing the Townshend import duty, would sell in the colonies more cheaply than ever. Whether or not Parliament intended a strategem to induce the colonials to deal in a taxed product, the Philadelphians immediately became alert to an apparent trick and took action which by this time had become nearly routine. They held a town meeting at the State House which demanded the resignation of agents who had been named to receive the tea. When news arrived that Captain Ayres would bring the tea ship *Polly* to Philadelphia about Christmas, 1773, handbills appeared on tavern bulletin boards signed by "The Philadelphia Committee on Tarring and Feathering," threatening the lives of river pilots who would dare to bring the ship up the Delaware. Mobs gathered around the homes of the three tea agents and forced their resignations.

On December 16, 1773, the Boston masqueraders held their famous Tea Party. News of this had scarcely reached Philadelphia when, on Christmas Day, riders brought news of the arrival of the *Polly* at Chester. Captain Ayres came ashore and on December 27 was brought to a town meeting of some 8,000 to 10,000 Philadelphians gathered in the State House yard. With events at Boston in everyone's mind, the meeting adopted resolutions by a general howl. The burden of the resolutions was, simply, that Captain Ayres should sail his ship out of Delaware Bay immediately, and that Pennsylvania approved the resistance of others to the tea duty.

Within a few months Parliament passed laws suspending the Massachusetts charter and closing the port of Boston until the city paid for the tea which had been thrown into the harbor. It also enacted laws establishing special courts for maritime cases and authorizing the use of private homes to quarter troops if Massachusetts did not provide them with barracks suitable for winter residence. Though these acts did not all relate to the tea episode, the colonists lumped them all together under the pejorative label "The Intolerable Acts." Boston promptly framed another Circular Letter calling for an intercolonial congress. Paul Revere delivered this letter to Philadelphia leaders on May 19, 1774. The following day the three major activists among the Pennsylvania radicals, Charles Thomson, Joseph Reed, and Thomas Mifflin, called a town meeting. By prearrangement, invitations did not reach men known to be sympathetic with the British, but the planners did invite some moderates, John Dickinson, Thomas Willing, and Edward Pennington, to serve as cochairmen. These men provided an aura of restraint and respectability to the proceedings, while from the floor the actual leaders gave fire-and-brimstone speeches. As both moderates and radicals demanded places on the resolutions committee, the meeting created a committee of both groups which drafted a reply to the Massachusetts letter, proposing that Parliament rescind its punitive acts, and that Boston pay for the tea its citizens had destroyed.

As talk about the calling of a Continental Congress spread, the German settlers of Hanover, on June 2, 1774, adopted the first Pennsylvania resolution supporting such a meeting. Within another week, Dickinson, Thomson, Reed, Mifflin, George Clymer, and some others called upon Governor Penn to convene the Assembly for the purpose of appointing Pennsylvania delegates to the Congress. Upon his refusal, they called another town meeting for

June 18. This meeting, nearly as large as the one which disposed of the ship *Polly,* represented all segments of the Philadelphia population and quickly endorsed the call for an intercolonial congress. It then appointed a large committee of correspondence which fed information into similar committees of the back country. Into this semiofficial communications system the Philadelphia leaders channeled their plan to convene the Pennsylvania Provincial Conference which would choose delegates for the approaching Continental Congress. Governor Penn now called the Assembly to meet on July 18, under the pretext of considering Indian problems, but really to forestall the seizure of initiative by the unofficial committees of correspondence.

The committees set July 15 as the day for town meetings to select delegates for their Pennsylvania Provincial Conference. This body, though no more representative of the whole population than the Assembly, did concentrate in one group the widespread sentiment for firm action. It met before the Assembly had gathered, and adopted resolutions calling for a general colonial congress in Philadelphia. It then moved into the Assembly hall where the regular government approved its action and appointed delegates to the coming Continental Congress: Joseph Galloway, Charles Humphreys, Samuel Rhoads, Thomas Mifflin, John Morton, George Ross, and Edward Biddle—the first three moderates and the others radicals.

THE PENNSYLVANIA REVOLUTIONARY ORGANIZATION

The First Continental Congress met at Philadelphia on September 5, 1774, with all the colonies represented but Georgia. Galloway presented the first important business to the body, a proposal to create a British commonwealth based on Franklin's Albany plan of 1754. Voting by colonies, the Congress rejected this, six to five. It asked John Dickinson to draw up a petition of rights and grievances to be sent to England, and then ordered a trade boycott which it organized under the label "The Continental Association." To enforce the boycott, Congress instructed all provinces to create a structure of central and local committees composed of "Associators." This request pointed particularly at Pennsylvania, whose government preferred compromise to direct attack on the mother country. Congress thus gave the appearance of official sanction to Pennsylvania committees which would function outside the framework of the provincial governmental machinery.

The Philadelphia Committee acted as headquarters for the Pennsylvania Associators and encouraged the formation of county committees, whose members soon undertook all kinds of functions. As their volunteer work expanded, they set up specialized committees of safety, of vigilance, and of inspection. They visited merchants, kept track of prices, inspected warehouses and ship cargoes, and reported on evasions of the boycott and their suspicions of their neighbors. These committees soon became a viable political entity known by the term "Associators." Conservatives, who had started the town meeting and committee procedure ten years before to force action by the Assembly, now complained bitterly that the "resolves of the people" had entirely supplanted "the laws and the constitution."

By 1775 the names Proprietary party and Antiproprietary party ceased to have any meaning, though some still used the terms. As the imperial problem now overshadowed all others, those who defied the Associators had either to abandon politics or to accept the role of Tories. Men like William Allen and Joseph Galloway entered this role very reluctantly, only because there was no longer any other place for them to stand. They both had been willing to resist particular policies of the British government, but neither could bring himself to make war on it. On the other side, people called themselves Whigs, but two groups of these existed. The Moderates like Dickinson supported the Association but wished by some compromise to continue living under the old Pennsylvania and British governments. The Radicals like Thomson hoped to upset the Pennsylvania constitution and declare independence from England. Both these groups answered to the name "Associators," but people soon began to call them "Moderates" or "Radicals" to distinguish their different objectives.

The Assembly elections of October 1774 brought victory for the Whigs. The new Assembly convened while the First Continental Congress deliberated, and promptly approved its actions—the first colonial legislature to do so. It also reappointed as delegates to the Second Continental Congress, scheduled to meet in spring, the same people who had served in the first, except that John Dickinson replaced Rhoads.

Despite the creation of Bedford County in 1771, Northumberland in 1772, and Westmoreland in 1773, the three original counties still elected twice as many assemblymen as all the others combined. Those denied equal representation resented the eastern monopoly of power. Many of the revolutionary committeemen began to think not only of challenging England, but also of ridding themselves of the proprietary government and setting themselves up in its stead. And the Radicals had discovered the tools to accomplish their purpose and were becoming expert in their use: town meetings, local committees, provincial conventions, and police power to enforce their edicts, the latter a device never adequately developed by the Assembly.

The Associators called the second Pennsylvania Provincial Conference to meet on January 23, 1775, with the object not so much of performing any business as of keeping alive public recognition of this form of meeting. It did exhort local committees to gather military stores, promote local manufactures, and hunt down profiteers or merchants who broke the boycott. Before adjourning, it named a Philadelphia Committee of Correspondence of some sixty members into whose hands it delivered authority to act in the name of the conference and to reconvene it when necessary. It had thus set up a quasi-legal body to function as a government alongside the constitutional one which sat as the Pennsylvania Assembly.

In April came news of the bloodshed at Lexington and Concord. In Philadelphia an excited public meeting resolved that all would join in arms to defend colonial liberty. This public pronouncement had the immediate effect of transforming the whole committee hierarchy of Associators into military units. The Assembly belatedly appointed its own Committee of Public Safety, assigning it authority to mobilize the Associators into a regular militia force. It appropriated money to defend Philadelphia, ordered county officials to outfit volunteer militia companies and to create mobile units of Minutemen, and before adjourning set up the General Committee of Safety to supervise all military activity and to defend the province as circumstances required. This committee, named by the Assembly and thus having a legitimate constitutional base, met for the first time on July 3, 1775, and named as its chairman Benjamin Franklin, who had just returned from England.

THE PROBLEM OF INDEPENDENCE

The Second Continental Congress had assembled in Philadelphia on May 10, 1775. Pennsylvania's delegation had changed when Galloway resigned, and the Assembly had added the names of Franklin, Thomas Willing, and James Wilson. By mid-June Congress had appointed

George Washington as commander of the Continental army, called for six companies of expert riflemen from Pennsylvania to serve at Boston, and put in motion extensive plans for the fortification of Delaware Bay. Washington reviewed the Pennsylvania troops in Philadelphia and set out for Massachusetts with George Ross as his secretary.

The twelve months from June 1775 to June 1776 brought utter political confusion to Pennsylvania. The Assembly, the Pennsylvania Provincial Conferences, several echelons of revolutionary committees, and the Second Continental Congress and its committees all gave orders which none had the means to communicate generally or to enforce. Local committees of patriots took the initiative in recruiting fifty-three battalions of Pennsylvania Associators, three battalions of state militia, and a special force of four battalions called the Flying Camp. Philadelphians hurried the creation of a makeshift Pennsylvania navy, and built defenses of the Delaware River which turned back an attack by several British ships-of-the-line. The year brought a spasm of witch hunting that humiliated Philadelphia Tories who paid for their declarations of loyalty to England by being carted through town by mobs. And it brought about a slow recognition that the old delicate political distinctions could no longer exist, but everyone had to join without any reservations either the revolutionaries or the loyalists.

The Tories had nearly been eliminated from politics by the fall of 1775. Their demise made more important the division among the Whigs between the Moderates, who were ready to resist the British threat to American liberties even to the point of war, but did not wish to separate from the Empire, and the Radicals or Independents who wanted exactly what the name "Independents" implied. The Moderate Whigs held a majority in the Assembly in 1774; in October 1775 the voters returned exactly the same men with the single exception of Galloway. The Assembly clearly proclaimed its moderate position when in November it instructed the Pennsylvania delegation to Continental Congress to "dissent from, and utterly reject, any Propositions . . . that may cause, or lead to, a Separation from our Mother Country." The Radicals fumed, but restrained themselves for they wished no fight at this stage with the powerful Moderate leaders.

When Thomas Paine, then a resident of Philadelphia, published the first edition of *Common Sense* there in January 1776, urging the prompt assertion of independence, the Moderates condemned it as a shocking and pernicious book. They became such a drag on the independence movement that the Continental Congress brought pressure on the Radicals to call another provincial conference to speak for Pennsylvania. Nothing demonstrated more clearly the reticence of Pennsylvanians to break ties with England than the special Assembly election of May 1776. When the Radicals charged that the victory of the Moderates in the October Assembly election resulted from inadequate representation of the revolutionary strongholds, Philadelphia, and the western counties, the Assembly voted four additional seats to the city and thirteen more to the west, and ordered a special Assembly election for May 10 to test public sentiment. The Moderates won, and pointed out that not a single supporter of independence had been elected by any western county, and only one from Philadelphia. The Continental Congress desired a Pennsylvania government managed exclusively by the Radicals.

On May 15, Congress adopted a resolution that citizens should create new provincial governments wherever the old ones seemed incapable of providing for the public welfare. The Philadelphia Radicals now called for the election of a Pennsylvania Provincial Conference to meet on June 18. This conference, created and controlled by Radicals, resolved that the proprietary government could not provide for the welfare of Pennsylvanians and issued a call for a constitutional convention. Rather than use the customary rules governing suffrage, the conference agreed that only persons approved by Associator committees could cast ballots for convention delegates; and no one could sit as a delegate until he had formally repudiated his allegiance to King George III and taken a religious oath. These procedures, by excluding Moderates and Quakers, assured that none but Radicals could vote or share in making the new constitution. The precautions gave prima facie evidence that the Radicals believed themselves in a minority.

The call for a Provincial Conference on June 18 fit into the time schedule which Congress had planned for declaring independence. On June 24, the Pennsylvania Conference approved a preliminary draft of the declaration, reversing the instructions of the Assembly that the Pennsylvania delegation in Congress should "dissent from and utterly reject" independence. On July 2, Congress called for a vote on the Declaration of Independence. The Pennsylvania delegation, now bound mainly by conscience since it had conflicting instructions, fairly reflected the state of the public mind. Franklin, Morton, and Wilson voted in favor of, Willing and Humphreys against, the declaration, while Dickinson and Morris absented themselves. Congress scheduled the great Philadephia celebration at which the Declaration of Independence would be publicly read for July 8, the day set for the election of delegates to the Pennsylvania Constitutional Convention.

The Assembly futilely protested. For some months it had ceased efforts at legislation and had confined itself, when it could muster a quorum, to passing resolutions. On July 15 the Constitutional Convention opened with Franklin in the chair. On July 23 it appointed its own Council of Safety with blanket authority to act as the government of Pennsylvania until a new government came into being. David Rittenhouse served as chairman, assisted by twenty-four others. The old Assembly, trying to preserve itself, met periodically until August 26 when, lacking a quorum, it adjourned never to meet again. On September 28, 1776, the convention proclaimed the existence of a new constitution of Pennsylvania creating a government which, after elections, would assume its responsibilities on November 28.

In the months before the new government came into being, the convention, and later the Radical Council of Safety, exercised dictatorial power. They directed military affairs, disarmed non-Associators, borrowed money, fixed commodity prices, defined offenses against the "state," prescribed oaths, called and supervised elections, and administered justice. The times required vigorous action. British victories in New York had both increased the strength of the Tories and weakened the Radicals by drawing off to the battlefields a great many of the Associators on whom the Radicals depended for political support. They had failed to reconcile the Moderates to independence, and feared the possibility of a counterrevolution which might wreck the whole independence movement. All these forces help to explain both the sudden seizure of power by the Pennsylvania Constitutional Convention and the very remarkable document it produced, a charter aptly described as "the most democratic constitution yet seen in America."

THE CONSTITUTION OF 1776

The new constitution which changed Pennsylvania from a British colony into an independent commonwealth had been drafted mainly by George Bryan, James Cannon, and Benjamin Franklin, although Samuel Adams gave advice so freely that he provoked some delegates at the convention "to drop distant hints of assassination." The preamble and declaration of rights repeated the classic statements of revolutionary rights proclaimed by the Stamp Act Congress, the First Continental Congress, and the Declaration of Independence. The structure of government consisted of a powerful unicameral legislature, called the Assembly; a weak administrative body, called the Supreme Executive Council; an appointed judiciary; and a troubleshooting committee, known as the Council of Censors, which met every seven years. All freemen had the right to vote, though at first the Assembly construed freemen to be only those who would take an oath supporting the revolution. Members of Assembly held office for one year, and each county initially would elect six assemblymen. Later, county representation would be in proportion to taxable population, which would be determined every seven years by a census conducted by the Council of Censors. The twelve members of the Supreme Executive Council, one from each county plus one from Philadelphia, were elected by the freemen to terms of three years. From these twelve, the Assembly and the Executive Council by joint ballot elected an officer called the President of Pennsylvania who served as chairman of the Council and as ceremonial figurehead for state occasions. The constitution assigned the Supreme Executive Council the usual administrative responsibility of executing the laws and gave it the power to appoint military officers, financial agents, and judicial personnel. The Council of Censors, elected by the freemen every seven years, had the duties to hold a census, reapportion the legislature, discover whether anyone had violated the constitution, and implement changes in the constitution if it thought them necessary.

For all the difficulties and bitterness which attended the adoption of the constitution of 1776, it did not appear to change very much the earlier instrument of 1701. The Assembly, still unicameral, retained the central position of power. The substitution of the Supreme Executive Council for the earlier appointed governor brought this function within control of the electorate; but it remained subordinate to the Assembly as the executive had been during the colonial era. The big change wrought by the 1776 constitution came not in the structure of government, but in the people who assumed the management of government. In place of the propertied men, the freemen Associators now had exclusive control of the ballot box, and they voted a new hierarchy of public servants into office, few of them experienced in administrative, legislative, or judicial work. This constituted the basic revolution in Pennsylvania.

Pennsylvania's achievement of independence suggests some observations. The local Associators conducted their major fight not against the British King or the Proprietor, but against the provincial Assembly. Yet, they never overthrew it, but permitted it to expire quietly of its own accord, while they created a new one, very like the old except for the membership. The Pennsylvania Radicals rebelled not against a form of government, but against a ruling clique, and the Radical minority might not even have moved to supplant the old Assembly except for pressure by the Continental Congress which, indeed, chose Philadelphia as its meeting place partly to give aid and encouragement to the Pennsylvania revolutionary party. Few Pennsylvanians of eminence had joined the Radicals by 1775. While many Radicals would later become prominent because of their contributions to the revolution, they had not yet attained notoriety, much less fame. Benjamin Franklin represented the old power structure, and while the Radicals used him in 1775 and 1776, they did not consider him one of the local activists, and thought him better suited to European duty as a diplomat. The revolutionary philosophy and techniques were first introduced to Pennsylvania politics by the Proprietary party leaders, most of whom later became Tories. And even after the Radicals had attained control, they recognized that the Moderates, who received independence reluctantly, continued to exercise a powerful influence throughout the new state.

BIBLIOGRAPHY

All the general histories of Pennsylvania deal extensively with the Revolutionary era. Of the monographs, Charles H. Lincoln: *The Revolutionary Movement in Pennsylvania, 1760–1776* (1901); and Theodore Thayer: *Pennsylvania Politics and the Growth of Democracy, 1740–1776* (1953) take the classic view that the people steadily pressed for and won democratic privileges. Two more recent studies, William S. Hanna: *Benjamin Franklin and Pennsylvania Politics* (1964); and David Hawke: *In the Midst of a Revolution* (1961), investigate the inner workings of revolutionary leadership and expose the conspiratorial aspects.

Specialized studies include Edmund S. Morgan and Helen M. Morgan: *The Stamp Act Crisis: Prologue to Revolution* (1953); Michael G. Kammen: *A Rope of Sand: The Colonial Agents, British Politics and the American Revolution* (1967); Culver H. Smith: "Why Pennsylvania Never Became a Royal Province," *Pennsylvania Magazine of History and Biography,* vol. 53 (1929), pp. 141–158; David C. Jacobsen: "John Dickinson's Fight against Royal Government," *William and Mary Quarterly,* vol. 19 (1962), pp. 64–85: Arthur D. Graeff: *The Relations between the Pennsylvania Germans and the British Authorities, 1750–1776* (1919); and George D. Wolf: *The Fair Play Settlers of the West Branch Valley, 1769–1784* (1969).

There are good studies of the Declaration of Independence by Julian P. Boyd, John M. Head, and David Hawke. For Pennsylvania's part in the Declaration, and the state constitution of 1776, see J. Paul Selsam: *The Pennsylvania Constitution of 1776, a Study in Revolutionary Democracy* (1936).

Biographies of the leading revolutionaries in Pennsylvania include Kenneth R. Rossman: *Thomas Mifflin and the Politics of the American Revolution* (1952); John F. Roche: *Joseph Reed, a Moderate in the American Revolution* (1957); Charles J. Stillé: *The Life and Times of John Dickinson, 1732–1808* (1891); J. Edward Ford: *David Rittenhouse, Astronomer-Patriot, 1732–1796* (1946); Nathan G. Goodman: *Benjamin Rush: Physician and Citizen, 1746–1813* (1934); Lewis R. Harley: *Life of Charles Thomson* (1900); and Charles Page Smith: *James Wilson, Founding Father, 1742–1798* (1956). In addition to Van Doren's biography of Franklin, Verner W. Crane: *Benjamin Franklin and a Rising People* (1954) will be of especial use for this period in Franklin's career.

CHAPTER EIGHT

The Revolutionary Era in Pennsylvania

The Declaration of Independence left military strategy primarily up to the British. The Americans had stated the fact of separation; to alter this the British had to take military initiative. British strategy developed three phases, all of them aimed at making maximum use of the loyalist support in the former colonies. The first phase projected the capture of seaboard cities starting with New York and proceeding to Philadelphia and then southward. A second phase, developed in 1777, planned to cut off New England by having British armies capture the Hudson Valley. The final phase of the war, from 1778 to its end, centered on conquering the South. Pennsylvania became a battleground as part of the first phase.

THE PHILADELPHIA CAMPAIGN

After Washington forced the British out of Boston in the spring of 1776, General William Howe retired to Nova Scotia. By September, aided by his brother Richard who commanded the British navy, Howe had occupied New York. The British forced the American army out of Long Island, Harlem Heights, and White Plains, and then began a march overland in December, heading for Philadelphia, but set up winter quarters in New Jersey. Washington had moved ahead of the British to protect Philadelphia, but the Continental Congress thought it prudent to move temporarily to Baltimore. As winter descended, Washington encamped his troops on the Pennsylvania shore of the Delaware, across from the Hessians in Trenton.

Washington's retreat through New Jersey in early December had become a flight by the time he reached Trenton, for Lord Cornwallis arrived there in time to watch the American rear guard rowing across the Delaware. Nearly half of Washington's troops had deserted, and his appeal for manpower brought little response. Washington wrote that, without reinforcements, "I think the game will be pretty well up." The same day that Washington moved into Pennsylvania, further discouraging news arrived that the British had captured Newport, Rhode Island, and again threatened Boston.

The need to restore morale figured in Washington's decision to launch a surprise attack on Trenton. With the arrival of 2,000 new militia from Pennsylvania, Washington was able to muster about 6,000 troops by Christmas. Local farmers reported that the Hessians had settled into the social routine of winter quarters and had few defensive outposts. On Christmas night, the Pennsylvania navy ferried Col. John Cadwalader's troops across the Delaware some miles south of Trenton, while General James Ewing with the Pennsylvania militia entered the city from a point directly opposite to prevent the enemy from escaping via a nearby bridge. A snow and sleet storm, heavy winds, and ice rendered the river crossing dangerous and dramatic. At eight in the morning the Continentals met the Hessian advance guard; within an hour and a half Washington routed the disorganized and half-dressed Hessian force and took nearly a thousand prisoners. When Cornwallis rapidly moved reinforcements from Princeton to Trenton, Washington eluded them, routed the British rear guard at Princeton, and then headed north to Morristown, New Jersey, where he spent the winter. The British returned to New York.

The British now undertook the second phase of their grand strategy, without, however, canceling the first. General John Burgoyne proposed to take the Hudson Valley by a three-pronged offensive from north, south, and west, converging on Albany. Lord Germain, in London, approved this plan in February 1777. General Howe proposed to capture Philadelphia in midsummer, in time to help Burgoyne by sending troops to Albany. Lord Germain approved this plan also, but failed to sign the orders that Howe should march to support Burgoyne after the Philadelphia campaign. Howe started late, embarked 15,000 troops at New York in July, sailed south to Chesapeake Bay, and then north in the bay to Elkton, Maryland, where the army went ashore during the last week of August.

Washington, already apprised of Burgoyne's intent, had sent 3,000 Continental troops north to reinforce General Horatio Gates in defending the Hudson. He moved the rest of his army into Pennsylvania and took up his position along the Brandywine Creek at Chadd's Ford, with Philadelphia at his back and Howe facing him. On September 11 the two forces met. While the British mounted a frontal attack, about half the army under Lord Cornwallis moved north along a route pointed out by local loyalists, crossed the Brandywine, and then marched south to strike the Americans from the rear. Washington was lucky to escape from the trap, and withdrew his troops to Chester without serious losses, but Philadelphia lay open.

The Continental Congress fled hastily to Lancaster where it met for one day, decided to place the Susquehanna River between it and the British, and traveled on to York where it held its sessions until July 1778. Washington marched to Philadelphia and then west toward Paoli. Howe followed him, more intent upon capturing the army than the city. At Warren's Tavern, just west of Paoli, on September 16 the two armies met in a skirmish often called the Battle of the Clouds. A driving rainstorm made gunfire impossible, whereupon both sides broke off the engagement. Howe turned back and entered Philadelphia without resistance on September 26. Most of the active patriots had fled, carrying the government records to Easton and the Liberty Bell to Allentown. The city's thousands of loyalists received Howe with demonstrations of joy.

Washington moved his army to Whitemarsh, northeast of Germantown, to await developments, while Howe, leaving most of his baggage near Paoli, posted part of his army in Germantown and the remainder in Philadelphia. General Anthony Wayne, who lived near Paoli and knew the countryside intimately, persuaded Washington that with fifteen hundred Rangers he could occupy the woods overlooking the British supply camp and destroy it in a surprise attack. When some loyalists in the vicinity informed the British of Wayne's whereabouts, they devised a countersurprise, sending their force by a back path into the American camp in the dead of night. To preserve silence, the British commander ordered flints removed from all weapons and depended on a bayonet attack. General Charles ("No Flint") Grey executed his mission with such success that the ensuing conflict became known as the Paoli Massacre, a hand-to-hand combat which cost nearly 400 American casualties and very nearly resulted in Wayne's capture.

Washington's command and, indeed, the survival of the whole revolutionary enterprise by this time looked gloomy. Rumors circulated of dissatisfaction among the higher officers with Washington's conduct of the war, for he had, with the exception of Trenton, lost every major battle since the occupation of Boston. A movement called the Conway Cabal to oust Washington from command came under discussion among the congressmen at York. The succession of military reverses also diminished the willingness of troops to stay in the ranks. Philadelphians described deserters entering the city as "almost naked, and generally without shoes—an old dirty blanket around them, attached by a leather belt around the waist." Continental currency had so depreciated that the $10 bounty which the army offered to soldiers who would extend their enlistment meant little; tea cost $60 a pound.

The Continentals desperately needed a military victory to counteract the growing despair. Under such pressure Washington planned the battle of Germantown, one of the most complex and daring operations to be attempted throughout the war. The plan incorporated highly sophisticated techniques: surprise, diversion, a multiple-column strike, precisely synchronized timing of troop movement, identification signals, careful map work, and rigid discipline. On paper, part of the army would move to the Delaware northeast of Philadelphia (Frankford) to begin a diversionary attack and draw the British in that direction. Meanwhile, at night, four separate columns would converge on Germantown by different routes and, after overpowering the enemy outposts, move into Philadelphia while the main British force was marching out to meet the simulated attack at Frankford. Had the fortunes of war gone in Washington's favor his plan might have succeeded, but the battle plan proved too complex for poorly trained troops to execute, and the army suffered another defeat. General Wayne said later, "We ran from victory."

VALLEY FORGE

For several months after the capture of Philadelphia, Washington had been besieged by advice from all sectors about where he should establish winter quarters. Lancaster and Reading, major supply depots, wished the army nearby for their protection, as did Wilmington and towns in New Jersey. Washington ultimately decided on Valley Forge, northwest of Philadelphia, which promised security, but was sufficiently close to the British that

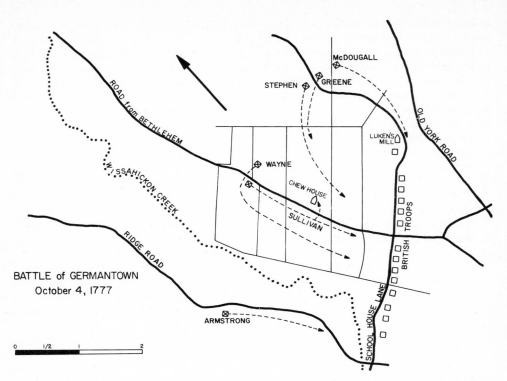

BATTLE of GERMANTOWN
October 4, 1777

Washington's complex battle-plan for the capture of Philadelphia via Germantown failed because dense fog shrouded troop movements and Stephen's brigade, becoming lost, approached and fired on Wayne's troops, thinking them the enemy. Sullivan's command delayed its advance in order to reduce a British stronghold in the Chew House. The British rallied rapidly and, after near defeat in the early stages of the battle, at length routed the disorganized Continentals, pursuing them back to Whitemarsh.

any move they made might be intercepted. The location also promised proximity to food and supplies which eastern Pennsylvania had in abundance. Surveyors had examined the Valley Forge site and marked off the plots which each company should occupy. The army began to move from Whitemarsh in early December in miserable weather. For two weeks, everyone was building shelters, and by Christmas most of the camp was under roof. At that moment, the food began to run short. The reasons why soon became apparent in ways most calculated to exasperate the troops. Profiteering and mismanagement, rather than actual scarcity, caused the trouble. The British paid gold for supplies; the Americans offered depreciating Continental notes or promises to pay later, and farmers and businessmen preferred the gold.

The winter at Valley Forge worked many changes in the American army. The severe hardships of the first month in some ways strengthened morale. Many malcontents and half-hearted patriots deserted and proved a good riddance. Those who stayed constituted a fully committed body of troops on whom officers could depend. News of Burgoyne's surrender gave heart to these toughening veterans, and the adoption of the Articles of Confederation by Congress on November 15 made them think seriously, for the first time, about their future as citizens of a new nation, rather than as state volunteers temporarily cooperating. The winter, after its first bitter onslaught, grew milder in the early months of 1778. A reorganization of the commissary and quartermaster departments improved the flow of supplies, so that the camp could settle down to a tolerable routine. The men talked a great deal among themselves of the meaning of the war, of the ideas of equality, of self-government, and of the inalienable rights of man. They developed into a crusading army, convinced of the important part they played in an unprecedented movement which might alter the world as people then knew it.

These changes in attitude and purpose laid the groundwork for the training and drill program begun in March by Baron von Steuben. Once impatient of drill and military discipline, the troops at last had begun to discover how largely the issue of victory or defeat rested upon their ability to respond correctly to standard orders. The defeat at Germantown had hammered home this lesson. By the time spring came, von Steuben had transformed the motley regiments of farm boys into soldiers, and the inexperienced officers into some semblance of a responsible and unified command.

While the Continentals worried away the winter at Valley Forge, the British spent a leisurely and sociable season in Philadelphia. Most of the officers quartered themselves in homes of the civilian population; the troops occupied barracks and camp grounds south of town. Many of the Philadelphians genuinely welcomed the troops as their own, and expressed relief that they had been rescued from "the rabble." Active patriots generally fled, but a considerable part of the population which sympathized with the revolutionary cause remained. Howe kept the army in restraint and appointed Joseph Galloway as superintendent of civilian activity in the city. Goods became scarce and costly, but shipments up the Delaware and a steady inflow of farm produce from the surrounding countryside kept the city well fed.

News arrived in early spring that the French had signed a treaty of alliance with the United States on February 6. General Howe had asked to be relieved of duty, and Sir Henry Clinton replaced him in command at Philadelphia. As soon as he learned of the French treaty, he prepared to leave the city for fear of being caught between a French fleet in Delaware Bay and General Washington at his rear. On June 18 he began moving the army into New Jersey for a march back to New York. Washington's army followed, crossed the Delaware above Trenton at Coryell's Ferry, and on June 28 engaged the British at the Battle of Monmouth in New Jersey. Here the work at Valley Forge proved itself. After a hard fight, the British withdrew from the field in the dead of night. The evacuation of Philadelphia brought military activity in Pennsylvania to a close, except for isolated attacks on frontier settlements.

WAR ON THE FRONTIER

At an Indian conference at Fort Niagara in May 1776, the British succeeded in gaining the support of many tribes. The Senecas, Wyandots, Shawnees, Delawares, and some other tribes joined the British, receiving from them gifts, weapons, the promise of plunder, and a bounty for scalps of white settlers. To counteract this, representatives of Pennsylvania and of the Continental Congress called an Indian conference at Easton in January 1777, at which they received assurances that the Six Nations planned to remain neutral. The results proved otherwise. Sporadic Indian raids occurred in nearly every western county during 1777. Washington had sent the Eighth Pennsylvania Regiment west to protect the frontier in the summer of 1776. It constructed a fort at Kittanning and planned to move up the Allegheny when orders came to rejoin Washington's army on the Delaware in January 1777.

Through the summer of 1778 the Indians, directed by British Col. Henry Hamilton, destroyed Pennsylvania frontier settlements at will. One series of raids destroyed farms in Penns Creek, Bald Eagle, and Kishocoquillas Valleys; another struck the West Branch of the Susquehanna, from Muncy and Williamsport to Northumberland, sending settlers flying eastward in the "Great Runaway," reminiscent of the months after Braddock's defeat.

Frontier warfare came to its bloodiest climax at Wyoming on July 3, 1778. The British Parliament had debated and approved the use of Indian warfare by army commanders in America. British Col. John Butler with some 400 Tory Rangers and about 700 Indians planned to destroy the Wyoming settlements. The Indians held a particular grudge against the Connecticut settlers of the Susquehanna Company who since 1754 had forced the Indians off the Wyoming hunting lands.

The leaders at Wyoming decided to meet Butler's advancing force with about 300 men, mostly too old or too young for the regular army. Under the command of Col. Zebulon Butler (no kin to his British namesake), this small detachment marched out to meet the British, found itself flanked by the Indians, and suffered a rout. The Indians scalped, tortured, and massacred all the soldiers they could capture; Indian Queen Esther Montour, in a wild war dance, tomahawked prisoners forced to their knees in a circle around a huge flat rock. Butler destroyed the Wyoming settlements and ordered the inhabitants to leave, but prevented any Indian assault upon the civilians. The Wyoming Massacre involved only the military force. The civilian population suffered great hardships on its flight toward the Delaware, and as word of the destruction spread, the whole nearby frontier gave way to panic and began a mass exodus to the south and east.

The Wyoming Massacre, bad as it was, became more horrible with each retelling until it became the major atrocity story of the Revolutionary War, and served a significant propaganda function at home and abroad. Represented in the American press as the wanton murder and torture of helpless women and children by Indians under the direction of British officers, the affair strengthened the American will to fight. It also raised a storm in the British Parliament. Lord Camden referred to Col. John Butler as "that hell-hound," while Bishop Hinchcliffe protested that nothing could justify such methods of war, and in anger pointed to an army appropriation bill which included crucifixes and scalping knives in the same column.

The Ohio country had so little protection that when Washington left Valley Forge in the spring of 1778, he sent the Eighth Pennsylvania Regiment under Col. Daniel Brodhead back to Fort Pitt. At Carlisle a force joined them under Captain Samuel Brady who had just learned of his brother's death at the hand of Chief Bald Eagle. Brady conducted many minor forays against the Indians from Fort Pitt and killed Chief Bald Eagle in an ambush near Kittanning, but the Mingoes, Delawares, Senecas, and Wyandots continued to terrorize the western counties. Brodhead launched a major invasion of the Seneca country southeast of Lake Erie. Leaving Fort Pitt in August, he proceeded up the Allegheny, destroyed Seneca towns and grainfields in what is now Warren County, moved west to French Creek, and returned to Fort Pitt by mid-September without losing a man or horse except for one rider whose mount lost footing at a place since called Slippery Rock.

After the Wyoming Massacre, the Indians continued their rampages in the northeast. Determined to stop the Indian forays, General Washington proposed a major expedition into Iroquois country to destroy the heart of the Six Nations and to capture Fort Niagara, the source of British supplies and leadership. He gave the command of 5,000 troops to General John Sullivan who mobilized his force at Easton and marched through Wyoming and Tioga into New York. On August 29, 1779, at Newtown he defeated Col. John Butler's Rangers and 1,500 Indians under Joseph Brandt, and systematically destroyed forty Iroquois towns and all the orchards, fields, and crops around them. Sullivan so denuded the countryside that he could not live by forage when his own supplies failed, and decided not to risk the march to Niagara. His position might have become serious except for Brodhead's march, which distracted the western Senecas at the very moment they might have moved against Sullivan. The ensuing winter of 1779–1780 brought 4 feet of snow to central Pennsylvania and New York. The Iroquois, deprived of their food stores, starved by the hundreds. The combination of Sullivan's raid and "the winter of the deep snow" so weakened the eastern tribes that they never seriously threatened the Pennsylvania frontier again, though sporadic raids continued throughout the war.

PENNSYLVANIA'S ROLE IN THE
REVOLUTIONARY WAR

Pennsylvania played a significant role in the American Revolutionary War and made many important contributions to the cause. Most of the state became a battlefield. It sent thirteen regiments to the Continental army, provided at least as many militiamen for limited service all over the commonwealth, and furnished many officers, including Generals John Armstrong, Philip Benner, John Cadwalader, James Ewing, Edward Hand, William Irvine, Thomas Mifflin, Peter Muhlenberg, James Potter, and Arthur St. Clair and Major General Anthony Wayne who commanded the Pennsylvania Line. Yellow Spring and the Moravian towns of Bethlehem and Lititz performed especially meritorious service in providing hospital facilities and caring for the wounded during the war. Reading, Lebanon, Downingtown, and Lancaster served as major supply depots, and the latter took care of large numbers of prisoners of war.

Pennsylvania provided great quantities of war materiel. Its many iron furnaces and forges produced cannon and shot. German craftsmen in Lancaster, Lebanon, and Reading turned out quantities of "Pennsylvania rifles," the weapon which frontiersmen used because of its range and accuracy. The rifle companies played havoc among British troops equipped with smoothbore muskets because the riflemen could direct deadly fire while safely out of range of musket balls. Conestoga horses and wagons became the primary carriers of supplies, and the German farms were a productive source of foodstuffs. General Thomas Mifflin for a time had charge of the Quartermaster Department, assisted by the Philadelphia merchant John Cox. Christopher Ludwig of Philadelphia became superintendent of bakers for the army. Dr. Bodo Otto of Reading served as surgeon general. Robert Morris, superintendent of finance for the Continental Congress, acted also as purchasing agent of Pennsylvania to provide the state quota of army supplies. As the Congress gave him little and the state no money to perform these duties, he employed his private credit and sought the cooperation of other wealthy men like Haym Salomon, who used their fortunes to underwrite the war

Some Leaders of the Revolutionary Era

John Dickinson, author of major state papers asserting American rights after 1765. (Pennsylvania Historical and Museum Commission)

Robert Morris, financier of the American Revolution. (Pennsylvania Historical and Museum Commission)

Thomas Mifflin, quartermaster-general of the Continental Army and Governor of Pennsylvania, 1790–1799. (Pennsylvania Historical and Museum Commission)

Rev. Richard Allen, founder of Bethel A.M.E. Church, Philadelphia, 1794, who, with Rev. Absalom Jones, gave leadership to blacks of the era. (Wesley: *Richard Allen*)

effort. Col. Ephraim Blaine, whose careful planning prevented a complete breakdown of supplies at Valley Forge, became commissary general in 1779. In the diplomatic field, Franklin played a crucial role in the French alliance of 1778. The list could be extended, but this will suffice to show that Congress relied heavily upon Pennsylvania for troops, ordnance, transport, supplies, medical service, financial backing, and administrative talent.

Pennsylvania also provided many of the patriotic symbols and traditions which grew from the Revolution. Philadelphia became a historic shrine as the seat of government, scene of the Declaration of Independence, possessor of the Liberty Bell and Independence Hall, and the home of such patriots as Franklin, Morris, Paine, Wilson, Matlack, Wayne, and Dickinson. Washington crossing the Delaware and events at Brandywine, Valley Forge, and Wyoming became classic examples of "the times that try men's souls." Traditions on a smaller scale grew and flourished: Betsy Ross and the first American flag; Molly Pitcher of Carlisle wielding a ramrod at the battle of Monmouth; Captain George Gibson and William Linn who, after incredible difficulties, provided George Rogers Clark with six tons of powder from New Orleans; the Pine Creek Declaration of Independence adopted by settlers of Clinton County on July 4, 1776; the dramatic escapades of Indian fighter Captain Sam Brady and his Tory counterparts, the Girty brothers, George and Simon—these created revolutionary traditions which became a permanent part of the national folklore.

A final aspect of Pennsylvania's contribution to the Revolutionary War involves the various loyalties of the citizens. A traditional estimate suggests that about one-third of Pennsylvanians remained Tories, about one-third became Patriots, and the remainder did not openly commit themselves. This ratio cannot be supported by hard quantitative evidence and must stand as a guess. But even the threefold division greatly oversimplifies the problem. Loyalties became extremely complicated, as responses to different test oaths demonstrated. The whole political faction of Moderates supported the war actively and showed enthusiasm for a strong Federal union; the faction called Radicals also supported the war but strongly opposed Federal union. Both groups supported the war effort, but they acted as rivals of each other. The Tories can most easily be identified. They remained loyal to England, aided the British war effort, and ultimately faced loss of their property and exile. Some 3,000 of them left Philadelphia with the British army in 1778. The German Plain Sects and Quakers received abuse as Tories, but most did not deserve the label because they opposed war, not independence.

The Radical party, which created the constitution of 1776, comprised mostly young militiamen, frontier farmers, city apprentices, and artisans. Almost none of their leaders such as James Cannon or Timothy Matlack had any public experience or reputation before 1775. The Moderates seem to have been the largest identifiable group. Their leadership carried over from earlier days and gives a clue to their followers. Men like John Dickinson, Robert Morris, Benjamin Rush, Joseph Reed, Thomas Wharton, Jr., and Anthony Wayne had a strong following among wealthy educated people. They supplied most of the high-ranking military officers, most of the money, and most of the materiel which Pennsylvania contributed to the war.

The real mystery surrounds those who changed sides as one or another army drew near, or as one side or the other showed a prospect of winning final victory. They plagued both armies, for no commander could be sure whether local intelligence he received came from friend or enemy. Each side experienced betrayal by persons presumably loyal to it. Many viewed the war with indifference, selling goods to whoever paid the best price and wishing, primarily, to avoid as far as possible any personal entanglement with it.

THE RADICALS IN POWER

Party conflict in Pennsylvania between 1776 and 1790 centered almost entirely on the revolutionary constitution of 1776. Its defenders, who had created it, called themselves the Radicals or the Constitutionalists. Its enemies, who had been ousted from office by it, adopted the names Anticonstitutionalists, Moderates, or Republicans. Both contending parties favored active prosecution of the war, but the Radicals jealously guarded their newly won power and distrusted the aristocratic attitude and the early resistance of the Republicans to independence, while the latter feared that the Radicals with their inexperience, wild talk, and ill-considered actions would ruin the economy and jeopardize the war effort. Each exaggerated the posture of the other. The Radicals whipped up hysteria by denouncing the Anti-constitutionalists as Tories; the Republicans played on the fear of mob rule by publicizing the Radicals as the party of violence and mobocracy. The oath required for suffrage and officeholding excluded everyone but the Radicals, for every voter and officeholder had to swear that he would not "directly or indirectly do any act or thing prejudicial or injurious to the constitution." No one who desired changes in the constitution of 1776 could conscientiously take the required oath.

The Republicans tried to undermine the Radicals before the first election in November 1776 by throwing doubt upon the legality of the new constitution. They called mass meetings to demand that another constitutional convention be held, and urged citizens not to take the required test oath. The Radicals won a majority in the first Assembly, but the Republicans elected enough members to control a quorum. Because no adequate machinery existed to police the polls, Republican strongholds permitted voting with a modified test oath. Republican assemblymen refused to take the oath of office, but the Radicals nonetheless seated them to create a quorum. Seeing the weakness of the new government, the Republicans now planned to force it to the ground unless the Radicals promised to alter the constitution; the Republicans withdrew, leaving the Assembly without a quorum. The Radicals countered by declaring the seats vacant and then filled them with their own people.

When the Radicals gained complete control in the Supreme Executive Council and the Assembly, they immediately appointed an all-Radical delegation to Continental Congress except for Robert Morris, whom they approved only after leaders in Congress vehemently insisted that they needed his financial aid. When the British threatened Philadelphia in December 1776 and again in the fall of 1777, the new Pennsylvania government appeared powerless to aid in its defense, having neither credit to obtain supplies nor any administrative staff to move men or goods in response to congressional requests.

The difficulties facing the Radicals stemmed partly from their own failure to comprehend the complexity of creating a new government, and partly from the exclusion of the Republicans from that government. The Radicals had few experienced people for government jobs, and the Republicans refused to take public office because of the oath. In the counties, experienced Radicals could seldom be found to serve as commissioners, lieutenants (in charge of militia), sheriffs, prothonotaries, or judges. Some of the old provincial officers would not turn over the local records to new officials. The Republicans served in many capacities for the Continental Congress; they gladly took the oath in support of the United States, but they refused to take an oath which barred them from trying to change the Pennsylvania constitution.

The Radicals insisted on the rigid application of the oath. By this device they could perpetuate their control of the government. The Radicals strengthened the oath system in June

1777 when the Assembly passed a new test act stating that nonjurors (those who would not take the oath) could not vote, serve on juries, sue in court, buy or sell real estate, or possess guns. They could, however, pay taxes from which the oath-taking Radicals exempted themselves.

The British attack on Philadelphia in the autumn of 1777 strengthened the Radicals, and they put fear to work in a campaign of proscription against alleged enemies. They compiled a list of suspicious people, mostly Quakers and wealthy Philadelphians, accused them of Toryism, and ordered them out of the state. Chief Justice Thomas McKean issued writs of *habeas corpus,* but no one paid any attention and the Radicals banished these people to New York or western Virginia. The Assembly then ruled that all former Crown officers in Pennsylvania should take the oath or forfeit their property. As public excitement mounted with the British invasion of Pennsylvania and the roundup of suspects, the Radicals gained strength, and in the October elections of 1777, by strict application of the oath at the polls, they elected nearly all the new assemblymen.

By mid-1778 the Radicals had established control in fact as well as in name; they ruled the state government and had made rapid headway in conducting the essential business of county government. Having consolidated their power, they began to abuse it by trying to force everyone in the state into their special political mold, or into silent submission. In September 1778, the Assembly legislated that no one could vote or hold office who had not taken the state oath prior to June 1, 1778—a law which placed most of the citizens in political exile. No one could engage in a trade or profession without taking the oath. Anyone charged with friendship for Britain should have his property confiscated and his name published. Lists growing from this order named not only the rich, but hundreds of laborers and artisans.

The hue and cry of "traitors" and "Tories" which the Radicals raised against the Republicans whipped up public hysteria. Mobs roamed the city of Philadelphia after the British left, holding kangaroo courts against engrossers and forestallers—merchants who were charged with profiteering, hoarding, or refusing to take paper money for goods at government-fixed prices. They attacked Levi Hollingsworth, who had gathered a quantity of flour for the French fleet, and threatened Robert Morris. After winning the election in October 1778, the Radicals pressed their attack further. They ousted the trustees and faculty of the College of Philadelphia, and created a new University of the State of Pennsylvania whose trustees would promote the Radical cause and whose professors would teach only approved political doctrine. They seized the lands of the Penns in the Divesting Act, and engaged in a power struggle with the Continental Congress.

The voting power of the Radicals rested primarily in the state militia, and the militia took its orders from the county lieutenants, who were appointed by the Supreme Executive Council and served as local political bosses. For this reason, the Radicals gave little support to the Continental army, but strongly encouraged everything which would strengthen the state militia. The Radicals told militiamen not to "receive any insults" from Continental officers, "even the greatest of them." Benedict Arnold, whose haughty arrogance when he took command in Philadelphia after Clinton's withdrawal infuriated Radical leaders, touched off an explosion when he ordered Timothy Matlack's son, a sergeant, to act as his valet. The Radicals soon gathered enough charges against Arnold for privately using public property to force Congress to order him court-martialed, and had the satisfaction of seeing him convicted, though he got off with a reprimand. This affair played a part in Arnold's later treason.

In October 1779, Radical mobs in Philadelphia finally touched off a local civil war. Having successfully cowed the merchants, they set out to intimidate the major Republican leaders.

An armed mob headed for the homes of James Wilson and Joseph Reed, and had begun to destroy them when the Republican "silk-stocking brigade" of City Light Horse rapidly converged on the scene, equipped with artillery. After a gunfight which killed several, the mob retreated and later sated its anger by assaulting General Arnold. The protracted rowdiness of the city mobs at length broke the Radical power, for everyone could see that the Republican warnings of mob rule had been proven true.

Within the next two years, the Radicals fell from power in Pennsylvania. By 1781 their paper money and legal tender system collapsed. They had tried to finance their regime by confiscating property, taxing everyone except themselves, and depending on legal tender money to make purchases and pay salaries. In January 1781, troops of the Pennsylvania Line at Morristown revolted because their requests for back pay had been repeatedly ignored. The Assembly by June had to acknowledge the obvious fact that no one would accept fiat money any longer, and passed a law abolishing the requirement that it be treated as legal tender. It then issued new paper money based upon a general state tax. These actions aided the Republicans for they had for years been preaching the necessity of exactly such sound fiscal practice.

In 1782 the triumph of Moderate John Dickinson as President of Pennsylvania over his Radical opponent, James Potter, concluded the era of Radical control. The defeat of Cornwallis on October 24 ended the war with England, and the coming of peace ended the psychological power of the chant, "Tories and traitors," on which the Radicals had relied so heavily for their strength. The new Assembly levied a broad general tax from which oath takers were no longer exempt. Attempts to collect it in western Pennsylvania led to a secession movement among settlers there who proposed to set up a new state called Transylvania, but the movement failed.

During their tenure of office, the Radicals had made three lasting contributions to Pennsylvania history. First, they carried independence to completion by creating the commonwealth of Pennsylvania under the constitution of 1776. Second, they obtained a great public domain by the Divesting Act of November 27, 1779, under which the state assumed ownership of all the unsurveyed lands of the Proprietors, paying them £130,000 sterling, and reserving to the Penns their private estates. The Divesting Act also abolished quitrents, and assigned to the commonwealth all money owing on land bought from the Penns. Third, the Assembly on March 1, 1780, passed the first state law providing for the abolition of slavery. Though the Radical leader, George Bryan, introduced and fought for this measure, his partisans in western Pennsylvania almost unanimously opposed it. The act passed by a vote of 34 to 21, in which the majority comprised a coalition of Constitutionalist and Anticonstitutionalist votes from Philadelphia and the German regions, whereas the opposition came primarily from the counties of the west. The Virginia settlers who in 1779 became Pennsylvanians brought their force to bear against the measure.

The abolition law provided for gradual emancipation. Persons bound to slavery when the act passed would remain slaves throughout life, but all children born after March 1, 1780, would become free upon reaching the age of twenty-eight. Masters had until November 1, 1780, to register their slaves; and any persons who were not entered on the slave register by that time were judged to be free.

The Radicals fell from power primarily because they failed to solve the economic problems of Pennsylvania. Their effort to manage an economy by edict alienated the people they most needed to assist them—the commercial and financial community. By taxing everyone except themselves, and ordering everyone to part with goods at a fixed rate for unsecured paper money, they exposed their inexperience. When the state proved unable to meet its quotas of goods and money for Continental Congress, and could not even pay its own soldiers, the Republican business community joined in a private effort, established the Pennsylvania Bank with a capital of $300,000, and through it provided the money which Congress needed and which the state government itself could not raise.

REPUBLICAN COUNTERREVOLUTION

Unlike the Radicals who had seized power in a swift *coup d'état,* the Republicans attained control of the Pennsylvania government by slowly building a majority in the Assembly. The war itself made most people acquiesce in the repressive measures of the Constitutionalists and forgive their inefficiency and mistakes in policy, for none could doubt their absolute commitment to military victory. But with the war over, tolerance of harsh wartime practices ended. If the Republicans had won a sudden and decisive triumph over the Radicals, they would have proposed a revision of the constitution of 1776, but because they achieved control in 1782 by a hairline majority they decided not to challenge the constitution, but first to strengthen their position within it.

In 1783 they obtained a majority of the Council of Censors but not the two-thirds necessary to enable that body to perform its function of amending the constitution. The Council of Censors took a population census which made possible legislative reapportionment, and the Republicans established nine new counties which helped to strengthen their Assembly majority. The Radicals, who for years had been protesting inadequate western representation, created only one new county—Washington in 1781. But the Republicans established Fayette (1783), Franklin and Montgomery (1784), Dauphin (1785), Luzerne (1786), Huntingdon (1787), Allegheny (1788), and Delaware and Mifflin (1789).

The Republicans launched a major attack against the test oaths which still prevented people inclined toward the Moderate policies from voting or accepting office. In September 1784, they mustered a tie vote in the Assembly for repeal of the oaths which the speaker broke in their favor, but at that point the Radical members withdrew and left the House without a quorum, which prevented a final vote on the measure. The Radicals again captured the Legislature in 1784, but they inaugurated policies which swiftly brought their final downfall. They required the state to assume the payment of principal and interest of all Federal certificates of indebtedness owned by Pennsylvania citizens. This proved a windfall to speculators, including a good many of the Radical leaders. Next, they voted another issue of paper money secured only by an unenforceable state tariff. Finally, they revoked the charter of the Bank of North America, successor of the Pennsylvania Bank and the one financial institution which had created a reservoir of credit and which encouraged business. The Radical program brought such immediate economic chaos that in October 1785 the voters turned the government back to Republican control.

The temper of the times changed significantly between 1783 and 1786. On June 21, 1783, several hundred Pennsylvania soldiers marched on the State House, surrounded it, posted armed guards at the doors, and then informed the Continental Congress that it had "only twenty minutes to deliberate" on demands for back pay. The Congress stalled and managed to disperse the mutineers, and then called on the Pennsylvania government for protection.

When the Pennsylvania response proved unsatisfactory, Congress left the city and moved to Princeton, and later to New York City where it remained until the Confederation government ceased to exist in 1789. This episode greatly distressed the Republicans, but it delighted the Radicals who seemed overjoyed to get rid of Congress and successfully balked all efforts to invite its return. The Radicals wanted state independence, not national union.

By 1786 such an event would hardly have been possible. The peace treaty had been signed in 1783, troops had been demobilized, separate states showed little capacity to stimulate their economies without some uniform policies on domestic and foreign trade, and enthusiasm for independence began to seem less vital than concern for economic survival. Hence the party that had demonstrated its capacity to handle economic crises became more popular, and the party which had thrived primarily upon emotional appeals to the revolutionary ideology grew weaker. Benjamin Franklin's return from Europe and his election as President of Pennsylvania in 1786 epitomized the change, for he represented the diplomat, the compromiser, and the practical man of affairs at the helm.

After 1786, the Republicans rapidly dismantled what remained of the Radical machinery of control. They repealed the test acts and opened the suffrage to the citizens for the first time since 1776. In March 1787, they rechartered the Bank of North America, which had continued to function in the interim under a Federal charter. They restored the University of Pennsylvania to its normal academic role. And, of most importance, they reconstituted the Pennsylvania delegation to the Continental Congress into a group vigorously determined to strengthen the Federal government by revising the Articles of Confederation.

NEW CONSTITUTIONS, FEDERAL AND STATE

The plight of the general government under the Articles of Confederation had become critical by 1786. Without authority to collect revenue of its own and without power to compel the member states to pay their quotas, the Congress of the Confederation had begun to lose the confidence of people at home and abroad. The threat of dissolution of the already weak Union became so imminent that in September 1786 a conference at Annapolis urged that all the states send delegates to a convention at Philadelphia in May 1787 to consider revising the Articles. Shays' Rebellion in Massachusetts, armed outbreaks in New Hampshire and Rhode Island, and continued threats of secession in western Pennsylvania all gave urgency to the proposal. Its language: "To render the Constitution of the Federal Government adequate to the exigencies of the Union," clearly forecast the need for a stronger national control; and this idea became the main point of controversy in Pennsylvania politics. The Radicals or Constitutionalists immediately expressed fear of any effort to strengthen the Union. The Republicans enthusiastically endorsed any move in this direction and on this issue won a majority of the Assembly in October 1786.

The new Assembly named as Pennsylvania delegates to the coming Constitutional Convention: Thomas Mifflin, Robert Morris, James Wilson, George Clymer, Thomas Fitzsimmons, Gouverneur Morris, Jared Ingersoll, and Benjamin Franklin, all men of property and political experience.

In the convention three Pennsylvanians played notably significant roles. Benjamin Franklin, when the meeting had nearly broken up in disagreement about the method of representation in Congress, guided a conference committee to the ultimate decision—the so-called Great Compromise between the large and small state factions by which states would have equal weight in a Senate, but voting strength in proportion to population in a lower House. During the debates on the executive office, James Wilson carried the main burden of argument that a vote of the entire population ought to undergird the office of president. The Convention assigned to Gouverneur Morris the task of writing the final draft of the document which became the Constitution of the United States. The delegates signed this copy, and the Congress on September 28, 1787, voted to submit it to the states.

The Assembly of Pennsylvania had planned to adjourn on September 29. Without any knowledge of the action by the Confederation government in New York, George Clymer, on September 28, moved that Pennsylvania call a ratification convention. This passed by a vote of 43–19, over vehement protests from the Radical minority. When in the afternoon the Assembly prepared to set a date and establish voting procedures for election of delegates, the Radicals absented themselves and forced the House to adjourn for lack of a quorum. That night word arrived from New York that Congress had invited states to ratify. Republican leaders carried this news to the recalcitrant Radicals but could not move them. On the last day of the session, the Assembly still could take no action until Republicans seized two Radical assemblymen, James McCalmont and Jacob Smiley, dragged them into the Assembly chamber, and held them in the hall while the Assembly, now legally constituted, proceeded to finish its plans for the ratification convention. Voters would elect delegates the first Tuesday in November, and the ratifying convention would meet in Philadelphia immediately thereafter.

The regular election for assemblymen in October foreshadowed a bitter fight over the proposed Federal Constitution and introduced some confusing new political terminology. The Republicans or Anticonstitutionalists were outspoken supporters of the national Constitution and began to adopt the name Federalists. The old Radicals or Constitutionalists were the bitter opponents of the Federal Constitution and became known as Antifederalists. The Assembly election in October 1787 of thirty-four Federalists and thirty-one Antifederalists foreshadowed a serious contest over ratification in Pennsylvania.

Until the election of delegates in November, Pennsylvania experienced one of the bitterest and most active political campaigns since 1776. Both sides bombarded the voters with newspaper articles, public letters, pamphlets, and speeches. The Antifederalist Radicals contended that Pennsylvania's delegates to the Constitutional Convention represented only easterners, Republicans, and businessmen; that the convention had exceeded its authority; that the proposed Constitution seized powers which belonged exclusively to the states; and that the ratification meeting had been called by an illegal quorum. The Federalists responded with the well-known arguments in favor of the Constitution. As the debate proceeded, the Federalists grew stronger. Most of the Germans seemed to favor the Federalist side; of twelve German assemblymen, only one had joined in the disruption of the quorum. But the western Scotch-Irish delegates largely opposed ratification.

Preelection prophets guessed that the two parties would show about equal strength in the ratifying convention, but the election brought a 46–23 victory for the Federalists. The counties of Berks, Bedford, Dauphin, Westmoreland, and Fayette sent full delegations of Antifederalists. After explanations by James Wilson and a brief debate, the Pennsylvania convention ratified the Federal Constitution on December 12, the second state to do so. On July 2, 1788, Congress announced that the ninth state had ratified and that the United States Constitution had become the frame of a new nation.

On July 4, Philadelphia held the biggest parade and celebration in its history, and towns throughout Pennsylvania generally celebrated. But there were exceptions. The unseemly haste of Pennsylvania's ratification stirred up wild resentment in Antifederalist areas. In at least one town, the effort of the Federalists to have a celebration provoked an assault on them by the more numerous Antifederalists, who seized copies of the new Constitution and threw them into the Federalist bonfire.

In the fall of 1788, state elections went nearly unnoticed in the excitement of choosing Federal officers for the first time. The outgoing Assembly named the first United States Senators, William Maclay and Robert Morris. The Federalists made a clean sweep of congressmen and presidential electors.

The Pennsylvania Federalists at this stage considered it time to proceed with the destruction of the state constitution of 1776. On March 20, 1789, as the new national government began to organize in New York, the Pennsylvania Assembly resolved on a popular referendum for changing the state constitution. If the voters approved, immediate action could be taken; if not, they would have to wait until the next meeting of the Council of Censors and follow the official amending procedure which might take four years. During the summer the Federalists busied themselves drumming up petitions until, by fall, they could present the Assembly with 10,000 signatures in favor of a change, to only 600 against it. The Assembly then voted to call a state constitutional convention in November 1789.

Interest in the fall elections of 1789 centered upon the delegates to the coming convention. Little party contention appeared, for the Federalists had triumphed and everyone seemed primarily interested in sending the most outstanding citizens to revise the frame of government. Both parties sent their best—the Federalists elected Thomas Mifflin, Thomas McKean, and James Wilson; the Antifederalists, Robert Whitehill, William Findley, John Smiley, and Albert Gallatin. Unlike the convention of 1776, that of 1789 contained mostly men of public experience, and within the meeting a highly conciliatory spirit prevailed.

The delegates used the United States Constitution as their pattern, modified to meet local needs. The new instrument provided for a powerful governor who should be elected by the people to a three-year term and could succeed himself twice. The governor held appointive power second only to that of the national president, could veto legislation, grant pardons, and control the militia. In place of the unicameral Legislature, the new constitution created a Senate and a House of Representatives. Senators served a term of four years, assemblymen one year. The governor appointed the judges and minor judiciary who served for life so long as they behaved well. The delegates abolished the Council of Censors. All male citizens over twenty-one who had paid a tax could vote, and the constitution, in a preamble and a bill of rights, guaranteed religious and civil liberty.

The convention completed its work and adjourned on February 26, 1790, with orders to reconvene on August 9. During the summer everyone had the opportunity to discuss the constitution. When the convention resumed its sessions it declared the new constitution to be in effect, without submission to a public vote. On September 3, the officers of the old government retired, and the new order took the helm. Thus, after a fourteen-year epoch of revolution, war, depression, and political passion, Pennsylvania had come nearly full circle back to managers very much like those who had governed during the latter years of the colonial era.

BIBLIOGRAPHY

Pennsylvania activities are covered in general histories of the American Revolution. Claude H. Van Tyne and George O. Trevelyan are the best of the older authorities; and John R. Alden, Edmund

S. Morgan, Richard B. Morris, and John C. Miller are the major recent authors. The military phases of the Revolution are emphasized in Willard M. Wallace: *Appeal to Arms: A Military History of the American Revolution* (1951); and John F. Reed: *Campaign to Valley Forge* (1965). Lynn Montross: *Rag, Tag and Bobtail* (1952) writes of the common soldier with chapters on Valley Forge and the mutiny of the Pennsylvania Line. Books entitled *Valley Forge* have been written by Harry E. Wildes (1938); Van Wyck Mason (1950); and Alfred Hoyt Bill (1952). Pennsylvania figures largely in Carl Van Doren's *Mutiny in January* (1943), and in his *Secret History of the American Revolution* (1941), the story of spying. Victor L. Johnson: *Administration of the American Commissariat during the Revolutionary War* (1941) is detailed and scholarly. Other important studies are Wayland F. Dunaway: *The Susquehanna Valley in the Revolution* (1927); Albert H. Wright (ed.): *The Sullivan Expedition of 1779* (1943); and Lewis S. Shimmel: *Border Warfare in Pennsylvania during the Revolution* (1901). Students should consult Wilkinson's previously cited *Bibliography of Pennsylvania History*, pp. 201–227, for an extensive listing of local military activities.

Political activities are treated generally in Allan Nevins: *The American States during and after the Revolution* (1924); and in detail in Charles H. Lincoln: *The Revolutionary Movement in Pennsylvania, 1760–1776* (1901); David Hawke: *In the Midst of Revolution* (1961); Robert L. Brunhouse: *The Counter-Revolution in Pennsylvania, 1776–1790* (1942); and E. Bruce Thomas: *Political Tendencies in Pennsylvania, 1783–1794* (1939).

On the Loyalists, the starting point is George W. Kyte: "An Introduction to the Periodical Literature Bearing upon Loyalist Activities in the Middle Atlantic States, 1775–1783," *Pennsylvania History*, vol. 18 (1951), pp. 104–118. The basic studies are William H. Siebert: *The Loyalists of Pennsylvania* (1920); and Henry J. Young: "Treatment of the Loyalists in Pennsylvania," (doctoral dissertation, Johns Hopkins University, Baltimore, 1955). See also Elmer E. S. Johnson: "The Test Act of June 13, 1777," *Pennsylvania German Society Proceedings*, vol. 38 (1927), pp. 9–22.

On the Liberty Bell, see Victor Rosewater: *The Liberty Bell* (1926): John Baer Stoudt: *The Liberty Bells of Pennsylvania* (1930); and Harold D. Eberlein and C. V. D. Hubbard: *Diary of Independence Hall* (1948). Details on the national flag appear in M. M. Quaife: *The Flag of the United States* (1942); and Edwin S. Parry: *Betsy Ross, Quaker Rebel* (1932).

Pennsylvania's role in the framing of the Federal Constitution may be followed in John B. McMaster and Frederick P. Stone: *Pennsylvania and the Federal Constitution, 1787–1788* (1888); Catherine D. Bowen: *Miracle at Philadelphia: The Story of the Constitutional Convention* (1966); Robert A. Rutland: *The Ordeal of the Constitution: The Anti-Federalists and the Ratification Struggle of 1787–1788* (1965); and Jonathan Elliott (ed.): *The Debates in the Several State Conventions on the Adoption of the Federal Constitution*, 5 vols. (1836), of which vol. 2 covers the Pennsylvania ratifying convention. See also Owen S. Ireland: "The Ratification of the Federal Constitution in Pennsylvania" (doctoral dissertation, University of Pittsburgh, Pittsburgh, 1966).

Biographies related to the revolutionary era in Pennsylvania are Joseph Gurn: *Commodore John Barry, Father of the American Navy* (1933); William B. Clark: *Captain Dauntless: The Story of Nicholas Biddle of the Continental Navy* (1949); Lawrence H. Gipson: *Jared Ingersoll, a Study of American Loyalism* (1920); Asa M. Stackhouse: *Colonel Timothy Matlack, Patriot and Soldier* (1910); Eleanor Young: *Forgotten Patriot: Robert Morris* (1950), a popular treatment; Clarence L. Ver Steeg: *Robert Morris, Revolutionary Financier* (1954), a sound and scholarly book; Edward W. Hooker: *The Fighting Parson of the American Revolution: A Biography of General Peter Muhlenberg* (1936); John F. Roche: *Joseph Reed, A Moderate in the American Revolution* (1957); Charles E. Russell: *Haym Salomon and the Revolution* (1930); Harry E. Wildes: *Anthony Wayne, Trouble Shooter of the American Revolution* (1941); Charles J. Stillé: *Major-General Anthony Wayne and the Pennsylvania Line in the Continental Army* (1893); Richard C. Knopf: *Anthony Wayne* (1960); and Charles Page Smith: *James Wilson, Founding Father, 1742–1798* (1956). W. H. Egle: *Some Pennsylvania Women during the Revolution* (1898) provides a handy source for this subject. On the role of the blacks, consult Benjamin Quarles: *The Negro in the American Revolution* (1953).

CHAPTER NINE

The Decline of Aristocracy: 1790–1808

Washington entered the Presidency in April 1789, without contest, and Thomas Mifflin won the governorship of Pennsylvania in 1790 with 27,725 votes to 2,802 for his opponent, General Arthur St. Clair. They ran as individuals rather than as party leaders; both supported the new Federal regime. But by 1792 the term "Federalist" had shifted its meaning from approval of the new national Constitution to endorsement of the policies of Alexander Hamilton. Mifflin became Governor because voters of both old parties trusted him. He possessed the experience and conservatism admired by the eastern Federalists, and as a revolutionary leader and a resident of the frontier, he held the respect of the old Radical or Constitutionalist party. He conducted himself with tact, avoided partisanship, and served for three terms.

Both the Federalists and the Antifederalists of Pennsylvania focused their attention primarily upon national issues to win public support. The Federalists endorsed strong national authority; they approved Hamilton's domestic program of funding the debt, a Federal bank, and national import and excise taxes. In foreign affairs, they approved neutrality in the war between England and France and the maintenance of trade with England. The Antifederalists feared the power of the Federal government. They opposed Hamilton's financial policy, and they disliked having the national capital at Philadelphia where wealthy urban aristocrats could exert their influence. Conversely they wildly celebrated the French Revolution and urged the United States to honor the French Treaty of 1778 by aiding France in her war with England. On the state level the parties fought not over substantive policy but over new political procedures.

NEW POLITICAL PROCEDURES

Nominating methods The state election of 1790 showed the weaknesses of the old way of nominating. Mifflin and St. Clair became candidates at the request of several informal meetings in Lancaster and Philadelphia, but such a haphazard method could not permanently be used to select nominees for Congress or the state Legislature. At first a few Federalist leaders picked all their party's nominees and called them the "Conference Ticket." The Antifederalists invited the old county Committees of Correspondence to forward names of nominees to a central committee, which framed their party ticket. Neither of these systems worked efficiently or obtained wide support.

The Philadelphia Federalists soon began to invite county representatives to attend the nominating conference, a practice which had the rudiments of a nominating convention. Their opponents formed political clubs, copied from the French revolutionaries. Democratic Societies and Democratic Clubs sprang up all over the commonwealth in 1793–1794 and often assumed the function of nominating candidates for their party.

Finally, the newspapers began to play an important part in the nomination procedure. Capable editors with strong partisan views used their papers to bring possible candidates into public view and to popularize them, thus influencing the nominating conferences or club meetings. Philadelphia published partisan papers which circulated throughout the nation. John Ward Fenno's *Gazette of the United States* supported the Federalist policies, while Benjamin F. Bache's *General Advertiser* and William Duane's *Aurora* became engines of propaganda for the Antifederalists, who soon took the name "Republicans." The newspapers served the Republican cause best, for they appealed to passion rather than to reason and reached many people who had not yet accustomed themselves to political activity except when summoned to mass meetings. The gradual change in nominating practices marked the beginning of wider public participation in naming candidates.

Conduct of elections The constitution of 1790 granted the right to vote to "every freeman" at the age of twenty-one who had resided in Pennsylvania for two years and paid a state or county tax within six months before the election. Except in Philadelphia, where different qualifications existed for voting in municipal elections, the popular balloting caused few problems even though the voters marked ballots openly at a table where all could see.

But serious problems arose in the state Legislature over rules governing the election of Federal officers within the state. United States senators, according to the state constitution, should be chosen by a vote of the two Houses of the Legislature; but the rules did not specify whether the Houses should poll their members separately, in which case a nominee would need a majority in each House to be elected; or whether they should vote jointly, in which case the Houses would meet together and a simple majority of all would elect. The Senate would have more influence under the first or concurrent voting system. The Assembly would dominate voting under the joint system. In 1791, when Senator William Maclay's short term expired, the Pennsylvania Legislature deadlocked for two years over this question, during which time Pennsylvania had but one United States senator. In 1793 the two Houses agreed on the joint ballot system, which was used until the Seventeenth Amendment to the United States Constitution in 1913 called for popular election of United States senators.

Another troublesome problem arose over the creation of election districts for various classes of officials. The Federalists in 1788 had passed a law providing for the election "at large" of presidential electors and congressmen; that is, candidates could reside anywhere in the state and every voter could choose among all of the candidates. This method favored the majority party. The Legislature set up eight congressional districts in 1790 but reversed itself in 1792 and ordered that congressmen and presidential electors should again be chosen "at large." Finally, in 1794, Pennsylvania created twelve congressional districts and enabled each district to nominate and elect its own local candidates.

A serious crisis arose in the presidential election of 1796 because the laws did not yet cover all the contingencies. That year marked the end of Washington's administration and brought a contest between Federalist John Adams and Republican Thomas Jefferson. Pennsylvania had by this time developed a fairly clear-cut division of opinion about these two. Governor Mifflin won a third term in the state election of October 1796, because neither party wished to unseat him, but they formed separate tickets for the presidential election of November and fought a bitter campaign.

State law required each county to send returns to the Governor within two weeks after the election; Mifflin would then announce the winning presidential electors. When the deadline arrived, three counties had not reported. Hesitant to announce a result which late returns might alter, he allowed another two weeks, which barely gave time for the winning electors to travel to Philadelphia to hold their poll for president. The second deadline arrived with all the returns in except those of Greene County. Mifflin now announced the election of thirteen Republicans and two Federalists. When Greene County finally reported, the Republicans claimed that they had won all fifteen electors and sent their whole ticket to Philadelphia, but the Electoral College honored Mifflin's list. This fracas very nearly cost John Adams the Presidency, for had Pennsylvania cast a solid Republican vote in the Electoral College, Thomas Jefferson would have become President in 1796.

Federal-state conflicts In addition to trying new modes of conducting nominations and elections, Pennsylvania politicians faced conflicts between national and state authorities. During Washington's Presidency the Whiskey Rebellion and the attempt to develop Presqu'-isle reflected such conflicts of interest. Pennsylvania became an early testing ground for trials of jurisdiction partly because Governor Mifflin ever since the Revolutionary War had never fully trusted General Washington. When western Pennsylvania rebelled against the excise tax on whiskey in 1794, Washington asked the Governor to call out the Pennsylvania militia to enforce the Federal law; but Mifflin refused, asserting that a president, in peacetime and in the absence of any local request for assistance, had no authority to direct a state governor to use state militia for any purpose. Mifflin established his point and set a precedent still honored.

The second conflict arose when Governor Mifflin sent state militia to protect surveyors of the Erie Triangle from Indian attack, in accordance with a Pennsylvania law of 1794. Washington, fearing that the appearance of state troops in this region would incite the Senecas to join the war already in progress between western Indians and the Federal troops, ordered Mifflin not to send militia to Presqu'isle. Mifflin challenged Washington's authority to "suspend the operation of a positive law of Pennsylvania" which conformed to all Federal statutes. Only the state Legislature could suspend the operation of its own laws. After a six-month controversy, the Pennsylvania Legislature did repeal the objectionable law, but Mifflin never acknowledged the right of a president to suspend the operation of a state law which might run counter to national policy.

While hopeful that the national government would succeed, Pennsylvania retained its century-old fear of centralized authority and directly challenged the power of the President of the United States on these occasions, setting early precedents in Federal-state relations.

THE FEDERALIST ERA IN PENNSYLVANIA: 1790–1800

The Whiskey Rebellion Secretary of the Treasury Alexander Hamilton devised a threefold program for national economic development which immediately became a center of controversy. To revive public credit, Hamilton drew up a funding bill which authorized the Treasury to issue new certificates for depreciated bonds of the states and of the old Confederation Congress at face value. Second, the Federalist Congress chartered the First Bank of the United States, located in Philadelphia, to mobilize private credit for government use. Third, Congress in 1791 passed a revenue bill which levied a tariff on foreign goods and placed an excise tax on certain domestic products including whiskey.

The whiskey tax required operators of stills under 400-gallon capacity to pay an annual tax of 54 cents for each gallon of the still's capacity, or they could pay 7 cents per gallon produced, or 10 cents per gallon of capacity for each month the still operated. However the distiller figured his tax, it seemed exorbitant in western Pennsylvania where nearly every farmer had a small still and where people thought of a gallon of whiskey as the equivalent of 25 cents.

The western Pennsylvanians petitioned for repeal of the Federal tax, asserting that it fell more heavily on the poor than on the rich; that it invited fraud and penalized honesty by asking distillers to certify their own production; that the westerners had no paper money or specie to pay the tax; that the tax rate on cheap western whiskey could run as high as 100 percent, though on expensive eastern whiskey it might be only 10 percent; that the tax therefore was unequal and unconstitutional; that in the west this tax would be four times as great as the aggregate of all existing real estate taxes; that while it might be a luxury tax in the east, it was a tax on a necessity (i.e., the exchange medium) in the west; that farmers could not transport grain in bulk, but could move it as whiskey; and, most important, that litigation arising from the tax had to be settled in Federal district court in Philadelphia, a trip that caused major hardship and actually deprived westerners of recourse to the courts.

Most westerners did not spin out such a long argument; from their habit of unfettered independence and their custom of using whiskey as money, they simply announced that they would not obey. After several mass meetings to denounce the law, local farmers took matters into their own hands. Groups of "Whiskey Boys" with blackened faces and rag masks beneath their eyes devised a standard treatment for revenue collectors: strip the officer, burn his clothes, shave his head, tar and feather him, tie him to a tree or deposit him somewhere deep in the woods, and make off with his horse. Passion ran so high that the "Boys" gave the full treatment to a man who merely rented a house to a revenue collector. Any farmer who paid the tax or spoke up for obedience to the law might expect neighbors to call to "mend his still" —that is, break it to pieces.

Such local militancy prevented the United States from collecting the excise tax in western Pennsylvania during 1792 and 1793. Governor Mifflin partially calmed the uproar by arranging to have Pennsylvania courts hold sessions in the west with authority to hear Federal excise tax cases. But unhappily, in July 1794, two months after Congress had agreed to court hearings in Pittsburgh, a Federal marshal, David Lenox, began to serve scores of writs which ordered defendants to Philadelphia for trial. His action detonated the Whiskey Rebellion.

When the news spread that, contrary to Mifflin's promise, the Federal agents planned to drag accused tax violators to Philadelphia, the countryside flew to arms and some 500 angry men marched to the home of Inspector John Neville near Pittsburgh. He happened to be away, but the Whiskey Boys burned the house and barns and shot an army officer who, with a few soldiers, tried to protect the residence. The object of the mob's ire, David Lenox, the writ-serving marshal, hurriedly escaped down the Ohio River.

Led now by David Bradford, often called "Tom the Tinker," in whose name a good many tar and feather parties had been called, the westerners vowed death to revenue collectors and withdrawal from the Union if President Washington tried to enforce the hated excise law. The failure of the government to open up the Spanish port of New Orleans to western river trade made Congress pay attention to the secession threats, for western Pennsylvania had been threatening to break away for a decade. Washington asked Governor Mifflin to employ the Pennsylvania militia to enforce the law, but the Governor declined. The Whiskey Boys moved the unsettled question off dead center by seizing a United States mail carrier to find out what the Federal people in Philadelphia might be writing about. This assault gave President Washington the opening he needed.

In Philadelphia, on August 2, Pennsylvania and Federal officials planned for a large-scale invasion, agreeing that the only way to enforce the law without bloodshed would be to send an army so large as to make resistance palpably futile. On August 4, United States Supreme Court Justice James Wilson reported to the President that regular court officers could not enforce Federal law in western Pennsylvania. This cleared the way for Washington to call up the militia. On August 7, Washington ordered the insurgents to disperse. The same day Secretary of War Henry Knox asked the Governors of Pennsylvania, New Jersey, Maryland, and Virginia to place 13,000 militia in Federal service, with 5,200 as Pennsylvania's quota.

Still hopeful that a military expedition might be avoided, Governor Mifflin and President Washington appointed a joint peace commission to make a final effort to bring the Whiskey Boys to terms. Thomas McKean and General William Irvine served for Pennsylvania, and United States Attorney General William Bradford, Senator James Ross, and Pennsylvania Supreme Court Justice Jasper Yeates for the United States. All five were Pennsylvanians. They observed mass meetings at Parkinson's Ferry and Redstone Old Fort in mid-August, talked with western leaders, and reported that there was no hope of peaceful settlement.

The Pennsylvania Legislature passed a four-month draft law with an appropriation of $120,000 on September 19, and by October 4 President Washington had joined the army which had gathered at Carlisle under the command of Virginia's Governor Henry Lee. Before the army marched, two western leaders, William Findley and David Redick, arrived to inform Washington that a meeting at Parkinson's Ferry on October 2 had agreed that the west would now scrupulously comply with the excise tax law, and that the army need not move. Washington gave them a curt dismissal. When the troops, now 15,000 strong, reached Parkinson's Ferry on November 8, General Lee issued a proclamation condemning the insurgents and calling upon all loyal citizens to take an oath in support of the Federal Constitution.

The army found no signs of belligerency or rebellion. The troops conducted a round-up of suspects, separated out twenty from several hundred caught in the dragnet, and marched them back to Philadelphia for trial. Observers along the line of march reported that they watched the army troop past their homes for two days, escorting in the center of the long column the twenty chained and forlorn suspects. The disproportionately large military force, though it provided a bloodless victory, had long-range political results, because the onlookers, in the words of one of them, "perceived, for the first time, with amazement and alarm, the immense power placed by the federal constitution practically in the hands of the leading advisors of the executive."

The Federal District Court in Philadelphia found most of the defendants not guilty. It sentenced to death two men accused of treason, but the President pardoned both. Of all the whiskey rebels, only David Bradford never received amnesty; he fled to Spanish Louisiana. The suppression of the Whiskey Rebellion strengthened the United States government, but not the Federalist party. Washington followed up his advantage by sending a message to Congress about the Whiskey Rebellion on November 14 in which he condemned the anti-administration Democratic Societies and placed on them the blame for stirring up the disorder and fomenting contempt for law. His address killed the societies but strengthened the resolution of their members to build the party they would call Republican to distinguish it from the aristocratic Federalist party.

The Gênet Mission and the Jay Treaty The foreign policy of the Federalists also sharpened partisan division in Pennsylvania. On July 14, 1789, three months after Washington's inauguration, Paris mobs stormed the Bastille and began the French Revolution. By 1793 the French attack on monarchy had provoked a war with England. In April 1793, Citizen Edmund Gênet, Minister of the First French Republic, came to America to seek aid in the war, and people who recalled French support of the American cause fifteen years earlier gave Gênet such a welcome that he believed they would joyfully help.

President Washington, moved by responsibility rather than emotion, carefully reviewed the alternatives and on April 22 issued a proclamation of neutrality. When Gênet reached Philadelphia in May, Washington received him with a calculated formality that was in marked contrast to the ecstatic reception given him by the citizens of Philadelphia. John Adams reported that "ten thousand people . . . day after day, *threatened to drag Washington* out of his house" to compel a declaration of war against England and the assumption of obligations to France under the Treaty of 1778. Gênet proposed to fit out privateers in America and to bring captured prize ships into ports of the United States, but Washington forbade such activity.

In July, Governor Mifflin learned that Gênet had armed a prize ship in Philadelphia and planned to send her to sea. Mifflin sent his secretary of the commonwealth, Alexander J. Dallas, to stop this enterprise, but Gênet angrily refused and announced that "he would appeal from the President to the people." Dallas reported the threat to the Cabinet officers, Knox and Jefferson, who also tried to dissuade Gênet, but he ignored them and ordered the privateer, *Little Democrat,* to sail. On August 1, 1793, Washington with the unanimous approval of the Cabinet ordered Gênet's recall. Gênet's disgrace forced those sympathetic to France out of the Washington administration.

In 1794, the signing of the Jay Treaty further widened the breach between the pro-British Federalists and the pro-French Republicans. This unpopular negotiation, weighted in favor of Great Britain, seemed to confirm earlier warnings of Pennsylvania Republicans that the Federalists were Tories and enemies of the objectives of the American Revolution. The treaty imposed restrictions on American trade with the West Indies, and gave promises but no guarantees of British withdrawal from military posts in the northwest.

The Whiskey Rebellion, the Gênet Mission, and the Jay Treaty all played an important part in reducing the large Federalist majority of 1790 in Pennsylvania, and in creating the nearly even division of the popular vote in the presidential election of 1796. The change of fewer than 150 votes out of some 24,000 could have altered the entire list of winning presidential electors.

Fries' Rebellion   France, in protest against the Jay Treaty, broke diplomatic relations with the United States before the inauguration of President John Adams. The new President dispatched commissioners to Paris to reestablish an exchange of ministers, but the French Directory insulted them with the extortion scheme called the XYZ affair. President Adams asked Congress to strengthen the army and navy as an undeclared war with France began.

In July 1798, when Congress passed a war-tax law, rebellion broke out in the Pennsylvania Dutch country where any kind of tax generally met opposition. The new law placed a tax on dwelling houses, reckoned by counting the number and size of windows. Congress designed it to spare the poor and require the rich to pay the heaviest fees. The German inhabitants of Pennsylvania had not become bilingual, did not understand the law, and believed false rumors that the new tax had some similarity to the hated salt or hearth taxes of the old country.

Ignorance of details of the law led to fear, and irresponsible utterance turned fear into violence. Strangely, much of the area affected—Northampton, Berks, Montgomery, and Bucks Counties—regularly voted Federalist, and the leader of the rebellion, auctioneer John Fries, was himself an outspoken Federalist. At first indignant householders poured boiling water on tax collectors who tried to measure ground-floor windows, bringing the term "Hot Water Rebellion" into currency. But "Fries' Rebellion" more accurately describes the resistance, for a loquacious auctioneer and former militia captain named John Fries set himself up as a popular leader and continually inflamed the people at public sales. After several tax agents had been assaulted and their records seized, the Federal District Court issued general warrants for the ringleaders. A marshal and his deputies arrested twenty-three men whom they jailed in the Sun Tavern at Bethlehem. Fries gathered a company, rode to Bethlehem, and forcibly freed the Federal prisoners on March 7, 1799.

President Adams, on March 12, gave the lawbreakers six days to disperse and called out the militia. The Pennsylvania militia cooperated with the Federal authorities in putting down the uprising. These troops set out from Philadelphia on April 4, marched through the German district seizing suspects, and ultimately captured John Fries by following his dog "Whiskey" into a swamp where Fries had hidden. Before the end of the month Fries had been indicted for treason, tried, found guilty, and sentenced to hang.

Fries' Rebellion came immediately to an end, but William Duane, new editor of the *Aurora,* kept it vividly alive everywhere his paper circulated. As one of the most trenchant political writers in the country, he seized upon the case of John Fries and made it a cause around which the Republicans could rally. Duane managed to obtain a new trial for Fries, but Federal Judge Samuel Chase handled the case with such bias that the lawyers withdrew and the judge again ordered the death penalty. President Adams then pardoned Fries.

Downfall of the Federalists The two trials of John Fries, one in April 1799, and the second in April 1800, coincided with the Pennsylvania campaigns for governor in 1799 and for U.S. president in 1800. At a meeting of their party's legislators, the Republicans nominated Thomas McKean for governor. The Federalists, also by legislative caucus, nominated James Ross of Pittsburgh. McKean had a long history of public service. He had fought in the Revolutionary War, signed the Declaration of Independence, served as President of Delaware, and been chief justice of Pennsylvania. He opposed the Jay Treaty, sympathized with the French revolutionaries, and denounced the Alien and Sedition Acts. Personally he had the aspects of a Federalist: wealth, aristocratic bearing, a conservative spirit, and some contempt for common people. His nomination caused consternation among western Republicans, but it also offered a tempting choice to dissatisfied Federalists there.

McKean won but the vote was very close. Fries' Rebellion probably spelled the difference, for the once-Federalist German counties gave McKean more than twice as many votes as Ross. The election demonstrated the political potency of the alliance between the western Scotch-Irish and the eastern Germans, both of whom had suffered from Federalist policies.

In December 1799, the Federalist senators rejected a House bill for choosing presidential electors "at large"—the same bill they had insisted upon in earlier years—for they feared that Jefferson's election would destroy the nation. The Legislature had to adjourn without providing for the popular election of presidential electors in Pennsylvania.

Governor McKean declined to call a special session, but said he would wait until the new Legislature met. This came too late for a popular vote for presidential electors and thus bypassed the procedural deadlock, but it placed the choice of Pennsylvania's electors in the hands of the Legislature itself. Under these circumstances, the election of state legislators in effect dictated the choice of presidential electors. The Republicans won handsomely, but even so the voice of the people did not carry into the Senate where the holdover Federalists maintained a slim majority. The issue now turned on whether the choice of electors would be made by joint or concurrent vote, and again a deadlock ensued.

As the time approached for the Electoral College to meet and the Legislature remained immobilized, the idea that the Federalist senators might be seeking to prevent Pennsylvania from participating in the presidential election spread abroad and aroused people to a frenzy. Circumstantial support of this charge developed when elections in other states brought news that without Pennsylvania's electors, Federalist Charles C. Pinckney would probably receive sixty-six votes, Jefferson sixty-five, and John Adams fifty-eight. The Legislature finally passed a compromise bill permitting each House to nominate eight electors, and from these sixteen the Houses by joint vote would choose the state's quota of fifteen. Practically this meant that the Assembly would nominate eight Republicans, and the Senate eight Federalists; and in the joint vote the legislators would choose eight Republican and seven Federalist nominees. Pennsylvania would thus cast one effective electoral vote for Jefferson.

In the Electoral College, Jefferson won seventy-eight votes, but his running mate, Aaron Burr, polled the same number. This threw the election into the national House of Representatives, where, voting by state, the congressmen on the thirty-sixth ballot delivered the Presidency to Jefferson. Governor McKean, terribly wrought up by the possibility of Burr's success, had asked the Pennsylvania Legislature to remain in session and prepared a proclamation pledging Pennsylvania's allegiance to Jefferson.

The frenzied election of 1800 illustrated qualities of party politics in Pennsylvania which had colonial precedent and would continue into the future. The intransigence of party leaders, the determination of a minority party holding power in one branch of government to serve its own presumed interests at whatever cost to the state or nation, the employment of tricky parliamentary maneuvers to obstruct action, the change of principle to serve immediate advantage, the tenacious and unshakable loyalty to party line regardless of larger public interests—these aspects of political behavior in Pennsylvania all clearly showed in the election of 1800. They failed to deprive Jefferson of the Presidency, but they embittered local politics for several generations.

THE JEFFERSONIAN ERA: 1800–1808

Pennsylvania in 1800 The major forces which had shaped Pennsylvania life during the eighteenth century seemed still to be at work at the beginning of the nineteenth: diversity, material development, and democracy.

Pennsylvania's major population groups remained culturally separate and still exhibited firmer loyalty to their local traditions than to the commonwealth. While statewide parties had begun to emerge, regionalism and cultural pluralism remained a potent and divisive force in them. Pennsylvania Germans often ran their own candidates separate from regular party tickets, and the hostility between western farmers and eastern city folk continued. Religious freedom fostered the multiplication of sects, and these became self-interested and jealous social units. The economy, growing more complex as it expanded, generated competitive and conflicting interests among farmers, shippers, land promoters, bankers, and manufacturers. All these constituted the diversity which characterized Pennsylvania, making it a land of dynamism, experiment, and opportunity, always full of turbulence.

The state continued its rapid development. From 1790 to 1800 the population grew from 400,000 to 600,000, and the number of counties from twenty-one to thirty-five. Foreign trade in the port of Philadelphia in 1800 reached $3,400,000, more than one-third of the national total. In 1806 foreign commerce into and out of Pennsylvania reached $17,000,000. Philadelphia, capital of the nation and the state, still held her place as the center of commerce and finance, serving as the home of the First Bank of the United States and of the major state chartered banks. But western demands forced the removal of the state capital from Philadelphia to Lancaster in 1799, and the national government moved its headquarters to Washington, D.C., in 1800.

Pennsylvania's diverse society and developing economy functioned in an expanding democracy. The state had abolished slavery; it had bestowed suffrage on almost all adult male citizens; it had achieved equal apportionment of legislators from all counties and districts; it directly elected its governor and the legislators of both Houses; and it had created a system of checks and balances which, while sometimes immobilizing the government, prevented the seizure of power by one branch. Only the judicial system remained outside the control of the voters; the governors appointed judges who held tenure for life.

The attack on the judiciary With the elections of Governor McKean and President Jefferson, the Republicans, who now controlled the executive and the legislative branches, tried to establish control also over the courts. But the life tenure of judges meant that the Federalist party would dominate the bench for years to come. Predictably, the Jeffersonians made their first order of business an attack on the Federalist judges.

The simple fact that nearly all the judges and lawyers of Pennsylvania were Federalists made it easy to stir up hatred of them as a group. Poor people knew only that when they took a case to law, they might not receive a trial for years and that they probably would lose. Squatters who lost a farm to a legal purchaser viewed the courts not as an arm of justice but as a tool of the rich to take advantage of the poor. Some of the Federalist judges brought political passion into the courtroom and let party feeling sway their conduct on the bench.

Governor McKean, a former chief justice of Pennsylvania, did not agree with his party about courts and lawyers. In his messages of 1801 and 1802 to the Legislature, he urged expansion of the judiciary as the best way to clear courts of their overcrowded dockets, speed trials, and reduce the cost of litigation. He hoped also to appoint new judges of the Republican persuasion to counterbalance the Federalist monopoly of the bench.

The Assembly, however, had other plans. Legislators began to exercise court functions by passing private bills to give individual constituents relief in cases which the courts ordinarily would have handled. Back-country people felt more confident of a Republican Assembly than of a Federalist judge.

Justices of the peace had jurisdiction over cases up to $20. In 1802, the lawmakers passed the $100 Act giving justices of the peace power to decide cases up to that amount. The governor appointed justices of the peace not for legal talent that they possessed, for few had any training, but because they worked locally for the party. Governor McKean vetoed the $100 Act in December 1802, saying that it would precipitate a flood of appeals. The Legislature then passed the Arbitration Act enabling litigants to seek an amicable settlement from an official referee before having recourse to courts. McKean vetoed this, pointing out that it would make more sense to come directly to court where a jury would decide facts than to have arbitration proceedings followed by a court trial. These measures signified public distrust of the Federalist-dominated courts.

On April 2, 1803, the Legislature reenacted the old law giving justices of the peace power to deal with $20 cases. When the Governor vetoed this, the lawmakers passed it over the veto. This gave them confidence to enact again the $100 Act which Governor McKean permitted to become law without his signature. The vote of 68–14 in the Assembly illustrated the degree of discontent with existing courts and lawyers.

A second phase of the attack on the judiciary came in the form of impeaching judges. Alexander Addison, president judge of the Fifth Judicial District in western Pennsylvania, brought his Federalist politics passionately into court, even after being reprimanded by the state Supreme Court. The infuriated Assembly ordered him impeached in 1802. Alexander J. Dallas prosecuted for the House, Addison defended himself, and the Senate voted him guilty in a partisan ballot. The House removed Addison in January 1803, and barred him from sitting as judge in any state court.

This success encouraged the House to more judge hunting. In 1802, the Supreme Court of Pennsylvania had sentenced a litigant, Thomas Passmore, to serve thirty days in jail for contempt. Passmore appealed to the Assembly shortly after it had disposed of Judge Addison. The Assembly thereupon impeached the three Federalist judges of the Supreme Court, Edward Shippen, Jasper Yeates, and Thomas Smith, in March 1803. The case against the Supreme Court rested upon such flimsy ground that no Pennsylvania lawyer would conduct the prosecution, and the House ultimately had to hire an attorney from Delaware. Dallas, who had prosecuted Addison, now defended the Supreme Court judges. The Senate acquitted them and they resumed their positions.

The Republicans next turned to revision of the constitution of 1790. William Duane used the *Aurora* to publicize this movement in 1805, making it a crucial issue in the election for governor that year. The revisionists demanded popular election of judges for a specific term of office, a one-year term for governor and for state senators, and a reduction of executive patronage.

This program reflected discontent with McKean's vetoes; suspicion that the incumbent Governor, senators, and judges all held aristocratic and Federalist attitudes; and a continued tinued growth of the demand for popular management of public affairs.

Split of the Jeffersonians: 1805–1808 In the election of 1802, McKean had beaten the Federalist gubernatorial candidate, James Ross, by 47,879 votes to 17,037. The Federalists elected no congressmen or state senators, and only 9 of the 86 assemblymen. The Republicans had raised their majority over the Federalists from 5,000 votes in 1799 to 30,000 in 1802. This result made the outcome of the presidential election of 1804 such a foregone conclusion in Pennsylvania that no campaign took place there. A legislative caucus named the Republican electors; the Federalists did not even choose a ticket.

Success, at first a cause of self-congratulation among Jeffersonians, soon became a source of disunity and factionism. Strong men in the dominant party fought each other for leadership, and the Federalist minority sought advantage by offering itself to whichever Republican faction would best serve its interests. The split in the Republican ranks became visible in the 1803 contest for control of Philadelphia where Dr. Michael Leib brought himself to power by demagoguery. Ambitious and adept at gaining popular support by stirring up hatred of others, Leib allied with William Duane and gained control of local nominations. To fight this political machine, A. J. Dallas and other friends of McKean formed their own faction, known as "Quids," admitting Federalists to their nominating meetings to gain strength. McKean aggravated the split by his repeated vetoes of Assembly bills, by his appointment of aristocrats to office, and particularly by a careless letter. Defending the state's right to have men of talent in office, he wrote a condemnation of "clodpoles, (or, if they please, clodhoppers)" as public servants. The letter leaked, and Duane published garbled versions portraying McKean as a man with utter contempt for common people.

In April 1805, the Republican legislative caucus nominated Speaker of the House Simon Snyder for governor, advertising him as a "clodhopper." Snyder, son of a poor German immigrant, had neither gentle breeding nor professional education. Starting as an apprentice to a tanner, he had worked his way up to storekeeper, miller, justice of the peace, and finally, assemblyman. He became the first common citizen and the first person of German descent to campaign seriously for the governorship. The same day that Duane's Republicans named Snyder, the Quids renominated McKean.

The campaign of 1805 aroused all the old class hatreds. Snyder's friends, calling themselves Democratic Republicans; called for revision of the constitution; and hammered at the high-toned Federalist quality of "His Super-Excellency" McKean and his Quid supporters. McKean's followers, adopting the name "Constitutional Republicans," publicized the remarkable progress of the state under the constitution of 1790 and warned that Duane's party proposed "an equal distribution of property." McKean won narrowly with 43,644 votes to Snyder's 38,483, but the Quid party fell into the hands of the anti-Jeffersonians and rapidly deteriorated.

In 1808 the elections of governor and president coincided in Pennsylvania. Snyder was nominated for governor, and the Republicans named James Madison for president. A new personality entered Pennsylvania politics at this time who would exert much influence in the next ten years. John Binns, an Irishman from Northumberland County, with all the pugnacity, polemical ability, and political cunning of Leib and Duane, established a new newspaper in Philadelphia, the *Democratic Press*. Binns, by trenchant writing and radical views, quickly supplanted Duane and established himself as Snyder's major advisor.

Snyder won the governorship by 67,975 votes to 39,575 for his Federalist opponent, James Ross. The large vote caused the chief surprise, for it exceeded by 40,000 the poll of 1805. The Federalists increased their strength in the state Legislature and the congressional delegation, but responded poorly in the presidential election, polling only 11,000 Pennsylvania votes for their candidate, Rufus King. James Madison claimed 53,000 Pennsylvania votes and won the Presidency.

The election of 1808 signified that the common people of Pennsylvania had abandoned their deferential attitude toward the rich and wellborn, and had themselves assumed the task of governing. The unprecedented turnout at the polls suggested that they looked on Snyder as representative of themselves and proclaimed that they need no longer rely upon an elite political aristocracy to serve their interests.

BIBLIOGRAPHY

Two detailed and scholarly monographs provide the best introduction to the Federalist and Jeffersonian periods of Pennsylvania history. They are Harry M. Tinkcom: *The Republicans and Federalists in Pennsylvania, 1790–1801: A Study in National Stimulus and Local Response* (1950); and Sanford W. Higginbotham: *The Keystone in the Democratic Arch: Pennsylvania Politics 1800–1816* (1952). More limited in scope but also useful are E. Bruce Thomas: *Political Tendencies in Pennsylvania, 1783–1794* (1938); J. Russell Ferguson: *Early Western Pennsylvania Politics* (1938), and Roland M. Baumann, "The Democratic-Republicans of Philadelphia: The Origins, 1776–1797" (doctoral thesis, Pennsylvania State University, 1970).

For special topics, see William Miller: "First Fruits of Republican Organization: Political Aspects of the Congressional Election of 1794," *Pennsylvania Magazine of History and Biography*, vol. 63 (1939), pp. 118–143; and in the same journal, Bernard Fay: "Early Political Machinery in the United States: Pennsylvania in the Election of 1796," vol. 60 (1936), pp. 375–390; and Elizabeth K. Henderson: "The Northwestern Lands of Pennsylvania, 1790–1812," vol. 60 (1936), pp. 131–160. Also interesting are Julian P. Boyd: "Attempts to Form New States in New York and Pennsylvania," *New York Historical Association Quarterly Journal*, vol. 12 (1931), pp. 257–270; and Harry M. Tinkcom: "Presque Isle and Pennsylvania Politics, 1794," *Pennsylvania History*, vol. 16 (1949), pp. 96–121. *The Journal of William Maclay, United States Senator from Pennsylvania, 1789–1791*, edited by Charles A. Beard (1927) gives an intimate picture of political controversy in these years.

On the Whiskey Rebellion, consult the *Pennsylvania Archives*, second series, vol. 4, "Papers Relating to What Is Known as the Whiskey Insurrection," for a collection of sources. The best scholarly work is Leland D. Baldwin: *Whiskey Rebels: The Story of a Frontier Uprising* (1939). Eugene P. Link: *Democratic-Republican Societies, 1790–1800* (1942); Frank Van der Linden: *The Turning Point: Jefferson's Battle for the Presidency* (1962), on the election of 1800; and Raymond Walters, Jr.: "The Origins of the Jeffersonian Party in Pennsylvania," *Pennsylvania Magazine of History and Biography*, vol. 66 (1942), pp. 440–458, are important, as is Charles A. Beard's classic, *The Economic Origins of Jeffersonian Democracy* (1915).

The relation of Federalist foreign policy to Pennsylvania affairs can be traced in Paul Varg: *Foreign*

Policies of the Founding Fathers (1963); Alexander De Conde: *Entangling Alliance: Politics and Diplomacy under George Washington* (1958); Joseph Charles: *The Origins of the American Party System* (1956); and Henry Budd: "Citizen Gênet's visit to Philadelphia," *Philadelphia City Historical Society Publications,* vol. 2 (1919), pp. 39–67. On the yellow fever epidemic of 1793 in Philadelphia, see John H. Powell: *Bring Out Your Dead* (1949).

The development of difficulties with France leading to Fries' Rebellion and the Alien and Sedition Acts may be studied in Mary E. Clarke: *Peter Porcupine in America: The Career of William Cobbett, 1792–1800* (1939); Frank M. Eastman: *The Fries Rebellion* (1922); W. H. H. Davis: *Fries Rebellion* (1899), the standard work on this topic; Andreas Dorpalen: "The German Element in Early Pennsylvania Politics, 1798–1800," *Pennsylvania History,* vol. 9 (1942), pp. 176–190; John C. Miller: *Crisis in Freedom* (1951); and James Morton Smith: *Freedom's Fetters: The Alien and Sedition Laws and American Civil Liberties* (1956). Frances S. Childs: *French Refugee Life in the United States, 1790–1800: An American Chapter of the French Revolution* (1940) deals largely with Pennsylvania.

On the Jeffersonian era, see James H. Peeling's doctoral dissertation, "The Public Life of Thomas McKean" (University of Chicago, 1929), and his article: "Governor McKean and the Pennsylvania Jacobins," *Pennsylvania Magazine of History and Biography,* vol. 54 (1930), pp. 320–354. In the same journal, see William M. Meigs: "Pennsylvania Politics Early in this Century," vol. 17 (1893), pp. 462–490; and Elizabeth K. Henderson, "The Attack on the Judiciary in Pennsylvania, 1800–1810," vol. 61 (1937), pp. 113–136.

In addition to standard biographies of key national figures such as Washington, Jefferson, and Hamilton, there are a number of biographies more closely related to Pennsylvania history. Among these are S. G. Kurtz: *The Presidency of John Adams: The Collapse of Federalism, 1795–1800* (1957); Raymond Walters, Jr.: *Alexander James Dallas, Lawyer, Politician, Financier, 1754–1817* (1943) and his *Albert Gallatin: Jeffersonian Financier and Diplomat* (1957); Claude M. Newlin: *Life and Writings of Hugh Henry Brackenridge* (1932); Samuel E. Forman: *Political Activities of Philip Freneau* (Johns Hopkins Studies in History and Political Science, ser. 20, nos. 9, 10, 1902); Philip M. Marsh: "John Beckley, Mystery Man of the Early Jeffersonians," *Pennsylvania Magazine of History and Biography,* vol. 72 (1948), pp. 54–69; and Paul A. W. Wallace: *The Muhlenbergs of Pennsylvania* (1950).

CHAPTER TEN

The Reshaping of Party Lines: 1808–1828

The governorship of Simon Snyder changed the focus but not the character of Pennsylvania political life. The controversies over judicial and constitutional reform which had disrupted McKean's administration were replaced by a new rupture over nominating procedures between the Leib-Duane faction of Jeffersonians, calling itself the Old School Democrats, and the followers of Snyder, taking the name New School Democrats. At the same time the non-intercourse policy of the national government during the Napoleonic War temporarily revived the Federalist party.

GOVERNOR SNYDER AND THE WAR OF 1812

The Olmsted case Shortly after Governor Snyder took office, Congress passed a harsh law giving customs officers power to seize goods anywhere in the country which they suspected of being destined for export in violation of the Embargo Act. When New England's Federalists threatened to leave the Union rather than submit to this law, the Pennsylvania Senate denounced the malcontents as "enemies and traitors." But at the same time, Pennsylvania itself became embroiled in a contest with the Federal government which brought a military confrontation. This was the Olmsted case.

Briefly, the trouble arose from the capture in 1778 of the British ship *Active,* which Gideon Olmsted and several other American prisoners aboard managed to seize at sea. While Olmsted was sailing the vessel to Philadelphia, the crew of the Pennsylvania ship *Convention* boarded her and took charge. Both Olmsted and the captain of the *Convention* claimed the prize money. A Pennsylvania admiralty court awarded one-fourth of the proceeds to Olmsted, one-fourth to the commonwealth of Pennsylvania, and the remainder to the captain of the *Convention* and to another vessel involved in the affair. The Continental Congress also heard the case and awarded the prize money to Olmsted. Pennsylvania authorities sold the *Active* and divided the cash as its court had decreed; but the state treasurer, David Rittenhouse, held the state's share until the legal controversy had been resolved. In 1795 a United States Supreme Court decision upheld the congressional award. Rittenhouse had died, but Olmsted in 1803 sued the executrices, two Philadelphia ladies, to obtain the money, and the United States District Court ordered the estate to pay Olmsted. The Pennsylvania Legislature then passed a law to prevent the Federal court from enforcing its judgment on the ground that the funds in question belonged to Pennsylvania.

In 1809, the United States Supreme Court issued a writ of mandamus to force the Rittenhouse estate to pay the prize money to Olmsted. Governor Synder called out the militia to protect the ladies in charge of the Rittenhouse estate from the Federal court order. In March 1809, a Federal marshal tried to serve writs on the ladies at their home, now called "Fort Rittenhouse," but the state militia turned him back with bayonets. The marshal then instituted proceedings against the militiamen for treason, and called up a Federal posse. Matters reached the point of mob violence a few weeks later, but the marshal did manage to serve the writs by guile and then arrested the ladies and the militia. At this point, Governor Snyder had to face squarely the issue whether he planned war with the United States, or would permit the Rittenhouse estate to pay to Olmsted the $18,000 it held in trust for Pennsylvania. Snyder directed the money to be paid to Olmsted. After a United States court tried and convicted the militamen, President Madison pardoned them. The affair demonstrated that no subordinate unit could challenge the Federal power with impunity, a lesson forcibly taught in the Whiskey Rebellion, Fries' Rebellion, and now in the Olmsted case.

The War of 1812 The excitement over the Olmsted case had scarcely died away before the nation became embroiled in a war with England. Governor Snyder, reelected to the governorship in 1811 almost without opposition, ended his feud with Madison over the Olmsted affair and agreed with the President that grievances against England could not be settled except by war. Pennsylvania gave sixteen votes in Congress for a declaration of war — more than any other state delegation. The congressmen supported the war primarily because the continued British violations of American neutral rights had outraged their Pennsylvania constituents. But the declaration of war in April 1812 raised alarm and resistance in commercial areas because foreign trade had been prospering and the government had made no preparation for a major conflict. Nearly all the Federalists and many city Republicans opposed it, but the great majority of the people favored Madison for president in 1812 against the antiwar candidate, DeWitt Clinton of New York.

Pennsylvania strongly supported the war effort. Even the Federalists, though they loudly complained about the inept conduct of the war, did not, like the New England Federalists, obstruct the war effort. They established volunteer units and joined their political rivals in the fighting. Snyder's call for the state quota of 14,000 volunteers brought out three times that number. The state contributed not only men, but leadership, money, and the staging area for a major battle. General Jacob Brown earned a congressional commendation for his important victories at Chippewa and Lundy's Lane. Among naval commanders, Captain Charles Stewart of the frigate *Constitution,* Captain James Biddle of the *Hornet,* and Commodore Stephen Decatur of the *United States* distinguished themselves in the war at sea.

The war nearly bankrupted the Federal government. The failure of Congress in 1811 to renew the charter of the First Bank of the United States deprived the Federal Treasury of its primary device to raise funds. Alexander J. Dallas, Secretary of the Treasury after Gallatin's transfer to the peace commission in 1813, found the public willing to purchase only $200,000 of a $5 million Federal bond issue in 1814. In this crisis, Philadelphia's merchant prince, Stephen Girard, stepped forward and bought the bond issue.

Pennsylvania sent men to all the various war fronts, but experienced only two contacts with the fighting on or near its own soil: the British blockade of Philadelphia and the Battle of Lake Erie. The Philadelphia episode caused nothing beyond temporary inconvenience, but the Battle of Lake Erie on September 10, 1813, proved of major strategic importance, guaranteeing continued American possession of the northwest territory. Commodore Oliver Hazard Perry assembled men and materials at Erie where Daniel Dobbin superintended the construction of a small fleet. With this hastily built navy, Perry defeated the British ships on Lake Erie and sent his famous dispatch: "We have met the enemy and they are ours."

On the whole, the war had gone badly. Detroit and Niagara had been lost, the Canadian expedition failed, and the British burned Washington in retaliation for American destruction of York (Toronto). Philadelphia, in a panic when the British attacked Washington and Baltimore, hastily tried to fortify itself, aided mainly by a volunteer force of 2,500 local blacks who in two days dug entrenchments around the city. The surrender of Napoleon at Waterloo opened the prospect that the full force of British arms in Europe would soon fall on the United States. Madison had already sent a peace commission to Europe including Albert Gallatin.

Gallatin and Dallas were Pennsylvania's highest ranking officers in the Federal government. Gallatin, a native of Switzerland, had settled in Fayette County, been elected to the United States Senate as an Antifederalist but was refused his seat, and had been appointed by President Jefferson as Secretary of the Treasury, a post he held until 1813. An able financier, full of large ideas and devoid of partisan pettiness, he served ably but gained little credit in his home state. His refusal to promote political jobs for henchmen of Leib and Duane aroused their hostility. One of Gallatin's most farsighted plans, a federally aided transportation grid of roads and canals for defense and commercial purposes, anticipated by a century and a half the national interstate highway system. Gallatin played a crucial role in negotiating the Treaty of Ghent which, on December 24, 1814, ended the war.

Alexander J. Dallas, who replaced Gallatin in the Treasury, belonged politically in the McKean wing of the Pennsylvania Jeffersonians. His wealth and financial understanding led him to perceive national needs and to propose measures which the Jeffersonians of 1800 had condemned. He achieved the establishment of the Second Bank of the United States in 1816, with its main office at Philadelphia, and devised the Tariff of 1816 to protect infant American industries, created by the war, from British competition after peace.

After the Treaty of Ghent had been signed, but before news of it had reached America, General Andrew Jackson met the flower of the British army in the Battle of New Orleans and cut it to pieces. The nation, after the series of military reverses and humiliations, responded to the astounding victory at New Orleans with such a frenzy of joy that the disappointing treaty terms, when they arrived, received scant attention. But General Jackson's name had indelibly impressed itself upon the national memory, and would shortly alter the course of Pennsylvania politics.

THE DEATH OF "KING CAUCUS"

In the election of 1814 for governor, the Federalists increased their strength, while the Snyderites suffered from the war and from Snyder's effort to control the mania for state banks which had flooded the country with shinplaster currency. The Governor showed his mettle by vetoing a popular bill to charter forty-one new state banks at the very moment the law-makers had assembled to make the 1814 nominations. They renominated Snyder, but then rebuked him by passing the Forty-bank Act over his veto. The Federalists nominated Isaac Wayne for governor, won the support of the Leib-Duane faction, and campaigned vigorously with the aid of Duane's *Aurora*. In the election, held just a few weeks after the British attack on Baltimore, Snyder won over Wayne, 51,099 to 29,566.

Snyder's final term brought marked changes to partisan politics in Pennsylvania which, since 1805, had centered mainly around the conflict between Binns and Duane. The resurgent Federalists had their hopes suddenly and irreparably smashed in January 1815 by the Hartford Convention and Jackson's victory at New Orleans. The New England conference verged on treason by attacking the Madison government at a time of grave national crisis; Jackson's triumph instantly deflated the movement. The Hartford Convention killed the national Federalist party and made its local adherents in Pennsylvania eager for alliance with dis-gruntled Democrats as their best hope of survival.

The collapse of the Federalists as a national party reduced Pennsylvania politics to a con-test between Jeffersonian factions. Snyder's friends, the "New School Democrats," ap-proved of new national policies which Jefferson had condemned: a federally chartered bank, a protective tariff, and Federal aid to road building. Snyder's enemies, the "Old School Democrats," claimed to represent the traditional Jeffersonian views. Actually the Old School Democrats cared little for principle, but comprised mainly former officeholders like Leib and Duane who wanted to get back on the public payroll. In 1820 the condition of parties in Pennsylvania was described by an assemblyman in the words: "When I say parties, I mean a division in the Democratic ranks."

The presidential election of 1816 highlighted the two problems which reoriented Pennsyl-vania politics: first, the idea that Pennsylvania's politicians had never received the Federal patronage due them for their loyal support of the Jeffersonians; and second, the belief that nominations by a legislative caucus enabled a dominant faction to perpetuate its power in disregard of the popular will. The nomination of James Monroe for president in March 1816 started a train of events in Pennsylvania which brought both these issues into focus.

For some years Leib and Duane had complained that while they had faithfully delivered the Jeffersonian electoral vote, they had been ignored in the distribution of Federal patron-age. Binns, too, though once at war with Leib and Duane in state politics, joined them in 1816 because he felt his service to Governor Snyder had been insufficiently rewarded. Thus, three factionists, one a demagogue and the other two cantankerous but powerful editors, had become enemies of Snyder as his term approached its close.

The *Aurora* and the *Democratic Press* hammered the theme that since 1789 Virginia always supplied the president while New York reaped the major patronage plums. For twenty-four of the twenty-eight years since 1789, Virginians had occupied the Presidency, and now Monroe would continue the dynasty. Before the congressional nominating caucus of 1816, Pennsylvania members understood that if they supported Monroe, the caucus would choose Snyder as the vice-presidential candidate. But once Monroe had been chosen, the caucus selected Daniel H. Tompkins, Governor of New York, for the second place. Outraged by the apparent betrayal, Pennsylvania politicians denounced the "New York–Virginia dynasty" and attacked the system of caucus nominations by which it maintained control. The uproar in Pennsylvania transcended factional lines, but only the Old School Democrats in coalition with the Federalists put it to immediate use. Condemning legislative caucuses as dictatorial and undemocratic, they called a special convention of delegates at Carlisle in September 1816, and placed in the field a set of unpledged presidential electors who, presumably, favored DeWitt Clinton for president. At the election in November, the depth of the split in the Jeffersonian party of Pennsylvania showed in the poll of 25,000 for the caucus (Monroe) ticket, and 17,000 for the convention (Clinton) ticket.

In the gubernatorial election of 1817, Snyder desired his state treasurer, William Findlay of Mercersburg, to succeed him. A legislative caucus dutifully nominated Findlay as the candidate of the New School Democrats in the spring of 1817. The Old School Democrats attacked the New School party for corruptly using "King Caucus" to perpetuate the succession, and demanded that voters participate in nominations. They called a second convention in Carlisle which excluded officeholders and admitted only delegates chosen by the voters at county meetings. The Carlisle convention of 1817 nominated for governor an old Federalist Revolutionary War veteran, Joseph Hiester of Berks County, and issued a statement demanding reform. The Old School Democrats, through the *Aurora* and the *Democratic Press,* created a widespread impression that the Snyder or New School party had become tyrannical and corrupt. Findlay barely won with 66,000 votes to 59,000 for Hiester.

Findlay's administration suffered both from bad luck and from the Governor's indiscretion. The Panic of 1819 struck in the last year of his term causing great distress in Pennsylvania, for which the Governor had to take the blame. At the height of the panic, Binns engineered impeachment proceedings against him. While the Senate refused to convict him, the trial exposed evidence that Findlay as state treasurer had used state funds for private purposes, and Binns therefore achieved his object—to convince the public that the New School administration had been corrupt.

These events immediately preceded the elections for president and governor in 1820. No one opposed Monroe for a second presidential term, a circumstance which gave rise to the misleading label "The Era of Good Feeling." In Pennsylvania, the Old School Democrats renominated Hiester at another delegate convention, and threw such fear into the Findlay people that the New School Democrats abandoned the legislative caucus and themselves employed a convention to renominate Findlay. This amounted to an admission that their opponents had been right in demanding reform. The bitterly fought campaign of 1820 nearly brought a tie, but Hiester won with 67,000 votes to 66,000 for Findlay—the largest vote ever to turn out in the state up to that time.

Governor Joseph Hiester, sixty-seven years old when he took office, had no further ambitions and determined to act without regard for party. He served the state by appointing competent officers from all factions, but in doing so he ruined his own organization. The ill-defined coalition of Old School Democrats, however, could not have survived long. Leib died in 1822, Duane went to South America, Binns became so erratic that he lost his former influence, and no new leadership emerged.

In 1823 the Old School Democrats wanted to renominate Hiester, but he declined. They then proposed reunion with the New School, but this effort failed. When the New School Democrats named John Andrew Shulze of Berks County as their candidate, the Hiester party

The old capitol building at Harrisburg was built in 1818 and burned in 1897. (Pennsylvania Historical and Museum Commission)

picked Andrew Gregg of Bellefonte who had served as secretary of the commonwealth under Hiester. Shulze's nomination constituted a bid for the Pennsylvania German vote which many people believed to be the factor which had elected Hiester. Shulze won, 93,000 to 64,000, and by the time his first term had ended in 1826, the old issues and personal conflicts which had formerly divided the Jeffersonians had so far burned themselves out that there was no opposition to his reelection.

THE QUEST FOR NATIONAL INFLUENCE

The Family party versus Amalgamation Monroe's reelection in 1820 without a contest made it clear that in 1824 all candidates for the presidential succession would be members of the same national party; and of these, only one would be the regular candidate—that is, be nominated by the traditional procedure of a congressional caucus. The New York–Virginia alliance which ran the caucus would choose William H. Crawford of Georgia as the nominee. But three others had a strong popular following: Henry Clay, Speaker of the House; John

Quincy Adams, Secretary of State; and John C. Calhoun, Secretary of War. In addition to these four experienced statesmen, promoted mainly by leading politicians, a fifth began to receive attention mainly at the grass roots—General Andrew Jackson, Senator from Tennessee. The new alignment of Pennsylvania parties in the 1820s grew directly out of the contest for the presidency among these men.

The first of the new factions became known as the Family party because its major leaders, George M. Dallas of Philadelphia, William Wilkins of Pittsburgh, and several others of the group, were related by marriage. These men, with influence in the two most populous counties, also inherited much of the voting strength of Snyder's New School Democracy. They placed the defeated Governor, William Findlay, in the United States Senate in 1821, and strengthened their influence by raising Shulze to the governorship in 1823. The Family Party early in 1821 settled on Calhoun as its favorite for the Presidency. Its plans projected an alliance of Pennsylvania, South Carolina, and Ohio to challenge the New York–Virginia dynasty. Since the latter would nominate Crawford in a congressional caucus, Pennsylvania would use its new convention system to place Calhoun's name in nomination. South Carolina and Ohio would then endorse Calhoun and other states would likely follow suit.

A second faction which at first favored Henry Clay began to evolve out of the Old School Democrats. It assumed the name "Amalgamation party," to signify a coalition of Federalists with Democrats who opposed the old Snyder or the new Family party leadership. The Amalgamators drew support largely from the rural areas, and condemned the Family party as an urban aristocracy. Democrats such as Henry Baldwin and Molton C. Rogers and Federalists such as young James Buchanan formed the core of the Amalgamation movement.

Neither Crawford nor Adams developed any strong support in Pennsylvania, and in 1823 it appeared that the state struggle would center around Calhoun and Clay. Then the unexpected happened. Without any apparent local leadership, Andrew Jackson began to take hold in the popular imagination. Jackson's unexpected emergence as the presidential candidate most attractive to Pennsylvanians grew partly from the system the state had inaugurated of bringing the electorate into the nominating procedures. As Jackson's popular strength became more evident, leaders of the major factions found it necessary to accommodate themselves to the rising grass-roots sentiment. The Amalgamation party made the first move, coming out for Jackson in 1823, with Clay as second choice. Because they had organization and leadership, the Amalgamators, or the Jackson-Clay men, successfully publicized the idea that they were the original Jackson party in the state.

The Family party still hoped to control the state nominating convention of March 1824 and to have it name Calhoun for president. Once the delegates had assembled, however, Dallas saw that he had miscalculated, for nearly all the delegates had been instructed for Jackson. To make the best of it, Dallas asked the convention to nominate Jackson as Pennsylvania's choice for president, with Calhoun as the vice-presidential nominee, a motion passed by 124 to 1. The Family party then proclaimed itself the major Jackson organization in the state.

The disputed election of 1824 An odd campaign ensued, for leaders of the two major parties in the state both supported Jackson for the Presidency. Each group really preferred a different candidate, but neither dared to challenge the public hysteria for Old Andy, and each tried to place itself before the public as the true Jacksonian party. The Amalgamators, who first came out for Jackson, called the Family party the "Eleventh-hour Men" or "Calhoun-

Jackson Men" to expose their tardy endorsement and their ulterior motive. The Family party condemned the Amalgamators as Federalists and friends of Clay. But both promoted Jackson with such effect that in the election of 1824 he polled in Pennsylvania a 20–1 victory over Clay, 9–1 over Crawford, and 7–1 over Adams. In the nation at large, however, the Electoral College gave Jackson 99 votes, Adams 84, Crawford 41, and Clay 37. As no candidate had a majority, the election went to the House of Representatives which had to select a winner from the three leading candidates. Calhoun became Vice President, and Clay, though out of the presidential race, controlled enough votes to determine the outcome.

Clay's friends, who had the power to choose between Adams and Jackson, naturally could be expected to favor the man who would treat their candidate best. A rumor arose that Jackson, if chosen, would appoint not Clay but Adams as Secretary of State. Congressman Buchanan, partisan of both Jackson and Clay, asked Jackson if he had pledged the Cabinet post to Adams. Jackson said he had decided nothing, and Buchanan repeated this to Clay.

Word of these interviews soon leaked and the Family party leaders used them to damage both the Amalgamation party and Clay. Congressman George Kremer of Selinsgrove published a statement that Clay had put his votes up for sale for the appointment as Secretary of State, that Jackson had spurned such a corrupt bargain, but that Adams would probably agree to it. Clay challenged Kremer to a duel, but withdrew when the Congressman chose squirrel rifles as the weapons. Shortly thereafter, the House elected Adams with the support of Clay's friends, and Adams announced Clay as his Secretary of State.

No one then or since could prove improper motive in these events, but the simple facts aroused widespread suspicion and the Family party did all it could to fix the charge of "corrupt bargain" on Clay and Adams, and later on Buchanan and his party. The Family party had also suffered an upset of plans from the election of Adams, but it could still maintain the Calhoun-Jackson alliance. The Amalgamation party, however, had to abandon all thought of further association with Clay, for the "corrupt bargain" charges made the continuation of a Jackson-Clay party an impossibility. The Amalgamators became exclusively a pro-Jackson party.

The two Jackson parties of Pennsylvania after 1825 had new tasks before them. Together they had to bring discredit upon the Adams administration and elect Jackson in 1828; and separately they had to discredit each other so that when Jackson did enter the White House he would favor one party but not the other as his true and loyal friends, entitled to patronage.

New parties in the election of 1828 Pennsylvania politics after the election of John Quincy Adams became increasingly complicated because national, state, and local party lines rested upon different considerations. On the national level, men had to choose between Adams and Jackson; in state politics they had to support or oppose the administration of Governor Shulze; and locally they still proclaimed themselves Federalists or Democrats. The Family party which had brought Shulze to power hoped to use his administration to promote the Jackson-Calhoun party nationally, but the Governor balked. He resented the pressure on him and deplored the obstructionist tactics of the Jacksonians in Congress, where they opposed all measures which might bring credit to Adams. In his message of 1826, Shulze said that Pennsylvania had no ambition "to be distinguished by extraordinary influence in the affairs of the general government," nor would the state "lend her strength for the advancement of individuals." This pronouncement directly contradicted the policy of the Family party.

The disputes among the Pennsylvania Democrats developed mainly over four issues between 1825 and 1828: revision of the state constitution of 1790, the internal improvements program, the protective tariff, and the presidential election of 1828. The pressure to revise the state constitution came mainly from the Old School men and Federalists who wished to weaken the hold of their enemies on the state government by curtailing the powers of the governor. The New School or Family leaders in 1825 passed a bill calling for a popular referendum on revision, but designed it to invite public rejection by giving the proposed convention unlimited power. The people defeated the proposal to revise the constitution by a vote of 59,000 to 44,000.

Also in 1825, the question of internal improvements began to grip the attention of the state so strongly that for some years the Legislature considered very little else. Until 1824 internal improvements had been constructed almost wholly by private enterprise. Although private citizens and the state government had bought over 10 million dollars worth of bonds by 1822 in 146 turnpike companies, 49 bridge companies, and 18 canal companies, the benefits remained local rather than general, for the units rarely interconnected. As the Erie Canal approached completion in 1824, a group of interested citizens mainly from Philadelphia formed the Pennsylvania Society for the Promotion of Internal Improvements, which demanded that the state build a canal system to connect the Ohio River and Lake Erie with the Delaware, and that no local canal projects be built until the entire Main Line had been completed. In response to this pressure, the Legislature on February 22, 1826, passed the bill which inaugurated the Pennsylvania State Works.

The people of Pennsylvania experienced a kind of hysteria about canal and road building in the late 1820s, and they also became fanatically attached to the idea of a protective tariff. The rapid growth of the coal and iron industries, and the craze for Merino sheep to supply the woolen mills brought farmers, manufacturers, and laborers into alliance in support of high protection. The tariff issue quickly attached itself to the larger presidential question and tended to polarize parties because Adams favored protection whereas Jackson had straddled the issue by advocating a "careful" tariff in 1824 and keeping silent thereafter. Adams and Clay, supported by the leading protectionists of the nation, occupied a position on the tariff much more appealing to Pennsylvanians than that of Jackson or Calhoun. This fact made the tariff a key problem for all the pro-Jackson politicians of the state. The voters wanted Jackson in the White House and wanted the tariff program of Adams and Clay in Congress.

In 1827 the Adams administration introduced the Woolens Bill into Congress. Except for a few Jackson men, Pennsylvania's congressmen voted for it, and it passed the House. In the Senate, Martin Van Buren shrewdly caused a tie by not voting, and forced Vice President Calhoun to cast the deciding vote. When Calhoun, following the wishes of his own section, defeated the Woolens Bill, he became the target of violent denunciation all over Pennsylvania.

Historians have so often heralded Pennsylvania as the center of Jacksonian Democracy that they sometimes forget how uncertain the outcome of the election of 1828 seemed to the people of that day. Jackson had been an overwhelming favorite in Pennsylvania in 1824, but only 40,000 people had voted. Between then and 1828 the Jackson forces did not appear to grow, but the Adams party made conspicuous headway. Distinguished Pennsylvanians such as Richard Rush, John Sergeant, Albert Gallatin, Amos Ellmaker, Joseph Hopkinson, and Charles Jared Ingersoll all accepted responsible positions in the Adams administration. Governor Shulze, abused by the Family party until he lost patience, finally came out openly for Adams and received an invitation from this party to accept the vice-presidential nomination in 1828, an offer he declined.

The Calhoun-Jackson party, driven to desperate measures, revived the old "bargain and sale" charge, through which they hoped to brand Adams and Clay as corrupt, show Jackson's aversion to intrigue, and destroy the political future of James Buchanan, head of the Amalgamators.

In the fall of 1827, Samuel D. Ingham and other Calhoun-Jackson leaders persuaded Jackson to accuse Clay of proposing to make him president in exchange for appointment to the State Department. Clay denied the accusation and demanded to know who made such a proposition on his behalf. Jackson named Buchanan. This forced Buchanan either to admit that he had been Clay's agent in a corrupt bargain, or to state that Jackson had not told the truth. In a public letter, Buchanan gave Jackson the lie, an act for which the General never forgave him. For a time Jackson's cause in Pennsylvania was severely shaken, for the Amalgamators saw little hope of continuing as Jackson supporters. Governor Shulze used his patronage liberally to ease their path into the Adams camp. But Buchanan kept his head, remained loyal to Jackson, and pointed out that the whole operation had been a Calhoun plot as it had hurt every presidential aspirant except the favorite of the Family party.

As the presidential contest of 1828 took complete possession of the popular interest, all local and state controversies became subordinate to it. Pennsylvania localities called meetings of the friends of Jackson or of Adams "without reference to the political distinctions which have hitherto divided us." When election day arrived, the tickets bore the simple labels "Adams party" and "Jackson party," and for the first time since 1800 Pennsylvania appeared to have developed a genuine two-party system. The state gave 101,652 votes to Jackson and 50,848 to Adams, a ratio which showed that Jackson retained his popularity with the rank and file. Few but the professionals paused to consider that the Jackson vote itself reflected two separate Jackson organizations which would now have to carry their respective claims for recognition and reward to the White House. For their steady support and resounding victory for the General, each felt entitled to high consideration; and from their steady and unabated hatred of each other, they promised little but grief to the newly elected President.

BIBLIOGRAPHY

The key books relating specifically to Pennsylvania in this era are Sanford W. Higginbotham: *The Keystone in the Democratic Arch: Pennsylvania Politics 1800–1816* (1952); Philip S. Klein: *Pennsylvania Politics, 1817–1832: A Game without Rules* (1940); and James A. Kehl: *Ill Feeling in the Era of Good Feeling: Western Pennsylvania Political Battles, 1815–1825* (1956). Significant books on the two major interests of the period, tariff and internal improvements, are Malcolm R. Eiselen: *The Rise of Protectionism in Pennsylvania* (1932); and Julius Rubin: *Canal or Railroad: Imitation and Innovation in the Response to the Erie Canal in Philadelphia, Baltimore and Boston* (1961). The two best general studies of this period have been written by George Dangerfield: *The Era of Good Feeling* (1952) and Shaw Livermore, Jr.: *The Twilight of Federalism: The Disintegration of the Federalist Party, 1815–1830* (1962). An extensive listing of materials relating to economic developments of the era will be found after Chapter 14 under appropriate topics.

On the Olmsted affair, see Mary E. Cunningham: "The Case of the *Active,*" *Pennsylvania History,* vol. 13 (1946), pp. 229–247.

The War of 1812 is best treated by Victor A. Sapio: *Pennsylvania and the War of 1812* (1970). See also Max Rosenberg: *Building of Perry's Fleet on Lake Erie, 1812–1813* (1950); and Harold L. Myers: *Pennsylvania and the War of 1812* (1964). C. L. Lewis: *The Romantic Decatur* (1937) is the standard biography of this naval hero from Pennsylvania.

Useful articles on political methods have been written by M. Ostrogorski: "The Rise and Fall of the Nominating Caucus, Legislative and Congressional," *American Historical Review,* vol. 5 (1899), pp. 199–283; and Joseph S. Walton: "Nominating Conventions in Pennsylvania," *American Historical Review,* vol. 2 (1897), pp. 262–278. Consult also biographies of notable Pennsylvanians of the era such as John H. Powell: *Richard Rush, Republican Diplomat, 1780–1859* (1942); Thomas Govan: *Nicholas Biddle* (1959); Harry E. Wildes: *Lonely Midas* [Stephen Girard] (1943); Raymond Walters: *Albert Gallatin* (1957); Philip S. Klein: *President James Buchanan* (1962); and William M. Meigs: *Life of Charles J. Ingersoll* (1897).

CHAPTER ELEVEN

The Jacksonian Era: 1828–1848

The election of Andrew Jackson inaugurated a new two-party system nationally, but in Pennsylvania the Adams-Jackson division showed a traditionally local pattern. The state Adams party, like the Federalists after 1800, was so small it could not possibly win; the Pennsylvania Jacksonian party, like the old Jeffersonian party, was so large that it remained split. This condition encouraged the development of coalitions against the dominant Jacksonian faction. Such coalitions appeared under the guise of anti-Masonry, anti-Catholicism, and antislavery.

RISE AND FALL OF THE FAMILY PARTY

Fight for the spoils The contest among the Jacksonians centered upon control of Federal patronage and capture of the state governorship in 1829. As the Pennsylvania Jacksonians would nominate a governor on the day of Jackson's presidential inauguration, March 4, 1829, each state faction considered it essential to have one of its leaders named to the national Cabinet before that date. Such a mark of favor from Washington would determine whether the Amalgamators or the Family party would name the Jacksonian candidate for governor, a choice which would be tantamount to election.

Buchanan's Amalgamators pressed Henry Baldwin on the President for a Cabinet post and planned to nominate Senator Isaac D. Barnard of West Chester, for governor. The Family party wanted a major Cabinet post for Samuel D. Ingham and promised to place its favorite, George Wolf, in the governor's chair. Just a few weeks before the Pennsylvania nominating convention Jackson named Ingham to the Treasury Department. This enabled the Family party, in a bitter convention contest, to nominate George Wolf of Easton, for the governorship.

For a time it appeared that no contest would develop over the governorship, as Shulze had determined not to run again and the Adams people had little strength in the state. Then an unexpected new issue called anti-Masonry entered the scene. The movement originated in the mysterious disappearance in 1826 of William Morgan of Batavia, New York, who planned to publish a book exposing Masonic secrets. The Anti-Masons alleged that an exclusive Masonic aristocracy, bound together by oaths and running the government by secret management in Masonic lodges, controlled the country from top to bottom. The Pennsylvania Germans, and particularly the Plain Sects who opposed oaths, proved especially susceptible to the anti-Masonic fever. In 1828 the *Anti-Masonic Herald* of Lancaster began publication, and Thaddeus Stevens, Amos Ellmaker, Thomas H. Burrowes, Theophilus Fenn, and Harmer Denny began to organize the movement into a political party.

In June 1829, the Anti-Masons nominated Joseph Ritner of Washington County, former Speaker of the House of Representatives, for governor. Since Ritner favored Clay's "American system" of bank, protective tariff, and internal improvements, whereas Wolf represented the Pennsylvania friends of Calhoun, the presidential question played an important part in the state election. The press widely proclaimed that a vote for Wolf in 1829 meant a vote for Calhoun in 1832, or conversely, that a Ritner ballot meant a Clay vote in 1832. Wolf won the governorship with 78,219 votes, but Ritner's 51,776 votes were a remarkable showing for a party just born.

Wolf's election signaled the high tide of success for the Family party. Two of its leaders soon entered the United States Senate, William Wilkins of Pittsburgh in 1830 to replace William Marks, and George M. Dallas in 1831 to fill the vacancy left by the resignation of Isaac D. Barnard. While the Family party consolidated its triumph, it also saw the apparent dissolution of the Amalgamation faction. Barnard died, Henry Baldwin announced his withdrawal from active politics, and Jackson sent James Buchanan on a genteel exile to St. Petersburg as United States Minister to Russia. In 1830 it appeared that when Jackson left office, Calhoun might succeed him in 1833 and Pennsylvania's turn would be next. But within a year, a series of events occurred which blasted the Family party and threw Pennsylvania politics into chaos. These events, engineered largely by Martin Van Buren, intimately affected the Pennsylvania scene.

The Family party ousted When Jackson rejected Federal aid to internal improvements, approved reductions in the tariff, and smashed the Second Bank, his Pennsylvania adherents reacted with incredulity and outrage. But they had stirred up such intense emotional commitment to General Jackson that they had to remain outwardly loyal to his administration even though its policies began to threaten Pennsylvania's major interests.

For years the promotion of internal improvements by the Federal government had been one of the favorite measures of the Keystone State. Such Pennsylvanians as William Strickland, Jonathan Roberts, Abner Lacock, John Sergeant, Samuel Breck, Charles Miner, and Mathew Carey were known in the United States and in Europe for their interest in improving overland travel. Pennsylvania congressmen backed the Maysville Road Bill and predicted that Jackson would not dare to veto it, but on May 27, 1830, he did.

Throughout the year 1830, tension built up between Jackson and Vice President Calhoun. Starting early in the year with the Webster-Hayne debate in which Calhoun strongly endorsed the states'-rights views of Senator Hayne, the difficulty expanded at a Jefferson Day dinner in April into a hostile exchange between the President and the Vice President over the protective tariff. Jackson's relations with Calhoun suffered another shock when the General learned that in 1818 Calhoun, while Secretary of War, had condemned Jackson's aggressive conduct in Spanish Florida. The formal break developed over the farcical but momentous Peggy Eaton affair. Jackson's friend, John Henry Eaton, Secretary of War, married a widow of questionable reputation. The aristocratic Mrs. Calhoun declined to associate with Mrs. Eaton socially, despite Jackson's insistence that she be given all the courtesy due a Cabinet member's wife. All the pro-Calhoun members of Cabinet, including Samuel Ingham, followed the Calhouns in ostracizing Mrs. Eaton. The incident drew national attention and forced a breakup of the Cabinet. Only Van Buren, a widower, emerged from the affair with augmented claims to Jackson's friendship. When Ingham refused to resign, Jackson fired him. The Eaton incident discredited Calhoun and his friends with Jackson, and Calhoun's major role in South Carolina's nullification attempt in 1832 further reduced the influence of the Calhoun-Jackson party of Pennsylvania.

Finally, Jackson's attack on the bank utterly confounded his partisans in Pennsylvania. The Second Bank of the United States under Nicholas Biddle's presidency had become a Pennsylvania institution, a Pennsylvania pride, and a Pennsylvania interest. All local parties approved it, and all but three Pennsylvania congressmen were for it. The state Legislature passed resolutions endorsing it, and Senator Dallas presented the memorial asking for its recharter. The bill passed, but on July 10, 1832, in the midst of the campaign for the Presidency, Jackson returned it with a stinging veto which stunned Pennsylvanians. Governor Wolf had openly backed the bank, and all the Jackson leadership had pledged loyalty to it. These people now had to abandon Jackson or eat their words. Most chose the latter course, and before long the campaign cry took the shape: "Hurrah for Jackson—he is all right; the Bank must be put down—the Tariff must be put down—and internal improvements is worse than bad."

But what rankled most was that Martin Van Buren, chosen as Jackson's running mate and now clearly heir apparent to the presidential chair in 1836, had emerged the winner. New York had triumphed and Pennsylvania's hopes lay in ashes. Yet, to keep alive politically, the Pennsylvania Jacksonians had to swallow their personal resentment and follow Van Buren or make a clean break from the party they had built. With reluctance and resentment, most of the Pennsylvania Jacksonians prepared to make the distasteful adjustment.

Governor Wolf and the bank issue The election year 1832, with campaigns for both governor and president, brought into the open the paradox that the dominant political force in Pennsylvania would have to promote a presidential candidate whose policies demoralized them and a vice-presidential candidate who had been unpopular in Pennsylvania since 1827. The anti-Jackson parties, that is, the National Republicans and the Anti-Masons, recognized the dilemma of Pennsylvania's Jacksonians and sought to capitalize on it. The National Republicans, soon to be called Whigs, nominated Henry Clay for president and picked Pennsylvania's John Sergeant for second place on the ticket. The Anti-Masons named William Wirt for president and Pennsylvania's Amos Ellmaker for vice president.

Within the state the same candidates for governor ran in 1832 as had competed in 1829: Wolf for the Jacksonians and Ritner for the combined Anti-Mason and Clay parties. Wolf studiously avoided the presidential question and rested his claims on his local performance.

The problems of the construction of the State Works and of maintaining the state's credit dominated the campaign. During his first term, Wolf had faced the consequences of the Legislature's decision to try to finance the public works by borrowing. The commonwealth now owed more than 8 million dollars, had levied no taxes to meet the interest payments, and thus could not find takers for new loans. The Second Bank had, indeed, been lending most of the cash to build the public works and for this reason, among others, had made itself indispensable to the Governor. Wolf either had to stop work on the canal system or devise sources of income to restore faith in the credit of the state and make further borrowing possible. He met the issue squarely by achieving the passage of a bill taxing mortgages, bonds, notes, and bank and turnpike stock, and raising county taxes. With this guarantee of income, he negotiated another loan of $3 million to complete work on parts of the canal already under contract, and established a special fund from the new taxes to apply to the payment of interest on the state debt. These sound measures saved Pennsylvania from bankruptcy at the same time that they enabled canal building to continue. The Anti-Mason party condemned Wolf's tax program and blamed him for extravagance and corruption in the State Works.

Wolf won over Ritner by the close vote of 91,144–88,072. The anti-Masonic hysteria and Jackson's repudiation of Pennsylvania interests showed clearly in this near defeat of the man who, but a few years before, had represented an apparently impregnable political party within the state. In the presidential election, Jackson polled 90,000 and the anti-Jackson ticket 66,000 votes. Pennsylvania's Jacksonians expressed their sentiments more clearly in the vice-presidential contest by casting the entire electoral vote of the state for William Wilkins. They would support Jackson but not Martin Van Buren.

Jackson's fight with Calhoun, his attack on Pennsylvania's favorite policies, his decision to run for a second term in 1832, his dependence on Van Buren for political strategy, and his use of Federal patronage to build a local Van Buren party created a leadership vacuum in Pennsylvania politics. Jackson's course undermined the old party managers before any new management had been established. A sense of angry frustration pervaded the politics of the commonwealth which soon nourished the growth of splinter parties based essentially upon hatred—the natural child of a sense of betrayal. Not only the Anti-Masons, but political groups opposing slavery, foreigners, and Catholics sprang up in Pennsylvania. Such a sudden growth of new parties based mainly upon prejudice or emotional outrage could scarcely have occurred if the Jackson movement had retained its once-strong leadership.

In December 1832, following his own and Jackson's reelection, Governor Wolf strongly defended the Second Bank and urged its support. Most of the state legislators at that time agreed with him even though his position explicitly repudiated Jackson's main presidential policy. Jackson, in an effort to start a pro–Van Buren, anti–Second Bank party in Pennsylvania, appointed William J. Duane of Philadelphia as Secretary of the Treasury, but when the President ordered Duane to withdraw Federal funds from Biddle's bank, Duane refused and Jackson had to fire him. During 1833, Nicholas Biddle began to call in loans, suspecting that the Treasury might suddenly demand the Federal money on deposit. The contraction of loans precipitated a panic which forced some state banks and private businesses to close, causing a rise in unemployment and a sharp drop in prices. Pennsylvanians generally blamed the depression on Jackson's war against the bank. The outcry against Jackson grew to such proportions that early in 1834 the Girard Bank of Philadelphia, which had been named as one of Jackson's "pet banks," returned all its Federal funds and gave up its "pet-bank" status.

The Pennsylvania attack on Jackson aroused the friends of the Second Bank in Congress to plan a new recharter move which, in January 1834, they believed would succeed. That month the next installment of interest on the Pennsylvania state loan fell due. Biddle offered to provide the necessary funds, but Governor Wolf said he would borrow the money from a number of state-chartered "country banks." Biddle then called on these banks for funds they owed to the Second Bank, leaving them without means to loan money to finance the public works. On February 22, 1834, bids for the new state loan were opened. No one had offered to take any of it. For the moment it looked as if the Second Bank had triumphed; that without its aid Pennsylvania could not pay its debts or finance its canal building.

Four days later, Governor Wolf sent a message to the Legislature attacking the Second Bank and sustaining Jackson's veto of the recharter bill. Underlying this remarkable somersault of the Governor lay the implication that the bank had overreached itself and had in fact demonstrated what Jackson had asserted—that it would use its power to control public policy; that, in this instance, it would force Pennsylvania into bankruptcy and stop canal building by making money scarce in a time of urgent need. Wolf's abrupt change of policy threw the friends of the bank into confusion. The recharter movement in Congress suddenly died. Local businessmen began to assert that Biddle and not Jackson had created the recent money panic. Jacksonians in the state Legislature praised Wolf and began to follow the national party line. Finally, Wolf, with help from banks outside the state, negotiated the sale of the state loan which had earlier gone without takers.

The outward appearance of renewed Jacksonian unity belied the actual condition. Some Jacksonians declared war on the Second Bank without quarter, whereas others including the Governor merely ceased to talk about it further. Wolf believed that Biddle's bank ought to be made less powerful, but he never approved of Jackson's summary withdrawal of Federal funds from it, nor did he think the Second Bank should be utterly destroyed. The Whigs and the Anti-Masons did their best to exploit the confusion among Jacksonians over the bank question. A Whig state convention at Harrisburg in May 1834 attracted one-third of the delegates from the ranks of pro–Second Bank Jacksonians.

During his second term, Governor Wolf succeeded in completing the building of the Main Line of the State Works from Philadelphia to Pittsburgh and in putting a portion of it into operation. He also accomplished one of his cherished goals, the establishment of a system of free public education, but neither of these accomplishments could be listed as a political asset. Counties remote from the Main Line complained of government extravagance and heavy taxes which they believed brought benefits only to others, and complaints came from the Pennsylvania Germans, the supporters of parochial schools, and factory owners about taxes for the public schools.

Governor Wolf had recommended a public school law in every message since 1829, and on April 1, 1834, he had the satisfaction of signing into law a bill creating a tax-supported system of public education which would become effective wherever established by local option. By December, however, a torrent of protest developed. The Senate thereupon passed a repeal, and the Assembly would probably have concurred except for an extraordinary forensic performance by Thaddeus Stevens who convinced a majority to sustain the bill. Wolf's leadership in promoting the public school system gained him an honored place in Pennsylvania history, but it cost him the support of many German voters in the election of 1835.

The Jacksonian Democrats convened at Harrisburg on March 4, 1835, to nominate their candidate for governor. Wolf hoped to be named for a third term, but the Amalgamation

Thaddeus Stevens, champion of the Negro, free public
schools, and Anti-Masonry; Republican dictator of Congress during the Civil War and Reconstruction period.
(Leo Stashin Collection)

faction had different plans. They wished to nominate Henry Muhlenberg of Reading, a pas-
tor-politician who had married the daughter of ex-Governor Hiester. Muhlenberg could obtain the German vote and, with unified support, easily win. But the convention deadlocked
between the friends of Wolf and those of Muhlenberg, nicknamed "Wolves" and "Mules" by
the press, and adjourned to meet at Lewistown in May. The Muhlenberg people construed
the postponement as a victory, but the Wolf delegates stayed on in Harrisburg and a day or
two later reassembled a rump convention which nominated Wolf. The furious Muhlenberg
partisans then met at Lewistown to nominate their man. With two Jacksonian Democrats
as candidates, the old factional split became an open public contest.

As the Anti-Masons saw victory within their grasp, they supplied leadership which the
Pennsylvania Whigs lacked. They again nominated Joseph Ritner for governor and invited
support of the Whigs and of bolting pro–Second Bank Jacksonians. Under the circumstances,
they could hardly lose. Ritner polled 94,023 votes, Wolf 65,804, and Muhlenberg 40,586. The
Jacksonians, not large-minded enough to subordinate their minor objectives to the larger
interest, gave the governorship to their adversaries.

THE RULE OF ANTI-MASONRY

The Ritner administration Governor Joseph Ritner continued the line of Pennsylvania German governors started with the election of Simon Snyder in 1808. A native of Berks County, Ritner had come from a poor family, worked as a weaver, and later migrated to Washington County where he became a farmer. He served as an assemblyman during the 1820s, became Speaker of the House, and supported the Jacksonians in 1824 and 1828. He kept the common touch, worked in the fields, ate with his own hired men, and took pride not in public office but in being a plain dirt farmer.

After his election, he found himself the head not of a party but of a loose, ill-defined coalition. The "Exclusives," that is, the hard-core Anti-Masons like Amos Ellmaker, Thomas Elder, and Thaddeus Stevens, shunned the Whigs and tried to form a working alliance in the Legislature with the Muhlenberg Democrats. The "Coalitionists" proposed a union of Whigs and Anti-Masons to defeat Van Buren for the Presidency in 1836.

Thaddeus Stevens soon seized management of Anti-Masons in the Legislature and instituted an investigation of the Masonic order. With intent to harass, he summoned prominent Democrats who were Masons, such as ex-Governor Wolf, Senator James Buchanan, George M. Dallas, and Judge Josiah Randall to appear before the Legislature. When Stevens's conduct provoked a riot in the Assembly hall, the disgusted Whigs joined the Democrats to discharge the witnesses. This terminated the witch-hunt and turned the anticipated exposure of Masonry into a political fiasco.

The anti-Masonic Legislature did take some politically effective action. It weakened the Democrats by requiring the personal registration of voters in Philadelphia and by reapportioning legislative districts to produce anti-Masonic majorities. The Legislature gave a Pennsylvania charter to the Second Bank of the United States, prolonging its life as a state institution after its Federal charter expired in 1836. The omnibus bank charter bill provided for a repeal of the tax laws enacted under Governor Wolf, the payment of a bonus of $4,500,000 to the state by the bank for its new charter, and a loan by the bank to the state of $7,500,000 for canal building. The bank employed a lobby of "borers" to promote the passage of this bill, and assemblymen friendly to the bank promised local canals to purchase votes that remained in doubt. Eight Democratic senators joined the Anti-Masons and Whigs in support of the bill.

The legislative session set the tone for the coming presidential election. The Democrats momentarily laid aside their internal disputes when the Muhlenberg faction endorsed the electoral ticket named by the Wolf faction. Both groups united in dismissing from the party the eight state senators who had voted for the recharter of the Second Bank. Since the bank now began to use its funds freely to strengthen the Anti-Mason–Whig coalition, the Democrats—no longer the recipients of its favors—embarked on an all-out attack against it, and made it the major issue of the campaign. Their strategy worked, for they won an overwhelming victory in the legislative election in October, and carried the state for Van Buren in November.

Some expected that the Democrats would now repeal the state charter of the bank, but this issue proved exceedingly touchy. Clearly, while the Democrats used the war on the bank as a device to gain votes, many of them had no more desire to destroy the institution in 1837 than they had had in 1833. They attacked for political effect, not for substantive cause, and remained its covert defenders.

The constitution of 1838 In 1835 a popular referendum had approved a revision of the state constitution of 1790. The voters elected delegates to a convention in 1836, choosing sixty-seven Democrats and sixty-six Whig–Anti-Masons, though the death of a Democrat and his replacement by a Whig reversed the majority of one before the convention began its sessions at Harrisburg on May 2, 1837. Under the chairmanship of John Sergeant, the convention worked until February 22, 1838, when it proclaimed the new document upon which people would vote in the fall elections.

The delegates faced four major problems: the power of the governor, the life tenure of judges, votes for nonwhites, and the power of the state over banks. Sentiment had grown that a governor ought not to serve three successive terms, and that his patronage should be curtailed. The fear of concentrated executive power, a tradition in Pennsylvania history, had strengthened after Snyder's administration and became one of the reasons for resistance to nominating Wolf for a third term in 1835. The constitution of 1838 provided that a governor should serve no more than two terms of three years each during any period of nine years. Also, the governor would no longer appoint county officers such as justices of the peace and clerks of court, who would now be elected by local voters. The governor would still appoint judges and district attorneys, but judges would no longer serve for life: justices of the state Supreme Court would hold office for fifteen years; other judges, for ten years. These provisions in general weakened the office of governor and transferred some of its former power to the electorate.

The question whether the constitution of 1790 entitled Negroes to vote came into prominence in 1836 and 1837 as a consequence of several lawsuits. In the absence of any explicit statement in the 1790 document, it appeared that blacks were indeed included in the suffrage. The rising crusade for the abolition of slavery and for the extension of rights of citizenship to free Negroes gave urgency to the problem. The discussion of Negro suffrage brought a nonpartisan vote of 77–45 in favor of writing the words "white freeman" into the article defining franchise. Robert Purvis, prominent Philadelphia Negro, wrote of this: "When you have taken from an individual his right to vote, you have made the government, in regard to him, a mere despotism."

The convention labored hard to devise rules governing the drawing of bank charters, but achieved little except to place a few new restrictions on legislative freedom to frame such charters. Popular ratification of the proposed constitution took place in the state election of 1838, but the bitter contest for the governorship nearly eliminated serious discussion of the constitution. It came into force on October 9, 1838, when 113,971 voters sustained it against 112,759 who opposed—a slim majority of 1,212 votes out of 225,000.

The Buckshot War Almost from the day of Ritner's election, politicians began to lay plans for his successor. The repudiation of anti-Masonry in the legislative elections of 1836 gave new heart to the Democrats, and the sudden onslaught of the Panic of 1837 in May further enlarged their hopes, for its unhappy local effects could be blamed on Ritner just as the 1819 panic had been laid at Findlay's door. When it appeared as if the old Muhlenberg-Wolf division would again plague the Democrats, Senator Buchanan worked out with Van Buren the means to remove both leaders from the 1838 contest by awarding them Federal jobs. Van Buren sent Muhlenberg abroad as United States Minister to Austria, and gave Wolf the choicest political plum in Pennsylvania, Collector of the Port of Philadelphia. With these men out of the way, the Democratic nominating convention of March 4, 1838, named David

R. Porter of Huntingdon County the party's candidate for governor. Porter had made a name for himself by winning a seat in the state Senate in 1836 in a district which the Anti-Masons thought they controlled.

The Anti-Masons, realizing that most of the emotional appeal had drained out of the Masonic issue, employed the internal improvements funds to buy votes. They promised public works projects and jobs to localities where they needed more support at the polls. Thaddeus Stevens, as chairman of the Canal Commission, arranged that the party leaders should travel over the State Works slowly, listen to local requests, and recommend the assignment of public works money where it appeared politically useful. Stevens strengthened his own control in Adams County by authorizing the building of a railroad out of Gettysburg over a route so winding that Democrats called it the "Tapeworm Railroad," designed to create political jobs rather than serve any transportation need.

The Anti-Masons actively attacked the Jacksonians for precipitating the Panic of 1837 by the Specie Circular, a proposition easier to defend than the assertion of Democrats that Ritner should be blamed. To enhance Ritner's image as a powerful executive, the Anti-Masons canvassed the banks of the state to learn when they planned to resume specie payments which had remained suspended since May 1837. They arranged with bankers that Ritner should issue a proclamation on July 13, 1838, ordering all banks to redeem their notes in coin on August 13. At Harrisburg, when the banks opened at nine o'clock on the appointed day, the tellers began to shell out "white boys and yellow boys" (silver and gold coins), and in celebration of it "the mountains and valleys of the Susquehanna resounded with the roar of cannon." The party staged the whole affair superbly and gained political credit for what the banks had already decided to do.

The election returns of October 9, 1838, showed that Porter had received 127,821 votes and Ritner, 122,325. In the legislative election, however, the seats of eight assemblymen from Philadelphia remained in contest because of alleged fraud and two delegations came to Harrisburg, each claiming legitimacy. The eight contested seats would determine which party held a legislative majority, and the Legislature would certify the vote for governor. The Anti-Mason leaders felt certain that if they controlled the Legislature, they could find means to invalidate the 5,000 odd votes which stood between Ritner and a second term as governor. Secretary of the Commonwealth Thomas H. Burrowes issued a statement calling for investigation of the whole election and urged Anti-Masons in the meantime to proceed "as if we had not been defeated."

Efforts to organize the House failed, street mobs invaded the legislative hall and started a riot, and soon two assemblies went into session, one composed of fifty-six Democrats called the "Hopkins House" and the other composed of fifty-two Whigs and Anti-Masons called the "Cunningham House." Each included its own set of eight disputed members without which neither had a legal majority. For a time, angry partisan mobs in Harrisburg threatened both chambers. The Governor called for Federal troops in Carlisle to keep order and, when they refused, ordered state militia from Philadelphia. Major General Robert Patterson told the troops to arm themselves with buckshot cartridges before they marched to Harrisburg, and this order gave currency to the term "Buckshot War" which the press put into circulation.

During the first week of December 1838, while the militia mobilized, thousands of armed Democrats began an unorganized descent upon the capital to fight, if need be, for Porter. Few at that time knew that Patterson had declined to use his force for any purpose beyond the protection of life and property, but many feared that Ritner proposed to seize the governorship. Shortly, however, five Whig and Anti-Mason senators, outraged by the entire proceeding, bolted and joined the twelve Democratic senators in recognizing the Hopkins House as legal. This 17–16 vote in the Senate broke Anti-Mason resistance. The Legislature certified the vote making Porter the next Governor and ended the Buckshot War barely in time for the inauguration ceremonies.

The reign of anti-Masonry in Pennsylvania produced few constructive accomplishments. It left the state deeply in debt and, after the repeal of the tax law, with no source of income to meet payments of interest or principal. It had spent the bank bonus money, the borrowed money, and the $3 million received from the Federal government as Pennsylvania's share of the national treasury surplus. It had used these funds to make the canal system produce votes rather than revenue. It turned over to Porter an empty treasury, ruined credit, an immediate threat of bankruptcy, and an expensive public works system geared to political patronage rather than to public transportation.

THE QUEST FOR SOLVENCY

Governor Porter's first term   David R. Porter started his administration auspiciously by avoiding the feud between the Wolves and the Mules. He chose personal associates for Cabinet, placing Francis R. Shunk, who had guided Democratic strategy during the Buckshot War, in the key position of secretary of the commonwealth. He appointed the neutral William F. Packer to chair the Canal Commission, assisted by a relative of Muhlenberg, Edward B. Hubley, and a friend of Wolf, James Clarke.

As had every governor since 1829, Porter faced a financial crisis from the moment of taking office. Needing $600,000 immediately to pay interest on the state debt, he offered a state loan of $1,200,000, but found no takers. A contemporary student of the state's resources and its financial difficulties, Charles Trego, summed up quite simply the problem and the answer. The state owed $40 million principal on which it had to pay $2 million interest annually. Income from the traffic on the canal system, which people had hoped would pay off the debt, scarcely paid for maintenance and upkeep. State borrowing to pay interest and to improve the public works kept the debt pyramiding and constantly raised the threat of bankruptcy and repudiation. But Pennsylvania had resources of $1,300 million in taxable real estate and $700 million in taxable personal property. A tax of 1 mill, or 10 cents on $100 would pay the annual interest. A 2 percent tax would liquidate the entire principal in a year. Obvious and essential as a tax appeared, the Governor avoided such a proposal, fearing injurious political consequences. But the only alternative, reliance upon bank loans, raised equally difficult problems since the national Democratic party had declared war on banks. Porter had to call for unpopular taxes, or curry favor with banks; if he chose the latter course he had to aid the bankers in return for loans but produce the popular impression that he remained their enemy. Such skilled tightrope walking constitutes part of the political craft. Porter, without much experience, determined to try it.

Unwilling to call for taxes, he made a quiet deal with Biddle's bank for a loan of $2 million, in return for which he promised not to hold the bank to some restrictive provisions in its 1836 Pennsylvania charter. When, in October 1839, another recession developed and many Pennsylvania banks suspended specie payments for their notes, Porter asked the Legislature to treat the banks with "forbearance and moderation" and to give them time. As the presidential campaign of 1840 had already begun, this pronouncement threw consternation into the Van Buren ranks, for these Hard-money Democrats had planned to submit a bill calling for immediate resumption of specie payments, with cancellation of the charter of any bank which failed to comply. Porter openly announced that without aid from the banks, Pennsylvania would become financially prostrate. The Hard-money men passed a bill calling for immediate resumption but, when faced with a Porter veto, changed the law to one legalizing the suspension of specie payments until January 15, 1841, with the proviso that non-specie-paying banks would have to subscribe to state loans, and would lose their charters if they failed to resume by the deadline. Thus Porter postponed the major issue until after the presidential election. He also made the desperate financial plight of the commonwealth so clear that the Legislature formulated and passed a bipartisan tax bill on June 14, 1840. So far he had faced his problems like a veteran, for he had obtained his loans, had saved the banks, and had obtained a tax bill, though no one could officially connect him with any of these results.

Meanwhile, the presidential election of 1840 developed. The Whigs held their national nominating convention at Harrisburg in December 1839 and nominated William Henry Harrison for president and John Tyler for vice president. In a wildly emotional campaign making Harrison into the military-hero–common-man image of Jackson, the Whigs held hard-cider, log-cabin, and coonskin-cap rallies, and developed most of the enthusiasm in the canvass.

The Pennsylvania Democrats ran quickly into difficulty over Van Buren, who had few devoted friends in the Keystone State. When the state nominating meeting convened on March 4, 1840, contesting delegations appeared from many counties, the Van Buren Democrats denouncing Governor Porter for his softness on banks, and the Porter men denouncing Van Buren. The Pennsylvania Democrats supported Van Buren's nomination, but by midsummer it had become apparent that the party had developed another split—this time between Porter's "Improvement men" who favored more spending for public works and cooperating with the banks, and Van Buren's Hard-money men who wished no mercy for the banks and cared little about the public works system. Buchanan and a few others tried desperately for harmony but met with little success. Harrison won Pennsylvania 144,018 to Van Buren's 143,675—a result remarkably close considering the intensity of the campaign for "Tippecanoe and Tyler Too," and the apathy of the Van Burenites. Governor Porter now had to look to his own prospects, for he would come up for reelection in the fall of 1841.

Solution of the state's financial crisis The Whig presidential triumph of 1840 carried the party to victory in the Pennsylvania Legislature, though its majority fell short of the votes needed to override a veto. If Harrison had lived, the Whigs would likely have elected a governor in 1841, but when the President died shortly after inauguration and Vice President Tyler entered the White House, the party suffered a severe setback. Tyler gave Federal patronage to Anti-Masons in Pennsylvania, and after he vetoed the Whig bill to recharter the Bank of the United States, Henry Clay's friends read him out of the Whig party. These events gave Porter hope of reelection to the governorship.

With the Democrats out of power in Washington and the Whigs in control of the Pennsylvania Legislature, Porter found conditions favorable for a reconciliation with the Van Burenites whose support he needed for reelection. He made his bid for their friendship in his annual message of January 1841, in which he called for state banking laws to contract the

William Still, one of the creators of the Underground Railroad (Still: *The Underground Railroad*)

Gov. David R. Porter bore the brunt of the state's financial collapse of the 1840s. (Pennsylvania Historical and Museum Commission)

David Wilmot introduced the Wilmot Proviso into Congress, 1846, and became a leader in the early Republican party. (Pennsylvania Historical and Museum Commission)

James Buchanan, fifteenth President of the United States. (Brady Collection, National Archives)

amount of bank capital and to revoke summarily the charter of any bank which suspended specie payments.

But the uncertainties of finance upset his plans. Just a few weeks after his message and the general resumption of specie payments by the banks, another money stringency developed which forced the Pennsylvania banks again to suspend payments. Porter's recommendation to revoke charters now embarrassed him, for he had power under the 1840 law to take such action. The state needed money to pay interest on its prior loans, but Porter could not now make concessions to institutions whose charters, he had just said, ought to be revoked. Porter let the Whig Legislature bear the brunt of the crisis and avoided the subject until after the Democratic convention of March 4, 1841, which renominated him for governor. The Whigs passed a bill on April 8 to prevent the revocation of bank charters and to give time for resuming specie payments, but Porter vetoed it to keep the good will of the Hard-money men.

On April 30, the Whig Legislature passed what it called the "Relief Bill," providing for additional state taxes, permitting banks to suspend specie payments, and requiring them to buy state bonds on the value of which they could issue low-denomination bank notes. This bill contained all the features most hated by the Hard-money men: it prolonged the life of Biddle's bank, expanded bank capital, and put banknotes which would depreciate into the pay envelopes of workmen. Porter vetoed it, as anticipated, but his friends in the Legislature, the Improvement men, joined the Whigs to pass the bill over the veto.

Porter won reelection in 1841, but his financial troubles continued into his second term. Shortly after his election a movement developed to sell the State Works and to repudiate the entire state debt. This served only to depress still further the value of the state's bonds and to frighten the holders of the debt at home and abroad. Porter, in his message of January 1842, pledged himself to oppose firmly either debt repudiation or sale of the canal system, and received a unanimous sustaining vote from the Legislature.

For two years the state failed to pay interest on the public debt, a serious blow to Pennsylvania prestige especially in foreign banking circles, but Porter ultimately paid the obligations of the commonwealth in full, including interest on the overdue interest. The bank struggle in Pennsylvania history exposed the proclivity of elected officials to buy the favor of constituents with borrowed money to be paid by later generations, rather than to place squarely on the shoulders of the beneficiaries the cost of current government programs.

The elections of 1844   In 1844 the people of Pennsylvania faced another of those convulsive political years in which they would ballot for governor in October and for president in November. The presidential canvass began early because Tyler's administration, representing neither major party, raised the hopes of would-be candidates in both. Senator James Buchanan had played a waiting game but thought he might win the 1844 nomination if a united Pennsylvania Democracy would support him. His friends called a state convention at Harrisburg which placed his name before the public on January 10, 1843, just a few hours after the state Legislature had reelected him to the Senate. Buchanan's early nomination as a favorite son brought his name to the masthead of many Democratic newspapers and provoked quick counteraction.

The Van Burenites, led by George M. Dallas and Henry A. Muhlenberg, stirred up a vigorous Philadelphia-oriented campaign for Van Buren. Governor Porter's Improvement men, who disliked both Buchanan and Van Buren, turned their attention to the renomination of Tyler as a Democrat, hoping thereby to gain Porter the vice-presidential place on the ticket. The Whigs, as expected, nominated Henry Clay on May 1, 1844.

By the time the Democratic convention assembled at Baltimore on May 27, both Clay and Van Buren had weakened themselves by public letters opposing the annexation of Texas. With Pennsylvania's Hendrick B. Wright in the chair, the Democrats chose the outspoken expansionist, James K. Polk, as the presidential nominee. To conciliate the disappointed Van Burenites and gain Pennsylvania support, the convention made George M. Dallas the nominee for vice president. The Pennsylvania delegation, and especially Buchanan's friends in it, played a significant role in Polk's success and had put Polk in their debt.

The state Democrats, meanwhile, had weathered another factional contest to nominate a governor in 1844. One leading candidate, Francis R. Shunk, had resigned as Porter's secretary of the commonwealth after the Governor's friends attacked Buchanan's presidential aspirations. Buchanan's friends now supported Shunk for the governorship. Henry Muhlenberg, backed by the Dallas people, also wanted the nomination. Contesting delegations nearly broke up the convention until Buchanan managed to persuade Shunk to withdraw to preserve party unity. The Democrats then nominated Muhlenberg. But on August 11, two months before election, Muhlenberg died, and a second Democratic convention gave Shunk the nomination. The friends of Muhlenberg acceded grudgingly after Shunk had promised to share the patronage with them.

Separate issues developed in the campaigns for governor and for president. The Native American riots in Philadelphia in 1844 made anti-Catholicism the major theme of the race for governor, whereas fears that Polk would repeal the popular Tariff of 1842 dominated the presidential canvass. For some years Philadelphia had experienced a heavy influx of Irish Catholics. Like many newcomers, they settled thickly together in one part of the city, retained their old-country habits and customs, and willingly obeyed the bidding of ward politicians who hurried them through the naturalization process and organized them into a voting bloc.

Ill feeling quickly developed in the public schools where the Protestants, as a matter of course, read their own version of the Bible. The parents of Irish-Catholic children, as a matter of course, objected. Fear and hatred of Catholicism, which had induced many earlier Europeans to come to America, still persisted. The rapid rise in Catholic immigration stimulated bigots to stir up Protestants against Catholics.

A political association of Native Americans developed in Philadelphia in the 1830s and revived strongly in the 1840s. A Native American party meeting in Kensington in May 1844 detonated a week-long riot in the Irish quarter. Mobs roamed the Kensington area burning Catholic churches and finally exploded into such violence that Governor Porter personally escorted the state militia to the city to restore order. The Nativists continued to hold massive demonstrations in Philadelphia and in July stirred up a second and more serious tumult which killed and injured many soldiers and rioters. The anti-Catholic disorders came prominently into the campaign for governor when Nativist newspapers reported that candidate Shunk had recommended an end to Bible reading in schools where it caused religious collision, and that Shunk himself was Catholic. Shunk denied membership in the Catholic church, but admitted that he had suggested that schools ought not to persist in a classroom custom which set children at each other's throats. The Native American issue brought little response from the rural regions where few Catholics lived, and Shunk won the governorship over the Whig candidate, Joseph Markle, by a small majority, 160,322–156,040.

The presidential candidates both posed in Pennsylvania as champions of protection for local manufactures. Clay had the better of the argument, but Polk, under heavy pressure, wrote a special letter to John K. Kane of Philadelphia for use in the Keystone State which the local Democrats paraphrased and editorialized into a stirring defense of protection. Polk's bold demand for the reannexation of Texas and the reoccupation of Oregon also appealed to many. For whatever reasons, Pennsylvania gave Polk a slim majority of 7,000 and the electoral votes of the state he had to carry to enter the White House. With Polk and Dallas elected, knowledgeable politicians considered it a foregone conclusion that Senator Buchanan would be offered the major Cabinet post, Secretary of State, in recognition of his services during the convention and the campaign.

PENNSYLVANIA POLITICS DURING THE MEXICAN WAR

The success of Shunk and Polk in 1844, both of whom emerged as surprise winners, set off another spirited factional scramble for influence and jobs. Polk, as expected, made Buchanan Secretary of State but did not gratify Buchanan's wishes for appointments for his friends. Dallas received so few patronage favors that he stopped making recommendations to the President in order to avoid the embarrassment of seeing his candidates rejected. Hendrick B. Wright's followers, the Muhlenberg Improvement men, and minor city cliques of Democrats all sought a share. But because Pennsylvania Democrats had no single spokesman, the patronage Polk did assign to the state carried little party value; rather the appointments served to strengthen the cliques, and this weakened the party as a whole.

Shunk, as Governor, adopted a different patronage policy. Rather than spread the appointments among many claimants, he concentrated them among his own friends. Had he served longer as a leader, this tactic might have brought him strength, but as a newcomer who had promised just a few months before to share patronage, his firm but exclusive policy solidified the Muhlenberg men and goaded them into an alliance with the Whigs. On March 14, 1845, they defeated Shunk's candidate for United States senator and elected Simon Cameron by allying with the Whigs and Native Americans. Cameron's defiance and his defeat of the Democratic caucus nominee led many party leaders to denounce him, but he proved too powerful to be ousted.

The Tariff of 1846 By the summer of 1846 the Mexican War had started, raising an outcry in the North that Polk had committed an aggression on a weak neighbor and planned to use the war to expand the slave area of the United States. Also, presumably to gratify the South, Polk desired a drastic reduction in the protective tariff rates of 1842. The national House of Representatives passed such a bill, the Walker-McKay Tariff, in July 1846, though every Pennsylvania congressman but David Wilmot voted against it. Wilmot, representing the Northern Tier lumbering district, felt little local pressure for protection.

In Harrisburg, both houses of the Legislature expressed disapproval. It seemed like another case of Jacksonian betrayal; Polk in 1844 had been described to the voters as more favorable to protection than Clay. Now he had offered, as a party measure, a tariff which the newspapers called free trade. When the vote in the United States Senate brought a tie, with both Pennsylvania's Senators opposing the bill, Vice President Dallas had to decide the issue. In one of the most courageous acts of his life, he cast the deciding vote which passed the Walker bill.

The Tariff of 1846 greatly embarrassed the Pennsylvania Democrats and gave the Whigs an easy target. They had only to contrast the pledges of Democrats with the performance.

The Whigs swept their candidates into state and national legislative posts in the fall, and hoped to oust Shunk the following year. But special factors prevented the low 1846 tariff from causing the anticipated slowdown of business. The demands of war, European crop failure, the stabilization of currency, and other events created a business upturn, so that the gloomy predictions of the Whigs never came to pass. The Democrats shortly took heart and began to praise the tariff bill they had so recently been condemning.

The Wilmot Proviso The return of prosperity saved Governor Shunk, for the Improvement men who had joined the Whigs to elect Cameron and planned now to shelve Shunk for their own candidate could not muster the necessary votes. The Democrats renominated Shunk at their convention of March 4, 1847. The Whigs named a Centre County ironmaster who had voted for the Tariff of 1842, James Irvin. The Native Americans made a separate nomination, Emanuel Reigart of Lancaster. For a time the Whigs set the campaign tone by vigorously attacking the Democrats for the Mexican War and the tariff, but major military victories began to make the war popular, and assaults on the tariff proved ineffective.

On August 8, 1846, David Wilmot proposed that Congress should exclude slavery from any Mexican territory acquired as a result of the war. The House of Representatives passed this, and the Pennsylvania House and Senate adopted bipartisan resolutions approving it. The United States Senate, however, rejected the Wilmot Proviso. From this moment the concept of "free soil" or no further extension of slavery began to spread widely in the North. But the Wilmot Proviso played little part in the Pennsylvania election of 1847. Buchanan worked out the Democratic answer to slavery in the territories in his "Berks County letter" of August 1847, proposing extension of the Missouri Compromise line westward as far as Federal territory should extend. Buchanan's suggestion received such widespread local endorsement that it crowded the Wilmot Proviso out of the press and neutralized its effect on the election. Shunk won an easy victory over Irvin, 146,000–128,000, while Reigart, the Nativist candidate, polled only 11,000 votes.

The downfall of the Democrats As the presidential election of 1848 approached with the certainty that Polk would step down, a crowd of Democratic hopefuls again initiated plans for the nomination. Dallas thought himself an obvious choice, for he was strong in Philadelphia and Pittsburgh, but he lacked a party organization in most of the central counties. Buchanan had a stronger position nationally, but needed the unified support of Pennsylvania to be seriously considered in a national convention.

After Shunk's reelection, the Legislature endorsed Buchanan as Pennsylvania's choice, and in March 1848 a state Democratic convention pledged the entire state delegation to him. Buchanan had a fair run for the 1848 Democratic nomination, losing eventually to Lewis Cass of Michigan. The Whigs, holding their national nominating convention in Philadelphia in June, named General Zachary Taylor. The issue of slavery in the territories figured largely in the campaign, for the friends of the Wilmot Proviso now formed a new national party, called the Free-Soil party, and nominated Martin Van Buren for president.

As the presidential campaign progressed, Governor Shunk suddenly resigned on July 9 because of an illness which made it impossible to perform his work. Acting-Speaker of the Senate, William F. Johnston, a Whig, became acting-Governor and immediately called for a general election on October 10 to fill the governor's chair. The law permitted him to remain acting-Governor for a year, but he preferred to have an early popular choice. The Whigs nominated Johnston, and the Democrats picked one of their canal commissioners, Morris Longstreth of Montgomery County. Johnston won the governorship with 168,522 votes to 168,225 for Longstreth—a majority of only 297. Pennsylvania gave General Zachary Taylor 185,423 popular ballots and the entire electoral vote of the state, while Cass trailed with 172,704 and the Free-Soil party mustered only 11,273 for Van Buren.

In the major contest, the Whig victory in Pennsylvania reflected popular response to the candidates as personalities rather than to issues. The Whigs won because of dissension among the Democrats and because General Taylor was a military hero. The Democrats lost because they had failed to resolve the continuing intraparty contest for leadership which now involved Buchanan, Dallas, and Cameron. In a half century of effort, Pennsylvania's dominant party had not yet succeeded in establishing effective discipline at either county or state levels.

BIBLIOGRAPHY

The most detailed studies are Klein: *Pennsylvania Politics, 1817–1832,* already cited, and Charles McCool Snyder: *The Jacksonian Heritage: Pennsylvania Politics, 1833–1848* (1958). E. Malcolm Carroll: *Origins of the Whig Party* (1925); Henry R. Mueller: *The Whig Party in Pennsylvania* (1922); Charles McCarthy: "The Anti-Masonic Party: A Study in Political Anti-Masonry in the United States, 1827–1840," *American Historical Association Annual Report,* vol. 1 (1903), pp. 365–574; and Sister M. Theophane Geary: *A History of Third Parties in Pennsylvania, 1840–1860* (1938) provide scholarly studies of the main parties. A modern reinterpretation has been prepared by Richard P. McCormick: *The Second American Party System: Party Formation in the Jacksonian Era* (1966), which analyzes party management and structure in each state.

Excellent contemporary accounts of Pennsylvania politics are given by Alexander K. McClure: *Old Time Notes of Pennsylvania,* 2 vols. (1905); and *A Philadelphia Perspective: The Diary of Sidney George Fisher Covering the Years 1834–1871,* edited by Nicholas B. Wainwright (1967).

The best books on the tariff are Malcolm R. Eiselen: *Rise of Pennsylvania Protectionism,* previously cited, and Frederick W. Taussig: *Tariff History of the U.S.,* 8th ed. (1931). On anti-Masonry see J. Cutler Andrews: "The Anti-Masonic Movement in Western Pennsylvania," *Western Pennsylvania Historical Magazine,* vol. 18 (1935), pp. 255–266; and William H. Egle: "The Buckshot War," *Pennsylvania Magazine of History and Biography,* vol. 23 (1899), pp. 137–156. The Constitution of 1838 is covered in *Pennsylvania Constitutional Convention, 1837–1838 Journal,* 2 vols. (1838); *Proceedings and Debates,* 14 vols. (1837); Roy H. Akagi: "The Pennsylvania Constitution of 1838," *Pennsylvania Magazine of History and Biography,* vol. 48 (1924), pp. 301–333; and Frank B. Sessa: "Walter Forward in the Pennsylvania Constitutional Convention of 1837–1838." *Western Pennsylvania Historical Magazine,* vol. 20 (1937), pp. 113–122.

On the Wilmot Proviso, see Richard R. Stenberg: "The Motivation of the Wilmot Proviso," *Mississippi Valley Historical Review,* vol. 18 (1932), pp. 535–541; and Chaplain W. Morrison: *Democratic Politics and Sectionalism: The Wilmot Proviso Controversy* (1967).

References on the State Works will be found at the end of Chapter 14. For sectional commercial rivalries, see James W. Livingood: *The Philadelphia-Baltimore Trade Rivalry, 1780–1860* (1947); Catherine E. Reiser: *Pittsburgh's Commercial Development, 1800–1850* (1951); Frank F. Crall: "A Half Century of Rivalry between Pittsburgh and Wheeling," *Western Pennsylvania Historical Magazine,* vol. 13 (1930), pp. 237–255; and Joseph S. Clark, Jr.: "The Railroad Struggle for Pittsburgh," *Pennsylvania Magazine of History and Biography,* vol. 48 (1924), pp. 1–38.

On the patronage, see Carl Russell Fish: *The Civil Service and the Patronage* (1905); Ralph W. Wescott: *The Customs Service in Philadelphia 1789–1834* (1934); and Donald W. Mumford: "Andrew

Jackson and the Executive Patronage in Pennsylvania," (master's thesis, University of Pittsburgh, Pittsburgh, 1949).

Biographies of important Pennsylvanians include: Lee F. Crippen: *Simon Cameron, the Antebellum Years* (1942); Charles B. Going: *David Wilmot, Free Soiler* (1924); Robert L. Mohr: *Thomas Henry Burrowes, 1805–1871* (1946); and the previously cited studies of Nicholas Biddle by Govan, of James Buchanan by Klein, and of the Muhlenbergs by Wallace.

CHAPTER TWELVE

Antislavery Politics: 1848–1861

The Quakers of Pennsylvania conducted a spirited and persistent campaign against human slavery from the earliest days of settlement. Friends and Mennonites of Germantown petitioned for the abolition of slavery in 1688. The Yearly Meeting of Friends condemned slavery in 1754 and urged general emancipation. The early Quakers took a leading part in the creation of the Pennsylvania Society for the Abolition of Slavery in 1775, and in 1776 the Philadelphia Friends' Meeting disowned slaveholders. In 1780, when about 6,000 Negro slaves lived in Pennsylvania, the state adopted the first abolition law in the nation. Although this gradual emancipation law had loopholes, the Pennsylvania courts so consistently supported the concept of personal freedom that local citizens found it nearly impossible to hold slaves after 1808.

THE ANTISLAVERY WHIGS

Antislavery in Pennsylvania   During the national excitement over slavery which accompanied the Missouri Compromise controversy in 1820, Pennsylvania passed "An Act to Protect Free Negroes and to Prevent Kidnapping," the first of the personal liberty laws to be enacted in the United States. This law gave to county judges the power to try fugitive cases, and made it a felony for anyone to capture an alleged fugitive slave unless he held a warrant from a judge. Maryland protested because under this act a Maryland slaveholder might be convicted of kidnapping if he recovered a runaway without having first obtained a warrant, and the time required to obtain a warrant usually enabled the fugitive to make good his escape. To ease growing tensions with Maryland, Pennsylvania adopted a new personal liberty law in 1826 which enabled a master to obtain a warrant from any member of the minor judiciary.

The smouldering resentment about slavery broke through the barriers of apathy in the early 1830s with Nat Turner's rebellion in Virginia and the publication in Boston of William Lloyd Garrison's inflammatory abolitionist newspaper, the *Liberator*. Led largely by James and Lucretia Mott, Quaker Philadelphia quickly became a focal point for abolitionist activity. A striking fact about Pennsylvania abolitionism was the active participation of Negroes in the movement. Philadelphia County had a Negro population of about 15,000 in 1830, many of whom were well-to-do and equipped for leadership. They promoted the first national Negro Convention there in the fall of 1830, stressing not only the abolition of slavery, but equally the improvement of the "forlorn and deplorable" conditions faced by Negro freemen. Three Philadelphia Negroes played a dynamic role in the national abolition movement: James Forten, wealthy sailmaker who made Philadelphia blacks the largest single bloc of subscribers to the *Liberator;* Robert Purvis, gentleman farmer who lived on a beautiful estate at Byberry and became president of the American Antislavery Society; and William Still, who promoted and wrote a famous history about the Underground Railroad.

In December 1833, a convention in Philadelphia organized the American Antislavery Society which, within a few years, had produced over a thousand local branches in Northern states. Four years later at Harrisburg, delegates from thirty local antislavery societies met to form the Pennsylvania State Antislavery Society.

Pennsylvania's population divided on the questions of the abolition of slavery and of race relations. Pennsylvania had taken its stand against slavery in 1780 and by 1831 no slave under fifty years old could have been legally held there. The colonial laws restricting Negroes had been removed and free Negroes after 1780 stood on a plane of legal equality with whites. Many became freeholders, attained economic security, and in some cases became wealthy like Joseph Casey, Philadelphia money broker, or Stephen Smith, lumber merchant of Columbia who was reputed to be the richest Negro in the nation. As blacks evolved from slaves into bondsmen or apprentices and then into freemen in Philadelphia, where they mainly congregated, they began at first to form a respected part of the community. But as their position improved, their future prospects declined for two reasons. First, their success attracted large numbers of Southern blacks who did not fit into the local economy and thus became a burden upon it. Second, new European immigrants resented competition from the better-trained, native-born Negroes and stirred up race prejudice in the city. Although state law did not restrict blacks, public custom excluded them from theaters, churches, meetings, Fourth of July rallies at Independence Square, public transport, intermarriage with whites, voting, militia service, and many jobs. Pennsylvania in the 1830s comprised a white society which detested slavery but also rejected free blacks as colleagues and neighbors. The new state constitution of 1838 excluded blacks from voting.

As the abolitionists and other reformers could not easily find meeting places in which to hold lectures and discussions, their leaders formed a stock company and erected a magnificent building in Philadelphia dedicated to free speech. With several auditoriums, offices for reform societies, a library, gaslight, a ventilating system, and other innovations, Pennsylvania Hall on the day of its dedication on May 14, 1838, was one of the finest edifices in the city. Three days later it was a smoking ruin, burned to the ground by an infuriated mob which had been inflamed by rumors and galvanized to action by the sight of blacks and whites walking arm in arm to a scheduled antislavery meeting. For a week the mob raged through the Negro district of the city, burning and pillaging.

In 1842 the Supreme Court of the United States in the decision *Prigg v. Pennsylvania* unanimously declared unconstitutional the Pennsylvania personal liberty law of 1826. This decision also voided the laws of other Northern states which had imitated Pennsylvania procedure. The justices wrote that the Federal Fugitive Slave Act of 1793 superseded all state laws and that this act did not require state assistance for its enforcement. As the 1793 statute had not created a Federal enforcement agency, *Prigg v. Pennsylvania* rendered the law almost useless, and the northward flow of fugitives set in more strongly than ever. The Underground Railroad sprang into being, composed of people of both races who received fugitives and secretly aided their flight north from slavery. The towns of Chester, Columbia, York, Gettysburg, and Chambersburg, all near the Mason-Dixon line, became important Southern terminals of the Underground Railroad which provided many alternate escape routes to Canada.

On March 3, 1847, Pennsylvania passed another personal liberty law which conformed to the *Prigg* decision. This act made it a crime for any state magistrate to hear a fugitive case, for a jailer to use a state prison to detain fugitives, and for anyone to capture an alleged fugitive from labor. The new law reflected in part the repugnance of Pennsylvanians to the whole process of slave hunting and in part the belief of Pennsylvania manufacturers that to oppose the economic policies of Southern Democrats, they also had to oppose slavery. Whatever the motives for its passage, the 1847 personal liberty bill effectively nullified the Federal Fugitive Slave Act of 1793 in Pennsylvania.

The Compromise of 1850 in Pennsylvania Governor William F. Johnston, a native of Westmoreland County, entered politics as a Democratic assemblyman, switched to the Whig party because he favored a high tariff, and became a Whig state senator in 1847. His election to the presidency of the Senate and to the governorship within the space of one year signified the high regard of his colleagues for his ability. Johnston began his administration at the moment that the United States entered the convulsive struggle over whether slavery should be permitted to enter any of the territory acquired from Mexico.

During the winter of 1849–1850, the nation approached the brink of secession over this issue, for California suddenly applied for admission as a free state. Her entry would force the slave states into the position of a perpetual minority, for by 1850 the South retained a veto power only in the Senate, with fifteen free and fifteen slave states. If California came in as a free state, the South would place itself at the mercy of the more populous free states in every branch of the Federal government.

This prospect highlighted the crisis and the drama of the Compromise of 1850. The South accepted the admission of California as a free state, with all its portentous implications, but demanded as its share of the compromise a new fugitive slave law. This part of the compromise—essentially the only concession the South gained—aimed not only at the physical delivery of fugitives but also at testing the good faith of the North. This good faith would be measured by the North's willingness to support the new law which gave force to Article IV, Section 2, of the United States Constitution.

The Fugitive Slave Law of 1850, to surmount the difficulties raised by the *Prigg* case, created a Federal enforcement agency. Federal commissioners could issue warrants for arrest, Federal marshals could deputize local citizens on the spot to assist in captures,

Federal officers would hear cases, alleged fugitives could not testify, and obstructionists faced stiff penalties. The new law threatened every Negro in the North, whether fugitive or resident freeman, and made a criminal of anyone who refused a Federal marshal's call to hunt down a fugitive.

Governor Johnston in his annual messages stated that although Pennsylvania disapproved of slavery, it would always rigorously protect all constitutional rights of the South, but the frenzied outcry against the Fugitive Slave Law caused him to hedge. Over 200 blacks fled from Pittsburgh within a week after the passage of the bill. Johnston, in his message of January 1851, said that Pennsylvanians would have to submit to the law, but that they ought to bestir themselves to make Congress change it. His statement ran directly counter to a strong national bipartisan movement to accept the 1850 Compromise as "a finality," a view shared by leading Whigs and Democrats who believed that the survival of the Union depended upon quieting the agitation about slavery.

The Christiana Riot and the election of 1851 The Pennsylvania election of 1851 quickly commanded wide national attention because it would test the Northern response to the compromise measures in a large and conservative state. Furthermore, it would provide an early indication of strength of presidential candidates in both parties. The Democrats, meeting at Reading on June 6, nominated William Bigler of Clearfield County for governor, a triumph for the faction which hoped to nominate James Buchanan for the presidency in 1852. But the Democrats still had to contend with the anti-Buchanan faction, now led by Simon Cameron, who strenuously endorsed Lewis Cass of Michigan for president. The convention adopted resolutions upholding the Compromise of 1850 as a final solution of the slavery controversy.

At Lancaster on June 24, a convention dominated by Free-Soil Whigs renominated Governor Johnston. Their resolutions called for a high tariff, supported General Winfield Scott for the presidency, declared opposition to any extension of slavery, and rejected a resolution to pledge support to the Fugitive Slave Law. These resolutions split the Pennsylvania Whigs between the "National" faction which followed President Fillmore in approving the 1850 Compromise measures as a finality, and the "Free-Soil" or "Conscience Whig" faction which proposed an alteration of the Fugitive Slave Law as soon as possible. Thus the Democrats had united on support of the finality of the Compromise of 1850, whereas the Whigs had divided over it. The parties seemed about evenly matched until the Christiana Riot on September 11. This local incident, just a few weeks before election, directed the national spotlight on Pennsylvania and sharply illuminated the emphasis which Bigler's Democrats had placed on enforcement of the Fugitive Slave Law.

The Christiana affair had been in the making for several years. In 1849 a free Negro named Abraham Johnson allegedly stole some grain from the Maryland farm of Edward Gorsuch with the aid of four of Gorsuch's slaves. When they became apprehensive that they would be discovered, they fled to Christiana, in southern Lancaster County, where a group of free Negroes pledged protection to the fugitives. In September 1851 Gorsuch received a letter advising him that he could easily reclaim his four slaves if he came to Philadelphia and used the procedures established by the new Fugitive Slave Law.

Gorsuch, with his son and four other Marylanders, then came to Christiana, Pennsylvania, and, in company with a Federal marshal armed with warrants, proceeded to the house of William Parker where the fugitives had gathered. In the meantime, William Still's vigilance committee in Philadelphia had alarmed the countryside. Local blacks assembled to aid Parker, and local whites would give the marshal neither information nor aid. On September 11, Gorsuch's party approached the Parker house where a violent verbal exchange occurred for about twenty minutes. The marshal, seeing his party outnumbered, wanted to withdraw, but Gorsuch refused. The blacks then emerged from the house and a fracas ensued in the course of which Edward Gorsuch was killed and his son Dickinson critically wounded by gunfire. One of the Negroes saved young Dickinson's life by throwing himself on top of him while infuriated women from Parker's house were hacking the older Gorsuch's body with corn cutters and scythes. The slave hunters now withdrew and many of the blacks fled to the home of Frederick Douglass in Rochester, New York, who shipped them on to Toronto, out of reach of United States law.

The Christiana Riot polarized thought on the slavery issue, each side exploiting it to the fullest. The Southern press dwelt on the fact that Gorsuch represented the highest type of manhood, a kindly master, an honest and generous employer, and the pride of his local community. That such a man, trying to perform an act in explicit accordance with the directions of the Federal Constitution and the law of the land, should be murdered in the attempt, meant only that the North no longer cared about the Constitution and the law. In short, the Compromise of 1850 had been a swindle; the North had seized the power and repudiated the responsibility. From this moment, serious thought of secession occupied many Southern minds.

The abolitionists, on the other hand, drew an equally vivid picture from their viewpoint. The Negroes at Christiana had defended "the just rights of man against manstealers and murderers." William Parker became the heroic figure, a living proof that Negroes understood the "sweetness of liberty" and were as ready as any to lay down their lives in its defense.

Coming just a few weeks before the state election, the riot had immediate political impact. Governor Johnston had ridden through Christiana on the train at the very time the riot had been in progress, but had not stopped. The conservative press condemned the Governor as a "reckless demagogue" whose course had led to "the bloody triumph of Abolitionism." The Democrats elected William Bigler by a majority of 8,500 and interpreted his success as a rebuke to abolitionism by Pennsylvania. President Millard Fillmore in his annual message of December 1851 expressed his concern about the riot at Christiana, warning that all articles of the Constitution including the one requiring rendition of fugitive slaves "must stand or fall together."

THE CONSERVATIVE DEMOCRATS

Governor William Bigler, born in Cumberland County, had worked on the *Centre Democrat* of Bellefonte and then became editor of the Clearfield *Democrat*. After amassing a fortune in the lumber business along the West Branch of the Susquehanna, he entered politics as a state senator in 1845. At the same time he was elected Governor of Pennsylvania, his brother John became Democratic Governor of California.

Bigler's election outwardly indicated solid Pennsylvania support of James Buchanan as the presidential favorite son in 1852, but within the Democratic party another factional contest had begun. Simon Cameron determined to thwart Buchanan's bid for the presidential nomination in 1852, and then to supplant him as party boss. He had a well-disciplined personal following and received encouragement from businessmen interested in the development of railroads, coal mines, and manufacturing who shared Cameron's desire to gain government support for their enterprises.

Cameron undermined Buchanan's presidential bid in the national Democratic convention of 1852. With his own chance dead, Buchanan promoted the nomination and election of Franklin Pierce who won a massive victory of 254 electoral votes to 42 for the Whig candidate, General Winfield Scott. Buchanan thus weathered Cameron's attack and expected Pierce to give him control of the Pennsylvania patronage. Pierce, however, sent him abroad as Minister to Great Britain, a post of distinction but politically almost useless.

Bigler conducted a conservative administration which served to strengthen the hopes of those who viewed the 1850 Compromise as a final settlement of the slavery issue. But although Bigler made it clear that he intended scrupulously to respect the Federal Constitution and laws, he could do nothing to prevent the growth of private resentment against slavery and slave hunting. Harriet Beecher Stowe's novel, *Uncle Tom's Cabin,* which appeared during the election of 1852, greatly expanded abolitionist sentiment in Pennsylvania, and this sentiment produced another confrontation between the state and Federal governments.

In September 1853 several Virginians and Federal marshals tried to arrest a fugitive slave, William Thomas, then a waiter in a Wilkes-Barre hotel. After a scuffle, Thomas fled and the marshals pursued and wounded him. Local abolitionists aided Thomas to escape, and then had the marshals arrested and imprisoned for assault and battery, under Pennsylvania law. The Federal court ordered their release. In a complicated legal contest between state and Federal courts the luckless marshals were three times imprisoned and three times released. Pennsylvania would not give in until the Federal court invoked the Force Act passed in 1833 to put down nullification by South Carolina.

In 1854 Governor Bigler approved a bill to consolidate the city and county of Philadelphia into a single body politic by making the city limits coextensive with the county. This simplified administration by eliminating some of the overlapping jurisdictions and offices. He carefully supervised the state finances and curtailed some of the worst abuses which had developed within the administration of the State Works, such as rigged bids and the unauthorized issue of scrip by canal officials to pay workers and contractors, which the Legislature had to redeem later. Canal division superintendencies changed so often that the auditors could not keep track of the state's obligations. Bigler tried to promote a sale of the state transportation system for $10 million but could find no takers. Near the end of his term Governor Bigler announced that he would no longer sign "omnibus" or "logrolling" proposals in which local pork-barrel projects appeared as riders to essential bills. The state-owned canal system had nourished this abuse to the point where Charles Ingersoll said of it: "Exchanges of local advantage are the levers that move the whole Commonwealth."

Governor Bigler looked forward confidently to reelection in 1854. The Democrats unanimously renominated him in March, and Cameron pledged his support. In return Bigler promised to promote Cameron's election to the United States Senate when James Cooper's term expired in 1855. The alliance between Cameron and Bigler led temporarily to a disruption of Buchanan's friendship with the Governor, but otherwise the Democratic prospects looked bright. Then, with little warning, the political outlook changed. In May 1854 Congress passed the Kansas-Nebraska Act repealing the Missouri Compromise and opening to slavery a vast western region from which it had been excluded since 1820. The law destroyed the "finality" aspect of the 1850 Compromise, threw the slavery issue back into the center of the political arena, and split every national party. The disruption of the major parties, in turn, opened the door to a discordant new political force—the Know-Nothing party.

THE KNOW-NOTHINGS

The Know-Nothing movement The Free-Soil Democrats of Pennsylvania so strongly opposed the Kansas-Nebraska Act that they abandoned the Bigler Democratic ticket and nominated David Wilmot for governor. Meanwhile the badly split Whigs named James Pollock, an avowed Free-Soiler, as their gubernatorial candidate. The Free-Soil Democrats then withdrew Wilmot's name and pledged their support to Pollock. A new anti-Catholic party, called the Know-Nothings, also endorsed Pollock and soon became the dominant element of the coalition.

In October 1854 Pollock defeated Bigler by 37,000 votes in one of the strangest elections in Pennsylvania history. The Know-Nothings, a political faction the very existence of which remained cloaked in mystery, distributed a large block of disciplined votes at will to elect whichever Whigs and Democrats they had designated. The Know-Nothings pledged themselves to fight "the nefarious designs of Jesuitism" and to destroy Catholicism in America, to stop foreign immigration, and to disfranchise naturalized citizens. They voted for anyone who agreed with these ideas.

The Know-Nothing hysteria mounted at a pace which completely confounded seasoned politicians in Pennsylvania. Since its members took an oath of secrecy, no one not in the group knew anything about it. The members themselves were under instructions to answer all questions relating to the movement with the words: "I know nothing." The Know-Nothings inducted thousands of Pennsylvanians who no longer felt at home in the Whig or Democratic parties. They formed secret lodges, acquired members only by invitation, swore them by oath to give up former allegiances, and required them to obey orders from the dictatorial state Know-Nothing council. The order devised a system of degrees to control the member as a voter and as a public officer. Lodges had secret passwords and signs to prevent infiltration. No public notice of meetings appeared; rather some secret mark placed at a predetermined spot informed the knowing ones of the time and place of a meeting.

On election day some officials were chosen whose names had never publicly been mentioned as candidates. To this day it remains a mystery who belonged to the lodges. Election returns showed clearly enough what candidates had Know-Nothing support, but not whether these candidates belonged to a lodge.

It is easy to explain why the Know-Nothings opposed Bigler and supported Pollock. The Democrats for years had depended upon the Irish vote of Philadelphia to produce needed majorities in statewide elections. In the Pennsylvania election of 1851, the Democrats made a clean sweep of major offices except for James Campbell, candidate for judge of the Supreme Court, who was a Catholic and whose defeat was caused by Nativist sentiment. Bigler appointed him attorney general, and, with Buchanan, successfully pressed Campbell's claims for recognition upon President Pierce, who named him Postmaster General in 1853. These acts inflamed the Nativists, and arrayed the Pennsylvania Know-Nothings against Bigler.

On the other side, Pollock, while serving as a congressman in 1844, had befriended Professor Samuel F. B. Morse, the inventor, who had written some vicious diatribes against the

Catholics. Pollock thus had a record of past associations which commended him to the Know-Nothings.

Still another political force affected the election of 1854—the temperance vote. Neal Dow, who had led Maine to adopt the first state prohibition law in 1851, continued his crusade into Pennsylvania. In January 1854 a huge convention in Harrisburg demanded action from the Legislature, which responded by putting the prohibition question on the ballot in the 1854 election. Pollock, himself a teetotaler, endorsed prohibition; Bigler, who was known to indulge, avoided the issue. Since prohibition lost by only 5,000 votes in a total referendum of 322,000, it was apparent that Pollock gained some support from the prohibitionists. His election stemmed from a combination of Anti-Nebraska Democrats, Whigs, Know-Nothings, and temperance people, but no one could tell with certainty the strength of any part of the coalition.

Bigler's unexpected defeat altered the plans which Cameron had made for election to the United States Senate, for the Know-Nothing coalition now controlled the state Legislature. Cameron had earlier flirted with the Nativists. He had used American (Know-Nothing) party votes to gain the senatorship in 1845, and had stirred up anti-Catholicism to defeat James Campbell. The day after Pollock's election, Cameron went to work to ingratiate himself with the new Legislature, cultivating the Know-Nothings by endorsing Nativist policies, appealing to Free-Soil Democrats by approving the Wilmot Proviso, and seeking Whig support by recommending an increase in tariff rates.

In February 1855 the Whigs and Know-Nothings picked Cameron for senator by a single vote over Andrew Gregg Curtin of Bellefonte, favorite of the Old Whigs. Then someone discovered that more votes had been cast than there were legislators present, and the meeting broke up in disorder. A deadlock between Cameron and Curtin continued throughout 1855 during which Pennsylvania had only one senator. Charges and countercharges between the two candidates aroused deep personal animosity which persisted throughout their lives. More than two dozen legislators publicly charged Cameron with bribery. By October 1855 the coalition which had elected Pollock had so disintegrated that the Democrats won back control of the state Legislature, which promptly ended the fight over the senatorship by naming ex-Governor Bigler to the vacancy. But more important, the events of 1855 permanently separated Simon Cameron from the Democratic party and propelled him into the new Republican party.

Sale of the Pennsylvania State Works   The continuing effort of the commonwealth to dispose of the public transportation system proved the most important local problem of the Pollock administration. The protracted negotiations focused on the Pennsylvania Railroad as the buyer, a corporation which had been the subject of violent sectional controversy from the time of its chartering on April 13, 1846. For years Pittsburgh had been hoping to be the western terminus of the Baltimore and Ohio Railroad, but in 1843 the Pennsylvania charter of the B&O had expired. The Philadelphia people in the Legislature prevented a recharter of the B&O, fearing the diversion of western trade to Baltimore. The Pittsburghers demanded the recharter because without it the B&O would alter its route, already completed to Cumberland, Maryland, and make Wheeling the western terminus. The defeat of the charter so outraged the western Pennsylvanians that they proposed to divide the state along the eastern boundaries of McKean, Clearfield, Huntingdon, and Bedford Counties, and petitioned the Legislature to give up its claims to the western counties. Instead, the Legislature provided for recharter of the B&O, unless the Pennsylvania Railroad acquired $1 million of capital and built 30 miles of roadbed toward Pittsburgh by July 30, 1847. If the Pennsylvania Railroad met the deadlines, the B&O charter would not take effect. By a furious subscription and building campaign, the Pennsylvania Railroad met the requirements, and thus rendered the B&O charter void. By 1854 the Pennsylvania Railroad was able to provide through traffic from Harrisburg to Pittsburgh.

As a part of its 1846 charter, the Pennsylvania Railroad had undertaken to pay a tax to the state of 5 mills per mile for each ton of goods carried between Harrisburg and Pittsburgh to compensate the commonwealth for the loss of receipts from traffic on the Western Division of the State Works, which the railroad paralleled. This tax was lowered to 3 mills in 1848 and rescinded on coal and lumber in 1855, but the company protested that no other railroad in the state had to bear such a tax burden.

We have seen that Governor Bigler found no takers for the State Works at $10 million in 1854. The following year, the commonwealth offered its Western Division directly to the Pennsylvania Railroad for $7,500,000, and asked $1 million more for repeal of the tonnage tax. The railroad rejected the offer. Finally, on May 16, 1857, Governor Pollock was authorized by the Legislature to offer the Western Division to the railroad for $7,500,000, plus $1,500,000 more upon payment of which the Pennsylvania Railroad would become perpetually tax exempt. The railroad would gladly have accepted this; in fact, it drew up the plan, but the courts struck down the perpetual-tax-exemption provision. The Pennsylvania Railroad then agreed to buy for $7,500,000, but to continue liable for the tonnage tax and any others which the state might levy. The Western Division of the Pennsylvania State Works passed to the Pennsylvania Railroad on August 1, 1857. Continuing pressure led the Legislature to rescind the tonnage tax later. By an act of August 21, 1858, the Sunbury and Erie Railroad purchased northern sections of the State Works for $3,500,000.

Before the end of 1857, the voters approved several amendments to the state constitution which prohibited the state or any minor civil divisions from extending credit or becoming a stockholder in any business corporation. This signified, along with the sale of the State Works, the final stage of disenchantment with public ownership, or mixed ownership of transportation ventures. The failure of many of these companies to provide either effective transportation or a financial return, even after liberal public subsidy, turned the people away from the concepts of direct government aid to private business and of state ownership.

THE REPUBLICAN PARTY

In Pennsylvania the Republican party began to take shape at the national Free Democratic party convention which met at Pittsburgh on August 11, 1852, to nominate John P. Hale for president and George W. Julian for vice president. Composed of old Liberty party men and Free-Soilers, its leadership carried over to the future Republican party. The passage of the Kansas-Nebraska Law brought the new party into existence. Several midwestern meetings adopted the term "Republican" early, and Horace Greeley made it national in June 1854 by substituting "Republican" for "Anti-Nebraska" in his *New York Tribune*. In November, David Wilmot began to organize a Republican party in his northeastern Pennsylvania district.

The following spring and summer, David N. White and Russell Errett, editors of the *Daily Pittsburgh Gazette,* promoted the formation of a Republican party in Allegheny County. In early fall of 1855 a group of delegates from ten counties met in Reading "to organize a republican party whose object shall be to place all branches of government actively on the side of liberty." Democrat David Wilmot, Anti-Mason Thaddeus Stevens, and other leaders called for a state Republican convention at Pittsburgh on September 5. The Republican leadership had expected to maintain the coalition which had elected Governor Pollock, but the abolitionists took charge. The radical Republican bravado frightened off the Whigs and the Know-Nothings and gave victory to the Democrats. After this, the Republicans in Pennsylvania usually campaigned under such labels as "Union party" or "Fusion Ticket" or "People's party"—names which emphasized their composite following and softened the divisive impact of antislavery.

On February 22, 1856, an informal Republican convention met at Pittsburgh to perfect a national organization and to lay plans for a summer convention to nominate a presidential candidate. Although Salmon P. Chase of Ohio, a pronounced radical, did much of the promotional work for the Pittsburgh meeting, the conservatives took control of the convention. They recognized that while antislavery sentiment provided a general basis of unity, the new party could not agree on any specific antislavery proposal, but it could appeal to the special interests and particular hatreds of many groups, Nativists, foreign-born, Protestants, businessmen, workingmen, and temperance people—all of whom might respond to attacks on the Democratic machine. The Pittsburgh convention achieved a remarkable degree of harmony considering the heterogeneous elements of which it was composed. It set up a national executive committee including David Wilmot and laid plans for the party's first presidential nominating convention to be held in Philadelphia in June.

The Pennsylvania delegates at Pittsburgh declined to endorse Republican attendance at a Union convention of all anti-Democratic forces already scheduled to meet in Harrisburg on March 26. Though they knew they had to unite with Americans (Know-Nothings), Whigs, and others to win offices, they were wary of any fusion which they could not dominate. The existing state Republican committee set up by Wilmot exemplified their fears: only six of the twenty-seven proclaimed themselves Republicans; the rest retained other party labels or were assumed to be enemies by the partisans at Pittsburgh. But Republican aloofness rested on sound strategy, for the passage of time would certainly bring slavery into sharper focus. This issue would divide every party except the Republicans.

As the presidential nominating conventions approached in the spring of 1856, the Republican party of Pennsylvania had achieved at least a working frame of thoroughly practical politicians who saw the new party as an opportunity to establish a new power structure in the commonwealth which they would control. They pulled back from close contact with abolitionists, fearing the political repercussions, and avoided radical expressions on the slavery question, emphasizing instead the corruption of the Democrats and their disregard of Pennsylvania's economic needs. The Pennsylvania Republicans during the succeeding four years followed the strategy initiated by the Jacksonians during the term of John Quincy Adams: they launched an unrelenting attack on the incumbent President in order to destroy his party at the next election. Ironically, they brought this disruptive strategy into play at the very moment that Pennsylvania, after years of frustrated hope, finally placed a native son in the White House.

BUCHANAN'S PRESIDENCY

The elections of 1856 and 1857: Buchanan and Packer The presidential nominations of 1856 fragmented every Pennsylvania party except the Democrats. The Know-Nothing or American party met in Philadelphia on February 22 to nominate Millard Fillmore and A. J. Donelson. Their action angered part of the delegates who, led by Pennsylvania's ex-Governor Johnston, bolted and formed the antislavery North American party. On June 2, the North Americans nominated John C. Frémont for president with Johnston as his running mate. The Republicans, holding their first national nominating convention on June 19 at Philadelphia, also picked Frémont to head their ticket with William Dayton for vice president. Neither choice pleased the Pennsylvania delegates, for they had preferred John McLean for president and Simon Cameron for vice president. But it is doubtful that any choice could have satisfied the Pennsylvanians, for the delegates of the Keystone State represented every political complexion. Thaddeus Stevens and Joseph Ritner had been Anti-Masons, Henry C. Carey was strong for high tariff, Free-Soiler David Wilmot was known as the "Free Trader," Passmore Williamson was a fanatical abolitionist, James Black a prohibitionist, E. D. Gazzam a hard-core Know-Nothing, and Andrew G. Curtin a Whig and personal enemy of that recently converted political maverick Simon Cameron. It was a motley group, still without effective leadership. While the full Republican convention proved to be a wildly enthusiastic and evangelical crusade to overcome those twin relics of barbarism, "polygamy and slavery," the Pennsylvania portion of it sought the less idealistic objective of overthrowing the Democracy which had become intrenched in the state and nation since 1828.

The Democrats in their Cincinnati convention, June 2 to 5, passed over Pierce and Douglas who both had suffered from their part in the Kansas-Nebraska crisis and chose Pennsylvania's James Buchanan, recently returned from the English mission. His absence during the troubles in Kansas made him acceptable to both Northern and Southern partisans, though the latter, preferring Douglas, accepted him reluctantly. With John C. Breckinridge of Kentucky as the vice-presidential nominee, the Democratic ticket signified an effort of the only national party remaining in the country to avoid sectional extremes and to present candidates representing the borderland that separated aggressive slavocrats from fanatical abolitionists.

After having been in contention for the Democratic presidential nomination in every contest since 1844, Buchanan finally achieved the prize at a time when he was less than eager to have it. He was sixty-five years old and had been in the thick of politics since he was twenty. Born in Franklin County in 1791, he attended Dickinson College and later practiced law in Lancaster. He had been a state assemblyman, a congressman for five terms, and a United States Senator for two terms; had served as Secretary of State under Polk; and had been Minister to Russia and Great Britain. At first a Federalist, he had become a leader of one of the two Pennsylvania Jacksonian factions. Buchanan had never lost a popular election, had avoided association with sectional extremists, and placed preservation of the Union first. He had no sympathy with Northern advocates of civil disobedience or with Southern fire-eaters. He believed that the survival of a nation comprising a multitude of conflicting interests depended upon mutual forbearance, mutual accommodation, the avoidance of extremes, the acceptance of compromise, and the willingness of a majority to give some consideration to the wishes of minorities. Only by such forbearance and restraint could the people avert civil war.

Buchanan's nomination and the fact that many politicians thought Pennsylvania's vote would determine the outcome of the presidential election focused national attention on the campaign in the Keystone State. Buchanan conducted a "front-porch campaign" from his Wheatland estate, conferring there with party leaders from every section. The conservative Old Line Whigs generally gave up their identity and came over to Buchanan. The sons of Daniel Webster and Henry Clay both came to Pennsylvania to campaign for Old Buck. The conglomerate opposition tried desperately to form a united front against the Democrats by promoting fusion tickets in all counties, but the attempt achieved only limited success. In the state election of October, the Democrats won the major state offices, fifteen of twenty-five congressional seats, and a majority in the state Assembly, though they lost control of the state Senate. But their victory was narrow and threw the Democrats into panic about the outcome of the presidential election in November. Buchanan carried the state with 230,772 votes, and this guaranteed his election. Frémont polled 147,963 and Fillmore, 82,202.

Buchanan's election paved the way for the state campaign for governor in 1857. The new President in some ways strengthened and in some ways weakened the Democratic party in his native state. He aroused a natural local pride which helped to unify the party, and conferred patronage lavishly upon Pennsylvania partisans, but his efforts failed to satisfy the massive and long-deferred political debts owed to Pennsylvania Democratic politicians. Furthermore, since Buchanan came into office succeeding one of his own party, he could make new appointments only by firing his own partisans.

In January 1857, two months before inauguration, the Pennsylvania Legislature had to choose a new United States senator. John W. Forney, a fiery and explosive newspaper editor who had been promoting Old Buck for twenty years, desired the place. Buchanan, agonizing over Cabinet choices, gave official endorsement but ineffective practical support to Forney's bid. Simon Cameron, in the meantime, captured the Senate seat by offering sufficient inducements to three pliant Democrats who held the deciding votes. No harder blow could have been given to the Buchanan Democrats. Forney angrily rejected Buchanan's proffer of a rich consular post and began to look elsewhere to advance his fortunes. A little later he would go over to Stephen A. Douglas, and then into the Republican ranks, using his newspaper, the *Philadelphia Press,* with telling effect. Cameron's election, while discomfiting the Democrats, raised problems also for the Republicans; for Cameron now became a major contender for the Republican party's leadership.

The Democratic state convention of March 2 nominated for the governorship William F. Packer of Lycoming County, editor of the *Lycoming Gazette.* Packer had been a Wolf Democrat, a canal commissioner, auditor general under Governor Porter, Speaker of the House, and a state senator, and he was an old friend of Buchanan's.

On March 25 the Republicans and Americans nominated David Wilmot for governor, giving minor places on the ticket to the Americans. As the Republicans dominated this meeting, they determined to endorse policies which would drive off the Americans, force them to stand alone, and thus expose their weakness; they drafted a platform scarcely mentioning nativism. As anticipated, the Americans chose not to support the Union ticket on these terms and held their own "straight-out" convention at Lancaster in June, at which they nominated Isaac Hazlehurst for the governorship and adopted an outright Nativist platform.

Wilmot carried his campaign directly to the people by a stump-speaking tour of the commonwealth. Packer declined an offer to debate Wilmot, but followed his footsteps through the state to refute his arguments. The Republicans generated an aggressive newspaper campaign fiercely attacking Buchanan, but they could not use the powerful tariff issue because their gubernatorial candidate, Wilmot, was notorious as the only Pennsylvania congressman to vote for the low tariff of 1846.

Packer won the election with 188,836 votes, as compared to 146,138 for Wilmot and 28,168 for Hazlehurst. The figures showed that the American party had run its course in Pennsylvania, and that the Democrats had managed to weather the recent storms and continued to be the strongest political entity in the state.

The disruption of the Democrats   The Democratic victories of 1856 and 1857 augured well for a revitalization of the party, but within a year the state organization had fallen to pieces. The slavery issue, the Panic of 1857, the consolidation of the opposition, and Democratic factional squabbles combined to reduce the Democracy to near impotence.

The Lecompton constitution of Kansas brought slavery again to the center of the political stage. Buchanan privately hoped that Kansas would seek admission as a free state, but as President he proposed to avoid sectional acrimony by playing the role of umpire, insisting upon the scrupulous adherence of all parties to legal procedure. As Congress had neglected to enact the usual legislation prescribing the method of summoning a constitutional convention, the territorial Legislature set up rules for voter registration and balloting in Kansas. Because many of the free-state Kansans boycotted both the registration and the delegate election, the Kansas voters chose a proslavery constitutional convention.

The convention at Lecompton produced two constitutions, one with slavery and another without, and in accordance with the Kansas-Nebraska Act, it submitted only the question of slavery to the electorate. Again the free-state people refused to vote, and the proslavery constitution won. The convention sent Buchanan this document for congressional approval. In the meantime, the new Kansas territorial Legislature called for a referendum on the entire constitution; and the free-state people now voted and polled a large majority against the constitution.

The country immediately flew into turmoil, the proslavery people demanding that Buchanan endorse the Lecompton constitution, and the antislavery partisans calling on him to reject it. Buchanan applied the rule book. Neither the President nor a territorial Legislature had authority to negate the will of a state constitutional convention or to repudiate a legally conducted popular election after it had been concluded. The people who had refused to vote when they had the opportunity had to abide by the decision of those who did vote. Buchanan sent the Lecompton constitution to Congress with his approval.

Congress and the nation experienced an emotional paroxysm over the Lecompton constitution from February until May when the compromise English Bill finally passed. Stephen A. Douglas broke with Buchanan over Lecompton, splitting off a segment of Democrats who cooperated with Republicans to defeat approval of the Lecompton document. Governor Packer, in his first message to the Pennsylvania Legislature in January 1858, took ground against Buchanan's position on Lecompton, and John W. Forney, editor of the powerful new paper, the *Philadelphia Press,* openly joined the Douglas dissidents. Although the delegates at the regular Democratic nominating convention at Harrisburg on March 4 endorsed Buchanan's Lecompton policy, the voters in municipal elections at Philadelphia and Reading in May brought defeat to the Democrats, an unheard-of result in these two traditional bastions of Democracy. Yet the Lecompton excitement, which the opposition press publicized as the "sole issue" from February until June, passed rapidly into oblivion in Pennsylvania. By July, Republican papers said little about it, transferring their primary attention to the tariff.

Packer met the financial panic in 1857 by recommending the passage of the Emergency Banking Act which enabled banks to open their doors without meeting the stringent specie requirements of the 1840 banking acts. But the Republican leadership focused directly upon the protective tariff as the issue most profitable to their cause. Morton McMichael, editor of the Philadelphia *North American,* became a blaring trumpet of protectionist doctrine, and Simon Cameron seconded this emphasis. Pennsylvania Republican leaders, recognizing the conservatism of the state on the slavery problem, discussed labels and agreed to drop the term "Republican" because of its national association with abolition, to discard the "Union party" label because it signified a coalition, and to inaugurate the use of the term "People's party." This attractive label implied a unified leadership and a Jackson-type constituency which could accommodate all shades of political opinion. The People's party directed the main emphasis to the need for a high tariff.

The Democrats became defensive on both Lecompton and the tariff. But more important, internal dissension began to rend the party at all levels. Governor Packer publicly disavowed Buchanan's Lecompton policy, and Forney worked on the Governor to widen the breach. Neither as yet became involved with the People's party, but they both separated from the Buchanan Democrats. Factional fights broke out in county after county. Democrat John Hickman led the anti-Buchanan movement in the Chester-Delaware County congressional district, J. W. Cake in the Schuylkill-Northumberland district, and Forney in the Philadelphia district. Democrat William Montgomery led a revolt in the Washington-Greene-Fayette district which Republican John Covode financed in part, and in the most serious fight of all, A. Jordan Schwartz declared war on and defeated Buchanan's most trusted subordinate, Congressman J. Glancy Jones of Berks County, the administration's floor leader in the House and chairman of the Ways and Means Committee. The Buchanan Democrats suffered a crushing defeat in the October 1858 elections, losing most heavily in the coal and iron counties where sentiment was strongest for a higher tariff.

By the beginning of 1859, national turbulence over slavery had quieted. Forney, in April, called a convention of States' Rights Democrats—actually a Douglas meeting—which castigated Buchanan but proved so weak that it dared not enter nominees for the October election. The People's party convened in June, came out for a protective tariff, and added its endorsement of a Federal free-homestead law. Significantly, newspapers favoring the People's party candidates condemned declarations of the Republican national committee against slavery, and emphasized that the People's party was not a Republican organization but a "unique" political phenomenon. In the October elections the People's party again won most of the contests, and beat the Democrats by about 18,000 votes in statewide balloting. The figures seemed innocent enough on the surface, but became alarming when viewed in historical perspective. For the first time since 1828, the Pennsylvania Democrats had lost two state elections consecutively. No one could brush away the evident fact that the power of the Democracy had been broken.

Pennsylvania in the secession crisis During the summer and fall of 1859 a man calling himself Dr. Smith had taken residence in Chambersburg, planning, he said, to start a mining enterprise in northern Virginia. He rented a farm in nearby Maryland to store equipment and received numerous visitors in Chambersburg, but aroused little notice or comment. On October 16, accompanied by thirteen whites and five blacks, Dr. Smith—actually John Brown, leader of the Potowattamie murderers in Kansas—invaded Harper's Ferry, seized the Federal arsenal, and called for a slave revolt. After Federal troops had ended Brown's effort and facts began to filter through, the slavery controversy blazed again with searing intensity. Brown had been financed by a half dozen well-known New England Republicans, some of whom knew in advance the purpose of their aid. Many claimed that the Republican party had a direct connection with the conspiracy, though its leaders hastily disclaimed any.

The Democratic majority in the United States Senate set up a committee to investigate the raid, with the obvious intent of implicating the Republicans. In the House, a coalition of Republicans and Douglas Democrats responded by setting up their own committee to attack President Buchanan. John Covode, Pennsylvania Republican congressman, initiated the House action and became chairman of the investigating committee. It met from March though June 1860, overlapping the meeting time of the Republican and Democratic nominating conventions and gravely affecting the latter. The Covode investigation, an assault by the Douglas Democrats allied with the Republicans against the Buchanan Democrats, contributed to the split of the Democracy that brought two Democratic presidential candidates into the field: Stephen A. Douglas representing the Northern wing; and Buchanan's vice president, John C. Breckinridge, representing the Southern wing. A moderate Constitutional Union party had selected John Bell and Edward Everett in early May. But most important, the Republican party settled on Abraham Lincoln and Hannibal Hamlin at their Chicago convention, May 16 to 18.

Pennsylvania played a major role at the Chicago convention. Its delegation, though divided between the friends of Cameron and the friends of Andrew G. Curtin, was pledged to Cameron as a favorite son. The Republicans generally recognized that the party could win only if it carried Indiana or Illinois and Pennsylvania, and that the nominee must be acceptable to these states. William H. Seward of New York could never carry the Keystone State, for Pennsylvanians had a long-standing resentment of New York politicians. Furthermore, Seward had made vehement antislavery pronouncements that alienated Pennsylvania's conservatives, and he also had angered the Native Americans.

The situation was that if the Republicans softened their position on antislavery and concentrated on the protective tariff and on a homestead law, they might win Pennsylvania. Cameron or Abraham Lincoln could be the standard bearer for such an appeal, but not Seward.

Pennsylvania in 1860 again engaged in one of its periodic dual elections, voting for a governor in October and a president in November. The People's party held the first state nominating convention on February 22 at Harrisburg where it chose Curtin to run for governor. Alexander K. McClure, a newspaper editor from Chambersburg and a partisan of Curtin, became state chairman in charge of campaign finance and strategy.

A week later, at Reading, the Democrats held a remarkably harmonious meeting which chose Henry D. Foster of Westmoreland County as candidate for governor, a man of unimpeachable character with good party connections and a reputation as a friend of the protective tariff policy. Even their opponents agreed that the Democrats could not have picked a stronger candidate.

In April, the new Constitutional Union party held a meeting in Lancaster, decided not to enter the governor's race, but made plans to organize in support of its presidential ticket, Bell and Everett.

The campaigns, as they developed into midsummer, exposed the fractures in both major parties. The split of the national Democracy between the Douglas and Breckinridge wings appeared certain to bring the defeat of both unless some accommodation could be reached which would deny Lincoln the electoral votes of Pennsylvania. On July 2, the Democratic state committee tried to unify the party by proposing that the regular electors, named at Reading in February, should vote for Breckinridge or Douglas, whichever could win. Forney, manager of the Douglas partisans, rejected this proposal ostensibly because it would give the Breckinridge Democrats the advantage, but also because Forney wished to protect himself in the event of Lincoln's success.

The Douglas national committee, however, viewed matters differently and called a meeting at Harrisburg in July which endorsed Foster for governor and asked that all Democrats meet again to reconsider the means of creating a fusion of presidential tickets. This meeting at Cresson on August 9 adopted the "Cresson Compromise"—essentially the same fusion proposal which had been rejected earlier. Most of the Douglas Democrats appeared satisfied, but Forney would not give in and set up a separate ticket of Douglas electors which weakened the fusion movement.

Outwardly, the Republicans seemed united and confident. They conducted a spirited campaign enlivened by torchlight parades organized by local clubs of "Widewakes." But internally the party was wracked by disagreement over issues and by an increasingly open fight between Cameron and Curtin for control. In the east, where antislavery doctrine hurt the Republicans, the press generally used the term "People's party," but in the west where antislavery and anti-Catholic doctrines were popular, editors employed the word "Republican."

McClure found his campaign efforts continually undermined by Cameron, who set up his own party task force to compete with McClure's local organizations and tried to seize the Republican party campaign chest. Matters grew so bad that Lincoln had to dispatch some of the national managers to try to patch up the Pennsylvania conflict. McClure retained control of the state committee and of the party treasury, but could not prevent Cameron from developing his personal following which acted independently of the state party chairman.

The October election gave Curtin an unprecedented majority of 32,000 over Foster. The Republicans won seventy-one of the hundred Assembly seats, ten of twelve state senators, and eighteen of twenty-five congressional contests. The portentous result made Lincoln's election almost a foregone conclusion. In November, as anticipated, Lincoln carried Pennsylvania by an astonishing majority of 60,000, and won the Presidency.

As soon as the results of the election had been confirmed, President Buchanan knew that he faced secession by South Carolina and possibly by other Southern states. He then proceeded according to deliberate plans which he believed best calculated to preserve the Union. He called for bipartisan support of a constitutional convention in his annual message in early December and, after the secession of South Carolina on December 20, sought Lincoln's endorsement of this recommendation. Lincoln at first acceded, but under pressure from advisers he finally withheld Republican support of this proposal, which killed it. Buchanan had hoped that a convention would encourage the Unionists in the South to resist secession, isolate South Carolina, and delay the secession movement in other states pending the outcome of the convention's work.

As the probability of civil war increased, many Pennsylvanians especially in the southern and eastern counties drew back and urged compromise or acquiescence in a peaceful separation from the South. In Philadelphia, with its heavy investment in Southern trade, a series of mass meetings called for conciliation, and streetside banners bore the motto: "Concession before secession." After secession had occurred, Cameron came out for compromise on slavery to preserve the Union and received praise for his stand in Philadelphia. But in Pittsburgh, public sentiment took a different cast. There, Russell Errett reported that resistance to compromise amounted "to almost a fury." Extremes of opinion could be found in every community, but a large segment of the population remained uncommitted and desired to tread cautiously, indicating that Pennsylvania bore the psychological as it did the geographic stamp of a border state. If war came, the Mason-Dixon line would be the military frontier, and people of this area with friends and relatives in Maryland and Virginia viewed the prospect with horror.

In January 1861, with the Republicans in Congress adamant against compromise, Buchanan undertook a new policy designed to prevent the outbreak of civil war before Lincoln took office. He avoided any provocative acts, encouraged the eight still loyal slave states to remain in the Union, made Washington secure for Lincoln's inauguration, and asked Congress to confirm his nominee for revenue collector at Charleston and to strengthen the armed forces. Congress declined to act, but Buchanan achieved his major objectives, turning over to Lincoln on March 4 a nation at peace, though fractured, with eight of the slave states still in the Union. Buchanan retired from office with a large share of public good will, having avoided the threatening onset of civil strife under the most harrowing conditions. Later, after the conflict began, he was subjected to merciless vilification by the Republicans.

Lincoln, as he prepared to assume power, found in Pennsylvania a political condition very similar to that which Andrew Jackson had encountered there in 1828. Two Republican parties existed, each demanding of him a primary share of the patronage. Lincoln early decided that, as Curtin had gained the governorship, Cameron should be mollified by receiving preference in the Cabinet, and offered him the Treasury Department. This threw the Curtin faction into consternation, and they remonstrated so strenuously that Lincoln asked Cameron to return the letter of invitation, but the wily Cameron declined to comply. Lincoln kept Cameron in the Cabinet, but changed his assignment from the Treasury to the War Department—a decision which provides some evidence that President Lincoln never dreamed, before he took office, that his administration would actually face a civil war. Thus the Pennsylvania Republicans began their days of power with Curtin managing the state administration and Cameron entrenched in the Federal administration, and each determined sooner or later to gain complete control. Lincoln wrote to a friend that his Pennsylvania partisans had given him "more trouble than the balance of the Union, not excepting secession."

BIBLIOGRAPHY

The major studies of the antebellum period by Roy F. Nichols and Allan Nevins contain much Pennsylvania material. The main monograph is John F. Coleman: "Pennsylvania Politics, 1848–1860" (doctoral dissertation, Pennsylvania State University, University Park, Pa., 1970). Mueller's *Whig Party in Pennsylvania;* Geary's *Third Parties in Pennsylvania;* and McClure's *Old Time Notes,* all previously cited, cover this era.

The response of Pennsylvania to the problems of race and slavery is exposed in such contemporary reports as: *History of Pennsylvania Hall Which Was Destroyed by a Mob, May 17, 1838* (1838); Pennsylvania Society for Promoting the Abolition of Slavery: *Present State and Condition of the Free People of Color of the City of Philadelphia* (1838); A Southerner: *Sketches of the Higher Classes of Colored Society in Philadelphia* (1841); and Benjamin C. Bacon: *Statistics of the Colored People of Philadelphia*

(1856). The important secondary works are Ira V. Brown: *The Negro in Pennsylvania History* (1971), with an excellent bibliography; Thomas E. Drake: *Quakers and Slavery in America* (1950); Merton L. Dillon: *Benjamin Lundy and the Struggle for Negro Freedom* (1966); Leon F. Litwack: *North of Slavery: The Negro in the Free States, 1790–1860* (1961); Ruth K. Nuermberger: *The Free Produce Movement* (1942); and Leonard L. Richards: *"Gentlemen of Property and Standing": Anti-abolition Mobs in Jacksonian America* (1970). Most important is Edward R. Turner: *The Negro in Pennsylvania,* cited earlier. See also Bella Gross: "The First National Negro Convention," *Journal of Negro History,* vol. 31 (1946), pp. 435–443.

Wilbur H. Seibert: *The Underground Railroad* (1899), long the standard work, is still useful but has been supplanted by Larry Gara: *The Liberty Line—The Legend of the Underground Railroad* (1961). Students will find much local color in the books by a planner of the escape system: William Still: *The Underground Railroad* (1883); and by Robert C. Smedley: *History of the Underground Railroad in Chester and the Neighboring Counties* (1883).

On *Prigg v. Pennsylvania,* see Richard Peters: *Report of the Case of Edward Prigg against the Commonwealth of Pennsylvania* (1842); Joseph Nogee: "The Prigg Case and Fugitive Slaves, 1842–1850," *Journal of Negro History,* vol. 39 (1954), pp. 193–194; and Joseph C. Burke: "What Did the Prigg Decision Really Decide?" *Pennsylvania Magazine of History and Biography,* vol. 93 (1969), pp. 73–85. The Christiana Riot has been treated by William U. Hensel: *The Christiana Riot and the Treason Trials of 1851* (1911); Roderick W. Nash: "The Christiana Riot: An Evaluation of its National Significance," *Lancaster County Historical Society Journal,* vol. 65 (1961), pp. 66–91; and Richard Grau: "The Christiana Riot of 1851: A Reappraisal," *Lancaster County Historical Society Journal,* vol. 69 (1964), pp. 147–175. Other fugitive slave episodes are discussed in Irene E. Williams: "The Operation of the Fugitive Slave Law in Western Pennsylvania from 1850 to 1860," *Western Pennsylvania Historical Magazine,* vol. 4 (1921), pp. 150–160; and Julius Yanuck: "The Force Act in Pennsylvania," *Pennsylvania Magazine of History and Biography,* vol. 92 (1968), pp. 352–364.

The political impact of the Know-Nothings has been best explored by Ray Billington: *The Protestant Crusade, 1800–1860* (1952). The Pennsylvania part of this story is told by Sister Theophane Geary: *Third Parties in Pennsylvania,* previously cited; Sister M. St. Henry: "Nativism in Pennsylvania with Particular Regard to its Effect on Politics and Education, 1840–1860," *American Catholic History Record,* vol. 47 (1936), pp. 5–47; and Warren F. Hewitt: "The Know Nothing Party in Pennsylvania," *Pennsylvania History,* vol. 2 (1935), pp. 69–85.

The growth of the Republican party in Pennsylvania is the subject of a doctoral dissertation by C. Maxwell Myers: "The Rise of the Republican Party in Pennsylvania, 1854–1860" (Pittsburgh 1940). Michael Fitzgibbon Holt: *Forging a Majority: The Formation of the Republican Party in Pittsburgh, Pennsylvania, 1848–1860* (1969), is an indispensable recent study. See also A. W. Crandall: *The Early History of the Republican Party, 1854–1856* (1930); Robert L. Bloom: "Kansas and Popular Sovereignty in Pennsylvania Newspapers, 1856–1860," *Pennsylvania History,* vol. 14 (1947), pp. 77–93; Charles W. Dahlinger: "Abraham Lincoln in Pittsburgh and the Birth of the Republican Party," *Western Pennsylvania Historical Magazine,* vol. 3 (1920), pp. 145–177; Reinhard H. Luthin: "Pennsylvania and Lincoln's Rise to the Presidency," *Pennsylvania Magazine of History and Biography,* vol. 67 (1943), pp. 61–82; and Edgar B. Cale: "Editorial Sentiment in Pennsylvania in the Campaign of 1860," *Pennsylvania History,* vol. 4 (1937), pp. 219–234.

The impact of the Kansas crisis on Pennsylvania receives attention in Reinhard H. Luthin: "The Democratic Split during Buchanan's Administration," *Pennsylvania History,* vol. 11 (1944), pp. 13–35. William Dusinberre: *Civil War Issues in Philadelphia, 1856–1865* (1965), summarizes public response to problems of the era. Much Pennsylvania material will be found in standard monographs on secession, particularly those by Kenneth M. Stampp and David M. Potter. Philip G. Auchampaugh: *James Buchanan and His Cabinet on the Eve of Secession* (1926) presents a spirited defense of Buchanan's policies. The best overall treatment of the Buchanan administration is Roy Franklin Nichols: *The Disruption of American Democracy* (1948).

Useful biographies include studies of Thaddeus Stevens by Thomas F. Woodley, Ralph Korngold,

Fawn Brodie, and Richard Current; of Simon Cameron by Lee Crippen and Erwin S. Bradley; of James Buchanan by Philip S. Klein; of David Wilmot by Charles B. Going; and of Jeremiah Sullivan Black by William M. Brigance. See also the doctoral dissertations on Charles R. Buckalew by William W. Hummel (University of Pittsburgh, 1963); on Hendrick B. Wright by Daniel J. Curran (Fordham University, 1962); and on Alexander K. McClure by William H. Russell (University of Wisconsin, Madison, 1953). Many social leaders are briefly discussed in Ira V. Brown: *Pennsylvania Reformers: from Penn to Pinchot* (1966).

Lincoln's exciting trip through Pennsylvania en route to his inauguration is narrated in Norma Cuthbert: *Lincoln and the Baltimore Plot* (1949); and Janet M. Book: *Northern Rendezvous: Harrisburg during the Civil War* (1951).

CHAPTER THIRTEEN

The Changing Economy: From Forest to Farm

An exposition of the major features of Pennsylvania's economic life during the first two centuries—the distribution of land, the settlement of boundaries, agriculture, trade and commerce, transportation, manufacturing, labor, and finance—will clarify the style of making a living in an earlier age, and will also expose the economic forces which affected political and social activities. The cardinal points of political change do not necessarily serve to mark points of economic change. Ways of making a living have a continuity which often overleaps politically significant compartments; economic institutions change very slowly. Each component of economic life has its own unique chronology of development. For this reason, elements of the Pennsylvania economy will be examined over a long period of time, to expose the changes that occurred from Penn's day until the Civil War.

THE DISTRIBUTION OF LAND

When its boundaries had been settled, Pennsylvania comprised nearly 30 million acres. Of this the Proprietors reserved half a million acres for themselves and disposed of 6½ million acres to others. In 1779 the new commonwealth of Pennsylvania, by the Divesting Act, assumed ownership of nearly 22 million acres which it then proceeded to sell or give away. The disposition of this vast domain constituted the largest economic activity of colonial days and one of the most important in the subsequent period.

Pennsylvania experimented with or adopted in desperation many distinct procedures to distribute land, but all of them rested upon a few underlying concepts. First, since Penn did not acknowledge that the King's Charter overrode Indian claims to the land, he ruled that no settler could buy land from an Indian, but that the province should acquire title to Indian tracts before putting land up for sale. This did not prevent settlers from squatting on Indian land, but it did prevent them, temporarily, from acquiring good title. Second, the government land offices from Penn's day until 1905 did not survey in advance the areas to be sold nor keep any record of plots still vacant, but made the purchaser responsible for finding out whether anyone else had bought the land earlier. As a result, many claims overlapped and Pennsylvania courts became burdened with litigation over original land titles. Third, the governments of the colony and the commonwealth normally placed the objective of settling people on the land ahead of the objective of acquiring revenue from its sale. Many actual settlers never paid either quitrents or the purchase price of the land they occupied, the authorities never tried very hard to oust them, and the courts regularly authenticated titles on the basis of the earliest date of possession rather than on the basis of payment of money owed to the land office.

The administration of land sales remained essentially the same from the establishment of a land office in 1732 until modern times. The colonial land office consisted of a secretary, a surveyor-general with deputies in the several counties, a master of the rolls who kept a record of deeds, a keeper of the great seal who authenticated deeds, and several commissioners who, acting with the other land officers, constituted the Board of Property which heard contests over titles and made decisions which could be appealed to the courts.

Pennsylvania disposed of its land in various ways. Some methods lasted for a century while others were in effect only a few years. During Penn's lifetime almost no system existed. The Proprietor himself sold land before he left England to European speculators called First Purchasers. These buyers bought thousands of acres at about 10 cents per acre and received a bonus grant of 100 acres in the new town, Philadelphia, for each 5,000 acres purchased. Since the grants required settlement in three years, many of them lapsed.

From Penn's death in 1718 until his male heirs became Proprietors in 1732, no land titles could be granted in Pennsylvania. The provincial government in these years issued land "tickets" which would be validated by deeds when a regular land office opened. When several ticket holders claimed the same property, the land office would settle the issue by priority of date.

After Penn's heirs, John, Thomas, and Richard, assumed the proprietorship in 1732, the province developed a routine for selling land called the application system which soon became the typical method. The system involved four steps. First, a prospective buyer made *application* to the land office for a stated number of acres in a roughly defined region. No money passed at this time, but the date of the application controlled the priority of the grant, and the earliest applicant had the best claim. Following application, a *warrant* was issued by the land office authorizing the applicant or a provincial officer to survey the tract. A *survey* was returned to the land office, including a precise description of the tract and a map containing the lines, angles, area, boundary markers, and if possible, names of adjoining owners. Six months after return of the survey, the applicant was supposed to pay for the land. Upon payment, the land office drew up a *patent* or *deed* which gave title to the purchaser.

This statement describes the system as it was intended to operate. In practice, however, it encountered all kinds of difficulty. New rules altered the time at which the purchase price had to be paid, and often settlers never paid for the land. Various applicants would take the first or the second or the third step, but would never complete the transaction by acquiring a deed. Yet priority in time of any step, whether application, warrant or survey, protected a settler against the claim of a later buyer who had paid for the land. Although the land office recorded surveys by counties, the entries of application, warrant, survey, and deed were listed by date and not by name or location. Until 1732, many land entries went into the provincial daybooks mixed up with all kinds of other records of receipts and disbursements, in the order that the transactions came to the bookkeeper's desk. Even the land office kept no master map, but only the sequential records.

Another difficulty of routine land purchase arose from the need to pay the annual quitrent to confirm good title. This required rent rolls by location of the tract so that a collector could proceed from one property to the next. But no such rolls ever came into being, and the Proprietors could only invite landowners to bring in the tax voluntarily upon penalty of losing their land. Few volunteered to pay, and the government hesitated to enforce its right to dispossess. Still, title to land upon which quitrent was owing was imperfect; a new buyer always had to assume responsibility to pay any arrears of quitrents without knowing what they might be. But the land office was in a weaker position than the landowner to prove the amount due. With the Divesting Act of 1779, quitrents were abolished, though purchase money owing to the Proprietors had to be paid to the commonwealth to acquire good title. Throughout the colonial era, the price of common land remained at about 25 cents per acre, with an additional fee of 10 cents per acre for costs—roughly 35 cents an acre plus the yearly quarter-penny per acre quitrent.

The system of routine purchase ran into trouble from the start because the land office had not the personnel to administer it. The system required agents, surveyors, and receivers of rent and purchase money scattered widely throughout the colony. But the agents were few and usually remote from actual settlements. Hence thousands of immigrants merely moved beyond existing county seats and set up farms where it pleased them. Often they gave some specific boundaries to their farm by marking trees along the line with a tomahawk. The so-called tomahawk right gave no title to land, but could often gain a settler a preemption or the first right to gain title by fulfilling the requirements of routine purchase. Such practice brought widespread acceptance of the "Law of Improvements," a term reflecting the willingness of the Board of Property and the courts to grant to squatters, that is, those who actually built houses and cleared land in areas where they had no legal claim, a right of preemption. If a settler could prove he had lived on and improved a tract of land, he acquired the first right to buy it, even though someone else might have applied for it at the land office.

From the time of the French and Indian War until early in the nineteenth century, special objectives of the government produced special devices of land distribution. The first of these, known as the *Campaign Lands,* gave commanders of forts the power to grant free land west of the Susquehanna to settlers who would occupy the region of Forbes's Road from Fort Bedford to Fort Pitt within five years of the expulsion of the French. The government wished to repopulate the region which had been emptied by Indian raids, partly for frontier defense and partly to strengthen claims of Pennsylvania in an area which Virginia considered hers. People who accepted this land had to pay only the small quitrent.

Pennsylvania more than doubled the land available for sale by two huge Indian purchases, the New Purchase of 1768 at Fort Stanwix incorporating a wide strip of land running from Wayne County in the northeast to Green and Washington Counties in the southwest; and the so-called Last Purchase in 1785, also arranged at Fort Stanwix, including the huge northwestern part of the state. Land in these areas was initially offered at 80 cents an acre in

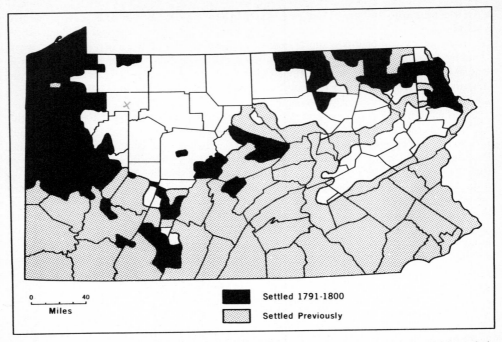

This map shows both the early settlement pattern along the southern part of Pennsylvania and the marked effect on settlement of the Land Act of 1792.

1,000-acre tracts. Between 1777 and 1785 the state reserved two huge tracts south of Lake Erie. The northern tract, in the area of Crawford, Mercer, Forest, Warren, and Venango Counties, was called the *Donation Lands,* to be given to revolutionary veterans of the Pennsylvania Line in plots from 200 to 2,000 acres depending upon rank. This land was surveyed in advance into rectangular numbered plots, the only place in Pennsylvania where this system was used. Soldiers had to apply for Donation Lands and applications were received until 1813.

Just south of the Donation tract, the state reserved a region in Allegheny, Armstrong, Lawrence, Butler, and Beaver Counties called *Depreciation Lands.* Plots were offered to veterans who applied for land in exchange for the depreciated certificates with which the Assembly had paid the troops during the Revolution. Grantees held Depreciation Land tax-free during their life.

The availability of millions of acres of rich land in the northwest encouraged other special land experiments. Between 1785 and 1792 the state established the *Academy Lands,* a grant of 112 tracts comprising 52,000 acres to various religious and educational institutions. Among the recipients were Dickinson and Franklin College, and the Pittsburgh, Washington, and Reading Academies.

The state also saw an opportunity to stimulate town growth and at the same time to increase the value of its land. Between 1783 and 1795, it created a number of *State Reservations* for town sites—that is, land which the state would survey as town plots and sell to people who would be required to build there within two years to perfect their title. The communities of Pittsburgh, Beaver, Allegheny, Erie, Franklin, Waterford, and Warren started in this way.

On April 3, 1792, the state passed a land-sale law which produced more litigation and chicanery than any land act in the history of the commonwealth. The act covered all the land included in the Old Purchase and the Last Purchase—nearly two-thirds of the state—except for the tracts reserved as Donation Lands, Depreciation Lands, Academy Lands, or State Reservations. It proposed to encourage settlement by offering land at reduced price to bona fide settlers. Land was reduced from 53 cents per acre to 6 cents per acre west of the Allegheny River, and to 2 cents per acre east of it, if the buyer settled and improved the land. A massive rush to buy ensued, and the commonwealth disposed of 5 million acres between 1792 and 1794, or almost as much as the Penns had sold in a century. Most of the purchases were made by a few land companies which, due to technicalities in the law, could evade the requirement for settlement.

The Holland Land Company, managed by Dutch merchants who had loaned the United States money during the Revolution, bought 1,500,000 acres in Pennsylvania south of Lake Erie at the reduced price, with Robert Morris acting as agent. The company set up a supply depot for new settlers at Meadville in 1795, built roads, offered 100 acres free to any homesteader who would buy 300 additional acres at $1.50 per acre, and invested a huge sum in the speculation. The 1792 law permitted granting warrants without settlement for two years after the cessation of Indian hostilities. But Anthony Wayne conquered a peace with the northwest Indians in 1795 in the treaty of Greenville after the Battle of Fallen Timbers, and in 1797 suits began charging that the Holland Land Company had forfeited its holdings. When Governor McKean took office in 1799 he gave clear orders that no deed should issue without proof of actual settlement. The Holland Company engaged in a lengthy and costly litigation, lost $1 million in the process, and disposed of its claims to the Lancaster Land Company, which later dissolved and divided its interests among the shareholders.

The North American Land Company acquired 250,000 acres in the same area, which it sold to Henry Baldwin of Pittsburgh in 1816 after an unsuccessful speculation. Astute John Nicholson, who personally owned 3 million acres in the northwest corner of the state, organized the Pennsylvania Population Company to which he sold a part of his holdings, but this company also went bankrupt mainly because it could not oust squatters from its land or collect a purchase price from them. The political change in 1799 militated against land hoarding and most of the hopeful real estate developers lost their investment.

Pennsylvania sold much of its land very cheaply, at 2, or 6, or 53 cents an acre depending upon the locality and proof of improvement. But even those who bought cheaply showed little inclination to pay. In 1805 the state asked for the execution of mortgages against money owing, but with little success. Subsequent laws seeking to extract payment for land were passed in 1820, 1835, 1858, and 1864, but none succeeded in frightening or forcing people into paying what they owed the state for their land. In 1874 the land office still recorded 2,365,000 acres for which it had never collected payment, and because of the inefficient method of bookkeeping, the true figure was undoubtedly larger.

THE BOUNDARIES OF PENNSYLVANIA

Every boundary of colonial Pennsylvania except the Delaware River raised a contest with neighbors. The boundary disputes arose from the vague wording of colonial charters and from the primitive state of geography. Trouble arose first with Maryland, then with Virginia, and finally with Connecticut, each confrontation leading to a boundary war. Pennsylvania achieved peaceable boundary settlements with New York, Massachusetts, and the Federal government.

William Penn recognized from the outset that he faced litigation with Maryland because of his Delaware grant which lay in the Delmarva Peninsula, between the Delaware and Chesapeake Bays, a region explicity given to Maryland in its 1632 charter. Penn also knew that depending upon interpretation of the charters, the southern boundary of his province might lie south of Baltimore, or north of Philadelphia.

After fruitless talks with Lord Baltimore, Penn returned to England in 1685 to defend his claim both to Delaware and to an advantageous southern boundary. The Privy Council awarded him Delaware without explicitly fixing its limits and postponed any decision on the Maryland line. During the next forty years, each province promoted settlement near the disputed boundary until it became apparent after the creation of Lancaster County in 1729 that a border war was brewing. In 1731, at Maryland's request, the Crown ordered the two colonies to negotiate a settlement. Commissioners from both sides reached an agreement in May 1732, covering both the Delaware and the southern Pennsylvania boundaries: A circle with a 12-mile radius should be drawn around New Castle. An east-west line should be surveyed across the Delmarva Peninsula, starting at Cape Henlopen on Delaware Bay. This line should be bisected, and a line run from this midpoint north until it formed a tangent with the New Castle Circle. It should be continued to a point 15 miles south of Philadelphia, and from here the southern boundary of Pennsylvania should be projected for 5 degrees westward. The commissioners from each province should be charged with executing the agreement.

Maryland, which had initiated the negotiations, soon began to delay execution. In 1736 a group of some fifty Pennsylvanians attacked a party of fourteen Marylanders who had settled ten miles south of Lancaster, and burned the house of Thomas Cresap, killing one Marylander in the process. Cresap's War, as the incident came to be known, precipitated the survey of a temporary boundary line. As the commissioners could not agree on many details, each side appealed to the British courts to resolve the issues. In 1750 Chancery Court ordered performance of the agreement, settling most arguments in favor of the Penns, but no action occurred until 1760 when Frederick, Lord Baltimore agreed with the Penns to proceed. David Rittenhouse, the Philadelphia astronomer, surveyed the New Castle Circle. He had so much trouble that the commissioners hired two professional mathematicians and astronomers from England, Charles Mason and Jeremiah Dixon, to survey and mark the Maryland-Pennsylvania boundary.

Their task was to establish a bench mark 15 miles south of Philadelphia and to survey a line west from this point for 5 degrees. Since a line running 15 miles south of the city ended in the middle of Delaware Bay, the surveyors projected a line west to the Brandywine, and then south the required distance where, after careful astronomical checking, they placed the "Stargazers' Stone," which served as anchor for the Mason-Dixon line. This stone came to have national significance, for it became the point on which future surveys of Federal land west of the Ohio-Pennsylvania line ultimately rested. Having fixed the latitude of the boundary at 39 degrees and 44 minutes, Mason and Dixon surveyed westward until, in 1767, they stopped some 30 miles beyond the present western terminus of Maryland.

The surveying party placed stones every mile, stopping at number 230. Later, during the negotiations with Virginia, Pennsylvania extended the Mason-Dixon line to 266.4 miles west of the Stargazers' Stone. The Crown ratified the boundary settlement in 1769, and from that date the Mason-Dixon line entered American history as the symbolic dividing line between the North and the South.

But one small detail remained unresolved. It was later discovered that the Stargazers' Stone did not lie on the New Castle Circle but was somewhat west of it. Consequently a narrow wedge of land whose ownership remained undefined had been created between the western limit of the circle and the northeastern corner of Maryland—a narrow triangle of some 800 acres known as the Delaware Wedge or the Thorn. In 1921 Pennsylvania agreed to have this area and its inhabitants, who technically had never been the citizens of any state, formally transferred to Delaware by projecting the Mason-Dixon line eastward to the circle.

The Virginia charters of 1606 and 1609 had roughly defined that colony's bounds as a strip of land between the 34th and the 45th parallels from sea to sea, and granted a tract "up into the Land throughout from Sea to Sea, West and Northwest." On the basis of this vague description, Virginians had organized the Ohio Company in 1749 to speculate in land between the western Potomac and Ohio Rivers. The assumption of Virginia that the Forks of the Ohio lay within its boundaries explains the readiness of its governor to take the initiative in protesting French intrusion and in sending Virginia militia to the scene in 1754. Discussions had already begun about the westward projection of the Mason-Dixon line when the French and Indian War intervened.

People moved rapidly into the area after the French and Indian War and the Indian purchase of 1768. Pennsylvania had already authorized settlement by means of the Campaign Lands. Virginia's Governor John M. Dunmore also asserted ownership, took control of Fort Pitt which he renamed Fort Dunmore, and disposed of land under Virginia title. The Pennsylvania Assembly established Bedford County in 1771 and Westmoreland County in 1773 to assert its claim to the southwest while the Penns petitioned the Crown to arrange a boundary settlement. Virginia countered by creating a District of West Augusta, setting up a local government and court system, and in 1776 organizing three counties, Yohogania, Monongalia, and Ohio. Between 1770 and the outbreak of the Revolution a number of conflicts among Indians, settlers, and peace officers of the rival colonies occurred, especially after John Connelly organized a Virginia militia company at Pittsburgh. Several years of sporadic fighting and arrests of settlers by both sides became known as Lord Dunmore's War.

The Declaration of Independence soon brought a stop to Lord Dunmore's War as state governments concentrated on the larger struggle. In 1779 a joint commission agreed to extend the Mason-Dixon line to the terminus described in Penn's charter—5 degrees west of the Delaware River. Virginia contended for a western boundary with Pennsylvania which would duplicate the contours of the Delaware River, but ultimately agreed to project a line due north to Lake Erie. The agreement validated land titles granted by Virginia in the area and provided for adjudicating title conflicts. Surveyors completed marking the southern and western borders of Pennsylvania in 1786.

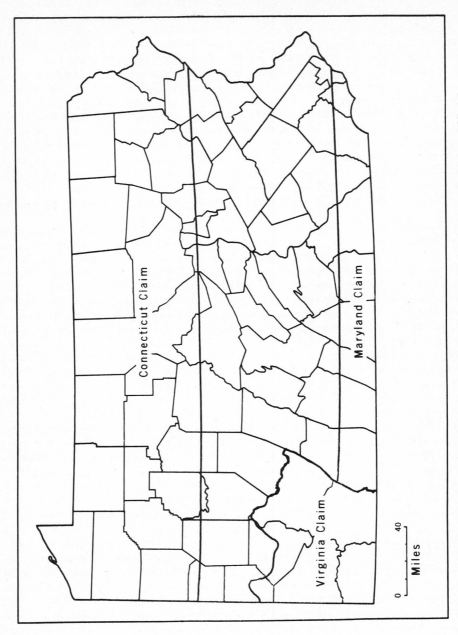

Map of the contested boundaries of Pennsylvania, showing areas claimed by Connecticut, Maryland, and Virginia.

The northern boundary of Pennsylvania caused the most trouble of all. Connecticut's charter of 1662 granted land from sea to sea, excepting only such territory as was then occupied "by any Christian prince or state." This excluded New York which had been settled by the Dutch, but granted land further west between the 41st and 42nd parallels, approximately the width of the Connecticut colony. The 41st parallel in Pennsylvania runs from the Delaware Water Gap in the east to New Castle in the west; two-fifths of the state lies north of it. The Connecticut charter created a prior claim to this portion of Penn's grant of 1681.

No one pressed the Connecticut government for western land until 1750 when people began to petition for grants. The authorities, uncertain of the status of the land, denied the requests until 1753 with the organization of the Susquehanna Company, a private land speculation enterprise financed largely by Connecticut people. Representatives of the Susquehanna Company negotiated a purchase of land in the Wyoming Valley from the Iroquois at the Albany Conference of 1754, a transaction of dubious legality as the Iroquois had already promised the Pennsylvania government not to sell this tract to anyone else. The Company began to promote settlement in 1755 but the Indian raids of the French and Indian War temporarily halted the effort.

After the war several hundred Connecticut families moved into the Wyoming Valley. The Penns protested and in 1763 obtained a British court order requiring Connecticut to prevent further occupation of the disputed territory by their people. In 1768 the Penns, in the "Old Purchase" Indian treaty at Fort Stanwix, had the Iroquois repudiate their 1754 sale of Wyoming land to the Susquehanna Company. This gave Pennsylvania good title so far as the Indians were concerned, but did not alter the colonial charter provisions.

Undeterred, the Susquehanna Company surveyed five townships in the vicinity of the present city of Wilkes-Barre, offering a plot 5 miles square to any group of forty settlers who would migrate and be prepared to defend the land against possible Pennsylvania claimants. The first group to migrate established a community they called Forty Fort in February 1769. Simultaneously, the Penns had made grants to Pennsylvanians on condition that they physically occupy the same area and defend it against Connecticut claimants. There promptly ensued the first of three boundary conflicts known as the Yankee-Pennamite Wars. The respective settlers engaged in sporadic raids on each other from 1769 until 1771.

At first the Connecticut government took no official notice of the activities of the Susquehanna Company, but in 1774 it formally recognized the Wyoming settlements by incorporating them in a new Connecticut county, Westmoreland, a name clearly indicative of the purpose. Connecticut, indeed, merely acted toward Pennsylvania as Pennsylvania had acted toward Virginia the year before when it created its own Westmoreland County in a disputed region at the opposite end of the province. The settlement of Muncy by Connecticut farmers detonated the second Yankee-Pennamite War which lasted from 1775 until the early years of the Revolution. About 5,000 Connecticut people inhabited the Wyoming Valley by that time.

Soon after the creation of the United States government under the Articles of Confederation, Pennsylvania appealed to Congress to settle the land dispute with Connecticut. A special commission heard arguments and on December 30, 1782, issued the Trenton Decree which rejected the Connecticut claims and confirmed Pennsylvania's title. The decree provided that Pennsylvania should sustain the land titles of the Connecticut settlers, but this proved easier to promise than to implement and the third Yankee-Pennamite War developed over conflicting titles of Pennsylvania and Connecticut settlers. The Pennsylvania controversy with Connecticut finally was ended in 1807 by a statute which confirmed the Connecticut titles and reimbursed the Pennsylvania claimants in cash for the loss of their land.

The Trenton Decree terminated the Connecticut claims but left unresolved the boundary between New York and Pennsylvania. Penn's charter granted him the land to the source of the Delaware River or to "the three and fortieth degree of Northerne Latitude," whichever proved to be furthest north. During the 1740s and 1750s New York's Governor George Clinton and the surveyor general, Cadwallader Colden, admitted that the language of Penn's grant gave title up to the 43rd parallel which runs from Albany to Buffalo. After the French and Indian War the Penns ceased to press for the 43rd parallel boundary. In 1774 they asked the Crown to approve a northern boundary line drawn along the 42nd parallel. Because of the Revolution, surveying did not begin until 1786, but the commissioners in charge reported on October 29, 1787, that the boundary line had been completed, running 259 miles from the Delaware River to the western border at Lake Erie.

Pennsylvania had now achieved, after 105 years, a completely closed and undisputed boundary, and land titles within it could at last be considered firm. One final negotiation was needed to construct the final shape of the commonwealth. Pennsylvania desired a port on Lake Erie which the boundary with New York did not provide. New York's western limits conflicted with the boundaries of Massachusetts, which held a sea-to-sea charter, and both claimed the Erie Triangle. New York ceded her claim to this area to the United States in 1781, and Massachusetts followed suit in 1786. Pennsylvania then purchased the Erie Triangle from the United States in 1792—a tract of 202,187 acres for $151,000. With this purchase Pennsylvania achieved the size and shape it has held ever since.

AGRICULTURE

Colonial farming Most people who came from Europe to colonial Pennsylvania hoped to make a living by farming. We have seen the various ways by which these immigrants acquired the land they planned to farm. The success they achieved depended in part upon the way their European farm habits worked in a different environment. Most of Pennsylvania was covered with forest which the first generations of farmers had to remove. The climate provided about 42 inches of rainfall per year, and temperatures which ranged from 22–32 degrees in January to 61–76 in July; the frostfree period varied from 207 days per year along the southern border to only 80 days along the New York line, a fact which partly explains the concentration of population in the south.

The main groups of settlers, English, German, and Scotch-Irish, each experienced a distinct farming history. The English created excellent farms in the southeast, but they wore out the soil, and the yield per acre of their farms had dropped alarmingly by the time of the Revolution. Many of the English families went into other occupations and sold off farmland at a profit as the region became more commercialized and the economy more metropolitan. The Pennsylvania Germans had the good fortune to find a region whose topography, climate, and limestone soil closely approximated those of their homeland. Their traditional methods of farming maintained the productivity of the soil; and this, plus their devotion to farming as a way of life, kept them firmly rooted to the area they first occupied. They are still there. The Scotch-Irish first settled in the limestone area adjacent to the Germans, but soon moved

Painting by Linton Park, *Flax Scutching Bee,* showing neighbors gathered to prepare flax for spinning. Many details of frontier life are evident. (National Gallery of Art, Washington, D.C. Gift of Edgar William and Bernice Chrysler Garbisch)

Frontier home along a turnpike, with land cleared and fenced. (Joseph Smith: *Old Redstone*)

westward into the slate lands along the mountains, watered by many surface springs. They often cleared fields and cropped them until they began to wear out, then sold to German families who clubbed together to buy the farms and rejuvenate them. Many Germans found their way into central and southwestern Pennsylvania in this way.

It has long been a cliché of colonial history that the frontier farmer wished to escape the pressure of population, and willfully set out to establish a lonely and independent existence in the heart of the wilderness. But most of the immigrants came from commercialized areas of Europe, had been accustomed to farming in relation to nearby village or city needs, and tried to reproduce this pattern in America. When farmers crossed the mountains, they looked for promising villages as much as for fertile soil, and wanted a location which offered the safeguards, the markets, and the social life that a village would provide. We should picture Pennsylvania colonial farming as primarily a village-oriented commercial venture, rather than merely a subsistence occupation.

Creating a farm out of the forest was the most arduous task of colonial agriculture. It took raw courage and firm faith to set out on such a venture, for it meant moving a family through an unmarked wilderness with no promise of surviving unexpected dangers or even of finding the expected destination. An observer in 1773 described a family of twelve on the trail, the man carrying an axe and gun, the wife a spinning wheel and a sack of bread, the children carrying bundles according to their size, two heavily loaded horses, one of them bearing an infant in a wicker cage strapped on top of the load, and a cow with bed cord wound around her horns and meal bags on her back.

At the chosen location, the family had to build temporary shelter and quickly clear some land for putting in a crop. Girdling the trees, Indian fashion, would provide a makeshift clearing, but chopping and burning the trees provided a much better initial field. Because of the prodigious effort required to clear land and to pull stumps, frontier farmers normally pooled resources. The difficulty of clearing land discouraged isolated settlement. Companies of men chopped big trees, grubbed small ones out by the roots, burned the piles of slashing, and stacked the trunks which would serve for fence rails or building logs. The newcomer provided enough whiskey to justify calling these occasions "log-rolling frolics." Fencing might be delayed for years but ultimately had to be done, especially on farms near the towns. One local ordinance defined the problem by requiring that fences be "horse-high, bull-strong, and hog-tight." Since timber was abundant most Pennsylvania farmers, when they reached the fencing stage, erected zigzag "worm" or "rattlesnake" fences. It took about 800 split rails to fence an acre in this manner. Farmers extracted a little money from "pot and pearl ashes" made from the residue of tree burning. They could sell potash commercially or keep it for rendering homemade soap by boiling it with animal fat.

Beyond a log-cabin home, the farmer had to have a smokehouse to dry meat, and a spring-house if he wished to keep milk or butter. He needed a barn for crop storage more than for animal care. The German farmers quickly built large bank barns to keep their animals under cover during the winter, but many frontier farmers let the animals roam the woods for forage, identifying them by clipping the ears with a brand mark.

Actual farming began with sowing the first crop. Among the cereals, wheat led Pennsylvania's colonial crops, with Indian corn second, and rye, oats, and barley following. The early farmers experimented to discover what crops yielded the highest return on their land. They often relied on foods which had grown well for the Indians, such as corn, beans, squashes, and melons.

Farmers used the time-tested ways of cutting hay and grain: the scythe, the sickle, and the cradle. They had their animals tramp out the grain on the barn floor or used a flail, and winnowed it by throwing it in the air in a breeze or before a man- or horse-operated fanning mill. The corn had to be cut and shocked, and the ears removed, husked, and then shelled. The farmer at this point either had to carry the grain to a nearby gristmill or had to make shift to pound out coarse flour and corn meal at home. The first few years would be a simple subsistence-type agriculture, but in time as new fields were cleared and old ones were made more suitable to the plow, the land would produce an excess for sale or barter. The natural increase of livestock relieved the family of dependence on hunting for meat and at the same time increased the urgency of developing pastures and raising fences. Pioneer farmers normally planted an orchard. The peach was native to the region, but apples, cherries, pears, and plums had to be grown from imported stock. Some of the fruit could be dried, like apple schnitz, and some was used to feed the pigs or left to rot, but most of it was made into various kinds of cider or brandy.

The age of experiment There was little about farming in colonial Pennsylvania that would not have been entirely comprehensible to any European peasant of the previous centuries, or that would seem very strange to a subsistence farmer today. But the political transition from colonial to independent status in 1776 brought changes in farming practice. Pennsylvania, as the seat of the first national capital, became a center of efforts to create a sense of national pride in agricultural production.

American farming practice had badly deteriorated during the eighteenth century, partly because farmers could afford to be prodigal with the land, and partly because the colonials failed to keep up with European methods. Farms around Philadelphia which in 1730 had been producing 30 bushels of wheat per acre could raise only 5 or 10 bushels in 1791. Western farmers systematically impoverished their fields by continuous cropping until it became cheaper for them to take up new farms than to rehabilitate the old. The Pennsylvania German farmers constituted a conspicous exception to the general practice. They fed their land by using manure, by rotating the land into pasture, or by permitting it to lie fallow, and succeeded in maintaining high yields. Pennsylvania's reputation as the "granary of the Revolution" came largely from the German farms, but the productivity of many eastern and western farms had declined by 1776. Seed deteriorated, the ill-kept and ill-fed livestock became smaller and more scrawny from neglect; and untended swine became wild.

The nation's leaders, notably George Washington and Thomas Jefferson, both gentleman farmers by vocation, vigorously exhorted Americans to prove their vaunted quality by improving their slovenly farming. Their outspoken interest gave a national urgency and a patriotic appeal to formal efforts, centering in the national capital at Philadelphia, to improve farming methods by the establishment of societies which would experiment with the latest concepts of soil treatment, crop rotation, seed varieties, new crops, and animal husbandry, and would disseminate the results of their findings. The time of this effort, from about 1780 to 1820, could be called an era of agricultural experimentation, conducted as a national patriotic endeavor.

The American Philosophical Society devoted much of its attention during the ensuing half century to the application of scientific knowledge to agriculture. In 1785, a group of Philadelphia professional men organized the Philadelphia Society for Promoting Agriculture. It drew its membership from all the states and served as a national clearinghouse of agricultural information. Its gentleman-farmer members conducted controlled experiments on their own lands and reported results in printed pamphlets. The society at first concentrated on the improvement of seed and the conservation of soil by various systems of crop rotation or the use of lime and fertilizer. Its interest in livestock led to the formation of another organization in 1809, the Pennsylvania Society for Improving the Breed of Cattle. This society promoted the importation from Europe of pure-bred stock such as Durham Short-horn and Guernsey cattle, Berkshire hogs, and Merino sheep. The magnificent Conestoga draft horses, so common in southeastern Pennsylvania, were a local breed.

The back-country farmers knew little of the activities of the "scientific farmers" who supported the societies, for they scorned "book farming." The societies, however, persuaded the state Legislature in 1820 to authorize county agricultural societies aided by state and county funds. The findings of the state societies then began to percolate down to the level of the working farmers through the county organization whose leaders had gained the re-spect of the local people. Almanacs like *Poor Richard's Almanac* or *Baer's Agricultural Almanac* found an honored place in almost every farm household and aided in the circu-lation of information to improve farming. After 1820, farm newspapers and periodicals played an important part in alerting the farm community to new ideas and practices. But farmers remained suspicious of new proposals, and it took a long time to alter traditional methods.

The impact of agricultural experimentation varied widely. Certain ideas which seemed to promise easy money seized the popular imagination and burgeoned into periodic "fevers" or "crazes" of one sort or another. The Merino sheep craze struck southeastern Pennsyl-vania between 1810 and 1816, and the silkworm craze between 1826 and 1829. There was a kind of mania for raising hemp to supply rope and cotton baling in the 1820s and 1830s, and an orgy of "Berkshire hog fever" between 1838 and 1842. These speculative fads ruined many farmers and tended to discredit sound proposals emanating from the scientific experi-menters in farming.

The age of mechanization Starting about 1840, Pennsylvania entered a new era of farming: the age of mechanization. Prior to it, any ancient farmer could have found tools on a Pennsyl-vania farm which would have been perfectly familiar to him. A generation later he would have been lost among the mowers, gang plows, spring-tooth harrows, hay rakes, seed drills, reapers, threshers, and other newly invented farm machines. These tools were still horse-drawn, but they introduced a strange and unprecedented new world of farming practice.

The rapid appearance of newly invented farm machinery forced farmers to seek informa-tion, and they now began to flock to county fairs to learn what the new devices could accomplish and how they worked. Machine farming introduced so many new complexities that special education of farmers became a necessity. The Pennsylvania State Agricultural Society was chartered in 1851 and became a kind of parent body and information center for the seventy-odd county and local farming societies which had come into being by 1857. It promoted county fairs and expositions and lent its powerful influence to the establishment of the Farmers' High School of Pennsylvania in 1855, the institution which in 1862 became the Agricultural College of Pennsylvania and later Pennsylvania State University.

For the most part, Pennsylvania farmers continued to use the old ways and adopted with reluctance the methods of scientific and machine farming. The ages of experiment and of mechanization had arrived in Pennsylvania by the time of the Civil War; but their most flourishing era lay in the future, and until then many farmers continued to imitate their grandfathers and to rely mainly upon human muscle and oxen or horsepower as in colonial days.

BIBLIOGRAPHY

General treatment of public land policy will be found in William R. Shepherd: *History of Proprietary Government in Pennsylvania* (1896); and vol. 2 of A. S. Bolles: *Pennsylvania, Province and State: 1609–1790* (1899). Specialized studies include Norman B. Wilkinson: "Land Policy and Speculation in Pennsylvania, 1779–1800" (doctoral dissertation, University of Pennsylvania, 1958); Harry R. Bivens: "Disposition of Lands in Provincial Pennsylvania" (master's thesis, Pennsylvania State University, 1932); and Joseph C. Ruddy: "The Policy of Land Distribution in Pennsylvania since 1779" (master's thesis, Pennsylvania State University, 1933). On western land, see Elizabeth K. Henderson: "The Northwestern Lands of Pennsylvania, 1790–1812," *Pennsylvania Magazine of History and Biography,* vol. 60 (1936), pp. 131–160; James N. Fullerton: "Squatters and Titles to Land in Early Western Pennsylvania," *Western Pennsylvania Historical Magazine,* vol 6 (1923), pp. 165–176; and in the same journal, John E. Winner: "Depreciation and Donation Lands," vol. 8 (1925), pp 1–11; Katherine M. Beals: "The Land Speculations of a Great Patriot [Robert Morris]," *Business History Society Bulletin,* vol. 3 (1930), pp. 1–9; Bertha S. Fox: "Provost William Smith and His Land Investments in Pennsylvania," *Pennsylvania History,* vol. 8 (1941), pp. 189–209; and Norman B. Wilkinson: "The 'Philadelphia Fever' in Northern Pennsylvania," *Pennsylvania History,* vol. 20 (1953), pp. 41–56.

Books dealing with land companies include Alfred P. James: *George Mercer of the Ohio Company: A Study in Frustration* (1963) and *The Ohio Company: Its Inner History* (1959); Julian Boyd and Robert J. Taylor (eds.): *The Susquehanna Company Papers,* 11 vols. (1962–1971); R. Nelson Hale: "The Pennsylvania Population Company," *Pennsylvania History,* vol. 16 (1949), pp. 122–130; and Paul D. Evans: *The Holland Land Company* (1924).

On the boundary lines, see William A. Russ: *How Pennsylvania Acquired Its Present Boundaries* (1966); and his article: "Exploring the Corners and Joints on the Pennsylvania Borders," *Susquehanna University Studies,* vol. 6 (1960), pp. 507–536.

The Maryland-Pennsylvania dispute is treated in Hubertis M. Cummings: *The Mason and Dixon Line: Story for a Bicentenary, 1763–1963* (1962); Thomas D. Cope: "The Stargazers' Stone," *Pennsylvania History,* vol. 6 (1939), pp. 205–221, and "Charles Mason and Jeremiah Dixon," *Scientific Monthly,* vol. 62 (1941), pp. 541–544: J. C. Hayes: "Penn vs. Lord Baltimore: A Brief for the Penns in re Mason and Dixon Line," *Pennsylvania History,* vol. 8 (1941), pp. 278–304, and "Delaware Curve," *Pennsylvania Magazine of History and Biography,* vol. 47 (1923), pp. 238–258; and W. B. Scaife: "Boundary Dispute between Maryland and Pennsylvania," *Pennsylvania Magazine of History and Biography,* vol. 9 (1885), pp. 241–271.

On the Pennsylvania-Virginia controversy, much source material will be found in Kenneth P. Bailey (ed.): *The Ohio Company Papers, 1753–1817* (1947). There are master's theses on this topic by Robert C. Noll: "Boundary Dispute between Pennsylvania and Virginia" (Pennsylvania State University, 1936); and William D. Barns: "Southwestern Pennsylvania during the Pennsylvania-Virginia Boundary Controversy, 1763–1784" (Pennsylvania State University, 1940). See also John E. Potter: "The Pennsylvania and Virginia Boundary Controversy," *Pennsylvania Magazine of History and Biography,* vol. 38 (1914), pp. 407–427.

On the Connecticut controversy, the major source is the *Susquehanna Company Papers,* cited earlier. *Pennsylvania Archives,* 2nd ser., vol. 16, gives the major Pennsylvania documents. See also Burke M. Hermann: "Pennsylvania-Connecticut Boundary Dispute," (master's thesis, Pennsylvania State University, 1916); and Oscar J. Harvey: "Some Phases of the Pennamite-Yankee Controversy," *Americana,* vol. 24 (1930), pp. 159–214.

On Pennsylvania agriculture, the indispensable books are by Stevenson W. Fletcher: *Pennsylvania Agriculture and Country Life, 1640–1840,* vol. 1, and *1840–1940,* vol. 2 (1950, 1955). On western Pennsylvania agriculture, Solon J. Buck and Elizabeth H. Buck: *The Planting of Civilization in Western Pennsylvania* (1939) is the essential treatise. Eastern agriculture is treated in books on the Pennsylvania Germans, listed in the Bibliography for Chapter 4.

One of the best sources on the farm life of early Pennsylvania is the Pennsylvania Farm Museum near Lancaster, under the direction of the Pennsylvania Historical and Museum Commission.

CHAPTER FOURTEEN

The Changing Economy: From Farm
To Factory

About 90 percent of the population of colonial Pennsylvania engaged in farming. The remaining 10 percent performed a wide variety of tasks, devoting their inventive efforts to transportation, commerce, and manufacturing, and to ways to organize, staff, and finance these enterprises. As the Industrial Revolution began, at the turn of the nineteenth century, these Pennsylvanians found themselves fortuitously in possession of all the basic ingredients to develop it: iron for machinery, coal for steam power, capital to finance experimental enterprises, skilled and resourceful people to manage and operate new factories, the geographical location to market their products, and a sympathetic and responsive government.

TRANSPORTATION AND COMMERCE

Colonial trade   Until the French and Indian War anyone traveling to the interior of Pennsylvania had two alternatives: the rivers or Indian paths. While the traveller would use both as convenience dictated, the settler generally sought farmland near a river, for water provided the safest and most certain contact with trading posts or villages. The population of the eighteenth century concentrated in river valleys, and until the end of Pontiac's Rebellion the inland farmers lived along streams which flowed either to Philadelphia or to Baltimore. By the time of the Revolution the southeasterly flow of commerce had become traditional; the back-country traffic trickled east to one or the other of these two seaport cities and converged there in a flood of produce, and the city merchants propelled the flow further east to Europe or south to the Caribbean islands. Commerce was water-borne from the point of origin to the point of overseas destination, and all along the route buyers and sellers looked oceanward.

When the frontiersmen finally moved over the Allegheny Mountains in the pre-Revolutionary era and began to settle along the tributaries of the Monongahela and Allegheny Rivers, they continued to think of Philadelphia and Baltimore as the normal outlets for their excess products. But the habit of trading to the east now encountered the barrier of the mountains, and little by little the westerly flow of water toward the Ohio and the Mississippi Rivers redirected the mental focus of the settlers. Philadelphia seemed increasingly remote, Europe inaccessible and unimportant. On the other hand, Cincinnati, St. Louis, and New Orleans became neighbors. Thus the flow of the rivers set Pennsylvanians trading in opposite directions.

The bulky products of the colonial frontier moved down streams from the farm to the mill to the village to the port of Philadelphia where the docks would be piled high with Pennsylvania cargo for export: wheat, corn, flour, biscuit, barreled beef, pork, bacon and ham, butter, cheese, apples, cider, leather, beer, whiskey, peltry, and lumber. On the Delaware River a kind of shallow-draft boat, pointed at both ends and capable of being poled laboriously back upstream, became the regional favorite. Called Durham boats from their orginal use by the Durham ironworks near Easton, they were about 60 feet long and could carry 15 tons. On the Susquehanna a motley array of produce-laden rafts floated to Baltimore at times of high water, to be broken up for lumber at the end of the journey. Western rivermen produced the keelboat which, like the Durham boat, could be poled back upstream.

The river commerce of colonial Pensylvania was nearly all one way—outbound with the current. The inbound trade followed the Indian paths, overland. While peddlers served the more heavily populated areas, packtrains generally carried the compact manufactured merchandise to the back country. They carried on much of the trade with the Indians, supplied frontier posts and villages with the things they needed, and normally returned east loaded with furs. Until 1818, packtrains were the only routine freight carriers across the mountains.

The packtrains used the Indian paths, as did the countless individuals migrating to new homes or moving about on business. These paths, a remarkable achievement in road engineering, constitute a lasting memorial to the Indians of Pennsylvania. The region was so crisscrossed by them that only rarely would a settler be further than 20 miles from one of them. Indian paths would usually be about 18 inches wide, well beaten, and unmistakable. They were dry, level, and direct. Rather than following the streams, they ran on higher ground, in the rise of valleys which farmers call a "ridge road."

The provincial authorities provided two special road systems: the King's Highways radiating for short distances out of Philadelphia, and the two westward-reaching military roads, Braddock's and Forbes's. The King's Highways, authorized in 1700, were 50-foot-wide dirt roads cleared of trees and brush. King's Road ran to Morrisville and connected Philadelphia with New York; Queen's Road ran to Chester; Old York Road to Doylestown, Allentown, and Easton; Egypt Road to Phoenixville; and the Old Conestoga Road to Lancaster, the largest inland town in America in colonial days.

The German farmers of the area found a major market for their produce in Philadelphia and at the many inns which sprang up along the pikes. By 1760 craftsmen of the area had developed a unique form of transport called the Conestoga wagon, pulled by six large Conestoga draft horses festooned with bells. These famous wagons, with a curved bed and sloping ends to prevent the shifting of the load on hills and to aid in fording streams, could carry three or four tons each. With their blue bodies, red wheels with wide iron tires, and white cloth tops stretched over hoops to keep the load dry, the Conestoga wagons became so numerous on the road from Philadelphia to Lancaster that they required traffic rules and introduced to America the custom of driving on the right. Later, slightly modified, they became the prairie schooners which carried migration across the Great Plains. Apart from their utility as frieght carriers, the Conestoga wagons became a kind of primitive art form inspiring skilled craftsmanship in decorative iron and woodcraft.

Stagecoach lines for passenger traffic sprang up wherever the existence of roads and the urban population justified them. From the 1730s onward, Philadelphia became a hub of stagecoach enterprises which fanned out in every direction along the King's Highways. It took two or three days to go to New York from Philadelphia, three or four to Baltimore, and a day and a half to Lancaster, depending on weather and road conditions.

The military roads built west of the Susquehanna by Braddock and Forbes provided the only wagon lanes over the mountains, and they became impassable when they fell into disrepair soon after the French and Indian War. With no army at hand to pull wagons over rocky inclines, they became impractical and lapsed into packtrain routes, though some parts remained usable for carts.

Competition of cities for trade   The seaport cities in colonial days served as sacks under a funnel, collecting the river-borne produce of the back country. Each port prospered by exploiting this natural monopoly. But as population grew, a strenuous commercial rivalry developed among New York, Baltimore, and Philadelphia. Looking seaward, New York had the best harbor for sailing ships, Baltimore less winter ice than the others, and Philadelphia the most troublesome port of entry.

But Philadelphia initially had a number of advantages. It tapped a larger farming community than the others and collected goods from two river systems, the Delaware and the Susquehanna. In the Federal era it was America'a largest city and enjoyed the added prestige of being capital of the state and of the nation. Early in the 1790s, Philadelphia had 42,000 inhabitants as compared with 33,000 for New York, her closest competitor; the city shipped more than one-third of all the exports of the United States, handled twice as much shipping as Baltimore and 25 percent more than New York. It had aggressive and wealthy merchants like Charles Willing, Thomas Willing, Robert Morris, George Clymer, Thomas Fitzsimmons, the Perots, and Stephen Girard, and firms like Levy, Franks, and Simon.

After 1800, when the national and state capitals moved elsewhere, Philadelphians began to worry about Baltimore; and when New York's Erie Canal neared completion in the early 1820s, the city fathers began a frantic effort to recapture their slipping commercial position, an effort which profoundly affected state politics up to the Civil War. Thomas F. Gordon's *Gazetteer of Pennsylvania* in 1832 stated:

> Philadelphia is not the port for one half of the State of Pennsylvania. The great valley of the Susquehanna pours a vast portion of its treasure into the city of Baltimore, and the Ohio and Mississippi bear away the whole surplus produce of Western Pennsylvania. Hence New Orleans and Baltimore are nearly as much ports of the State as Philadelphia itself.

Philadephia's exertions to promote her own trade aroused a competitive response from Pittsburgh which by the 1830s had achieved economic and political power. Thus the rivalry of major cities for commercial advantage existed not only between states, but in Pennsylvania within the state. The inside struggle between Pittsburgh and Philadelphia weakened the latter's response to the challenge of New York and Baltimore. It also delayed Pennsylvania's decision to build a first-rate trade artery to the west and aroused sectional rancor and obstructionism. By the time the state finally completed its canal system from Philadelphia to Pittsburgh, New York had already achieved primacy in commerce. By the 1850s, both Philadelphia and Pittsburgh had begun to turn from commerce to manufacturing as their main economic thrust.

The turnpike era   From 1790 to 1830 Pennsylvania concentrated its transportation effort on roads and bridges. It seems now that regional planning of through routes, as advocated by Albert Gallatin's report of 1808 on Federal internal improvements, would have saved a great deal of time, money, and effort. But people feared to give state or national authorities broad power over transport routes. Consequently each town promoted a road to connect it with a near neighbor and Pennsylvania soon had hundreds of short turnpikes which did not interconnect and served only a local function. With 3,000 miles of turnpikes by 1832, Pennsylvania led all the states, but the mileage was split up among some 220 local companies. The busiest through road was built by the state, extending the Philadelphia-Lancaster pike westward to York, Chambersburg, Bedford, and Pittsburgh. Completed in 1818 as an all-weather macadam pike, the Pennsylvania Road carried nine-tenths of all the transmontane traffic of the nation until the opening of the Erie Canal. A northern branch connected Harrisburg with this road via Carlisle and Chambersburg.

The turnpike road companies were mostly mixed corporations; that is, the state or local government pledged to buy part of the capital stock, and private buyers took up the rest. This provided a partial public subsidy to the companies and encouraged promoters to undertake ventures which private capital would not have sustained. When construction costs exceeded the estimates, the companies often issued additional stock which the Legislature authorized the state to buy.

The builders experimented with many types of roads. The Lancaster-Philadelphia pike, one of the best, used the ideas developed by Telford and MacAdam in England: a base of 7-inch stone topped with a layer of 3-inch stone and the whole capped by a layer of fine crushed rock. The Americans added a high crown to carry off the water. This construction, later adopted for the Cumberland Road, provided an all-weather surface. But most of the turnpikes were merely a dirt surface cleared of boulders and stumps, and these quickly developed huge chuckholes from the action of spring thaws. Traffic wore ruts, exposed subsurface rocks, and subjected vehicles to constant pounding and occasional upset. To prevent chuckholes and ruts, some road companies laid split logs perpendicular to the right of way, like closely laid railroad ties, and covered them with dirt. These log or "corduroy" roads served well until the dirt sifted through the chinks. Near the end of the era, a few plank roads were built. Such smooth, all-wood highways gave a luxurious ride, but many companies went bankrupt because they had underestimated the maintenance costs.

The tolls, collected every five or ten miles, ranged from about 40 cents per gate for a four-horse coach to 3 cents for a wagon with 15-inch-wide tires, which flattened the ruts. Drovers taking animals to market paid about 12 cents per gate for twenty sheep or hogs and twice that rate for cattle. Different rates applied at different seasons, and local farmers had free use of the roads near their land.

Innumerable taverns sprang up along the turnpikes, identified by painted signs depicting the crowned heads of Europe, Indian chiefs, and national heroes; the whole animal kingdom of lions, stags, bulls, horses, swans, and eagles; and symbols of nature and the crafts, like the white oak, the grape, the plow, the wheat sheaf, or the Pennsylvania farmer. At dusk the main road inns became a bedlam of travellers, horses, stages, freight wagons, and drovers with hundreds of unruly animals in their charge.

Turnpike companies generally built their own bridges over small streams, but separate bridge companies financed the larger ones over major rivers like the Susquehanna. Pennsylvania's many streams focused interest on bridges and brought forth many experiments. By the 1820s travellers commented on the especially elegant and substantial bridges of the region. The Philadelphians, when their city was national capital, built floating bridges across the Schuylkill by chaining logs together and fastening planks across them, but the weight of a wagon sank the roadway several inches under the water. In 1796 Judge James Finley of Fayette County invented a chain suspension bridge which he patented in 1801 and which spread all over the nation. A Philadelphia company erected such a bridge over the Schuylkill in 1809, but a faulty chain coupling broke under the weight of a herd of cattle in 1811 and the structure collapsed. The Lancaster Pike boasted three "great bridges": a wooden "Permanent Bridge" across the Schuylkill, a three-arch limestone bridge over the Brandywine at Downingtown, and the magnificent nine-arch Witmer's Bridge over the Conestoga at Lancaster which was built and owned by the man whose name it bore.

The name Theodore Burr is indelibly associated with bridging the Susquehanna. This Connecticut Yankee came to Northumberland in 1811 to build his first huge, multispan, arch-truss, covered bridge across the river; and by the time of his death in 1822 he had constructed five more such bridges, four in Pennsylvania and one in Maryland: Nescopek Falls (Berwick), Harrisburg, Columbia, McCall's Ferry, and Rock Run, Maryland. The Columbia-Wrightsville bridge used twenty-seven spans to bridge 5,690 feet of water. Burr performed his greatest engineering feat in the McCall's Ferry bridge, floating prefabricated spans into position on pontoons and hoisting them onto the piers. Burr's bridge at Harrisburg remained in use until the twentieth century. In the west, Pittsburghers had completed bridges across the Allegheny and the Monongahela by 1819. All these bridges were financed by private corporations, and they charged toll independently of the turnpikes which they served.

The steamboat and canal era Although Pennsylvanians planned throughout the colonial period to build canals, they acted first to produce an entirely new kind of water transport, the steamboat. William Henry built an experimental steamboat on Conestoga Creek in 1763, and Oliver Evans demonstrated his strange-looking steam amphibian vehicle to Philadelphians in 1804. But two other names have attached themselves most firmly to the early steamboat: John Fitch and Robert Fulton. Fitch, a Connecticut-born jack-of-all-trades, came to Philadelphia and in 1787 launched a boat propelled by banks of steam-driven oars. In 1788 and 1790 he produced two paddle-wheel steamboats which offered regular commercial service between Philadelphia and Burlington, New Jersey. People ridiculed his achievement and so discouraged him that he finally abandoned his efforts. He lives in history as "Poor John Fitch," a man whose vision reached ahead of his time.

Robert Fulton completed Fitch's work. Born in Lancaster County, he became an artist, a civil engineer, and an inventor. He wrote treaties on canal construction, built a successful

William Frick's Boat Yard at Highspire. Building canal boats was a large industry. This yard built boats for the privately operated Schuylkill Canal. (Pennsylvania Historical and Museum Commission)

submarine and underwater torpedoes, designed bridges, and after 1800 began work on steam navigation. As with most so-called inventions, his steamboat, *Clermont,* which in 1807 paddled up the Hudson River at 4½ miles per hour, represented not a new idea but the solution of technical difficulties. Fulton placed a lighter engine in a stronger hull, and started the steamboat age.

In 1811 a partner of Fulton's in Pittsburgh built the first Mississippi River steamboat. It was called the *New Orleans* and it proved itself by going to its namesake city and back on its maiden voyage. Pittsburgh soon built a thriving steamboat industry, producing some 2,000 of these famous rivercraft before the Civil War. The proven success of steamboats excited people along the Susquehanna to dream that they could establish two-way transport between Maryland and New York. A York firm in 1825 built an iron steamboat, the *Codorus,* which steamed to Binghamton and back and raised wild enthusiasm. The Baltimore-built steamboat *Susquehanna* successfully plied between the Conewago Falls and Berwick until, in 1826, it exploded at Nescopeck Falls. Sporadic efforts to navigate the Susquehanna by steam continued into the 1850s.

Pennsylvania chartered fifteen private companies to build canals and improve rivers between 1791 and 1819. Some of these never completed their projects and others merged. The privately run canals which became operational were the Lackawaxen Canal of the Delaware and Hudson Company which carried coal from Honesdale, Wayne County, to the Delaware River; the Lehigh Navigation Company whose canal tapped the coal region of Luzerne County and joined the Delaware at Easton; the Schuylkill Navigation from Pottsville to Philadelphia; the Union Canal which connected the Susquehanna River at Middletown with Philadelphia by intercepting the Schuylkill Navigation near Reading; the Wiconisco Canal on the east bank of the Susquehanna from Millersburg to Clark's Ferry; the Conestoga Slackwater Navigation from Lancaster to the Susquehanna at Safe Harbor; and the Codorus Canal from York to the Susquehanna. Private companies also ran the two major interstate canals: the Susquehanna and Tidewater Canal from Wrightsville to Havre de Grace along the west bank, and the Chesapeake and Delaware Canal from the head of Elk River to the Delaware Bay. In the 1850s, river improvements made the Youghiogheny River navigable to the Monongahela, and the Monongahela navigable southward to Virginia. Enough privately financed canal building had been done by 1825 to make it clear that this method would produce only scattered short lines to serve special local purposes, and that more centralized planning and much greater resources would be needed to create routes from one end of the state to the other which could compete with New York's Erie Canal.

Pennsylvania passed the law which inaugurated the huge state transportation system, called the State Works, in February 1826, a week after the *Susquehanna's* disaster exploded the dream of inland steam navigation. The state system would comprise six divisions: the Main Line from Philadelphia to Pittsburgh; the North Branch from Clark's Ferry to Athens, connecting with the New York canals; the West Branch, from Northumberland to Bellefonte; the Delaware Canal from Easton to Philadelphia; the Erie Extension from Pittsburgh north; and the French Creek Feeder linking the Erie Extension with the Allegheny River. These systems provided about 800 miles of waterway and 117 miles of railroad. They interlocked not only with each other, but with most of the private canals and state systems of New York, Maryland, and Virginia.

Travelers described the trip on the Main Line as an engineering marvel and a scenic wonder. Construction of the canals required digging a ditch 40 feet wide and 4 feet deep and giving it a watertight lining, walling one bank against erosion wherever the canal adjoined a river, building bridges to accommodate intersecting roads, locating towpaths on both sides of the canal, providing innumerable locks, devising various means to carry the canal and towpaths across small intersecting streams, digging feeder canals to maintain proper water level in the transport canals, locating and building the sluices to raise or lower the water level, building aqueducts like the double-decker at Clark's Ferry or the Conemaugh Viaduct at Johnstown to carry the canal and towpath across large rivers and ravines, devising the mechanics and the hydraulics of the locks, gates, and sluices, and solving a host of other practical problems. Such work had to continue after the canals had been completed, for winter ice and summer cloudbursts often brought diaster. In the spring of 1838 a mountain cloudburst washed out the whole system from Hollidaysburg to Huntingdon and stopped traffic for nearly a year.

The railroad part of the State Works formed its unique and most famous engineering achievement. The railroad from Philadelphia to Columbia was mostly routine construction, but the line from Hollidaysburg to Johnstown, known as the Allegheny Portage Railroad, provided five double-tracked inclined planes on each side of the mountain on which cars were hauled by stationary steam engines. Cars on adjoining tracks moved up and down simultaneously to balance the load. Nine short railroads using horses first and locomotives later hauled cars over the level planes between inclines. The cars had to be coupled and uncoupled

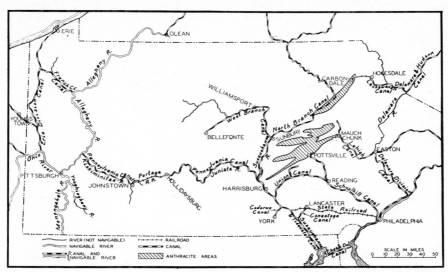

The canal system of Pennsylvania showing the Main Line and various divisions of the State Works and the private canals, many of which were built to tap the anthracite coal fields.

thirty-three times on the thirty-six-mile transit over the mountains. Later canal boats were built with two or four watertight sections each of which rode on a special railroad car from Philadelphia to Columbia. The rejoined sections traveled as a boat to Hollidaysburg where, taken apart again, the sections were hoisted onto flatcars and carried over the Portage Railroad. Thus a passenger or a load of grain might proceed from one end of the line to the other without leaving the boat.

The State Works provided a training school for inventors and transportation men. The high cost of the hemp hawsers used on the inclines and their occasional breakage led John A. Roebling of Mercer County to propose wire rope. The experimental rope he supplied for the Portage Railroad launched him into the business which later produced the wire-suspended Niagara and Brooklyn Bridges and speeded the other inventions dependent on flexible metal wire. Famous railroad men like Moncure Robinson, Mathias Baldwin, William Norris, Phineas Davis, Thomas A. Scott, Andrew Carnegie, and Simon Cameron gained experience as planners, designers, suppliers, or managers for the State Works.

The state owned and scheduled the locomotives on the railroad portion of the Main Line, but the shippers owned the cars and paid for use of the line and the motive power. Canal boats were privately owned. As enterprisers gained experience, they introduced canal boats with sleeping and dining facilities for passengers instead of stopping overnight at the canal inns which dotted the line as did the stagecoach taverns on the pikes. In the heyday of the State Works, a passenger could board a sectional boat in Philadelphia and never leave it until he disembarked at Pittsburgh four days later—a trip of 394 miles for $7. Freight cost about 3 cents per ton mile on the canal in 1853 as compared with about 15 cents by wagon. The Main Line was admittedly an engineering wonder, but except for the railroad line from

A sectional canal boat being hauled up the incline to Plane #6 on the Allegheny Portage Railroad between Hollidaysburg and Johnstown. (Pennsylvania Historical and Museum Commission)

Philadelphia to Columbia, it was a financial disaster. Even with the sectional boats, the mountain passage required too much car handling to compete with the Erie Canal.

Railroads Railroad development in Pennsylvania went through three stages: the early horse-powered tramways, the short coal railroads, and the trunk lines. Quarries and mines began to use tramways as early as 1809. In 1827 the Lehigh Coal and Navigation Company built a 9-mile gravity railway at Mauch Chunk, where loaded coal cars at the hilltop mine entrance coasted downhill carrying the mules who would haul the empties back up the hill. The Delaware and Hudson Company built a 16-mile railroad from Carbondale to the head of their canal at Honesdale in 1829, and purchased an English locomotive, the *Stourbridge Lion,* to haul the cars. Other coal railroads began operation soon thereafter. The Philadelphia and Reading Railroad, chartered in 1833, was carrying more tonnage by 1858 than the Erie Canal. The Philadelphia and Sunbury; the Mount Carbon; the Delaware; the Lehigh; the Schuylkill and Susquehanna (Lehigh Valley); the Delaware, Lackawanna and Western; and many other coal railroads were chartered before 1860. Some of them carried coal only from the mines to the nearest canal port, but others, like the Reading Railroad, paralleled a canal and put it out of business. In 1856, coal composed 42 percent of the Pennsylvania Railroad's tonnage.

By the 1850s the railroad builders were still duplicating the procedure of the turnpike builders—chartering scores of companies committed to build local lines. As the folly of this became apparent, a few major railroads began to buy up short lines and to concentrate their effort on building trunk lines. The Pennsylvania Railroad had acquired so many of the short lines by 1860 that it obtained a near monopoly of rail traffic through Pennsylvania from Chicago. Several competing trunk railroads of adjacent states, mainly the Erie, the New York Central, and the Baltimore and Ohio, gained some branch-line traffic from Pennsylvania, but the Pennsylvania Railroad carried the main flow.

Pennsylvania reached its maximum of 954 miles of canal in 1840. Railroad trackage had nearly attained this point by 1850 but by 1860 had grown to 2,598 miles. Railroaders in Pennsylvania from 1830 to 1850 faced the resistance encountered by most innovators. Farmers complained that locomotives frightened the animals; teamsters and boatmen foresaw the destruction of their livelihood; villagers denounced the threat to public safety; and those who had invested their money in turnpikes and canals cried in anguish. But by 1850 railroads had proved their superiority. Cities, counties, and local citizens invested in the first railroads, and towns became so eager to have a railroad that local governments in Pennsylvania invested $14 million in railroad securities by 1840. Pittsburgh's massive investment in railroads became the major political issue of the city in the late 1850s. But the longer lines strained local resources, and British capitalists soon became the largest investors in the Philadelphia and Reading company and the Pennsylvania Railroad company.

Scene along the West Branch of the Susquehanna, showing turnpike, telegraph, railroad, canal, and river in close proximity. (Pennsylvania Historical and Museum Commission)

As railroad building expanded, new problems and new solutions grew apace. A war of gauges developed in the early 1850s when railroads of Ohio and of Pennsylvania each provided seven different widths of track. In 1852 the Pennsylvania Legislature required all railroads to use the 4-foot, 8½-inch width as a standard gauge. John B. Jervis of the Delaware and Hudson line contrived the pilot truck or four-wheel bogie which guided the locomotive smoothly into curves and greatly reduced derailments. William Norris, Philadelphia locomotive builder, gained international fame in 1836 by demonstrating to an audience of incredulous railroadmen that his engine, the *George Washington,* could pull a loaded train up the steep Belmont incline. Joseph Harrison of Philadelphia invented the equalizing beam which kept all driving wheels of a locomotive in contact with the track and thus increased traction and reduced accidents. The Cumberland Valley Railroad introduced a sleeping car in 1836. Manufacturing establishments for locomotives and railroad equipment sprang up all over the commonwealth, chief among them the Baldwin Locomotive Works in Philadelphia.

MANUFACTURING

Before the Industrial Revolution, manufacturing in Pennsylvania meant home and village crafts. The only common machines before the era of steam and iron were spinning wheels, hand looms, bellows, flax and hemp brakes, and simple mills to grind flour, saw logs, or card wool and full cloth. But Pennsylvania possessed features which stimulated more complex manufacturing techniques. Cosmopolitan Philadelphia brought active thinkers into contact with one another and provided the financial resources for experiment. Its close ties with Europe kept the people acquainted with new products and methods in England and on the Continent. Its proportion of skilled artisans to the total population gave it as high a concentration of mechanics as could be found anywhere. And it could furnish the transportation, the markets, and the variety of materials which its craftsmen needed. By 1810, Philadelphia was the source of one-third of all the manufactures of the state.

Beyond the city, Pennsylvania had rivers for power and transportation, and such basic raw materials as wood, fibre, iron ore, stone, and clay. The province had a stable government whose laws generally encouraged manufacturing and did not inhibit the movement of products. All these factors gave an impetus to manufacturing in preindustrial Pennsylvania. But most important of all were the Embargo, the Nonintercourse Acts, and the War of 1812 which, coming at the very moment the new technology of the Industrial Revolution was appearing, shifted the emphasis from shipping to manufacturing.

In the colonial era, most manufactured products were made at home: cloth, furniture, preserved food, utensils, implements, and building materials like brick and boards. The products from the farms were the largest part of the manufactures of the province in money value, but they were the least important in terms of complex machinery or organized production. Household manufactures were supplemented by village manufactures from the shops of blacksmiths, shoemakers, coopers, and other skilled craftsmen. When villages developed into cities, merchant mills undertook larger production by hiring workbench craftsmen or small shops to deliver their products to a central location for distribution. The craftsman did not now sell his product directly, but became a supplier to a larger enterpriser. From this stage to the factory system was but a short step.

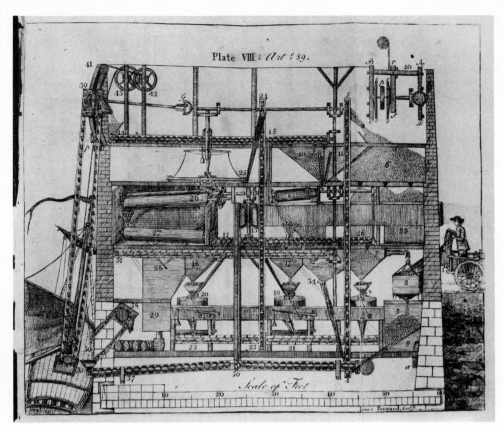

Diagram prepared in 1795 by Oliver Evans for his automated grist mill which received grain from wagons or ships and, using water power and gravity, moved it through the grinding process into barrels without human intervention. Numbers show the movement of the grain. (Oliver Evans: *The Young Millwright*)

Water-powered mills became the most widespread mechanical contrivance before the Industrial Revolution. On a frontier farm a sawmill was a pit and a saw which enabled one or two men to cut a log into planks. At the village, a sawmill might use waterpower to move a bank of saws through a log. Philadelphia craftsmen produced the saws and by 1820 had made this city the national center of that industry. Carding mills to comb tangles out of flax or wool to prepare it for spinning, and fulling mills to soften the woven cloth became common village establishments. But gristmills were the most numerous, for farmers needed a mill close to home.

At the end of the War for Independence Oliver Evans, a versatile inventor of Philadelphia, revolutionized gristmilling. In his prophetic book, *The Young Mill-wright and Miller's Guide,* he presented detailed instructions for building an automated gristmill. After the farmer delivered his grain, the waterpowered mill weighed it, carried it aloft to a hopper, released it by gravity to millstones on the lower levels, raised it again to cool, and directed it into chutes to be sifted on the way down and barreled at the bottom. The Evans-type mill came into wide use throughout the Middle Atlantic region after 1800 and became a distinctive architectural as well as mechanical landmark. It was an early example of a continuous-flow mill, receiving raw material, carrying it through a sequence of processes, and delivering a finished product with little human intervention.

The iron business of colonial Pennsylvania, more than any other, presaged the Industrial Revolution. In an era of small farms, wooden implements, and workbench manufacturing, the ironmasters forged the guidelines for the factory system of the future: massive capital investment; detailed cost accounting; development of far-off markets; division of labor by precise job definition; invention and crafting of machinery, as none could be bought ready-made; standardization of product; and personnel management of a complex order. The charcoal iron business meant not a mansion and a furnace stack, but the creation and smooth coordination of half a dozen businesses: mining, limestone quarrying, woodcutting and char-coal burning, working in the furnace, and possibly forging. In addition to these, it meant the artisans to supply the whole complex establishment: farmers, coopers, wagonmakers, tanners, blacksmiths, wheelwrights, millers, storekeepers, and perhaps a teacher and preacher. These had to work in close coordination or the enterprise would fail, as many did.

Thomas Rutter built a crude bloomery on Manatawny Creek in 1718 to start a business which has been growing in Pennsylvania ever since. By the time of independence the Schuyl-kill Valley had become the heart of the American iron industry, and soon thereafter the furnaces began to spread along the valleys of the Susquehanna, the Monongahela, and the Allegheny Rivers. By 1800 at least 167 furnaces and forges had been established, and their owners represented economic and civic leadership in the persons of such men as James Logan, William Bird and Mark Bird, the Potts family, Robert Coleman, James Wilson, James Ross, William Henry Steigel, and Peter Grubb, whose Cornwall furnace has been preserved by the state.

The early iron business had two distinct parts: the furnace which produced pigs or castings; and the forge which fashioned the reheated pigs into rods, straps, and plates that a blacksmith could use. The furnace operation required about 10,000 acres of land providing iron ore, limestone, hardwood, and a swift-flowing stream all in close proximity, normally a wilderness location. Miners dug surface ore with pick and shovel; ore burners baked it to remove impurities and to fuse the ore into pellets. Quarrymen blasted limestone and broke up large rocks by sledge into fist size. Making charcoal required the most effort, for it took 400 bushels of charcoal to make a ton of iron. An average furnace denuded an acre of woodland every day and consumed around 6,000 cords of wood a year. These raw materials had to be carried in carts or baskets from the point of production to the furnace stack. The forge sometimes was part of a furnace operation, but more commonly was a separate enterprise, for it required much more water to lift a ¼-ton forge hammer than to operate a furnace bellows.

The rapidly rising demand for iron products kept continual pressure upon ironmasters to improve their production methods. Isaac Meason's Plumsock Works near Uniontown introduced the process of making bar iron by using a puddling furnace and grooved rolls. By the

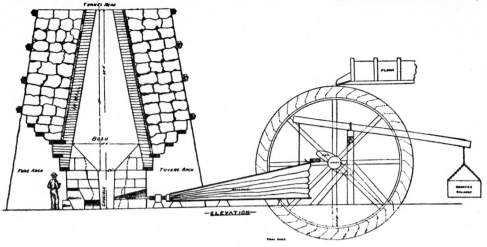

Diagram of a charcoal iron furnace stack showing the tunnel head, bosh and crucible, and water-driven bellows with counterweights. (Arthur C. Binning: *Pennsylvania Iron Manufacture in the 18th Century*)

An early water-driven forge, where pig iron from the furnace was refined and shaped. (Arthur C. Bining: *Pennsylvania Iron Manufacture in the 19th Century*)

1820s Pennsylvania had eight rolling mills, mostly steam-powered, which made both bar and sheet iron. As railroading expanded, England supplied most of the improved T rails until the United States captured this market in the late 1850s when George Fritz at the Cambria Iron Works in Johnstown replaced the two-high rolls of the mill with a three-high train which doubled production. The new system permitted workmen to lower hot rolled iron from the top set of rolls and send it back through the bottom set, instead of carrying the piece back through the mill after each successive passage through the two-high rolls. At about the same time Bernard Lauth, a Pennsylvania mill owner, discovered that iron could be cold-rolled and would emerge a tougher, smoother product. By 1860, Pennsylvania mills rolled more than half the iron of the nation, and had become the center of creative activity in iron and steel manufacture.

Charcoal iron dominated the industry up to the Civil War. Until 1840 the main production remained concentrated in Lancaster, Berks, and Chester Counties; after that the Juniata district of Mifflin, Huntingdon, and Centre Counties became the most productive. The ores of this region were especially rich and produced a high-quality iron which craftsmen like gun and tool makers required. At its peak in 1840, the charcoal iron business represented a capital investment of nearly eight million dollars, employed 11,522 workers, and operated 113 furnaces and 169 bloomeries, forges, and rolling mills.

The advent of coal brought major improvements to smelting. The Franklin Institute of Philadelphia in 1826 offered gold medals to iron masters who smelted with anthracite, and in 1836 the state legislature urged that new iron companies turn from charcoal to coal. The Lehigh Coal and Navigation Company offered its dams for power and pledged $30,000 to any new iron companies that would use anthracite. Many furnaces experimented with the new fuel in the 1830s without solving the problems until David Thomas, a workman of the Lehigh Crane Iron Company near Allentown devised worktable techniques and earned for himself the title "Father of the American Anthracite Iron Industry." A reverberatory furnace which separated the fuel from the ore solved the main problem. By 1860, Pennsylvania produced over half the anthracite iron in the United States, most of it in the Lehigh Valley.

The introduction of coal as a smelting fuel forced the improvement and general use of the hot blast. And all these developments, together with the improvement of transportation facilities, combined to relocate the iron industry from the wilderness into cities like Pittsburgh and Johnstown. Large iron-sheathed furnaces flanked by heaters replaced the old stone stacks and gave the iron business a new appearance. At the very end of the antebellum period, William Kelly at the Cambria Iron Works proved the practicability of making steel by his "air-boiling" process, for which he received a patent as original inventor in 1857 despite a contest with Britain's Henry Bessemer over priority. The new process, soon to be backed by a powerful financial pool known as the Pennsylvania Group, ushered in the age of steel.

In the century between the French and Indian War and the Civil War, during which the Industrial Revolution wrought its changes, Pennsylvania adapted in a way which preserved its major colonial industries and kept their production in first or second place among the states of the nation, depending upon the decade. The major industries were processed foods like flour, meat, whiskey, and beer; textiles in the form of homemade linsey-woolsey until 1820, and factory-made woolen and cotton cloth thereafter; iron and its products; paper,

Canal boats at the Nanticoke Breaker waiting to be loaded with coal. (Pennsylvania Historical and Museum Commission)

mainly for the publishing business; tanned leather; and wood and its products. Philadelphia led the nation in shipbuilding for most of the century, and by 1850 the lumber business of the upper Susquehanna, centering around Lock Haven and Williamsport, became the largest in the country. In 1860, Pennsylvania held first place nationally in the production of cloth, iron, leather, and wood.

Many other types of manufacturing existed on a smaller scale. Baron Henry William Stiegel began the production of glass in Manheim in colonial days. This industry later grew rapidly in the vicinity of Philadelphia and Pittsburgh. The Pennsylvania Germans produced colorful pottery which attained wide distribution. Philadelphia's artisans made the luxury articles which the inhabitants of a great city always wanted: silver, brass, and pewter work; clocks; fine furniture and carriages; books; and special articles of clothing such as hats or hosiery. Each of these industries, whether major or minor, has a story of its own which cannot be told here.

But three important aspects of manufacturing remain to be examined: the concept of protection, the chartered corporation, and diversification. We commonly accept that shippers opposed and manufacturers sought a protective tariff in the early national period of American history; and that in the mid-1820s, as the New England manufacturing interests began to outweigh the commercial interests, protection became the major political issue. But this shift of emphasis did not occur in Pennsylvania, which strongly supported the protective principle from the days of Washington for a variety of reasons. Farmers wanted protection of wool and hemp; workers thought protection would raise wages; iron producers needed protection against stiff British competition; Philadelphia, the main shipping point, also contained most of the early manufacturing establishments; and finally a group of eminent Pennsylvania economists developed cogent arguments in favor of the protective system.

Tenche Coxe of Philadelphia became Alexander Hamilton's assistant during the period when he was preparing his *Report on Manufactures* in 1790. Coxe held farsighted economic views, advocating industrial planning by cities, conservation of natural resources, and the protective principle to aid infant industries. Mathew Carey became the ideologist and statistician for Henry Clay's American System. He published a stream of books and pamphlets full of hard arguments and persuasive figures to support his advocacy of a mutually beneficial alliance between government and business—an American mercantilism. Carey had a special interest in promoting high protection for Pennsylvania's iron industry. Mathew Carey's son, Henry Charles Carey, continued his father's protectionist crusade. Finally, the German economist, Friedrich List, came to Reading where he edited a newspaper which sustained the protective argument.

Pennsylvania congressmen regularly supported protective tariff bills. They backed Hamilton's *Report on Manufactures* in 1791. Philadelphia's Alexander J. Dallas, as Secretary of the Treasury, devised the Tariff of 1816. Henry Baldwin of Pittsburgh served as chairman of the Ways and Means Committee in Congress and tried unsuccessfully to raise the tariff in 1820. We have already discussed how Pennsylvania congressmen supported the high tariff bills of 1824, 1827, 1828, 1832, and 1842; and how all but David Wilmot voted against the low tariff of 1846. The Republicans used the widespread sentiment for higher tariff as a political tool in Pennsylvania to elect Lincoln in 1860.

The second theme, state chartering of manufacturing corporations, introduced the problem of institutional change. The old partnership or joint stock company worked for small and simple projects like a bridge or turnpike, but fell far short of the needs for massive capital investment, long-range continuity, limited liability, and the flexibility of function demanded by the new factory system. The Pennsylvania Legislature at first looked with suspicion upon applications for chartering manufacturing concerns, especially when the incorporators sought broad powers. But as products began to flow from the factories, charters began to multiply. Pennsylvania issued five charters to manufacturing corporations before 1815, eighty-one from 1815 to 1850, and ninety-three from 1851 to 1860. Most manufacturers operated without charters, but the above figures illustrate the trend toward the corporate system of organization under state charter which would characterize the future.

The third theme, diversification, suggests some useful comparisons. Pennsylvania by 1860 had developed traditional products and skills: food processing, textiles, iron, leather, and wood. These started early in the 1700s and remained of major importance; that is, the Industrial Revolution did not curtail any, but expanded each of these major industries. The state thus gained much of its wealth from a few continuing products. But at the same time it produced a wide variety of minor manufactured products. It never held the position of a single-product economy like some of the cotton and corn states. The diversification of enterprise gave the commonwealth great resilience to depressions and reduced the impact of dislocations brought by the rapidly changing technology.

LABOR

Pennsylvania's colonial work force rapidly broke away from the menial status which the European class structure had assigned to its laborers. Artisans and mechanics filled such a vital need in the new province that they quickly gained respectability and influence.

Children probably formed as large a labor group as any because so much of the population lived on farms. Large farm families were the rule, and the number of children determined how fast the woodland could be transformed into tillable fields, how much livestock a farmer could manage, how much grain he could plant and harvest, or how much cloth he might have for sale. In the cities, children who followed their father's trade served as helpers and apprentices until they reached maturity.

Those who already had a trade were always in demand; the skilled artisans and mechanics moved rapidly from the status of employee to employer. Anyone who began as an apprentice or journeyman found wide opportunity to set up business for himself. Franklin, John Fitch, and Oliver Evans all followed this route. The artisans commanded not only high wages but a great deal of independence and respect. It is impossible to tell their exact number at any given time because they changed their status and location, but these workers formed the largest part of the population of the towns and of the iron plantations.

Pennsylvania never welcomed slave labor. During Penn's lifetime the Assembly entertained motions periodically to declare all slaves free, but did not act. In 1712, however, the Assembly placed a duty on the importation of slaves to discourage the traffic. Very few slaves were brought to Philadelphia from Africa, but a good many came from Barbados and were sold in the city coffeehouses, mostly for house servants. Negro craftsmen provoked protests from European immigrants to Philadelphia who in 1722 demanded legislation to prevent the employment of blacks. The Assembly resolved "that the principle was dangerous and injurious to the Republic, and ought not to be sanctioned," but nonetheless passed laws in 1725 and 1726 which made special rules for Negroes and set them apart, by law, as a separate class. About 6,000 slaves had entered Pennsylvania by 1750; thereafter their number grew mainly by natural increase as importation declined. The Census of 1790, a decade after the passage of Pennsylvania's abolition law, recorded 6,537 free Negroes and 3,737 slaves residing in the state, out of a total population of 434,373.

Most of Pennsylvania's early work force came through the process of indentured servitude by which an immigrant obligated himself to service for a period of years to whoever paid his passage. The ship captain generally held the original indenture papers and sold the services of his passengers to buyers upon arrival at Philadelphia.

A second type of indenture provided education and apprentice training for young people whose parents sold their labor for up to eight years in return for introduction into the "mysteries" of some craft and "six months day schooling and six months evening schooling, to learn to read, write and cipher."

Finally, many people imprisoned for debt sold themselves as indentured servants to their creditors or to people who would pay the debt. This procedure, with the consent of the debtor, was formalized by acts of Assembly in 1700 and 1731. Under certain circumstances the jailer could sell the services of prisoners. Such indenture ceased when Pennsylvania abolished imprisonment for debt in 1833.

The indenture contract imposed obligations upon the master to feed and house the servant, and to provide "freedom dues" such as clothing, shoes, or money when the term of service had expired. The servant bound himself to serve his master, keep his secrets, not lend or waste his goods, not commit fornication, marry, play cards or dice, buy or sell his own or anyone else's goods, absent himself without leave, or "haunt ale-houses, taverns or play-houses."

The involuntary indentured servants entered the same contract, but against their will. Unscrupulous ship captains associated with "Newlanders" or "Crimps," who either sand-bagged and kidnapped unsuspecting people on European waterfronts, or worked out elaborate confidence schemes to swindle scores of people at once. No one knows how many Pennsylvanians joined the labor force under such unhappy circumstances, but the number probably was large because the profits were great. One shipload might net hundreds of thousands of dollars.

With the advent of the factory system and machine technology, a great gulf developed between skilled and unskilled workers. The craftsmen in the building trades and the factories became highly articulate and formed nearly all the unions in Pennsylvania before 1860. The day laborers on the turnpikes and canals, the miners, the domestic servants, and the women and children in factories rarely attempted to organize or to force any change in their condition. The charcoal iron workers in Pennsylvania formed a special category because they lived on many separate plantations. A great many of them were skilled artisans, but they escaped the dehumanizing influence of the factory and remained in a paternalistic system which by 1860 had become an anachronism.

In a typical Philadelphia factory of the 1830s work began at sunup and continued until sundown in summer, or until eight o'clock in the evening in winter, six days a week, with one hour a day off for a meal. Workers were forbidden to carry into the factory any tobacco, drinks, paper or reading matter, or loose food. They were docked at the rate of a half day's pay for each half hour of lateness, though some foremen docked this much for tardiness of five minutes. Workers had to give two weeks notice of quitting or would receive no pay for the period. Foremen whipped or beat people who made mistakes in their work but mostly reserved this treatment for women and children.

Factory managers, often by agreement among themselves, adopted practices which angered the workers. They hired their hands individually, would not permit any collective bargaining, and retained an absolute right of summary and arbitrary dismissal without any advance notice. Factories gave certificates of honorable discharge to workers who left under the rules, but any hand who was fired because he had irritated his boss for any reason did not receive such a certificate and had his name recorded on a blacklist which was circulated among other employers. A man without a discharge certificate had a hard time finding employment. Factories very early used the speedup for operatives paid by piecework, and inflicted both corporal punishment and money fines for slow or sloppy work or on the whim of the foreman.

The wages for factory hands cannot easily be summarized for they varied a good deal at different times and places. We know that the highest wage scale existed in the decade before the Panic of 1819, and that except for a few years, wages declined continually into the 1850s. Real wages are difficult to compute before the Civil War because employers paid their employees in depreciated state bank notes, or partly in orders on local or company stores. Since this was an era before the fixed-price system began, stores often charged workingmen more for things paid by these company certificates. Artisans such as carpenters or bricklayers commonly received half their wages in paper money and the rest in leftover lumber or bricks.

Cotton mills in Philadephia, two-thirds of whose workers were women, paid from $1 to $3 per week. In 1832 the wage scale ran from $12 to $20 a month, but by 1840 it had dropped and ran between $7 and $13 per month. Small children earned 1 cent an hour, or 75 cents a week; older children made between $1 and $2 per week. Mill owners answered complaints with the argument that the children caused more trouble than they were worth, and that they hired them only as a charity to keep them in view while their parents worked, but the local humane societies believed otherwise. The pressure mill owners brought against passage of the public school law of 1834 belied their protests of charitable intent.

Day laborers who had been earning 75 cents a day before 1819 saw their pay drop to 12½ cents a day in the following decade, and then stabilize at 50 cents a day, which the contractors on the State Works generally paid. Coal miners in the 1840s were receiving $5.25 per week, paid entirely in company store orders. Skilled workmen like masons, carpenters, and bricklayers received between $1 and $2 per day. Workers in the building trades received the highest pay of all, but they suffered from seasonal unemployment, which reduced their yearly income to the level of some factory workers. The continuing decline in their wages between 1810 and 1850 led these highly articulate workmen to organize trade unions for their protection.

Pennsylvania trade unions began with the formation in 1794 of the Federal Society of Journeymen Cordwainers of Philadelphia. It lost a strike against wage reductions in 1799 and collapsed. The printers of the city formed a union in 1802 to raise wages by collective bargaining, with no better result. These early efforts induced the masters to make a collective agreement among themselves for blacklisting. The general decline of wages in the 1820s precipitated the unionization of many crafts, mostly in Philadelphia: the carpenters, hatters, tailors, bricklayers, house painters, masons, shoemakers, cabinetmakers, and others. The building trades unions formed a confederation in 1827 called the Mechanics Union of Trade Associations. The idea of wider organization took hold and produced the Trades Union of Philadelphia in 1834 which loosely united some fifty separate trade unions. The leaders then went on to found a National Trades Union in the same year, but the effort dissolved in talk.

Workingmen's parties sprang up between 1827 and 1834 in Philadelphia, Pittsburgh, Harrisburg, Lancaster, Carlisle, and a few other towns, but they confined their activities to local issues and personalities. The workingmen demanded the repeal of laws permitting imprisonment for debt, and the Legislature abolished this practice in 1833. They wanted free public education, which the state undertook in 1834. They called for a ten-hour day and succeeded in obtaining a Philadelphia ordinance for it in 1835. They asked for a law which would give mechanics the first claim on the assets of bankrupt builders, so that they could collect wages owing. In 1854, Pennsylvania adopted a law assigning a prior claim up to $100 to each unpaid workman from the remaining assets of insolvent contractors. As Pennsylvania entered the period of the Civil War, its craftsmen had acquired fifty years of experience in union organization.

CREDIT AND BANKING

Colonial Americans normally exported low-value raw materials and imported high-value merchandise, a practice which drained them of specie. Consequently they devised a make-shift system of barter and credit. Philadelphia merchants normally received a year to pay London bills. They consigned merchandise to back-country traders and storekeepers on credit, and the latter disposed of it to local farmers who paid in produce such as flour and grain. The storekeepers returned this to Philadelphia, and the city merchants used it to meet their European obligations. The barter system generally prevailed in colonial Pennsylvania, and because of the difficulty of setting up the proper credit arrangements at points along the line, a trade connection, once established, was likely to continue for a generation.

The barter system sharply curtailed the freedom of choice among buyers and sellers and grew more cumbersome as the population grew. Out of this condition the pressure arose in the 1720s for the issue of paper currency by the province. Franklin proposed this in his *Modest Inquiry into the Nature and Necessity of Paper Currency* in 1729, and reiterated his view that sound paper money increased economic development in his *Remarks and Facts Concerning American Paper Money* in 1767. Many provinces issued poorly secured paper which rapidly depreciated and caused complaints in Parliament, but Pennsylvania currency represented an actual reserve of silver and land with which to redeem the paper.

During the Revolution the need for money became critical. Pennsylvania's new government as well as the Continental Congress issued fiat paper currency, based on nothing more substantial than a promise to pay later. This fluctuated with the fortunes of war and ultimately became almost worthless. In 1780 after the British had captured Charleston and the American army was destitute and starving, a group of Philadelphia merchants agreed to mobilize their private credit by forming the Pennsylvania Bank, a nonprofit, patriotic scheme to provide Congress with funds to supply the army. The bank rapidly accumulated £300,000, mostly from Philadelphia subscribers, and met the military supply crisis.

In 1781, Congress appointed Robert Morris its superintendent of finance, and Morris proposed the creation of a chartered Bank of North America. Congress incorporated this institution on December 31, 1781, but problems arose over the power of Congress under the Articles to take such action, and the bank directors obtained a Pennsylvania charter in April 1782. Private subscribers paid in specie for bank stock or transferred their funds in the Pennsylvania Bank to the new institution. The arrival of specie from France and the capture of coin from the British put the institution on a sound footing. Thomas Willing, a leading Philadelphia merchant, became the president. When the Pennsylvania Radicals won control of the Assembly in 1785, they repealed the bank's charter, but the Federalists reinstated it in 1787. The Bank of North America, though first chartered by Congress, was not a Federal bank in the usual sense. It operated as a private institution, made money for its managers, and continued in business until its merger with a Philadelphia insurance company in 1929. It may be considered the first chartered bank in America.

On December 12, 1791, the federally chartered First Bank of the United States opened its main office in Philadelphia. Thomas Willing became its president and nine of its directors came from Pennsylvania, more than from any other state. In 1793, the state chartered and subscribed one-third of the capital of a new Bank of Pennsylvania, also located in Philadelphia, which opened branch offices in Harrisburg, Lancaster, Reading, Easton, and Pittsburgh.

In 1813 Pennsylvania passed a law to charter twenty-five new banks. Governor Snyder vetoed it, but the legislature passed another bill over the Governor's veto, authorizing the charter of forty-one new banks. Thirty-five of them were in business within two years. In addition to this sudden sevenfold increase in the number of chartered banks, an unknown number of unchartered or freebooter banking institutions had started operations. The chartered banks held more public confidence because of the restrictions imposed by the state: a limit on debts, a set specie reserve, limits on the amount of money that could be loaned to one borrower, an obligation to lend 20 percent of the capital within the bank's home district, a requirement to loan money to the state, and ultimately, in 1838, a forfeiture of the charter if the bank could not redeem its notes in specie. The existence of such restrictions, however, did little to prevent the banks from doing business as they pleased.

The development of state chartered banks inaugurated a habit of government financing that lasted for a century in Pennsylvania. The state legislature had developed an aversion to taxation which went back to early colonial days, and the lawmakers of the nineteenth century sought every device to meet the financial needs of government by means other than taxing. They tried land sale, fiat money, and lotteries after 1776, and then hopefully experimented with the investment of state money in transportation companies and banks. The charter of the Bank of Pennsylvania in 1793, requiring that the state purchase one-third of the capital stock, set a precedent for such investment. Albert Gallatin pointed out that until the completion of the State Works, Pennsylvania had managed "to defray out of the dividends all the expenses of government without any direct tax." The state continued to accept cash bonuses from banks seeking charters, such as the $4,500,000 which Biddle's Bank of the United States paid for its state charter of 1836, and required banks to pledge loans to the government at low interest. Pennsylvania banks always maintained a close tie with state politics in this era by helping the party in power to surmount financial crises without taxation, and occasionally by using their power to extend or withold credit as a political weapon.

National political managers regularly turned to Pennsylvanians for banking leadership. Pennsylvanians held the secretaryship of the Treasury for twenty-five of the fifty years between 1800 and 1850. Albert Gallatin served under Jefferson and Madison, Alexander J. Dallas under Madison, Richard Rush under John Quincy Adams, Samuel D. Ingham and William J. Duane under Jackson, Walter Forward under Tyler, Robert J. Walker under Polk, and William Morris Meredith under Taylor. Pennsylvanians also held the presidency of both Banks of the United States, Thomas Willing for the First Bank, and William Jones and Nicholas Biddle for the Second. The commonwealth provided more leadership in the financial than in the political field in the pre-Civil War era.

BIBLIOGRAPHY

Specialized studies of commerce include Frederick B. Tolles: *Meeting House and Counting House;* James W. Livingood: *Philadelphia-Baltimore Trade Rivalry:* and Catherine E. Reiser: *Pittsburgh's Commercial Development,* all previously cited. In addition, see Mary A. Hanna: *Trade of the Delaware District before the Revolution* (1915); Curtis P. Nettels: "Economic Relations of Boston, Philadelphia and New York, 1680–1715," *Journal of Economic and Business History,* vol. 3 (1931), pp. 185–215; Marion V. Brewington: "Maritime Philadelphia, 1609–1837," *Pennsylvania Magazine of History and Biography,* vol. 63 (1939), pp. 93–117; Harry D. Berg: "The Organization of Business in Colonial Philadelphia," *Pennsylvania History,* vol. 10 (1943), pp. 157–177; Arthur L. Jensen: *The Maritime Commerce of Colonial Philadelphia* (1963); and David T. Gilchrist et al. (eds.): *The Growth of Seaport Cities, 1790–1825* (1968).

On transportation, a convenient starting point is George Swetnam: *Pennsylvania Transportation* (1964). Balthaser H. Meyer and Caroline E. MacGill: *History of Transportation in the United States before 1860* (1917) includes much Pennsylvania material. On turnpikes, see Thomas B. Searight: *The Old Pike* (1894); Philip D. Jordan: *The National Road* (1948); Charles A. Hanna: *The Wilderness Trail,* 2 vols. (1911); John T. Faris: *Old Trails and Roads in Penn's Land* (1927); William C. Plummer: *The Road Policy of Pennsylvania* (1925); Joseph A. Durrenberger: *Turnpikes: A Study of the Toll Road Improvement in the Middle Atlantic States and Maryland* (1931); Charles I. Landis: "History of the Philadelphia and Lancaster Turnpike," *Pennsylvania Magazine of History and Biography,* vol. 42 (1918), pp. 1–28, 127–140, 235–258, 358–360, and vol. 43 (1919), pp. 84–90, 182–190; Julius Sachse: *The Wayside Inns on the Lancaster Roadside between Philadelphia and Lancaster* (1913); John Omwake: *The Conestoga Six Horse Bell Teams of Eastern Pennsylvania* (1930); and George Shumway et al.: *Conestoga Wagon, 1750–1850: Freight Carrier for 100 Years of America's Westward Expansion* (1966).

On bridges, see Richard S. Allen: *Covered Bridges of the Middle Atlantic States* (1959); and Hubertis Cummings: "Theodore Burr and His Bridges across the Susquehanna," *Pennsylvania History,* vol. 23 (1956), pp. 476–486.

River transportation receives attention in histories of the various rivers. In addition to these, see Leland D. Baldwin: *The Keelboat Age on Western Waters* (1941); Louis C. Hunter: *Steamboats on the Western Rivers* (1949); Richmond E. Myers: "The Story of Transportation on the Susquehanna River," *New York History,* vol. 29 (1948), pp. 157–169; W. E. Albig: "Early Development of Transportation on the Monongahela River," *Western Pennsylvania Historical Magazine,* vol. 2 (1919), pp. 115–124; and in the same journal, Leland D. Baldwin: "Rivers in the Early Development of Western Pennsylvania," vol. 16 (1933), pp. 79–98.

Study of canal transportation should begin with Carter Goodrich (ed.): *Canals and American Economic Development* (1961); and Julius Rubin: *Canal or Railroad? Imitation and Innovation in the Response to the Erie Canal in Philadelphia, Baltimore and Boston* (1961).

The State Works of Pennsylvania are described briefly in Theodore B. Klein: *Canals of Pennsylvania and the System of Internal Improvements* (1901); and more extensively in Avard L. Bishop: "The State Works of Pennsylvania," in *Transactions of the Connecticut Academy,* vol. 13 (1907), pp. 149–297. See also Bishop's "Corrupt Practices Connected with the Building and Operation of the State Works of Pennsylvania," *Yale Review,* vol. 15 (1907), pp. 391–411.

The Wilkinson *Bibliography of Pennsylvania,* pp. 306–309, lists many articles on specific canals. Book-sized treatments include Chester L. Jones: *The Economic History of the Anthracite-Tidewater Canals* (1908); Gerald Smeltzer: *Canals along the Lower Susquehanna* (1963); Edwin D. Leroy: *The Delaware and Hudson Canal* (1950); Manville B. Wakefield: *Canal Boats to Tidewater: The Story of the Delaware and Hudson Canal* (1965); Robert J. McClellan: *The Delaware Canal: A Picture Story* (1967); Ralph D. Gray: *The National Waterway: A History of the Chesapeake and Delaware Canal, 1769–1965* (1967); and Anthony J. Bryzski: "The Lehigh Canal and Its Effect on the Economic Development of the Region through Which It Passed, 1818–1873" (doctoral dissertation, New York University, 1957).

The two general histories of state railroads are Jules I. Bogen: *The Anthracite Railroads: A Study in American Enterprise* (1927); and Roger B. Saylor: *The Railroads of Pennsylvania* (1964). There are many histories of individual lines. Histories of the four great trunk lines traversing Pennsylvania include William B. Wilson: *History of the Pennsylvania Railroad Company,* 2 vols. (1899), the best study of this line; Edward H. Mott: *Between the Ocean and the Lakes: The Story of the Erie* (1902); Frank W. Stevens; *Beginnings of the New York Central Railroad* (1926); and Edward Hungerford: *Story of the Baltimore and Ohio Railroad* (1928).

The standard general histories of manufacturing are James L. Bishop: *History of American Manufac-*

tures from 1608–1860 (1860); and Victor S. Clark: *History of Manufactures in the United States, 1607–1860* (1916). For manufacturing in Pennsylvania, see Charles Robson (ed.): *Manufacturies and Manufactures of Pennsylvania in the Nineteenth Century* (1875); James M. Swank: *Progressive Pennsylvania* (1908); and Sylvester K. Stevens: *Pennsylvania: Titan of Industry,* 3 vols. (1948). Histories of major cities tell of their particular industries.

Special industries have been treated in Carl Bridenbaugh: *The Colonial Craftsmah* (1950); George H. Eckhardt: *Pennsylvania Clocks and Clockmakers* (1955); Henry J. Kauffman: *The Pennsylvania-Kentucky Rifle* (1960); Charles B. Kuhlman: *The Development of the Flour Milling Industry in the United States* (1929); William S. Lesh: *A History of the Tanneries of Monroe County* (1947); C. W. Summerfield: *The Shoe Industry in Pennsylvania* (1902); Samuel Batchelder: *Introduction to the Early Progress of the Cotton Manufactures of the United States* (1863); J. R. Kendrick: *The Carpet Industry of Philadelphia* (1890); Charles L. Chandler: *Early Shipbuilding in Pennsylvania* (1932); David Hunter: *Papermaking in Pioneer America* (1952); G. D. Boardman: "Early Printing in the Middle Colonies," *Pennsylvania Magazine of History and Biography,* vol. 10 (1887), pp. 15–32; Dudley Tonkin: *My Partner, The River: The White Pine Story on the Susquehanna* (1958); "When Timber Was King," *Pennsylvania History,* vol. 19, no. 4 (October, 1952), pp. 391–507; F. W. Hunter: *Stiegel Glass* (1914); George L. Heiges: *Henry William Stiegel and His Associates: A Story of Early American Industry* (1948); Harrold E. Gillingham: a series of articles on the manufacture of pottery, glass, bricks, and instruments in *Pennsylvania Magazine of History and Biography,* vols. 51, 52, 53, 54 (1927–1930); Frederick D. Suydam: *Christian Dorflinger: A Miracle in Glass, 1828–1915* (1950); William Bining: "The Glass Industry of Western Pennsylvania, 1797–1857," *Western Pennsylvania Historical Magazine,* vol. 19 (1936), pp. 255–268; Lowell Inness: *Early Glass of the Pittsburgh District* (1949); Paul C. Dewhurst: *The Norris Locomotives* (1950); and Malcolm C. Clark: "The Birth of an Enterprise: Baldwin Locomotives, 1831–1842," *Pennsylvania Magazine of History and Biography,* vol. 90 (1966), pp. 423–444.

The early iron industry of Pennsylvania can be traced in James M. Swank: *Introduction to a History of Iron Making and Coal Mining in Pennsylvania* (1878), and *History of the Manufacture of Iron . . . from Colonial Times to 1891* (1892); and in Arthur C. Bining: *Pennsylvania's Iron and Steel Industry* (1954), and *Pennsylvania Iron Manufacture in the Eighteenth Century* (1938). Other useful works are *Forges and Furnaces in the Province of Pennsylvania* (1914), prepared by the historical committee of the Pennsylvania Society of Colonial Dames of America; Frederick K. Miller: *The Rise of an Iron Community: An Economic History of Lebanon County, 1740–1865* (1952); Alfred Gemmell: *The Charcoal Iron Industry in the Perkiomen Valley* (1949); Henry J. Kauffman: *Early American Ironware, Cast and Wrought* (1966); Henry C. Mercer: *The Bible in Iron* (1961); and Joseph E. Walker: *Hopewell Village: A Social and Economic History of an Ironmaking Community* (1966).

The most important books on the early coal industry are Howard Eavenson: *The First Century and a Quarter of the American Coal Industry* (1942); R. D. Billinger: *Pennsylvania's Coal Industry* (1954); C. K. Yearley: *Enterprise and Anthracite: Economics and Democracy in Schuylkill County, 1820–1875* (1961); and Frederick M. Binder: "Pennsylvania Coal: An Historical Study of its Utilization to 1860" (doctoral dissertation, University of Pennsylvania, 1955).

On slave labor, see Darold D. Wax: "The Demand for Slave Labor in Colonial Pennsylvania," *Pennsylvania History,* vol. 34 (1967), pp. 331–345. The main works on indentured servants are K. F. Geiser: *Redemptioners and Indentured Servants in the Colony and Commonwealth of Pennsylvania* (1911); and Cheeseman A. Herrick: *White Servitude in Pennsylvania* (1926).

The basic scholarly work on industrial labor is William A. Sullivan: *The Industrial Worker in Pennsylvania, 1800–1840* (1955). Other useful items in this field are Augusta E. Galster: *The Labor Movement in the Shoe Industry with Special Reference to Philadelphia* (1924); Edgar B. Cale: *Organization of Labor in Philadelphia, 1850–1870* (1940); Leonard Bernstein: "The Working People of Philadelphia from Colonial Times to the General Strike of 1835," *Pennsylvania Magazine of History and Biography,* vol. 74 (1950), pp. 322–339; Alexander Trachtenberg: *History of Legislation for the Protection of Coal*

Miners in Pennsylvania, 1824–1915 (1942); and David Montgomery: "The Working Classes of the Pre-industrial American City, 1780–1830," *Labor History,* vol. 9 (1968), pp. 1–22.

Pennsylvania banking is generally covered in B. M. Nead: *Brief Review of the Financial History of Pennsylvania, 1682–1881* (1881); and John T. Holdsworth and John T. Fisher: *Financing an Empire: History of Banking in Pennsylvania,* 4 vols. (1928). Wilkinson's *Bibliography of Pennsylvania History* lists histories of many individual banks and biographies of leading bankers.

CHAPTER FIFTEEN

Clues to a Regional Culture: Church and School

In colonial times the churches served as the major determinant of motives and mores, the foundation of community loyalty and cohesion, and the ultimate source of answers to questions of right and wrong. Although nearly all the churches of early Pennsylvania grew from the background of western European Christianity, and most of them from the Protestant segment of this religion, they emphasized their differences more than their similarity. Penn's province, in an era generally marked by the requirement of strict conformity to one state church, welcomed variant expressions of Christian belief and became a magnet and a haven for European nonconformists. After the Revolution, many of the American churches declared their ecclesiastical independence from European mother churches. Since the churches took responsibility for governing human conduct, they played the leading role in education until the Industrial Revolution introduced the need for training in vocational skills, and at that point the state stepped in to institute secular public education.

THE RELIGIOUS COMMUNITIES

Religious diversity The theme of diversity which appears in so many aspects of Pennsylvania life stands out sharply in the history of its churches. Four features of the colony encouraged religious diversity. First, William Penn invited it. "We must give the liberty we ask," he wrote, and the Rhine Valley responded, for it already knew his reputation for tolerance and his respect for freedom of conscience. Second, the people who came were mainly the poor from many lands. They found no churches or ministers of their communion in Pennsylvania, and they either had to create a homemade religious life based on their recollections or have none at all. Third, the government of Pennsylvania encouraged and protected the widest variety of religious activity. The first article of the Charter of 1701 which Penn ordered to be kept "without any Alteration, inviolably forever," gave as impregnable a guarantee of religious liberty as has ever been written. Fourth, most of the religious groups which came to Pennsylvania invited fragmentation because they were freedom-seeking and congregationally oriented; that is, they were the groups most dedicated to religious liberty and most opposed to conformity.

The early religious communities of Pennsylvania like the Friends, the Mennonites, the Dunkers, and the Amish had little difficulty in adapting to their new wilderness home because none of them needed buildings or ordained ministers. They often came as a group, settled as a group, and continued to hold services in private houses as they had done in Europe. But the much larger number of German Reformed, Lutheran, and Presbyterian people who came in after 1720, not as congregations but as individuals, faced a different problem. No church facilities existed in Pennsylvania nor did it appear likely that the overseas mother churches would provide them. In consequence, a motley array of self-appointed clergymen made the rounds of the back country, preaching, baptizing, marrying, burying, and offering prayers and communion. Some of these undoubtedly were dedicated, sincere, and able, but many others were vagabonds and imposters who made a mockery of their alleged ministry.

The Great Awakening A young Presbyterian, Gilbert Tennent, brought the Great Awakening to Pennsylvania from New Jersey where it had started. His father, William Tennent, had founded Log College at Neshaminy in Bucks County to train Presbyterian preachers. Pennsylvania leaders in the Great Awakening were often called the Log College revivalists. The Tennents and others, disgusted with complacent orthodoxy, violently attacked conventional churchgoing and demanded that parishioners pay less attention to the ceremonies and begin to live the life they piously talked about. They sought converts, held home meetings, and often turned church services into bedlam, raging, shouting, stamping, and roaring at the congregation, who were meanwhile shouting, groaning, or rolling on the floor. While the revivals were at their height in Pennsylvania, George Whitefield, the famous English evangelist, arrived in Philadelphia in 1739 and gave his prodigious qualities as a preacher to the movement.

The Great Awakening in Pennsylvania first proved a divisive force. The Presbyterians expelled the revivalist congregations in 1741; these organized a separate church called the New Side or New Light Presbyterians in 1745. In 1758, after the fire had burned out, they rejoined the parent church which in the interim had called itself the Old Side or Old Light Presbyterians. The revival movement also split the Dutch Reformed Church and caused dissension in all. On the other hand, the Great Awakening temporarily reinforced the ecumenical movement, for it appealed to people as followers of a single faith, not as rival sectarians. The Moravians, whose leaders in the 1740s hoped to unite all Protestants, found Whitefield's ecumenical views congenial to their own. Henry Melchior Muhlenberg, organizer of the Pennsylvania Lutherans, worked in cooperation with the leading revivalists, for he wanted conversions and approved the humanitarian thrust of the movement.

The Great Awakening stirred David Brainerd to direct the Presbyterians to religious work among the Pennsylvania Indians, and aided the Moravian missionary, David Zeisberger, in his dramatic career among the natives. By strengthening the idea of social responsibility, the

Great Awakening played an early role in the slow, hard task of uprooting slavery. Finally, the movement had possibly its greatest impact on the unchurched, the thousands who in the absence of regular churches had drifted away from the religious associations they had known in Europe.

The Plain Sects The Plain Sects had the least institutional complexity because they looked to no governing body in Europe and because they remained small and managed their affairs in Pennsylvania with a minimum of organizational apparatus. Their leaders often came with them to the province. The sects opposed church structure and emphasized individual commitment and responsibility, they generally permitted self-government at the local meeting level, they emphasized the simple life, and they remained small because their concern with freedom of conscience and the right of dissent encouraged secession.

The Friends built their first meetinghouse in Philadelphia in 1682. Their numbers increased rapidly during the next three decades, but in 1691 they suffered a split over the ideas of George Keith, contentious master of the Penn Charter School, who considered the inner light an insufficient guide to salvation and proposed that Quakers celebrate communion. The Philadelphia Yearly Meeting disowned him in 1692, but he attracted many to his views and formed the faction called Keithian or Christian Quakers. Keith joined the Anglican church in 1700 and persuaded many of the Quakers to follow his example. During the French and Indian War the Quakers divided between the "soft" and the "stiff" members, the former desiring to bend slightly on pacifism to retain political power, and the latter withdrawing from politics rather than compromise their conscience. Another split occurred during the Revolutionary War when the Monthly Meetings expelled Quakers who supported the war effort, like Thomas Mifflin and Betsy Ross. Those who had been disowned formed the Free or Fighting Quakers who held meetings in Philadelphia until 1836.

The Quakers increased from about 30,000 at the time of the Revolution to some 60,000 in 1850. From the earliest days until the Civil War the Society of Friends stood in the vanguard of humanitarian projects such as a milder penal code; prison reform; education for all regardless of race, sex, or creed; temperance; the abolition of slavery; equality for women; concern for the Indians; improvement of working conditions in factories; care of the poor, the crippled, the blind, the deaf and dumb, the insane, the widows, the orphans; and the establishment of libraries.

Quaker Pennsylvania quickly attracted sects from continental Europe which had suffered persecution for views and customs comparable to the Friends: pacifism, quietism, opposition to oaths, a distinctive plain dress, informal worship, and personal humility and piety. Among these, the most important were the Mennonites, the Amish, the Dunkers, the Schwenkfelders, and the Moravians. Some Mennonites settled at Germantown in 1683 and brought others to the locality. In 1708 they erected a church and organized the first American congregation. In 1710 Hans Herr and Christian Kendig brought a group of Mennonites from Switzerland to the Pequea Valley, a settlement which, had grown to 1,000 by the time Lancaster County was set up in 1729. Other Mennonites found homes along the Skippack, the Swatara, and the Tulpehocken. Most of the Mennonites came in the first half of the eighteenth century, nearly all of them settled in Pennsylvania, and most of these found their way to Lancaster County where they became farmers. They were fervent and loyal supporters of the Quakers in their opposition to war, but the Revolution split the Mennonites as it had the Quakers though the breach did not last as long. But fear of similar difficulties in the future led a portion of the Pennsylvania Mennonites to emigrate to Canada between 1790 and 1810. The Mennonites condemned worldly pleasures and tried to keep themselves apart. They avoided politics, settled disputes among themselves instead of going to court, cared for their own aged and unfortunate, and dedicated their lives to their own farm communities. They did not seek wealth, developed no internal caste system, and held honesty, integrity, and simplicity as cardinal virtues.

The Amish had split off from the Swiss Mennonites when Jacob Amman (Amen) in 1693 demanded stricter enforcement of Meidung or ostracism as a disciplinary measure. The Amish people altered some Mennonite practices by introducing the ritual of foot washing, adding color to their plain dress, and having the married men grow long hair and beards. They began settlement in Berks County in 1714 and continued to come until 1764 when they had spread into Chester, Lancaster, and Somerset Counties. Most of them, however, took up land in Berks County and devoted themselves exclusively to farming which they considered a part of their religious life. The durability of the simple Amish life through years which changed America beyond belief became a wonder of the nineteenth and a miracle of the twentieth century.

The Dunkers, or German Baptist Brethren, formed in Germany as followers of Alexander Mack in 1708. They began coming to Pennsylvania in 1719 to escape persecution, arriving in several church groups over the next ten years and settling mainly in Germantown and in Montgomery, Berks, and Lancaster Counties. Peter Becker accompanied the first settlers to Germantown where, in 1723, he established the first German Baptist Brethren Church in America. Alexander Mack, the founder, brought all his followers from Europe to Pennsylvania in 1729. Like other Plain Sects, the Dunkers dressed simply, avoided rough language, were pacifists, did not go to law, worshipped in quiet, informal meetings, and had only congregational government. They grew slowly and numbered only about a thousand at the end of the colonial period.

One of the Dunkers, Conrad Beissel, drew a small body of followers with him to the Cocalico Creek in Lancaster County in 1728 where he started a monastic experiment known as the Ephrata Cloister. His people erected a number of large buildings and attracted several hundred converts, men and women, who lived in celibacy and devoted themselves to an ascetic existence of communal living. Beyond group farming, they spent much time in prayer, in writing and singing hymns, and in producing the famous Bibles and religious books which bear the mark of their Ephrata press. The Cloister community, sometimes known as the Seventh Day Baptists, experienced varying schisms over leadership in colonial days, but survived into the twentieth century. Some of the buildings have been restored by the commonwealth to help the modern visitor sense something of the outward and the inner life of these colonial mystics.

A small German sect founded by Kasper Von Schwenkfeld developed in Silesia, faced persecution by both Catholics and Lutherans, and finally fled to Pennsylvania in 1734 and made its home mainly in Bucks and Montgomery Counties, though some went to Berks and Lehigh. They were plain folk following many of the patterns of the others except that they brought along an excellent library and welcomed rather than shunned book learning. They numbered only about 400 in 1790 but maintained their customs and identity and grew slowly through the nineteenth century.

The Moravians grew out of the Hussite movement and began as the Bohemian church. During the Reformation they broke away from Catholicism and became the *Unitas Fratrum,*

Restored group of buildings of the Ephrata Cloister which reflect the features of German architecture of the colonial era. (Pennsylvania Historical and Museum Commission)

a church organized on the episcopal system. They declined in Europe in the seventeenth century, and revived again in the eighteenth, when persecution drove them to the estate of Count Nicholas Ludwig von Zinzendorf in Saxony, who had earlier given sanctuary to the Schwenkfelders. Zinzendorf, a Lutheran, tried to convert the Moravians but instead they brought him into their church as a bishop. The Count obtained land for the Moravians in Georgia. When this colony failed, the survivors came to Philadelphia in 1740 with George Whitefield. He sold them land near Easton where the Moravians set up their first Pennsylvania community. Count Zinzendorf came to the new Moravian town just before Christmas, 1741, and named it Bethlehem.

The Moravian church under Zinzendorf had two major goals: to unite all the German sects and churches into one, and to do missionary work among the Indians. The first stirred up a great deal of opposition and came to nought, but the Moravians achieved remarkable success among the Indians. Such men as David Zeisberger, Frederick Christian Post, and John Heckewelder earned the confidence and respect of the Indians to a degree few Europeans ever enjoyed. The Moravians built their major community at Bethlehem where they practiced a quasi-communal life, and started churches in Lititz, York, Lebanon, and Philadelphia. They bore some similarity to the sects in their pietism, their simple life, and their unique customs, but they maintained an episcopal church structure.

The German churches: Lutheran and Reformed   The Swedes had set up the first Lutheran church on Tinicum Island in 1643, and in 1700 built Gloria Dei—Old Swedes Church—in Philadelphia. The German Lutherans started with the New Hanover Church of 1703 under the pastor Justus Falkner. After 1720 the Lutherans immigrated in increasing numbers, not as congregations but as individuals. Lacking ordained ministers, they depended upon volunteers or vagabond preachers, and set up churches on their own initiative. In the 1730s as the Great Awakening began to spread, some Philadelphia congregations sent a delegation to Europe to plead for ministers from the mother synod at Halle. The demands of orphan churches and the activities of the Moravians finally spurred the Halle authorities to send the Reverend Henry Melchior Muhlenberg to Pennsylvania. Arriving in 1742, he visited congregations, selected men he thought qualified as their pastors, fought against the union of churches, and used the Great Awakening to serve the purposes of his mission. At his request, more ministers came and in 1748 he established a Lutheran Ministerium in Pennsylvania which ordained pastors. Thereafter the Lutherans experienced an orderly growth under the watchful eye of Muhlenberg, the "Father of American Lutheranism."

The German Reformed people came about the same time and in the same way as the Lutherans—not as congregations but as individuals. John Philip Boehm organized one of the earliest German Reformed churches at Falkner's Swamp in 1725, but most of the Reformed people had to manage on their own. Following the Lutheran pattern, the Reformed Synod of Holland sent the Reverend Michael Schlatter to Pennsylvania to organize the scattered churches, evict charlatan pastors, and serve as widely as he could. Like Muhlenberg, with whom he was on good terms, he rode thousands of miles through Pennsylvania and adjoining colonies to start new congregations and to bring order to established ones. He organized the Reformed Coetus or general church assembly at Philadelphia in 1747 and traveled back to Europe in 1751 to present at headquarters the needs of Pennsylvania for ordained ministers and funds. The Reformed Church had set up over a hundred congregations in Pennsylvania by 1790.

The Scotch-Irish Presbyterians   The Presbyterians became the largest church in colonial Pennsylvania. The Reverend Jedidiah Andrews organized the first Presbyterian church in Pennsylvania at Philadelphia in 1698, and a growing membership led to the creation of the Philadelphia Presbytery in 1706 and Synod in 1717. A wave of immigration in the 1720s required the erection of the Presbytery of Donegal in 1732, in the heart of the new settlements of Lancaster County. The rapid Scotch-Irish influx of the 1740s and the simultaneous revivalist activities of the Tennents brought about the rift between the Old and the New Lights, but that had healed before the great migration over the Alleghenies after the French and Indian War. Into this wilderness the Presbyterians in 1766 sent two missionaries, the Reverend Charles Beatty and the Reverend George Duffield. Meanwhile, the Presbytery of Donegal supplied ministers from the east, notably the Reverend John McMillan, who became a legend among western Presbyterians for the fire of his sermons and the scope of his circuit riding. In 1781 the Presbytery of Redstone was set up to serve the southwest, and in 1786 the Presbytery of Carlisle to serve the Cumberland Valley and central Pennsylvania. Unlike the

Estimated size of Pennsylvania churches

Church	Estimated membership, 1776-1790	Seating capacity of churches, 1850	Times increase, 1850 over 1776-1790	Number of churches, 1850
Presbyterian	80,000	359,000	4.5	775
Methodist	1,500	341,000	227.3	889
Lutheran	60,000	261,000	4.3	498
Baptist	5,000	128,000	25.6	320
German Reformed	35,000	105,000	3.	209
Roman Catholic	10,000	89,000	8.9	139
Episcopal	3,000	67,000	22.3	136
Friends	30,000	61,000	2.	142
Moravians	2,500	32,000	12.8	84
Mennonites	4,000	23,000	5.8	92

Figures for 1850 from *Eighth Census of U.S., Pennsylvania* (1853), pp. 200–203, are rough estimates based on capacity of existing church structures. The estimates for 1776–1790 have been derived from William W. Sweet, *The Story of Religions in America* (1930), and *Religion in Colonial America* (1942), passim.

Lutheran and Reformed churches whose ecclesiastical authority rested in Europe, the Presbyterians held control of their own activities in Pennsylvania through the Philadelphia Synod, which could ordain ministers. The church structure was highly democratic, for congregations voted for their pastors and handled their own finances.

Separation of Pennsylvania churches from European ties Political independence brought in its train a movement of American churches to separate from the European mother churches to which many Pennsylvania denominations had looked for funds and management. Most of the sects had no problem because their leadership came to America with them. The Quakers continued to send a delegation to the London Yearly Meeting to maintain personal contact, but the American Yearly Meeting had long exercised authority among colonial Quakers. Only the Moravians remained under European control, and their German governing body, by resisting American national trends such as the use of English and the admittance of laymen to church management, slowed the growth of the Pennsylvania church.

The Lutherans established the Pennsylvania Ministerium in 1748; they created the Pennsylvania Synod for clergymen in 1781, and admitted laymen to it in 1796 so that the church had a central government within the state. Lutherans established other state synods on the Pennsylvania pattern until 1820 when all united in a general synod which became the national ruling body. The nationalized church took the name "German Lutheran church" and used the German language in services until the Civil War era. The German Reformed people, after the Synod of Holland failed to act, met at Lancaster in 1793 where they created the Synod of the Reformed Church in the United States which became the American government for this Pennsylvania-centered denomination. John Winebrenner, German Reformed pastor in Harrisburg, established the Church of God, also called the Winebrennerians, which attracted many German church people after 1830.

The Presbyterians had become accustomed to regional self-government, but had no national structure. In 1786 the Synods of New York and Philadelphia drafted plans for the government of all American Presbyterian churches. At Philadelphia in 1787, while the Founding Fathers were drafting the Federal Constitution, Presbyterian delegates wrote their American church constitution which took effect in 1788.

The Church of England held services in Philadelphia as early as 1696 under the ministry of the Reverend Thomas Clayton, and many Keithian Quakers became Anglicans after 1700. Philadelphia remained the center of Anglicanism in Pennsylvania where the communicants included such aristocrats as Robert Morris, Richard Peters, Judges Benjamin Chew and William Tilghman, Francis Hopkinson, and Provost William Smith. The Revolution much weakened the Anglican church because many of its members remained loyal to England and had to leave Pennsylvania. Interestingly, most of the initiative and leadership to create an American Episcopal church came from the states where it had not been established by law. Pennsylvania's Dr. William White, rector of Philadelphia's Christ Church, and Provost William Smith, who had moved to Baltimore, led the movement for several conventions which met in Philadelphia in 1785 and 1786. The attending clergymen adopted a constitution for a new Protestant Episcopal Church of the United States in America, which by 1789 had become a functional American institution.

The American Methodists grew from the work of John Wesley in England who, as an Anglican, stressed the need to bring morality and religion to the masses and emphasized the human role and emotional response as tools of salvation. Wesleyan missionaries conducted services in Philadelphia in 1768, and the following year the congregation erected St. George's Methodist Church, the first of that denomination in America. But only a few hundred Methodists lived in Pennsylvania before the Revolution, and after it the number declined because of the flight of Anglican clergymen on whom these people depended. The Methodist Episcopal church achieved its national organization in 1784, and thereafter grew more rapidly than any other church in Pennsylvania, achieving a membership in 1850 of nearly 350,000 which made it second in size of all the churches in the state. Only the Presbyterian church was larger. An offshoot of the Methodists developed in the 1790s when Jacob Albright started a reform movement which grew into a new German sect, the Evangelical Association.

The Baptists in Pennsylvania organized at Cold Springs, Bucks County, in 1684 under the leadership of the Reverend Thomas Dungan. The First Baptist Church of Philadelphia, founded in 1698, attained a considerable accession of Keithian Quakers, but few Baptists migrated to Pennsylvania and the church grew slowly. Not until 1770 was the first Baptist church established west of the mountains, in Uniontown. The Baptists, numbering about 5,000 in 1790, were strongest in the east and west, but had few churches in the central section of Pennsylvania. The Baptist church was congregational and did not depend on Europe for direction. After the Revolution the Baptists created general committees for exchange of information which were similar to the Philadelphia Baptist Association of 1707. Like the Methodists, the Baptists grew very little in Pennsylvania until after the Revolution, and then flourished mightily, increasing from 5,000 in 1790 to nearly 130,000 in 1850. Like the Methodists, the Baptists had no traditional ties to break with Europe and therefore set up church organizations that can be considered indigenous.

The Roman Catholics had the opposite experience. During the colonial era they were under the jurisdiction of the Vicar Apostolic of London. Father Joseph Greaton held the first Catholic services in Philadelphia in 1720, and in 1733 built St. Joseph's chapel there, the first Catholic edifice in Pennsylvania. Fathers William Wappeler and Theodore Schneider served the German Catholics. The former established the first Sacred Heart Mission in Pennsylvania at Conewago, now Adams County, in 1730, and in 1742 built a stone chapel at Lancaster. Most Catholics in colonial America resided in Maryland and Pennsylvania. In 1784, on petition by Catholics from both states, the Pope terminated the American jurisdiction of the London vicar. In 1789 John Carroll of Maryland became the first Catholic bishop in America, and Pennsylvania Catholics then looked to their neighbor state for guidance.

There were five priests and about 10,000 Catholics in Pennsylvania in 1790, but their number grew rapidly. Philadelphia became a separate diocese in 1808, Pittsburgh in 1842, and Erie in 1853. In the mountains of central Pennsylvania, Prince Demetrius Augustine Gallitzen became a legendary figure. This wealthy Russian abandoned a life of ease to found a Catholic colony at Loretto in 1799, and for thirty years endured the harshest personal privation to serve, without pay, the people of this rough mountain district.

The rapid influx of Catholics from Ireland after 1830 soon aroused among Protestants all the latent suspicion, fear, and bigotry of Reformation days. Hatred of Irish immigrants exploded in a furious outburst against the Catholics which Protestant clergymen aggravated and which the Native American party leaders carried to the point of riot, bloodshed, and arson, at Kensington in 1844. The disorders did not discourage immigration, however, for the Irish continued to arrive, as did German Catholics, and the state had around 100,000 Catholics by 1850.

Few Jews came to colonial Pennsylvania, but they slowly entered the commonwealth after 1776. They located mostly in Philadelphia and Pittsburgh, very few farmed, and most entered business activities. The large Jewish immigration came in the post-Civil War period.

Pennsylvania Negroes, most of them Philadelphians, had long wished for their own churches, but generally attended white churches, sitting in a designated section. In 1787, in protest against the seating restrictions, Negroes in St. George's Methodist Church withdrew from the service. Under the leadership of Richard Allen and Absalom Jones, founders of the Free African Society of the city, the black community raised funds for a church of their own, aided by Dr. Benjamin Rush who had regarded the blacks highly ever since their courageous service during the yellow fever epidemic. Jones and Allen disagreed over religious affiliation, but Jones organized and became the pastor of the St. Thomas Protestant Episcopal Church in 1794; and Allen in the same year created the Bethel African Methodist Episcopal Church which Bishop Francis Asbury dedicated. By the 1850s the Philadelphia Negroes had created eighteen churches, nine of them Methodist, three Baptist, three Presbyterian, two Episcopal, and one Congregational.

EDUCATION

The religious base of colonial education The churches dominated education in Pennsylvania from its founding until the establishment of free public schools in the 1830s, mainly because early immigrants tended to settle among people of their own religion and their local schools naturally reflected that faith. The transition from religious to secular public education coincided with the Industrial Revolution which altered social mores, moved people about more rapidly, and demanded more specialized knowledge for employment. Students trained in the modern public schools may ponder with Alexander Meiklejohn "the terrifying question what a nation or state or town or village believes, if it believes anything"; and might ask whether a school district possesses any beliefs comparable in explicitness or durability to the teachings of churches about what a human being should or might be. In the preindustrial era, the schools generally taught the beliefs of the local church about God and man, sought to arouse a sense of man's responsibility to his Creator, and tried to established moral guidelines for personal behavior.

Few children in colonial Pennsylvania studied beyond the three R's. Reading received first priority for it held the key to the one book likely to be in a provincial home, the Bible. The Assembly in 1683 ordered all parents to teach their children "to read the Scriptures and to write by the time they attain to twelve years of age," and levied a fine for noncompliance; but this charge was not enforced and the province merely encouraged and did not provide education. Pupils of a scholarly bent might pursue a fourth R, religion, if they seemed likely candidates for the ministry, but those who continued beyond reading, writing, and arithmetic either went to European universities if their fathers had the means, or studied privately with local scholars.

Colonial primary education   Colonial Pennsylvanians developed several methods of primary education: the pay or subscription schools, usually called "dame schools" in the city and "neighborhood schools" in the country; the church schools; and the apprentice contract. The pay schools were informal arrangements among neighbors to hire a schoolmaster and set up a classroom for their children. Widows or maiden ladies generally taught "dame schools" in the larger towns, providing a schoolroom in their home. In the country, neighborhood schools held sessions in a room in a farmer's home where the teacher lived, conducted classes in winter, and worked as a farm hand in other seasons. As the school population increased, the subscribers often built small school buildings as a cooperative community effort. By 1834 when tax-supported public education began, about 4,000 such private schoolhouses had been erected in Pennsylvania by neighborhood action.

The several churches held different views about the purposes and content of education. The Quaker schools aimed to direct children toward self-support in order to serve society, and toward self-command in order to live uprightly in response to the dictates of conscience. The Friends fostered education for boys and girls, for Quakers and non-Quakers, and for persons of every race. They opposed government management or control of education for they wished both to avoid taxation and to keep an exclusive hold on the religious training of their children. Each Quaker Meeting normally set up its own school.

The Germans lagged in establishing schools, especially the sectarians who opposed an educated ministry. Fathers taught their sons to work on the farm, and mothers instructed their daughters in spinning, weaving, managing a household, and being a wife. The German church people depended on their ministers for education, and as the latter wanted mainly to train additional preachers, they concentrated on carrying select pupils into advanced schooling rather than directing their energies toward setting up elementary schools. Lutheran and Reformed churches often united their efforts to start subscription schools which held sessions in the church, but the European bodies did not finance church schools in Pennsylvania and the local parishioners of the German churches rarely undertook the task as a congregational responsibility. The British Society for Propagating Christian Knowledge sent funds to set up English language schools among the Pennsylvania Germans, but these people, sensing a threat to their own culture, would not cooperate even though their ministers encouraged the effort and Michael Schlatter was put in charge of the plan. Of all the German people, the Moravians proved most dedicated in providing schools for their young.

The Scotch-Irish Presbyterians, the most active in creating schools, aimed in part at improving opportunities for their children and in part at providing the base for catechizing. Their elementary schools usually took the form of subscription schools in that they were privately financed and managed, but they were mainly religious in spirit and purpose. The churches played an advisory role and exercised influence by indirection at the elementary level of schooling; their direct participation in education came at the secondary and college levels.

To visualize a primary school in colonial Pennsylvania we should picture from six to thirty students, aged five to twelve, in a room equipped with benches for the students and a rostrum for the teacher. The teacher might have some books, but the students did not, except for hornbooks containing the alphabet and key words. Some schoolbooks came into general use late in the colonial era such as the *New Pennsylvania Spelling Book* of 1754, or the *New England Primer* which began to be printed in quantity in Philadelphia in the 1770s. This Puritan alphabet book and first reader dwelt almost entirely on religion, including a catechism; a dialogue among Christ, Youth, and the Devil; and an assortment of hymns, prayers, and moral maxims. It remained a standard beginner's book until 1795 when Pennsylvania-born Lindley Murray produced his famous *English Grammar.* In the 1830s another Pennsylvanian, William McGuffey, produced the series of *McGuffey's Readers* which soon became the best-selling American book, next to the Bible.

Male teachers had little social status, for their occupation appeared an admission of incapacity to hold a better-paying job. As with the early self-proclaimed clergymen, some teachers were imposters and degenerates, but many others had both excellent academic qualifications and deep dedication. In cosmopolitan Philadelphia, immigrants who had been educated in Europe often became private schoolmasters, advertising in the newspapers that they would teach algebra, geometry, trigonometry, surveying, navigation, French, Latin, Greek, rhetoric, English, belles lettres, logic, philosophy, and other subjects. Women advertised schools in which young ladies could learn manners, French, instrumental music, singing, and dancing.

Some of the early teachers had high qualifications. It would have been hard to find better minds or more devoted scholars than Francis Daniel Pastorius, Robert Proud, George Keith, Provost William Smith, Anthony Benezet, John Todd, the Reverend Gilbert Tennent, James Wilson, and others. One of the most effective of these early teachers was Christopher Dock, kindly Mennonite teacher of Skippack who, at the request of his friends, left a detailed description of his methods. Dock rewarded pupils who excelled, and mobilized the good students to encourage and aid those who had trouble with the lessons. Unlike most of his contemporaries, he rarely used the switch, twisted noses and ears, made students kneel on dried peas, or rapped their knuckles with a ruler. A student in trouble had to find a classmate willing to sign bond for his subsequent good behavior, the bondsman to be punished for any transgression by his friend.

Beginning of the public schools The attainment of independence brought little change in educational practices. The constitution of 1776 included a general provision that the Legislature should establish schools in each county to furnish instruction "at low prices" financed "by the public," but no action followed this vague directive. The constitution of 1790 stated that the Legislature should provide education "in such a manner that the poor may be taught gratis." This article, by focusing exclusively on education of the poor, disapppointed those who wanted a system of general public education. In 1794, the two Houses passed separate bills authorizing counties to finance elementary schools by a local tax, and pledging the state to appropriate one-fifth of the total cost, but the measures failed in conference committee. The rejected bills contained all the main elements of the plan that was adopted forty years later.

The state finally passed laws in 1802, 1804, and 1809 which for the first time implemented the provisions of the constitution by requiring county overseers of the poor to pay regular tuition at subscription schools for poor children, collecting the money by a "poor tax." This law created no schools but enabled children of parents who declared themselves paupers to attend existing pay schools. As the parents resented making the declaration of poverty and the children disliked the stigma of being paupers, the new laws did very little to augment the number of pupils and nothing to increase the number of schools or teachers in the state.

A decade of experience with the pauper laws proved their inadequacy and aroused a tremendous surge of interest in the experiments of the English Quaker Joseph Lancaster, whose model schools in London promised a cheap and quick answer to the shortage of schools and teachers in Pennsylvania. The Lancastrian schools used a student-monitor system; that is, the teacher instructed a corps of older and brighter students who then instructed classes of younger pupils. Wild hopes spread that one teacher, working in a specially designed building, could provide instruction for upwards of 1,000 pupils. Roberts Vaux of Philadelphia headed the movement to build such a model school in that city in 1817, and in 1818 Joseph Lancaster arrived to give personal advice and supervision. Between 1817 and 1828 several monitor schools existed in Philadelphia and one began in Lancaster. Their experience demonstrated that the Lancastrian method did not work.

Responding to its traditional fear of taxes, Pennsylvania had thus far avoided a tax-supported school system, but just as the Lancastrian system collapsed many forces and events coalesced to bring state action. The rapidly expanding population, the growing complexity of economic life as the Industrial Revolution progressed, the rise of the penny press, the demands of the city workingmen, the equalitarian ideas of the Jacksonian age, the wider participation of people in politics, and the recognition by political leaders that the electorate needed to be literate all had a pervasive and cumulative impact. The formation in 1827 of the Pennsylvania Society for the Promotion of Public Schools in Philadelphia became the signal for massive pressure on the Legislature. Civic leaders like Roberts Vaux, John Sergeant, Samuel Breck, and John Wurts and politicians of all parties gave voice to the growing demand. Every Pennsylvania governor since Thomas McKean had called for the creation of a tax-supported public school system, but it was Governor George Wolf who finally persuaded the Legislature, on April 1, 1834, to pass the "Act to Establish a General System of Education by Common Schools."

The public school law of 1834 used existing political units as the base for local school administration, establishing the counties and larger towns as school divisions, and the townships, boroughs, and wards as school districts. Citizens in the districts could vote whether or not to join the new school system. If they decided to participate, they elected a local school board which had power to set the school tax rate and made the district eligible to receive state funds in proportion to the local contribution. The local school boards were responsible for erecting school buildings, hiring teachers, determining the curriculum, and supplying equipment; county inspectors periodically certified teachers and reported on school operation to the secretary of the commonwealth who now assumed the added title of state superintendent of public schools. State appropriations came from a school fund of $2 million; the interest of $100,000 per year would be distributed annually among the qualifying school districts. All children could attend these schools free.

The passage of the public school law brought a swift reaction by its opponents which nearly caused its repeal. Its enemies included many wealthy and conservative people who desired no change in the status quo, leaders of some churches who viewed state education as a double cost to them and a threat to religious instruction in parochial schools, a large part of the German population who wanted to raise their children in the old language and tradition, and many ignorant and indigent people who generally opposed anything which required taxation. But the attack failed, and the Legislature passed additional school laws in 1835 and 1836 which corrected some minor flaws in the original act and gave a permanent foundation to the Pennsylvania system of public schools. The main elements of the plan were: free tuition, school districts coextensive with existing political subdivisions, the right of any district to accept or reject the system, state aid only to accepting districts, and the concentration of power in the local school boards.

The existence of permissive laws did not at once create schools. Governor Wolf deserves major credit for passage of the school law, but his successor, Governor Ritner, did most to translate the law into reality. His secretary of the commonwealth, Thomas H. Burrowes, did the practical work, visiting nearly all the counties, talking with innumerable local meetings to explain the new system, instructing new school boards on their duties, and even designing a one-room school the plans for which he distributed widely and which became the pattern for buildings which dotted the countryside for a century. Appointed as the first superintendent of common schools in 1835, Burrowes dedicated the rest of his life to developing the Pennsylvania public school system.

Secondary education: the academies Secondary education in Pennsylvania became the special province of the academies. In colonial days the churches established most of these to train young men for the ministry, and clergymen generally served as teachers. The Quakers started the William Penn Charter School in 1689 and other such schools were established at Germantown, Abington, and Gwynedd. Of the German-speaking people, the Moravians took the lead in secondary education, founding Linden Hall Seminary at Lititz in 1747, a Seminary for Young Ladies at Bethlehem in 1749, and Nazareth Hall for Boys in 1759. Among the Presbyterians, William Tennent's Log College of 1726 set a pattern for such academies as the Derry Church School in Dauphin County (1732), Fagg's Manor in Chester County (1740), the Pequea Academy in Lancaster County (1752), and the Marsh Creek School in Adams County (about 1770).

After the Revolution, public-spirited citizens of nearly every community established local academies, frequently as a county enterprise with the school bearing the county name and locating at the county seat. The Legislature chartered about 150 academies between 1784 and 1861, and county courts after 1840 granted charters to fifty more. In addition to the 200 chartered academies, about 325 of these institutions functioned without incorporation. In 1850 there were 524 academies in Pennsylvania but only a few experimental public high schools.

The academies emphasized scholarly rather than vocational or practical education, stressing denominational religion, gentlemanly behavior, oratory, debating, composition and rhetoric, the Greek and Latin languages, classical history and literature, mathematics, and science. The individual capabilities of teachers determined the curriculum at a particular academy and the students took what was offered and stayed as long as their parents paid the fees.

The state gave land grants to many academies between 1784 and 1800, and thereafter the Legislature usually gave each newly chartered institution $2,000 if the school promised to enroll four or five poor children without tuition charge. In 1838 the Legislature granted chartered academies $500 per year for ten years; when these annual grants stopped, many closed. The incorporators of academies capitalized them usually at $5,000 or $10,000 and issued stock in denominations as low as $5 per share to gain the widest possible local support. Some counties conducted lotteries to aid their local academy. Tuition charges varied widely, and payments were accepted not only in money but in farm produce, supplies, work, or services. In the 1830s, academies charged from $100 to $150 per year for room, board, and tuition, while day schools charged separately for each course. The costs remained low enough that the academies could serve the entire community. These institutions attained an elite status partly because of the pride people took in having created a symbol of culture in their midst, but mostly because their students so often became distinguished civic leaders in later life and shed luster on the schools which had trained them.

Collegiate education Pennsylvania colleges all developed after the Revolution with the exception of the University of Pennsylvania. The line distinguishing the early academies and colleges is not always easy to draw, and as the need for higher education developed the academies tended to grow into collegiate institutions. Franklin's Philadelphia Academy and Charitable School of 1749 became the College of Philadelphia in 1755 and the University of Pennsylvania in 1779, the only nonsectarian college to be chartered in the state until the founding of the Agricultural College, now Pennsylvania State University.

The Presbyterians created the largest group of colleges. Dickinson College, chartered in 1783, grew from the desire of the church to have a college-trained clergy and the interest of Dr. Benjamin Rush who wanted to improve the educational facilities of the state. The Pittsburgh Academy of 1787 developed into the University of Pittsburgh. Washington Academy, chartered the same year, became Washington College in 1806; the Canonsburg Academy of 1791 became Jefferson College in 1802; and these later merged as Washington and Jefferson College. Presbyterian groups also chartered Allegheny College (1815), Lafayette College (1826), Geneva College (1848), Waynesburg College (1850), and Westminster College (1852). The Ashmun Institute at Oxford, chartered by the Presbytery of New Castle, Delaware, in 1854 and considered the oldest college for Negroes, became Lincoln University in 1866.

Franklin College, chartered in 1787, grew out of the desire of Philadelphia Federalists to provide an advanced school for Lancaster County Germans whose political support they needed. The German Reformed Church founded the Classical Institute in York in 1832 and moved it to Mercersburg in 1835 where it took the name Marshall College. A merger in 1853 created Franklin and Marshall College in Lancaster.

The Lutherans established Gettysburg College in 1832 as an outgrowth of the earlier Gettysburg Academy which had prepared students for the Lutheran Theological Seminary at Gettysburg. In 1858 the Lutherans chartered Susquehanna University in Selinsgrove as a classical and theological institution. The Moravians started their Women's College in 1742, and obtained a charter for Moravian College, Bethlehem, in 1807. The Quakers created Haverford College, chartered in 1833, and the Baptists started Bucknell University at Lewisburg in 1846. The Methodists established Madison College at Uniontown in 1827 and Avery College for Negroes in Allegheny in 1849, but neither of these survived. The rapid influx of Irish into Pennsylvania in the 1840s led to the opening of four Catholic colleges: Villanova in the town of Villanova, St. Francis College in Loretto, St. Vincent College in Latrobe, and St. Joseph's College in Philadelphia. All these had begun instruction between 1842 and 1851, but because of opposition by the Native Americans in the state Legislature some of them had to operate without charters during their early years.

By 1860, Pennsylvania had established twenty-four colleges with 156 faculty members. In addition to these institutions, numerous female colleges and seminaries had opened, notably the Pennsylvania Female Seminary, Collegeville (1853), Beaver College, Jenkintown (1853), Pittsburgh Female College (1854), and Irving Female College, Mechanicsburg (1857). Teachers colleges had just begun to appear before 1860. The Legislature passed the Normal School Act in 1857 providing for the establishment of teacher-training colleges or normal schools in each of twelve districts of the state. Millersville began its career as the first of these institutions in 1855, followed by Edinboro in 1861.

The educational facilities of Pennsylvania from the time of William Penn until the Civil War had undergone several major changes. During the colonial period the government played no part, and what few schools there were owed their existence either to churches or to neighborhood initiative. From the Revolution to 1834 the state talked of free public education but provided none except to offer to pay tuition in private schools for children whose parents declared themselves paupers. The school laws of 1834, 1835, and 1836 inaugurated elementary schooling for all children, financed mainly by local taxation. Education beyond this level remained in private hands, for the academies and colleges either had church financial support or tried to succeed as private business enterprises. By the 1850s, the commonwealth had begun to experiment with the public school system at the secondary school level, and in the normal schools and the Agricultural College of Pennsylvania had taken a first step into the collegiate domain.

BIBLIOGRAPHY

Religious developments may be broadly traced in the works of William W. Sweet. The Great Awakening is examined by C. H. Maxson: *The Great Awakening in the Middle Colonies* (1920). For the post-Revolutionary period, see Ray A. Billington: *The Protestant Crusade, 1800–1860* (1952); and Bernard A. Weisberger: *They Gathered at the River* (1958), the story of the revivalists.

There is no general history of religion in Pennsylvania, but the literature on religious topics is extensive. The Wilkinson *Bibliography of Pennsylvania History* lists references chronologically on pp. 127–131, 271–272, 329–332, 398, and 483–485, and materials on the several denominations on pp. 641–693. Dietmar Rothermund: *The Layman's Progress: Religious and Political Experience in Colonial Pennsylvania, 1740–1770* (1961) is an effort at synthesis.

The basic books on the early Quakers in Pennsylvania are listed in the Bibliography for Chapter 2.

For religious communities in Pennsylvania, see Arthur E. Bestor: *Backwoods Utopias* (1950). Julius F. Sachse: *German Pietists of Pennsylvania* (1895), and *German Sectarians of Pennsylvania, 1708–1800: A Critical and Legendary History,* 2 vols. (1899–1900), are excellent. On Ephrata, see Walter C. Klein:

Johann Conrad Beissel (1942); Felix Reichmann and Eugene E. Doll: *Ephrata as Seen by Contemporaries* (1954); Madison E. McElwaine: *Faith and Works at Middle Octorara since 1727* (1956); Eugene E. Doll: *The Ephrata Cloister* (1958); and James E. Ernst: *Ephrata: A History* (1963). On Old Economy, see Karl J. R. Arndt: *George Rapp's Harmony Society, 1785-1847* (1965).

The best introduction to the Amish is Calvin G. Bachman: *The Old Order Amish of Lancaster County* (1942). Other dependable works are H. M. J. Klein: *History and Customs of the Amish People* (1946); A. Reed Hayes, Jr.: *The Old Order Amish-Mennonites of Pennsylvania* (1947); Elmer L. Smith: *The Amish People* (1958); and John A. Hostetler: *Amish Society* (1963).

A handy reference for Mennonite history has been provided by C. Henry Smith and Harold S. Bender (eds.): *The Mennonite Encyclopedia,* 2 vols. (1955-1956). Other standard references include J. G. Scheffer: "Mennonite Emigration to Pennsylvania," *Pennsylvania Magazine of History and Biography,* vol. 2 (1878), pp. 117-138; C. Henry Smith: "Mennonite Immigration to Pennsylvania in the Eighteenth Century," *Pennsylvania German Society Proceedings,* vol. 35 (1929), pp. 1-412; C. Henry Smith: *Mennonites of America* (1909), and *The Story of the Mennonites* (1941); J. W. Hoover: *Social Attitudes of the Mennonites* (1915); and John C. Wenger: *History of the Mennonites of the Franconia Conference* (1937).

The key history of the Schwenkfelders is H. W. Kriebel: *Schwenkfelders in Pennsylvania* (1904).

On the Church of the Brethren, the following are the standard works: Martin G. Brumbaugh: *History of the German Baptist Brethen in Europe and America* (1899); G. M. Falkenstein: "German Baptist Brethen or Dunkers," *Pennsylvania German Society Proceedings,* vol. 10 (1899), pp. 5-148; John S. Gillin: *The Dunkers: A Sociological Interpretation* (1906); W. J. Hamilton (ed.): *Two Centuries of the Church of the Brethren in Western Pennsylvania, 1751-1950* (1953); and Russell W. Gilbert: "Blooming Grove, The Dunker Settlement of Central Pennsylvania," *Pennsylvania History,* vol. 20 (1953), pp. 23-39.

Much has been written about the Moravians, of which the following will be most serviceable: E. A. de Schweinitz: *History of the Church Known as Unitas Fratrum or the Unity of the Brethren* [Moravians] (1901); J. M. Levering: *History of Bethlehem, Pennsylvania, 1741-1872* (1903); John R. Weinlick: *Count Zinzendorf* (1956); and Gillian L. Gallin: *Moravians in Two Worlds* (1967).

The student can obtain good perspective on Lutheranism in early Pennsylvania in Lucy F. Bittinger: *German Religious Life in Colonial Times* (1906); and especially L. Pederson Qualben: *The Lutheran Church in Colonial America* (1940). The standard work is Theodore E. Schmauk: *The Lutheran Church in Pennsylvania, 1638-1820* (1903). The basic biographies are Margaret Seebach: *An Eagle in the Wilderness: The Story of Henry Melchior Muhlenberg* (1924); Theodore G. Tappert and John W. Doberstein (trans.): *The Journals of Henry Melchior Muhlenberg,* 2 vols. (1942-1945); and Delber W. Clark: *The World of Justus Falckner* (1946).

The early history of the Reformed church has been written mainly by James I. Good in a series of volumes. The major books on the Reformed church in Pennsylvania are H. S. Dotterer: *Historical Notes Relating to the Pennsylvania Reformed Church* (1900); and Joseph H. Dubbs: *The Reformed Church in Pennsylvania* (1902). The most important biographical studies are Henry Harbaugh and Daniel U. Heisler: *Fathers of the Reformed Church in Europe and America,* 6 vols. (1857-1888); William J. Hinke: *Ministers of the German Reformed Congregations in Pennsylvania and Other Colonies in the Eighteenth Century* (1951); and Henry Harbaugh: *The Life of Michael Schlatter* (1857), which, on pp. 87-234, contains a transcript of Schlatter's "True History of the Real Conditions of the Destitute Congregations in Pennsylvania," a major source about German church people in colonial Pennsylvania. Several doctoral dissertations deal with the Reformed people, notably Charles H. Gladfelter: "The Colonial Pennsylvania German Lutheran and Reformed Clergymen" (Johns Hopkins, 1952); and John B. Frantz: "Revivalism in the German Reformed Church in America to 1850" (Pennsylvania, 1961).

The standard scholarly work on the Presbyterians is Guy S. Klett: *Presbyterians in Colonial Pennsylvania* (1937). An introduction to original material is provided by M. W. Armstrong, A. L. Lefferts, and C. A. Anderson: *The Presbyterian Enterprise: Sources of American Presbyterian History* (1956). The two indispensable biographies are Dwight R. Guthrie: *John McMillan, The Apostle of Presbyterianism in the West, 1752-1833* (1952); and Guy S. Klett: *Journals of Charles Beatty, 1762-1769* (1961).

The beginnings and early history of the Protestant Episcopal church in Pennsylvania are included in S. M. J. Anderson: *History of the Church of England in the Colonials and Foreign Dependencies of the British Empire,* 3 vols. (1845); William S. Perry: *Historical Collections Relating to the American Colonial Church,* 4 vols. (1885), in which vol. 2 deals with Pennsylvania; Edgar L. Pennington: "The Beginning of the Church of England in Pennsylvania," *American Antiquarian Society Proceedings,* vol. 51 (1941), pp. 95–159; and Clara O. Loveland: *The Critical Years. The Reconstruction of the Anglican Church in the United States of America, 1780–1789* (1956). Other useful works are Louis C. Washburn: *Christ Church, Philadelphia: A Symposium* (1925); and Albert F. Gegenheimer: *William Smith: Educator and Churchman, 1727–1803* (1943).

The standard work on pre-Civil War Methodism is Abel Stevens: *History of the Methodist Episcopal Church in the United States,* 4 vols. (1864–1867), which should be supplemented by W. C. Barclay: *Early American Methodism, 1769–1844* (1949). For the local story, see S. M. Stiles: *Methodism in Pennsylvania* (1871); Jacob S. Payton: *Our Fathers Have Told Us: The Story of the Founding of Methodism in Western Pennsylvania* (1938); Louis D. Palmer: *Heroism and Romance: Early Methodism in Northeastern Pennsylvania* (1950); and Wallace G. Smeltzer: *Methodism on the Headwaters of the Ohio* (1951). The key biography is Stuart C. Henry: *George Whitefield: Wayfaring Witness* (1957).

On the Baptists, see *Centenary of Organized Baptist Work in and about Pittsburgh* (1913); and Robert G. Torbet: *A Social History of the Philadelphia Baptist Association, 1707–1940* (1944), a book which explains the church position on problems such as war, slavery, industry, and morals.

On Evangelical groups, see S. C. Breyfogel: *Landmarks of the Evangelical Association, 1800–1887* (1888); and Raymond W. Albright: *A History of the Evangelical Church* (1942).

Some of the more important materials on Catholicism in Pennsylvania before 1860 are Leo G. Fink: *Old Jesuit Trails in Penn's Forest: The Romance of Catholicity Told in the Footprints of Pioneer Missionaries of Eastern Pennsylvania* (1933); Anna D. Gamble: *Conewago Chapel Sesquicentennial* (1937); D. H. Mahoney: *Historical Sketches of the Catholic Churches and Institutions of Philadelphia* (1909); J. L. Kirlin: *Catholicity in Philadelphia* (1909); and A. A. Lambing: *History of the Catholic Church in the Dioceses of Pittsburgh and Allegheny* (1880). The key biography is Hugh J. Nolan: *The Most Reverend Patrick Kenrick: Third Bishop of Philadelphia, 1830–1851* (1948).

On the Jews, see H. P. Rosenbach: *History of the Jews of Philadelphia prior to 1880* (1883); Edwin Wolf and Maxwell Whiteman: *The History of the Jews of Philadelphia from Colonial Times to the Age of Jackson* (1957); and Sidney M. Fish: *Aaron Levy, Founder of Aaronsburg* (1951).

The best work on the Unitarians is Elizabeth M. Geffen: *Philadelphia Unitarianism, 1796–1861* (1961).

Education in Pennsylvania before the 1830s was so closely tied to religious denominations that the bibliography above on religion will apply. In addition, see F. Thomas Woody: *Early Quaker Education in Pennsylvania* (1920); Howard H. Brinton: *Quaker Education in Theory and Practice* (1949); Mabel Haller: "Early Moravian Education in Pennsylvania" (doctoral dissertation, University of Pennsylvania, 1951); Margaret A. Hunter: *Education in Pennsylvania Promoted by the Presbyterian Church, 1726–1837* (1937); Charles L. Maurer: *Early Lutheran Education in Pennsylvania* (1932); and Frederick G. Livingood: *Eighteenth Century Reformed Church Schools* (1930). On early schoolmen, see William Riddle: *Nicholas Comenius; or Ye Pennsylvania Schoolmaster of Ye Olden Time* (1897); Martin G. Brumbaugh: *Life and Works of Christopher Dock* (1908); Gerald C. Studer: *Christopher Dock, Colonial Schoolmaster* (1967); and Robert F. Seybolt: "Schoolmasters of Colonial Philadelphia," *Pennsylvania Magazine of History and Biography,* vol. 52 (1929), pp. 361–371.

Lawrence A. Cremin: *The American Common School* (1951) carries the story to 1850 and lays a broad background against which to view public education. Pennsylvania receives considerable attention. The important local studies are James P. Wickersham: *A History of Education in Pennsylvania: Private and Public, Elementary and Higher* (1886), a sound study; Louise Walsh: *History and Organization of*

Education in Pennsylvania (1930); James Mulhern: *A History of Secondary Education in Pennsylvania* (1933), a scholarly treatment; Charles C. Ellis: *Lancastrian Schools in Philadelphia* (1907); and Joseph J. McCadden: *Education in Pennsylvania, 1801–1835, and Its Debt to Roberts Vaux* (1937).

For private or church academies and colleges the student is referred to the Wilkinson *Bibliography of Pennsylvania History,* pp. 113–119, 273–275, and especially 332–343. The basic general histories of higher education are Charles H. Haskins and William I. Hull: *History of Higher Education in Pennsylvania* (1902), which is done by institution; D. G. Tewksbury: *The Founding of American Colleges and Universities before the Civil War* (1932); and Saul Sack: *History of Higher Education in Pennsylvania,* 2 vols. (1963).

CHAPTER SIXTEEN

Clues to a Regional Culture: The Professions and the Arts

Pennsylvanians made notable contributions to the professions of law, medicine, science, and journalism. All these, between 1681 and 1861, changed from European-type elite groups into more open professional communities in which admission rested on proven talent rather than family background. Pennsylvania also produced large numbers of creative artists in the fields of architecture, painting, music, the theater, and literature. The art forms became highly refined in the major cities, and developed indigenous primitive forms in the back country. The Quakers frowned on most artistic activity as a useless diversion of energy which should have been directed to aid the unfortunate. They slowed artistic development during the colonial era, but Pennsylvania enjoyed a phenomenal growth in the arts from the time of Washington's Presidency, when Philadelphia, as the national capital and the most cosmopolitan city of the Western world, became the "Athens of America."

THE PROFESSIONAL COMMUNITY

Law The history of the bench and bar in Pennsylvania before 1861 presents the odd paradox that, although the people hindered and discouraged the development of the legal profession from the earliest days, the state developed or attracted a fraternity of lawyers unequalled, as a group, anywhere in the nation. Penn had little regard for lawyers, and the Quakers considered them a source of mischief and evil. The Friends and the German Plain Sects wished to settle their differences out of court. The Assembly in 1686 passed a law forbidding lawyers to receive "any reward whatsoever" for representing a client, under penalty of a fine of £5 for taking pay. In 1705 another statute authorized people to settle contests over monetary claims by choosing a mutually agreeable arbitrator whose decision would be as legally binding as an award by a court. As the population grew and the society became more complex, court litigation increased, but the idea persisted that courts and lawyers were tools of the rich and powerful to take advantage of the poor and weak. Such thinking underlay the Whiskey Rebellion, the attack on judges between 1801 and 1820, the pressure to give local magistrates summary jurisdiction over cases formerly tried in court, and the tendency of people to avoid the courts for redress of grievances and to appeal to the Legislature for relief by private bills.

The judicial structure of Pennsylvania remained basically the same from the early 1700s until the Civil War. The Provincial Assembly in 1722 provided for a supreme court, for county courts of common pleas, of quarter sessions, and for orphans; for courts of oyer and terminer when needed, and for a special city court in Philadelphia. Lay judges, that is, people not learned in the law, could serve all these courts except the supreme court and the court of oyer and terminer where, because of the importance of the cases coming before it, a supreme court judge had to join others on the bench. Justices of the peace often held additional commissions to serve as county judges, and supreme court judges commonly rode circuit to sit as the learned members of panels of local lay judges for certain cases. The province also established the position of attorney general to represent the legal arm of the provincial authorities. These offices and functions carried into the commonwealth era with little structural change until the constitution of 1838 reduced the life tenure of judges to ten years for county courts and fifteen years for the supreme court. In 1850 the judgeships became elective instead of appointive.

Young men normally trained for law in the office of an established barrister who acted as preceptor. During the colonial period, sons of the wealthy commonly went to England to be trained at the Inns of Court, which meant not a law school, but a more prestigious preceptorship. Among the distinguished Pennsylvania jurists who received their training in England between 1760 and 1783 were Pennsylvania Chief Justices Benjamin Chew, Thomas McKean, Edward Shippen, and William Tilghman; Justice Jasper Yeates; Presidents of the Supreme Executive Council Joseph Reed and John Dickinson; and such famous leaders of the bar as Nicholas Waln, Edward Tilghman, Richard Tilghman, William Rawle, Jared Ingersoll, and Peter Markoe. But most started as clerks in some Philadelphia lawyer's office.

Philadelphia became the heart of the legal profession in Pennsylvania, not because all the lawyers resided there, but because all who gained distinction had to practice there since the most important courts held their sessions in that city, including the Supreme Court of the United States during the 1790s. In 1735 Andrew Hamilton traveled to New York to win a verdict for Peter Zenger, and the legend of the "Philadelphia lawyer" as one extraordinarily shrewd was begun. A delighted crowd carried Hamilton from the courtroom on their shoulders, New York gave him a key to the city in a golden box, and many acclaimed him as champion "of the rights of mankind and the liberty of the press."

The names of distinguished Pennsylvania lawyers in the era before 1861 are legion. Among those who served in national office, we may mention Federal Attorneys-General William Bradford (1794–1795), Richard Rush (1814–1817), Henry D. Gilpin (1840–1841), Jeremiah S. Black (1857–1860), and Edwin M. Stanton (1860–1861); and United States Supreme Court Justices James Wilson (1789–1798), Bushrod Washington (1798–1829), Henry Baldwin (1830–1846), and Robert C. Grier (1846–1870).

Philadelphia's Peter S. Du Ponceau tried to systematize and apply professional criteria to the apprenticeship method of training for law by organizing a law academy in 1821. The lawyers resisted, but the students maintained pressure for formal schooling. In 1850, George Sharswood took charge of the newly established law department of the University of Pennsylvania which soon developed into a law school. This significant innovation broke the hold of the elite barristers over legal training and replaced the long apprenticeship period with a two-year university course. In 1856 the supreme court of Pennsylvania accepted a degree from the law department as evidence of qualification of the applicant for admission to practice. The democratization of the legal profession followed. In 1800, 72 percent of all the Philadelphia lawyers came from high-income, upper-class families; in 1860 only 44 percent had this origin. None of the lawyers in 1800 came from families of clerks, shopkeepers, or non-English immigrants; by 1860, more than a quarter of practicing lawyers in Philadelphia had such family origins. Admission to the bar on the basis of the personal relationship between preceptor and student, which had been the norm in 1800, was in 1860 being replaced with empirical standards demanded by the faculty of a school of law.

Medicine The medical profession in the early eighteenth century was composed of practitioners occupying different levels of prestige. At the top stood the academically trained physician, and below him came the surgeon, the apothecary, and the midwife. By the middle of the nineteenth century the medical schools had admitted surgery, pharmacy, and obstetrics to the status of professional respectability. Between 1750 and 1850, a galaxy of brilliant physicians and a concentration of clinical and educational facilities made Philadelphia the center of medical activity in America.

In eighteenth century Pennsylvania, trained physicians served the upper classes, while most people relied mainly on Old World superstitions, patent medicines, and family cures. The doctrine of signatures still had wide currency in William Penn's lifetime, a belief that God had created an antidote for every human malady by placing a curative power in every plant, animal, or rock; and man had only to learn to associate the right object with each disease to cure it. America opened to Europeans a whole untapped source of natural remedies for their ills, and this hope stimulated a massive campaign of classification of flora, fauna, and minerals. Indian knowledge of the curative powers of certain American herbs strengthened the belief of settlers in the doctrine of signatures, and even local preachers proclaimed that the country "has native remedies against its natural defects." Franklin in the 1730s published three editions of the book *Every Man His Own Doctor,* which enumerated what native plants would cure American distempers, and William Bradford and Christopher Sauer published almanacs which included all sorts of medical nostrums.

Throughout the Pennsylvania Dutch regions in the eighteenth and nineteenth centuries, people often sought treatment by powwow doctors, or used their own knowledge of hexerei whose charms in one form promised safeguard against evil, and in another might cast a spell on an enemy. In 1820, John George Hohman of Reading published the *Long Lost Friend,* a compilation of mysterious arts and remedies rooted in medieval times, which exposed the charms, amulets, palindromes, herbs, elixirs, potions of animal parts, incantations, and the like which might cure all manner of human afflictions and protect cattle and crops.

In the towns, however, and especially in Philadelphia, major advances within orthodox medicine occurred. Philadelphia ranked first among American colonial cities as a center of medical learning. Fourteen of its seventeen leading physicians at the time of the Revolution had studied in the European medical capitals of Paris, Leyden, London, and Edinburgh.

The European-trained Thomas Bond (1712–1784) developed the idea of the Pennsylvania

Hospital which Franklin successfully promoted, and gave the first clinical lectures in America. Dr. Thomas Cadwalader (1708-1799) wrote *An Essay on the West Indian Dry Gripes* (lead poisoning) in 1745 which is considered to be the first American medical book. Two of the most highly regarded colonial physicians were Dr. William Shippen (1712-1801) and his son of the same name (1735-1808). The younger Shippen's lectures at the College of Philadelphia in 1762 mark the beginning of formal medical education in America. Dr. John Morgan (1735-1789) was active in the establishment of a medical school at the College of Philadelphia in 1765, and became the first professor of medicine in the country.

Dr. Benjamin Rush (1745-1813)—friend of Jefferson; member of the Continental Congress and signer of the Declaration of Independence, advocate of prison reform, temperance, and abolition of slavery and capital punishment; and surgeon general during the Revolution—was the first American to achieve an international reputation as a physician. He believed that all disease arose from excitement within the blood vessels, and he achieved notoriety for his insistence upon bloodletting and purging as the general cure-all. He worked valiantly to control the yellow fever epidemic in Philadelphia in 1793. Dynamic, versatile, contentious, and often deluded, Rush is most favorably remembered in the world of medicine for his interest in the care and treatment of the insane.

In the period of the early nineteenth century a group of young doctors began to supplant the colonial worthies. Dr. Caspar Wistar (1761-1818), professor of anatomy and chemistry at the University of Pennsylvania, held Sunday night "Wistar parties" at his home where for years the leaders of the arts and sciences and visiting scholars exchanged ideas and developed new concepts. Dr. Philip Syng Physick (1768-1837) occupied the first chair of surgery at the University of Pennsylvania and gave professional status to this branch. By 1810, obstetrics had been included as a department in the medical college. Dr. Nathaniel Chapman (1780-1853), a pupil of Rush, wrote the first American book on *materia medica*. He founded the still-existing *American Journal of Medical Science* in 1820 and became the first president of the American Medical Association. Dr. Thomas S. Kirkbride (1809-1883) was interested in the care and treatment of the insane in hospitals especially designed for this purpose.

The doctors of Philadelphia formed the College of Physicians in 1786, the oldest medical academy in the nation, and took the initiative in creating the American Medical Association, organized at the Philadelphia Academy of Natural Science in 1847. The medical department of the College of Philadelphia started a decade before the Revolution, and ultimately grew into the Medical School of the University of Pennsylvania. The Philadelphia College of Pharmacy was chartered in 1821, Jefferson Medical College was founded in 1825, and the Pennsylvania College of Dental Surgery received its charter in 1850. In the same year the Legislature chartered what became the Woman's Medical College of Pennsylvania, the first such institution to go into actual operation.

The Pennsylvania Hospital came into existence in 1751 to begin a long and distinguished service to the medical profession and the state. Dozens of other hospitals were created in the years before the Civil War by private philanthropy, by churches, by government agencies like the Navy Department, by groups of doctors interested in special types of treatment, and by some nationality groups.

Science　In the seventeenth and early eighteenth centuries, the word "science" did not describe a vocation with structured content and method, and few people devoted their time exclusively to it. The word "scientist" did not come into use until the 1840s. Men studied "natural philosophy" mainly as an intellectual hobby in conjunction with their established professions as clergymen, politicians, teachers, or lawyers. The physicians formed the largest single group of Pennsylvanians who applied themselves to inquiry and rational explanation of the natural world in colonial days.

Intellectual curiosity and the world of ideas cannot be confined to any geographical region, and for this reason it is not entirely realistic to speak of the growth of science in Pennsylvania. We do recognize, however, that the free interchange of thought among people of scholarly interests promotes the work of all. The pace of inquiry quickens when members of a scholarly community live in close proximity, as happened in colonial Philadelphia. This city became the focal center of scientific exploration in colonial America for several reasons. The town was relatively free of the kind of narrow sectarians who would oppose the discussion of scientific theories which might challenge any part of their religious dogma. Benjamin Franklin, through his discoveries about electricity, gained the attention of the European world of science and opened the door of communication. And finally, many of the Philadelphia doctors had studied at European universities noted for their scientific activities, and these contacts continued. Pennsylvania men of science corresponded regularly with important figures in Europe such as the Swedish botanist, Carolus Linnaeus, and the Englishmen John C. Lettsom, John Fothergill, and Peter Collinson. Joseph Priestley and Thomas Cooper brought their scientific knowledge and reputations from England to Pennsylvania in 1794 and strengthened the already established bonds between European scholars and those of Pennsylvania.

Penn's secretary, James Logan (1664–1751) who saw the drama of discovering and identifying the plants of a new world with all their potential as sources of new foods and medicines became a friend and collaborator of John Bartram (1699–1777) of Philadelphia, often called the first American botanist. Bartram traveled between New York and Florida; recorded his botanical observations; experimented with seeds, bulbs, and hybridizing; started a botanical garden in Philadelphia; and achieved international recognition. His son, William Bartram (1739–1823), continued his father's work and published important botanical treatises on the region from the Carolinas to Florida. Benjamin Smith Barton (1776–1815), a physician, wrote the first American textbook on botany and published an early American *materia medica*. Gotthilf Henry Ernest Muhlenberg (1786–1815), a pastor from Lancaster and first president of Franklin College, wrote extensively on the botany of his area and received the plaudits of Linnaeus. Thomas Nuttall (1786–1859) explored the Mississippi River valley as a botanist and ornithologist. He named the Wisteria vine in honor of his scientific colleague, Dr. Caspar Wistar. Constantine Samuel Rafinesque (1783–1840) eagerly observed and catalogued all natural phenomena, but had a special interest in plant life and fish. Born in Turkey, he made Philadelphia his headquarters and undertook numerous scientific explorations into the area immediately west of the Appalachians.

In the field of mathematics, David Rittenhouse (1732–1796) held the most distinguished reputation. We have already encountered him as a surveyor, but his main interest lay in astronomy. His calculations of the parallax of the transit of Venus in 1767 was the most accurate made in America. He made several mechanical orreries to reproduce the movement of the planets, invented scientific devices such as a collimating telescope, a metallic thermometer, and a plane transmission grating, and devised a number of demonstrations of proof in pure mathematics. Hugh Williamson (1735–1819), a physician and friend of Franklin's, applied his mathematical knowledge to the study of meteorology. Andrew Ellicott (1754–

1820) surveyed most of the boundaries of Pennsylvania, designed the "Federal City" of Washington after L'Enfant's plans had to be modified, and became professor of mathematics at West Point.

Benjamin Franklin (1706–1790) is best known to the modern world for his amazing versatility, but he achieved his reputation in the European scientific community of the 1700s by showing the identity of electricity and lightning, an empiric demonstration which quickly outmoded the theoretical debate then raging. Franklin's fame obscured somewhat the electrical experiments of Ebenezer Kinnersly (1711–1778), a Baptist minister and English teacher of Philadelphia who prepared a college course on electricity in 1764, invented an electrical thermometer, and developed more systematic though less theatrical evidence of the properties of electricity than his famous fellow citizen.

In chemistry, Joseph Priestley (1733–1804) had already established his scientific fame in England by discovering oxygen prior to his removal to Northumberland, Pennsylvania, in 1794. He fled England to escape political persecution for his sympathy with the French revolutionaries, and was attracted to Pennsylvania by the scientific activity there. He set up his laboratory in the wilderness in order to work without disturbance, but visited Philadelphia frequently to participate in meetings of the American Philosophical Society. Priestley discovered eight gases and experimented also with electricity and optics. An associate, Thomas Cooper (1759–1839), came to Pennsylvania the same year as Priestley, practiced law and medicine in Philadelphia, became a violent political activist against the Federalists, and served as professor of chemistry at Dickinson College from 1811 to 1815, and at the University of Pennsylvania from 1815 to 1819. He later moved to South Carolina, but not before publishing important scientific books on Priestley's work and on the relationships between chemistry and medicine. Caspar Wistar (1761–1818), the physician who did so much to develop a community of scientists in Philadelphia, devoted his efforts to promote chemistry as a specialized area of science. Thomas Woodhouse (1770–1809), also a doctor, concentrated on chemistry and in 1792 founded the Chemical Society of Philadelphia, one of the first such organizations. Woodhouse pioneered in plant chemistry, industrial chemistry, and chemical analysis.

Of many Pennsylvania scientists who shared an interest in geology, two may be selected for special comment. William Maclure (1763–1840) mapped the geology of the United States east of the Mississippi River, and served as president of the Academy of Natural Sciences in Philadelphia from 1817 to 1840. James Mease (1771–1846), a physician, published the pioneer work on the geology of the nation in 1807.

Although we have classified the foregoing men according to specific areas of inquiry, all of them had multiple interests, and some, like Franklin, Priestley, and Cooper, may be considered universal geniuses. In the early days of science, each inquirer had a uniquely personal approach. Charles Willson Peale, the artist, was also an amateur naturalist who avidly collected scientific artifacts and curios such as the bones of a mastodon which he exhibited along with his paintings at his Philadelphia museum. His son, Titian, became an entomologist. He explored the upper Missouri with the expedition of Stephen H. Long in 1819–1820, and visited the Polynesian Islands with the Wilkes Expedition of 1838–1842, writing and illustrating scientific reports of his observations. Elisha Kent Kane, a physician, accompanied the first Grinnell Arctic Expedition and commanded the second, 1853–1855, becoming the first American to chart a route to the North Pole.

These men, whether pursuing a specialty or following multiple interests, worked mainly as scholars, classifying, cataloging, and theorizing. Other scientific workers devoted themselves more to the practical applications of existing scientific knowledge, such as Thomas Godfrey (quadrant), Robert Fulton (steamboat), Oliver Evans (gristmill), Mathias Baldwin (locomotive), John A. Roebling (wire rope), William Kelly (steel), and Joseph Saxton (photography).

The several learned societies, located mainly in Philadelphia, were probably the most important promoters of science before 1860. The American Philosophical Society ranked first among these. Growing out of a proposal of Franklin in 1743 "for Promoting Useful Knowledge among the British Plantations in America," the Society received a charter in 1780, built its quarters on Independence Square in 1785, and provided a forum for distinguished scientists to disseminate their ideas.

In 1812, several Philadelphians interested in natural history founded the Academy of Natural Sciences which by 1826 had acquired a building, established a museum, and become a clearinghouse and reference point for catalogers and classifiers. The Athenaeum for the promotion of science and literature began in 1813 and acquired a building in 1847. The Franklin Institute was founded in 1824 and provided exhibits, training, and encouragement for inventors and mechanics. It brought into membership such men as Mathias W. Baldwin, William Strickland, and Isaiah Lukens, and set up a schedule of awards for worthy inventions. Specialized societies like the Philadelphia Society for Promoting Agriculture, the Chemical Society of Philadelphia, and the College of Physicians played a part in encouraging scientific inquiry.

Libraries also rendered assistance. Some of the best colonial libraries in Pennsylvania were in the homes of private individuals, but Franklin's Junto inspired the creation of the Library Company of Philadelphia which came into existence in 1731 and has served the state ever since. The Mercantile Library (1821) and the Historical Society of Pennsylvania (1824) provided large collections of scholarly books. The early colleges, especially the University of Pennsylvania and Dickinson, also developed outstanding scientific libraries.

Journalism Pennsylvania, although still 69 percent rural in 1860, contained an unusually large number of towns big enough to support a local newspaper. The state led all others in the number of newspapers published from the Revolutionary War until the 1840s. There were 9 Pennsylvania newspapers in 1776, 72 in 1810, 185 in 1828, 229 in 1840, and 310 by 1860. In that year, Pennsylvania circulated 85 million newspapers, more than the combined total of the fifteen Southern states.

Newspaper publication in Pennsylvania began on December 22, 1719, when Andrew Bradford released the first issue of his *American Weekly Mercury* in Philadelphia. It was the first paper of the middle colonies and the third in America, missing second place by one day to the *Boston Gazette.* Samuel Keimer started the *Pennsylvania Gazette* in 1728, a paper which Benjamin Franklin purchased in 1730 and made famous. Franklin turned the editorial management over to his partner, David Hall, in 1748 but maintained his financial interest. Christopher Sauer began the first German-language newspaper, *Die Germaner Zeitung,* at Germantown in 1739. By 1775, Philadelphia was publishing six English newspapers; Lancaster, one English and one German; and Germantown, one German.

During the 1790s when Philadelphia was the national capital, the city became the home of journals with national circulation and impact, such as John Fenno's *Gazette of the United States* (1790–1847), William Cobbett's *Porcupine's Gazette* (1797–1799), and the famous

Aurora (1790–1835) edited first by Benjamin Franklin Bache and then by William Duane. In 1786, John Scull of Pittsburgh transported the first printing press over the mountains and began publishing the *Pittsburgh Gazette,* a journal which under a succession of distinguished editors like Neville Craig, David N. White, and Russell Errett, became a major voice for the people of the West. John Dunlap's *Pennsylvania Packet,* antedating the Revolution, became the first American daily in 1784, and had the further distinction of printing the first broadsides of the Declaration of Independence and the United States Constitution for distribution to the people. The *Packet* later became the *North American,* managed by one of the outstanding American editors of the Civil War period, Morton McMichael. The Jeffersonian era brought the *Democratic Press* into being, a Philadelphia paper edited by John Binns who, for the first time, used the word "Democratic" in the name of an American newspaper.

In addition to the political papers, various commercial, religious, and reform organizations produced numerous journals for both instruction and indoctrination. Benjamin Lundy and John Greenleaf Whittier served as editors of the *Pennsylvania Freeman,* an abolitionist paper based in Philadelphia. The Colonization Society produced the *Colonization Herald* from 1835 until 1865, and the temperance societies and woman's rights supporters also established journals. The *Woman's Advocate* of the 1850s was the first newspaper printed and published by women.

Philadelphia became a center of magazine publishing from the Revolution to the Civil War. In the 1750s, Franklin's Junto started the *American Magazine;* just before the Revolution, Thomas Paine edited a periodical he called the *Pennsylvania Magazine,* and from 1787 to 1792 *Carey's American Museum* appeared. These short-lived efforts were followed by a group of literary magazines which sought to stimulate American letters and to counteract European sneers at Americans as uncultured illiterates. The *Port Folio,* edited by Joseph Dennie who was hailed as the "American Addison," ran from 1801 to 1827 and sought "elegant literature" by Americans. The *American Quarterly Review* (1827–1837) also emphasized the publication of serious literary efforts.

Godey's Lady's Book (1830–1898) published works by eminent American writers like Edgar Allan Poe, Nathaniel Hawthorne, and Washington Irving, but also included sections of women's fashions and light reading which had wide appeal. Its success brought competitors into the field, notably *Peterson's Ladies' National Magazine* (1842–1898). *Graham's Magazine* (1841–1858) and *Sartain's Magazine* (1849–1852) sought to advance the prestige of American literary men by offering a medium of publication which would be attractive to the intelligentsia. All these magazines had their headquarters in Philadelphia.

THE COMMUNITY OF ART

Architecture Buildings reveal much about the character of a people or a region. We will first look at the homes of common people, built by the owners and neighboring craftsmen without the aid of architects, and second, consider architectural showpieces such as the mansions of wealthy individuals or impressive public and institutional buildings. The former will expose more about Pennsylvania, the latter more about architecture.

Early Pennsylvania homes fall into three easily distinguishable categories: log houses, homes based on German origins, and those of the British Isles. Outside of a few large towns, the log house was the almost universal first dwelling for Pennsylvanians simply because

The Hans Herr house, built in 1719, showing the major features: steep roof, chimney in center, small windows, thick masonry walls. (Hans Herr Restoration Committee, Lancaster)

trees were everywhere. Log construction methods were first imported from Scandinavia and Germany. So many people built log houses over so long a span of time that these structures attained a kind of genealogy, traceable by the ways the corner logs were interlocked. The earliest or the crudest builders used round, unbarked logs with the ends roughly notched. The next generation of cabins displayed axe-dressed beams joined by interlocking squared notches. As better tools and more skilled workmen became available, the logs might be sawed to shape and joined at the corners by dovetail notches, or be mortised into upright cornerposts and pegged into place. Chinks between the logs were filled with wooden wedges, grass, and mud, and better cabins rested on a stone foundation. The fireplaces which dominated one gable end were at first made of heavy green logs plastered with mud; later rough stone fireplaces became standard, and in the best-crafted cabins the fireplaces might contain some dressed stone and a special baking oven built into the interior structure, along with hooks and an iron crane for hanging kettles.

The Germans who came to Pennsylvania brought with them a style of home building which harked back to the Middle Ages and reflected something of the simplicity, the frugality, and the resistance to change which characterized these people. The European tradition dictated buildings of stone, but Pennsylvania could provide also logs and brick. The German homes may be found in any of these materials or in combinations of them—one of the unique marks of Pennsylvania colonial homes which used not the traditional but the available building materials. German houses had a steep roof often terminating at the eaves in a "kick" or slight flare which threw water outward away from the walls. The chimney protruded from the center of the tiled roof; the gable ends were faced with vertical siding and punctured with a tiny square window, or several if the gable rose two stories. The windows throughout were small and set flush in the thick walls with a wide sill inside. Most of the outside space appeared as wall, with a few randomly placed squarish windows framed austerely by undecorated wood or stone.

German colonial houses were usually built over a spring with the entrance to it on the outside to keep dampness out of the living quarters, but sometimes the spring was accessible by an inside doorway. An unpretentious doorframe held a heavy oak door, often with a design of inverted V's formed by the planking. The door swung on decorative wrought-iron hinges and might be cut in half horizontally to make a "Dutch door." Some two-story houses had a "pent roof," or a small apronlike roof encircling the house between the first and second stories to deflect rainwater away from the foundation. But most commonly the early Germans built the front and back walls only one story high, and the steep roof enclosed the second story and attic. The Moravian buildings at Bethlehem and the Ephrata Cloister complex, both dating from the 1740s, illustrate the various features of Pennsylvania German colonial architecture.

In contrast to the German houses, people from the British Isles, whether English, Scotish, or Welsh, tended to build houses reflecting Georgian or late Renaissance or Baroque architecture. A characteristic rectangular Georgian dwelling presented its long side to the street. The front door opened to a central hall running through the house to a rear door, and the main stairway curved upward from one side of this hall. Two rooms opened on either side of the hall, all with fireplaces which required these houses to have double chimneys at each gable end. Large windows with ornamented lintels flanked the main doorway, normally two on each side. The doorway itself commanded primary attention, for a Georgian entrance was ornately embellished with columns on either side of the entry, a lintel with rectangular or half-moon glass lights, and a large portico surmounting the whole. Because all these houses had a basically similar floor plan, the doorways became the main focus of individuality. The second floor presented five large windows aligned symmetrically with the ones below. The gable ends had two windows for each floor, and two small quarter-round or horizontally rectangular windows in the attic, or a single half-moon window, depending upon how the chimneys had been located. The roof pitch was usually shallow unless the house included third-floor rooms with dormer windows. Houses of this general design could be found all over Pennsylvania normally built of the traditional brick, but also of local stone or wood.

The foregoing brief descriptions portray typical German and English houses as an experienced builder might have constructed them. But local circumstances continually altered the plans and intermixed the German and English features. Variations in building materials and the application of the details of one European style to the floor plan of another tell a story of independent craftsmen, indulging individual preferences. This feature of Pennsylvania regional architecture followed the tradition of diversity which appears in so many aspects of Pennsylvania life and culture.

The architectural showpieces were the mansions of the wealthy and the structures which housed public and private institutions. These were carefully planned, tended to reflect the changing trends in architectural style, and were the products of particular architects and designers. It will be simplest to view this realm chronologically, proceeding from one dominant style to the next, or, specifically, from Georgian which dominated the colonial era, to the Federal style which was a simplified Georgian of the early Republic, to the Classic Revival from the early 1800s to the 1840s, and finally to the Gothic Revival which developed before and continued through the Civil War. This national progression had some unique regional aspects.

Philadelphia produced the architectural gems of the colonial era. Christ Church, begun in 1727, became upon its completion in 1755 one of the most notable Palladian edifices of its day, displaying a richly detailed early Georgian exterior and rearing a Christopher Wren steeple higher than any other building of its time in America. In 1732 work began on the State House which, with the later additions, became Independence Hall as it has been known since 1776. The actual designers of these notable buildings remain uncertain. The lawyer, Andrew Hamilton, has often been credited with designing the State House and Dr. John Kearsley with Christ Church, but probably they promoted the construction, whereas two master carpenters, Edmund Woolley and John Harrison, respectively, drew the plans for these two famous buildings. The Pennsylvania Hospital by Samuel Rhoads, constructed between 1755 and 1800, and Carpenters' Hall of 1770, by Robert Smith, also became architectural landmarks of colonial Philadelphia. All of these buildings were in the Georgian style, built of brick.

The mansions of the wealthy in colonial days provide insight into both the architecture and customs of the age. Many Philadelphia colonial country houses have survived by being incorporated in Fairmount Park. The commonwealth of Pennsylvania, through its Historical and Museum Commission, has restored or preserved others, and historical groups in many counties have performed a similar service so that we still have many opportunities to observe at first hand colonial ways of living. Among the state-maintained properties are the Swedish log house on Upper Darby Creek in which John Morton, signer of the Declaration of Independence, lived; the recreated Pennsbury Manor, William Penn's mansion north of Bristol; Graeme Park near Neshaminy, built by Governor William Keith in 1721; Hope Lodge near Fort Washington, built in 1723; the homes of Conrad Weiser at Womelsdorf, of Daniel Boone near Birdsboro, and of iron-master John Potts of Pottstown; the Ephrata Cloister at Ephrata; and the village of Old Economy at Ambridge, built after 1824 but reflecting much of colonial architectural practice.

After a brief era known as the Federal period of architecture, from the Revolution until about 1810 during which buildings of the late Georgian style predominated, the Classic Revival began. This became the strongest influence on public and private building from about 1800 until the 1840s. Both Roman and Greek forms emphasizing the use of columns became popular, but from the late twenties adaptations of the temple form of the Greeks dominated the architectural scene. Benjamin Henry Latrobe, Pennsylvania's first architect in the professional sense, gave impetus to the Classic Revival in his Bank of Pennsylvania, 1798, employing the Roman dome and a portico of columns derived from the Greeks. William Strickland followed with the Second Bank of the United States, the Merchant's Exchange, the United States Mint, and many other Philadelphia buildings in the classic mode. This form reached its purest expression in the work of Thomas U. Walter who applied the Greek temple form to Nicholas Biddle's home, Andalusia.

The Greek Revival worked its way to the west after the east had abandoned it. The lovely

Baker Mansion, home of the Blair County Historical Society, one of the outstanding examples of the Greek revival style applied to a private residence. (Harold E. Dickson)

Independent Congregational Church at Meadville, an outright Greek temple, was designed by George W. Cullom and built in 1836. In Pittsburgh, Samuel Church's home, "Woodlawn," of 1833 and Judge William Wilkins "Homewood" of 1835 offered notable examples. Erie had a Greek temple bank. The Elias Baker mansion of Altoona, built in 1844, survives as a major example of the Greek temple theme applied to a residence. The Greek Revival found its expression in dozens of county courthouses, churches, and residences, particularly west of the Susquehanna. Its popularity had passed by 1850.

Between about 1840 and the Civil War, the Gothic Revival appeared. The use of forms derived from European Gothic cathedrals had made occasional appearance in Pennsylvania buildings since colonial days, but the architects John Notman in Philadelphia and John Chislett in Pittsburgh made full-scale use of this style and brought it into fashion. Notman's St. Mark's Church in Philadelphia, 1848, was a frankly medieval cathedral. This era saw the building of courthouses and prisons copied from medieval castles, with their turrets and castellated battlements.

Along with the Gothic Revival came the Italianate-Renaissance Revival, and eclectic architecture drawing its models from every land and using every conceivable form and material for building. Civic buildings appeared in the design of Egyptian temples and homes began to display a wild assortment of turrets, balconies, lookout towers, multishaped windows, heavy overhanging cornices, and roofs with gables everywhere, as if a rebellion had broken out against the earlier symmetry of the Georgian and the Classical styles.

Painting, sculpture, and the decorative arts   Painting may be considered according to the canons of art and also as a portrayal of the character of a locality by a regional community of artists. Painters often provide clues to a regional culture by their choice of subject and their mode of treating it.

Until 1750, the only significant Pennsylvania painters had been European-trained immigrants. Gustavus Hesselius (1682–1755), a Swedish "face painter" who came to America in 1712, is valued for his portraits of several Delaware Indian chiefs. Robert Feke (ca. 1705–1750) spent his last years in Philadelphia painting local portraits some of which, in more recent times, were mistakenly thought to be the work of John Singleton Copley. John Valentine Haidt (1700–1780) studied painting at the Berlin Academy, followed Count Zinzendorf to Bethlehem in 1754, became a Moravian minister, and executed a number of religious paintings for Moravian churches. These men, with John Meng (1734–ca. 1754), were the precursors of the community of Pennsylvania painters.

During the second half of the eighteenth century a group of Pennsylvanians became professional painters, most of them working in portraiture because this provided the best means of obtaining a steady income. Philadelphia became the center of their activity partly because its size and wealth provided patrons on whom the artists depended for a livelihood. Of all the Pennsylvania artists, two dominated this era: Benjamin West (1738–1820) and Charles Willson Peale (1741–1827).

West, a Quaker, began painting likenesses of people around his home while still a small boy. His remarkable natural talent attracted the interest of several knowledgeable friends who provided him with professional brushes and paints, and with books of engravings. The Quaker Meeting disapproved, but West nonetheless persisted, painted portraits in Lancaster for several years, and at length went to study in Italy, financed by sympathetic Philadelphians including William Allen and Provost William Smith. West went to England in 1763, quickly became one of the most sought-after portraitists in London, was given a generous commission by King George III to provide paintings for the royal residences, founded the Royal Academy of England in 1768, and became its president in 1792 on the death of Sir Joshua Reynolds. Successful and wealthy, West remained in England until his death in 1820, and became a generous host to aspiring American painters. He welcomed them, housed, fed, financed, and taught them, and soon came to be spoken of as the "Father of American Painting." Although West stands on his own merit as a painter, regarded mainly as an innovator of realism, his greatest contribution lay in his encouragement to American students. Among those who studied at the West mansion were John Singleton Copley, Gilbert Stuart, Charles Willson Peale, Matthew Pratt, Robert Fulton, Washington Allston, John Trumbull, James Earle, William Dunlap, and Samuel F. B. Morse.

Charles Willson Peale, a dynamo of a man, was raised in Maryland; was schooled as an indentured apprentice to a saddler; worked as a gunsmith, coachmaker, silversmith, and clockmaker, and later came to Philadelphia where he worked as a painter and indulged his hobby as a naturalist. Peale studied under Copley and West. He served with Washington during the Revolutionary War, employing his graphic talents to sketch fortification plans and paint numerous portraits of revolutionary leaders whose appearance would otherwise

Painting by Edward Hicks, *The Residence of David Twining, 1787,* showing a Quaker farm near New-town. (Abby Aldrich Rockefeller Folk Art Collection, Williamsburg, Va.)

remain unknown. In 1785 he established the Museum of Natural History in Philadelphia; ten years later he took the lead in preparing the first public art exhibit in American history; and in 1805 he was a leader in founding the nation's first institution of art, the Academy of Fine Arts in Philadelphia, which held annual art exhibits starting in 1811.

Among other Pennsylvania painters who may be placed in the "portrait" era of the late eighteenth and early nineteenth century were Gilbert Stuart (1755–1828), celebrated during his Philadelphia period for portraits of Washington; Matthew Pratt (1734–1805); Robert Edge Pine (1730–1788), who produced an important historic painting of "Congress Voting Independence"; Thomas Sully (1783–1872), probably the leading portrait painter of the age; and John Neagle (1796–1865), a student of Sully. Jacob Eichholtz (1776–1842) of Lancaster painted portraits of many early political leaders, and Joshua Shaw (ca. 1777–1860) performed a similar function in Pittsburgh.

As the nineteenth-century cities grew larger and private wealth increased, painters found a rising demand for their work and could break away from portraiture into other forms.

Painting by John Lewis Krimmel, *Fourth of July in Centre Square,* showing part of the Philadelphia Water Works and the statue of the Nymph of the Schuylkill by William Rush. City Hall now stands at this spot. (The Pennsylvania Academy of Fine Arts)

Artists like Thomas Birch (1779–1851) of Philadelphia painted seascapes and naval scenes from the War of 1812, and winter landscapes of eastern Pennsylvania. Thomas Doughty (1793–1856) became a pioneer American landscape painter devoting his attention to scenes along the Susquehanna and Juniata and becoming one of the founders of the Hudson River school. W. T. Russell Smith (1812–1896) of Pittsburgh painted excellent western Pennsylvania landscapes. George Catlin (1796–1872) of Wilkes-Barre became a nationally acclaimed painter of the Plains Indians, depicting them generally against the dramatic background of a western landscape.

A number of significant painters of the pre-Civil War era followed their special interests. John Lewis Krimmel (1787–1821) worked in genre, painting street scenes in Philadelphia. In Pittsburgh, James Reid Lamdin (1807–1889), a fine portrait painter, also contributed socially expressive scenes from his native city. Several primitive painters who worked as signmakers produced works of art which have endured, such as Edward Hicks, the Quaker from Newton, who painted many versions of *The Peaceable Kingdom;* and John A. Woodside (1781-1852) of Philadelphia who has left admirably detailed paintings of country life.

Although most painters produced many different kinds of work, Severin Roesen (1815–ca. 187†), a German immigrant who settled in Williamsport, devoted himself exclusively to still-life paintings of fruit and flowers, done with emphasis on realism.

Both the number and the quality of the artists who made Philadelphia their home in the early days of the Republic added luster to the fame the city had long enjoyed as "The Athens of America." The arts tended to flourish in the cities, and Pittsburgh's James Lamdin established the first art gallery there in 1828. After 1832, J. J. Gillespie's art shop in the city became the center of the art world of western Pennsylvania. These early Pennsylvania pioneers in painting provided the roots of a rich artistic tradition.

Sculpture did not flourish in early America, and only one Pennsylvanian, William Rush (1756–1833), attained a major reputation in this field. Rush worked in impermanent wood, producing numerous busts of contemporary men, figureheads for sailing ships, and life-sized eagles. His most pretentious work, *Leda and the Swan,* formed the center of a fountain in front of the Centre Square Water Works in Philadelphia, a Classic Revival structure by Benjamin Latrobe which provided a dramatic background and made this civic expression of the fine arts a favorite resort of townspeople after its completion around 1812.

Early Pennsylvanians produced many forms of decorative or folk art. The field is nearly limitless, for folk art includes objects useful in daily life for which people acquire a special appreciation because of their beauty of form, color, finish, or craftsmanship. Fine furniture produced by city cabinetmakers and the more simply styled but gaudily painted benches, boxes, and chairs of the Pennsylvania Germans became objects of art in the eyes of their fabricators and owners. Among the gems of the late colonial and early Republican period were the grandfather clocks, marvels not only of woodwork but of mechanical ingenuity. David Rittenhouse, Odran Dupuy, Christopher Sauer, and the Gobrecht family produced some of the best of these majestic timepieces.

Pennsylvanians played a significant part in the production of artistic glass and ceramics. Baron Henry William Stiegel of Manheim began to make his now-famous "Stiegel glass" in the 1760s. Albert Gallatin, in western Pennsylvania, opened the New Geneva Glass Works in 1797, and later the Craig and O'Hara Company of Pittsburgh became a center for the production of decorative cut and pressed glass. In the field of ceramics, the Tucker family of Philadelphia began producing the first American porcelain in the 1820s, making exquisite white tableware with delicately decorated borders and embellished sometimes with views of Philadelphia in the center. The Pennsylvania Germans made cruder but better-known ceramic ware, such as stoneware, slip-ware, or sgraffito. Stoneware in the shape of jugs, bowls, and other heavy tableware was highly glazed usually in brown but occasionally in black or blues. Slip-ware and sgraffito were colorfully decorated in the traditional Dutch designs. On slip-ware, special designs or personalia were applied atop the glazed surface, whereas on sgraffito the inscriptions were cut down through the unbaked glaze into the red clay base. These two Pennsylvania German pottery forms were sometimes lumped under the name "tulip ware."

Metalcraft was an important decorative art. Many persons worked in silver, copper, brass, and pewter with results that achieved recognition as art forms. Silversmiths Philip Syng and Cesar Ghiselin of Philadelphia made many of the most highly regarded pieces. The coppersmiths made weather vanes into shapes that took their place as folk art, and the ironworkers provided artistic forms peculiar to them. Firebacks, stove plates, and chunk stoves displayed intricately cast designs, including such detailed religious scenes in relief that these stoves have been called "The Bible in Iron." There was scarcely a furnace that did not engage in competition for excellence of decorative design in its patterns of stoves and iron-fronted Franklin fireplaces. The makers of wrought-iron hardware at the forges also brought art into their designs for strap hinges, locks, shutter clamps, foot wipers, and other common household necessities. In a more specialized art, gunsmiths cut and etched designs onto gun barrels and stocks. Between 1800 and 1850, tinsmiths supplied an eager Pennsylvania German population with household tinware, painted for their particular market with the favorite colorful themes: tulip, heart, and bird. Women in Pennsylvania households from the Delaware to the Ohio made quilts which were original works of art, meticulously planned and painstakingly executed; or produced equally original designs in braided and hooked rugs. To reduce such various exercises in native art to categories is nearly impossible, but visits to some of the many state and local museums of Pennsylvania, such as the Pennsylvania Farm Museum near Lancaster, the Mercer Museum at Doylestown, the William Penn Memorial Museum at Harrisburg, the Hershey Museum, the Westmoreland County Museum of Art at Greensburg, or some of the county historical society museums will illustrate the dominant themes of Pennsylvania folk art.

Music and the theater The Quakers opposed music, but all the other Pennsylvania settlers brought with them a European tradition of religious music and engaged in hymn writing, choral singing, and instrumental music during colonial days. Francis Daniel Pastorius of Germantown wrote hymns, and John Kelpius and his Wissahicken hermits brought musical instruments to Pennsylvania, and composed the text and music for many hymns. The Amish had the sixteenth-century martyr hymnbook *Der Ausbundt* reprinted in Pennsylvania, and used it widely. The Mennonites sang psalms, and their Skippack schoolmaster, Christopher Dock, taught singing to the children. The Schwenkfelders composed more than 1,500 hymns and had them printed into a hymnbook by Christopher Sauer in 1762. The Presbyterians considered the precentor, who led the congregational singing, nearly as important as the minister.

Of all the early settlers, the Germans most actively incorporated religious music into their lives, and three particular German communities became centers of music in Pennsylvania: the people of Ephrata, the Moravians, and the Harmony Society at Old Economy. At Ephrata, Conrad Beissel, possibly the first composer of religious music in America, developed an original system of harmony, measure, and musical notation. His choral compositions ran to seven parts and covered the entire voice range. The Ephrata community produced over 1,000 hymns with original musical scores which Franklin published in 1730, and which the Ephrata brothers printed in 1747 in a book made at their local press.

The Moravians brought a love of music and a variety of instruments to Pennsylvania, and quickly became one of the most widely known musical communities in colonial America. The Moravian bishops were normally fine instrumentalists, and the men and women performed not only as choirs but with violins, oboes, flutes, French horns, trumpets, and trombones. They used music to celebrate many special religious occasions, and pioneered in musical education. The Moravians formed the Collegium Musicum in 1744 and in 1820 created the Philharmonic Society. They were early recipients in America of compositions by Mozart, Haydn, Mendelssohn, Handel, and Bach, and gave the premiere American performances of some of the works of these composers.

In the early 1800s the Harmony Society settled in western Pennsylvania under the leadership of George Rapp. Music formed a basic element of this communal religious society, for its members sang not only in their religious services, but had special songs for walking to the fields, and for each type of work.

Until the end of the colonial era, most musical development in Pennsylvania was associated with churches. The growth of secular music began with the achievement of independence and in Pennsylvania became closely associated with the theatrical world. The Quakers tried to restrain both musical and dramatic entertainment, but condemned the latter particularly because they considered plays and actors a threat to morality and decency.

Concerts and the theater naturally flourished first in Philadelphia, the cultural capital of the province. Interested citizens formed the Orpheus Club in 1759, and opened the Southwark Theatre on Society Hill the following year for operas, ballets, and concerts. Such performances were quickly outlawed, but the legal prohibition was lifted in 1766. After a decade of growing theatrical activity, both the Continental Congress and the Pennsylvania Assembly ordered the closing of playhouses as frivolous in a time of crisis, a prohibition which remained in force until these blue laws were repealed in 1789. In 1793 Philadelphia obtained its own theatrical company, Wignell and Reinagle, who in that year built the famous Chestnut Street Theatre, familiarly called Old Drury. Until its demolition in 1855, Old Drury was the heart of the city's theatrical world. Other theaters followed—the Walnut, the Arch, the Pennsylvania, the Olympic, the New National, and many more. By the 1820s these theaters presented more drama and less music until, in the two decades before the Civil War, they had become self-sustaining as theaters exclusively for stage plays. Among them, they offered in the years 1835–1855 nearly 13,000 plays. The Walnut Theatre alone ran fifty-six performances of Shakespeare's Richard III between 1835 and 1841.

The theater achieved independence from the primarily musical world after the musicians set up their own concert halls. A group of talented Philadelphians who were instrumentalists, composers, conductors, and enthusiasts, notably Benjamin Carr, Raynor Taylor, Charles Hupfeld, and Benjamin Cross, established the Musical Fund Society in 1820 and constructed a concert hall in 1824. The society began a regular program of operas in 1828, and arranged concerts by the many European virtuosos who had begun to take American concert tours. It also trained conductors and encouraged composers. The society remained musically active, but by the 1850s its Music Fund Hall had become outmoded. In 1857, Philadelphia's music lovers built the palatial opera house at Broad and Locust Streets known as the American Academy of Music, later to be the home of the Philadelphia Orchestra.

As musicians tended to be itinerant, it is difficult to name composers who can be considered Pennsylvanian, but several names should be introduced. Francis Hopkinson, who in 1759 wrote "My Days Have Been So Wondrous Free," is generally acknowledged as the first American secular composer. Hopkinson's son, Joseph Hopkinson, wrote "Hail Columbia" in 1798, and Philadelphia's Thomas à Becket wrote "Columbia, the Gem of the Ocean," which had its premiere performance in the Chestnut Street Theatre. Apart from such productions, many men composed operatic and orchestral works, notably the harpsichordist John Bentley, French horn player Victor Pellissier, organist Raynor Taylor, singer and pianist Benjamin Carr, cellist Henry Capron, violinist Anton Philip Heinrich, and finally, William Henry Fry who discarded his dependence on European musical tradition and wrote the first opera indigenous to America, *Leonora*. All these men had their major roots in Philadelphia.

In the 1840s and 1850s, interest in music moved westward, and inland cities began to produce local musical organizations. The Pittsburgh Harmonic Society, a concert group, was active from 1812 until 1818, and the Mozart Society was organized there in 1838. In Williamsport, J. T. Mussina established the Repasz Band in 1831, inaugurating a type of American musical activity which spread rapidly throughout the country until nearly every town had its band to welcome visiting dignitaries, march in parades, celebrate patriotic days, and provide local musical entertainment.

As interest in music developed, a wave of European instrumentalists and singers came to America for concert tours and brought to many Pennsylvania communities, for the first time, high-quality musical performances. Among the scores of visitors, two gripped the public imagination and aroused universal enthusiasm in the 1840s and 1850s: Jenny Lind, the "Swedish Nightingale," and the Norwegian violinist, Ole Bull. The latter, delighted with Pennsylvania, purchased a 10,000-acre tract where in the 1850s he built the town of Oleana, Potter County, hoping to create a Norwegian colony devoted to music. Unhappily, he bought land to which the seller had no title and his plans collapsed, but he continued his concert work and became one of the best-known and best-loved performers of the antebellum era.

The classical forms of music engaged the interest of the most serious students and performers, but only a small portion of the population ever became acquainted with their work. Another form of music, less highly regarded but more widely spread, took root in antebellum Pennsylvania—folk songs and ballads. There were the songs of the mine patch; the labor union songs; Indian ballads; the songs of the loggers, the rivermen, the wagoners, the canallers, and the railroaders; and the farm and mountain ballads. The nationality groups had their own particular balladry and folk tunes: the Germans, the Scotch-Irish, the Welsh, the Irish, and the Negroes all contributed songs richly expressive of their joys, hopes, and sorrows in Pennsylvania. No one person stands out as composer or performer in this area of music, but one Pennsylvanian created songs which later became folk music: Stephen Collins Foster. Born in 1826, the son of a mayor of Pittsburgh, Foster gave up life as a bookkeeper to write popular music for the minstrel troupes which had come into vogue in the 1850s. His nostalgic songs of the Old South, full of romantic melancholy for the plantation blacks, brought him little income but became a national institution. "O Susanna," "Old Black Joe," "My Old Kentucky Home," and others equally well known, worked their way into the hearts of people in many nations and remain songs which are immediately recognized nearly anywhere in the world.

Literature In colonial Pennsylvania the Quakers exerted as strong an influence on writing as they had on the graphic and performing arts, but in a different way. Their ideas of tolerance and freedom of expression encouraged literary effort, but for social betterment rather than for entertainment, diversion, or escape. Most Pennsylvania colonial writers used the instructional, polemical, or descriptive forms, buttressed by scholarship, satire, and logic. They produced promotional and historical books about the province; religious treatises; persuasive or contentious books about the Indians, slavery, science, and politics; and a few notable poems and autobiographical memoirs. After the Revolutionary War the literary men turned to the more imaginative realms of the romantic novel, lyric and pastoral poetry, and the drama.

Among the earliest writers about the province of Pennsylvania were William Penn; Thomas Holme, the city planner of Philadelphia; and Gabriel Thomas, who in 1698 published a delightfully witty *Historical and Geographical Account of the Province and Country of Pennsylvania and of West Jersey*. Francis Daniel Pastorius, whom Whittier called the

"Pennsylvania Pilgrim," published seven books and left forty-three more in manuscript form, including descriptions of the province, poems, childrens' books, and scholarly works on religion and the Indians, written in Latin, German, or English. His descriptive writings drew many of his European countrymen across the Atlantic to Pennsylvania. Benjamin Rush, a prolific writer on science, philosophy, education, and religion, also wrote an excellent descriptive treatise on the Pennsylvania Germans. Robert Proud, master of the Friends Public School, wrote the first systematic history of Pennsylvania in 1798. David Ramsay of Lancaster published several books in the 1780s on the history of the American Revolution.

Many Pennsylvanians wrote about religion and theology, often contentiously in pamphlet wars over some local controversy. Others, like William Penn and John Kelpius, produced works of lasting theological consequence. Several men wrote memoirs of their own lives which earned them contemporary fame and have remained in circulation ever since. Most famous was Benjamin Franklin's *Autobiography.* Two Revolutionary War veterans, Alexander Graydon and Christopher Marshall, wrote illuminating diaries of their experiences in the field. One writer of the late 1700s deserves to be remembered if only because he anticipated by two centuries the later practice of identifying bureaucratic programs by their initial letters. He wrote a witty book about colonial Philadelphia in the form of letters by "Tamoc Caspipina," a name derived from his position as "The assistant minister of Christ Church and St. Peter's in Philadelphia in North America."

Political themes inspired literature of importance in the years before and after the Revolution. John Dickinson in 1765 produced his *Letters of a Pennsylvania Farmer to the Inhabitants of the British Colonies,* a careful analysis of the problem of imperial taxation which earned him the nickname of "Penman of the American Revolution." Benjamin Franklin published effective short polemical pieces, and Thomas Paine, temporarily a Philadelphian, anonymously published his famous and incendiary pamphlet, *Common Sense,* in that city in 1776. Pittsburgh's Judge Hugh Henry Brackenridge published several inspirational books about the American Revolution during the conflict, and later wrote the barbed and witty picaresque novel, *Modern Chivalry,* satirizing social and political customs of his day.

The post-Revolutionary era brought acclaim to several Pennsylvania authors primarily for their literary craftsmanship, rather than for the relevance of their subject matter to current affairs. Charles Brockden Brown (1771–1810) became not only the first American novelist, but the first to pursue a professional career based exclusively upon writing. He wrote six novels between 1798 and 1801 of which *Arthur Mervyn,* a story of the yellow fever epidemic in Philadelphia, has been judged the best although some critics prefer *Wieland,* an imaginative suspense tale set in Philadelphia which abounds in seduction, murder, and suicide. Edgar Allan Poe cannot be considered a Pennsylvanian, but he lived in Philadelphia from 1838 until 1844, a period of illness, penury, and frustration at his failure to create a new literary magazine. He wrote some of his best-known works during his Philadelphia sojourn, including "The Raven," "The Gold Bug," and "Murders in the Rue Morgue." Bayard Taylor (1825–1878) of the town of Kennett Square wrote several novels the best of which was a tale of the Revolutionary War entitled *The Story of Kennett.* He achieved widest renown for his books and lectures on foreign travel. Taylor traveled extensively, and on his return to America appeared on the lecture platform in the various native costumes of the countries he had visited.

Pennsylvania's poets during the first 150 years achieved a limited following. In the early days, Quaker restraint placed reins on poetic ambition, and in the nineteenth century the New England poets became the center of national attention. But a number of Pennsylvania poets played an important role among their contemporaries. Acquila Rose (1695–1723), one of the earliest American lyric poets, warmed the hearts of Philadelphians and brought general grief to the city when he died at the age of twenty-eight, having demonstrated, like the painter John Meng, a rich talent cut short before it had time to mature. A trio of Philadelphians of the pre-Revolutionary era encouraged each other in poetic writing: Nathaniel Evans (1742–1767), Thomas Godrey, Sr. (1736–1763), and Francis Hopkinson (1737–1791). The first two wrote lyric poems on classical themes in a manner suggestive of that which Keats later perfected. Their published work did not circulate very much beyond the city literati, but Hopkinson gained a wide audience by writing patriotic doggerel like "The Battle of the Kegs," making fun of the British in 1777.

Philip Freneau (1752–1832), a revolutionary naval veteran who suffered brutal imprisonment at the hands of the British, became a passionate democrat, a Jeffersonian editor in Philadelphia during the 1790s, and the outstanding American poet of his era. He wrote bitingly satirical poems about the British, and on American politics during Washington's presidency, but his most enduring poems vividly recreated the life of the sea, a world he knew intimately as a wartime sailor and later as the master of a brig. William Cliffton (1772–1799), though he died at twenty-seven, proved a worthy foil for Freneau, for he wrote stinging political satires in the poetic manner of Dryden in support of the Federalists and flaying the Jeffersonians. Thomas Dunn English (1819–1902), an almost unlettered Philadelphia Irishman, wrote thousands of poems and more than fifty plays, most of which showed his lack of literary training. But he produced one poem which caught the public fancy and made him famous: "Ben Bolt." Thomas Buchanan Read (1822–1872) of Chester County was another prolific Pennsylvania poet of the mid-nineteenth century with little early training who was judged by critics of his time to be an imitator of Wordsworth. The literary magazines eagerly published his poems, and those published in book form sold well. Like English, Read perpetuated his name primarily through one poem, "Sheridan's Ride," which he wrote in less than a day in November 1864, after seeing a newspaper account of the actual event.

Pennsylvania had few playwrights before 1790 because the development of the dramatic arts had been stunted by restrictive laws, but when the Philadelphia theater began to flourish in the early nineteenth century a number of significant authors appeared. In the colonial period, only Thomas Godfrey achieved importance. His romantic tragedy, "The Prince of Parthia," was the first play written by an American and professionally produced. David Douglas's American Company first staged this drama in Philadelphia in 1767, and gained for Godfrey the title "Father of the American Drama."

In the years between 1790 and 1860, six Pennsylvania playwrights produced worthy scripts: James N. Barker (1784–1858), Richard Penn Smith (1799–1854), John A. Stone (1800–1834), Robert T. Conrad (1810–1858), Robert Montgomery Bird (1806–1854), and George Henry Boker (1823–1890). Barker's play of 1808, *The Indian Pricess,* for the first time used an American Indian theme, dramatizing the Pocahontas story. Richard Penn Smith, grandson of Provost William Smith, wrote a number of American historical and patriotic plays such as *William Penn, The Eighth of January* commemorating Jackson's victory at New Orleans, and *"The Triumph at Plattsburgh."* His best plays, however, were two melodramas, *The Deformed or Woman's Trial* and *The Disowned, or the Prodigals,* which played in many American cities and in London. John A. Stone came to Philadelphia to produce a play he had written, *Metamora, or the Last of the Wampanoags,* in a prize contest initiated by America's most popular actor, Edwin Forrest, who was seeking plays in which he could take the leading role. The four winners, all Pennsylvanians, included Stone,

Smith, Conrad, and Bird. Stone's *Metamora* reflected deep understanding of Indian character and, when played by Forrest, held audiences transfixed. Conrad also attained fame through Forrest who portrayed the outlaw Jack Cade in Conrad's play *Aylmere, or the Bondman of Kent.* In this story of an English revolt against the feudal system, the gigantic Forrest brought his audiences into convulsions with his roaring, ranting, screeching personification of the hero, Cade.

Of all the Pennsylvania playwrights of the antebellum era, George Henry Boker was the most accomplished. He dealt with European themes and gained his reputation through skilled dramatic craftsmanship rather than because of the local appeal of his subject matter or the association of his plays with a famous actor like Forrest. His Spanish tragedy, *Calaynos,* written when he was twenty-five, established him as a leader of his field. His *Francesca da Rimini* was judged by the profession as the best American play of its kind in 1860. Boker's major contributions continued into the post-Civil War period, but he had firmly established his reputation before that struggle began.

BIBLIOGRAPHY

A great deal of material on the professions, arts, and sciences will be found in the county and city histories.

On the legal profession generally, see George A. Billias: *Law and Authority in Colonial America* (1965); and Daniel J. Boorstin: *The Americans, The Colonial Experience* (1958), book 2, part 7. For Pennsylvania, the basic colonial study is William H. Lloyd: *The Early Courts of Pennsylvania* (1910). Other more specialized works are Thomas R. Meehan: "Courts, Cases and Counselors in Revolutionary and Post-Revolutionary Pennsylvania," *Pennsylvania Magazine of History and Biography,* vol. 91 (1967), pp. 3–34; Elizabeth K. Henderson: "The Attack on the Judiciary in Pennsylvania, 1800–1810," *Pennsylvania Magazine of History and Biography,* vol. 61 (1937), pp. 113–136; and J. Paul Selsam: "A History of Judicial Tenure in Pennsylvania," *Dickinson Law Review,* vol. 38 (1934), pp. 168–183. The most useful biographical studies are Isaac Sharpless: *Political Leaders of Provincial Pennsylvania* (1919), which treats such men as Logan, the Lloyds, Kinsey, and Dickinson; Frank M. Eastman: *Courts and Lawyers of Pennsylvania: A History, 1623–1923,* 3 vols. (1922), the standard work; and Horace Binney: *The Leaders of the Old Bar of Philadelphia* (1859). Gary B. Nash: "The Philadelphia Bench and Bar, 1800–1860," *Comparative Studies in Society and History,* vol. 7 (1965), pp. 203–220, exposes the early legal fraternity as a closed cultural elite.

For developments in medicine see Frederick P. Henry: *Standard History of the Medical Profession of Philadelphia* (1897); Theodore Diller: *Pioneer Medicine in Western Pennsylvania* (1927); and Richard H. Shryock: *Medicine and Society in America, 1660–1860* (1960). An introduction to medical education and institutions will be found in George W. Corner: *Two Centuries of Medicine: A History of the School of Medicine, University of Pennsylvania* (1965); and Gulielma F. Alsop: *History of the Women's Medical College, Philadelphia, Pennsylvania, 1850–1950* (1950). The epidemics are covered by John H. Powell: *Bring Out Your Dead: The Great Plague of Yellow Fever in Philadelphia in 1793* (1949); and Charles E. Rosenberg: *The Cholera Years* (1962). Biographies of important Pennsylvania physicians have been written by Irwin Richman: *The Brightest Ornament: A Biography of Nathaniel Chapman, M.D.* (1967); James E. Gibson: *Dr. Bodo Otto and the Medical Background of the American Revolution* (1937); Earl D. Bond: *Dr. Kirkbride and his Mental Hospital* (1947); Whitfield J. Bell, Jr.: *John Morgan: Continental Doctor* (1965); Carl Binger: *Revolutionary Doctor: Benjamin Rush, 1746–1813* (1966); Betsy C. Corner: *William Shippen, Jr., Pioneer in American Medical Education* (1951); and Andrew S. Berky: *Practitioner in Physick* (1954), a biography of Dr. Abraham Wagner, colonial doctor among the Pennsylvania Germans.

Books on early American science that will provide background have been written by Brooke Hindle,

Whitfield J. Bell, Jr., and Nathan Rheingold. Useful biographical works include Merle M. Odgers: *Alexander Dallas Bache, Scientist and Inventor, 1806–1867* (1947); Ernest Earnest: *John and William Bartram* (1940); Josephine Herbst: *The New Green World. John Bartram and the Early Naturalists* (1954); Bernard I. Cohen (ed.): *Benjamin Franklin's Experiments* (1942), though the student should refer to Wilkinson's *Bibliography of Pennsylvania History,* pp. 189–200, for extensive Franklin listings; J. A. Leo Lemay: *Ebenezer Kinnersley, Franklin's Friend* (1964); Talbot Hamlin: *Benjamin Henry Latrobe* (1955); Jessie Poesch: *Titian Ramsay Peale, 1799–1885, and His Journals of the Wilkes Expedition* (1961); Ira V. Brown (ed.): *Joseph Priestley: Selections from His Writings* (1962): Edward Ford: *David Rittenhouse, Astronomer-Patriot. 1732–1796* (1946); Brooke Hindle: *David Rittenhouse* (1964); Eugene S. Ferguson: *Early Engineering Reminiscences (1815–1840) of George E. Sellers* (1965); and Robert Cantwell: *Alexander Wilson, Naturalist and Pioneer* (1961).

There are few published histories of newspapers, but a model of such a history is J. Cutler Andrews: *Pittsburgh's Post Gazette: The First Newspaper West of the Alleghenies* (1936). Among the biographies, students should note A. J. DeArmond: *Andrew Bradford, Colonial Journalist* (1949); and Ward L. Miner: *William Goddard, Newspaperman* (1962), on the editor of the *Pennsylvania Chronicle,* largest of the colonial newspapers.

In the broad field of the arts, Walter M. Whitehill (ed.): *The Arts in Early American History: Needs and Opportunities for Study* (1965); and Louis B. Wright et al.: *The Arts in America: The Colonial Period* (1966) provide background. On the arts in Pennsylvania, see Anna M. Archambault (ed.): *Guidebook of Art, Architecture and Historic Interests in Pennsylvania* (1924); and Harold E. Dickson: *A Working Bibliography of Art in Pennsylvania* (1948).

Histories of early American architecture by Fiske Kimball, Joseph Jackson, Howard Major, Talbot F. Hamlin, and Carl W. Condit contain much Pennsylvania material. Studies of Pennsylvania architecture have been made by Alfred L. Kocher: "Early Architecture of Pennsylvania," *Architectural Review,* vol. 48 (1920), pp. 513–530; vol. 49 (1921), pp. 31–47, 135–155, 233–248, 311–330, 409–422, 512–535; vol. 50 (1921), pp. 27–43, 147–157, 214–226, 397–406; vol. 51 (1922), pp. 507–520; vol. 52 (1922), pp. 121–132, 435–444; Philip B. Wallace: *Colonial Churches and Meeting Houses, Pennsylvania, New Jersey and Delaware* (1931); Eleanor Raymond: *Early Domestic Architecture of Pennsylvania* (1931); and Harold E. Dickson: *One Hundred Pennsylvania Buildings* (1954).

The history of Philadelphia architecture appears in Frank Cousins and P. M. Riles: *The Colonial Architecture of Philadelphia* (1920); Theodore B. White (ed.): *Philadelphia Architecture in the Nineteenth Century* (1953); Philip B. Wallace: *Colonial Houses, Philadelphia, Pre-Revolutionary Period* (1931); Harold D. Eberlein and C. Van Dyke Hubbard: *Portrait of a Colonial City, 1670–1838: Philadelphia* (1939); and George Tatum: *Penn's Great Town: 250 Years of Philadelphia Architecture* (1961).

On characteristic architecture of the German regions, see G. Edwin Brumbaugh: "Colonial Architecture of the Pennsylvania Germans," *Pennsylvania German Society Proceedings,* vol. 41 (1933), part II, pp. 5–60; and William J. Murtagh: *Moravian Architecture and Town Planning, Bethlehem, Pennsylvania, and Other 18th Century American Settlements* (1967). On western Pennsylvania, consult Charles M. Stotz: *The Architectural Heritage of Early Western Pennsylvania* (1966). Helpful biographies are Joseph Jackson: *Early Philadelphia Architects and Engineers* (1922); Talbot F. Hamlin: *Benjamin Henry Latrobe* (1955); and Agnes A. Gilchrist: *William Strickland: Architect and Engineer* (1950).

Pennsylvania painters are the subject of books by Harold E. Dickson: *Pennsylvania Painters* (1955); and Paul A. Chew (ed.): *250 Years of Art in Pennsylvania* (1959). Biographies of early Pennsylvania painters have been written by Dorothy Miller: *The Life and Works of David G. Blythe* (1950); John W. Jordan: "Gustavus Hesselius: The Earliest Painter and Organ Builder," *Pennsylvania Magazine of History and Biography,* vol. 29 (1905), pp. 129–133; Alice Ford: *Edward Hicks: Painter of the Peaceable Kingdom* (1952); Charles C. Sellers: *Charles Willson Peale, 1741–1827,* 2 vols. (1947); William Sawitzky: *Matthew Pratt* (1935); Edward Biddle and Fielding Mantle: *The Life and Work of Thomas Sully, 1783–1872* (1921); and H. E. Jackson: *Benjamin West* (1900).

On the early sculptor William Rush, see Henri Marceau: *William Rush, 1756–1833: The First Native American Sculptor* (1937).

Folk art is a topic with so extensive a bibliography that only a few of the basic books can be given here. In general, see Carl Bridenbaugh: *The Colonial Craftsman* (1950); Jean Lipman: *American Folk Decoration* (1951); and R. C. Steinmetz and C. S. Rice: *Vanishing Crafts and Their Craftsmen* (1959). On Pennsylvania, consult Frances Lichten: *Folk Art of Rural Pennsylvania* (1946), and *Folk Art Motifs of Pennsylvania* (1954); John J. Stoudt: *Pennsylvania Folk Art* (1948), and *Early Pennsylvania Arts and Crafts* (1965); Edwin A. Barber: *Tulip Ware of the Pennsylvania German Potters* (1903); Earl F. Robacher: *Pennsylvania Dutch Stuff* (1944); Henry Kauffman: *Pennsylvania Dutch American Folk Art* (1946); and Solon Buck and Elizabeth Buck: *The Planting of Civilization in Western Pennsylvania* (1939). Paul Chew's *250 Years of Art in Pennsylvania,* cited earlier, contains an excellent section on folk art.

Books on early Pennsylvania music include *Church Music and Musical Life in Pennsylvania in the Eighteenth Century* (1926), issued as publication no. 4 of the Pennsylvania Society of Colonial Dames; Gertrude M. Rohrer (comp.): *Music and Musicians of Pennsylvania* (1940); George Korson: *Pennsylvania Songs and Legends* (1949); Don Yoder: *Pennsylvania Spirituals* (1961); and William H. Armstrong: *Organs for America: The Life of David Tannenburg* (1968).

On Pennsylvania German music, see Rufus A. Grider: *Historical Notes on Music in Bethlehem, Pennsylvania, 1741–1871* (1873). Julius F. Sachse: "Music of the Ephrata Cloister," *Pennsylvania German Society Proceedings,* vol. 12 (1903), pp. 9–108; R. R. Drummond: *Early German Music in Philadelphia* (1910); Claude M. Rosenberry: "The Pennsylvania German in Music," *Pennsylvania German Society Proceedings,* vol. 41 (1933), part 1, pp. 27–44; W. E. Boyer et al. (eds.): *Songs along the Mahantongo* (1951); and George Korson: *Black Rock: Mining Folklore of the Pennsylvania Dutch* (1960), and *Minstrels of the Mine Patch: Songs and Stories of the Anthracite Industry* (1964). Also of interest will be John T. Howard: *Stephen Foster: America's Troubadour* (1934); Thomas W. Lloyd: *Ole Bull in Pennsylvania* (1921); and Norman B. Wilkinson (ed.): "'New Norway'—A Contemporary Account," *Pennsylvania History,* vol. 15 (1948), pp. 120–132.

The theater in Pennsylvania, centering in Philadelphia, may be studied in Reese D. James: *Old Drury of Philadelphia: A History of the Philadelphia Stage from 1800–1835* (1932); Thomas C. Pollock: *Philadelphia Theatre in the 18th Century* (1933); Arthur H. Wilson: *A History of the Philadelphia Theatre, 1835–1855* (1935); and Reese D. James: *Cradle of Culture: The Philadelphia Stage, 1800–1810* (1957). See also Joseph Jefferson: *Autobiography* (1899); Gladys Malvern: *Good Troupers All: The Story of Jo Jefferson* (1945); M. J. Moses: *Fabulous Forrest: The Record of an American Actor* (1929); and Richard Moody: *Edwin Forrest: First Star of the American Stage* (1960).

The following will provide material on the pre-1860 literary scene: A. H. Smyth: *Philadelphia Magazines and Their Contributors* (1892); Francis H. Williams: "Pennsylvania Poets of the Provincial Period." *Pennsylvania Magazine of History and Biography,* vol. 17 (1893), pp. 1–33; E. P. Oberholtzer: *Literary History of Philadelphia* (1906); Minerva K. Jackson: *Outlines of the Literary History of Colonial Pennsylvania* (1906); Nancy H. McCreary: "Pennsylvania Literature of the Colonial Period," *Pennsylvania Magazine of History and Biography,* vol. 52 (1928), pp. 317–341; H. R. Thayer: "Pittsburgh Authors," *Western Pennsylvania Historical Magazine,* vol. 2 (1919), pp. 149–160; E. P. Anderson: "Intellectual Life of Pittsburgh, 1796–1836," *Western Pennsylvania Historical Magazine,* vol. 14 (1931), pp. 9–27, 92–115, 225–236, 289–309; Claude F. Lytle: *Pennsylvania Song and Story: A Critical Evaluation of the Work of Pennsylvania's Writers* (1932); Henry Harrison: *Pennsylvania Poets* (1936); Earl F. Robacher: *Pennsylvania German Literature: Changing Trends from 1683 to 1942* (1943); and John J. Stoudt: *Pennsylvania German Poetry, 1685–1830* (1955). Some Pennsylvania material will be found in Richard M. Dorwon: *Burying the Wind: Regional Folklore in the United States* (1964).

3

Laboratory of Industrial Society: 1861–1900

CHAPTER SEVENTEEN

The Civil War and the Rise of the Republican Party

On April 12, 1861, Southerners opened fire on Fort Sumter in the harbor of Charleston, South Carolina, and plunged the United States into war. States' rights, nationalism, economic sectionalism, irresponsible agitators (Northern abolitionists and Southern "fire-eaters"), blundering politicians, and especially slavery as a moral issue have been called the cause of that war. The experience of Pennsylvania does not completely support any of these suggested causes—not even the moral issue of slavery. Many Pennsylvanians were hostile to slavery and slaveholders, but the hostility was more economic than moral. Slavery was an alien labor system and the Negro slave (allied in many minds with the Southern master) was a potential rival. Initially, few Pennsylvanians fought to free slaves; more fought because they did not want Pennsylvania to be dominated by the South; but most fought because the South's attack on Sumter both challenged them and convinced them that the Union was worth preserving.

MOBILIZING MEN AND MACHINES

Despite strong economic ties that bound many merchants to the South, Philadelphia responded enthusiastically to the Southern challenge. Large crowds besieged newspaper offices for the latest word and forced them to fly the American flag.

In other cities wild enthusiasm greeted news of the attack on Sumter. "I'm a Democrat," shouted a Pittsburgh theater patron, "But three cheers for Major Anderson [the commander of Sumter]." Men gathered in barrooms, halls, and offices to celebrate, and there was so much flag-waving that Pittsburgh developed a shortage of bunting. In Lancaster the crowds

247

about the bulletin boards boasted they would go South and wipe out "those damned nigger drivers" in a month and muttered that former President Buchanan, their erstwhile hero, better not show his face in town. In all Pennsylvania, men flocked to the colors. Reading's Ringgold Light Artillery Company, the first Pennsylvania company in the field, arrived at Harrisburg on April 17. The Logan Guards (Lewistown), the Washington Brigade (Philadelphia), the National Light Infantry (Pottsville), and the Allen Rifles (Allentown) were quickly mustered. It was clear that Pennsylvania would furnish its 14,000-man share of Lincoln's ninety-day volunteers, but, as Sidney George Fisher noted, "Everything else was deficient—discipline, clothing, weapons, & ammunition."

"God knows where it may end," exclaimed Buchanan on hearing news of Sumter. His pessimistic view was unpopular but accurate. A long, costly, extended war had begun. The keystone of the old Federal Union, Pennsylvania now proved the keystone of the Union war effort. In 1860 Pennsylvania's mechanical industries were twice as productive as those of the entire South with Philadelphia the North's largest manufacturing center. The war was fought with iron, and Pennsylvania, preeminent in metallurgy, produced 80 percent of the North's pig iron. Pittsburgh was the principal iron center, but the Lehigh, Schuylkill, and Susquehanna Valleys also produced sizable quantities. Despite labor shortages, production expanded. The Fort Pitt Works in Pittsburgh made mammoth castings for giant howitzers, while the Phoenixville Iron Works devised the process for manufacturing a widely used 3-inch rifled fieldpiece. Machine shops made guns, saw factories made sabers, and the government-owned Frankford Arsenal produced ammunition. Pennsylvania doubled its output of iron rails and supplied the Pennsylvania Railroad—a vital link between East and West—with locomotives and freight cars. Pennsylvania also contributed expert railroad personnel including Assistant Secretary of War Thomas A. Scott (and his aide Andrew Carnegie), who frequently expedited troop movements by rail, and Herman Haupt, who coordinated Union rail facilities. Haupt was a wizard who untangled traffic snarls on single-track lines to supply a 100,000-man army, and repaired lines and constructed bridges with fantastic rapidity. "That man Haupt," Lincoln boasted, "has built a bridge across Potomac Creek [Run], about 400 feet long and nearly 100 feet high, over which loaded trains are running every hour, and, upon my word, gentlemen, there is nothing in it but beanpoles and cornstalks."

The war effort called for more than iron rails and guns. Coal, food, clothing, and other supplies were needed, and Pennsylvania produced them. All the Union's anthracite and most of its bituminous coal was supplied by Pennsylvania, as was a large share of its flour and meat, textiles and clothing. The fact that Pennsylvanians secured lucrative contracts to supply Union armies and headed the Department of War throughout the entire struggle aroused both the jealousy and the suspicion of those from other states. Jay Cooke, a Philadelphia banker, also became renowned as the financier of the Civil War. Only a fraction of the war's cost was collected in taxes; the rest was borrowed for varying time and interest rates. Bankers and wealthy individuals were the first and best source for money, but they insisted on short-term and high-interest loans. In 1865 almost one-quarter (about $800 million) of the national debt was in three-year treasury notes paying 7.3 percent interest. In December 1861, fear of a war with England and the government's failure to plan an adequate tax program prompted bankers and men of wealth to refuse loans to the government. At this juncture the Lincoln administration turned to Jay Cooke and made his firm the sole subscription agent for United States bonds. Getting a commission and dealing through subagencies, Cooke successfully used newspaper advertisements and appeals to workingmen to market the bonds.

Painting by unknown American artist, *Fourth Pennsylvania Calvary,* 1861. (Philadelphia Museum of Art, The Edgar William and Bernice Chrysler Garbisch Collection)

Mobilizing men proved more difficult than mobilizing money and machines. On both sides the war was fought by state emergency forces. Pennsylvania raised one-sixth of the Union armies, and its experience in securing these men was typical. Enthusiastically responding to Lincoln's call for 75,000 militia, enough Pennsylvanians rendezvoused at Harrisburg and Philadelphia to form thirty-nine three-month regiments, whereas the state was initially required to supply but fourteen. At assembly points confusion was rampant. "The absence of arms, ammunition, and equipments of all kind," exclaimed Fitz John Porter, the first Federal officer to arrive at Harrisburg, "could not have been worse had it been premeditated. The State had no arms whatever or equipments for cooking purposes . . . and I had to resort to extraordinary expedients of hotels and restaurants to feed the men till the commissary department could be organized." When on May 3 Lincoln called for 42,000 three-year volunteers, Pennsylvania readily formed the ten regiments required with its surplus of three-month volunteers.

By late July an act of Congress authorized the President to accept as many as 500,000 volunteers with six-month to three-year terms. When troops were needed the President was to set population-based state quotas. The law empowered governors to commission field, staff, and company officers, causing incompetent political generals to abound. Vacancies among regimental officers were filled by enlisted men electing officers up to the rank of captain, and commissioned officers electing higher officers. The War Department shortly placed Curtin in command of all recruiting in Pennsylvania. "One of the greatest perplexities of the government," Lincoln reported to Congress in July 1861, "is to avoid raising troops faster than it can provide for them." The War Department ordered governors to cease recruiting in December 1861 and to sell recruiting equipment on April 3, 1862. But after the bloody Seven Days Battle on the Peninsula much of the glory departed from military life. Young men had come to realize that those who lived by the sword frequently perished by it; and that even more soldiers died from pneumonia, dysentery, and other camp diseases. Rehabilitating the recruiting service, Lincoln faced the greater perplexity of raising troops as fast as they were annihilated.

When his call for 300,000 fresh troops was unsuccessful, Lincoln resorted to drafting. In July 1862 Congress authorized a state draft of able-bodied men from age eighteen to age forty-five. Commencing in October 1862, this draft was resisted. Armed riots involving 1,000 to 5,000 men in Schuylkill County were cooled by feeble enforcement of the draft law. Ever the pragmatic politician, Lincoln informed authorities by confidential messenger, "I am very desirous to have the laws fully executed, but it might be well, in an extreme emergency, to be content with the appearance of executing the laws." The shortage of volunteers and the failure of the state draft produced a Federal draft law signed by Lincoln on March 3, 1863. Service still could be avoided by hiring a substitute or by paying a $300 commutation fee. Since the draft was only resorted to when a subdistrict failed to raise its quota of volunteers and since men were credited to the subdistrict in which they volunteered, rich subdistricts offered higher bounties, got more volunteers, and had fewer drafts making true the old saw, "a rich man's war, but a poor man's fight."

Everywhere in Pennsylvania the draft was unpopular. Balls, parties, and raffles helped raise commutation money. When that escape was eliminated in July 1864, a draftee's only way out was the substitute system. Those eager to avoid service often foisted upon the army "the most cadaverous and unsuitable, profligate and vicious" characters, and substitute brokers earned fat commissions supplying "lawless and desperate characters" at enormous figures. Desertion, common enough in Civil War armies, was rife among substitutes. Conscientious objectors added to the draft problem. Noting "the rapid increase" in Pennsylvania of noncombatant sects, a provost marshal jested, "The Quakers, Dunkards, and Mennonites are having more than a revival." Draft resistance centered in three mountainous areas: the hard coal region, the central counties, and the counties bordering Virginia. The most serious disturbances were in Schuylkill, Carbon, and Luzerne Counties where coal miners had formed a union, gone on strike, and shut down the collieries. Needing both coal and men, Lincoln dispatched troops to break the strike and kept them in Schuylkill County until the end of the war. It was not the spirit of rebellion that prompted men to resist the draft as much as the spirit of individualism that insisted one should not be made to fight against his wishes.

Conscription in Pennsylvania, however, met with indirect success. As a provost marshal observed, ". . . without an impending draft, no local bounties would have been raised, and without local bounties no volunteers could have been obtained." In some subdistricts bounties were so generous that no draft was necessary. Bounties were raised by local taxation, and the decision whether to raise a bounty was decided by majority vote. Most soldiers volunteered (only about 6 percent were conscripts and substitutes), but their enlistment was stimulated by the draft law, which directly or indirectly was responsible for most of the 338,000 Pennsylvania enlistments.

GETTYSBURG

Pennsylvania's military contribution to the Union was great. Officers and men from this state served in every major campaign, but it was in Virginia and on their own soil at Gettysburg that Pennsylvanians made their greatest contribution. One-third of the Union troops at Gettysburg were from Pennsylvania, as were their commander, George Gordon Meade, and two of his lieutenants, Generals John F. Reynolds and Winfield Scott Hancock. A representative campaign, Gettysburg had interminable marching, constant maneuvering, daring cavalry dashes, furious artillery barrages, desperate frontal assaults, clever flanking movements, and hogsheads of spilt blood. It was at Gettysburg that the tide of the Confederacy began to ebb.

After defeating the Army of the Potomac at Chancellorsville, Virginia, in early May 1863, Robert E. Lee, Confederate commander, made plans to invade Pennsylvania. Not only did Lee hope to obtain provisions for his army and to disrupt rail transportation, he also hoped to win a battle on Northern soil both to strengthen the Northern peace party and to force Ulysses S. Grant away from Vicksburg, Mississippi. On June 3 Lee put his army in motion; by mid-June the vanguard composed of Richard Stoddert Ewell's corps pushed into Pennsylvania. Ewell's task was primarily foraging; if he could garner enough horses, cattle, and flour, the rest of Lee's army would follow. Upon reaching Pennsylvania, Ewell divided his corps so as to better accomplish his goal. Between June 23 and 29 his men captured Chambersburg, Carlisle, Gettysburg, York, and Wrightsville on the Susquehanna River. Confederates had a marvelous week eating ripe cherries, burning Thaddeus Stevens' ironworks at Caledonia, magnanimously allowing local ministers to pray for Lincoln though the Confederate flag waved over Carlisle barracks, and sending captured Pennsylvania militia home with bare feet "instead of the expected trophies of war." Besides providing for themselves, they sent Lee 5,000 barrels of flour, 3,000 cattle, and a trainload of ordnance and medical supplies.

On June 26 Lee entered Pennsylvania and pushed toward Harrisburg, hoping to draw out the Union army and to cut the Pennsylvania Railroad. Until the evening of June 28, Lee assumed that the Union army was south of the Potomac. His flamboyant cavalry chief, James Ewell Brown ("Jeb") Stuart, had taken advantage of Lee's vague orders and had abandoned scouting for a spectacular wagon raid. When the guns of Gettysburg sounded, Lee, still without a report from Stuart, lamented, "I am in ignorance as to what we have in front of us here. It may be the whole Federal army, it may be only a detachment."

Although Joseph Hooker, commander of the Army of the Potomac, skillfully got his troops across the Potomac just twenty-four hours after Lee's army crossed, his superiors had lost confidence in him at Chancellorsville. When General in Chief Henry W. Halleck would not let him abandon Harper's Ferry, Hooker offered his resignation, which was readily accepted. At about three A.M. on June 28 a special messenger awakened and notified General George Gordon Meade that he had been given command of the Army of the Potomac. "Considering the circumstances," Halleck remarked, "no one ever received a more important command." Since Meade was a Pennsylvanian, Lincoln remarked that he should fight well. Meade moved his well-concentrated army north and on the eve of the Battle of Gettysburg had it scattered north and south of the Maryland-Pennsylvania border.

The Battle of Gettysburg began west of that city when John Buford's First Cavalry Division ran afoul of A. P. Hill's corps advancing from Cashtown. Alerted of the Confederate advance, General John F. Reynolds, commander of the First Corps, observed the battle with Buford from the belfry of the Lutheran Theological Seminary. It was Reynolds, a fighter and a Pennsylvanian, who chose the battlefield. Meade would have preferred fighting to the south along Pipe Creek, but Reynolds saw that the Gettysburg terrain was good for the Union. Rather than withdraw, Reynolds brought up infantry, which forced back the Confederates, but he was killed by a sharpshooter.

Desultory fighting continued west of Gettysburg until three P.M. when Ewell's corps arrived. In the severe fighting which followed, O. O. Howard commanded the outnumbered and outflanked Union forces which repulsed several Confederate assaults. With no reinforcements at hand, Howard withdrew his troops through Gettysburg and reorganized them south of the town on Cemetery Hill and in its vicinity. Both the battle and retreat were costly; Howard's First Corps began the day with almost 10,000 men but ended it with only 2,400.

The first day of Gettysburg was crucial; it ended with the battered Union army occupying strong positions, which the Confederates would never capture. Credit for the Union's advantageous position goes to Reynolds who decided to stay and fight and to Howard who stationed his reserves on Cemetery Hill. Meade's effect was largely negative. The Union army was scattered when the day began and failed to smash Lee's army as it emerged from Cashtown Gap; and Meade complicated the defense of Cemetery Hill by telling Winfield Scott Hancock (Howard's junior) to take command, with the result that Howard and Hancock were commanding simultaneously. Finally, though he could have reached the battlefield by 4:30 in the afternoon, Meade waited until after midnight to reconnoiter the field.

By nine o'clock the next morning (July 2) Meade had skillfully distributed six corps along a fishhook running west from Culp's Hill to Cemetery Hill and curving south along Cemetery Ridge to the base of unoccupied Little Round Top. If artillery were placed on Little Round Top, however, it could enfilade and render useless the Union line on Cemetery Ridge. The Union line had another drawback; the Third Corps commanded by Daniel Sickles, a political general, had occupied an exposed low marshy section just north of Little Round Top, but Sickles without Meade's approval moved his corps to an advanced position running from the rocky Devil's Den to the Peach Orchard and along the Emmitsburg Road.

At about four P.M. Longstreet's corps attacked Sickles (the Union left), commencing the second day's battle. Shocked to discover the extent of Sickles' advanced positions, Meade threw in reinforcements since withdrawal was now impossible. Sledgehammer blows by the Confederates smashed the Third Corps back from the Devil's Den, the Peach Orchard, and the Wheat Field. Sickles fought hard and well, selling his ground dearly and losing his right leg in the bargain. Shortly after Longstreet began his attack, General Gouveneur K. Warren, chief engineer of the Army of the Potomac, made the appalling discovery that Little Round Top, the key to the Union left flank, was not defended. Warren hastily ordered troops and Lieutenant Charles E. Hazlett's battery of six 3-inch guns to Little Round Top just as Confederates swarmed over the Devil's Den and charged. With no road, Hazlett and his men performed a minor miracle to get their pieces and caissons to the top of the hill, and in the bitter hand-to-hand combat that followed they hung on to Little Round Top.

Confederates also attacked the Union right. Following an artillery duel won by Northern guns, Confederate infantrymen occupied positions abandoned by the Union and in places reached the top of Cemetery Hill, from which they were swept by a spirited counterattack at dusk. When night enveloped the battlefield, Union forces held the line they had occupied that morning except for a few abandoned positions. Having successfully met a series of crises, Meade modestly reported, "The enemy attacked me about 4 p.m. this day, and after one of the severest contests of the war, was repulsed at all points." Yet Meade apparently had some doubts about the battlefield. That evening he sounded out his subordinates on the wisdom of withdrawing closer to the army's base of supplies. They emphatically wished to remain both at Gettysburg and on the defensive.

On July 3 Confederates renewed the battle at four A.M. While Ewell dissipated his strength on the Union right during five hours of desperate fighting, Lee assembled 130 guns on Seminary Ridge. Having failed on both the Union left and the Union right, Lee obviously planned an unprecedented artillery barrage before unleashing his infantry on Cemetery Ridge, the Union center. At one P.M. Confederate batteries opened fire. For two hours they blasted Cemetery Ridge, but aimed too high. Although horses and wagons behind Union lines were destroyed and Meade was forced to move his headquarters, Union infantry and artillery were only moderately damaged and conserved most of their long-range projectiles for the expected assault. "They are moving out to attack," signaled Warren from Little Round Top. As the smoke cleared, Union forces watched 15,000 Confederates form three lines. Commanded by George Pickett, they began the most famous and perhaps most foolish charge in American military history. Across the beautiful 1-mile valley they marched, re-forming their neat parade lines after climbing fences. As they reached the gentle slope of Cemetery Hill, Union artillery on the left opened up forcing the Confederate right toward the Union center. Hancock's artillery in the center, however, out of long-range ammunition, withheld fire until Confederates were in canister range and then opened with terrible effect.

On Cemetery Ridge, Union infantry, withholding fire until Confederates were within 100 yards, unleashed a devastating volley. Along part of the line the attackers fell back in disorder, but where they were most concentrated they halted, fired, and marched on. Forming a blunt wedge, they struck General Alexander S. Webb's brigade of Pennsylvanians. Union troops attacked and surrounded the Confederate wedge on three sides. Although Webb was forced back, he was reinforced and Pickett's men were driven off, leaving hundreds of prisoners, dead, and wounded. Union artillery and 9,000 to 10,000 infantry had broken Pickett's charge. Of Pickett's survivors, the historian Douglas Southall Freeman wrote, "The enemy had beaten them back, they could do no more. The rest of it—war's decision, America's destiny, the doom of the Confederacy—all this was read afterwards into the story of their return."

Lee feverishly prepared his weakened and disorganized army for a seemingly inevitable counterattack which could well destroy it. Meade, however, sent out and then pulled back a line of skirmishers, and refrained from further attack. The Battle of Gettysburg was over. The bill was high. Of 90,000 Union effectives 23,049 were gone: 3,155 killed, 14,529 wounded, and 5,365 captured or missing. Though Confederates reported that 20,451 of Lee's 75,000 effectives were lost, that figure is probably low. A more realistic figure is 28,063 with 3,903 killed, 18,735 wounded, and 5,425 missing.

The battle was over but not the campaign. Lee bent every effort to escape south of the Potomac, while Meade, whose army also had been severely punished, conceived that his task was to drive the invader "from our soil." "Will our Generals," Lincoln exploded, "never get that idea out of their heads? The whole country is our soil." With Meade, prodded by Lincoln, in cautious pursuit, Lee headed for the Potomac. Swollen by heavy rains, it was impossible to cross. On July 7 Lee dug a semicircular beachhead protecting the crossings between Falling Waters and Williamsport. Lincoln and Halleck repeatedly urged Meade to destroy Lee's army, but only minor cavalry clashes and skirmishes ensued. On the evening of July 13 under cover of rain, Lee escaped with his entire wagon train and virtually all his men. "We had them within our grasp," Lincoln lamented and oversimplified. "We had only to stretch

Andrew Gregg Curtin, Republican war
Governor of Pennsylvania. (Leo Stashin
Collection)

forth our hands and they were ours. And nothing I could say or do could make the army
move."

Ultimately the North was victorious, but the Civil War profoundly affected the history of
Pennsylvania and of all states by destroying states' rights constitutional arguments. No longer
was Federal supremacy questioned, and the trend to centralize and to increase functions at
Washington was accelerated. Though the state government would play an increasing role in
the lives of Pennsylvanians, the Federal government would grow even faster. While Sidney
George Fisher was "more impressed than ever with the wealth, resources, and beauty of
Pennsylvania," he perceived also that the "war indeed has revealed to us & to the world the
immense power & unbounded resources of the nation."

THE POLITICS OF WAR

The Civil War transformed Pennsylvania politics. Consistently Democratic until 1860—
except for a few elections the Whigs won with anti-Masonic or Nativist support—Pennsylvania emerged from the war and its aftermath a Republican state. The People's party of 1860,
a loose agglomeration of old Whigs, new Republicans, antiforeign Nativists, and antislavery
Democrats, placed Republican Andrew Gregg Curtin of Bellefonte in the governor's chair,
and Pennsylvania cast its electoral vote for Abraham Lincoln, just as Republican platform
builders had hoped when they included a protective tariff plank.

Curtin (1861–1867) became the first Northern governor to advocate force to keep the South in the Union. He took Lincoln's advice to express "without passion, threat, or appearance of boasting, but nevertheless, with firmness" his purpose "to maintain the Union at all hazzards." The new Republican Legislature followed Curtin's lead. It passed the Smith resolutions, which recognized the right of the South to hold slaves but refused to condone secession; pledged Pennsylvania's faith and power to support the Union; and selected two uncompromising Republicans for the United States Senate: Edgar Cowan, a Cameron man, and David Wilmot, a Curtin man. In addition both Curtin and the Legislature helped doom the February Washington Peace Convention by sending an unsympathetic delegation and by severely restricting its maneuverability.

When Cameron became Lincoln's Secretary of War, a new dimension was added to the Curtin-Cameron feud. Since states recruited Civil War soldiers, Cameron constantly dealt with Curtin and clashed frequently with him. When Baltimore rioting stopped communications with Washington, Curtin called for 25,000 additional troops, which Cameron haughtily refused until after the disaster at Bull Run. Probing for a weak spot, the Cameron faction vociferously attacked Curtin for providing troops with inferior supplies, undermined confidence in his administration, and temporarily endangered the state's credit.

While Cameron attacked Curtin for mismanaging troop supplies in Pennsylvania, Cameron was attacked for mismanaging the War Department. Cameron's task of organizing immense armies was colossal, and McClellan's huge, well-equipped, and admirably supplied army was a solid accomplishment, but wasteful administration and cheating contractors marred Cameron's and the War Department's achievement. Though Cameron in this instance was personally free from corruption, allegations to the contrary damaged the credit of the government. Lincoln replaced him with Edwin M. Stanton, a Pennsylvania Democrat, and sent Cameron to St. Petersburg as Minister to Russia. The Curtin forces received word of Cameron's exile with ill-concealed glee.

Already hurt by the Curtin-Cameron feud, Pennsylvania Republicans further estranged their constituents by repealing the tonnage tax on the through traffic of the Pennsylvania Railroad. Railroad lobbyists argued that the tax injured both the railroad and the Pennsylvania economy, but many Democrats and farmers insisted that the railroad should continue to pay for the privilege of paralleling, competing against, and in 1857 purchasing at a fraction of its worth the state-owned Main Line of the public works. While Republicans favored repeal in 1860, they dared not agitate for it lest they lose the state for Lincoln. Nevertheless on April 28, 1861, the Commutation Act repealed the tonnage tax, thanks to the campaigning and lobbying of Thomas A. Scott, vice-president of the Pennsylvania Railroad; the support of Cameron; the clever debating of Curtin's lieutenant, Senator Alexander K. McClure; and the willingness of some legislators to sell their votes. That act also saved the Pennsylvania Railroad $650,000 in canal payments over a thirty-year period and erased the $700,000 it owed in back tonnage taxes as long as it used that sum to develop feeder lines.

Whatever merit repeal had, its passage added to the woes of the People's party. Opposition was particularly strong in Allegheny County, where hatred of the Pennsylvania Railroad was strong, and among farmers, who feared increased taxes would result. The unpopularity of the repeal coupled with war weariness following the defeat at Bull Run seriously weakened the People's party. Realizing that a military victory would produce a political victory in the October 1861 elections, Curtin urged that the war be prosecuted vigorously. With neither action nor victory forthcoming from General George B. McClellan, Curtin and McClure decided to nominate War Democrats on Union party tickets in doubtful contests. The plan successfully prevented Democratic control of the House. Although War Democrats elected on the Union party ticket held the balance of power, they worked with Republicans to elect as Speaker of the House John Rowe, a War Democrat and a close friend of McClure.

Investigation of alleged corruption attending the passage of the Commutation Act proved impossible to avoid. But the Pennsylvania Railroad succeeded in getting the investigating committee stacked in its favor. Except for Chairman William Hopkins, an honest and politically ambitious Democrat, and for Thomas Williams, an Allegheny County Republican whose hatred of the Pennsylvania Railroad was boundless, Speaker Rowe chose committee members from a list handed him by McClure and compiled by Scott. Though the committee was subsequently enlarged, its character did not change. Nevertheless, its findings were damning. The Pennsylvania Railroad through Scott and his aides had bribed both newspapers and legislators; and legislators, in turn, had blackmailed the railroad. The Hopkins committee was unable to get either J. Edgar Thompson, president of the Pennsylvania Railroad, or Scott to testify. Thompson pleaded illness; and Lincoln and Stanton made Scott a temporary colonel and ordered him to the West to prevent Democrats from gaining political capital from his testimony.

As the war progressed, abolition replaced the tonnage tax as the leading issue in Pennsylvania politics. In 1861 Cameron espoused abolition in an unsuccessful attempt to shore his eroding position, but his failure should not obscure growing sentiment in favor of abolition. When the war began almost all agreed that it was being fought to preserve the Union rather than to wipe out slavery. Lincoln particularly stressed this view to prevent border states from seceding. After the border states were secured, the idea of converting slaves into soldiers gained adherents. Thaddeus Stevens helped prepare the nation for emancipation and pushed Lincoln toward this goal.

Republicans clearly had their work cut out in 1862. Continued Union defeat led to war weariness and made appealing the Democratic slogan, "The restoration of the Union as it was and the preservation of the constitution as it is." With their white-supremacy platform denouncing Republican plans to turn "the slaves of the Southern States loose, to overrun the North and enter into competition with the white laboring classes," Democrats successfully played upon the fears of workingmen. Joined by former Douglas Democrats, such as Editor John W. Forney of the Philadelphia *Press,* Republicans formed the National Union party and gained adherents by accusing Democrats of treason, of starting and protracting the war, and of making a draft necessary by not volunteering.

During this difficult campaign, Curtin played a leading role at the Altoona Governors' Conference. With Lee invading Maryland and with pressure mounting on Lincoln to emancipate and arm slaves and to remove McClellan, Curtin urged governors to meet on September 24, 1862, at Altoona to prosecute the war more vigorously. The Radical governors planned to demand their goals, but McClellan checked Lee at Antietam on September 17 and Lincoln cut the ground from under the Radicals by issuing the preliminary Emancipation Proclamation two days before they met. Consequently the conference rubber-stamped Lincoln's policies, thanked him for the proclamation, urged him to create a 100,000-man reserve corps, and recognized him as commander in chief. To Curtin's relief, no public demand was made to replace McClellan with John Charles Frémont, the incompetent darling of the Radicals. Philadelphia-born McClellan was popular in Pennsylvania, and Curtin realized that Frémont would be a political as well as a military disaster.

Whatever prestige the Altoona conference brought the Republican party, it did not prevent Democrats from winning the election of 1862. On the state level they picked up three seats in the dominantly Republican Senate, ruled the House by eight seats, and controlled by one vote a joint session making it possible for them to name the United States senator. Furthermore, despite Republican gerrymandering making the population of some districts only one-third that of others, Democrats won half the twenty-four Pennsylvania seats in the United States House of Representatives. Cashing in on weariness with defeat, Democrats won their first clear-cut victory in five years on an antiabolition, white-supremacy platform.

Electing a senator was the major task facing the new Legislature. Simon Cameron, whose stay in St. Petersburg was nearly as brief as a guided tour, resigned his post in November 1862 and returned to Pennsylvania to become senator. Adept at manipulating the Legislature, Cameron in 1863 prepared to sacrifice the Republican incumbent David Wilmot and to induce a Democratic Legislature to name him senator. Campaigning for unanimity, Democrats were victorious after openly threatening that any Democrat voting for Cameron rather than their party's candidate, Charles R. Buckalew, would be carried feet first from the House chamber. Before the election a Democrat announced that Cameron forces had offered him $100,000 for his vote. A second Democrat, T. Jefferson Boyer, subsequently confessed that he had agreed to vote for Cameron for $20,000 to $25,000 but only to deceive Cameron's agents and to prevent them from debauching someone else. Investigators later disagreed over Boyer's role but clearly established that Cameron had attempted to bribe him.

The important gubernatorial campaign of 1863 began with Democrats attacking Republican arbitrary arrests. Democrats capitalized on the fact that for criticizing the Lincoln administration the Democratic editors of the Harrisburg *Patriot and Union* were upon an hour's notice and without preliminary hearing arrested and imprisoned in Washington for sixteen days, and that the Democratic editor of the Philadelphia *Evening Journal* was imprisoned at Fort McHenry for the same reason. While Radicals argued that the executive had the power to suspend the writ of habeas corpus and make arbitrary arrests, Curtin took the wind out of Democratic sails and enhanced his chances for renomination by maintaining that Congress alone had power to suspend the writ.

Throughout the first half of 1863 Democrats continued to exploit increasing war weariness. Repeated defeat, particularly in Virginia, led the Democratic House to draw up resolutions condemning secession, unconstitutional acts by Congress, executive usurpations, arbitrary arrests, the Emancipation Proclamation, compensated emancipation, the administration, and abolitionists; inviting the South back to allegiance; calling for a convention to amend the Constitution; and praising the boys in blue. These resolutions formed the base of the 1863 Democratic platform upon which a stalwart opponent of state conscription, Justice George W. Woodward of the state Supreme Court, ran for governor.

Though Curtin was the strongest Republican candidate, he was seriously ill and the Radical-Cameron faction supported John Covode. Curtin wished to have both parties nominate General William B. Franklin, who was both an ardent Democrat and a supporter of the war, but Franklin was unacceptable to some Democratic leaders, who wanted the war ended by compromise. Seeking a graceful way to retire, Curtin was delighted when Lincoln assured him he could have a first-class mission abroad. But Republicans would not let Curtin retire. County after county elected delegates to the Union Party State Convention pledged to Curtin. Pleased by this support, he decided to accept the nomination ten days before the convention was to meet.

During the campaign that followed, Northern victories heartened Republicans and Cameron men swung into line claiming, "It is a question now only between a *loyal man* and a *Copperhead.*" Renowned as the soldier's friend, Curtin urged that Pennsylvania soldiers be furloughed for thirty days in time for the October election, and according to the hostile New York *Herald,* Pennsylvanian civil servants working in Washington were given a fifteen-day leave to return home to vote. Along with the Ohio election, the Pennsylvania contest was a test for the Lincoln administration. A Union party victory would ensure vigorous prosecution of the war and continue the trend toward abolition; while a Democratic victory would strengthen hostile congressional elements. Amid charges and countercharges of buying and importing voters, Curtin was elected by a margin of 15,000 out of more than 500,000 votes. With an equally slim margin, the Union party gained control of both houses of the Legislature.

Curtin's health failed after his second inauguration. On Lincoln's order a naval vessel carried him to Havana where he recuperated the rest of the winter. By mid-March 1864, he returned to Harrisburg to wrestle with the problems of his second administration. Though his physical strength grew, Curtin's political strength ebbed during his second term. When it ended, Cameron controlled the Pennsylvania Republican organization.

CAMERON'S TRIUMPH

Excelling in "spoilsmanship, opportunism, and political chicanery," Simon Cameron deserves much but not all of his dubious reputation. From the early 1820s his business and political ventures—the former very much dependent upon the latter—were almost always successful. Beginning as a printer and branching out into construction, Cameron received lucrative state printing as well as canal-building contracts from his friend Governor John A. Shulze. As Cameron moved into railroading, iron, and banking, his political power enhanced his business interests, while these interests, in turn, influenced his political behavior. It was no accident that Cameron's one consistent political principle was the protective tariff.

A perfect illustration of the practical politician, Cameron remained publicly devoted to Lincoln, who had dealt him a serious political blow by exiling him to Russia, even while privately working for the nomination of Benjamin F. Butler for the presidency. Cameron also kept on good terms with another presidential hopeful, Salmon P. Chase. Realizing by January 5, 1864, that Butler's chances were nil and that there was no serious opposition to Lincoln in Pennsylvania, Cameron confounded Curtin's lieutenant McClure and Chase supporters by inducing all Republican state legislators to endorse Lincoln's renomination. Later Cameron not only secured for Lincoln a unanimous Pennsylvania delegation, but also managed the ensuing campaign in which Lincoln carried the state by 20,000 votes. Cameron's tactics included suspending the draft until after the election, sending 100 "reliable" men to visit Pennsylvania soldiers recently enabled to vote in the field, and obtaining furloughs for 10,000 Pennsylvania troops. By the end of 1864 Cameron had made a remarkable political recovery.

Though neither legislation nor policy is associated with his name, Cameron was an astute

Simon Cameron, Lincoln's Secretary of War, senator, and ultimately Republican boss of Pennsylvania. (Leo Stashin Collection)

and imaginative political organizer and leader. He built his machine from the ground up because control of the state convention depended on control of county and ward conventions, which in turn depended on control of local precinct or township meetings which were open to all party members. His lieutenants had prestigious Federal offices, while Curtin could offer his helpers only state offices. Despite his disgrace in 1862, Cameron remained Lincoln's chief consultant on Federal patronage in Pennsylvania; and patronage maintained his political machine. McClure complained to Lincoln that he slighted the Curtin forces, and Wayne MacVeagh noted to Cameron, "Mr. Lincoln listens to nobody else from Pennsylvania as he does you." Lincoln's assassination left Cameron's strength unimpaired. When the martyred president was deified, Cameron was renowned as his man in Pennsylvania. Until he deserted President Andrew Johnson in the summer of 1866, Cameron received Johnson's support, and even after their break he retained control of Federal officials in Pennsylvania.

The reaction against Johnson helped Republicans win in 1866 over the combined Johnson-Democratic forces. Republicans had a majority of thirty-five on a joint ballot in the Legislature, eighteen of twenty-four congressmen selected were Republicans, and John White Geary defeated the Democratic nominee Hiester Clymer for governor. Though the Republican victory was complete, it was deceptive; a shift of 1½ percent of the voters would have produced a Democratic victory.

A War Democrat, John Geary by 1866 agreed fully with Stevens on Reconstruction and with Cameron on the tariff. Having been San Francisco's first mayor, governor of "bleeding Kansas," and a Union general, Geary (1867–1873) won Pennsylvania's governorship through the efforts of John Covode and John W. Forney with the blessing of Cameron. Radical acceptance of Geary reflected the public's desire for a soldier-statesman, especially one of proven administrative abilities. Though McClure and others opposed Geary's nomination, all Republican factions worked for his election. That Geary was against Johnson was clear, but what he was for remained cloudy. In contrast, everyone knew where his opponent Clymer stood. A civilian who had opposed war measures and was attacked as a Copperhead, Clymer narrowed his appeal by running on a white-supremacy platform and supporting Johnson's Reconstruction policies.

With Republican rule assured, the big question was who would rule the victors. The power of Cameron—rather than the popularity of Curtin or the prestige of Stevens—decided that question. A most successful war governor, Curtin was Pennsylvania's most popular Republican, while Stevens was the nation's leading Radical and its most powerful political figure. Despite his disgrace as Secretary of War and his blemished reputation, Cameron easily defeated both Curtin and Stevens in the 1867 senatorial race.

Although Cameron was the victor, his rivals had not been eliminated. Nevertheless he rapidly consolidated control of the Pennsylvania Republican party. Expending too much energy on the issues of Reconstruction, the aged Thaddeus Stevens died soon after he failed to impeach Johnson. Indeed the shift from Stevens, an inflexible champion of Negro rights, to Cameron, a Radical only when expedient, as the leading Pennsylvanian in Congress personified the change in Republican attitudes during the post-Civil War years. Curtin experienced a brief revival of influence in 1868 when the McClure-dominated Republican State Convention supported him as Ulysses S. Grant's running mate, but the national convention cut him down. Ironically Cameron, a power in the new Grant administration, influenced Grant to appoint Curtin Minister to Russia in 1869. Curtin's exile to St. Petersburg left his young lieutenant Matthew Stanley Quay fighting a losing campaign for his absent leader. Quay was an extremely resourceful political fighter and personally a brave man, but he was not a martyr. When Cameron beckoned him to join his organization, Quay abandoned Curtin and his lost cause. By 1871 Quay was Cameron's trusted lieutenant.

Cameron led the party; Governor Geary did not always follow. Geary owed his nomination to the Cameron wing of the party, but as Cameron's power grew, Geary became increasingly independent. Presidential aspirations, no doubt, led him to transcend the machine and to develop a personal following. He gave his sympathies for temperance and the working-man free play and attacked the power of special interests. Over a four-year period, Geary vetoed 268 private bills, many of them granting favors to an individual or corporation. Two bills he vetoed in 1871, for example, would have exempted the Mechanics National Bank and the Girard National Bank, both of Philadelphia, from state taxes totaling $55,000. Despite Geary's vetoes, over a thousand private bills passed; legislators were publicly accused of bribery and even Geary was attacked. Attempting to check the burgeoning power of the Pennsylvania Railroad, Geary vetoed both legislation allowing its directors to expand its stock indefinitely and a bill no longer requiring the railroad to guarantee the bonds it paid the state for the Main Line canal. Geary's independence did not endear him to Cameron, who was close to Scott of the Pennsylvania Railroad, but it did secure his renomination and reelection without Cameron's help. Geary in 1869 defeated by only 4,600 votes the Democratic nominee Asa Packer, a millionaire who controlled the Lehigh Valley Railroad. During his second term, Geary refused to recognize any Republican faction and by the end of that term supported neither the regular Republican ticket nor that of the Liberal Republican insurgents.

Cameron's control was challenged in 1872. The normal opposition of the outs among Republicans, particularly Curtin's disappointed followers, was accentuated by Quay's desertion and by widespread reports of corruption. Cameron frequently advised Grant and shared in his administration's reputation for venality. More damaging to Cameron even than national scandal were reports of political corruption in Pennsylvania. According to these accounts, gangs of repeaters rolled up Republican majorities and business interests paid legislators to vote for and against bills. It was also alleged that the state treasurer, Cameron's lieutenant Robert W. Mackey, realized about $150,000 annually on the banking operations of the treasury and distributed a portion to the Legislature, that the commonwealth paid a George O. Evans a 10 percent fee of almost $300,000 for collecting Pennsylvania claims on the Federal government, and that Governor Geary himself set the exorbitant fee and was given $52,000 of it. Municipal reform movements developed in Philadelphia and Pittsburgh, and in October 1871, after a reluctant Legislature gave them the opportunity, Pennsylvania voters emphatically called for a revision of the state constitution.

It was McClure who organized Republican opposition against his ancient foe Cameron. In a special January 1872 election McClure ran for the state Senate against Henry W. Gray who had regular-Republican and Philadelphia-machine backing. With strong business support and Democratic endorsement, McClure lost to Gray by only 900 votes and contested the election. In a series of spectacular hearings, the Democratic state Senate tossed out enough illegal Republican ballots to give McClure the victory and to make him leader of antimachine Republicans in Pennsylvania.

McClure and other dissident Republicans had little interest in the developing national Liberal Republican movement until Horace Greeley, who would later be its nominee for the presidency, paid a visit. Discreet inquiries by McClure revealed that many prominent Republicans, including members of the Curtin faction and others who had had their political or business ambitions frustrated by the Cameron machine, were ready to bolt. Pennsylvania Liberal Republicans were basically political outs who had nothing to lose by revolt. Though the national Liberal Republican movement was anti-Grant and favored amnesty for the South and civil service and tariff reform, the Pennsylvania movement was simply an attempt to defeat Cameron.

In April, McClure headed the Liberal Republican State Central Committee, and in May he led the Pennsylvania delegation at the Cincinnati Liberal Republican Convention. There, without authorization, McClure permitted the Pennsylvania delegation to support Curtin for the presidency on the first ballot. In this way McClure identified Curtin, who was still in Europe, with the Liberal Republican movement and effectively killed his chances for the Republican vice-presidential nomination. Efforts to support Curtin failed, and the Pennsylvania delegation ultimately joined the stampede that nominated Greeley.

The Liberal Republican revolt further complicated Pennsylvania politics. The Cameron machine stood by Grant and nominated Auditor General John J. Hartranft for governor. Smelling victory thanks to the Republican split, Pennsylvania Democrats reluctantly accepted Greeley as their presidential nominee and named former United States Senator Charles R. Buckalew for governor. With Democrats backing the Liberal Republican candidate for the presidency, Liberal Republicans were expected to support the Democratic state ticket. Although McClure and Samuel J. Randall, the Democratic state chairman, did cooperate, fusion existed in name only. Liberal Republicans were less intent upon electing either Greeley or Buckalew than upon defeating Cameron's reelection to the Senate by returning an anti-Cameron Legislature. "Gentlemen, be not deceived," warned a Liberal Republican, "the question . . . is not whether Greeley or Grant shall be president; it is whether the corrupt cabal, Cameron, Hartranft, and Mackey shall continue to exercise imperial power in Pennsylvania."

The Pennsylvania revolt worried Grant. Not only did it jeopardize the second largest number of electoral votes but, occurring in an October election state, its success or failure in the gubernatorial contest would influence the November presidential vote. Reflecting that anxiety, Republicans poured $75,000, innumerable speakers, and tons of campaign literature into Pennsylvania. In October Hartranft defeated Buckalew (353,387–317,760). Regular Republicans gained control of the Legislature (of Liberal Republicans only McClure survived) and won a majority of delegates to the forthcoming constitutional convention. If thousands of Democrats had kept diaries as did William G. Armstrong, they too might have recorded on November 5, 1872: "Election day. The first time I failed to vote—could not bring myself to do it. . . . The election has gone by default." The Liberal Republican movement was smashed, and Democrats were "disorganized and demoralized." Grant overwhelmed Greeley 349,689–211,961, and Republicans elected twenty-two members of Congress while Democrats elected but five. Cameron's tool Hartranft would succeed Geary as Governor, the comfortably Republican Legislature would reelect Cameron to the United States Senate without a serious struggle, and his archenemy Curtin would flee to the Democratic party. Cameron had achieved his lifelong ambition; he was undisputed chief of the ruling party in Pennsylvania.

BIBLIOGRAPHY

The best single volume on the Civil War is J. G. Randall and David Donald: *The Civil War and Reconstruction,* 2d ed. (1961). No volume integrates excellent photographs with illuminating quotations as well as David Donald: *Divided We Fought: A Pictorial History of the War, 1861–1865* (1961). See also Donald's *Lincoln Reconsidered: Essays on the Civil War Era* (1956).

For the reaction of Pennsylvania to the war, see William Dusinberre: *Civil War Issues in Philadelphia, 1856–1865* (1965); Winnifred K. MacKay: "Philadelphia during the Civil War, 1861–1865," *Pennsylvania Magazine of History and Biography,* vol. 70 (1946), pp. 3–51; in the same magazine, Nicholas B. Wainwright: "The Loyal Opposition in Civil War Philadelphia," vol. 88 (1964), pp. 294–315; Sidney George Fisher: *A Philadelphia Perspective: The Diary of Sidney George Fisher Covering the Years 1834–1871,* edited by Nicholas B. Wainwright (1967); Lee E. Corter: "The Part Played by Pittsburgh in the Civil War" (master's thesis, Pennsylvania State University, 1935); Bernard Levin: "Pennsylvania and the Civil War," *Pennsylvania History,* vol. 10 (1943), pp. 1–10. On the raising of troops in Pennsylvania, see the informative William A. Itter: "Conscription in Pennsylvania during the Civil War" (doctoral dissertation, University of Southern California, 1942).

For the Gettysburg campaign, see Douglas Southall Freeman: *R. E. Lee: A Biography,* 4 vols. (1935), vol. 3, pp. 8–161; Freeman, *Lee's Lieutenants: A Study in Command,* 3 vols. (1942–1944), vol. 3, pp. 1–205; Bruce Catton: *Glory Road: The Bloody Route from Fredericksburg to Gettysburg* (1952), pp. 269–383; Kenneth P. Williams, *Lincoln Finds a General: A Military Study of the Civil War,* 5 vols. (1950–1959), vol. 2, pp. 606–754; Edwin B. Coddington: *The Gettysburg Campaign: A Study in Command* (1968); Warren W. Hassler, Jr.: *Crisis at the Crossroads: The First Day at Gettysburg* (1970); and Edward J. Nichols: *Toward Gettysburg: A Biography of General John F. Reynolds* (1958).

The basic book on Pennsylvania politics during these years is Erwin Stanley Bradley: *The Triumph of Militant Republicanism: A Study of Pennsylvania and Presidential Politics, 1860–1872* (1964). Also consult Stanton Ling Davis: *Pennsylvania Politics, 1860–1863* (1935); and the less reliable but often revealing Alexander Kelly McClure: *Old Time Notes of Pennsylvania,* 2 vols. (1905). For further information on the Liberal Republican movement in Pennsylvania, see Frank B. Evans: *Pennsylvania Politics, 1872–1877: A Study in Political Leadership* (1966). On voting patterns, see Walter Dean Burnham: *Critical Elections and the Mainsprings of American Politics* (1970).

Biographies are also helpful, but there has been no good one written on Curtin. Many and varied biographies of Stevens have been done; three of the better recent ones are the scholarly and hostile Richard N. Current: *Old Thad Stevens: A Story of Ambition* (1943); the uncritically laudatory Ralph Korngold: *Thaddeus Stevens: A Being Darkly Wise and Rudely Great* (1955); and the scholarly and sympathetic Fawn M. Brodie: *Thaddeus Stevens: Scourge of the South* (1959). Particularly useful for Pennsylvania politics is Erwin Stanley Bradley: *Simon Cameron, Lincoln's Secretary of War: A Political Biography* (1966). Worthwhile biographies of less-known figures include Harry M. Tinkcom: *John White Geary: Soldier-Statesman, 1819–1873* (1940); and William A. Russell: "A Biography of Alexander K. McClure" (doctoral dissertation, University of Wisconsin, 1953).

CHAPTER EIGHTEEN

Basic Industries

Pennsylvania was the keystone in the arch of post-Civil War American economy. In 1860 it had 2,598 miles of railroad track, making it fourth in the nation; in 1900 it was in second place with 10,311 miles. Although Pennsylvania from 1860 to 1900 was the second manufacturing state in the Union, it was the chief producer of coal, iron, and steel, the basic ingredients of industrialism, and for much of this period it was the main source of petroleum and lumber. Despite the expansion of the country westward and improvement of transportation facilities which opened up new sources of raw materials, Pennsylvania retained its preeminence in coal, iron, and steel. Those basic industries attracted and sustained a variety of manufactures and maintained Pennsylvania's position as a leading industrial state.

RAILROADS

The Pennsylvania Railroad provides an appropriate transition from politics to industry since it was basic to both. Secretary of the Navy Gideon Welles perceived in 1869 that: "The railroad controls Pennsylvania, and Cameron has had the adroitness to secure it." By 1871 the Pennsylvania Railroad dominated Pennsylvania transportation; the monopoly feared by Governor Geary had become a fact. As C. Vann Woodward observes:

> The biggest freight carrier in the world and probably the most powerful business corporation in America, the Pennsylvania moved 31,000,000 tons of freight and reported net earnings of $22,000,000 in 1876, a depression year. It stood astride the heart of the iron, coal, steel, and petroleum districts of the country and stretched out mighty arms in all directions.

With western trade its chief objective, the Pennsylvania Railroad operated a line from Philadelphia to Pittsburgh in time to meet the demands of the Civil War, but it lacked feeder lines; its charter forbade the construction of branches beyond the counties its main track crossed. The 1861 Commutation Act, however, required the Pennsylvania Railroad to develop feeder lines. These feeder lines, roughly a dozen railroads varying from 1 to 90 miles in length, which the Pennsylvania Railroad operated and ultimately owned, enabled it to tap coal, timber, and iron resources.

The Pennsylvania Railroad soon gained significant branches. In 1859 it acquired the Cumberland Valley Railroad, traversing that valley rich in both soil and iron ore, and a year later began to buy into the Cameron's Northern Central Railroad (whose stock it controlled by 1900) running from Baltimore to Sunbury, which through leases ultimately connected with the New York Central at Canandaigua. Other lines acquired, the Philadelphia and Erie (1861) and the Allegheny Valley (1868), proved less advantageous to the Pennsylvania Railroad.

The Pennsylvania Railroad also hoped to connect with Cincinnati, Cleveland, St. Louis, and Chicago. Although it invested heavily in three railroads consolidated in 1856 as the Pittsburgh, Fort Wayne & Chicago, the Pennsy lacked sufficient stock to control reorganization when that road failed shortly after reaching Chicago in 1859. To reach St. Louis the Pennsylvania Railroad invested in three additional railroads united in 1868 under the ambitious name Pittsburgh, Cincinnati and St. Louis, but known as the Panhandle, whose tracks extended only to Columbus. The critical year for the Pennsylvania Railroad was 1869. Dissatisfied with the Pennsylvania Railroad as its only eastern outlet and fearful that the Pennsy-controlled Panhandle had designs on Chicago and would prove a difficult competitor, the prosperous and ambitious Fort Wayne considered connecting with the Baltimore & Ohio to the east and tapping St. Louis to the west. The Pennsylvania and Fort Wayne railroads, however, quickly reached an agreement in 1869 when Jay Gould, president and chief stock manipulator of the Erie Railroad, began looking for western connections for his road. Through the Panhandle, the Pennsylvania Railroad hastily acquired another track to Chicago by outbidding Gould for a lease of the Columbus, Chicago and Indiana Central. When Gould tried to buy control of the Fort Wayne, the Pennsy leased it for 999 years and took possession on July 1, 1869. In January 1869 the Pennsy's track went as far west as Columbus; within the next two years it had reached Cleveland and Chicago on the Great Lakes, St. Louis on the Mississippi, and Cincinnati and Louisville on the Ohio River, and it controlled a network of midwestern branches; by 1873 it had shorter routes than its rivals to Chicago, Cincinnati, and St. Louis and routes to all major centers in the West except Detroit.

While the Pennsylvania Railroad pushed west, it could not ignore New York City, America's leading seaport. In 1867 it connected with a group of New Jersey railroads (the Joint Companies) to form a through route to Jersey City at the port of New York. Disregarding its original purpose to divert traffic away from New York, the Pennsylvania Railroad helped make that port more attractive to shippers. No longer the great terminal, Philadelphia was merely another station along the line. Freight could be moved by car floats about New York harbor, but ferrying passengers placed the Pennsylvania Railroad at a disadvantage. To remedy the difficulty, it drove two single-track tunnels under the Hudson River and four tracks under the East River connecting with the Long Island Railroad (acquired by the Pennsy in 1900). After the Hell Gate Bridge was built, the Pennsylvania Railroad had a through line between New England and the West via New York. The magnificent Pennsyl-

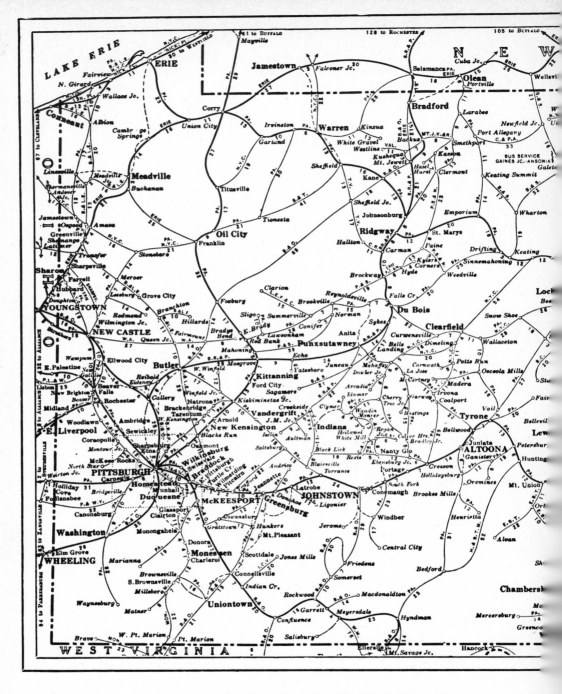

Railroad map of Pennsylvania, 1928. (Copyright by Rand McNally & Company)
Main line railroads with through service: ——————
Other railroads: _____
Interurban Electric Lines: _ _ _ _ _ _ _ _ _

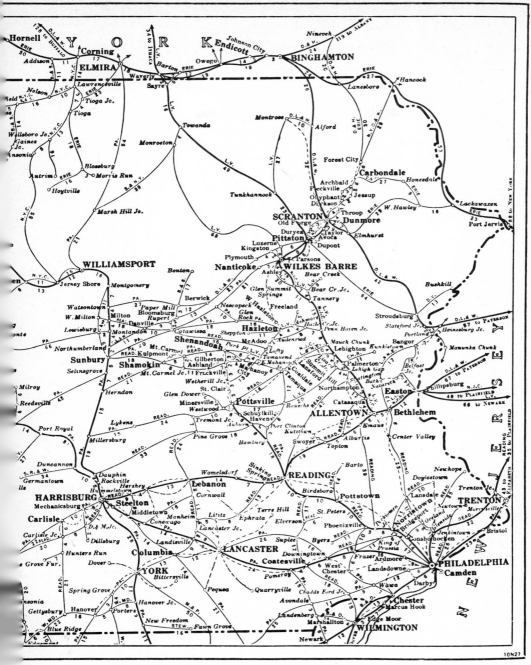

Figures along railroads indicate mileage between towns. All towns of 5,000 population or over on railroads are shown on this map, except in the vicinity of Pittsburgh. Their relative local commercial importance is indicated by graded type thus: **ABCDE, Abcde,** Abcde.
Junctions and terminals of less-than-above population are shown in italic.

vania Station, modeled upon the Baths of Caracalla and opened in 1910, remained a New York landmark until an unappreciative generation destroyed it in 1963 for a new Madison Square Garden.

The Pennsylvania Railroad owed much to cautious J. Edgar Thompson, but Tom Scott, his hard-driving vice president, also deserves credit for the road's tremendous growth. Scott's greatest contributions to the railroad were in politics and in empire building. He knew the Pennsylvania Legislature and could secure friendly laws and defeat hostile ones. Enthusiastically participating in the expansion of the railroad, in 1870 he became president of the Pennsylvania Company, which controlled lines northwest of Pittsburgh, and in 1874 president of the entire road. Falling in depression years, Scott's presidency of the Pennsylvania Railroad was marked by consolidation. He suffered a paralytic stroke in 1878 and retired in 1880, when prosperity was returning. He died less than a year later at the age of fifty-eight.

Pennsylvania Railroad finances were managed conservatively. Since railroad construction was financially hazardous, the Pennsy wisely tried to avoid it and concentrated on acquiring existing lines; 129 of them had a separate corporate existence in 1899. If a new line had to be constructed, the Pennsylvania Railroad organized a subsidiary corporation and bought enough stock and bonds to ensure control and completion of the project. But whether conservatively managed or not, the railroad desperately needed capital, and Europeans helped meet its needs. Although Americans owned 80 percent of the Pennsylvania Railroad's stock in 1902, only seven years earlier British investors had owned nearly half its stock. Unlike the Gilded Age railroads renowned for stock manipulation and mismanagement, the Pennsylvania Railroad usually plowed a dollar back into property for every dollar paid in dividends.

One of the hazards of railroading was competition, particularly in the trunk-line territory between midwestern cities and Atlantic seaports. Railroads with their heavy fixed costs engaged in rate wars and gave rebates and drawbacks to attract freight from other lines. Rebates as high as 50 percent of the published freight rates were returned to powerful shippers, such as Andrew Carnegie and John D. Rockefeller. In 1877 the Pennsylvania joined with other railroads to set rates, divide traffic, and pool receipts in an effort to eliminate cutthroat competition. At first resulting in an unprecedented period of rate stability, the scheme proved short-lived and impossible to enforce. Still hoping to eliminate competition, Alexander J. Cassatt of the Pennsylvania Railroad originated the community-of-ownership principle. To prevent further demoralization of bituminous coal rates, Cassatt induced the New York Central to join the Pennsy in purchasing control of the Chesapeake & Ohio. Under his leadership the Pennsylvania Railroad also bought into other coal carriers—the Baltimore & Ohio, the Norfolk & Western, and the Reading railroads—in this way creating a community of interest.

Competition both reduced freight rates and improved the speed and comfort of passenger service. To meet the challenge of the New York Central, the Pennsy inaugurated 18-hour service between New York and Chicago in 1905. Freight rather than passengers, however, was of prime importance to railroads in the nineteenth century, as it is in the twentieth. Despite the steady reduction of rates, shippers resented their unequal treatment. Cities, towns, and villages without competing lines had to pay higher rates; the Pennsylvania Railroad charged Pittsburghers 25 cents per 100 pounds of grain shipped from Chicago while New Yorkers paid only 15 cents. On the other hand, New Yorkers were angry when cheaper trunk-line rates to Philadelphia enlarged its foreign commerce. Even more galling were drawbacks, rebates, and special contracts. After state regulatory laws were invalidated by the Supreme Court's 1886 *Wabash* decision that forbade states to set rates even within their borders on railroad traffic entering from or bound for other states, Congress enacted the Interstate Commerce Act of 1887. It made rebates, drawbacks, long and short hauls, and pools illegal; required the publication of reasonable rate schedules; and created a five-man Interstate Commerce Commission. Even so, it was largely ineffectual. Railroad regulation was a mockery until passage of the Elkins Act of 1903 and the Hepburn Act of 1906. The Pennsylvania Railroad easily adjusted to these regulatory acts, many of whose features were advantageous (after the Hepburn Act the Pennsy felt free to sell its interest in the Chesapeake & Ohio), and continued to prosper.

Although the Pennsy was by far the most important line in Pennsylvania, in 1869 there were eighty-three other railroads in the state. The New York Central, the Erie, the Baltimore & Ohio, and the Western Maryland all served Pennsylvania as did numerous smaller roads including the following anthracite railroads: the Philadelphia & Reading, the Delaware, Lackawanna & Western, the Lehigh Valley, the Jersey Central, and the Delaware & Hudson.

The Reading—as the Philadelphia & Reading Railroad was commonly called—was the greatest of these anthracite roads. Chartered in 1833 it had a well-built line from Philadelphia through Reading to Pottsville by 1842 and within a few years carried annually over a million tons of anthracite. A policy of expansion begun in 1861 had by 1868 resulted in 532 miles of main track going from Reading to Philadelphia, to Columbia, to Harrisburg, to Pottsville, and to Allentown. The Reading Railroad's great strength and weakness was its dependence on anthracite, which gave it an unusually large volume of tonnage but made it dependent on the vagaries of the coal trade. To alleviate that dependence and to compete with trunk lines, the Reading Railroad sought connections with western and eastern roads. Until 1869 it was conservatively managed, but in that year thirty-four-year-old Franklin Gowen became president and altered the company's policies. After 1871 Gowen bought the coal lands served by his railroad, arguing that "a road which owns its own traffic, . . . is absolutely free from the danger of competition of rival lines." By 1874 the Reading Railroad owned 100,000 acres of coal land, had erected iron furnaces in the Schuylkill Valley, and had acquired a fleet of colliers to transport anthracite up and down the Atlantic seaboard.

Gowen ran into problems. He bought coal lands at inflated greenback prices with bonds payable in gold; he built iron furnaces when the substitution of coke for anthracite was shifting iron production from the Schuylkill Valley to Pittsburgh. The ban on mining and manufacturing by railroads in the constitution of 1873 came too late to save Gowen from himself; the Reading and other carriers already controlled most of the anthracite produced. An imperious man who brooked no opposition, Gowen wasted at least $4 million in crushing the Workingmen's Benevolent Association, a miners' union that was destroying itself through internal dissension. In five years Gowen multiplied the bonded indebtedness of the Reading Railroad twelve times, forcing it to manipulate statements and to borrow to pay interest on the debt. These efforts could not save the Reading from receivership in 1880, though Gowen's contagious enthusiasm saved him the presidency. His subsequent attempt to convert the Reading into a trunk line failed when the Vanderbilt–New York Central interests ceased their support and work on the South Pennsylvania Railroad paralleling the Pennsy's main line stopped (fifty years later the commonwealth converted it into part of the Pennsylvania Turnpike). Again bankrupt, the Reading was reorganized in 1886 by J. P. Morgan, who made certain that Gowen would not manage it. Another adventurer, A. A. McLeod, bankrupted the Reading once again trying to realize Gowen's last dream—a monopoly of anthracite railroad companies. Completely reorganized again by Morgan, the Reading Railroad in the twentieth century has been conservatively managed and dominated by the Baltimore & Ohio.

Whatever their methods and their merits, Gowen, Scott, Thompson, Cassatt; other dreamers, schemers, planners, and builders; their companies; and their faithful followers bound Pennsylvania in a network of rails that paradoxically freed its coal, its iron and steel, and its oil and timber to the outside world.

COAL

Pennsylvania and coal are virtually synonymous. Anthracite (hard-coal) deposits found almost exclusively in eastern Pennsylvania and extensive bituminous (soft-coal) fields in western Pennsylvania have made this state the nation's leading coal producer. Though coal has been formed over a 250-million-year period by subjection of buried vegetation to intense pressure and heat, man has extensively utilized the coal of Pennsylvania for only 150 years.

Cheap, adequate transportation facilities by canal and rail stimulated anthracite production and divided the anthracite fields into the Wyoming, Lehigh, and Schuylkill regions. Anthracite production multiplied in tons from 11 million in 1860 to 28.6 million in 1880 and 57.4 million in 1900, while workmen in the industry increased from 35,600 in 1870 to 144,206 in 1900.

Since very little anthracite is near the surface, small-scale, independent miners quickly gave way to large-scale operators who utilized elaborate, extensive, and expensive slope, shaft, and to a lesser extent strip mines. In contrast to strip mines in which steam shovels scraped away the overlay of earth and then scooped up the entire coal bed, slope and shaft mines required that 20 to 50 percent of the coal be left as pillars. Found in the Lehigh and Schuylkill regions, slope mines were downward pitching tunnels driven into workable coal seams less than 200 feet beneath the surface, but most anthracite seams, particularly in the Wyoming region, were mined by shafts which averaged 400 feet deep, although some went down 2,000 feet. These shafts contained elevators for men and coal as well as equipment for pumping seepage from and ventilating the gangways and adjacent chambers where the coal was mined. When rich veins became exhausted, coal that was deeper, thinner, dirtier, less accessible, and more difficult to blast loose was exploited. By 1900 a large percentage of coal came from veins 3 to 4 feet thick. Pennsylvanians offset these disadvantages through technological improvements. Explosives employed to blast coal loose steadily improved; in 1887 an electric locomotive, instead of mules or horses, was first used to move coal along the gangways to the shaft; and by 1900 compressed-air drilling machines had largely replaced hand drills.

Anthracite had been used to smelt iron since the 1840s, and during the 1860s and 1870s it was the chief furnace fuel, but in the 1880s coke made of bituminous coal displaced it. The Appalachian bituminous region—which covers 14,200 square miles of western Pennsylvania, stretches as far south as northern Alabama, and totals 69,000 square miles—is the most important bituminous coal deposit in the world. Mechanization in this region has been at a high level because the seams are extensive, are found at shallow depths, have few faults,

Engraving, *Descent of a Horse down a Mine-Shaft.* (New York Public Library, Astor, Lenox and Tilden Foundations)

and are relatively flat. As industry developed, the demand for bituminous coal increased. Bituminous coal not only fed the fires of the western Pennsylvania salt industry, which flourished until 1870, but also the steam engines in nineteenth-century factories and on railroads, and subsequently the steam turbines that produced electricity. In 1860 Pennsylvania mined 4,710,400 tons of bituminous coal; after the Civil War, production expanded to 21,280,000 in 1880 and to 79,842,326 in 1900. Since the last decades of the nineteenth century, great quantities of bituminous coal have been converted into coke. Produced by heating coal out of contact with air, coke has had many industrial uses, particularly in smelting and making steel. In 1880 Pennsylvania produced 84 percent of the nation's coke, or about 3 million tons. Most of it was produced in colorful, flaming beehive ovens that wasted invaluable by-products, such as gas, benzene, ammonia, and napthalene, which later slot-type ovens saved. By 1900 Pennsylvania had increased production to 13 million tons.

Pittsburgh owes its growth as a manufacturing center to its strategic location in the midst of bituminous coalfields where the Monongahela and Allegheny Rivers form the Ohio River. As James M'Killop, a Scottish professor, observed in 1869:

> No city in America contains more solid wealth, in proportion to its population, than Pittsburgh. Its growth and prosperity has been rapid and permanent. Possessing in its coal the creative power, it stretches out its mighty arms and gathers the wealth of half a continent into its midst. . . . An observer is amazed at the gigantic establishments. There are iron mills, lead factories, raileries, glass works, potteries, gun smitheries, tobacco factories, tanneries, shipbuilding, &c.; yet all these, from the most delicate ornaments of glass to the ponderous cannon and steam-engine, result from the coal which underlies the smoky hills of Pittsburgh.

Indeed the industrial might of post-Civil War Pennsylvania was founded on coal.

IRON AND STEEL

Abundant supplies of iron ore, limestone, and fuel made Pennsylvania the world center of the iron and steel industry. Blessed with a variety of iron ores, hematite, brown ore, magnetite, and carbonate, Pennsylvania—along with New York and New Jersey—was the chief American source of iron before 1860. As significant to the industry as the ore itself were Pennsylvania's resources of first charcoal, next anthracite, and finally coke for fuel and reducing agents.

By the Civil War Pennsylvania mills rolled more than half the 500,000 tons of American iron (most of it for rails), and the Lehigh Valley became the center of the American anthracite iron industry. Western Pennsylvanians, though possessing ideal coke from the Pittsburgh bituminous seam in the Connellsville region, could not smelt iron successfully with it until they substituted a hot blast for a cold one. Not until 1883 did coke-produced iron exceed anthracite-produced and charcoal-produced iron combined. With mineral fuel, larger steam-powered blast furnaces lined with firebrick replaced water-powered stone furnaces. Later, with railroads to bring in raw materials and to carry off finished products, iron and then steel blast furnaces were constructed not on remote hillsides but in urban centers near labor markets. Perhaps the greatest technological advance in the iron and steel industry was the Kelly-Bessemer discovery in the 1850s that steel could be made inexpensively by blowing cold air through molten iron. Because of the time lag between a discovery and its widespread application, the Civil War was fought with iron rather than with steel, and large-scale, inexpensive steel production was not realized until the 1870s. Among the early users of the Bessemer process were the Pennsylvania Steel Company at Steelton, the Freedom Iron and Steel Works at Lewistown, and the Cambria Iron Company at Johnstown.

Superior in the long run to the Bessemer process and almost simultaneously introduced from Europe was the open-hearth process. It employed a large shallow-bowled reverberatory furnace from which samples of the molton metal could be taken so that the refining could be stopped when the desired quality of steel appeared. The open-hearth furnace, however, was much slower than the Bessemer process in which the proper carbon content was judged by the color of the converter's flame. American manufacturers initially preferred speed and guesswork, but open-hearth steel exceeded Bessemer steel in 1908. Production skyrocketed. By 1900 Americans were fabricating over 10 million tons of steel a year; and despite the westward migration of the industry Pennsylvania contributed over 60 percent of the total.

Painting by S. B. Shiley, *Teeming Ingots, Bessemer Converter.* (Bethlehem Steel Corporation)

Technological innovations were expensive and led to large-scale business organization. The obvious efficiency and power of the corporation swept before it the traditional hostility of Pennsylvania to the corporate form of business organization. Long after other industrial states had acted, Pennsylvania passed in 1873 an incorporation law for the iron and steel industry and in 1874 a general act of incorporation with generous provisions allowing limited liability and borrowing of money through bond issues. Ironically Andrew Carnegie, that colorful, controversial, contradictory, and most successful steelman, neither utilized the corporate form nor depended very long on the tariff in building his empire.

Carnegie is one of the few men who rose from rags to riches. Born and bred in poverty-stricken, radical Scotch working-class surroundings, Carnegie migrated with his family to the Mecca of nineteenth-century radicals, the United States of America. The Carnegie family settled in Allegheny City (now part of Pittsburgh). At thirteen Andrew Carnegie became a bobbin boy at $1.20 a week, and later he was an engine tender. Unhappy in the latter job, he became a messenger in the Pittsburgh telegraph office for $2.50 a week. Thanks to Colonel James Anderson, who opened his private library of 400 volumes to working boys, Carnegie read widely in politics, history, science, and philosophy.

Carnegie's economic rise was phenomenal. Listening in his spare moments to the Morse code he was among the first to take messages by sound. After his promotion to operator, Carnegie met Tom Scott, a frequenter of the telegraph office who was beginning his spectacular career with the Pennsylvania Railroad; at the age of eighteen Carnegie became Scott's private secretary. From 1853 to 1865 Carnegie remained with the Pennsylvania Railroad, becoming supervisor of the Pittsburgh division and organizing the military telegraph for the Union during the Civil War.

Carnegie left railroading to enter the iron industry. In 1865 he joined the Keystone Bridge Company and with the help of his railroad contacts was instrumental in its success. He also made small fortunes in oil and in selling railroad securities in Europe before the Panic of 1873 and earned a dubious reputation among conservative Pittsburgh businessmen as a dashing entrepreneur. The crucial year in Carnegie's life was 1873. A friend of Bessemer and in close contact with English steelmakers, Carnegie put all his money and efforts into steel. He began construction of the J. Edgar Thompson steel mills (named for the president of his best potential customer—the Pennsylvania Railroad). Carnegie's connections with steel and with philanthropy began the same year. His first public gift was baths for his native Dunfermline, Scotland. For the next thirty years the triumph of the Carnegie Steel Company was a large part of the triumph of the American steel industry and of all American industry.

There are several reasons for Carnegie's success; incomparable Lake Superior ore, the most valuable of which he purchased or leased by the 1890s; the protective tariff, initially helpful but subsequently opposed by Carnegie; the Connellsville coke area developed by Henry Clay Frick, who joined Carnegie in 1882 and became his chief executive officer in 1889; but above all else Carnegie's organization. Men in his organization included Frick; Charles M. Schwab, who started as a dollar-a-day laborer; and the legendary Captain William R. ("Bill") Jones, ingenious inventor and inspirational leader who was later burned to death at Carnegie's Braddock works by molten metal while trying to clear a jammed furnace. The Carnegie Steel Company was for almost its entire existence a limited partnership, not a corporation. Its stock was not publicly sold but given to a few promising men in the organization, and every dollar made by the Carnegie Steel Company was retained by active partners.

In addition to his organizational ability, Carnegie had optimism, enthusiasm, courage, and daring. These traits made him experiment with new techniques and expand despite hard times. During the depression from 1893 to 1897 Carnegie expanded his holdings at a very low cost while his competitors declined. With the return of prosperity he could undersell other steelmakers and had a stranglehold on the industry. At the turn of the century Schwab estimated that the Carnegie Company produced between 25 and 30 percent of the nation's steel including half the structural steel, half the armor plate, and 30 percent of the rails fabricated in the United States. In 1900 the company's profits were $40 million, of which Carnegie's personal share was $25 million. Yet he never forgot his radical background; his ambition transcended mere moneymaking; in 1901 he sold out for $250 million to the United States Steel Corporation organized by J. P. Morgan. Conceiving of himself as a trustee of wealth that others helped create, Carnegie, in the remaining two decades of his life, gave $350 million to philanthropic projects in both the United States and Great Britain for the "improvement of mankind." The innumerable public libraries which he established were his way of paying his debt to Colonel James Anderson.

The United States Steel ("Big Steel") merger of ten great steel companies, several of which were the products of earlier mergers, is the classic example of industrial consolidation and economic integration. Capitalized at $1.4 billion, or nearly twice its actual worth, United States Steel comprised 149 steel plants, 84 blast furnaces, 1,000 miles of railroad,

Andrew Carnegie, industrialist. (Historical Society of Pennsylvania)

and 112 Great Lakes vessels, in addition to vast coal, ore, and limestone deposits. Though its holdings were far-flung, most of its works were less than a hundred miles from Pittsburgh.

OIL

Unlike railroading, coal mining, and the iron and steel industry, the petroleum industry originated in America. Though petroleum was known in Pennsylvania as early as 1755 and was bottled for medicinal purposes in the early nineteenth century, the age of petroleum really began in 1859. In that year Edwin L. Drake drilled the first successful oil well; all oil previously used had seeped to the earth's surface. Having several years before invested his $200 life savings in the Pennsylvania Rock Oil Company, Drake journeyed to Titusville for the company and stopped en route to observe salt-well-drilling operations. Believing that a fortune could be made in oil, he persuaded the Rock Oil Company to lease its land to him and to another stockholder, and they formed the Seneca Oil Company in 1859. Drake became its general manager and began drilling operations. To eliminate seepage, Drake invented, but neglected to patent, the drive pipe (10-foot sections of 6-inch pipe battered down through sand and clay to rock), which is still used. With his money almost exhausted, Drake struck oil at 69½ feet on August 27, 1859. The people of Titusville who had once quipped derisively over Drake's folly now whooped joyfully over Drake's genius.

The impact of the discovery was instantaneous. Petroleum could be refined into superior lubricants and into kerosene, which provided excellent lamplight. The demand for these products, particularly kerosene, was immediate and soon became worldwide. Speculators rushed to secure leases along Oil Creek between Titusville and Oil City; when 1860 ended there were seventy-four oil wells daily producing a total of 1,165 barrels. Though well-heeled speculators used steam power, many of the earliest wells were kicked down by men stepping on stirrups attached to an elastic pole utilizing its spring and their weight to drive the attached drill through rock. Subsequent wells were deeper than Drake's; he had had the incredible luck to drill where oil was closest to the surface.

Drake's subsequent career was tragic. That his discovery left him the calmest man in Titusville was the product of his own complacency. "I have tapped the mine," he said, and went off fishing while others scurried for oil leases. With his prestige Drake could have associated himself with several oil companies, but he was content to be the Titusville justice of the peace and an oil buyer for a New York firm. Drake moved to New York in 1863, became a stockbroker, lost his fortune, suffered a spinal affliction, and died in 1880.

At first 75 barrels a day was the top output for a Titusville well, but on April 17, 1861, the Little and Merrick Well began gushing 3,000 barrels daily, and this output was matched by the Empire Well. These wells not only exhausted the supply of barrels and wasted a fantastic amount of oil but also glutted the market, forcing the price of oil per barrel down from $10 to 10 cents.

To be useful petroleum had to be refined. A refinery in the 1860s was simply an inexpensive distillery comprising an iron drum for the still and a worm in which the vapor condensed. When crude oil was heated in the still, first naphtha would distill, at 180° F; next kerosene; and last a heavy oil containing paraffin, at about 1000° F. The naphtha, heavy oil, and tar left in the still were dumped into Oil Creek as worthless; after treatment with sulphuric acid and caustic soda the kerosene or lamp oil was marketed.

Transportation was a problem. Before 1860 Titusville's nearest railroad stops were at Corry, Union Mills, and Garland, about 20 to 25 miles to the north over dirt roads renowned as

> Wholly unclassable
> Almost impassable
> Scarcely jackassable.

The cost, about $2.50 a barrel, was high; indeed it cost more to ship oil from Oil Creek to Union Mills than to ship it from Union Mills to New York City. Nevertheless, prior to 1862 about 6,000 teams of horses with a capacity of about six barrels each were hauling oil to the railroad. Spilled oil gave horses a caustic, low-grade burn, leaving them hairless below the neck as they pulled their loads through this mucky hell for horses.

Another early method of oil transportation was by water. Since Oil Creek was frequently too shallow for navigation, a pond freshet was created by damning up branches of Oil Creek and cutting the dams in careful sequence to raise the water level for flatboats. At the height of the busy season two freshets a week were the rule. Riding the crest of a pond freshet required skill. Striving to avoid rocks, bridges, and each other, 150 to 200 flatboats manned by 500 boatmen and carrying a total of 10,000 to 30,000 oil barrels would ride the crest down narrow Oil Creek to the Allegheny River at Oil City.

The difficulties of transporting oil hastened the coming of railroads and pipelines. After

Engraving by H. F., *The Hippopotami of Petroleum Centre,* capturing the micabre atmosphere of the early oil fields. (New York Public Library, Astor, Lenox and Tilden Foundations)

the broad-guage Oil Creek Railroad connected Titusville with Corry in 1862, wagon and water transportation declined. By 1865 the tank car was introduced and rails encircled the oil region, freeing it from rapacious teamsters, who charged individuals $2 to $3 for a muddy ride from Oil City to Franklin. The same trip in elegant railroad cars took twenty minutes and cost 35 cents. Despite the reduced rates, the huge oil traffic made these railroads very profitable. Pipeline transportation proved feasible in October 1865, when Samuel Van Syckel operated the first commercially successful oil pipeline.

The bonanza element in the early oil industry gave it a flavor similar to that of Western goldmining. Land values skyrocketed and oil companies multiplied with Philadelphia, New York, and London speculators gobbling up their stock. Pithole City was the classic oil town. In early 1865 a series of oil strikes were made on the 65-acre Holmden farm; by May one building was under construction; three months later Pithole had 15,000 people with fifty hotels, two banks, two telegraph offices, two churches, the third-largest post office in Pennsylvania, a newspaper, a theater, and innumerable bars and bawdy houses. In September the Holmden farm sold for $2 million. Although robbery was common and men were armed, there was little violence in Pithole City. Only one killing occurred and it appeared to be in self-defense. Pithole declined as fast as it had grown. When, in the autumn, wells began to dry up, speculators lost heart and left in search of oilier rock. By January 1866, Pithole was a ghost town.

By 1865 increasing supplies of crude oil, more refineries, better transportation, and the growing demand for kerosene convinced John D. Rockefeller, a Cleveland produce merchant, that oil was worthy of his undivided attention. With characteristic energy and efficiency, Rockefeller bought oil directly from producers, hauled it in his own wagons, refined it in his own refineries, and made his own barrels and acid. Nevertheless, Rockefeller could not compete advantageously for seaboard markets because of his Cleveland location. To offset this disadvantage, in 1868 Rockefeller secured from the New York Central Railroad system a rebate, or a reduced freight rate, on all oil shipped by his Standard Oil Company. Building on this advantage, Rockefeller controlled in less than two years the largest refineries in the world and exclaimed, "The oil business is mine." To prove his statement, Rockefeller had to fight independent Pennsylvania refiners.

The antagonists used a variety of weapons. With refining capacity about double that of crude oil production, Rockefeller and Tom Scott of the Pennsylvania Railroad in 1872 secretly reorganized the abandoned South Improvement Company to control the oil industry and to systematize rebates and traffic. Composed of thirteen refiners from Cleveland, Pittsburgh, and New York (ten of them from the Standard Oil group), the South Improvement Company agreed to ship 27½ percent of its freight on the New York Central, an equal amount on the Erie, and 45 percent on the Pennsy. In return, railroads agreed to double their oil rates but to allow a 50 percent rebate for members of the South Improvement Company and even to allow drawbacks, whereby the company would receive rebates on oil shipped by competitors. Facing ruin, many independent refiners sold out to Standard Oil, but other outraged refiners and producers organized a Petroleum Producers' Union. This union refused to sell crude oil to members of the South Improvement Company, refrained from drilling new wells for sixty days, and pressured the Legislature for relief. When other independents joined the struggle, Tom Scott deserted Rockefeller, met with the independents, and actually lowered freight rates to less than they had been before the South Improvement Company was created; and the Pennsylvania Legislature revoked the South Improvement Company's charter.

Rockefeller, however, continued to eliminate competition. His 1872 and 1873 attempts to set a quota of crude oil for each refinery and to set kerosene prices by cooperative agreement failed. Given his goal, coercion was necessary. Abandoning the pooling device in June 1873, Rockefeller acquired barreling and shipping facilities in New Jersey, giving him control of the export market. He persuaded railroads to equalize the freight rates of crude oil and kerosene per barrel, and gained control of the largest pipelines. When Standard Oil began to buy out refineries in 1874, it was able to coerce unwilling owners to capitulate by underselling, by rebates, and by creating tank car and barrel shortages. Soon Standard Oil owned twenty of the twenty-one Pittsburgh refineries, ten of the twelve in Philadelphia, and all of those in the oil region. When the Pennsylvania Railroad, through its Empire Transportation Company, tried briefly in 1877 to halt Rockefeller's drive by adding New York refineries to its pipelines and tank cars, Rockefeller boycotted the Pennsylvania Railroad and rallied to his cause the New York Central and Erie railroads. Scott surrendered the Empire Transportation Company to Rockefeller for $3 million when the

1877 railroad strike hit the Pennsylvania Railroad with force. By the summer of 1878 when he was only thirty-eight, Rockefeller controlled 97 percent of all refineries.

Pennsylvania oil men did not give up. In May 1879 they began operating the Tidewater Pipe Company's line from Corryville in the Bradford oil field to Williamsport, where the Reading Railroad carried the oil to the few independent Philadelphia and New York refineries. The cost of shipping oil by the new route (17 cents a barrel) was one-fifth the cost by rail. When Rockefeller countered by buying out the independent refineries, Tidewater built its own refineries; but Rockefeller bought sufficient Tidewater stock to convert it into an ally with whom in 1883 he divided crude oil traffic—88½ percent for Standard Oil and 11½ percent for Tidewater. During the 1890s Pennsylvania oil region independents organized the Producers Oil Company, the United States Pipe Line Company, and the Pure Oil Company to fight Standard Oil; and in 1900 the three merged as Pure Oil, which remained independent.

The automobile generated an enormous demand for petroleum in the twentieth century, but the discovery of new oil fields relegated Pennsylvania to a subordinate position in oil production. A Rockefeller associate had once rashly promised to drink all the oil found outside Pennsylvania, but by 1970 the state's share in producing the nation's annual 3½ billion barrels of crude oil had dropped to one-ninth of 1 percent. Despite small production, however, Pennsylvania crude oil is prized as a source of lubricating oil. Although oil production no longer centers in Pennsylvania, the state has developed its refining capacity, which is exceeded only by that of Texas. And as deep drilling testifies, men still seek petroleum reserves far beneath Pennsylvania's surface.

TIMBER

In the 1860s Pennsylvania was the nation's leading lumbering state. The value of sawed lumber and containers (staves, headings, and so forth) was $35 million in 1870 as compared with $13 million for pig iron and $7 million for steel. But Pennsylvania did not long maintain primacy; in 1870 it was already in second place and by 1900 it was in fourth place.

An orgy of unbridled private enterprise, early lumbering left Pennsylvania with extensive stands of saplings and many nostalgic memories. Before railroads, motortrucks, and portable sawmills, the lumber industry was more exciting, with loggers using ingenious and dangerous methods to bring timber to market. Lumber camps were primitive and isolated, food was coarse but plentiful, and shelves with straw mattresses served as bunks. Exposed to the elements and to danger, lumberjacks were a tough, hardy breed with gargantuan appetites for food, cheap whiskey, and fighting. A lumberjack would deliberately court battle by sitting in another's place in the mess hall or by walking around town with a chip of wood on his shoulder. When lumberjacks fought, the victor often jumped on the face of the vanquished and sometimes permanently maimed him by chewing off his ear.

Besides drinking and fighting, logging involved lumberjacks in constant danger and backbreaking toil. Their work included felling trees, trimming their limbs, sawing them into 8 to 20-foot logs, snaking them to the water's edge using a chain and horses along slope runways, piling them in enormous heaps, stamping their ends with the owner's brand, launching them in the spring, and freeing their inevitable jams with either a cant hook or dynamite.

Williamsport's giant log boom made it the lumber capital of the world from the 1860s to the 1880s. Stretching diagonally from shore to shore, the boom was a 6-mile string of logs linked by iron chains and anchored with stone-filled log cribs. At the lower end of the boom, "boom rats" with long pikes and sharp calked boots sorted the logs according to Williamsport's 1,700 registered brands, before they were sawed or made into huge rafts and floated downstream. Williamsport's best year was 1885: almost 2 million logs passed through its boom, and its twenty-five sawmills and numerous planing mills produced 226 million board feet. Lining the river at Williamsport and for miles beyond were mammoth mountains of sawed lumber and manufactured wooden items.

As its many ghost towns mutely testify, Pennsylvania's timber kingdom is but a memory. Yet Pennsylvania permanently influenced the lumber industry by schooling many of the nation's outstanding lumber barons. Frederick Weyerhaeuser, John DuBois (founder of Du Bois), Harry McCormick, and William E. Dodge used their Pennsylvania experience in harvesting the forests of the West and South. But thanks to government controls these forests were not as ruthlessly exploited as were Penn's woods.

BIBLIOGRAPHY

Statistical information on Pennsylvania's industries can be readily found in U.S. Bureau of the Census: *Historical Statistics of the Unites States: Colonial Times to 1957* (1960); Pennsylvania Bureau of Statistics: *Pennsylvania Statistical Abstract* (annual); U.S. Bureau of the Census: *Twelfth Census of the United States . . . 1900: Manufactures,* part 2; U.S. Bureau of the Census: *Statistical Abstract of the United States, 1901.*

The best work on industrial development during the Gilded Age is Edward C. Kirkland: *Industry Comes of Age: Business, Labor, and Public Policy, 1860–1897* (1962). More valuable than one would assume on the basis of its publisher (the Pennsylvania Railroad Company) is George H. Burgess and Miles C. Kennedy: *Centennial History of the Pennsylvania Railroad, 1846–1946* (1949). C. Vann Woodward: *Reunion & Reaction* (1956) is concerned with Thomas Scott's efforts to make Rutherford B. Hayes president of the United States. On the Reading Railroad, see Marvin W. Schlegel's excellent *Ruler of the Reading: The Life of Franklin B. Gowen, 1836–1889* (1947); and Jules I. Bogen: *The Anthracite Railroads: A Study in American Railroad Enterprise* (1927). On coal, see Peter Roberts: *The Anthracite Coal Industry . . .* (1901); Samuel H. Daddow and Benjamin Bannon: *Coal, Iron, and Oil . . .* (1866); Robert D. Billinger: *Pennsylvania's Coal Industry* (1954); Howard N. Eavenson: *The First Century and a Quarter of American Coal Industry* (1942). Arthur C. Bining: *Pennsylvania's Iron and Steel Industry* (1954) is an excellent short survey. On Carnegie, see the uncritically sympathetic Burton J. Hendrick: *The Life of Andrew Carnegie,* 2 vols. (1932); and the balanced Joseph Frazier Wall: *Andrew Carnegie* (1970). The oil industry is discussed in Paul H. Giddens: *The Birth of the Oil Industry* (1938); Ernest C. Miller, *Pennsylvania's Oil Industry,* rev. ed. (1959); John J. Abele: "Oil Empire Split Fifty Years Ago," *New York Times,* May 21, 1961; Allan Nevins: *Study in Power: John D. Rockefeller, Industrialist and Philanthropist,* 2 vols. (1953); and Ralph W. and Muriel E. Hidy: *Pioneering in Big Business, 1882–1911: History of Standard Oil Company (New Jersey)* (1955). See also Charles D. Martens: *The Oil City* (1971). The best sources on the lumber industry in Pennsylvania are a special issue of *Pennsylvania History,* vol. 29 (October 1952); and R. Dudley Tonkin, *My Partner, the River* (1958).

CHAPTER NINETEEN

Immigration and Labor

"It may be doubted," reformer Henry George stated of Pennsylvania in 1886, "if there is on the earth's surface another area of 43,000 square miles, which, considering all things, is better fitted by nature to yield large returns to labor." The building and operation of railroads, the mining of coal and iron, the production of steel, oil, lumber, and textiles was impossible without the labor of thousands of men, women, and children. Although by twentieth-century standards post-Civil War workers labored long hours for low pay under wretched conditions, people from adjacent rural areas and from faraway Europe flocked to industrial centers because their lot as industrial workers was better than their former condition. Pennsylvania's vast labor force made it a part of all significant labor movements, but the struggle to improve laboring conditions was marked by strikes and occasional violence. Motivated by greed, to be sure, but also by the doctrines of social Darwinism and Christian steward-ship, management attempted to protect what it thought was the natural or divine order of things and fought the labor movement.

IMMIGRATION

Until after World War I immigration to the United States was nearly unrestricted. But the poverty-stricken recent arrival began close to the bottom of the social order, toiled at tough, poorly paid "foreign jobs," and achieved upward mobility only with unusual effort. Vast differences, not merely economic but ethnic, linguistic, and religious, separated later arrivals from the descendents of earlier immigrants. These differences were especially pronounced between the Civil War and World War I when an increasing number of migrants arrived from eastern and southern Europe. The result produced a heterogeneous labor force divided by animosities between native and foreign-born laborers and among various immigrant groups.

The number of migrants fluctuated from year to year depending on war and economic opportunity. Migrants to the United States numbered 92,000 annually in the early years of the Civil War and 1,285,000 in 1907. In the seventies they averaged 281,000 annually, in the eighties 525,000, in the depression-wracked nineties 369,000, and in the first ten years of the twentieth century 880,000. In the decade preceding World War I (1905–1914) over one million people arrived annually, and more than half the wage earners in the nation's twenty-one leading industries were immigrants. From the beginning of World War I immigrant domination of labor declined, and it continued to drop after Congress in 1921 under the national-origins quota system both restricted the number of migrants and favored those from northwestern Europe.

Pennsylvania attracted more immigrants than any other state except New York. In 1860 over 430,000 (15 percent of Pennsylvania's population) were foreign-born, while in 1920 almost 1,400,000 (16 percent of the people) were foreign-born. Both the ultimate destinations of immigrants and their percentage of the total population remained relatively constant in Pennsylvania. Particularly after 1890 few immigrants farmed despite their agrarian backgrounds; most worked in mines, mills, and factories. Immigrants flocked to the anthracite and bituminous coal regions and to Philadelphia, Pittsburgh, and other urban centers. Confronting a strange and often hostile society, most immigrants segregated themselves into ethnic subdivisions. In 1920 natives of Russia were the largest immigrant group in Philadelphia, with Irish and Italians vying for second place; Poles the largest group in Allegheny, Luzerne, Lackawanna, and Schuylkill Counties and in the cities of Wilkes-Barre and Chester; Italians in Washington, Fayette, and Montgomery Counties and in the city of Scranton; natives of Austria in Westmoreland and Cambria Counties and in Johnstown; Hungarians in Northampton County and the cities of Bethlehem and McKeesport; Irish in Delaware County; Yugoslavians in Beaver County; and Germans in Erie County and in the cities of Pittsburgh and Erie. Italians and Germans very nearly shared the lead with Poles in Allegheny County. Almost half the 30,000 Lithuanians in Pennsylvania located in Schuylkill and Luzerne Counties; Czechoslovakians were second and third in Washington and Fayette Counties, respectively, while Welshmen were second to the Poles in Wilkes-Barre.

Miners, ironworkers, and steelworkers reflected the shifting patterns of immigration. Before 1880 these workers were native Americans or immigrants from the British Isles and northern Europe. After 1880 a few southern and eastern Europeans broke into these occupations, and after 1890 they took over the most difficult and worst-paying "hunky" jobs. The older groups which they displaced moved into higher-skilled, better-paying tasks. Most old-stock American, English, German, Scottish, Welsh, and Irish miners felt that an intimate working association with new immigrants brought a "sort of reproach." In iron and steel new immigrants were not merely segregated from the old but were further differentiated among themselves.

Despite dire predictions, Pennsylvania rapidly assimilated its new citizens. The slowest to be Americanized were the remote colonies of Polish and Croatian anthracite miners, many of whom came in the early eighties as contract laborers. Joseph H. Senner, a friend of the immigrant and secretary of the Immigration Protective League, observed that those

Photo study by Lewis W. Hine, *At a Russian boarding house, Homestead, Pa.—1909.* (Lewis W. Hine Collection, Local History and Genealogy Division, New York Public Library, Astor, Lenox and Tilden Foundations)

miners "could be Americanized very much quicker if they were not treated as a kind of an outcast; . . . They are left alone too much, . . . a good many of them; and especially their children would like very much to go out and mingle among the Americans, but they have no opportunity." Furthermore, in the anthracite regions there were few public schools, and the Pennsylvania compulsory school law was not enforced in that area notorious for child labor. Despite these obstacles, Senner optimistically and correctly predicted that these miners would be assimilated.

The immigrant's saga is impressive and instructive. Wrenched from the home of his fathers, shipped under vile conditions across the sea, cast on a foreign shore and cheated all the way, the uprooted found immigration a brutal, searing experience. More poignant and tragic, the immigrant was thrust into an alien culture that simultaneously demanded he integrate, merge, or melt while it segregated him, separated him, and attempted to keep him out of the melting pot. The gap between immigrant parents clinging to Old World ways and their Americanized children multiplied communication difficulties parents and children usually experience. A leading immigration historian, Oscar Handlin, however, has pointed out that the immigrant's alienation, though extreme, was shared by many native Americans. Migration from East to West and from country to city has always been a fact of American life.

LABORING CONDITIONS

Since Pennsylvania has many industries demanding diverse skills, the wages and hours, working and living conditions of its laborers have varied. Skilled laborers—glass blowers, workers in the building trades, and railroad engineers, for instance—were much better off than unskilled laborers, who in addition to other disadvantages had low social status and little sense of accomplishment. Finally, because they occupied a secure niche in their community, small-town laborers could often deal with the impersonality of industrialism better than laborers in large cities.

Of all workers in Pennsylvania, the coal miner has attracted the most interest. Often drenched with seepage and blackened with powder smoke and coal dust, the Pennsylvania miner risked death in some of the world's most dangerous mines. Although members of the Senate Committee on Education and Labor in 1883 thought that miners were "seduced . . . by extraordinarily remunerative wages," the average miner earned only about $350 a year at that time. Daily pay was good, but chronic overproduction forced miners to be idle nearly half the time. In 1898 the average number of days worked in forty-seven Pennsylvania industries was 298, while the anthracite miner worked only 148 days. Bituminous miners fared better. Their wages were higher and they worked more frequently (209 days in 1898).

Photo study by Lewis W. Hine, *Slavic Coal Miner in Pittsburgh District—1910*. (Lewis W. Hine Collection, Local History and Genealogy Division, New York Public Library, Astor, Lenox and Tilden Foundations)

Indeed, necessity compelled miners to get their very young sons jobs picking slate from the coal.

Pennsylvania mining towns in 1886 gave Henry George the impression "of a hard, dull, monotonous struggle for mere existence; of human life reduced to little more than animal terms, and shorn of all that gives it dignity and grace and zest." Miners lived in company-owned, unpainted, two-room row houses and paid from 10 to 40 percent more than regular market prices for provisions at a company store.

Unskilled iron and steel workers were "huddled together in tenement houses and no more comfortable than the miners," but working and living conditions were better for the skilled. They usually enjoyed more room (a three-room row house with a basement kitchen), had better furniture and carpets, ate fresh beef more often, and clothed their families in neater, better-quality garments than miners could afford. Some steelworkers' houses, however, were so close to the mills that in summer the noise made conversation difficult. Furthermore, ironworkers and steelworkers frequently suffered from rheumatism caused by the temperature contrast between the severe roastings received when loading furnaces and the cooling-off periods, many had their eyesight affected by looking into the heat, and injuries were common. They also worked long hours; most steelworkers put in a 12-hour day and many a seven-day week as late as the 1920s.

Recreational facilities were nonexistant. "If there is any grass on the south side of Pittsburgh attached to a tenement house," Robert D. Layton, a former secretary of the Knights of Labor, claimed in 1883, "it is in a little box sitting on the windowsill." For children too small for factory work there was only the street for play, and Sunday in Pittsburgh was dismal for adult workers who had a day off but found places of amusement closed and shop windows curtained.

With their city ranking third in garment manufacturing, Philadelphia garment workers toiled at home and in sweatshops. While the trend in the late nineteenth century was toward factories equipped with elaborate machinery and employing large numbers of people, the reverse was true in the garment industry. The manufacturer reduced his overhead by cutting out garments and contracting with sweatshops and home workers to assemble them by piece rate. In 1895 Pennsylvania sweatshops had to meet a standard of cleanliness to earn a permit and could no longer operate in private homes. The law, however, did permit families to manufacture in their own homes, and the worst sanitary conditions often prevailed in these family shops. During the two annual rush seasons, men worked until they dropped from exhaustion, and wives and children pitched in with all their strength. Cutthroat competition from farmers' wives, with even lower rates, further reduced the income of city garment workers. At the turn of the century conditions in sweatshops were better than in family shops but left much to be desired. Garment workers could earn $8.50 for a 60-hour week but had work only about half of the year and averaged only $188.10 annually. Out of these earnings, the average garment worker with a family of five paid $9 a month rent for three rooms.

THE NATIONAL LABOR UNION

Organized industry produced organized labor. Eroded bargaining power forced workingmen to abandon individualism and embrace unionism. Craft unions grew rapidly during the Civil War, and in 1866 a number of them formed the National Labor Union. Its leading spirit was William H. Sylvis, who became its president in 1868. Born in Armagh the son of a poor, footloose wagonmaker, Sylvis started his iron-molder apprenticeship at eighteen and later began his own foundry. Failure, ill-health, and injury—when molten iron poured down his boot—made him strive to improve the lot of workingmen. During an 1857 strike protesting a 12 percent wage cut, Sylvis joined the Philadelphia Stove and Hollow-ware Moulders' Union. As its secretary, Sylvis was instrumental in establishing the National Molders' Union in 1859 and became its treasurer in 1860. While holding these offices, Sylvis supported himself by working ten hours a day at his trade.

In 1863 Sylvis was largely responsible for reorganizing the Iron Molders' International Union and was elected its president. In 1867, with from 75 to 85 percent of all iron molders union members and most of the foundries closed shops, the Iron Molders' Union, Sylvis proudly maintained, was the "most prosperous, successful and perfect union on the American continent." In 1866 Sylvis helped establish the National Labor Union and in 1868 became its president.

The National Labor Union's strategy was defensive. It sought to preserve or, more precisely, to reestablish relationships between master and workman upon mutual and reciprocal obligations. To achieve that end and enable workers to share the profits, Sylvis induced the iron molders to set up a cooperative foundry, but for want of capital it failed. Sylvis then decided that labor had to organize politically to induce the state to finance cooperatives. He also called for a government-regulated paper currency (greenbacks) that would stabilize and remove control of interest rates from "bankers, brokers and other gamblers"; for a tax on uncultivated property, forcing speculators to sell unused acres and enabling labor to escape west; for an eight-hour day; and for international cooperation between European and American labor, particularly in controlling immigration for the benefit of both groups. Sylvis also worked to organize labor unions for women and encouraged woman's rights and woman suffrage. Despite an anti-Negro bias, he wanted blacks in the labor movement. "If workmen of the white race do not conciliate the blacks," he warned, "the blacks will vote against them."

Sylvis never realized his dreams. Shortly after becoming president of the National Labor Union, he died suddenly at the age of forty. The National Labor Union did enter politics in the 1872 campaign, but without Sylvis's dynamic leadership efforts to implement his program proved disastrous and the union melted away.

THE KNIGHTS OF LABOR

Nine Philadelphia tailors on December 9, 1869, started the Noble and Holy Order of the Knights of Labor. Its first head was Uriah S. Stephens, who set the humanitarian and idealistic policies of the organization. Stephens, who had been educated for the Baptist ministry but apprenticed to a tailor after the Panic of 1837, wished to consolidate "all branches of labor into a compact whole," and his organization helped restore the sense of community, which the industrial order was destroying. By January 1, 1878, the Knights had established enough local assemblies to hold their first general assembly in Reading and to form a national labor organization. The Knights was not an affiliation of trade unions; membership was on an individual basis and open to all except lawyers, doctors, bankers, liquor dealers, stockbrokers, and professional gamblers. The Knights favored boycotts and arbitration but discouraged strikes. Its platform demanded the eight-hour day, weekly pay laws, equal pay for equal work, and health and safety legislation for miners, manufacturers, and builders; it demanded laws prohibiting children under fourteen from working, laws ending the contract system on municipal, state, and national works, and laws ending both the importation of contract labor and the use of convict labor. Above all, the Knights of Labor, which was also defensive, wanted to form cooperatives, which it thought would make labor "independent of bosses" and create a society free of the injustices of the individualistic industrial order.

To protect members from the prejudice of their employers, the organization was kept secret. In all public notices its name was indicated by five stars. It expanded rapidly after its first general assembly, but declined when the Catholic church and the general public linked it with the Molly Maguires and other secret societies. After the Knights of Labor forsook its secrecy, received the Pope's approval in the early eighties, and won strikes in 1884 and 1885, it grew phenomenally; by 1886 its members numbered over 700,000.

A year after the first general assembly, Stephens retired; his successor was Terence V. Powderly. Born in Carbondale, Powderly as a young man had seen "the blackened, charred bodies of over one hundred men and boys . . . brought to the surface" at Avondale after a tragic mine disaster and had heard John Siney's speech on the desolate hillside. "You can do nothing to win these dead back to life," Siney had said, "but you can help me to win fair treatment and justice for living men who risk life and health in their daily toil." Powderly, who never forgot Siney's speech, remained at the head of the Knights of Labor until 1893. A man of tremendous energy and varied interest, Powderly lived until 1924. He was mayor of Scranton during six of the fourteen years he headed the Knights of Labor; later Powderly practiced law, did considerable writing, and served the government as commissioner-general of immigration and as chief of the Division of Information in the Bureau of Immigration as well as in other posts.

A series of unsuccessful strikes, frequently called by local leaders against Powderly's advice, led to the swift decline of the Knights. By 1893 many skilled industrial workers had left it for trade unions affiliated with the American Federation of Labor, membership had dropped to 75,000, and the agrarian element in the organization had become dominant. The much-feared, overgrown giant had shrunk to a pigmy. "The last important manifestation of middle-class reform philosophies in the American labor movement," the Knights of Labor impressed the general public with the importance of organized labor and made workingmen realize the importance of solidarity—that "an injury to one is the common concern of all."

THE MOLLY MAGUIRES

Organized labor eschewed violence, which most frequently occurred where unions were weak or nonexistent and grievances were many. Amid the heyday of Native Americanism, the Irish became a majority in the anthracite region. Participants in the 1857 St. Patrick's Day parade in Schuylkill County were shocked to see their saint hung in effigy to a telegraph pole with a string of potatoes about his neck. During this year the Schuylkill County press first mentioned Molly Maguires, but it was not until the Civil War that this secret organization was linked with terrorism in Pennsylvania. Although in the majority, Irish were at this time underdogs in the anthracite area. They were the laborers assigned to the English and Welsh miners; they were the doers of unskilled jobs. Even the coal patches, the small towns surrounding the mine shafts, were divided along ethnic lines. Already bruised by past prejudices, Irish miners turned to protective secret societies which had helped them fight landlordism and anti-Catholicism in Ireland. By the 1870s the Ancient Order of Hibernians (AOH), affiliated with the parent organization in Ireland, was the most powerful benevolent and immigrant-aid society in America.

The class nature of Civil War conscription measures infuriated Pennsylvania miners. At a Carbon County meeting in 1862 to plan a public Fourth of July celebration, Copperhead sentiments prevailed, and a youthful miner, John Kehoe, added action to words by spitting on the flag. When a mine foreman, F. W. Langdon, denounced the group, Kehoe reportedly flung back, "You son of a bitch, I'll kill you." Langdon, part of whose job was to determine whether coal loads had too much refuse, was unpopular with the miners. He was attacked and stoned that evening and died the next day. Violence continued to grow with the Civil War. On November 5, 1863, George K. Smith, a mine owner and operator in Carbon County who was openly sympathetic to the draft, was shot by a band of men with blackened faces who entered his home. When arrests were made for the killing, a mob released the suspects. In Schuylkill County alone, according to the *Miners' Journal,* there were fourteen unsolved murders apiece for 1863 and 1864, twelve for 1865, and six for 1866.

With peace and the organization of a miners' union, violence in the area slackened. Despite its rule prohibiting violence, the new union, the Workingmen's Benevolent Association (WBA), was associated by the public with the Molly Maguires. Actually most Schuylkill County Hibernians were also members of the WBA, but the inner circle—the real Molly Maguires—was composed primarily of tavern keepers and hangers-on who had nothing to do with the union. The WBA led by John Siney originated in Schuylkill County in 1868 and became a loosely federated, general union on March 17, 1869, though its main strength remained in Schuylkill County. Aiming for higher wages and safer working conditions, the WBA worked to control coal production and ran afoul Gowen of the Reading Railroad, who also wanted to control production.

Gowen initially tried to gain that control by mediating between the WBA and mine owners. He appeared successful until 1871 when Schuylkill miners joined Luzerne miners in suspending production. Unable to rule the WBA, Gowen moved to control production by owning mines. Knowing that the long suspension had brought many mine operators close to bankruptcy, Gowen kept them from accepting union terms by boosting freight rates. From 1871 to 1874, he purchased 100,000 acres of coal lands. He also hired Pinkerton detectives to infiltrate both the WBA and the Ancient Order of Hibernians and by 1874 resolved to smash the union. The WBA, however, was destroying itself. During its first three years it had maintained three strikes for a total of sixteen months, but by 1873 it was weakened by ethnic clashes, by differences between contract miners and wage earners, and by lack of cooperation among miners from different anthracite regions. In early 1874 the WBA lost John Siney and whole districts to a competing union, the Miners' National Association of the United States. Decimated and nearly broke, the WBA could not survive the Long Strike of 1875.

Gowen's most successful detective, James McParlan, entered the Schuylkill region as James McKenna in late October 1873. Initiated into the Hibernians by April, McParlan remained with the Molly Maguires until March 1876. He found that violent acts were seldom discussed in open lodge but were planned by an inner circle of officers. "The Bodymaster," he reported, "receives the grievance and complaint and appoints the man or men privately and secretly notifies them of what they are required to do and then the 'job' is done."

Not only did the WBA die during the Long Strike of 1875, but a rash of killings during that struggle led to the destruction of the Molly Maguires. Ironically, Gowen, having pressed no murder charges when he was district attorney in Schuylkill County from 1862 to 1864, now neglected the overextended Reading Railroad to prosecute the Molly Maguires. Twenty men were hanged in 1877 and 1878 for Molly Maguire crimes. Twelve of these men were convicted on information or testimony provided by McParlan and eight on testimony that came out of the trials in which McParlan had testified. Despite conflicting testimony over his part in murdering F. W. Langdon in 1862, John Kehoe, the "King of the Mollies," was hanged; and with his death Molly Maguirism ended.

As Harold Aurand observes:

Historians have debated whether the Mollies were hardened criminals or innocent labor leaders; many, in the heat of argument, have completely neglected the episode's true significance. The Molly Maguire investigation and trials were one of the most astounding surrenders of sovereignty in American history. A private corporation initiated the investigation through a private detective agency; a private police force arrested the alleged offenders; and coal company attorneys prosecuted them. The state provided only the courtroom and hangman. The fate of the Molly Maguires taught the people of the anthracite regions that the Coal and Iron Police were supreme within the area.

THE GREAT STRIKE

In 1877 Pittsburgh proved the anthracite region had no monopoly on violence. It was a workingmen's town in which all classes were united in hatred of the Pennsylvania Railroad. Pittsburgh felt itself the victim of this railroad—whose high rates had cost Pittsburgh its preeminence in oil refining. Freight rates from Pittsburgh to Philadelphia were identical with the 100-mile-longer run from Oil City to Philadelphia. In 1877 freight shipped on the Pennsylvania Railroad to San Francisco cost 20 percent more from Pittsburgh than from New York.

When Robert Pitcairn, superintendent of the Pennsylvania Railroad's Pittsburgh division, ordered that all eastbound through freights be doubleheaders as far as Conemaugh starting Thursday, July 19, 1877, he was asking for trouble. Although some double-engined trains had been used on this uphill run, many single-engined trains were still in use. The new order would lay off fifty or sixty conductors and brakemen, and those remaining would have to handle twice as many cars. Not only did double-engined trains mean more work, they also meant more danger from cars breaking loose and crashing. The time was inauspicious for Pitcairn's doubleheader order. Having just received their first paycheck since a 10 percent wage cut, workmen on the Pennsylvania Railroad were furious; the Trainmen's Union was active and trouble was already brewing over a salary slash on the Baltimore & Ohio. The first of the new doubleheaders left on schedule, but the flagman on the second train refused to budge and the rest of the crew joined him. When an alternate crew of yardmen was collected, other trainmen refused to let freight trains leave. "It's a question of bread or blood," one protested. Sympathizers quickly gathered. The Pittsburgh police force, which a few days before had been cut in half because of insufficient funds, was unable to disperse angry crowds.

The Trainmen's Union called a meeting that evening. Amid assurances from other Pittsburghers that "We're with you" and announcements that the work stoppage was growing both on the B & O and on the Pennsylvania, the union agreed to strike and demanded no more doubleheaders, pay restored to pre-June levels, the rehiring of dismissed trainmen, and abolishment of pay grades. The Great Strike was on.

No freight trains ran on Friday, but passenger trains with one exception left on schedule. The strikers' committee presented its demands to Superintendent Pitcairn, who discussed them with Alexander Cassatt, the vice-president of the Pennsylvania Railroad who had arrived in Pittsburgh that morning. "Have no further talk with them," Cassatt said. "They've asked for things we can't grant them at all."

When local militia called out on Friday afternoon fraternized with the crowds, Cassatt suggested Philadelphia troops. In 1846 Philadelphians had influenced the state Legislature against a B & O right of way to Pittsburgh; the memory of this injury increased hostility to the home of the Pennsylvania Railroad. When Philadelphia troops arrived on Saturday afternoon pulling two Gatling guns, the crowds grew denser. Pelted with coal and actually fired upon, the troops turned their guns on the hillside crowds, killing about twenty and wounding many more.

The troops retreated to a nearby Pennsylvania Railroad roundhouse where, hungry, tired, and frustrated, they pleaded with their officers to let them fire into the angry mob surrounding them. "We'll have them out if we have to roast them out," yelled a rioter. Strikers sent burning oil and coal cars into the roundhouse while Pittsburghers watched the glow from the hillside. Sunday morning the troops retreated from the blazing roundhouse, were attacked by rioters, fled to the arsenal and sought refuge there unsuccessfully, and finally found shelter at the Allegheny County Workhouse 12 miles from town.

With the retreat of the Philadelphia militia, looters scrambled for goods tossed from railroad cars by their cohorts. Into the crowd vanished food provisions, clothing, glassware, whiskey, coal, Bibles, and assorted volumes of *Chamber's Encyclopedia.* Fires trailed looters and moved toward the Union Depot. The depot went up in flames Sunday afternoon, as did the Adams Express Company, the Panhandle freight depot buildings, and a 150-foot-high, slate-sided grain elevator. Suddenly fearful that Pittsburgh would become another Chicago, the crowd began helping firemen fight the blaze which had also consumed 104 locomotives and 2,152 railroad cars. These were the burned-out sights that greeted United States troops who arrived from Ohio on Monday morning.

The strike, which was virtually nationwide, almost succeeded. Labor became aware of its strength but fumbled in the use of it. Local leaders were weak and soon lost control of the strike, while central organization was nonexistent. More united than strikers, management refused to discuss grievances until lawlessness and insubordination stopped. A doubleheader freight left Pittsburgh on Sunday, July 29, and trainmen complied when Pennsylvania Railroad officials asked them to report for work by the following Tuesday morning.

THE AMERICAN FEDERATION OF LABOR

While the Knights of Labor worked to reform society, national trade unions strove to improve working conditions for laborers in their own trade. "We have no ultimate ends," Adolph Strasser, president of the International Cigar Makers Union, testified in 1885. "We fight only for immediate objects—objects that can be realized in a few years." While the membership of the Knights of Labor dwindled and its program failed, trade-union membership slowly increased. "Practical" men, who were wage-conscious rather than class-conscious, had replaced the old labor movement dreamers.

A move to align skilled trade unions, made at a meeting of labor leaders in Pittsburgh in November 1881, resulted in the Federation of Organized Trade and Labor Unions, a weak and transitional organization whose treasury and records were taken over in 1886 by the American Federation of Labor (AFL). Samuel Gompers was elected the AFL's first president and devoted his full energy to it until his death thirty-eight years later. Promising "strict recognition of the autonomy of each trade," the AFL issued charters for constituent unions, settled jurisdictional disputes, and formed city centrals and state federations to promote labor legislation. Member unions paid a per capita tax which financed strikes and lockouts.

The Homestead strike   The largest and strongest trade union affiliated with the AFL was the Amalgamated Association of Iron, Steel and Tin Workers of America,whose 24,000 taxable members accounted for roughly one-tenth of the total 1891 AFL membership. The year of the Homestead strike the Amalgamated Association's total receipts were over a quarter of a million dollars, and about one-fourth of the skilled steelworkers belonged to the association. The union was stronger in mills where ironworks had been converted to steel than in works originally built as steel mills. Of the three Carnegie plants built as steelworks, only the one at Homestead, a typically drab, saloon-filled industrial town 10 miles east of Pittsburgh on the left bank of the Monongahela River, was controlled by the Amalgamated Association. The plant, employing about 4,000 workers, operated continuously with two 12-hour, seven-day shifts, and monthly produced 25,000 tons of steel. Wages ranged from 14 cents an hour for the humblest laborers (usually recent immigrants) to $14 a day for a few highly skilled workers (usually native Americans), with skilled workers generally working fewer than the standard 84 hours a week. Skilled and unionized workers despised unskilled laborers who, in turn, hated them, while ethnic differences reinforced divisions in the labor force.

On June 30, 1892, the Amalgamated Association's three-year contract covering the Homestead plant and affecting 325 workers would expire. Two months before that date and shortly before he departed for his annual six-month stay in Scotland, Andrew Carnegie drafted a notice to Homestead workers and submitted it to Henry Clay Frick, manager of the plant and chairman of the Carnegie firm. "As the vast majority of our employees are Non-Union," Carnegie wrote, "the firm has decided that the minority must give way to the majority. These works will necessarily be Non-Union after the expiration of the present agreement."

Although Frick, who had broken the Connellsville coal strike in 1890, was no friend of labor, he thought Carnegie's antiunion notice premature. Frick insisted, however, that if the Amalgamated did not accept his terms by June 24, its members would be dealt with as individuals; and he also prepared for trouble. He enclosed the plant with a 3-mile-long board fence with barbed-wire topping and regularly spaced 3-inch holes, and requested Pinkerton guards should a strike materialize. These arrangements were complete when he conferred with labor leaders on June 23. The three issues discussed were the minimum steel price on which the sliding wage scale would be based, the terminating date of the new contract, and tonnage rates. Although Frick wanted the sliding-scale minimum reduced from $25 to $22 a ton, he increased his figure to $23 during the negotiations, and the union lowered its figure to $24. Frick, however, was determined to change the contract's termination date to December 31, while the union, fearful of winter strikes, held out for June 30—the date that had been in effect for twelve years.

When the June 23 conference ended in a stalemate, the union expected negotiations to continue, but Frick was through. Two days later he arranged with Pinkerton's National Detective Agency for 300 armed guards to arrive on July 6 when he planned to reopen the works. On June 28 he shut down the armor-plate mill and the open-hearth department, locking out 800 workers. Effigies of Frick and John A. Potter, the plant superintendent, were hanged that night, and the next morning Homestead laborers, both native and foreign-born, answered the lockout with a strike. By July 2, when strikers were paid off and discharged, union recognition and collective bargaining had become the real issues.

Aware of laborers' loathing for Pinkertons, Frick arranged for his guards to arrive in the early-morning darkness of July 6. Near Pittsburgh they and their Winchester rifles were loaded on two barges for the trip up the Monongahela River. News of the barges reached Homestead before the Pinkertons. They were greeted by a mob which fought two landing attempts. During these two encounters three Pinkertons and seven people in the crowd were killed and many were wounded. Both times after the firing the crowd dispersed to seek shelter and to care for the dead and the wounded; both times the Pinkertons refused to land protesting that they had not been hired to fight and that "they would be damned if they would fight." At four P.M. the Pinkertons surrendered with the understanding that they would receive safe conduct through Homestead. But the mob would not adhere to the agreement. As the unarmed Pinkertons marched through the streets, men, women, and children robbed and assaulted them until nearly half of them suffered injuries.

Despite the suffering of the Pinkertons, public opinion condemned Frick's actions. A Boston minister exulted, "Workmen have met and defeated the . . . hirelings of capital, and for their victory we need to thank God." On July 7 in the nation's Capitol senator after senator condemned the use of armed Pinkertons. Governor Robert E. Pattison rebuked the Allegheny County sheriff for not accepting the union Advisory Committee's offer to guard the plant. Late on July 10, convinced that intervention was necessary, Pattison called out the entire militia. In 12 hours 8,000 men marched on Homestead. On July 15 the plant furnaces were lit, but strikebreakers could not make steel without skilled workers. Sympathetic strikes occurred at other Carnegie plants. Even the nonunion mill at Duquesne struck for a week, while the Beaver Falls mill struck for four months.

On July 23 Alexander Berkman, a revolutionary anarchist who had been active in New York, overpowered Frick in his office, shot him twice, and stabbed him repeatedly with a file. Although Frick lived and the Advisory Committee condemned Berkman's act, the assault brought Frick a measure of public sympathy and stiffened his opposition to the union. One week later he declared, "If it takes all summer and all winter, and all next summer and all next winter, . . . I will fight this thing to the bitter end. I will never recognize the union, never, never!"

It took all summer and most of the fall. Homestead workers continued their remarkable display of solidarity. Despite the management's invitation to sign individual contracts, only about 300 strikers had returned to work after two months. Although it was apparent by mid-October that the strike had been lost, the Amalgamated did not declare the mill open until November 20. The showdown had cost three-fifths of the strikers their jobs, and workers had lost about $1,250,000 in wages. In two years membership in the Amalgamated Association fell to less than half its prestrike strength. The Carnegie firm continued its war on organized labor; union membership became grounds for dismissal, wage scales were kept secret, and grievance procedures and extra pay for Sunday work disappeared.

The strike was lost and the cause of labor, especially in the Pittsburgh area, was set back for years; yet, despite the defeat and Berkman's act, certain gains were made. The solidarity displayed heartened the friends of labor and distressed its enemies. The AFL, whose total 1892 receipts were less than $16,000, raised over $11,000 for the relief and legal aid of the strikers; the Knights of Labor, though warring with the AFL, printed circulars and held picnics to aid the people of Homestead, and Pittsburgh merchants helped sustain strikers with money, food, and clothing. The *Nation,* complaining that "the rioters at Homestead" were objects of sympathy, declared that in no previous large-scale industrial conflict had the workers received so much support from "the classes socially above them." The use of Pinkertons had robbed Carnegie and Frick of would-be sympathizers. For the first time Protestant opinion significantly divided in an important labor dispute. Also for the first time it was argued in the United States Senate (by John M. Palmer of Illinois) "that society could properly limit the employer's freedom of action" and that "the organization of labor" should be promoted "as we have heretofore encouraged the organization of capital."

The anthracite strike "Several times I have been asked," wrote Samuel Gompers, "what in my opinion was the most important single incident in the labor movement of the United States and I have invariably replied: the strike of the anthracite miners in Pennsylvania." In 1899 the United Mine Workers (UMW) earnestly turned to the anthracite area because organized bituminous miners realized the importance of a united coal front for future bargaining. The chief organizer was John Mitchell, who had become president of the UMW the year before at the age of twenty-eight.

Even though the entire anthracite industry was concentrated in 500 square miles, organization was difficult. The memory of the futility of the Long Strike of 1875 was vivid. Anthracite lands were largely owned and controlled by coal-carrying railroads, which were dominated either by J. P. Morgan or by the Vanderbilt combination. Divided into nearly twenty cultural groups, miners of the area had only despair in common. Many of the non-English-speaking, unskilled miners had come as strikebreakers in 1875 and 1887 and were still despised as scabs by skilled workers, who almost invariably were English, Welsh, Scottish, or Irish. The "foreigners" in turn hated skilled miners almost as much as they hated operators.

Quickly designating leaders to organize skilled workers, Mitchell turned to developing leaders among foreign-born, unskilled miners. To them this serious young man, "dressed in the long miner's coat worn by the westerners, and buttoned up to a straight clerical collar" seemed like a priest. After selecting and training men in each ethnic group who knew both their ethnic group and the meaning of unionism, Mitchell placed them on a par with English-speaking organizers. Miners of all groups and languages thronged to hear Mitchell, and as he talked with them he used coal as the great leveler. "The coal you dig," he insisted, "isn't Slavish or Polish or Irish coal, it's coal."

Mitchell realized that the miners needed allies as well as hope. He pleaded the cause of unionism not only with foreign-language editors but with clergymen and priests in the area; and he pleaded with tradesmen, arguing that general prosperity depended upon miners receiving an adequate wage and carefully pointing out that he was not asking for favors but for justice. Miners in the area had received no increase for twenty years and worked fewer than 200 days a year.

When the UMW asked for a pay increase in 1900, operators ignored it. The union then called out its 10,000 members in the anthracite area, and 100,000 miners responded. Operators prepared to bring in strikebreakers, but the second McKinley-Bryan presidential campaign was in full swing and Republicans did not want a long coal strike to interrupt their proclamations of prosperity. Marcus Alonzo Hanna, McKinley's strongest backer and a power in the industrial peacemaking National Civic Federation, appealed to operators for a settlement and then went over their heads and arranged for J. P. Morgan to meet with Mitchell. Pressured operators grudgingly gave the miners a 10 percent wage boost but refused to recognize the union.

In 1902 the UMW made further demands. Miners' yearly earnings averaged less than $300; 441 men and boys had been killed in mining accidents the previous year; and paternalism was rife. When operators ignored miners' grievances, a strike was called on May 9, 1902, with 150,000 miners responding. Calling the strike an uprising against property rights and public order, operators brought in 3,000 coal and iron police and deputized 1,000 other individuals. Expecting violence, the public witnessed what was probably the most orderly strike the coalfields had experienced. John Mitchell was against radicalism and violence, and anthracite miners were content to do things his way. Mitchell remained moderate in his statements and constantly expressed a willingness to accept arbitration. He pointed out in a Philadelphia speech:

> The present miner has had his day. He has been oppressed and ground down; but there is another generation coming up, a generation of little children prematurely doomed to the whirl of the mill and the noise and the blackness of the breaker. It is for these children that we are fighting. We have not underestimated the strength of our opponents; we have not overestimated our own power of resistance. Accustomed always to live upon a little, a little less is no unendurable hardship.

Mitchell's foil was George F. Baer, president of the Philadelphia & Reading Railroad and spokesman for the operators. When a local citizen appealed to him to end the strike, Baer's reply shocked the country. "I beg of you not to be discouraged," he wrote. "The rights and interests of the laboring man will be protected and cared for—not by the labor agitators, but by the Christian men to whom God has given control of the property rights of the country. . . ."

With winter approaching and the price of coal climbing, Theodore Roosevelt, who had been made President by McKinley's assassination, requested a meeting with Mitchell and the operators on September 29. While Mitchell impressed the President with his quiet dignity and willingness to arbitrate, Baer lectured Roosevelt for wasting time "negotiating with the fomenters of this anarchy" and angered him so that he wished to take Baer "by the seat of the breeches and the nape of the neck" and chuck him out the window.

Even when 10,000 state militia arrived to protect strikebreakers, miners refused to go back to work. The generous contributions of the bituminous districts, other trade unions, and the general public enabled Mitchell to announce that they had money enough to strike all winter. Indeed, a few months after the strike ended, over a million dollars remained in the treasury. Strikers could go without pay longer than people could go without hard coal. The public grew more impatient. Roosevelt informed Morgan that if the operators would not arbitrate he would order the army to dispossess them and run the mines as a receiver. Under this pressure, operators agreed to arbitrate. Miners returned to work on October 23, ending their more than five-month strike.

Mitchell and the union carefully gathered witnesses to testify before the arbitration commission. Chief of the miners' lawyers was Clarence Darrow, who eight years before had defended Eugene Debs in the Pullman Strike and twenty-two years later would defend evolution in the famous "monkey trial." Skilled miners, laborers, breaker boys, and miners' widows who had not been compensated for their husbands' deaths all passed in procession. Andrew Chippie, a twelve-year-old boy, testified that his 40 cents a day earnings were not given him but were applied to the debt left by his father who had been killed in a mine accident four years before. Members of the commission had seen and heard enough; they announced their award on March 23, 1903. Anthracite miners were granted a 10 percent wage increase, their working day was reduced to 8 or 9 hours depending on their class of work, discrimination against union members was prohibited, and the Anthracite Board of Conciliation was established to settle disputes during the three years of the agreement. The board has continued to arbitrate labor-management grievances, and through the years has been remarkably successful in reducing tensions.

A statue of John Mitchell still stands in Scranton; on its marble base is written "Champion of Labor—Defender of Human Rights."

BIBLIOGRAPHY

For immigration statistics, consult the appropriate census. U.S. Bureau of the Census: *Thirteenth Census of the United States, 1920: Population,* vol. 3, pp. 883–886, is very useful for determining where ethnic groups settled. Two excellent sources are Industrial Commission: *Reports . . . on Immigration . . . and on Education . . .* (1901), vol. 15; and Immigrant Commission, *Immigrants in Industries,* 61st Cong., 2d Sess., 1910, S. Doc. 633. See also Sarah Florence Elliott: "Immigration to Pennsylvania, 1860–1920" (master's thesis, Pennsylvania State University, 1923); Oscar Handlin: *The Uprooted: The Epic Story of the Great Migrations That Made the American People* (1951), and "Immigration in American Life: A Reappraisal," in Henry Steele Commager (ed.), *Immigration and American History: Essays in Honor of Theodore C. Blegen* (1961).

Two histories of labor are particularly useful: Foster Rhea Dulles: *Labor in America: A History* (1949); and Joseph G. Rayback: *A History of American Labor* (1959). On laboring conditions, see in particular vols. 7 and 14 of the work by the Industrial Commission cited above; the four-volume report of the Senate Committee on Education and Labor: *The Relations between Labor and Capital . . .* (1885); Henry George: "Labor in Pennsylvania," *North American Review,* vol. 143 (1886), 165–182, 268–277, 360–370; vol. 144 (1887), pp. 86–95; and Herbert G. Gutman: "The Worker's Search for Power: Labor in the Gilded Age," in H. Wayne Morgan (ed.), *The Gilded Age: A Reappraisal* (1963), pp. 38–68. For details on Sylvis and the National Labor Union, see Jonathan Grossman: *William Sylvis, Pioneer of American Labor: A Study of the Labor Movement during the Civil War* (1945). On the Mollies, see the well-written and thoroughly researched Wayne G. Broehl, Jr.: *The Molly Maguires* (1964). On the WBA and the plight of the anthracite miner, see Harold W. Aurand: "The Workingmen's Benevolent Association," *Labor History,* vol. 7 (1966), pp. 19–34, and *From the Molly Maguires to the United Mine Workers: The Social Ecology of an Industrial Union, 1869–1897* (1971). Information about the most important Knight of Labor may be found in Terence V. Powderly: *The Path I Trod* (1940), edited by Harry J. Carman, Henry David, and Paul N. Guthrie; the best source on the Great Strike is Robert V. Bruce: *1877: Year of Violence* (1959). Alfred P. James covers in detail "The First Convention of the American Federation of Labor, Pittsburgh, Pennsylvania, November 15th–18th, 1881," *Western Pennsylvania Historical Magazine,* vol. 6 (1923), pp. 201–233; vol. 7 (1924), pp. 29–56. On the AFL in general, see Samuel Gompers: *Seventy Years of Life and Labor: An Autobiography,* 2 vols. (1925). Valuable testimony on the Homestead strike may be found in U.S. Congress: *Employment of Pinkerton Detectives: Labor Troubles at Homestead, Pa.,* 52nd Cong., 2d Sess., H. Rep. 2447; and an excellent concise discussion is Henry David: "Upheaval at Homestead," in Daniel Aaron (ed.), *America in Crisis: Fourteen Crucial Episodes in American History* (1952). A fuller treatment may be found in Leon Wolff: *Lockout: The Story of the Homestead Strike of 1892: A Study of Violence, Unions, and the Carnegie Steel Empire* (1965). For a discussion of Pinkertons, see J. Bernard Hogg: "Public Reaction to Pinkertonism and the Labor Quuestion," *Pennsylvania History,* vol. 11 (1944), pp. 171–199. On the legendary John Mitchell, see Elsie Glück: *John Mitchell, Miner: Labor's Bargain with the Gilded Age* (1929).

CHAPTER TWENTY

From Farm to City

With a romantic tendency to emphasize rural rather than urban roots, Americans forget that their cities are older than their farms. Philadelphia, Lancaster, Wilkes-Barre, Harrisburg, and Pittsburgh were all bases from which first traders and then agriculturalists subdued the surrounding countryside. From the beginning these cities were centers of political, economic, social, and cultural life. Nevertheless with agriculture a vital industry, Pennsylvania remained overwhelmingly rural throughout most of the nineteenth century. The industrial takeoff beginning about 1840, however, was accompanied by an urban upsurge in Pennsylvania converting it into a predominantly urban state by the mid-1890s.

DIVERSIFIED FARMING

Good transportation plus varied topography, soil, and climate made Pennsylvania agriculture more diversified and consequently more stable than that of states where farms yielded a limited number of crops. Agricultural production in Pennsylvania grew steadily. Until 1879 increased production resulted from increased acreage. In 1880 Pennsylvania had 213,542 farms averaging 93 acres and totaling 19,791,341 acres (of which 13,423,007 acres were of improved land). After this date fewer acres were cultivated, but better farming methods continued to increase Pennsylvania's productivity. Diversified farming meant less stress on grains such as wheat and corn, which had long been the staples of Pennsylvania agriculture, and more stress on dairy farming, poultry husbandry, livestock raising, truck gardening, and fruit growing. The most significant step toward diversification and the most important agricultural development in late-nineteenth-century Pennsylvania was the rise of the dairy industry.

The rapid development of Pennsylvania dairy farming after 1870 was made possible by state disease-control programs. The eradication of bovine tuberculosis serves as an example. Tuberculosis among dairy cattle in Pennsylvania became a serious problem about 1880. An effective control program was undertaken in 1896 when Leonard Pearson, professor of veterinary medicine at the University of Pennsylvania, was appointed state veterinarian. Pearson had studied with Robert Koch, the noted German bacteriologist, and in 1892 was the first veterinarian in the United States to use tuberculin as a diagnostic agent on an entire herd. Out of seventy-nine registered Jersey cattle tested in Villanova, fifty-one cows reacted. When their owner consented to their slaughter to prove the reliability of the test, disease was found in every animal.

Pearson condemned the bank barn as conducive to bovine tuberculosis. "The most cheerless place on many a farm," he said, "is the basement of the old barn—dark, damp and forbidding. The place is so dark that patches of manure on the udders, flanks, hips and sides (of the cows) are rarely seen." This type of barn, the most common in eastern Pennsylvania, was built into a bank with an overhang on the south side and was introduced by early German and Swiss settlers. Pearson's attack on bank barns did not endear him to Pennsylvania farmers.

The long and arduous fight against bovine tuberculosis was matched by that against milk adulteration. In 1896 the Pennsylvania Department of Agriculture found milk adulterated by adding water "more or less at every change of ownership," by skimming off the cream, by adding skimmed milk, and by adding powdered chalk or flour to watered milk. To prevent souring, milk dealers frequently added preservatives, such as formaldehyde or boric acid. The fight against adulterated milk, however, would not be won until the 1930s.

The production of other commodities usually duplicates patterns found in the dairy industry. The vicissitudes of Pennsylvania fruit growers, for example, not only demonstrate that increased quantity and improved quality resulted from organization, mechanization, government aid, and regulation, but also reflect—or even magnify—the ups and downs of all Pennsylvania farmers.

The golden era of fruit growing in Pennsylvania started about 1845, lasted until 1872, and matched a period of general agricultural prosperity. Although the heaviest planting was apples, pears also did well in Pennsylvania. In 1870 Tobias Martin, a noted pear grower in Mercersburg, got $1 to $1.50 a dozen for extra-fine Bartletts and $4 a bushel for first-grade fruit. But the first transcontinental railroad, the Union Pacific, had been completed the previous year, and in 1873 Martin accurately predicted "that California was going to knock our pear market all to smash." What was left of the fruit market after competing with well-organized Western producers was glutted by overproduction. A Berks County apple grower lamented in 1881 that "it scarcely paid to haul them from the orchard . . . to the cider-mills, . . . where six cents per bushel was all that was paid." In 1887 the State Horticultural Association concluded, "Fruit grown in Pennsylvania is not now a profitable business," and in the particularly disastrous year of 1891 apple prices were so low that hundreds of thousands of bushels rotted on the ground.

Hard times were nearly universal for Pennsylvania farmers from 1873 until about 1896. A farmer's income depended not only upon soil fertility, rainfall, hard work, and skill but also on the demand for his produce, the competition both from his neighbors and from farmers thousands of miles away, the interest paid his banker for loans to buy land and machinery, the freight rates paid railroads for transporting crops, and the middleman's fee for handling produce. Commencing with the failure of the Philadelphia banking house of Jay Cooke & Co., the Panic of 1873 plunged the nation into a long and serious depression. Overexpansion of railroads, manufactures, and agriculture had caused the depression; and overexpanded farmers who had contracted large debts at high rates of interest were seriously hit. In the 1880s with the continual expansion of agriculture in the West, many Pennsylvanians (particularly young ones) abandoned their farms and moved either to the West or to the city.

Although "no" was the inevitable answer to the perennial question, "Does farming pay?" it did pay for most farmers. "Notwithstanding this depression," the secretary of the State Board of Agriculture reported in 1890, "we find in every community farmers who are quietly making money." Pennsylvanians, particularly those close to cities, generally earned more money when they grew less wheat and corn, and concentrated more on perishables, such as milk, vegetables, and fruit. After 1891, agricultural conditions improved even during the depression following the Panic of 1893.

Although Western competition hurt fruit growers, they were able to survive. Developments in the 1880s and 1890s improved their position and enabled them to enter the twentieth century in a prosperous condition. Insoluble technical problems became soluble after the organization of the State Agricultural Experiment Station in 1887. That same year brought refrigerator railroad cars and with them more profitable long-distance fruit transportation. In 1890 sprays were introduced to kill multiplying fruit insects, and the last years of the nineteenth century brought the general use of cold storage and commercial canning. The agricultural depression ended and farming prosperity began in 1897.

THE EDUCATION OF THE PENNSYLVANIA FARMER

The most salient characteristic of Pennsylvania agriculture since 1879 has been the declining amount of farmland coupled with increased overall production. Ingenious mechanical advances in the nineteenth century helped increase production. In 1877 James Oliver patented the first successful chilled-iron plow, "which brought complete turning of the soil to perfection." With the introduction of the twine knotter in the late 1870s, the self-binder for wheat and other small grains achieved real efficiency. The lister, which both made a furrow and planted corn in it, appeared about 1880, and improvements were made on harrows, seed broadcasters, and drills. By 1890 a combined rake, carrier, and loader was developed which could load a ton of hay in five minutes. An hour's labor in the best-managed wheat fields of 1896 equalled 18 hours in 1830.

Into the twentieth century, animal power propelled plows and more elaborate machinery. In the decade following the Civil War, oxen predominated on Pennsylvania farms. "All the theory is in favour of the ox," it was said. "He costs little, works hard, eats little, and when we have done with him he is worth more than when we began—whereas a horse costs much, eats much, and when he dies is worth comparatively nothing. . . ." In the next decade, however, the slow-moving ox fell out of favor. Improved roads, cleared fields, and more farm machinery made the faster horse of prime importance on Pennsylvania farms for the next half century. In 1910 horses were Pennsylvania's most valuable livestock; they were appraised at $68,055,000 while cattle were valued at $47,229,000.

The tractor ultimately replaced the horse during and after World War I. In 1853 Joseph W. Fawkes, a mechanic of Lancaster County, invented the first steam plow to achieve popular acclaim. Fawkes's steam plow and its early competitors were "cumbersome monsters" weighing from 6 to 8 tons, requiring coal and a crew of two to four men, and costing between $10,000 and $15,000. Despite these disadvantages a number were used in the wheat fields of the prairie states and in California, and over a 20-year period in the late nineteenth century Pennsylvanians annually manufactured at least 1,800 steam tractors. It was not until the twentieth century that lighter gasoline tractors proved more practical than steam tractors on the rough-contoured and modest-sized farms of Pennsylvania.

Machinery enabled farmers to cultivate more acres, but the increase in yield per unit resulted primarily from advances in agricultural science. The nineteenth century witnessed great strides in the science of agriculture, but its greatest utilization has been in the twentieth century. Farmers have adopted new machines more readily than new ideas. Their education has been a slow process. Though they have been society's leading individualists, farmers paradoxically have been deeply indebted to state and Federal scientists and to governmental aid for their gains since the late nineteenth century.

Pressure from the Pennsylvania State Agricultural Society (formed in 1851) led the state Legislature to appropriate $10,000 in 1855 to establish the Farmers' High School, which eventually evolved into Pennsylvania State University. In 1862 the institution's name was changed to Agricultural College of Pennsylvania, and it received additional support that same year from the Federal Morrill Land Grant Act for the establishment of state agricultural and mechanical colleges. Pennsylvania received 780,000 acres in the West from this act (30,000 acres for each congressmen and senator) but sold the land hurriedly for only $438,186. Three experimental farms were purchased with $43,866 of this money and the remainder was invested in an endowment fund. In 1887 the Federal government established the Agricultural Experiment Station at the college and an era of good feeling between farmers and the college began.

Pennsylvania farmers have also profited from the work of scientists employed by the United States Department of Agriculture, the Pennsylvania Department of Agriculture, and other universities. Congress created the Department of Agriculture in 1862, but it was not until the 1880s that it made extensive contributions. In 1895 Pennsylvania established its own Department of Agriculture. Reorganized in 1919, it has served farmers by increasing production and has aided consumers by maintaining high-quality farm products and processed foods.

Governmental support is in proportion to a group's political power, and farmers have had power in Pennsylvania. Rural representatives have influenced the Legislature, and its hesitation to reapportion seats to reflect urban growth has made the farmer's vote more valuable than the city dweller's. Farmers have concentrated their efforts and made their desires more explicit through their main organization, the Grange.

Oliver Hudson Kelley, founder of the National Grange, was a clerk in the newly established Federal Agricultural Bureau at the close of the Civil War. A tour through the South convinced him that a secret, fraternal organization would help boost Southern farmers' morale, restore harmony, and promote prosperity among farmers. Joined by others, Kelley on December 4, 1867, established the National Grange of the Patrons of Husbandry. In April he purchased a ticket to Harrisburg and with $2.50 in his pocket embarked on an organizing trip. At Harrisburg he secured $15 to continue his journey but was unable to organize a subordinate grange. "It is useless," he despaired, "to try to save the American farmer, because he will do nothing to save himself." Buoyed by his wife's faith in the Grange idea and by her contribution of a small personal legacy for expenses, Kelley continued his organizational work. Pennsylvania's first local Grange was organized on March 4, 1871, at Montgomery in Lycoming County; the Pennsylvania State Grange was established at Reading on September 18,1873. Pennsylvania has consistently been a strong granger state, with more members concentrated in northern counties than in other sections of the state. Among other things, the Pennsylvania Grange sponsored lectures, called for higher state appropriations for public schools (but opposed centralizing control of the school system at Harrisburg), crusaded for better roads, worked for timber and water conservation, raised $100,000 for a girls' dormitory (Grange Hall) at Penn State, and actively supported the Hatch Act (1887) establishing agricultural Experiment Stations.

COUNTRY LIFE AND TOWN LIFE

Though we would like to think of the nineteenth-century farm as a lost Eden, it was far from paradise. The farmer, his wife, and his children worked long, hard hours; lacked the conveniences of urban housing; and suffered from isolation, inadequate medical facilities, and inferior schools. Many of the beautiful brick and limestone Pennsylvania farmhouses that we admire today were built between 1860 and 1873 when agriculture was especially prosperous. Although these farmhouses generally possessed museumlike parlors reserved for Sunday and company use, the kitchens, where for all practical purposes the families lived, had few conveniences and plumbing was nonexistent. It has been estimated that the average 1870 farm woman lifted in the course of her daily chores a ton of water. Added to the household tasks of farm women was dairying, which was frequently considered women's work. "The 'Pennsylvania Dutchman,' whatever his virtues may be," it was observed in 1901, "has a terrible aversion to milking a cow. He looks upon it as a disgrace to his manhood, and all the milking done in this section of Pennsylvania [around York] for many years was done by the female portion of the family."

Despite the purer air, outside work, and open spaces, country people were not as healthy as city people. Before 1880 sick rural people usually were treated with tonics of sulphur and molasses and concoctions of wild cherry bark. If the sickness persisted, elaborate rituals, dating back to the Middle Ages, would frequently be prescribed to remove the hex causing the sickness. Little was known about sanitary measures, and home cures and conjures failed to halt infant mortality and diseases fostered by contaminated water. In the last two decades of the nineteenth century, rural people became dependent upon the country doctor, only to have him begin disappearing with the new century.

Better roads not only made better-trained doctors and better-equipped hospitals more accessible to country people but also led to consolidated and improved schools. Not until 1874 were public schools provided for all school-aged children in Pennsylvania, and free textbooks were not authorized until 1893. In 1895 state aid for public high schools was added, and school attendance was made obligatory for children between eight and thirteen. Two years later transportation was provided for rural students. In 1915 Pennsylvania had 10,606 one-room rural schoolhouses and 886 of these had fewer than eleven pupils. Although Pennsylvania had begun consolidating its elementary schools in 1892 (schools in Linesville, Crawford County, and Russell, Warren County, were consolidated that year), change was slow. By 1900 there were only eight consolidated schools in the state. Although transportation was to be provided for pupils living more than a mile and a half from schools, farmers, valuing home rule in school administration more than improved education through consolidation, clung to the little red schoolhouse.

The drudgery of nineteenth-century farm life was relieved by Saturday night in town, Sunday morning in church, and the agricultural fair. Preparations for the fair were many, as a contemporary describes them:

> The calendar was . . . built around fair week. . . . For thirty days before the great event, work was planned to have the wheat sowed, the corn shocked, the Sunday vehicles washed, . . . the harness blacked and nothing left in the way of an early-morning . . . start to the fair to get the buggy or surrey or spring wagon located in the "first row" so the women folks when tired out could sit and watch the endless crowd that milled around. . . . More than one farm wagon, bedded with timothy or fresh straw and carrying a cargo of wide-eyed family and home-grown food, rolled out of the barnyard soon after midnight and rumbled into the fair ground at break of day. . . .

Agricultural fairs were held almost yearly in various counties starting in 1851. By 1870 they had taken on an amusement-park atmosphere with farmers leaving "stock pens and agricultural halls nearly empty" in their eagerness to bet on horse races and gawk at lurid sideshows.

An occasional sideshow or horse race, however, simply did not compare with the recreational opportunities afforded by cities. Whether native or foreign-born, Americans preferred city to country life for economic, social, and cultural reasons. The city offered a greater variety of better-paying jobs, making it possible for the laborer to double his income by moving to the city. Around 1900 agricultural laborers averaged about $215 yearly while those engaged in manufacturing and mechanical industries averaged $445. Frederick Law Olmsted, a pioneer urban landscape architect, observed in 1871 that women were even more eager to leave the farm than men.

Cultural advantages were greater in the city with its superior school system and its libraries, museums, and concert halls. Philadelphia boasted beautiful churches and talented clergymen; Fairmount Park (the largest park within any American city) with its blend of woods, fields, water, and statuary and the oldest zoo in the United States, and also one of the best; the Academy of Music; the Library of the American Philosophical Society; the Free Library Company; the Pennsylvania Academy of Fine Arts; Memorial Hall in Fairmount Park (long an art museum); the University of Pennsylvania; the national shrine of Independence Hall; the imposing City Hall; and many examples of fascinating architecture.

Though during the late nineteenth and early twentieth centuries relatively few migrants to the city were attracted by books, artifacts, and music, many were attracted by other recreational opportunities. Melodrama and slapstick comedy were available for a dime in urban theaters, and after the nation's first modern movie theater opened in Pittsburgh in 1905, capacity crowds jammed the nickelodeons. Professional baseball could be enjoyed in Philadelphia and Pittsburgh, as well as in other Pennsylvania towns. People were also attracted to cities by department stores and shops with intriguing display windows. The bustle of city streets was an attraction, as were saloons. With one saloon for every 870 persons, Philadelphia lagged behind neighboring New York and Baltimore, which had one for every 200 and 229 persons, respectively. Brothels and gambling dens were more dubious resorts, but they, too, added to the fascination of urban life. Rural boys and girls, hoping to escape dull lives,

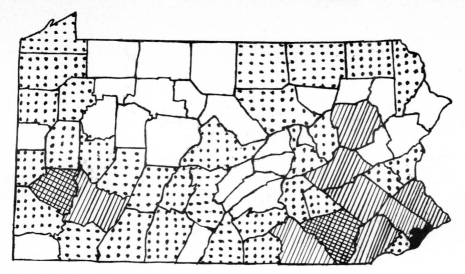

Population by county, 1860.

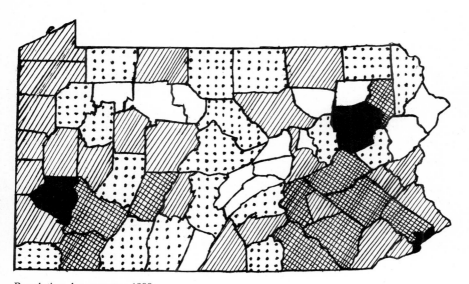

Population by county, 1900.

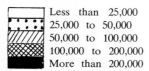

Less than 25,000
25,000 to 50,000
50,000 to 100,000
100,000 to 200,000
More than 200,000

fled to the city and thought its opportunities for recreation and companionship worth the long hours of labor at bench and sewing machine. Finally, the city with its hospitals, dispensaries, organized charities, and settlement houses offered more services for the poor than did the country.

URBAN BUSINESS

Industrial development and urban growth proceeded side by side and reinforced each other. The coming of the railroad and the rise of the coal, iron, steel, oil, and lumber industries all contributed to the urbanization of Pennsylvania. In general, rail transportation made possible the feeding, clothing, sheltering, and employing of large numbers of people in one location. Indeed, dependence upon transportation facilities for access to raw materials and markets encouraged factories to cluster in towns and cities, particularly at junctions of competing rail lines. Specifically, the growth and prosperity of Altoona were largely dependent upon the carshops maintained there by the Pennsylvania Railroad. Anthracite mining was largely responsible for the urbanization of the Scranton and Wilkes-Barre area as well as for that of Hazleton, Pottsville, and a number of other mining communities, while greater Pittsburgh, Johnstown, and other towns developed because of bituminous coal, iron, and steel production. The oil industry produced Oil City, and lumbering contributed greatly to the growth of Williamsport.

Spectacular industries—wresting and processing raw materials from the earth—have overshadowed industries that convert the coal, iron, steel, oil, lumber, fiber, and grain into finished products. The growth of these manufactures, however, has been important to the national economy and to the growth of Pennsylvania cities. The number of Pennsylvania wage earners employed in manufacturing—including iron and steel—multiplied five times from 1850 to 1900 (growing from 147,000 to 734,000), while total earnings multiplied nine times during the same years. Eighty percent of these wage earners were employed in urban industries by 1900. Manufacturers' growing demand for labor and a rising scale of wages—almost doubling from 1850 to 1900—ensured rapid urban growth.

Cities specialized in certain manufactures. Philadelphia, the state's leading manufacturing city, in 1900 specialized in foundry and machine-shop products, sugar and petroleum refining, and in the manufacture of carpets and men's clothing, while Pittsburgh specialized in manufacturing iron and steel, foundry and machine-shop products, electrical apparatus, railroad cars, and glass, as well as pickles and sauces and meat packing. Among smaller cities, Erie made foundry and machine-shop products, paper, planing-mill products, flour, and malt liquors; Lancaster manufactured umbrellas and canes, tobacco, confectionery, cottons, and iron and steel; Williamsport produced lumber products, rubber boots and shoes, silks, men's clothing, and leather; while Wilkes-Barre manufactured silks, cottons, foundry and machine-shop products, malt liquors, and wire.

Pennsylvania's leading urban manufacture in 1900 was iron and steel; textiles ranked second in Pennsylvania, and Pennsylvania also ranked second in the nation in textiles. The late-nineteenth-century trend in textiles away from hand looms and household manufactures toward power machinery housed in factories increased urbanization. Philadelphia was the country's greatest textile center, and silk, in which Pennsylvania ranked second in national production, was the state's most valuable textile, with production centers at Philadelphia,

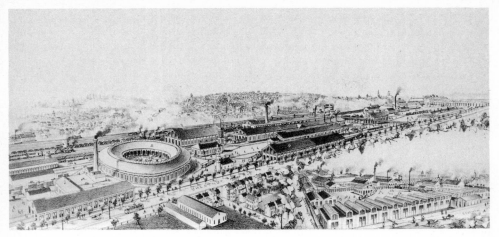

Print by T. M. Fowler, *Penn'a R. R. Car Shop's, Altoona Pennsylvania, 1895.* (Historical Society of Pennsylvania)

Scranton, Allentown, and Easton. Silk manufacturing had grown steadily during the last decades of the nineteenth century, and it concentrated on threads to be woven into cloth outside the state. Cotton was almost as important to the Pennsylvania textile industry as silk. Pennsylvania cotton production ranked sixth in the nation by 1880, and fifth by 1900, with Philadelphia cotton manufacturers originating and perfecting decorative cotton fabrics such as tapestries and chenille curtains. Pennsylvania's woolen manufactures, which in 1900 ranked second in the nation, were virtually confined to Philadelphia. In 1860 Philadelphia turned out large quantities of all-wool and mixed cassimeres, satinets, Kentucky jeans, twills, tweeds, and flannels for sale in the West, and by 1900 it was renowned for women's dress goods novelties. Pennsylvania ranked first in carpet production both in 1870 and in 1900, when it produced almost half the nation's carpets. The Pennsylvania carpet industry in 1900 was almost entirely confined to Philadelphia. Until the Murkland power loom was introduced in 1868, Philadelphia could not compete successfully with wily New England manufacturers, who refused to share the design of their power looms that successfully wove ingrain carpets. The Murkland machine coupled with the importation of some "remarkably beautiful specimens" from England in the 1880s helped Philadelphians become preeminent in both the weave and the design of ingrain carpets. Philadelphia was also the center for the production of Pennsylvania worsteds as well as hosiery and knit goods. Pennsylvania was the second state in worsteds in 1870 and the third in 1900, while after 1870 it was second in the production of knit goods and hosiery. The worsted industry became important about 1860 with the introduction of power-combing machinery, particularly the noble comb from England utilizing short fine wools for worsted yarns. Numerous knitting machines were invented in Philadelphia and many large knitting plants were located there, but a large number of household manufacturers utilizing hand frames persisted as late as 1900.

Scarcely less important than textiles to Pennsylvania and its urban development was the growth of the foundry and machine-shop industry. Pennsylvania manufactured (primarily in Philadelphia and Pittsburgh) half the nation's steam locomotives built in 1900 and was second in production of metalworking and pumping machinery. Pennsylvania produced an incredible variety of iron and steel items ranging from hollow ware to bridges.

Other industries, ranked in the order of their importance in 1900, contributed to the growth of Pennsylvania cities. Pennsylvania led the nation in tanning leather. Although much of the industry—utilizing hemlock bark—centered in Tioga, Elk, Potter, and Clearfield Counties, Philadelphia was a major center of leather production. Railroad shopwork and car construction were carried on in Reading, Philadelphia, Pittsburgh, and Berwick as well as in Altoona. Though western competition caused flour milling to decline, the printing and publishing industry continued to grow, enabling Pennsylvania to maintain second place behind New York. Largely confined to Philadelphia, Pennsylvania's sugar refineries were small, unscientific plants located in back alleys until a new refinery was built in 1866 on the banks of the Delaware marking the beginning of mechanized and scientifically operated plants consuming huge quantities of Caribbean, Brazilian, and East Indian raw cane sugar as well as tons of European raw beet sugar. An infinite variety of other industries ranging from cigar making to shipbuilding have contributed to the growth of Pennsylvania cities.

The city was not only a center of manufacturing but also of finance and trade. Although by the time of the Civil War Philadelphia had lost its banking preeminence to New York, it remained a major center of national finance. In the post-Civil War boom, the Philadelphia banking house of Jay Cooke & Company extended credit to railroads (particularly the Northern Pacific) and to industries that speculated in and exploited natural resources. So entwined in national finance was Cooke's bank that its failure in 1873 precipitated one of America's worst economic depressions.

The career of Pittsburgh's Andrew W. Mellon illustrates the interplay among banking, industry, urban growth, and politics. With interests in real estate, coal, lumber, and building materials, Judge Thomas Mellon established the banking firm of T. Mellon & Sons in 1869 when he retired from the Allegheny County court of common pleas. After seasoning in the lumber and building business, Mellon's son Andrew joined the family bank in 1874 and a year later became a partner. Through his father, who had lent money to both Carnegie and Frick, Andrew Mellon associated with Pittsburgh's ablest entrepreneurs. In 1882 Judge Mellon, recognizing that his twenty-seven-year-old son Andrew possessed the "best business brains of the family," transferred ownership of the bank to him.

Pittsburgh and the Mellon bank grew together. Mellon had a genius for recognizing new talent and ideas, for investing in small businesses that would become great corporations. Seeing that chemist Charles M. Hall's electrolytic process for manufacturing aluminum merited support, Mellon and his family became principal stockholders in the Aluminum Company of America (Alcoa). Mellon also helped Edward Goodrich Acheson place the Carborundum Company on a sound basis and to Acheson's dismay controlled that company by 1898. In 1901 Mellon helped found the Gulf Oil Corporation, whose Texas and Oklahoma oil fields soon proved prosperous. Mellon also helped establish the Union Steel Company, which later merged with United States Steel, the Standard Steel Car Company, and the New York Shipbuilding Company. Recognizing the value of Heinrich Kopper's by-product coke ovens that recovered vast quantities of gas, sulfur, coal tar, and other materials that had previously been lost, Mellon converted this small business into a rich corporation. In 1918 Mellon and three associates purchased Kopper's American assets from the alien

John Wanamaker, merchant. (Library of Congress)

property custodian for an absurdly low price. With two young engineers trained by Lehigh College, Howard McClintic and Charles Marshall, Mellon formed a construction partnership which built Panama Canal locks, the Hell Gate and George Washington Bridges, and the Waldorf-Astoria Hotel. At one point in his career Mellon was active in sixty different corporations. Political involvement also boosted Mellon's fortune; he was a generous supporter of both the Quay and Penrose Republican machines, and they, in turn, supported the high tariff which particularly aided Mellon's monopolistic Alcoa Corporation. Mellon's later service as secretary of the treasury in the 1920s did not hurt his business interests. Mellon and Pittsburgh prospered together, each spurring the other's growth.

The retailing of goods also developed cities, and in John Wanamaker, Philadelphia produced one of America's leading retailers. An innovator with boundless energy, nerve, and optimism, Wanamaker was the owner of a fashionable and profitable men and boys' clothing store on Chestnut Street. In 1876 he moved his store to the rambling old Pennsylvania Railroad freight station (boasting two acres of floor space) and within a few months added women's apparel to his line. Opening the same year as Philadelphia's Centennial Exhibition, the "Grand Depot" attracted thousands of centennial visitors. When after the fair Wanamaker failed to interest other merchants in leasing space in the Grand Depot, he made it into the world's first department store, a cluster of specialty shops all under one roof with 129 counters and 1,400 stools on which customers could sit while selecting their purchases. An unqualified success, Wanamaker's store became one of the largest in America employing 5,000 workers by 1885. Wanamaker utilized newspaper advertising, eliminated haggling by charging one set price that was clearly marked on merchandise, gave money-back guarantees, and offered customers monthly charge accounts.

A committed Christian and Republican as well as storekeeper, Wanamaker worked to strengthen the Young Men's Christian Association and Sunday schools, fought for prohibition and Pennsylvania's blue laws, and came out against the Quay Republican machine. President Benjamin Harrison rewarded Wanamaker for contributing to his 1888 campaign by appointing him postmaster general. Though Wanamaker's spoils methods offended civil service reformers, he was an imaginative administrator who effected several technical improvements, experimented with rural free delivery, and favored parcel post and postal savings, both of which were later adopted.

As urban industrial, commercial, and banking organizations became more complex, they attracted white-collar office workers and managers as well as blue-collar laborers. By the last half of the nineteenth century, industrial corporate management had outgrown factory quarters and preferred locating near bankers, salesmen, and buyers. Like other cities, Pittsburgh met demands for business contacts through its communications network and its high-rise office buildings, which changed the central business district. Beginning in 1874, Pittsburgh businesses communicated with each other through a telegraph service. Telephones were introduced in 1877 and their business use became widespread by 1879. In Pittsburgh the population of the four central wards declined from 21,439 in 1850 to 8,217 in 1900. In 1870 the same wards had thirty-four churches; by 1910 there were only eleven and school population was cut in half. On the other hand, tax assessment figures rose sharply during the late 1880s. Pittsburgh's first high-rise office building went up in 1895, and by 1912 twenty-seven had been constructed. Industry, commerce, and finance nourished the sprawling metropolis, and those who managed the huge organism congregated at its center.

URBAN PROBLEMS

The transformation of the inner city accelerated the growth of the outer city, where the increasing army of white- and blue-collar workers were housed. Finding the economic, social, and cultural advantages of the city superior to life in the country, late-nineteenth-century Americans surged into cities, creating or accentuating problems that have not been solved. Rapid expansion usually meant inadequate housing, water, sewage disposal, sanitation, streets, transportation, police and fire protection, parks, and playgrounds. Not all city dwellers bore equally the brunt of these problems. Poverty-stricken, unskilled recent arrivals huddled in slums and suffered, while the vast majority of city dwellers were more inconvenienced than victimized by the disadvantages of urban life. Nevertheless both for those whom it inconvenienced and for those whom it victimized the city usually offered a better way of life than they had formerly experienced.

Transportation to the inner city was the major problem for outer-city dwellers. Commuter trains and trolley lines in the nineteenth century—and in the twentieth century elevated railroads, subway systems, bus lines, and ultimately superhighways—failed to provide adequate transportation because each improvement stimulated population growth and created an even greater demand. Suburban commuter trains, though they helped move metropolitan masses, hauled only a fraction of the human freight packed into trolley cars. Philadelphia boasted horse-drawn street railway cars after the late 1850s, but prior to 1867 regular service was not permitted on "the Lord's Day, commonly called Sunday" and Negroes were not allowed in the cars but were forced to ride on the outside platforms.

Engraving by C. R., *Broad-Street, Philadelphia* (1876). (New York Public Library, Astor, Lenox and Tilden Foundations)

A breakthrough in urban transportation came in the 1890s when the larger, faster electric trolley replaced the horsecar. Nevertheless, service was far from ideal. Although the transit systems of both Philadelphia and Pittsburgh were monopolized around 1900, both were consolidated from numerous separate companies. In 1874 thirty-nine companies operated lines in Philadelphia; and Pittsburgh, at one point, had ninety-six different transit companies. Innumerable companies simply meant that neither city had an overall, rational system for transporting its citizens.

The suburbanite was cursed by a transportation problem but was better housed than the denizen of the inner city. By the first decade of the twentieth century the rich built spacious houses in Pittsburgh's East End and spread out on the hills of Avalon, Crafton, and Sewickley; on Philadelphia's Chestnut Hill and its sprawling Main Line suburbs; and in Harrisburg's Front Street mansions overlooking the Susquehanna River. Good housing outside and within the city was not limited to the wealthy. In the Pittsburgh district, for example, many wage earners enjoyed comfortable company houses located in the industrial satellites of Vandergrift (laid out by the noted landscape architect Frederick Law Olmsted), Ambridge, and Midland. Five- to seven-room stucco and frame houses with inside toilets, running water, and electricity rented for from $12 to $20 a month in Midland. Many streets and sections of both Pittsburgh and Philadelphia contained comfortable detached houses where clerks, mechanics, and shopkeepers lived. Clearly most skilled laborers and some unskilled laborers enjoyed adequate housing, but both geographically and financially these houses were beyond the reach of most unskilled workers.

Neither Philadelphia nor Pittsburgh suffered from a serious tenement house problem, but both had serious housing problems. Indeed, the relative scarcity of tenements, which by definition have three or more families to a house, deceived some reformers into exclaiming about "the happy condition of Philadelphia" housing. In Philadelphia the worst housing was in tenements and in the scattered alleys. When William Penn laid out Philadelphia in large blocks he intended each house to be surrounded by gardens making the whole a "green country towne which might never be burnt and might always be wholesome." Penn's large blocks were cut up by alleys and ultimately crowded with houses. Many alley houses received no light or air from the rear or sides, and frequently the court they faced was dark and narrow. One row of five houses faced a court whose width varied from 3 feet 2 inches to 3 feet 11½ inches. Contemporaries noted the relationship between the lack of fresh air and sunlight and the prevalence of tuberculosis—the great killer of that age.

Residents of Philadelphia's 4,000 tenement houses were if anything worse off than occupants of alley houses. Despite Philadelphia's low population density, serious overcrowding was common. A 1905 investigation of one block revealed five instances of "as many as seven persons of all ages and both sexes" living and sleeping in one room which also served as the kitchen, and "one family was found sharing three rooms with eighteen lodgers." With many families using common hydrants and toilets, no one felt obliged to clean them. In the houses investigated, 41 percent of the sinks were not connected to sewers but emptied into yards, courts, or alleys, and an additional 15 percent were not trapped, thus directly connecting the sewer with the air of the room. Tenements were also dangerous firetraps. Of sixty-five tenements inspected in 1905, fifty-five "made no pretense of complying with the law requiring fire-escapes."

Housing in Pittsburgh was worse than in Philadelphia. Though Pittsburgh had sewers, many houses were not connected with them. Privies were often built over long wooden chutes, such as those emptying into Saw Mill Run, a stream which drained the sections of Montooth, Beltzhoover, Mt. Washington, West Liberty, and Elliott and theoretically carried the sewage of 35,000 people into the Ohio River. Much sewage, however, remained on the banks of the run, which was a shallow stream in dry weather. Overcrowding was also common in Pittsburgh tenements. One room in Soho slept ten boarders, two of whom were on the night shift, and accommodations in Pittsburgh's satellite mill towns, such as Homestead, were scarcely better.

Though some companies maintained model homes for their employees, other companies neglected to repair their houses. When the Carnegie Steel Company (which became part of the United States Steel Corporation in 1901) acquired the old Painter's Mill on Pittsburgh's South Side, it modernized the plant but did nothing to Painter's Row, actually six rows of dilapidated brick and frame company houses. In 1907 and 1908 a detailed investigation "found half a thousand people living there under conditions that were unbelievable,—back-to-back houses with no through ventilation; cellar kitchens; dark, unsanitary, ill-ventilated, overcrowded sleeping rooms, no drinking water supply on the premises; and a dearth of sanitary accommodations that was shameful." The report of this investigation aroused a New England stockholder and alerted Pittsburgh health authorities, forcing U.S. Steel to tear down three rows of these houses and to improve others.

Water, as well as housing, has been a persistant urban problem. By utilizing handy rivers, Pennsylvania's chief cities had an adequate volume of water, but many residences were without running water and all who depended on the public supply were without pure water. Pittsburgh utilized the Allegheny and Monongahela Rivers, which carried "in solution the soluble chemical products of the mills along their shores, . . . as well as the off-scourings of iron and steel mills, tanneries, slaughter houses, and similar industries." The sewage of 350,000 inhabitants along the Allegheny and of Swissvale, Homestead, Braddock, Rankin, and McKeesport along the Monongahela further poisoned Pittsburgh's water. The prevalence in Pittsburgh of typhoid fever, a direct result of impure water, became a national scandal. "For every case of typhoid fever," an eminent English sanitarian had pointed out, "somebody ought to be hung." From 1898 to 1907 the annual typhoid death rate per 100,000 was 130 in Pittsburgh, 104.4 in Allegheny City (Pittsburgh's North Side), 54.7 in Philadelphia, 27.3 in Chicago, 18.2 in New York, 11.7 in London, and 4.2 in Berlin. Over a twenty-five year period, from 1883 to 1908, almost 55,000 Pittsburghers suffered from typhoid fever and 7,422 of them died. Finally in 1908, twelve years after Pittsburgh established a filtration commission and after political squabbling caused tragic delays of at least four years, Pittsburgh's filtration plant began to operate and the incidence of typhoid fever dropped markedly.

Late-nineteenth-century Philadelphia and Pittsburgh combined bad housing and water with inadequate park and playground facilities. In a macabre sense these facilities were unnecessary for workers and their children since long hours in steel mills and glass factories left no time for recreation. With the decline of child labor and the winning of a somewhat shorter workday for many adults around 1900, cities began to build parks and playgrounds. Ironically and unfortunately these facilities were frequently built only in affluent neighborhoods. In 1896 Pittsburgh had but two parks, Highland and Schenley, both out of reach of the poor, who had only streets and alleys in which to play. In 1895 Burd S. Patterson of Pittsburgh secured passage of a state law authorizing the use of schoolyards as playgrounds. Philadelphia quickly utilized this law with the board of education maintaining school playgrounds. In Pittsburgh playgrounds came more slowly and from public-spirited private groups. The Civic Club in 1896 opened the first school playgrounds and paid for all expenses including that of a janitor.

Poverty, crowding, substandard housing, few recreational facilities, and a boss-ridden political system bred drinking, gambling, and crime. In poor and crowded wards, where voting lists could easily be padded and repeaters were readily available, political bosses built substantial majorities by combining haphazard charity, occasional parties, a few jobs, and help (not justice) for those in trouble. Containing crime in poverty-stricken wards, rather than eliminating it, seems to have been the objective of the machine, and many citizens of those wards joined the underworld because for them crime paid. Though risks were involved, there appeared to be greater upward mobility in vice and crime than in steel mills and coal mines.

Local police were but reflections of local bosses in their efforts to contain rather than to eradicate crime. Police tenure was insecure and dependent on service to the faction in power. Completely dominated by the political machine, Philadelphia police perpetuated its power by protecting voting repeaters from "intimidation." Philadelphians reported "that they had seen the police help to beat citizens or election officials who were trying to do their duty, then arrest the victim."

WHITE AND BLACK GHETTOS

Representatives of many races, religions, and ethnic groups have congregated in cities. The degree to which they have become segregated has depended on how hostile they found the American society and that in turn has depended on how strange the strangers were. Thus the alienated of each generation, whether Irish or German, Italian or Serbian, Pole or Hungarian, Jew or Negro, have congregated together. Their easiest choice was to cluster and form their bonds with one another. As strangers have lost their strangeness, they have been accepted in the larger society. Differences in religion and color, however, have proved more difficult to tolerate than new customs, dress, or language. Jews with what was initially a strange religion, Negroes with their different color, and both groups with a long history of slavery, persecution, and prejudice remained longer in the inner cities than other groups.

Philadelphia's Jewish community dates to the colonial period when many of its members attained elite status. The first Jews in America were Sephardic (Iberian or Western European) in origin, religious ritual, and language. Before the end of the colonial period, however, Ashkenazic Jews, who were German and central European in origin and spoke Yiddish, were in the majority. They were delighted to join the more aristocratic Sephardic congregations and by 1882 had an upper class of their own. These established Jews despised the thousands of fellow Ashkenazic Jews who in the late nineteenth century, fearing death in a pogrom, fled Russian dominions. Jews described these new arrivals with names ending in "ki" or "ky" as kikes and a young Jewish immigrant exclaimed, "We've never had to take half the insults from Gentiles we've taken from Jews."

In both Philadelphia and Pittsburgh, Russian Jews crowded into ghettos. From 1882 to 1914 thousands of pious, orthodox, Eastern European Jews "with their own religious ritual, language, and traditions" poured into the Philadelphia area south of Pine Street along Fourth and Fifth Streets. There they worked in the garment and handicraft industries or earned a precarious living as shopkeepers, drummers, or peddlers. In Pittsburgh the Jewish community congregated in the Hill District, where a study of two blocks revealed that 817 out of 1,080 residents were Jewish and that out of the 143 Jewish families 110 were from Russia and 27 from Romania. Most of these families were from small towns, two-thirds of them had been in America less than ten years, and though the majority had remained in Pittsburgh they had moved frequently within their area. Eighty-seven of the families had lived in their homes less than two years. For ninety-two of these families migration to America had been for economic reasons, and for forty-one the search for religious and political freedom had motivated their journey. For most, there was an anguished period of poverty and insecurity before they made economic headway, and for some, hard times never ended. In America there were fewer openings for craftsmen and farmers than in Europe, and it was necessary for many to become peddlers, hucksters, factory workers, and laborers. As a contemporary wrote, the people of these blocks, "who have suffered oppression and borne ridicule; who in the face of insult and abuse have remained silent . . . have stamped on their countenances a look of stubborn patience and hope—always hope—and of capacity to overcome."

And overcome they did. By the 1920s the Eastern European Jewish community had leaped from the ghetto into the middle class. To be sure anti-Semitism in America—the rise of which coincided with the Eastern European influx in the 1880s and 1890s—remained and, indeed, grew more pronounced in the 1920s, but American prejudice and Russian Jewish prosperity gradually eroded the caste barriers between Russian and German Jews. The

Octavius V. Catto, educator. (Pennsylvania Historical and Museum Commission)

more successful moved out of South Philadelphia into West Philadelphia and Germantown or in Pittsburgh from the Hill District to Squirrel Hill.

While the Russian Jew escaped the ghetto, the Negro became trapped. Religion and customs could be altered to blend unobtrusively with the dominant background, but the black man has always been visible in America. As the Negro population of Philadelphia and Pittsburgh multiplied, the black ghetto developed. In both Philadelphia and Pittsburgh the story is similar, but in Philadelphia it has been written on a larger scale. While the Negro population of Allegheny County grew from 10,357 in 1890 to 144,545 in 1970, Philadelphia's Negroes jumped from 39,371 to 653,791. In Philadelphia Negroes numbered one-tenth of the population in 1810, but their number remained relatively static between 1830 and 1870. Negroes could not vote in Pennsylvania from 1837 to 1870, and in Philadelphia, race riots occurred before the Civil War and again in 1871 when incumbent Democrats tried to keep newly enfranchised blacks from voting. The riots of 1871, culminating in the assassination of several Negroes including Octavius V. Catto, a prominent teacher who had declared, "I would not stultify my manhood by going to my home in a roundabout way," ironically marked the beginning of better race relations in Philadelphia. Outraged by Catto's murder, prominent Philadelphians gave him the most imposing funeral since that of Abraham Lincoln. Restrictions on personal liberty gradually relaxed. Discrimination had ended on Philadelphia streetcars in 1867, in Pennsylvania theaters in 1874, and on Pennsylvania railroads in 1878; and Philadelphia schools had been desegregated by 1881. The Pennsylvania civil rights act of 1887 outlawed Jim Crow discrimination in "any restaurant, hotel, railroad, street railway, omnibus line, theatre, concert hall or place of entertainment or amusement."

By the 1890s the Negro population of Philadelphia was significant enough for W. E. B. DuBois to make his pioneering study *The Philadelphia Negro*. DuBois's purpose was to ascertain "what the real condition of the Negro is and what movements would best be undertaken to improve the present situation." He was disturbed by the slow advance, if not "actual retrogression," of the Negro since the Civil War. DuBois's investigation of Seventh Ward Negroes between Spruce and South Streets and Seventh and Twenty-fifth Streets confirmed his forebodings.

By obtaining the vote in 1870 blacks achieved a small measure of political power, but they were usually not essential to perpetuate the machine's power. Black voters could be divided into three categories: the great majority who blindly followed the Republican party hoping for offices or influence, a considerable group in the worst sections that sold their votes to the highest bidder, and a very small group of independents who voted for reform. Most Negroes supported the machine because the "very reformers who want votes for specific reforms, will not themselves work beside Negroes, or admit them to positions in their stores or offices, or lend them friendly aid in trouble." Furthermore even if some of the few Negroes who became councilmen or policemen had achieved that high level through political deals, all Negroes took pride in their exalted position and refused to turn them out of office.

In the 1890s few black children attended predominantly white schools, but with 94 percent of Negro youth from ten to twenty years of age able to read and write, Philadelphia Negroes were more literate than Italian, Russian, Polish, Hungarian, and Irish immigrants living there. Yet few Negroes entered high school, and by 1896 fewer than a hundred Philadelphia Negroes had graduated from college or a professional school. Poverty and lax attendance frequently kept children out of school, and motivation was lacking because of limited opportunity. "What's the use of an education?" asked a black graduate of Central High School who could find only menial employment. Even a University of Pennsylvania graduate in mechanical engineering with an excellent record was reduced to waiting on the tables of his white fellow graduates at the University Club. Henry O. Tanner, a distinguished painter who won honors in France and whom Philadelphia now proudly acknowledges as a son, had to abandon both his city and his country to "find room for his talents." "How long," asked DuBois, "can a city teach its black children that the road to success is to have a white face? How can a city do this and escape the inevitable penalty?"

DuBois discovered that the Negro's quest to earn a living was complicated by his lack of training, by stiff competition for jobs from better-trained and more aggressive white natives and immigrants, and by his need to raise his standard of living. That Seventh Ward blacks were practically excluded from the trades and industries of Philadelphia in 1896 is shown by the following figures comparing them with the city residents as a whole: 74 percent of Seventh Ward blacks were engaged in domestic and personal service as compared with 23 percent of Philadelphia residents as a whole; 15 percent were in trade and transportation as compared with 25 percent; 8 percent were in manufacturing and mechanical industries as compared with 47 percent; and 2 percent were in professional service as compared with 4 percent. Sixty to 100 ministers, 40 teachers, 15 physicians, 10 lawyers, and 3 dentists composed the little group of Negro professionals in Philadelphia. A small but growing number were businessmen, but their businesses were mostly restaurants, barber shops, and grocery, cigar, and candy stores representing little capital. Fewer than 1 percent of Philadelphians employed as clerks, semiprofessionals, and civil servants were black. Black policemen were first employed in 1884; there were 60 of them in this group and there were 30 Federal employees. The high percentage of black laborers and servants in the 1890s indicates that little progress had been made since midcentury. With large numbers competing for the few jobs open to them, wages remained low. When industrial employment was found, the tendency to segregate gangs of laborers hurt both blacks and whites and fanned existing prejudice since employers frequently hired blacks below the wage scale and forced whites to work for the same wage.

Even in the 1890s, however, Frederick W. Taylor, the progressive manager of the Midvale Steel Works, found integrated gangs of workmen more productive than those segregated by nationality or race. Later renowned as the father of scientific management, Taylor recognized that the damage resulting from cliques formed in separate gangs outweighed the advantages that ethnic dividing might produce. Furthermore, he discovered that Negroes made efficient skilled workmen. "They do all the grades of work done by the white workmen," Taylor observed. "Some of this work is of such a nature that it had been supposed that only very intelligent English and American workmen could be trusted with it. We have 100 colored men doing that skilled work now, and they do it as well as any of the others."

Poor health, low income, and high rent plagued Philadelphia Negroes. From 1884 to 1890 the white death rate was 22.69 per 1,000 while the black death rate was 31.25. During these same years the death rate for children under five was 94 per 1,000 for whites and nearly double for blacks (171.44). Hereditary disease, neglect of infants, poor food, insufficient clothing, and bad sanitary conditions accounted for the high Negro death rate. Incomes were much lower for blacks. Forty-eight percent of black families earned between $5 and $10 a week. For rent, Negroes frequently paid from one-fourth to three-fourths of the family income. Since they were restricted to certain areas, a housing shortage kept rents high. Blacks earned less, lived in worse quarters, and paid relatively more rent than whites.

It was often difficult for Negroes to achieve a close-knit family life. The heritage of slavery included "unregulated polygamy and polyandry," exaggerated the role of women, and centered life outside the immediate home around the big house. Among Philadelphia Negroes there was an "unusual excess of females." Twenty-one percent of women from thirty to forty were unmarried and 20 percent were either widowed or separated, indicating the "widespread and early breaking up of family life." Working mothers left "children without guidance or restraint for the better part of the day," and the combination of low pay and high rents often necessitated taking in lodgers, which destroyed the privacy and intimacy of home life.

The church played a major role in the lives of Philadelphia Negroes. Each church represented a social circle and provided entertainment and amusement ranging from concerts to picnics. Held both in the morning and in the evening, Sunday services were social as well as religious events. Basically democratic, churches tended to conserve old standards rather than to strive for new ones. "On the whole," DuBois remarked, "the average Negro preacher in this city is a shrewd manager, a respectable man, a good talker, a pleasant companion, but neither learned nor spiritual, nor a reformer." Even so, most efforts to promote general intelligence and social betterment were church-centered.

Crime was prevalent among Philadelphia blacks—particularly among young, untrained men, whose chief offences were stealing and assault. If lack of harmony with social surroundings leads to crime, clearly, people occupying the lowest social strata are predestined to be the greatest offenders. Negroes, furthermore, were products of slavery, migration, and poor environment. Slavery fostered ignorance and lack of self-discipline, while migration uprooted raw country people and forced them to adjust to crime-ridden ghetto life. Negro criminals were products of homes "badly situated and badly managed, with parents untrained for their responsibilities"; they were part of a total milieu which caused them to lose aspiration, self-respect, and their sense of manhood. DuBois realized that the real foundation for the wide disparity between black and white environments was "the widespread feeling . . . that the Negro is something less than an American and ought not to be much more than what he is."

BIBLIOGRAPHY

For Pennsylvania agricultural statistics, see E. L. Gasteiger and D. O. Boster: *Pennsylvania Agricultural Statistics, 1866–1950* (1954). The major source on rural life and agriculture in Pennsylvania is Stevenson Whitcomb Fletcher: *Pennsylvania Agriculture and Country Life, 1840–1940* (1955). The course of agriculture in the nation at large may be observed in Fred A. Shannon: *The Farmer's Last Frontier, Agriculture, 1860–1897* (1945), and to a lesser extent in Shannon's *The Centennial Years (1967)*. See also Arthur S. Young, "Pennsylvania's Part in Developing Power Machinery," *Pennsylvania Farmer* (Jan. 10, 1948), pp. 18, 20, 31. The best sources on the Pennsylvania Grange are Solon Justus Buck: *The Granger Movement: A Study of Agricultural Organization and Its Political, Economic and Social Manifestations, 1870–1880* (1913); and Fred Brenckman, *History of the Pennsylvania State Grange* (1949).

On American cities in general, see Blake McKelvey: *The Urbanization of America: 1860–1915* (1963). The splendid photographs in Lawrence Lafore and Sarah Lee Lippincott, *Philadelphia: The Unexpected City* (1965), are an excellent introduction to the architectural beauties of that city. Much information on post-Civil War urban manufactures may be found in U.S. Bureau of Census: *Twelfth Census of the United States . . . 1900, Manufactures, part 2, States and Territories* (1902), p. 8. On banking, see John Thom Holdworth: *Financing an Empire: History of Banking in Pennsylvania*, 4 vols. (1928), p. 2. On Andrew Mellon, see Harvey O'Connor: *Mellon's Millions: The Biography of a Fortune, the Life and Times of Andrew W. Mellon* (1933); as well as Allan Nevins: "Andrew William Mellon," *Dictionary of American Biography*, vol. 22, pp. 446–452. For the life and work of a great retailer, see Joseph J. Senturia: "John Wanamaker," *Dictionary of American Biography*, vol. 19, pp. 407–408; Joseph H. Appel: *The Business Biography of John Wanamaker: Founder and Builder . . .* (1930); and Herbert A. Gibbons: *John Wanamaker*, 2 vols. (1926). On the development of Pittsburgh's inner city, see Samuel P. Hays: "Historical Social Research in the Process of Urbanization: The Case of Pittsburgh" (paper read before the Pennsylvania Historical Association Convention, Oct. 20, 1967, Beaver Falls, Pa.). A mine of information on franchises in general and streetcar lines in particular may be found in Delos F. Wilcox: *Municipal Franchises . . .* , 2 vols. (1910–1911).

Much data on slums and their residents can be found in Paul U. Kellogg (ed.): *The Pittsburgh Survey,* 6 vols. (1909–1914). Also see Emily Wayland Dinwiddie: "Housing Conditions in Philadelphia," *Charities,* vol. 14 (1905), pp. 631–638; Lincoln Steffens: *The Shame of the Cities* (1957); Philip Goodman: *Franklin Street* (1942); and E. Digby Baltzell: *Philadelphia Gentlemen: The Making of a National Upper Class* (1958). A most revealing study is W. E. B. DuBois: *The Philadelphia Negro: A Social Study,* introduction by E. Digby Baltzell (1967). Also see DuBois: "The Black Vote of Philadelphia," *Charities,* vol. 15 (1905), pp. 31–35; and William J. McKenna, "The Negro vote in Philadelphia Elections," *Pennsylvania History,* vol. 32 (1965), pp. 406–415; and Ira V. Brown: "Pennsylvania and the Rights of the Negro, 1865–1887," *Pennsylvania History,* vol. 28 (1961), pp. 45–57, and *The Negro in Pennsylvania History* (1970).

CHAPTER TWENTY-ONE

The Evolution of a One-party State

The Cameron machine moved quickly to consolidate its victory over the combined forces of Liberal Republicans and Democrats. In 1873 the Legislature enacted and Governor John F. Hartranft signed a congressional reapportionment act, a model of gerrymandering which would hobble the Democratic party for the next fourteen years. By gathering populous Democratic counties into large districts and by creating small Republican districts, Republicans limited Democrats to a maximum of nine out of twenty-seven seats. Democratic Bucks County was partitioned among three neighboring counties, and a Democratic ward of Scranton was annexed to a rural Republican district. But the 1873 Legislature is most notorious for approving 1,389 special and local acts as compared to only 63 general acts. Most of these special acts remained buried in committees until the closing moments of the session when they were rushed through. One such bill, passed unanimously in both houses, permitted the Pennsylvania Railroad to increase its capital stock without limit. Hartranft insisted on a ceiling but was agreeable to a high one, and the final act prohibited increase beyond 100 percent.

Both Republican and Democratic newspapers condemned the Legislature. Its severest critic, however, was its lone Liberal Republican member, Senator Alexander K. McClure, whose position outside both parties inspired him to espouse reform. Near the end of the session, the House in a jovial mood invited McClure to address it on reform. McClure, who had spent most of the session fruitlessly sponsoring reform legislation, "was greeted with a barrage of printed bills, documents, newspapers, and cigar boxes." Knowing "no other body of men, either present or past, that needed instruction on the necessity of both public and private morality so much" or which had "so broadly or deeply experimented in the line of individual and official profligacy," McClure was grateful that it had "called the confessor." There was, he noted, "a faint silver lining on the deep cloud" that "gladdened the hearts of the whole people of the State and reinspired hope"—the Legislature had voted for an early adjournment. "Hoping, gentlemen, if I may be pardoned the use of the term, that the length of your lives may correspond with the measure of your virtues and that you will be succeeded by better men than yourselves, I bid you good night." McClure left the chamber "amid uproarious applause and another barrage of paper."

THE CONSTITUTION OF 1873

Reform was far from dead in Pennsylvania. Indeed Pennsylvania simultaneously supported reform and the Cameron machine. To put it another way, Pennsylvanians balanced the scales by voting both to reform the machinery of government and to keep Cameron and his lieutenants operating that machinery. Pennsylvania's tendency to opt for both reform and the machine is illustrated by the voters' reaction to State Treasurer Robert W. Mackey, a trusted lieutenant of Simon Cameron who had been elected by the state Legislature in 1869 and had deposited state funds (approximately $2 million worth) interest free in certain pet banks. Grateful bankers utilized this free capital and split their profits with the treasury ring. The Legislature in 1871 and 1872, reacting to popular demand, passed a proposed amendment to the 1838 constitution that required the election of the state treasurer by the people. When in October 1872 the people overwhelmingly ratified the amendment (681,620–4,394), it appeared that Mackey and the treasury ring were on the way out. The reverse was true. In the spring of 1873 the Legislature extended Mackey's term, and when the first election for state treasurer was held in October of that year, Mackey triumphed.

The Pennsylvania Legislature was notoriously corrupt; and the absence of a general incorporation law and the practice of special and local legislation were responsible for much of the corruption. Legislators sold their votes to grant corporations privileges and then blackmailed these corporations by threatening to pass strike bills depriving them of their advantages. Out of 9,230 acts passed between 1866 and 1873, 8,700 were special and local acts. These bills were passed with little study or debate. So confused and unconcerned were legislators that on two occasions in 1870 they passed bills that were identical with previously passed bills. The Legislature also reputedly auctioned the offices of United States senator and state treasurer to the highest bidder. Furthermore the Legislature would not change the 1869 Registry Act, which enabled the ring-dominated Philadelpha Board of Aldermen to appoint election officials who in turn controlled the registration of voters, supervised elections, and disposed of any challenge to the ring. Pennsylvanians hoped a new constitution would curtail legislative license, municipal corruption, corporate power, and the governor's liberal distribution of pardons.

By the early 1870s there was a significant groundswell for constitutional revision. Having failed to dislodge the Cameron machine by other means, both Democratic and Republican political outs hoped to curtail its power by adopting a new constitution. Businessmen objected both to legislative blackmail and to favors given corporations with power or inside connections. Reformers, many of them members of distinguished families with deep roots in Pennsylvania, were appalled both by corruption and by the reputation it gave the state their fathers had made the keystone of the Federal arch. Diverse forces including the Union League of Philadelpha, the Allegheny County Republican organization, numerous Democratic organizations, the conservative Philadelphia *Public Ledger,* a variety of Democratic papers, former Governor Andrew Gregg Curtin, and Governor John W. Geary all called for constitutional revision. In the face of such sentiment, the Cameron machine did not seriously oppose a constitutional convention. When given the opportunity (by a Democratic Senate and a Republican House resolution) to determine whether a constitutional convention should be called, voters in October 1871 overwhelmingly voted approval (332,119–69,738). The election was followed by a legislative struggle over how and where delegates should be chosen. Ultimately Republicans agreed to substantial minority representation, and in the October 1872 elections Republicans won sixty-nine, Democrats sixty-one, and Liberal Republicans three delegates to the convention. Several independent-minded delegates nullified the slight Republican advantage.

The constitutional convention was in session for 180 days spread from November 12, 1872, to December 27, 1873. Distinguished Democrats present were former State Chief Justices Jeremiah S. Black and George W. Woodward and former United States Senators Charles R. Buckalew and William Bigler; Curtin was one of the three liberal Republicans. The most distinguished Republican there was Wayne MacVeagh who was both a reformer and Simon Cameron's son-in-law and would become President Garfield's attorney general. Railroads were directly represented by two Democratic delegates Theodore Cuyler, a Pennsylvania Railroad lawyer, and Franklin B. Gowen of the Reading Railroad. Other delegates with business interests were M. Hall Stanton, Philadelpha merchant, and E. C. Knight, sugar refiner. Three iron manufacturers were delegates compared to only one full-time farmer, and no one represented either skilled or unskilled labor. Henry C. Carey, a champion of the protective tariff and the inflationary interconvertible bond theory, was the convention's leading political and economic theorist. The Pittsburgh *Gazette* reported: "In respect of wealth it is the heaviest deliberative body that ever met in Pennsylvania. Hence its eminent respectability is apparent. No trifling with the conservative principles of society here. No experimentation outside the well established usages and laws, from which has grown this great individual prosperity."

Bent on reform, the convention agreed to draw up a new constitution. Reasoning (with dubious validity) that it is more difficult to bribe a larger group, it virtually doubled both the House and the Senate, to 200 and to 50 members, respectively. The seats in both houses would be apportioned according to population, with each county entitled to at least one representative; senators would serve four years and members of the House two; and biennial elections and meetings of the Legislature would be held. By preventing amendments that would alter the original purpose of bills, by limiting all but appropriation bills to a single, clearly titled subject, by requiring that each bill be read in its entirety on three separate days, and by insisting that all its amendments be printed and distributed before the final passage of a bill, the convention sought to prevent treachery in passing legislation. The new constitution forbade special and local legislation on twenty-eight subjects and required thirty days' notice in the locality affected before permitted local legislation could be introduced. Taxation was to be equal on the same types of property, and in an effort to eliminate a future "Credit Mobilier" (whose vague Pennsylvania charter insiders utilized to build and plunder the Union Pacific Railroad), charters under which no bona fide corporation existed when the constitution went into effect would be voided.

The new constitution was designed to curtail political machines. State elections would be held in November rather than in October, and local elections would be held in February. To prevent frauds at the polls, the constitution required that all ballots be numbered, defined bribery and provided for its punishment, guaranteed minority representation on election boards, and provided that contested elections (similar to McClure's in 1872) be decided in the courts. The new constitution nullified Philadelphia's notorious Registry Act by instituting statewide registration requirements. In addition, the convention attacked both the Philadelpha and the Allegheny County machines by demanding that all officials of counties with more than 150,000 population be salaried, in this way eliminating the costly practice of allowing some officers fees based on a percentage of the vast sums they received.

The convention was especially sensitive to the handling of finances. No city commission could contract debt unless specifically approved by the city government, and all cities had to establish sinking funds pledged to paying off their funded debts. The constitution required that the state sinking fund be used only to pay off the public debt, limited the use of reserve funds to current operations, and decreed that no elected or appointed official could make a profit from these funds (as Mackey had done), and to keep stealing at a minimum placed a low ceiling of $1 million on the state debt. Subsequent amendments raised the debt ceiling to $50 million in 1918 and $100 million in 1923, but from the 1930s the commonwealth circumvented unrealistic constitutional debt requirements by setting up numerous authorities to finance its programs.

The convention designed many provisions as positive improvements rather than as negative responses to abuses. The suffrage was no longer restricted to free whites. The governor would serve four instead of three years, the state treasurer two years, the auditor general three years, and the newly created lieutenant governor four years. None of these officers could immediately succeed himself. A second important new officer, the secretary of internal affairs, would serve four years and could immediately succeed himself. The constitution enlarged the state Supreme Court, whose members served twenty-one-year terms, and arranged their selection to achieve bipartisanship. Amendments to the constitution, which if approved would go into effect on January 1, 1874, had to be passed by two successive Legislatures and meet with voter approval.

The only significant opposition to ratifying the constitution came from the Republican machine, but most rank-and-file Republicans did not follow their leaders. Despite Chris Magee's opposition, Allegheny County voted 10–1 for the constitution, which won in Philadelphia as well. Although central Pennsylvania Republicans heeded Cameron's voice, their opposition was insignificant. On December 16, 1873, the new constitution triumphed 253,774–108,594. For Liberal Republicans like Curtin, repeatedly defeated and humiliated by Cameron, victory was sweet. "The result," he gloated, "means reform and the people will have it." *Penn Monthly* rejoiced in "the beginning of a new era" for Philadelphia because the new constitution had "broken into pieces the chains by which the city . . . was bound."

The result, however, did not mean reform for Pennsylvania, nor did a new era begin for Philadelphia and Pittsburgh. In February 1874, to the dismay of some Philadelphia reformers, McClure—whom they considered a "reckless political adventurer" who would "pollute and betray" the cause of municipal reform—headed the Democratic opposition ticket against Mayor William S. Stokley, the machine candidate for reelection. With reformers divided over McClure, the Philadelphia machine triumphed. Firmly controlling the Legislature, the Republican machine gerrymandered the reapportionment of the Senate and House under the new constitution, created a sinking fund to pay Philadelphia's debt as required but acceded to a ring request to increase that municipal debt, and by failing to set up a reasonable salary schedule for county officers in Philadelphia, Allegheny, and Luzerne Counties defied a constitutional provision and continued the lucrative fee system. "Reform," Governor Hartranft perceived, "cannot be obtained by mere constitutional enactment, nor by surrounding offices and trusts with additional restraints. . . . It will not suffice to enact that integrity and fitness are essential qualifications for office, unless the people see to it that none without these qualifications are selected."

THE PENNSYLVANIA REPUBLICAN MACHINE

Simon Cameron constructed and Matthew Quay and Boies Penrose successively and successfully operated the Pennsylvania Republican machine from the 1860s to the 1920s. Though renowned by its enemies as the classic smoothly functioning American political machine, it was—as were other so-called machines—actually a confederation of local party chieftains who generally followed but occasionally opposed the boss. The Cameron-Quay-Penrose organization was so successful and long-lived that more than any other organization it deserved the title "machine," which expressed the mingled hatred, despair, and admiration of its enemies. Nevertheless its independently powerful parts (local machines controlled by local bosses) could become unhitched and cause the machine to function badly. It was powerful but not omnipotent. It is true that its task was easier because Pennsylvania was decisively Republican—from 1861 to 1935 only one Democrat served as governor—but it is also true that the machine helped make and keep Pennsylvania decisively Republican. Republican domination of Pennsylvania owed much to the exploitation of Civil War hatreds, to support from businessmen, farmers, and immigrants, and above all to superb political leadership and organization.

During and after the Civil War, Republicans wished to tar all Democrats as Copperheads and traitors. They succeeded to a remarkable degree because many Pennsylvania Democrats had opposed the war and resisted the draft, and some, it was rumored, had even joined the subversive and in fact mythical "Fishing Creek Confederacy." True and fabricated stories of Ku Klux Klan atrocities committed upon Negro Republicans during Reconstruction further infuriated Pennsylvanians and determined them to vote Republican. White Southerners were virtually all Democrats and to Pennsylvanians appeared unrepentant, unreconstructed, and anxious to reenslave the Negro. The Grand Army of the Republic (the Union veteran organization) was overwhelmingly Republican, and men who joined the army as Democrats shifted after the war to the popular party of loyalty.

Businessmen also tended to support the Republican party. Iron and steel, textile, and other manufacturers craved a protective tariff that would eliminate foreign competition and enhance profits for American manufacturers while increasing prices for American consumers. Pennsylvania was heavily involved in manufacturing, and Pennsylvania Republicans were more conspicuously identified with protection than were Democrats. Indeed Simon Cameron combined careers in business and politics, and his successors were friendly to large-scale enterprise. Kept busy with state politics, United States senators from Pennsylvania from the 1860s to the 1920s rarely affected legislation, but when they did it was almost invariably with regard to the tariff. Quay influenced the 1890 McKinley tariff, Philander C.

Knox the 1909 Payne-Aldrich tariff, and Penrose championed the high tariff and generally opposed progressive legislation. In return, many businessmen gave generously to finance campaigns and often influenced their employees to vote Republican. An increasing number of these employees came from southern and eastern Europe where democracy and self-government were poorly developed. Not having participated significantly in the political process before their arrival, these immigrants tended to support the existing power structure by voting with their employers, who before Pennsylvania adopted the secret ballot in 1891 could easily ascertain how their men voted.

Yet, other Northern states experienced the Civil War, industrialization, and immigration without being dominated for generations by the Republican party. Most political leaders failed to create an organization comparable to the Pennsylvania Republican machine which had little trouble controlling nominations and winning elections. The key to its success was its control of local leaders, for the machine's power to nominate and to elect was lodged on the local level. Cameron, who designed the machine, strove to be in contact with every voter in the commonwealth through local political leaders. The machine supported these local bosses in a variety of ways. A local boss could be a state or Federal officeholder, a contractor whose firm would receive lucrative government contracts, a banker in whose bank state funds would be deposited, or perhaps a tavern keeper whose license, issued by a local judge, gave him a neighborhood monopoly. The machine gave the local boss political, economic, and social power, which he utilized to enhance majorities at primary and regular elections. Rural leaders tended to be loyal to the machine, but urban bosses with considerable local sources of revenue and growing constituencies were apt to be more independent.

The procedure of nominating candidates illustrates the importance of local control. Precinct or township Republicans would meet to select nominees for local offices and delegates to ward or county conventions which selected nominees for the state Legislature and delegates to the state nominating convention. In this nominating process rank-and-file party members could participate only on the lowest step. And it was on that step that local bosses demoralized and defeated reform Republicans by packing precinct or township meetings with their ardent—and frequently beholden—supporters. A reform Republican primary victory could hurt the party more than a Democratic triumph in the regular election.

Controlling the vote was as important to the machine as naming the Republican candidate. The machine could not afford complacency. Until 1894 Pennsylvania was a two-party state, though its voters had a distinctly Republican bias. Democrats could and did win if enough reform Republicans bolted. To maintain its majority support, the machine used repeaters and if necessary falsified returns. Before 1874 fraud was relatively simple. Anyone the election judges permitted to mark and toss a ballot into the box could do so; and at many polling places election judges, either members of the machine or paid-off Democrats, were cooperative. After the Uniform Elections Act of 1874 registered voters, the art of repeating became more complex. The machine padded registration lists of living residents with those who had died and with those who had never lived. Founding fathers continued to vote in Philadelphia a century after they completed their work. When just before an election, Rudolph Blankenburg, a political reformer, sent registered letters to each enrolled voter in a selected division, 63 percent of the letters were returned marked "not at," "removed," or "deceased." On election day, party workers toured the city with a list of names including their own, voting in various districts. A Philadelphia man admitted having voted the Republican ticket thirty-seven times in the election of 1899. Before the advent of the secret ballot in 1891, the machine kept close track of votes and held back the tally in precincts it most effectively controlled. If, despite repeating, the machine needed several thousand votes to win, these controlled precincts would falsify the needed votes.

Political campaigns were expensive and were financed by assessing officeholders approximately 3 percent of their annual salary and by contributions from businessmen. The Republican machine's support of protection, and its reluctance to tax high incomes paid off in generous business support. Special favors granted by state and local bosses to specific businessmen also garnered large dividends. Money derived from dispensing patronage and franchises gave the machine a measure of independence that twentieth-century reform has denied contemporary politicians. The machine, however, used its power and relative independence not for the commonweal, but to perpetuate itself.

With a vicelike grip on nominations and elections, the well-financed machine developed leaders, but Cameron, Quay, and Penrose can hardly be termed statesmen. The machine required so much attention that it dominated them. Apart from their interest in the tariff, they were identified with no important legislation or policies. Their main interest and talent lay in tinkering with party mechanism, nominating candidates, and managing campaigns. For example, Quay managed Benjamin Harrison's 1888 campaign and in 1900 conspired to shelve Theodore Roosevelt in the vice presidency. At best Cameron, Quay, and Penrose were behind-the-scenes powers in national Republican councils. On the state level, they were powerful enough to prevent the growth of other leaders. There was no place in the Republican machine or even in machine-dominated Pennsylvania for either popular or issue-oriented political leaders.

THE MACHINE IN ACTION

The interplay during the late nineteenth century among the political boss, the local organization, and the governor in their quest for power illustrates the operation of the machine. Cameron and Quay could not dictate to all governors, nor could they boss all local Republican organizations. The machine was not monolithic; quasi-independent local Philadelphia and Pittsburgh machines were important components and at times the boss faced serious revolts. Nevertheless, the boss and his chief lieutenants, through their control of the nominating procedure, decided who should be governor; and the governors, appointed because they were followers rather than leaders, were beholden to the machine in varying degrees. Whether Republican or Democratic, late-nineteenth-century Pennsylvania governors had limited powers. Apart from appointing the secretary of the commonwealth, the attorney general, and some minor posts, the governor had little patronage. Local and Federal civil servants were far more numerous than state officers. Nineteenth-century Pennsylvanians favored local government and through the new constitution jealously restricted the power of state government. When it became necessary to bequeath some of their power, local politicians preferred giving it to the Legislature, which was more responsive to local pressure. Finally, the constitution crippled Pennsylvania governors by denying them two consecutive terms.

General John F. Hartranft—a Civil War hero and Governor Geary's auditor general—as the last governor elected under the 1838 constitution, could and did serve two consecutive terms (1873–1879). Most of his administration coincided with a severe depression that brought unemployment and unrest and culminated with the great 1877 strike. Though he later doubted that in the long run bayonets effectively maintained industrial peace, Hartranft frequently utilized the state militia to quell violence (incidently quelling strikes as well) and in 1877 not only called for but also personally commanded Federal troops at Pittsburgh. When not involved with turmoil, the Hartranft administration began a series of geological surveys, provided for more effective state regulation of banking, and reorganized the state militia as part of the National Guard.

During Hartranft's term, Cameron's power was great but not absolute. In 1878, for example, Simon Cameron and his son Donald, who had succeeded him in the United States Senate, agreed with their lieutenants to partition the state; the Camerons would continue to rule the center and Mackey the West, but Quay would be installed in the East. At their behest, the Legislature created and Hartranft gave Quay the lucrative office of recorder of Philadelphia, but opposition by James McManes—ruler of the gas trust and boss of Philadelphia—and by Philadelphians, who were incensed by what amounted to a $30,000 tax, forced Quay to resign his Philadelphia foothold the following year.

Quay constantly struggled for power. Under Hartranft's successor, Henry M. Hoyt (1879–1883), who since 1875 had been chairman of the Republican State Committee, Quay initially was successful. He and Mackey succeeded, over Cameron's opposition, in nominating Hoyt, and after Quay abandoned his plan to control Philadelphia, Hoyt reappointed him to his old position, secretary of the commonwealth. Quay, however, soon suffered a series of reverses. Independent Republicans forced Cameron and Quay to accept their candidate for the Senate in 1881, and Hoyt took an independent reform tack and by 1882 broke with the Cameron-Quay organization. Hoyt reduced the state debt, prosecuted railroads for freight-rate discriminations (particularly in oil) until they settled out of court, promoted public health by annulling the charters of quack medical schools that had been selling diplomas and by establishing a state medical board, and advanced penal reform (to which he was deeply committed) by promoting reform institutions for young offenders.

Quitting his post as secretary of the commonwealth in 1882, Quay remained out of office for three years and lost considerable power. Not only had Democrat Robert E. Pattison been elected governor in 1882, but within the Republican party Pittsburgh's boss Chris Magee (Mackey had died) was in the ascendancy. In 1885 an old treasury scandal broke; it became known that Quay had lost state money on the New York stock market in the late 1870s. Technically he had borrowed the money from banks where state funds were deposited, but Quay had promised that the state would not ask for the money he had borrowed until it was repaid. To make up the loss of $250,000 and keep the scandal quiet, Don Cameron had put up $100,000 and Quay had pledged securities worth $150,000. By incredible political alchemy, Quay converted this last disaster into a victory. He denied nothing, declared himself a candidate for state treasurer, and reminded his political debtors that he needed and expected repayment. On the back of former Governor Curtin's request for his help two decades earlier, Quay penned, "I am a candidate for the Republican nomination for State Treasurer, I ask your support." Quay not only smashed Magee's candidate for the nomination but in the ensuing election defeated the Democratic candidate by a 50,000 majority. The election choked Republican insurgents and made Quay the leader of Pennsylvania Republicans. They elected his man James A. Beaver governor in 1886, and in 1887 Quay joined Don Cameron in the United States Senate.

General Beaver, whom independent Republicans had rejected in 1882 as the Cameron-Quay nominee, was a thoroughly respectable Civil War hero. Four years later the independents returned to the Republican party and supported Beaver even though he was still Quay's nominee. Beaver, who served as governor from 1887 to 1891, has been overshadowed by Pattison who both preceded and followed him, but Beaver both advanced industrial education (leading ultimately to the establishment of manual training schools) and increased good roads in Pennsylvania. He also advocated (but the people overwhelmingly rejected) a constitutional amendment to prohibit the manufacture and sale of intoxicating beverages, and after the Johnstown Flood (May 31, 1889), caused in part by irresponsible logging, Beaver urged that Pennsylvania create adequate forest reserves. He quickly responded to the Johnstown tragedy by appointing a flood-relief commission and placing Adjutant General Daniel H. Hastings in command. Hastings brought order and relief to Johnstown and became the hero of rank-and-file Republicans and their choice as Beaver's successor. Quay, however, offended many Republicans by refusing to nominate Hastings, and Pattison again triumphed.

Four years later Quay could not ignore the popular Hastings, who was elected governor in 1894 by a 240,000-vote margin. In the depression following the Panic of 1893, Pennsylvania had become a one-party state, and it would remain so for forty years. Quay's control of the Republican party, however, was not assured, for Hastings proved as independent as Hoyt. The positive accomplishments of Hastings' administration (1895–1899)—which created the Superior Court to relieve pressure on the Supreme Court, the state Department

Matthew S. Quay, Republican senator and boss.
(Library of Congress)

of Agriculture to aid farmers, and the first state forest reserves to foster conservation—were overshadowed by his struggle with Quay.

In 1895 insurgents led by Hastings, David Martin of Philadelphia, and Chris Magee and William Flinn of Pittsburgh, formed an anti-Quay combine to capture the Republican State Convention. Once again Quay wrote to hundreds of Republicans, "I am a candidate for chairman of the Republican State Committee, and if I have any friends in Pennsylvania I ask them to stand by me at this time." Taking a distinctly reform tack, Quay struck at the combine's vitals when he deplored the use of money in politics, corporate control of government and elections, exclusive franchises, and favoritism in letting contracts. Strongly supported by rural delegates, Quay had a majority when Israel Durham and Boies Penrose won for him a third of the Philadelphia delegates. Quay remained in control, Martin's power eroded, and Durham became the new boss of Philadelphia.

Quay survived the combine challenge only to be more severely tried by insurgents including a Business Men's Republican League led by merchant prince John Wanamaker. In his attacks, Wanamaker described the perfectly operating machine, but by revolting he demonstrated that Quay could not count on a perfectly operating machine. Quay, Wanamaker asserted, not only controlled the Republican State Committee, two United States senators, thirty congressmen, and the Pennsylvania Senate and House of Representatives, but also thousands of Federal and state officeholders and the employees of institutions—such as mental hospitals and normal schools—dependent on state appropriations. Wanamaker damned corporations as the "principal allies and partners of the machine" and described Carnegie's workmen being "marched to the polls under the supervision of superintendents and foremen" and voting for Quay candidates "under penalty of losing their jobs."

Wanamaker's accusations won more adherents when just before the election of 1898 a new scandal broke. The Peoples Bank of Philadelphia (long a depository of state funds) failed in 1898, and papers revealing that its cashier and Quay had speculated with state funds fell into the hands of Quay's enemies. Furthermore, Quay, rather than the commonwealth, had received interest on state funds deposited in the Peoples Bank. Quay was arrested in October 1898, a damaging hearing followed, and he was released on bail. Quay's man William A. Stone nevertheless easily became governor (1899–1903), but insurgents carried enough legislative districts to hold the balance of power between the machine and Democrats. A few weeks after the election a Philadelphia grand jury indicted Quay on four counts involving the misuse of state funds, and his effort to quash the indictment in the state Supreme Court failed. When the Legislature assembled in January 1899, insurgents led by Senators Flinn of Pittsburgh and Martin of Philadelphia prevented Quay's reelection to the Senate but failed to agree on his successor. Quay's trial began on April 11, the deadlocked Legislature after sixty-six fruitless ballots adjourned on April 20, and on April 21—thanks to the judge's exclusion of evidence relating to Quay's dealings with earlier state treasurers and the heavy reliance by the defense on the statute of limitations—the jury declared Quay not guilty. Within an hour Governor Stone had appointed Quay to the Senate, but insurgents carried their fight there, and on April 24, 1900, Quay was refused a seat. The day following the Senate vote, the Republican State Convention met, endorsed Stone's appointment of Quay 280–69, insisted Quay remain a candidate, and named him a delegate to the Republican National Convention. Quay vigorously campaigned for a friendly legislature, but when the Legislature convened in January 1901, insurgents led by Flinn and Martin fused with Democrats to command a majority. On the crucial vote for Speaker of the House, Quay managed to dislodge five Democrats from the fusion and his man won by one vote. Some insurgents then moved over to Quay, and the Legislature reelected him to the Senate with twelve votes to spare. The six-year struggle to overthrow Quay was over; the "Old Man" was victorious.

Quay was an unusual man. A Congressional Medal of Honor winner for valor at Fredericksburg, who championed the American Indian, he read widely in several languages and owned one of the finest libraries in America. Devoid of hypocrisy, he was blatantly cynical. "Providence has given us the victory," exclaimed Benjamin Harrison in 1888. "Think of the man!" commented National Chairman Quay, "He ought to know that Providence hadn't a damn thing to do with it." Quay later added that Harrison "would never know how close a number of men were compelled to approach the penitentiary to make him President." Quay combined the personal qualities essential to a political boss. He was diplomatic, secretive, audacious, decisive, indefatigable, but not vindictive, and above all loyal to his party, friends, and organization.

The city machine Urban politics during Quay's day was frequently complex. Local politicians, state bosses, businessmen, and reformers fought to control the lucrative franchises and contracts awarded by expanding cities. Two such struggles—one over Philadelphia street-railroad franchises and the other over Pittsburgh water-supply contracts—produced chaos and illustrated that while the Republican party dominated both those cities and the state, no one had complete control of the machine. Most of those struggling for power preferred to profit from the cities' problems rather than to solve them.

The evolution of the monopolistic Philadelphia Rapid Transit Company was inextricably involved in municipal and state politics. By 1881 a trio of influential Republicans, Peter A. B. Widener, William H. Kemble, and Matthew S. Quay, controlled three of the most important Philadelphia lines and aimed to establish a monopoly. Widener had served Philadelphia as city treasurer and was a member of the machine, while Kemble was a former state treasurer and Republican national committeeman who had recently been in prison for questionable financial practices. After influencing the 1883 Legislature to permit the creation of traction companies anywhere in Pennsylvania, this trio immediately established the Philadelphia Traction Company combining their holdings into one system. Additional properties were acquired, and the Philadelphia city councils vied with the state Legislature in showering blessings upon this politically powerful company. In the 1890s Philadelphia Traction electrified its lines and battled its two rivals, Peoples' Traction and Electric Traction, until they capitulated in 1896 and helped form the Union Traction Company. The Wideners—father Peter and son George—and their associates William L. Elkins and Thomas Dolan (who also ran the United Gas Improvement Company) quickly dominated the new company and through it Philadelphia's 447-mile street-railway system. But Widener's relations with Quay deteriorated after Kemble died and particularly after 1898 when Widener abandoned Quay who was struggling to get reelected to the Senate while under indictment for misappropriating state funds.

Quay carefully planned his revenge. He allied himself with ruthless, ambitious John M. Mack who had made a fortune mixing paving and electric lighting with political connections. On May 28, 1901, as Widener and his associate Elkins embarked on a European tour, Quay's henchmen introduced bills in the state Legislature creating underground and elevated street railways which could enter upon existing street-railway lines if the city approved. The franchises were both exclusive and perpetual, and the companies were to have unlimited power to borrow money on bonds. Clearly destroying the franchise rights of the Widener-dominated Union Traction Company, these ripper bills were quickly rammed through the Senate and House and received the approval on June 8 of Governor William A. Stone, a loyal machine man. Spurning John Wanamaker's offer to pay the city $2.5 million, the city councils and Mayor Samuel H. ("Stars-and-Stripes Sam") Ashbridge awarded thirteen franchises to Mack on June 14, only seventeen days after Widener and Elkins had left the country.

The ripper bills and the "Philadelphia franchise grab" did not demolish Widener. Mack had the franchises but lacked capital. The rumor that the Pennsylvania Railroad would join Mack in building a Broad Street subway inspired Widener to seek an accord. The result was the emergence in 1902 of the ultimate in traction holding companies, the over-capitalized Philadelphia Rapid Transit Company. The new company agreed to lease Union Traction for an annual cost beginning at $900,000 and doubling to $1.8 million by 1908, in addition to guaranteeing the rentals of Union Traction's underliers, bringing the total to about 8 million dollars. The deal was enormously profitable for the Wideners since Union Traction, a waterlogged holding company saddled with innumerable leases and unable to pay dividends, was now guaranteed over 17 percent annually on its paid-in capital. Mack also made a killing on the deal when Philadelphia Rapid Transit paid $2 million for his thirteen ripper companies capitalized at $7.4 million, of which only $3.4 million was subscribed and a mere $338,400 paid in. Philadelphians, however, paid for that waterlogged pyramid in high fares for poor service.

In Pittsburgh the fight for pure water tragically became part of a long and arduous see-saw struggle between rival Republican factions. By the early 1890s a Republican ring headed by Boss Christopher L. Magee and William Flinn dominated Pittsburgh. Apart from the lucrative sources of franchises and vice, the Pittsburgh ring grafted considerable sums from public contracts. Chris Magee's cousin, E. M. Bigelow (known in Pittsburgh circles as "the Extravagant"), served the ring as director of public works. Bigelow awarded contracts to the lowest *responsible* bidder and with striking regularity Bigelow judged that the construction firm of Booth & Flinn, Ltd., made up for its high bids in responsibility. As a matter of fact, a municipal reformer Oliver McClintock insisted, and backed his charge with photographs, that Booth & Flinn did abominable work while charging outrageous prices.

Reformers challenged the ring in the February 1896 mayoralty election. George W. Guthrie, leader of the Democratic remnant Magee did not control, headed the ticket. Supported by McClintock and other municipal reformers he came within a thousand votes of upsetting the ring and forced the promise of a filtration plant. In June 1896 the Filtration Commission began its investigation. Its report of February 1899 recommended construction of a slow-sand-filtration plant. Though the money was on hand by May 1, 1900, a political squabble delayed work for four years. Magee aspired to Quay's United States Senate seat at the same time that E. M. Bigelow and Flinn clashed over contracts. Flinn induced the councilmen to fire Bigelow as director of public works. This move inspired Bigelow's brother Thomas to help Quay defeat Magee. Tom Bigelow also tried to smash the Magee-Flinn ring by inducing the Legislature to grant Pittsburgh a new charter. The new charter temporarily gave the governor the right to appoint the recorder and the recorder the right to appoint the director of public works. Thanks to Tom Bigelow's lobbying and Governor Stone's appointment of a friendly recorder, E. M. Bigelow was back in office a year after Flinn had tossed him out. Bigelow then fired his predecessor's engineer who was planning the filtration plant. Comprised of Magee-Flinn men and hostile to Bigelow, the councils of Pittsburgh attacked him for delaying the filtration plant. Furthermore the ring convinced the agreeable Governor Stone to name a new recorder. To his letter of removal, Stone added the unique postscript, "I was not bribed." Once again Bigelow was out and the ring was in control. It attempted to move fast but was stymied by the Bigelow or reform faction whose delaying tactics included injunction proceedings and quibbles over mechanical details and legal technicalities. Magee subsequently died, and in April 1903 the Bigelow faction defeated Flinn. Serious opposition to the sand-filtration plant ceased, and in March 1905 the final contract was let. Political squabbling caused four years of unnecessary delays, from April 1900 to April 1904, and sacrified at least 1,538 lives to typhoid fever.

THE LOYAL OPPOSITION

Until 1894 the Democratic party threatened the Republican machine. It controlled the Legislature that elected William A. Wallace to the United States Senate in 1875; and in both 1882 and 1890 Pennsylvanians chose a Democrat, Robert E. Pattison, as their governor. After these victories it was not until 1934 that Pennsylvanians elected a Democrat as either governor or senator. Though they failed to carry the state for a presidential nominee from 1860 to 1932, Democrats from 1876 to 1892 came reasonably close. Rutherford B. Hayes defeated Samuel J. Tilden by only 19,000 votes in 1876, and the Republican plurality in those years did not exceed 85,000. Republicans, however, were steadily gaining; and in 1896 William McKinley received 300,000 more votes than did William Jennings Bryan. From that date until 1932 no Democratic presidential candidate came close to carrying Pennsylvania except Woodrow Wilson in 1912; and though Republicans split their vote between Theodore Roosevelt and William Howard Taft, Wilson lost to Roosevelt by 50,000 votes. The Democrats from 1876 to 1892 usually won about one-third of the congressional contests, but in 1894 Democrats won only two of Pennsylvania's twenty-eight seats in the House of Representatives. Clearly from the late 1870s to the early 1890s Democratic opposition in Pennsylvania reflected the resurgent national party led by Tilden and Grover Cleveland, but the Panic of 1893 virtually destroyed both the state and the national Democratic parties. Woodrow Wilson finally in 1912 and 1916 revived Democrats on a national level, but to resurrect them in Pennsylvania required both the Great Depression of the 1930s and Franklin D. Roosevelt.

In the late nineteenth century, sources of Democratic strength in Pennsylvania were essentially the same as in the nation. The party suffered from what has been called political schizophrenia. The conservative, rural, agrarian, Protestant part of the Democratic party was chiefly composed of German and Scotch-Irish groups in interior counties, while the liberal, urban, laboring, Catholic element was primarily made up of Irish groups in Philadelphia, Allegheny County, and the coal areas. Although great blocks of Democrats voted in Philadelphia and Pittsburgh, from 1880 to 1896 they carried neither city in any election for governor or president.

Both issues and party organization help explain why Democratic power gradually eroded until the Panic of 1893 suddenly washed it almost entirely away. A minority party cannot afford bickering leaders, factionalism, or poor organization, and all three cursed Democrats. Furthermore, the Pennsylvania Democratic party had the uncanny knack of coming up on the wrong side of current issues. It abandoned the high tariff when protection was most popular; espoused free silver when bankers, industrialists, laborers, and farmers came to loath inflation; and failed to embrace reform despite numerous, prominent, reform-minded, independent Republicans. The Democratic party declined because it failed to adjust to the post-Civil War world of Pennsylvania. Visions of great antebellum triumphs under Jackson, Polk, and Buchanan, which had occurred during the lives of many postwar leaders, burdened the party and kept it looking backward.

Not only did Democrats come up on the wrong side of issues but they could match neither Republican organization nor Republican financial resources. With few officeholders to assess, few businessmen to contribute, and little prospect that expenditures would produce victories, Democrats were handicapped. Democratic leaders did not wield power comparable to that of Cameron or Quay, because they headed an agglomeration of independent county organizations whose Jeffersonian principles made them more opposed to central authority. State leaders cajoled rather than ordered county leaders, who were primarily interested in carrying local elections.

Worse yet, Democrats bickered incessantly over the little power state leadership afforded. In the 1870s and 1880s William A. Wallace and Samuel J. Randall struggled to control Pennsylvania Democrats. After the Liberal Republican debacle in 1872, Wallace, who had opposed fusion with that movement, emerged triumphant. In 1875 he went to the United States Senate, and though Randall achieved power on the national level as Speaker of the House of Representataves from 1876 to 1881, Wallace remained top dog in Pennsylvania until the close of 1880. In that year Wallace suffered a double defeat; Republicans prevented his return to the Senate, and the Democratic presidential candiate, General Winfield Scott Hancock of Pennsylvania, lost to James A. Garfield. After the defeat of Wallace, Randall's power grew.

Thanks to the mugwump Republican revolt against Cameron and Quay, Democratic prospects, so dismal in 1881, brightened in 1882. Independent Republicans nominated Senator John Stewart of Franklin County for governor in opposition to the machine candidate James A. Beaver, while Democrats, sensing victory, overcame their antiurban and antireform bias and nominated the reforming city controller of Philadelphia, Robert E. Pattison. The Democrats triumphed; Pattison won the governorship with a minority of the votes cast.

Economy and reform characterized the first Pattison administration (1883–1887). Pattison reduced the debt, eliminated useless offices, and appointed qualified civil servants. He also insisted that corporations—particularly railroads and canal companies—obey the constitition and the laws, and he urged the Legislature to reapportion legislative, congressional, and judicial districts as the 1873 constitution required. Although they reapportioned judicial districts, neither the Democratic House nor the Republican Senate (even in special session) would agree to legislative and congressional redistricting. Incensed that the special session cost half a million dollars and accomplished nothing, Pattison pushed through a law eliminating per diem allowances and compensating legislators $1,500 for regular sessions and $500 for special sessions. Pattison also personally investigated and reformed the neglectful, inhumane, and corrupt administration of soldiers' orphan schools.

Independents liked Pattison, but they did not like the Democratic party. They realized that Pattison was at odds with spoils-minded Democratic state leaders who wished to

Robert E. Pattison, Democratic governor. (Pennsylvania Historical and Museum Commission)

fire Republican officeholders and that corruption was rampant in Lehigh, Schuylkill, and Philadelphia Counties. The Schuylkill County directors of the poor, for example, used county funds to perpetuate the local Democratic machine, and to prevent genuine opposition several Philadelphia leaders were financed by the dominant Republican machine.

Still persisting in their predilection for faction, Pennsylvania Democrats by 1886 had formed three distinct groups. The most powerful group followed Randall, who championed protection and dispensed patronage in Pennsylvania after Cleveland became President in 1885. Another group continued to support Wallace, an excellent organizer who inspired personal loyalty, and a small group with reform proclivities followed Pattison. Randall dominated the 1886 convention, which nominated Chauncey F. Black as Pattison's successor, but Wallace, who wanted the nomination himself, refused to campaign for Black, independents supported Beaver, and the Democrats were defeated. Though Randall continued to lead the party, his days were numbered. As Cleveland's interest in lowering the tariff quickened, so did his friendship with the Erie industrialist William L. Scott. In 1887 Cleveland deprived Randall of patronage and invited Scott, rather than Randall, to the Oak View Conferences that determined Democrats' stand on revenue reform. With his power slipping, Randall's lieutenants William F. Harrity (whom he had made postmaster of Philadelphia) and William U. Hensel (state chairman) abandoned him.

Scott's short-lived leadership was followed by Harrity's disastrous reign. Since he was one of the three largest coal operators in western Pennsylvania, Scott was unpopular with laborers. Realizing that his support would bring defeat to any candidate, he refused to take part in the 1890 gubernatorial campaign. Scott, Cleveland, and particularly Harrity supported Pattison for the nomination, while Wallace united his supporters with what was left of Randall's following. Realizing that Pattison could attract independent votes necessary for victory, Democrats once again nominated and elected him governor. With Harrity both nominating him and serving as his campaign manager, Pattison during his second term (1891–1895) recognized his debt to Democratic politicians. Unlike his first term when he appointed his minister as his private secretary, Pattison now named to that post H. D. Tate, leader of Bedford County Democrats, and further dismayed reformers by appointing Harrity secretary of the commonwealth and Hensel attorney general. Nevertheless during his second administration Pattison continued to stress the reduction of taxation, economy, reform, and obedience—particularly by large corporations—to the state's constitution and laws. Although the Republican-dominated Legislature hampered his efforts, Pattison in 1891 procured enactment of the secret ballot. Reformers, however, remained aloof and would not join the party led by Harrity. Democratic national chairman from 1892 to 1896, Harrity consolidated his power during Pattison's administration, but the depression following the Panic of 1893 demoralized and disintegrated his party. Though Cleveland lost Pennsylvania by only 64,000 votes in 1892, Republicans after the Panic of 1893 swept the state by previously unheard of majorities. Democratic losses between 1892 and 1896 ranged from a substantial 4.4 percent of the voters in totally rural counties to an enormous 13.9 percent in metropolitan Philadelphia and Allegheny Counties.

Laborers became distinctly cool to Democrats in the 1890s. Laborers were convinced not only that Democratic tinkering with the protective tariff had caused the Panic of 1893 and their distress but also that the Democratic party was hostile to their aspirations. Scott, an enemy of organized labor, had led Pennsylvania Democrats, and two years before Cleveland broke the 1894 Pullman Strike with Federal troops, Pattison had broken the Homestead Strike with state militia.

Free silver dealt Democrats a devastating blow. Though the Pennsylvania Republican congressional delegation, reflecting the desires of Pennsylvania iron manufacturers, favored the 1875 inflation bill thirteen to five, by the 1890s laborers, farmers, and businessmen— whether bankers, manufacturers, or merchants—opposed the free coinage of silver. Though it advocated a number of fundamental reforms, the Populist party was not popular in Pennsylvania. Only about 8,000 Pennsylvanians supported James B. Weaver, the Populist presidential candidate in 1892, whereas twelve years earlier 20,643 had supported him as a Greenbacker. Populists' candidate for governor in 1894 won only 2 percent of the votes, and their candidate for state treasurer in 1895 only 1 percent. Populists received little support from urban wage earners or from coal miners, and their sparse rural support concentrated in underpopulated and less-prosperous areas such as Crawford, Indiana, and Potter Counties. When Democrats embraced part of the Populist program by adopting free silver in 1896, their losses were accentuated in the prosperous eastern farming counties. German farmers were hostile to inflation; in many Lehigh County townships the Republican vote grew from 30 to 50 percent. Democratic stands on the tariff and silver drove laborers and farmers to the Republican party. With Democrats leaderless, divided, and impotent, Pennsylvania had become a one-party state.

BIBLIOGRAPHY

Frank B. Evans: *Pennsylvania Politics, 1872–1877: A Study in Leadership* (1966) discusses the last years of Simon Cameron's regime in Pennsylvania. On the constitution of 1873, see Mahlon H. Hellerich: "The Pennsylvania Constitution of 1873" (doctoral dissertation, University of Pennsylvania, 1956). On Quay and his machine, consult Leila H. Rupp: "Matthew Stanley Quay in Pennsylvania State Politics" (master's thesis, University of Pittsburgh, 1928); James K. Pollock: "Matthew Stanley Quay," *Dictionary of American Biography,* vol. 25, pp. 296–298; Matthew Stanley Quay: *Pennsylvania Politics: The Campaign of 1900 as Set Forth in the Speeches of Hon. Matthew S. Quay* (1901); John Wanamaker: *The Speeches of John Wanamaker on Quayism and Boss Domination in Pennsylvania Politics* (1898).

For municipal politics, see Lincoln Steffens: *The Shame of the Cities* (1957). Philadelphia traction matters are discussed in Delos F. Wilcox: *Municipal Franchises . . . ,* 2 vols. (1910–1911); in Gustavus Myers: "The Most Corrupt City in the World," *Living Age,* 7th ser., vol. 22 (1904), pp. 449–464; and especially in Harold E. Cox and John F. Meyers: "The Philadelphia Traction Monopoly and the Pennsylvania Constitution of 1874: The Prostitution of an Ideal," *Pennsylvania History,* vol. 35 (1968), pp. 406–423. Pittsburgh's fight for pure water is detailed in Frank E. Wing: "Thirty-five Years of Typhoid," in Paul U. Kellogg (ed.): *Pittsburgh Survey,* 6 vols. (1909–1914), vol. 5, pp. 63–86.

For information on Democrats during these decades, see Lewis Wesley Rathgeber: "The Democratic Party in Pennsylvania, 1880–1896" (doctoral dissertation, University of Pittsburgh, 1953). Consult Irwin Unger: *The Greenback Era: A Social and Political History of American Finance, 1865–1879* (1964); and Ralph R. Ricker: "The Greenback-Labor Movement in Pennsylvania, 1870–1889" (doctoral dissertation, Pennsylvania State University, 1955) on the inflationary mood of Pennsylvania in the 1870s and 1880s. On the Pennsylvania Populists, see William E. Lyons: "Populism in Pennsylvania, 1892–1901," *Pennsylvania History,* vol. 32 (1965), pp. 49–65. On the Bryan campaign, see S. K. Stevens: "The Election of 1896 in Pennsylvania," *Pennsylvania History,* vol. 4 (1937), pp. 65–87.

On the realignment of Pennsylvania parties in the 1890s, see Walter Dean Burnham, *Critical Elections and the Mainsprings of American Politics* (1970).

CHAPTER TWENTY-TWO

Society and Culture in the Gilded Age

Pennsylvania transformed itself in the decades following the Civil War. The twin forces of rapid industrialization and urbanization affected businessmen and laborers, farmers and politicians, and also influenced education and scholarship, religion and thought, journalism and literature, drama and music, architecture and art. Public education expanded; dilettante scholars gave way to specialists attached to universities; and secularism, Darwinism, and the social gospel struck at fundamental religion. Partisan, personal journalism succumbed to impersonal, "independent" newspapers dominated not by politicians but by advertising businessmen; realistic and even naturalistic writers began to challenge romantic escapist authors; taste in drama and music improved; and Pennsylvanians experimented in new forms and won international homage in architecture, painting, and sculpture.

Though cultural and intellectual changes may be delineated, they portray mere (albeit important) segments of society. Extraordinary events and crises, however, frequently concentrate and capsule society's accomplishments and behavior and can reduce society's portrait to manageable proportions. Focusing on two such events—the joyous 1876 Centennial Exhibition in Philadelphia and the cataclysmic 1889 Johnstown Flood—illustrates some characteristics of Pennsylvania and American society in the Gilded Age.

THE CENTENNIAL EXHIBITION

Eighteen seventy-six, the centennial year of American independence, opened with the ringing of almost every bell and the blowing of almost every whistle in and around Philadelphia. That night while the old colonial flag flew over Independence Hall, Dwight Moody and Ira

Construction site in Fairmont Park for the 1876 Centennial Exhibition. (Historical Society of Pennsylvania)

Sankey staged three staggered revival meetings and wished everyone a "Happy Eternity." Held for nine weeks in the huge freight depot John Wanamaker was converting into the country's first department store, this revival attracted preexhibition crowds and excursion trains to Philadelphia and helped prepare America's soul for the centennial celebration.

The nation's birthday party lasted from May to November and was attended by 8 million people, or one out of every five Americans. It took place in Fairmount Park, where 236 acres were enclosed for what was officially called the United States International Exhibition. Because the 100 years being celebrated had seen America change from an agrarian country to an industrial nation, the center of the exhibition was the great Corliss engine, whose geared flywheel and two huge walking beams dominated Machinery Hall and symbolized the nation's technological growth. On opening day George H. Corliss, designer of the machine, directed President Ulysses S. Grant and Emperor Dom Pedro of Brazil as they each turned a lever to start the huge steam engine which powered surrounding machines. Crowds cheered as 13 acres of machines began spinning cotton, printing newspapers, making shoes, pumping water, and performing other tasks. Calling the Corliss engine "an athlete of steel and iron," William Dean Howells said, "It is in these things of iron and steel that the national genius most freely speaks; by and by the inspired marbles, the breathing canvases, the great literature; for the present America is voluble in the strong metals and their infinite uses."

Shortly after the Corliss engine was put in motion, Brazil's Empress Theresa pulled a tasseled gold cord which started a 6-horsepower steam engine in the Woman's Pavilion. Looms started and a weekly magazine, *The New Century for Woman,* streamed from a press. Women not only operated all machines in the building but were responsible for everything shown, from statuary to corsets. Etchings by Queen Victoria occupied the place of honor. Benjamin Franklin's great-granddaughter, Mrs. Elizabeth Duane Gillespie, had toured the country organizing tea parties to raise money for these exhibitions. So successful were her efforts that the Women's Centennial Committee also financed other parts of the exhibition including weekly symphony concerts during the centennial summer.

Other pavilions included Industrial Hall, whose central attraction was a fountain designed by Frederic Bartholdi, creator of the Statue of Liberty; and twenty-four buildings representing various states and numerous buildings representing foreign countries. Memorial Hall and Horticultural Hall were intended as permanent additions to Fairmount Park and were planned by the engineer and landscape architect Herman J. Schwarzmann. Designed from European models and costing $1.5 million, Memorial Hall had 2½ miles of picture-covered walls. Unfamiliar with nude art, Puritanical Americans were shocked by many of the paintings and statues from France and Italy but still pushed and jammed so much that exhibition goers found it difficult to view the artwork. Cast in the Moorish style of the twelfth century, Horticultural Hall was a "de lux greenhouse, a glazed iron cage." Banded in gay colors inside and out, with ornamental stairs leading up to galleries painted blue and gold, it typified both the period's interest in new materials and its love of the romantic and exotic. With industrialism taking precedence over agriculture, it was probably the last great building of its kind devoted to horticulture.

Across from the main entrance of the exhibition, the Pennsylvania Railroad built a depot where excursion trains arrived and departed every 30 seconds. From all points west, train fares were reduced as much as 30 percent. Exhibition visitors paid 50 cents admission, and most took a 5-cent ride through the exhibition grounds on one of ten narrow-gauge trains. Each train had a locomotive and four open-air cars, which were so packed that as one centennial goer complained, "you have to hang on by your eyelids."

Especially impressive to exhibition crowds were the technological innovations. These included the new typewriter on which for 50 cents one could have a letter written, a lamp burning electricity rather than gas or oil, and Alexander Graham Bell's telephone. Among other popular items were the hand and torch of the not-yet-completed Statue of Liberty, 6,000 Chinese silkworms busily producing silk, 10,000 newspapers from every state in the union, each in its own pigeonhole and available for free reading, fountains with ice water (furnished primarily by the Temperance Society), and a "plaster cast of George Washington riding heavenward on the back of an eagle." *Harper's Weekly* quoted Fukui Makoto, Japanese commissioner to the exhibition, who captured the crowds in words vivid to all visitors of subsequent fairs:

> The first day crowds come like sheep, run here, run there, run everywhere. One man start, one thousand follow. Nobody can see anything, nobody can do anything. All rush, push, tear, shout, make plenty noise, say damn great many times, get very tired, and go home.

In the midst of the exhibition Philadelphia's greatest moment was July 4. The Centennial Committee planned a special celebration at Independence Square. Made bold by the success of the Woman's Pavilion, suffragettes asked to present, but not to read, their special Declaration of Independence for Women. When their request was turned down, they grew militant. Secretly they planned for five prominent members possessing press cards to read their declaration. As 150,000 people jammed the area around Independence Square, the day's program began. Honored guests included presidential candidate Rutherford B. Hayes and Civil War Generals William T. Sherman and Philip H. Sheridan. Band music was fol-

Woman's Pavilion at the Centennial Exhibition (1876). (Historical Society of Pennsylvania)

lowed by a chorus singing a hymn composed for the occasion by Oliver Wendell Holmes. Next William S. Stokley, the mayor of Philadelphia, handed the original manuscript of the Declaration of Independence to Richard Henry Lee of Virginia, who had been chosen to read it. As Lee finished, Susan B. Anthony, Matilda Gage, Sara Spencer, Lillie Blake, and Phoebe Couzins walked to the front and with a few carefully chosen words Miss Anthony introduced to the stunned crowd the suffragettes' declaration. The five determined women next distributed copies as they marched to the musicians' platform (opposite the speaker's platform), where the others clustered about Miss Anthony who read their entire declaration while the Poet Bayard Taylor simultaneously read his National Ode from the speaker's platform. Most men present saw little connection between Thomas Jefferson's declaration and that of the women who had marred the centennial Fourth of July celebration. But for women who could not vote and had difficulty keeping property after marriage the connection was apparent and made them determined to strive for their freedom during the centennial year.

THE JOHNSTOWN FLOOD

On May 31, 1889, the South Fork Dam broke and poured 20 million tons of water into the populated valley where Johnstown stood, not quite 15 miles below. According to David G. McCullough, historian of the disaster, at least 2,209 men, women, and children perished in this terrible flood, the worst this country has had. Dominant themes of the Gilded Age are demonstrated by the Johnstown Flood and its aftermath. The doctrine of laissez-faire, very much in vogue, discouraged inspection or regulation of the dam. Belief in individualism insisted that people could do what they wished with their property even to the point of endangering others. Widespread casualness bordering on callousness was rampant. Because the Pittsburgh men who owned the South Fork Dam (and were most responsible for the disaster) were both wealthy and prominent, they were never held accountable for the results of their carelessness. But once the disaster struck, a spirit of cooperation prevailed. Men who were ordinary the day before proved themselves heroes, and almost everyone put aside his personal tragedy and loss to help care for the injured and homeless, bury the dead, and clear away the debris. People from other parts of the state, the nation, and the world warmheartedly responded with $3,742,818.78 for the area plus thousands of workmen and trainloads of provisions.

Part of the Main Line of the public works (Pennsylvania's answer to the Erie Canal), the South Fork Dam was built to keep the canal west of Johnstown supplied with water during dry summers. Built of horizontal layers of clay, the dam had a 72-foot-wide spillway cut through the rocky hillside to which the dam's eastern end was secured. The length of the breast was slightly over 930 feet, the top width was about 20 feet, and the thickness at the base was 270 feet. There were five large cast-iron pipes in the stone culvert at the center of the base. Controlled from a nearby wooden tower, these pipes could release water down to the South Fork, where it flowed down the Little Conemaugh to the Johnstown basin. Shortly after the dam's completion on June 10, 1852, the Pennsylvania Railroad rendered it obsolete, and it was left to weather in the woods.

By 1879 when the South Fork Fishing and Hunting Club acquired possession of the dam it had been seriously weakened. The dam had been partially washed out in 1862, the control tower subsequently had burned to the ground, and in 1875 the discharge pipes (which when opened in 1862 had averted a tragedy) had been removed and sold for scrap. The club restored the dam, but the work, supervised by a man with no engineering credentials, was poorly planned and executed and cost a mere $17,000. The discharge pipes were not replaced, and rock, mud, brush, hemlock boughs, hay, and even horse manure were dumped into the washed-out portion of the dam.

Rumor had it that all club members were millionaires. Membership in the club, which owned the dam, the lake, the boats, and about 160 additional acres, cost $800, and the sixty-one members were an elite group. Andrew Carnegie, Henry Clay Frick, and Henry Phipps, Jr., a Carnegie partner, were all members of the club, as were Robert Pitcairn of the Pennsylvania Railroad and Andrew Mellon. The membership also included Philander C. Knox, who would become secretary of state; George F. Huff, a future congressman; John G. A. Leishman, who would become the first United States ambassador to Turkey; and Samuel Rea, a future president of the Pennsylvania Railroad. Apparently none of these men, despite their expertise in related fields, gave a moment's thought to the strength of their dam, nor did the club take action when the Cambria Iron Company protested the want of a discharge pipe and the unsubstantial repairs and offered to contribute liberally to make the dam "absolutely safe."

Flashfloods were synonymous with spring for the people of Johnstown, and, with a head of water behind the earthen dam high above them, rumors that the dam would break accompanied the floods down the valley. Unaware that they were creating part of their problem, people of the valley continued stripping their mountains and hills for lumber and narrowing their river channel for new buildings and bridges. There were bad floods in 1885, 1887, and 1888, for each year "there was a little less river to handle more runoff." And each spring as they waded in the streets of Johnstown residents greeted each other with, "Well, this is the day the old dam is going to break." Years later Victor Heiser, who was his family's sole survivor of the flood, recalled, "The townspeople . . . grew calloused to the possibility of danger. 'Sometime,' they thought, 'that dam will give way, but it won't ever happen to us!'"

The night before the flood brought the worst rains that anyone could remember. As doomsday dawned club members and employees worked feverishly to prevent what they feared was inevitable. Local people stood by shouting suggestions. Colonel Elias J. Unger, the current president of the club, refused to increase the output of the spillway by tearing out the iron screen that prevented black bass from escaping. Later he became reconciled to sacrificing the fish, but by then the screen was so jammed with debris it would not budge. Three times warnings were sent to Johnstown, but the telegraphers laughed and did not sound a general alarm.

The dam broke and a roaring torrent sped into the valley. The flood rushed past South Fork, which was built on the hillside and through Mineral Point where it claimed sixteen victims and raced on. East Conemaugh was the only town to get a real warning—the tied-down whistle of a work train—which gave the inhabitants 2 minutes to scramble for the hills. Woodvale, the company town for Cambria Iron, came next. The flood took 314 lives, or one out of every three residents. With a "roar like thunder" the water struck Johnstown hardest of all. Preceded by mist "like dust . . . precedes a cavalry charge," it devastated the city in 10 minutes.

"For most people," McCullough states, "they were the most desperate minutes of their lives, snatching at children and struggling through the water, trying to reach the high ground, running upstairs as houses began to quake and split apart, clinging to rafters, window ledges, anything, while the whole world around them seemed to spin faster and faster." Most of the debris from the valley piled up at the stone railroad bridge on the other side of Johnstown. Rescuing people from the wreckage was slow work since few tools were available. Then suddenly in the dark and rainy night the debris at the bridge caught fire. Bystanders rushed to help the 500 to 600 people who were enmeshed in the tangled mass at the bridge. About 80 of the men, women, and children who had miraculously escaped drowning perished in the fire while rescuers tried frantically to save them.

Those who survived the flood and the fire at the bridge woke to a dismal, cold morning; the bodies of men and horses mingled with the debris were already beginning to smell. By noon rafts had been built to aid in the rescue operations, and by midafternoon committees were organized to bury the dead and to care for the living. Early Sunday morning, June 2, a relief train from Pittsburgh got through to the stone bridge. Track had been laid though it was impossible to tell where the roadbed had been, and food was passed out as the train made its way through the devastated valley. By Sunday night more than a thousand doctors, undertakers, workmen, and newspapermen had come, and more were arriving each hour. That night it was decided to request troops to help with the situation, and Governor Beaver quickly appointed a relief commission headed by Adjutant General Daniel H. Hastings.

The Johnstown Flood was the biggest news story since the assassination of Abraham Lincoln, and many of those who read about it rushed to the scene of the disaster. Clara Barton brought her newly organized American Red Cross, and Booth & Flinn, the Pittsburgh

The Johnstown Flood, John Schultz house. Six people were in this house when the flood struck and all survived. (Library of Congress)

contractors, brought 1,000 of their workmen to the area. Rumors of plundering Hungarians who severed dead fingers for diamond rings and further rumors of lynchings of Hungarians for their "fiendish work" made everyone concede that martial law was necessary. When eager reporters gave credence to these unfounded reports, they inflamed latent prejudices and added new wounds to the stricken area. Filled with fear by their neighbors' abuse, many of Johnstown's 500 Hungarians let their children go hungry rather than venture out to collect relief food. When a group of Hungarians, who had dug graves all day, were ambushed and clubbed en route home after dark, newspapermen denied the reports of atrocities they had earlier propagated, and Johnstown citizens let their better instincts triumph.

Gradually Johnstown resumed normal activities. Five months after the flood, Clara Barton and the Red Cross left, taking with them the heartfelt gratitude of Johnstown people. Andrew Carnegie visited the area and characteristically promised a new library, and Robert Pitcairn and the Pennsylvania Railroad were praised for the tremendous feat of reaching Johnstown almost immediately with supplies. But the gratitude that Johnstown felt toward Pittsburgh for responding in its time of need was tempered by the knowledge that Pittsburgh men had been primarily responsible for the disaster. It became apparent that not one penny would be realized from the damage suits that followed the flood, and many people in the valley resented the sacrifice of thousands of lives "to preserve game for some Pittsburgh swells."

THE PUBLIC SCHOOLS

When the Civil War began, Pennsylvania's public system of primary and secondary education had barely begun either to function or to evolve into modern form. Public school facilities expanded after the war, but public high schools encountered opposition from private, non-sectarian, academies with moderate tuition charges that had flourished during the first half of the nineteenth century. These private institutions opposed the growth of high schools until the 1890s when public secondary schools were obviously successful. Most academies then closed, selling their property to the public schools. Many Pennsylvanians opposed high schools, claiming that they were too expensive to maintain, that they benefited the rich (most of whose children attended) at the expense of the poor (few of whose children attended), and that they made children idle, useless, discontented, and unfit for farm labor. Nevertheless by 1900 Pennsylvania had about 300 high schools with 27,412 students. These students made up, however, only 2 percent of the state's total public school enrollment, and Pennsylvania in 1897–1898 ranked lowest among North Atlantic states in high school enrollment. Low high school enrollment resulted automatically in low college enrollment. Massachusetts had 4.19 college students for 1,000 population, while Pennsylvania had only 1.83. Significant strides in providing general high school education were not made until the second decade of the twentieth century.

Although Philadelphia's Central High School was excellent, many Pennsylvania high schools in the last part of the nineteenth century were little more than overgrown grade schools. In 1898 only 102 out of 226 high schools in fifty-nine counties had four-year programs; while 84 were three-year schools. Seventy-four of these three-year schools and 54 of the four-year schools had but one to three teachers; while 12 four-year schools, 24 three-year schools, and 16 of the 19 two-year high schools had only one teacher.

Districts followed their own organizational pattern. Pennsylvania had everything from one- to six-year high schools, and districts frequently created distinct units by dividing the elementary grades into four schools: primary, secondary, intermediate, and grammar. Gaps or breaks between these divisions coupled with a rigid grading and examination system eliminated most students before high school. By 1900 educators recognized that eliminating students and leaving them back had to be stopped, that nonessentials must be removed from the curriculum, and that more flexibility in grading was necessary. These ideas led to the establishment of junior high schools in the twentieth century.

Subject matter and teaching methods proved as important as establishing schools. All agreed that the primary grades should stress the three R's and that high schools should prepare students for life or the "pursuits of commerce, manufactures, and the useful arts," but many debated what best prepared students for teaching (high schools trained elementary teachers) and particularly whether high schools should attempt to prepare students for college. These debates reflected a conflict between the disciplinary and the utilitarian theories of education.

The disciplinary theory which stressed the study of the classics and mathematics to strengthen mind and morals dominated school curriculum and teaching methods in the 1860s. One exercised the mind as a muscle, it was thought, by conjugating ancient verbs and by memorizing the steps in solving mathematical problems. "A blacksmith's arm," remarked James P. Wickersham, state superintendent and the dominant figure in late-nineteenth-century Pennsylvania education, "and the mind of a Bacon grew virtually by the same process. We learn to remember by remembering . . . and in no other way." The disciplinary theory affected the teaching of all subjects. Rules, definitions, and forms had to be memorized from textbooks whether or not they were understood or useful. Stringent examinations required students, for example, to know the highest mountains, largest lakes, longest rivers, and deepest coastline indentations, to date and identify events but not to explain them, to memorize titles and authors, to write a sentence "containing a relative pronoun in the possessive case, a pronominal adjective, and a verb in the subjunctive form of the potential mood."

After 1860 advocates of a utilitarian philosophy of education challenged promoters of the disciplinary theory. Speaking in Kingston, Pennsylvania, Horace Greeley, editor of the *New York Tribune,* anticipated a future trend in education. "The mind," he said, "is disciplined best by its own proper work; and not by making this discipline the great end." Greeley protested that "poring over Greek verbs and Hebrew roots and accents" for mental discipline was a "waste of time and energy." As education became more widespread and democratized, educators reflected the basic utilitarianism of American society and the needs of an industrial state. They demanded more science, more industrial arts, and more experimentation in teaching methods. The utilitarians, however, had little impact on education before the 1876 Centennial Exhibition. Exhibits there proved that Europe had outdistanced the United States in technical and industrial education and touched off a two-decade debate on whether manual training belonged in the schools. Before the debate ended, Philadelphia had opened manual training schools and other districts had introduced industrial arts courses.

Reactions to educational exhibitions at the Centennial Exhibition also clarified methodological thinking. "One believes himself in a dream," remarked the French critic F. Buisson, "when he sees . . . in the copybooks of Pennsylvania schools, entire pages of words selected from the sciences—words which the scholars will never employ a single time in their whole lives, and which they are required to learn with great trouble—such words as 'inexpungability,' 'incommunicability,' 'protozoa,' and hundreds of others more difficult and more useless." Buisson, however, was quick to commend those Pennsylvanians who had introduced new teaching methods:

> It is remarkable that in places where the textbook and literalism have not stunted the mental growth of children, . . . we find that their compositions and other original exercises prove that they possess an intelligence and a vivacity of mind perfectly charming; while in other places where the mania of learning answers "by heart" still reigns, the scholars even at the age of fifteen or sixteen years are scarcely able to express their thoughts upon the most familiar subjects, to write a letter, to give an account of a walk, or, without help, to describe a scene that they have witnessed.

Enlightened teaching methods made slow headway. In the 1880s and 1890s criticism of the Pennsylvania educational system was rife. The Erie superintendent of schools denounced it in 1887 for its rigidity and uniformity, for its inclusion of nonessentials in the curriculum, and for its failure to keep in mind that schoolchildren differ "more or less widely in race, heredity, surroundings, strength, health, and faculty of learning." As late as 1900 most state high schools offered only one curriculum but placed less emphasis on the classics than they formerly had.

While high schools slowly introduced new subjects and methods, primary schools remained traditional. J. M. Rice investigated the Philadelphia school system in 1893 and found primary schools in a "chaotic" condition, while grammar schools were "uneven" with many "still very poor" but some "very excellent." This investigation revealed the difficulties many children experienced:

> The lower grades are as a rule divided into sections of from ten to fifteen pupils. While some of the lessons are . . . given to the whole class, most of them are given only one section at a time, so that in many of the grades the children receive direct instruction for no more than two or two and a half of the five hours that they spend in school, the little pupils being engaged in busy-work more than half the time. . . . A favorite occupation appeared to be the drawing of borders consisting of moons and half-moons around their slates.

Rice discovered that most teachers did not plan or prepare lessons and the results were mediocre. "I found the reading very bad," he noted, "the arithmetic not very much better, and beyond that but little was attempted." For the 20 percent who survived the primary schools, there was the possibility of better grammar schools, but, as the report pointed out, progressive teachers were few and the curriculum narrow. Grammar schools had neither music nor natural science, and not until 1892 was a special supervisor hired for drawing and modeling.

Politics as well as traditionalism dominated Philadelphia schools. By creating a central board and appointing a superintendent in 1883, Philadelphia eliminated some of the chaos in its system. Although each ward (there were thirty-six wards in 1893 and forty-two in 1904) had a local school board of thirteen members, the ward boss appointed principals and teachers on the basis of politics and pull. In 1902 teachers paid to three directors of the Twenty-eighth Ward Board $100 to $160 for appointments, $15 for transfers, and $10 for raising their rating. The janitor, with whom the ward boss usually could communicate more readily than with the principal, frequently ran the school. When a janitor asked a substitute teacher what she could do "in the way of votes" for the "organization," and she replied, "What sort of a teacher do you suppose I am?" "You ain't the kind we want here," he shot back. Within hours a more pliable candidate had taken her place.

Parsimony also destroyed effective teaching in Philadelphia. Schools became old and run-down. For each child in the first and second grades principals were allowed only 40 to 45 cents annually to replace books, stationery, and material. The city furnished schools with neither a piano nor a telephone. Classes for lower grades sometimes ran to seventy-seven children, and teachers were dropped if the register fell below forty. Salaries were low with those of Philadelphia's women teachers placing last and those of men teachers placing thirty-fourth on a list comparing salaries in forty-three cities. In this way the nation's third city neglected both its children and its founder's advice on their education. "For their learning be liberal," William Penn had exhorted. "Spare no cost; for by such parsimony all is lost that is saved."

HIGHER EDUCATION AND SCHOLARSHIP

A glance at several colleges founded during and after the Civil War reveals continuities and changes in higher education. Religious groups continued to establish colleges, but once established, these colleges frequently drifted into secularism. Quakers established Swarthmore College in 1864 and Bryn Mawr College in 1885; Catholics, Duquesne University in 1878 and the University of Scranton in 1888; Brethren, Lebanon Valley College in 1866, Juniata College in 1876, and Elizabethtown College in 1899; Episcopalians, Lehigh University in 1866; Presbyterians, Wilson and Chatham colleges in 1869 and Grove City College in 1876; Lutherans, Thiel College in 1870; and Baptists, Temple University in 1884. Though most private colleges originating during the Gilded Age were church-related, Drexel Institute of Technology, established in 1891 by the munificence of Anthony J. Drexel, was nonsectarian. Furthermore between 1859 and 1893 Pennsylvania established thirteen state normal schools for the training of teachers. After the Civil War, ties between denominations and colleges began weakening, and by 1900 clergymen were no longer universal favorites for college presidents, nor were they as powerful on boards of trustees as they had been. The establishment of Bryn Mawr, Wilson, and Chatham colleges for women, and of Drexel Institute of Technology and Lehigh University with its stress on engineering underscored two other significant trends in late-nineteenth-century Pennsylvania colleges. The state's most outstanding institution of higher learning, the University of Pennsylvania, was from its colonial inception utilitarian in its curriculum and nonsectarian in its control. In the latter respect it was almost unique. Virtually all other nonsectarian colleges were established as either normal schools or technological schools.

Although the most striking characteristic of late-nineteenth-century higher education in Pennsylvania was the growth of secularism, sectarianism was far from dead. The municipal reformer Frederic C. Howe later illustrated this point when he wrote of his college days (1884–1889):

Allegheny was thoroughly sectarian. Progress toward a degree was made easy for men who said they were going into the church or into foreign missions. . . . Professions of faith were rather more important than scholarship, and revival meetings were the great events of the winter. . . . Freshmen and sophomores were allotted to the seniors, who took us on long walks, during which they inquired about our souls. Night after night they herded us into the Stone church. There revivalists prayed, worked on our fears, made us feel that we were eternally damned if we went without their particular brand of religion.

Despite Howe's experience, secularism was growing. Besides fostering new colleges, it changed the curriculum of established schools. In 1868 the president of Dickinson College persuaded the trustees to adopt an elective system after the freshman year by arguing that better Methodist ministers would be trained by falling in "with the drift of modern culture and modern needs toward the Scientific & Literary Studies." Endowments and the elective system hastened the secular trend. The tie binding Lafayette College to Presbyterianism never appeared more blessed than when the 1864–1865 catalog declared "the Bible the central object of study in the whole college course." Trustees, however, accepted with delight $400,000 from a Hazleton coal baron, Ario Pardee, to establish and house a "scientific course in the College." Another Presbyterian school, Washington and Jefferson College, in 1871 accepted a $20,000 endowment for a scientific professorship from an alumnus, Dr. Francis J. LeMoyne, who attached progressive strings to his gift. LeMoyne insisted that the "Dead Languages (Latin, Greek, Hebrew)" receive no more emphasis than other branches of study, that these languages not be required for "a diploma of highest grade," and that the college "make no distinction whatever, on account of *race, color* or religious views, in the selection or admission of Trustees, teachers or pupils." Latin, Greek, and Hebrew gave way to the sciences and to French and German under the elective system. When Swarthmore College opened in 1869 it allowed some electives in all four years, while Bryn Mawr College in 1885 required only English, science, history, and philosophy, allowing students to choose their major and minor studies from various disciplinary groups. Many colleges gave ground grudgingly, but by 1895 even the adamant Franklin and Marshall College had yielded to the elective system.

Pennsylvania has had a long tradition of subsidizing institutions of higher learning. Though hard times in 1844 forced the state to terminate this well-established program, in the 1860s and 1870s Pennsylvania again aided technical and medical education and in 1895 broadened the aid to include the general educational program of selected schools and universities. The 1873 constitutional provision prohibiting state contributions to sectarian institutions advanced secularism.

The rise of scientific, technical, medical, and legal education also advanced secularism. Despite the high cost, several Pennsylvania colleges during this period followed the example of Lafayette and Washington and Jefferson colleges and instituted courses of study in science and engineering. In addition, Lehigh University, Drexel Institute of Technology, and Carnegie Institute of Technology (first projected in 1900, opened in 1905, and now known as Carnegie-Mellon University) were established primarily as schools of engineering and applied science. Though most lawyers in the nineteenth century read law in an established lawyer's office and then passed bar examinations, as the century progressed formal training in a law school attached to an existing college or university became common. Perhaps the most arresting developments in special scientific and technical schools occurred in schools of medicine.

Medical education markedly improved after Abraham Flexner's devastating report, *Medical Education in the United States,* appeared in 1910. The fact that progress had been made before that report simply emphasizes how abysmal medical education was in the mid-nineteenth century. Quack medical schools specializing in unorthodox approaches to medicine abounded, and instruction in better medical schools, such as the University of Pennsylvania and Jefferson Medical College, left much to be desired. Requirements for the medical degree were substantially the same in 1865 as they were in 1790. Students had to attend a two-year, ungraded curriculum (four or five months to a year), study an additional year with a medical preceptor, write a thesis, and be at least twenty-one years of age. Though Hahnemann and Women's Medical colleges in 1869 and Jefferson Medical College in 1872 had instituted an optional three-year, graded curriculum, the old two-year course with various professors delivering unintegrated, didactic lectures remained the rule. In 1876, however, the University of Pennsylvania required the progressive three-year curriculum and abandoned "exclusively didactic teaching," and by the 1890s all four of these Philadelphia schools and the University of Pittsburgh adopted a four-year course.

By midnineteenth century, Pennsylvanians conceded the necessity for special teacher training and established normal schools. When existing private colleges made only feeble attempts to train teachers, state action became necessary. The Normal School Act of 1857 divided Pennsylvania into districts with a projected school for each district and provided for uniform admission, curriculum, and graduation standards. The act required a faculty of at least six professors specializing in practical content and methods subjects. Between 1859, when the state superintendent of common schools accepted the Lancaster County Normal School at Millersville as a state normal school for the second district, and 1893, when he accepted East Stroudsburg State Normal School for the fourth district, the state recognized thirteen normal schools. In 1920 the state accepted Cheyney Training School as the fourteenth. Originally established in 1840 by Quakers as the Institute for Colored Youth, Cheyney had since 1857 specialized in training black teachers. Though the state contributed heavily to these normal schools, it initially did not own, manage, or control them. But the state increased its role, particularly in 1874 and 1875, and between 1913 and 1922 it purchased and took complete control of these schools.

Nineteenth-century state normal schools were essentially secondary schools. Most students took a two-year course preparing them to teach in the common schools. By 1895, to the dismay of the state superintendent of education, normal schools were also preparing students for college and for commercial life. By 1900 normal schools had added a year of study but were still below the college level. Pennsylvania converted all fourteen normal schools into state teachers colleges between 1926 and 1932, and into state colleges in 1960.

The Gilded Age expanded higher education not only by establishing new liberal arts and professional schools but by making a college education available to more young people. Americans recognized dimly, yet more clearly than before, that all capable students, even if they were poor, black, or female, deserved a higher education. The Pennsylvania State University and the state normal system widened educational opportunities, and some special provision for higher education for blacks was made with Cheyney State College and with Lincoln University, a Presbyterian institution which granted its first B.A. degree in 1868. Despite repeated petitioning by alumni, whites dominated the administration and faculty of Lincoln University until 1932 when trustees appointed the first Negro to the faculty. Few blacks attended predominantly white institutions of higher learning. Not only were these schools reluctant to recruit blacks, but slavery's legacy of economic and cultural poverty had prepared few blacks for college. A small breakthrough was made in 1875 when the University of Pittsburgh accepted Charles Avery's $25,000 gift for the free education of twelve Negroes each year.

Greater progress was made in educating women. Reputable late-nineteenth-century circles no longer believed in the superiority of the male mind. After the Civil War many colleges became coeducational. Pennsylvania State University admitted women in 1871, women first attended the University of Pennsylvania in 1877 (though it was not until 1938 that all branches of that university were open to them), and the University of Pittsburgh admitted women in 1893. Most schools admitting women offered them "ladies' courses" that were less arduous and academically less rigorous than regular college courses. Indeed, for this reason the United States commissioner of education eliminated from his list of bona fide liberal arts colleges all Pennsylvania women's colleges except Bryn Mawr. The Pennsylvania Hospital admitted women medical students to clinical lectures in 1869, but male students made their resentment evident:

> When the ladies entered the amphitheatre they were greeted by yells, hisses, "caterwaulings," mock applause, offensive remarks upon personal appearance, etc. . . . During the last hour missiles of paper, tinfoil, tobacco-quids, etc., were thrown upon the ladies, while some of these men defiled the dresses of the ladies near them with tobacco-juice.

The development in the late-nineteenth century of the German-style graduate school, where professional specialists awarded Ph.D.'s to narrower specialists, doomed broad-ranging dilettante scholars, of whom Henry Charles Lea is an especially diligent and talented example. Philadelphia born in 1825 of amateur scholar parents, Lea received a broad education. His proficiency in literature and languages (he knew at least eleven), chemistry, conchology, botany, and drawing was great. He published papers on the salts of manganese, on mollusks, and on Tennyson, Leigh Hunt, Elizabeth Barrett Browning, and others, and translated Greek poetry. At eighteen he entered the family publishing business, where he worked forty-two years. Lea took an active part in public affairs, crusading against local, state, and national corruption and for civil service reform. His main interest, however, was medieval history. After publishing articles and books on church history, he wrote his monumental three-volume *History of the Inquisition of the Middle Ages* (1887–1889) and later published volumes on the Spanish inquisition.

Though many Pennsylvania colleges early offered graduate training, most of them quickly returned to undergraduate courses exclusively. The University of Pennsylvania, however, formed an early and genuine graduate school, formalized its Ph.D. requirements by 1882, and awarded its first Ph.D. under the new program in 1889. The beginnings of graduate-school specialization can be illustrated by another distinguished Pennsylvania historian, John Bach McMaster, born twenty-seven years after Lea. Although he was professor of American history at the University of Pennsylvania, McMaster had been trained as an engineer and wrote the first of the nine volumes of *History of the People of the United States* (1883–1927) while an engineering instructor. A third distinguished Pennsylvania historian, Ellis Paxson Oberholtzer, sixteen years the junior of McMaster, with whom he studied, earned his Ph.D. in 1893 with a dissertation on the referendum in America and later wrote the five-volume *History of the United States since the Civil War* (1917–1937). Subsequent Pennsylvania historians—trained in the twentieth century—worked in narrower and narrower fields, illustrating the trend toward specialization and professionalization. In that trend, history has been similar to other disciplines in the arts and sciences.

RELIGION AND NEW IDEAS

New ideas swept America during the Gilded Age. Developments in the social, biological, and physical sciences excited intellectuals within and outside the academic community and when coupled with changes in American society, struck heavy blows at supernaturalism and absolutism. Not only did urbanization break down Sabbath keeping and church ties, but cities also were centers of scientific advance. Higher critics of the Bible denied the infallibility of the literal scriptures; anthropologists, archaeologists, and students of comparative religion suggested that Christianity had natural rather than supernatural origins; astronomers recognized that the heavens were changing and not permanently fixed by laws of gravity; physicists decreed that force and matter were indestructable, that new energy could not be created, and that existing energy was constantly being dissipated; and biologists following Charles Darwin's theory of organic evolution undermined the idea of fixed species, broke down the wall between animals and men, substituted the slow rise of man from humble biological origins for his sudden fall from Eden, and severely limited if not eliminated God's creative role by proposing that man evolved through mutation of species and natural selection (including a struggle for existence and the survival of the fittest). To a people being torn from their rural roots and in the throes of an industrial revolution, evolution smashed the heretofore eternal fixed verities.

Yet Darwinism proved the cornerstone for a new order and gave men new perspectives. By 1900 virtually all scientists, most intellectuals, and many theologians accepted evolution as God's design and tailored their Christianity to fit it. Darwin's impact extended far beyond biology and religion. In the last decades of the nineteenth century, philosophers, historians, economists, lawyers, political scientists, anthropologists, sociologists, psychologists, educators, architects, and artists utilized evolutionary concepts to revolutionize their disciplines. Indeed even businessmen found Darwinism a convenient justification for eliminating their weaker competitors. Optimistically believing that "all is well since all grows better," Andrew Carnegie welcomed "the concentration of business, industrial and commercial, in the hands of the few, and the law of competition between these, as being not only beneficial, but essential to the progress of the race." By the end of the nineteenth century, these social Darwinists were attacked and refuted, but—significantly—within a Darwinian framework. Reformers suggested that mutual aid and cooperation were more important in organic evolution than struggle, and in 1907, economist Simon N. Patten of the University of Pennsylvania (Wharton School of Finance) anticipated twentieth-century welfare economics when he argued that struggle bred emotion, not strength, and primitivism, not progress; that there were no inherent differences between the rich and the poor; and that scientific utilization of resources could abolish poverty and achieve equality and progress. Yet for the average Pennsylvanian, struggling in the mill or on the farm, the impact of Darwinism meant little.

Nevertheless there were alterations in the sectarian balance and religious mood of Pennsylvania. The host of immigrants produced the tremendous growth of the Roman Catholic and Greek Orthodox churches and Jewish congregations. New denominations in the Protestant spectrum—including Mormons, Seventh-day Adventists, Christian Scientists, and Jehovah's Witnesses—converted many Pennsylvanians. On the other hand, older groups like the Quakers and the German Plain Sects did not increase as rapidly. Among the larger Protestant denominations no one better expressed the predominant religious mood of Americans and Pennsylvanians during the Gilded Age than evangelists Dwight L. Moody and Ira Sankey. A former Chicago shoe salesman who vowed to "reduce the population of hell by one million souls," Moody and his singing partner Sankey, a former New Castle, Pennsylvania, bank clerk whose "sweet voice rang out pure and clear like the notes of a silver flute," were the nineteenth century's most successful evangelistic team. Fresh from a triumphant tour of the British Isles and a short run in Brooklyn, Moody and Sankey accepted

John Wanamaker's invitation in late 1875 to use his Grand Depot for evangelistic meetings. In Wanamaker's scheme of values, converting sinners took precedence over converting a freight station into a department store. The meetings were an enormous success and ran nine weeks in the dead of winter. Moody augmented the huge crowds (lines formed at 4:30 some January mornings) by introducing and perfecting new publicity techniques. The pair affected both the small and the great. President Grant, his cabinet, and a number of distinguished public servants attended one meeting after officially inspecting the Centennial Exhibition. Grant praised Moody mildly, but extravagantly commended Sankey, possibly because his songs had the flavor of Civil War ballads.

Moody and Sankey tailored old-time religion to appeal to a gilded, urban age. Where earlier rural camp-meeting revivalists utilized fear and exuberance to convert sinners, Moody and Sankey were sentimental. Moody stressed the beautiful life with God that awaited the redeemed rather than the everlasting horror of hell that would swallow sinners. His sermons were filled with tales of deathbed repentances and stories of miraculous answers to prayer. Though he himself would shout and jump about the pulpit, Moody did not want his converts to jump, shout, writhe, jerk, or dance in the aisles as had been customary in rural camp meetings. He was the first prominent revivalist to utilize music psychologically in persuading sinners to repent. In place of the camp-meeting folk hymns that narrated Biblical stories with shouting and hallelujahs, Sankey substituted sentimental melodies which suited the urbanites of his day.

In 1900 Pennsylvania's outstanding clergyman was Russell H. Conwell. Called to Philadelphia's moribund Grace Baptist Church in the early 1880s, Conwell soon had a thriving congregation and in 1891 moved it to the 3,000-seat Baptist Temple. Conwell admired Moody and like him stressed salvation, believed in miraculous answers to prayer, and was sentimental. The Baptist Temple had its beginning when a deeply touched Conwell told his congregation that six-year-old Hattie Wiatt with her dying breath had given 57 cents in a red pocketbook for a new church building. But unlike Moody, Conwell was concerned about the earthly condition of his predominantly humble parishioners. Utilizing volunteer instructors, he organized a night school for working people in the basement of his church. Out of these modest beginnings sprang Temple University, one of the major institutions of higher learning in Pennsylvania. Conwell also helped found three Philadelphia hospitals. He did not, however, espouse the social gospel with its thorough commitment to social justice and its criticism of unregulated private enterprise and corporate wealth. Indeed Conwell celebrated materialism in his "Acres of Diamonds" lectures: "I say you ought to be rich, you have no right to be poor. . . . Philadelphia furnishes so many opportunities. . . . Money is power; money has powers; and for a man to say, 'I do not want money' is to say, 'I do not wish to do any good to my fellowmen.'" Even Andrew Carnegie did not celebrate the gospel of wealth more effectively.

JOURNALISM AND LITERATURE

Political parties dominated American newspapers in the 1860s and 1870s, but by 1900 businessmen controlled the press through advertising, loans, or outright ownership. Both political parties and business enterprises, anxious for public support, attempted to control the press, but businessmen ultimately won. During the Civil War, Philadelphia newspapers with two exceptions followed the dictates of party leaders. While defending war profiteers and public officials and charging the Democratic opposition with treason, Republican papers were subsidized by the Lincoln administration with appointments and public advertising. The *Evening Journal,* missing the patronage it had enjoyed under Buchanan, complained, "We do not think much of those newspapers which are very loyal indeed, when we discover that they are excellently well paid for their loyalty, when we ascertain that two or three of one newspaporial family have been very handsomely provided for, and will be the better off the longer the war lasts." The *Inquirer* shared some Republican patronage and generally supported the Lincoln administration but criticized "party tricksters" and corrupt contractors, while the *Public Ledger* supported Lincoln but disdained partisanship. The relatively independent *Inquirer* and *Ledger* were connected with banking and large financial interests—Anthony J. Drexel and Francis A. Drexel bought the *Ledger* in 1864—and foreshadowed the future trend of American journalism. By 1900 newspapers had become big businesses, and the favors a political party could offer them were insignificant. A veteran Philadelphia journalist noted: "Every man who advertises largely in the newspapers is one of the masters of the press. . . . Moneyed corporations (to which many of the editors are deeply indebted, and which actually *maintain* not a few of them), possess unlimited authority over the 'free and independent' newspaper press of our country."

Newspapers in the 1860s and 1870s were personal vehicles for outstanding editors, but by 1900 personal journalism had given way to yellow journalism. Before the turn of the century we normally think of editors and papers as inseparable. In Philadelphia it was John W. Forney's *Press,* Morton McMichael's *North American,* and Alexander K. McClure's *Times;* in Harrisburg, George Bergner's and then Charles Bergner's *Telegraph,* and Benjamin F. Meyers' *Patriot;* and in Pittsburgh, Russell Errett's *Gazette,* later his *Commercial,* and James P. Barr's *Post.* By 1900 one man could no longer dominate a large newspaper printing wire-service reports on fast presses. When newspapers divided editorial functions among faceless, specialized editors, the papers lost much of their character and reader appeal. In 1900 about a third of the nation's metropolitan press was attempting to arouse lost interest through yellow journalism. Both the Philadelphia *Inquirer* and the Pittsburgh *Commercial Gazette* used scareheads shrilly screaming about unimportant news and pictures. Papers indulging in yellow journalism sometimes faked pictures and fabricated interviews and stories, issued Sunday supplements with colored comics and superficial articles, and ostentatiously sympathized with the underdog and crusaded for the comman man.

Although slowly losing ground, Philadelphia ranked third, behind New York and Boston, as a magazine-publishing city in the last decades of the nineteenth century. Two general magazines, *Lippincott's* and *Penn Monthly,* aided Philadelphia's literary reputation, while *Peterson's, Godey's, Arthur's,* and beginning in the 1880s the *Ladies' Home Journal* continued Philadelphia's preeminence in ladies' magazines. Philadelphia also published many professional magazines—particularly legal, medical, and religious ones.

Established in 1868, the handsomely printed and illustrated *Lippincott's* was a distinguished magazine. Excellent contributors made its articles on travel and art and its literary criticism and book reviews unusually good. Unfortunately, however, it failed to make money, and its editors began to make changes in the 1880s. In 1881 it became a bit lighter and lowered its price, in 1885 it dropped illustrations, and after 1887 it carried an entire novel in each issue. Though some of its novels were excellent (Oscar Wilde's *The Picture of Dorian Gray,* for example) and many of its contributors outstanding (Bret Harte, Paul Lawrence

Dunbar, Arthur Conan Doyle, Owen Wister, and Stephen Crane, for instance), the magazine declined slowly in the 1890s. In 1914 it changed its name to *McBride's Magazine* and moved to New York, where it lasted but two years.

Another distinguished Pennsylvania magazine, the *Penn Monthly,* published by Wharton Barker from 1870 to 1882, was the organ of the Philadelphia Social Science Association. Along with the social sciences, it discussed literature, science, art, philosophy, education, and travel; printed some poetry and University of Pennsylvania news; and numbered Henry C. Carey, Henry C. Lea, and S. Weir Mitchell among its contributors. Narrower but not as narrow as its name, the *Pennsylvania Magazine of History and Biography,* started in 1877 by the Historical Society of Pennsylvania, focused on history but offered contributors ranging from humorist Mark Twain to chemist Benjamin Silliman.

Apart from its successful Sunday school and professional journals and apart from the *Ladies' Home Journal,* Philadelphia periodicals declined in the 1880s and 1890s. Although the old trio of ladies magazines wandered off to New York to die in the 1890s, the *Ladies' Home Journal* became a smashing success. Started in 1883 by Cyrus H. K. Curtis's wife Louisa Knapp, the *Journal* published fiction, household hints, recipes, and fashions that appealed to middle-class housewives. Curtis built its circulation to 270,000 by 1886 and obtained Louisa May Alcott and other big-name contributors. Through inducements and advertising, he continued to increase the circulation, size, and cost of the *Journal.* In 1889 Mrs. Curtis relinquished the editorship to Edward Bok. Because he designed the magazine for "what . . . women wished to be rather than . . . what they actually were," Bok was tremendously successful. His formula was intimacy, service, idealism, reform, excellent contributors on a variety of subjects, and handsome typography and art. He established regular departments called "Side Talks to Girls," "Side Talks to Boys," and "Heart to Heart Talks," and ran series such as "Unknown Wives of Well Known Men." The *Journal* pioneered the practice of a new cover for each issue and the use of four-color artwork, and retained distinguished illustrators (such as Howard Pyle and Charles Dana Gibson) and contributors. William Dean Howells, Rudyard Kipling, Mark Twain, Bret Harte, and Hamlin Garland all wrote for the *Journal.* Benjamin Harrison described his life in the White House, Dwight L. Moody edited the Sunday school department feature, and John Philip Sousa, Reginald de Koven, Sir Arthur Sullivan, Ignace Jan Paderewski, Johann Strauss, and Pietro Mascagni published music in the *Journal.* Starting in 1895 the *Journal* printed plans for houses in the $1,000 to $5,000 bracket and provoked the architect Stanford White to remark, "I firmly believe that Edward Bok has more completely influenced American domestic architecture for the better than any other man in this generation." Bok furthermore worked to improve interior decoration, taste in art (by providing portfolios of prints at low prices), and the landscape (by working to eliminate billboards and ugliness). He continued his crusade in the twentieth century and saved the beauty of Niagara Falls from power companies that would have despoiled it, tried unsuccessfully to wean American women from Paris fashions, and shocked countless readers by mentioning syphilis in his struggle for sex education. Bok, however, was not a crusader for women's rights. "Perambulating encyclopedias in the guise of women" made him uncomfortable, and he attacked woman suffrage. When he retired in 1919, Bok was one of the nation's leading editors and the *Journal* was the most valuable monthly in the world. It had achieved a two-million circulation, with each issue running to about 200 pages and grossing over $1 million in advertising.

In the late nineteenth century Pennsylvania's predominantly romantic writers gave little inkling of the realistic and naturalistic trends shaping American literature. "Here," lamented prominent Philadelphian Sidney George Fisher, "there is no literature or appreciation of it or literary men or appreciation of them." Bayard Taylor's travel books were much better than the shallow poetry which earned him the title "Laureate of the Gilded Age," George H. Boker wrote good romantic tragedies but produced his best work in the 1850s, S. Weir Mitchell specialized in historical romances, and Charles Godfrey Leland's literary fame rested on his dialect ballads as Hans Breitmann. Rebecca Harding Davis in the sixties did write realistic fiction "to dig into this commonplace, this vulgar American life, and see what is in it," but her later novels tended to be sentimental, while her son Richard—though a superior war correspondent—wrote flashy superficial novels. Another Philadelphia writer was Frank Stockton, who in 1902 satirized historical romances about seventeenth-century piracy but is chiefly noted for his juvenile, whimsical, and humorous stories. Philadelphia even had difficulty keeping authors of modest talents, for they wandered off to New York, which had become the literary capital of America. A literary giant, Walt Whitman, lived in poverty across the river in Camden, New Jersey, and though he constantly rode the Philadelphia and Camden ferry (on which he had a pass), members of the Centennial Commission ignored this neighbor who celebrated America as no other poet has done. Whitman indeed personally published and sold a centennial edition of *Leaves of Grass* and offered a "Song of the Exposition" to newspapers for $50.

MUSIC AND DRAMA

Perhaps the least-developed fine art in Pennsylvania and the United States during the late nineteenth century was music. Led by Clement Tetedoux, Pittsburghers established the Cantata Society in 1869, and out of it grew the Gounod Club which in the 1870s performed *Martha, Bohemian Girl,* and *Rose of Castile.* Tetedoux also helped organize and direct the 400-voice chorus and 100-piece orchestra for the 1878 Messiah Festival. Pittsburghers achieved social as well as musical fulfillment in this Messiah Festival, in the Mozart Club, which continued to flourish, and in the Tuesday Musical Club organized in 1889. In the fifteen years beginning with 1896 Pittsburgh came of musical age with its symphony orchestra, directed by Victor Herbert, Frederick Archer, and Emil Paur; although disbanded for a period, the symphony was revived by a later generation.

When in 1857 Philadelphians built for $250,000 the Academy of Music—the oldest and handsomest large concert hall still in use as such in America—they offered tangible evidence of their commitment to music. As the nineteenth century wore on and Philadelphians enjoyed both orchestras and operas, German rather than Italian influences became dominant. From 1856 to 1895 Philadelphia had the Germania Orchestra, whose musicians were then absorbed by the Thunder Orchestra (with Henry G. Thunder conducting), which became part of the Philadelphia Orchestra in 1900. Philadelphia not only heard symphonies but also the operas of Bellini, Verdi, Meyerbeer, and Wagner soon after their premieres abroad. During the winters of the 1870s and 1880s, Philadelphia had almost weekly opera performances. The New York Metropolitan Opera Company began its Philadelphia tours in 1885, making it possible for Philadelphians to enjoy even better opera but preventing the formation of a strong local company.

In the Civil War era and immediately afterwards two theaters—the Arch Street and the

Walnut Street—dominated Philadelphia drama. Resident stock companies were responsible for most productions at these theaters. Each season, company members played more parts than modern performers play in a lifetime and had the experience of acting with at least a dozen of America'a best actors including Edwin Forrest, one of the greatest tragedians of his time, who was a Philadelphian and often performed in his native city. Philadelphians were fond of spectacles. Popular during the early Civil War years was *The Southern Rebellion by Land and Sea,* which closed with a triumphant Union cavalry charge. In 1868 the extravagant production of *A Midsummer Night's Dream* cost $35,000 and played at the Walnut from August 12 to September 28, and in 1876 *Around the World in Eighty Days* also enjoyed a long run.

Resident stock companies provided an intimate theater to which the public returned again and again to see its favorites in various roles. Some of these actors had started at the bottom of the ladder, while others, frequently members of theatrical families, had started near the top. Born in Philadelphia in 1808, John R. Reed started as a lamplighter at the Walnut in 1824, became a general utility actor, and ended by bequeathing his skull to the property room for use in *Hamlet.* During the Civil War era the Drews were the most important family in the Philadelphia theater, with Mrs. John Drew, a superb Lady Teazle in *The School for Scandal,* ably managing the Arch.

Philadelphia's favorite actor John Sleeper Clarke was married to Asia Booth, sister of the famous tragedian Edwin Booth. Clarke joined the stock company at the Arch in 1855 as the leading comedian and remained all but two years of his career in Philadelphia, where at various times he managed the Arch, Walnut, and Broad theaters. Clarke varied his acting at first but soon found that his success depended on his portraying the comic characters with which his audience identified him. Lincoln's assassination by Clarke's actor brother-in-law John Wilkes Booth brought a violent outburst against theaters and actors in general and in Philadelphia against Clarke in particular. After being detained for questioning by Federal officials in Washington from April 27 to the end of May, Clarke returned to Philadelphia and gradually regained his old place in the hearts of theatergoers.

The play *Black Crook,* popular for its notorious ballet and cancan, packed the better theaters of this era with leg-conscious men. But in the spring of 1869 the London Burlesque Combination, with its blondhaired girls who talked slang and sang coarse songs in a cultured English accent that had always been associated with refinement, really excited the Philadelphia male. Though a causal relationship may not have existed, sex entered the theater at the same time that Negroes, who had attended Philadelphia theaters before the Civil War, were excluded from all theaters except the Academy of Music. Even the academy had a special "colored" section divided from other seats by a board fence across the lobby and entered by a separate door and stairway. Negroes frequently sat elsewhere in the gallery without incident, but the fence remained a stark monument to the racism of the period.

Like most Gilded Age theatergoers, Pittsburghers were restless and demonstrative. They were fond of melodrama, broad farce, and elaborate revues abounding in unexpected and overpowering stage effects. On the Pittsburgh stage horses, dogs, waterfalls, and steam launches always brought applause. One of the most talked-of spectacles was the death scene from Sardou's *Cleopatra* played by Fanny Davenport in 1891 and described by the *Gazette:*

Instead of a fake serpent she drew from a basket of flowers a live, crawling snake about a foot in length and tenderly placed it in her bosom, telling it to bite and bite again. As the poison began to work, the reptile crawled upon her shoulder and passed its head through her earring, its fiery tongue flashing threateningly and its black beady eyes glistening in the bright light.

The main attraction was usually accompanied by a farce, skit, or pantomime featured at the beginning or close of a performance. Comedies brought bigger crowds than tragedies, and the galleries frequently were packed when other areas of the theater were sparsely populated. Proud of the saying that an actor who could please the Pittsburgh gallery could succeed anywhere, the gallery clapped and even broke into pandemonium when moved, showed its disinterest by noisy interruptions, and frequently hissed rather than joining claques.

Pittsburgh boards boasted something for everyone. Civil War audiences never tired of *Uncle Tom's Cabin* and enjoyed *The Octoroon,* a tragic drama in which a young man falls in love with a lovely woman with the "gentlest of bosoms" who is damned "because out of eight parts of her nature one was derived from African blood." Pittsburgh audiences were fond of low-comedy portrayals of Irish, Yankee, German, and Jewish characters of marked eccentricities, and also appreciated local and state subjects. In 1876 they saw *The Molly Maguires* and in 1878 *The Lower Million* based on the great Pittsburgh railroad strike the year before. The riot scene featured 150 men, some veteran rioters from the strike. Shakespeare and other classics were sandwiched on the Pittsburgh boards with current fare both domestic and imported.

Among the actors visiting Pittsburgh during these years was Edwin Booth. In 1887 he brought in $17,000 in one week at the Pittsburgh Opera House, but since Booth received 90 percent of the gross receipts little of the money remained in Pittsburgh. Maggie Mitchell came to Pittsburgh again and again, and although a chauvinistic Union captain interrupted one of her 1861 performances with the accusation that she had trampled on an American flag while playing in the South, Pittsburghers applauded her on return engagements. James O'Neill, the father of the noted playwright Eugene O'Neill, was also a favorite with Pittsburgh audiences, as was Joseph K. Emmet, a former resident who frequently kept playgoers waiting for his often unrehearsed antics while he sobered up enough to stagger on stage.

During the Civil War years and those immediately following, Pittsburgh theater was at its peak. Pittsburgh was filled with industrial activity and money flowed freely, but following the Panic of 1873 theater managers had a difficult time. In the midseventies traveling companies began superseding visiting stars, and by 1879 the Pittsburgh Opera House, the city's most important theater during this period, found it no longer profitable to employ a resident stock company.

ARCHITECTURE

When Americans tired of the Greek designs which had dominated the early nineteenth century, architects turned to Gothic and Italian styles. John Notman (1810–1865), who designed the Athenaeum of Philadelphia (1845–1847), was chiefly responsible for bringing Italian styles to Philadelphia. And, as St. Mark's Church (1848–1851) shows, Notman was also a profound student of the Gothic Revival. From the cities, the Italian influence—later called Victorian—spread to smaller centers. A visitor found the Italian-style buildings in the prosperous lumbering center of Williamsport "generally superior to those of any other

Jayne Building (1849–1850), Philadelphia, William L. Johnston, architect. Though built entirely of masonry, this building's vertical lines prophesized the skyscraper. (Historical Society of Pennsylvania)

borough in the Commonwealth—many of them indeed models of architectural taste."
Samuel Sloan (1815–1884), a prominent Philadelphia architect who published builders' books
which popularized Victorian architecture, planned Williamsport's Lycoming County Courthouse which was built in 1860 and duplicated five years later in Sunbury. One of the best
Gothic Revival churches in Pennsylvania is the trim and sophisticated St. Mark's Episcopal
Church (1867–1869) in the town of Jim Thorpe (Mauch Chunk), designed by the elder
Richard Upjohn (1802–1878), the country's leading church architect. Another splendid example is the round-arched First Presbyterian Church of York (1860) planned by the Philadelphia architect Joseph C. Hoxie (1814–1870) with its lofty, well-proportioned spire. William
L. Johnston (1811–1849) utilized Gothic architecture's vertical lines—an ideal design for tall
structures—in his innovative Jayne Building (built in 1849–1850; demolished in 1958) in
Philadelphia. Costing over half a million dollars, the Jayne Building was the biggest and
most expensive business building in the United States and one of the first protoskyscrapers
built in America. With eight stories above the street level and three below, it also had an
underground tunnel to a nearby post office. Though built of solid masonry, its Gothic granite
front with large window areas and doorways and the new emphasis on vertical lines made
the Jayne Building light in feeling.

When plans for Philadelphia's City Hall could go forward after the Civil War, earlier
classical designs gave way to the new enthusiasm for the French Renaissance. An early

Philadelphia City Hall (1871–1881), John
McArthur, Jr., architect, an elegant structure
that deservedly dominates Philadelphia. (Historical Society of Pennsylvania)

Philadelphia City Hall tower and sculpture of William Penn by Alexander Milne Calder. [Lawrence Lafore and Sarah Lee Lippincott, *Philadelphia: The Unexpected City* (Doubleday)]

example of this popular style, sometimes called the Mansard Madness, is the Philadelphia Union League Club (1865) designed by John Fraser. Built of red brick and brownstone, its mansard roof, ornate detail, and curving exterior stairs made it both handsome and hospitable. As designed by John McArthur, Jr. (1823–1890), assisted by the venerable Thomas Ustick Walter (1804–1887, who had designed the National Capitol dome and the House and Senate wings), City Hall secured the title "Age of Elegance" for the last half of the nineteenth century. Handsomely detailed and with effective handling of space, its interior court, council chamber, and mayor's apartments are especially noteworthy and place it on a par with the world's best architecture. City Hall was started in 1871 and when occupied ten years later was the largest office building in the world and the largest building of any kind on this continent. It covers 4½ acres (a greater area than the Capitol in Washington), has over 600 rooms, and cost $25 million. It is enriched both inside and out with sculpture by Alexander Milne Calder (1846–1923), the father and grandfather of prominent sculptors of the same name, who topped its 547-foot tower with a 37-foot bronze statue of William Penn.

The Pennsylvania Academy of Fine Arts (America's oldest existing art institution) moved into its third and present Philadelphia home during the centennial year 1876. Designed by Frank Furness (1839–1912), who was probably the boldest and most inventive architect

Engraving, *New Building of the Pennsylvania Academy of Fine Arts, Philadelphia* (1876). Architect Frank Furness planned this building's French mansard roofs, Gothic forms, and the mingling of rough brown stone, patterned brick, smooth lighter stone, and polished granite columns. (New York Public Library, Astor, Lenox and Tilden Foundations)

of his day, this "romantic fantasy of a building" shows his love of contrast. As he would do time and again, Furness combined historic details in an original fashion that made the building very much his own creation and difficult to classify. Now cherished as "a superb period piece," the Pennsylvania Academy of Fine Arts Building was upon its completion pronounced a failure by the *American Architect and Building News,* which complained that the building's ornament pestered rather than accentuated its lines but admitted it was full of life which "would atone for much worse faults."

A Philadelphia native—the son of Dr. William H. Furness, the abolitionist minister of the First Unitarian Church—Frank Furness rarely took a commission outside the city. Even though he was controversial and ignored contemporary standards of beauty, Philadelphia supported him. The daring Provident Life and Trust Company (built in 1879; demolished in 1960) was but one of the many banks Furness planned. Prominent among his other buildings were the Library Company Building (built in 1878–1880; demolished in 1940), which was described as a tour de force and which housed the oldest circulating library in the country (founded by Benjamin Franklin in 1731), and the robust Library of the University of Pennsylvania, which was opened in 1890. The largest commission of Furness's firm was the addition to the Broad Street Railroad Station (built in 1893; demolished in 1953), which was several times the size of the original station built a decade earlier. Furness's plan was remarkably modern and functional. With a "courage to believe that anything was possible to the architect who willed it," Furness profoundly influenced Louis Sullivan, whose emphasis

Allegheny County Courthouse tower.
(County of Allegheny)

on functionalism set the direction of world architecture and who became the only man whom Frank Lloyd Wright called master.

While Philadelphia's City Hall was a statement of the past, Pittsburgh's Allegheny County Courthouse (1884–1888) pointed to the future and proved that great civic structures could both be practical and monumental. It was designed by Henry Hobson Richardson (1838–1886), a great-grandson of Joseph Priestley and the best-trained American architect of his day. He dominated his age so completely that when the ten finest American buildings were chosen in the eighties, five of them were his. Richardson, who died before the Pittsburgh Courthouse was completed, considered it and the Marshall Field Store in Chicago his greatest triumphs and wished posterity to judge him by them. Built of light-colored granite in the Romanesque style which Richardson had popularized, the Allegheny County buildings exhibit a refreshing restraint and bluntness of modeling. Symmetrically built around a central court, the courthouse's interior walls have numerous, varied, but rhythmically grouped arches and linteled windows which give it a pleasing, open look. Joined to the courthouse by the bridge of sighs, the jail "achieves a power, a grim magnificence" new to American architecture. The granite wall enclosing the jail yard is considered "one of the most magnificent displays of fine material in the world." Almost as much admired is the purely functional yet abstract-appearing, cylindrical, rock-faced chimney shaft rising above it.

Architectural firms became both common and popular during the late nineteenth century. Even an individualist like Frank Furness found it convenient to be part of an organization of specialists. The head of the outstanding American architectural firm in the 1890s was

Allegheny County Jail and Courthouse (1884–1888), Henry H. Richardson, architect. This building is his masterpiece and Pittsburgh's greatest structure. Note the workmen in this 1888 photograph putting finishing touches on the tower. (County of Allegheny)

Charles Follen McKim (1847–1909), who was born at Isabella Furnace (Chester County), the son of abolitionist James Miller McKim. Although McKim had worked in Henry H. Richardson's office, he leaned strongly on classical and Renaissance models. His firm, McKim, Mead, and White, designed numerous public and private buildings from New England to Florida and was largely responsible for the turn-of-the-century classical revival in American architecture. Standing out among the drab office buildings around it, the Girard Trust Corn Exchange Bank (1905–1908), Philadelphia's grand example of McKim's art, helps City Hall and the Union League Building lift Broad Street above the aesthetic level of most commercial streets in the nation.

PAINTING AND SCULPTURE

Considered the greatest American painter of all time and lauded for the psychological realism of his work, Thomas Eakins (1844–1916) was not a popular painter during his lifetime. He was born in Philadelphia, where he lived all his life except for his years of European

The Girard Trust Corn Exchange Bank (1905–1908), Charles Follen McKim, architect. This building combines squares, rectangles, triangles, cylinders, and spheres to form a classic temple of unsurpassed beauty. (Girard Bank)

study. At sixteen Eakins, who made science the foundation of his art, began studying anatomy at Jefferson Medical College and drawing at the Pennsylvania Academy of Fine Arts. For most of his career he dissected cadavers "to increase his knowledge of how beautiful objects are put together," and his experiments with muscles disproved the theory held by physiologists that each muscle had a single function countered by an opposite muscle. A lover of mathematics and also an excellent photographer, Eakins did a series of experiments that proved important in the development of the motion-picture camera. When he was twenty-two, he went to Paris and remained in Europe for over three years building the groundwork of his style. Returning to Philadelphia, he first painted his family and his friends. In these portraits Eakins discovered the vitality of an ordinary situation. Honesty was a striking feature of his work, but Eakins was also concerned with the meaning of a

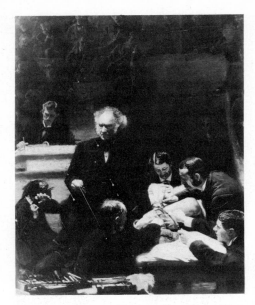

Painting by Thomas Eakins, *The Gross Clinic* (1875). (Jefferson Medical College, Thomas Jefferson University)

pose. He was eager to communicate a mood and a sense of design involving both restraint and movement.

Eakins was a great teacher, and his hours with students cut his output as a painter. He began teaching at the Pennsylvania Academy of Fine Arts in 1876, the year that its new building was opened. In 1879 he was named professor of drawing and painting and in 1882 director of the Art School at the Pennsylvania Academy, a responsibility he had in fact been filling since 1876. Eakins' position was weakened in 1883 when a new chairman of the School Committee took office. After "a decade of teaching essentially in conflict with the mores and desires" of those controlling the academy, Eakins was forced to resign in 1886. The immediate cause was his removing a loincloth from a male model to demonstrate the origin of a muscle for a women's class. In order to continue studying with him, Eakins' pupils formed the Art Students' League, which functioned until 1892 with Eakins as unpaid teacher.

In 1875 Eakins completed *The Gross Clinic* (Jefferson Medical College), which is now judged the most important work by an American artist in the nineteenth century. Eakins had counted on this painting to establish his reputation and had expected it to be prominently hung in Memorial Hall during the Centennial Exhibition. Five of Eakins' pictures were hung there, and one of them, *The Chess Players* (The Metropolitan Museum of Art), was especially commended, but *The Gross Clinic* was relegated to the medical section of the exhibition, where it was surrounded by "trusses, artificial limbs, and ear cleaners." The painting focuses with "bold and grail-like light" on Samuel Gross, a famous Philadelphia surgeon, pausing in the midst of an operation in his charity clinic. A team of assisting surgeons are surrounding the patient, who is almost completely covered with operating cloths. Nearby is seated the patient's mother, wanting to be near yet shrouding her eyes from the scene taking place a few feet away. Filling the amphitheater are numerous medical students who complete the picture without competing with the drama below. *The Gross Clinic* raises "realistic American subject matter to the level of myth with a broad and profound power and an intelligence that had never been approached before." But human suffering as well as the blood on Dr. Gross's hand and scapel proved offensive to nineteenth-century viewers. "The more one praises it," a Philadelphia critic said of the painting, "the more one must condemn its admission to a gallery where men and women of weak nerves must be compelled to look at it, for not to look at it is impossible." Some seventy-five years later when the Philadelphia Museum celebrated its seventy-fifth anniversary, *The Gross Clinic* ranked third in a most-popular-painting contest, but Philadelphia's appreciation came three-quarters of a century too late. Lacking an audience equal to his performance, Eakins turned from the broad course he had charted and spent most of his career painting realistic portraits, which frequently disappointed his sitters. It took the honest and perceptive Walt Whitman to be pleased with his portrait, which he said, "sets me down in correct style, without feathers—without fuss of any sort." If it caught "too much Rabelais instead of just enough," Whitman said, it was because Eakins "faces the worst as well as the best." Unlike Whitman, society for decades refused to forgive Eakins for facing, accepting, and picturing things as they were.

A year younger than Eakins, Mary Cassatt (1845–1926), the most eminent American woman painter, was born in Allegheny City and had girlhood residences in Lancaster County and in Philadelphia. Coming from a prominent Pennsylvania family (her brother became president of the Pennsylvania Railroad), Cassatt spent her childhood from seven to fourteen getting continental culture in France. From fourteen to twenty-one she lived in Philadelphia, where she studied three years at the Academy of Fine Arts. Against her parents' wishes, she then returned to France, where she remained the rest of her long life except for three visits to America. Cassatt studied the great European collections untiringly and was a superb critic. Her sure judgment virtually formed the collection of her New York friends the Havemeyers, which when given to New York's Metropolitan Museum established it as a great international institution.

Mary Cassatt was thirty-two and had exhibited for five years in the Paris Salon when Edgar Degas, noticing that she had something special, asked her to join the impressionists. As she later said, "At last, I could work with absolute independence without considering the opinion of a jury. I had already recognized who were my true masters. I admired Manet, Courbet and Degas. I hated conventional art—I began to live." Cassatt's paintings and graphic art reflect her realism. She successfully fused the new impressionistic values with the old ones she knew so well. She was an impressionist in her color, in her use of light, and sometimes in her brushwork, but she remained a careful draftswoman and was never reconciled to the dissolution of form. A tremendously industrious artist with a feeling for individual character, Miss Cassatt left about 300 oil paintings, 225 prints, 400 pastels, and numerous watercolors and drawings. Like the life she lived, her pictures have balance, reserve, charm, and warmth. Her subject was the human figure; she is best known for her pictures of girlhood, womanhood, and motherhood in which the relationship between mother and child is deeply felt.

Like Eakins and Cassatt, Henry Ossawa Tanner (1859-1937) studied at the Pennsylvania

Gouache by Mary Cassatt, *Self-Portrait* (1878).
(Collection of Mrs. Richman Proskauer)

Academy of Fine Arts. He was born in Pittsburgh and was the son of Benjamin Tucker
Tanner, a black Methodist minister. Young Tanner moved to Philadelphia with his family
when he was seven. At twenty-one, after being educated in the Philadelphia schools, Tanner
entered the Pennsylvania Academy, where he studied under and was encouraged by Eakins.
After two years at the academy, Tanner tried for seven years to earn a living in Philadelphia
by painting. When this proved impossible, he moved to Atlanta and attempted to support
himself as a photographer. Tanner's luck turned when one of his paintings attracted a
Methodist bishop's wife, Mrs. Joseph C. Hartzell, who with her husband arranged a one-man
show in Cincinnati. Not one painting was sold to the public but the Hartzells bought them
all for $300, enabling Tanner to go to France. Acutely aware of racial injustice in the United
States, Tanner enjoyed the company of people in Paris who made no distinction between
races. He took little interest in movements in modern art, and at thirty-five had his first
painting accepted in the Salon. Three years later his painting "The Raising of Lazarus" won
a gold medal in the Salon and was purchased for the Luxembourg Museum. Tanner, who
primarily painted Biblical subjects, received this good news while touring the Holy Land to
study his backgrounds firsthand. The trip was made possible by a Philadelphia patron,
Rodman Wanamaker, who like his father John Wanamaker, seldom missed a chance to aid
the cause of religion. Tanner grew more successful each year. In 1900 he visited Phila-

Painting by Thomas Eakins, *Portrait of
Henry O. Tanner* (1900). (Hyde Collection,
Glens Falls, New York)

delphia, where Eakins painted his portrait. As time progressed, Tanner's subjects became
more mystical and his manner less realistic, and around 1907 he began painting with multiple
glazes in a technique similar to that used by Albert P. Ryder. Although his later paintings
sold well, his earlier free, direct, and more personal paintings probably represent him at his
best. Interest in Tanner declined after his death, but he later received the attention he deserves, and Philadelphia is proud of its once-forgotten son.

A major American sculptor and a great collector of medieval art, George Grey Barnard
(1863-1938) was born in Bellefonte, the son of Joseph H. Barnard, a Presbyterian minister
with deep roots in Pennsylvania. Although he early moved to the Middle West and spent
his productive years as a sculptor in Paris and in New York, George Barnard wrote in his
will, "my remains on earth to rest near my Beloved groups on the capital of my native state
of Pennsylvania." At his first public showing in 1894 Barnard was the most discussed man
in Paris. The jury of the Salon of the Champs de Mars including Auguste Rodin applauded
his six entries.

Early in his career Barnard had aspired "to make his life's task a succession of related
works." His opportunity came in 1902 when Joseph M. Huston, designer of the present
capitol at Harrisburg, gave Barnard the largest commission ever received by an American

Sculptures by George Grey Barnard, *Love and Labor: The Unbroken Law* (1911) on the north side of the main entrance to the Pennsylvania State Capitol. (Pennsylvania Historical and Museum Commission)

sculptor. From the beginning there were misunderstandings and differences between Barnard and officials at Harrisburg. The amount to be paid and the number of figures to be made were reduced several times during the nine years that it took to complete the project. Funds were cut off when a capitol graft scandal hit the newspapers even though Barnard was not involved. To keep work on the project going in France, Barnard mortgaged his possessions and dropped his life insurance and when still more money was needed became a dealer in medieval sculpture but managed to keep many items for his own collection, now housed in the Metropolitan Museum's Cloisters. A second collection was later sold to the

Philadelphia Museum of Art. Unable to go ahead with his capitol groups and barter antiques simultaneously, Barnard returned in 1907 to the United States, where he hoped to come to an agreement with Harrisburg officials.

In 1908 Boston enthusiastically received a showing of twenty-five of Barnard's works. Barnard and his sculptures were immensely popular, and the press was soon reporting how "a crowd of vultures" was wronging him in Pennsylvania. Fearing a national scandal if the project should fail, Barnard's friends interceded with anyone they could reach in Harrisburg and subscribed funds for Barnard's immediate aid. In 1910 with his Pennsylvania statues exhibited in the Spring Salon, Barnard was again the sensation of Paris. Auguste Rodin pronounced the work "magnificent," and Theodore Roosevelt on viewing the groups, which weighed over a hundred tons, said, "I am proud of this work—proud—thrice proud." After the sculptures crossed the Atlantic, it took eighteen railroad cars to get them to Harrisburg. When the final trimmings and installation had taken place, "Barnard Day" was proclaimed and Harrisburg got a half holiday.

While the sun shone on his white marble bas-relief and pedestal groups portraying "man's suffering or prospering in measure with his fulfillment of the laws of God and nature," Barnard and his statues were eulogized. Music composed for the occasion included the still-familiar "Pennsylvania." "Doffing his soft black hat," Barnard bowed repeatedly as the multitude cheered. These Harrisburg statues are still renowned as masterful achievements, "products of an artist of extraordinary imagination and technical powers."

BIBLIOGRAPHY

Dee Brown: *The Year of the Century: 1876* (1966) provides much information about the centennial celebration; and David G. McCullough: *The Johnstown Flood* (1968) is the best book on that subject. For information on both grade schools and high schools, see James Mulhern: *A History of Secondary Education in Pennsylvania* (1933); J. M. Rice: "The Public-school System of Philadelphia," *Forum,* vol. 15 (1893), pp. 31–42; and Adele Marie Shaw: "The Public Schools of a Boss-ridden City," *World's Work,* vol. 7 (1904), pp. 4460–4466. For data on colleges, see Saul Sack: *History of Higher Education in Pennsylvania,* 2 vols. (1963); and Frederic C. Howe: *The Confessions of a Reformer* (1967). The careers of the three historians used to illustrate changes in scholarship may be explored in Edward S. Bradley: *Henry Charles Lea, 1825–1909: A Biography* (1931); "Henry Charles Lea," *National Cyclopaedia of American Biography* vol. 23, pp. 17–19; and in the *Dictionary of American Biography:* Dana C. Munro: "Henry Charles Lea," vol. 6, pp. 67–69, William E. Lingelbach; "John Bach McMaster," vol. 12, pp. 140–142; and Roy F. Nichols: "Ellis Paxson Oberholtzer," vol. 22, pp. 495–496.

On religion, philosophy, and new ideas, see Merle Curti: *The Growth of American Thought,* 3d ed. (1964), pp. 517–519. For information on Conwell, see Frederick T. Parsons: "Russell Herman Conwell," *Dictionary of American Biography,* vol. 4, pp. 367–368; and Agnes Rush Burr: *Russell H. Conwell and His Work: One Man's Interpretation of Life* (1926). On Pennsylvania newspapers, see Elwyn Burns Robinson: "The Public Press of Philadelphia during the Civil War" (doctoral dissertation, Western Reserve University, 1936); Frank B. Evans: *Pennsylvania Politics, 1872–1877: A Study in Political Leadership* (1966), pp. 22–24; and Frank Luther Mott: *American Journalism, A History: 1690–1960* (1962). Frank Luther Mott: *A History of American Magazines,* 4 vols. (1930–1957), is the standard work.

On Philadelphia, see Sidney George Fisher: *A Philadelphia Perspective: The Diary of Sidney George Fisher Covering the Years 1834–1871,* edited by Nicholas B. Wainwright (1967); Dorothy E. C. Ditter: "Cultural Climate of the Centennial City, Philadelphia, 1875–1876" (doctoral dissertation, University of Pennsylvania, 1947); and Nathaniel Burt: *The Perennial Philadelphians: The Anatomy of* an *American Aristocracy* (1963). On Pittsburgh in general, see Leland D. Baldwin: *Pittsburgh: The Story of a City* (1937). On literature, see Ellis Paxson Oberholtzer: *The Literary History of Philadelphia* (1906). The development of the theater may be seen in William Dickey Coder: "A History of the Philadelphia Theatre, 1856 to 1878" (doctoral dissertation, University of Pennsylvania, 1936); Thomas F. Marshall: "A History of the Philadelphia Theatre, 1878–1890" (doctoral dissertation, University of Pennsylvania, 1941); and James Allison Lowrie: "A History of the Pittsburgh Stage, 1861–1891" (doctoral dissertation, University of Pittsburgh, 1943). On music, consult Edward Gladstone Baynham: "The Early Development of Music in Pittsburgh" (doctoral dissertation, University of Pittsburgh, 1944).

On Pennsylvania architecture in general, see Harold E. Dickson: *One Hundred Pennsylvania Buildings* (1954); Irwin Richman, *Pennsylvania Architecture* (1969). On Philadelphia architects and architecture, see Theo B. White (ed.): *Philadelphia Architecture in the Nineteenth Century* (1953); George B. Tatum: *Penn's Great Town* (1961); Louis H. Sullivan: *The Autobiography of an Idea* (1957); Homer T. Rosenberger: "Charles Follen McKim (1847–1909)," *Cosmos Club Bulletin,* vol. 14 (March 1961), pp. 2–6. On H. H. Richardson and the Pittsburgh Courthouse, see Henry-Russell Hitchcock, Jr.: *The Architecture of H. H. Richardson and His Times* (1936).

For an introduction to Pennsylvania artists, see Harold E. Dickson: *Pennsylvania Painters* (1955). On Eakins, see Sylvan Schendler: *Eakins* (1967); and Fairfield Porter: *Thomas Eakins* (1959). On Cassatt, see Adelyn Dohme Breeskin: *Mary Cassatt: A Catalogue Raisonné of the Oils, Pastels, Watercolors, and Drawings* (1970); *The Graphic Art of Mary Cassatt* (1967); and John Canaday: "Mary Cassatt: Two Worlds in One," *New York Times* (Feb. 6, 1966). On Tanner, see Marcia M. Mathews: *Henry Ossawa Tanner: American Artist* (1969); Patricia Read: "Henry Ossawa Tanner," *Dictionary of American Biography,* vol. 22, pp. 648–649; and John Canaday: "A Poor Deal for a Good Man," *New York Times* (Nov. 19, 1967). On Barnard, see the following items by Harold E. Dickson: Introduction to *George Grey Barnard, Centenary Exhibition, 1863–1963* (1964), pp. 6–9; "Log of a Masterpiece: Barnard's 'The Struggle of the Two Natures of Man,'" *Art Journal,* vol. 20 (1961), pp. 139–143; and "Barnard's Sculptures for the Pennsylvania Capitol," *Art Quarterly* (1959), pp. 127–147.

PART

4

An Age of Transition:
1900 to the Present

CHAPTER TWENTY-THREE

Penrose and Progressivism

The Progressive era in Pennsylvania is an era of paradox. Pennsylvania adopted genuine social and political reforms. Municipal reform movements bore fruit in both Philadelphia and Pittsburgh. Aroused citizens protested corruption on the state level, and the exploitation of labor—particulary child labor—awakened Pennsylvania's social conscience. Yet the machine paralleled these reform movements and indeed reached new heights of efficiency during the Progressive years while management—supported by both the Pennsylvania state government and society at large—smashed labor's efforts to unite.

PENROSE

When Quay died in 1904, Boies Penrose became leader of the Cameron-Quay machine. A Philadelphian of Philadelphians, Penrose boasted, "I can trace my ancestry clear back to the first Adam, and I wouldn't be surprised if I didn't inherit some of his original sin." Penrose's father was descended from the Biddles and his mother from Lord Baltimore, founder of Maryland. Privately tutored until he was an adolescent, Penrose grew up undisciplined, robust, and lazy. He was trained further at the Philadelphia Episcopal Academy and Harvard College, where he narrowly missed election to Phi Beta Kappa "because he preferred dominance and his own way." A physically imposing youth (6 feet 4 inches tall) of courage and incredible energy when interested in a project, Penrose was brilliant, cynical, and taciturn. He was also an arrogant, aloof, irreverent individual who indulged his appetites. Lack of social contacts as a child probably account for his aloofness, lack of close friends, uneasiness with women who were his social equals, boorishness, vulgarity, and abhorrence of physical contact with males. Though physically he was the answer to a football coach's dream, he refused to "brush against the messy, smelly bodies of *those* fellows." Penrose hated to shake hands and refused to do so when older and established. Gluttony eventually built up his weight to 350 pounds. His breakfast sometimes consisted of a dozen fried eggs, a huge ½ inch-thick slice of ham, a dozen rolls, and a quart of coffee, and for lunch he frequently shared a whole stuffed turkey with a friend.

Returning to Philadelphia from Harvard, Penrose read law in the office of the distinguished reformer Wayne MacVeagh, was admitted to the Philadelphia bar in 1883, and with his law partner Edward P. Allinson published studies called *Ground Rents in Philadelphia* (1884) and *Philadelphia, 1681–1887: A History of Municipal Development* (1887), which sympathized with administrative reform. Penrose began his political career as a reformer by successfully and courageously managing the reform campaign of LaBarre Jayne for the city council seat from the aristocratic north end of the Eighth Ward. Though Penrose was interested in administrative reform, it was a minor interest. He was not committed to reform; the Jayne campaign was simply an opportunity to demonstrate his prowess. When, with a shrewd eye for talent, local Republican leaders—his erstwhile enemies—invited him to join their organization, Penrose gladly accepted. His early and constant obsession with power proved indispensable to his political rise. Penrose went to the state Legislature in 1884, switched to the state Senate in 1887, and ten years later succeeded Don Cameron in the United States Senate.

Penrose proved himself in the state Legislature. After Quay went to the Senate, Penrose visited all sixty-seven counties to establish a personal relationship with the state's more than 20,000 Republican political workers. Penrose used the same formula that Cameron and Quay had used. Like them, he dispensed contracts, patronage, and campaign funds, but he was much more systematic. Accurate, precise, and meticulous in attending to political matters, Penrose constantly impressed on every locality the necessity of electing legislators who would be loyal to the organization. More than Quay, Penrose was in tune with the industrialists who dominated Pennsylvania. Quay was content to make money with the state's funds on the stock market, but not Penrose. He later said, "I decided to get far enough along to be able to control legislation that meant something to men with real money and let them foot the bills. Never commit yourself but always be in a position where you can if you choose. The men with money will look you up then and you don't have to worry about campaign expenses." Independently wealthy, Penrose disapproved of making money from politics. "Take it from me, Mr. Quay," he warned, "this petty thievery won't pay. You almost went to the pen for a measly hundred thousand. . . . Look at all the things these corporations can do; all the millions they can uncover, with a little encouragement from legislatures." Penrose took the lead in establishing closer relations between large business interests and the Republican machine in Pennsylvania. He wrought a change from 1887, when Pennsylvania legislators individually extracted from swarming lobbyists thinly veiled bribes, to 1897, when the boss or his agent arranged legislation. After Penrose went to Washington, he continued through his lieutenants to increase his control and to watch the Legislature.

Despite tremendous ability, Penrose was content to follow Rhode Island's powerful senator, Nelson W. Aldrich. Penrose was a high-tariff man, generally opposed to Progressive legislation and causes such as woman suffrage and prohibition. He hoped to shelve Theodore Roosevelt—whom he thought something of a demagogue—in the vice presidency, and he helped the old guard make Warren G. Harding President. Poignantly and tragically, he made

Boies Penrose, Republican senator and boss.
(Historical Society of Pennsylvania)

a shrewd prediction that he would have a mediocre senatorial career. "What's the use?" he asked Talcott Williams, who had urged him to take up the day's great issues of railroads, labor, and imperialism:

> I propose to stay senator. I want power. It is the only thing for which I care. I have it. I shall keep it. There are about five thousand election divisions in this State. They hold from twenty thousand to twenty-five thousand Republican workers who carry the division and bring out the vote. I must know all these men. They must know me. If I do not meet them and never see them, I must know what they are, what they want, and how and when. . . . The interests of the State? Of course I look after those. But the job is managing and knowing the . . . men who run the election divisions. As for great measures and great issues such as you talk about, no senator of a State of this size, run as it is, has the time to take them up. I am always glad to hear suggestions. Come to me, write to me. I shall always be glad to hear you, but staying senator is my job.

PROGRESSIVE CRITICS OF SOCIETY

Despite Penrose, the Progressive movement affected Pennsylvania. Originating in the late nineteenth century and blossoming in the first two decades of the twentieth century, the Progressive movement challenged the nation's dominant political and economic forces. Progressives sought to break alliances between political bosses and economic monopolists and to deprive both groups of power. Many Progressives sprang from prominent families and were disturbed by their impotence in contrast to the importance of their parents. The powerful boss winning elections with huge majorities from overpopulated, poverty-stricken wards, destroyed their political power, and the powerful businessman crushing smaller competitors destroyed their economic power. To combat both economic and political monopolists, Progressives reluctantly abandoned the laissez-faire philosophy and small-government notions of their fathers and utilized local, state, and Federal government to regulate both political and economic systems. Indeed, Progressives were so impressed by effective and efficient corporations that they wished to apply the same techniques of scientific management to public administration. Conceiving of themselves as underdogs, Progressives also fought for disadvantaged elements in society. They were not revolutionists but worked to achieve orderly social change.

Progressivism had its precursors and none was more important than Henry George. Born in Philadelphia and educated at Central High School, George moved to San Francisco at eighteen. There he personally experienced the poverty—"all the dull, deadening pain, all the keen, maddening anguish, that to great masses of men are involved in the words 'hard times'"—and brilliantly contrasted it with prosperity in his classic work *Progress and Poverty* first published in 1879. Where "population is densest, wealth greatest, and the machinery of production and exchange most highly developed," George found "the deepest poverty, the sharpest struggle for existence," and the most enforced idleness; and he thought it a monstrous evil that "amid the greatest accumulation of wealth, men die of starvation, and puny infants suckle dry breasts."

Copies of George's book sold by the millions, and he was acclaimed at home and abroad. His primary contribution was as a critic of society who tried to restore man as the measure of all things, who emphasized human and humane values, and who introduced economics not only to humble men but also to distinguished business and professional people. Joseph Fels, a Philadelphia soap manufacturer who generously supported George's single-tax cause, serves as an example. George also influenced George Bernard Shaw, Sidney Webb, H. G. Wells, and other Fabian Socialists in Great Britain.

Although George's solution—a single tax on increases in land values—was not widely adopted, his program has had more practical significance than most historians realize. Nations may have ignored the single tax, but Pennsylvania (and more recently Hawaii) has modified and utilized George's ideas. In 1913 Progressives and Georgists, primarily from Pittsburgh, induced the state Legislature to institute a graded tax in Pittsburgh and Scranton (the two second-class cities of the commonwealth), which between 1914 and 1925 lowered in five graded steps the building tax rate to 50 percent of the land rate. In recent years many urban tax experts and urban renewal authorities have agreed that lowering taxes on improvements while raising taxes on land values would have the effects of causing land to be put to economic use, discouraging urban sprawl, encouraging improvements, and discouraging land speculation.

Muckraking journalists in the Progressive era continued the work Henry George began. Their sensational and somewhat exaggerated exposés of the evils of American political and economic life aroused the public. The most outstanding muckraker of political institutions, Lincoln Steffens, exposed both "Philadelphia: Corrupt and Contented" and "Pittsburgh: A City Ashamed," while the most distinguished muckraker of economic institutions, Ida M. Tarbell, idealized the individualistic Pennsylvania oil man while damning John D. Rockefeller in her *History of the Standard Oil Company*.

Born on an Erie County farm, brought up in the oil city of Titusville, and educated at Allegheny College, Ida Tarbell in 1900 was forty-three, a feminist, and an editor and contributor to what became the leading muckraking journal, *McClure's Magazine*. Tarbell began research on her exposé of Standard Oil in the fall of 1901 and the articles appeared between 1902 and 1904. "The time, the magazine, and the writer," observes Rockefeller's sympathetic biographer Allan Nevins, "combined to make this serialized book the most spectacular success of the muckraking school of journalism, and its most enduring achievement."

Tarbell's *History of the Standard Oil Company* has both the virtues and the vices of muckraking literature. Although passionate and morally outraged, she based her work primarily on facts and figures. She carefully documented her hypothesis that Standard's power derived from its favorable shipping arrangements (rebates and drawbacks) with railroads, which smaller producers and refiners could not match. She was, however, a muckraking journalist and a reformer, prone to exaggeration and loathe to pass up a good if doubtful story. Muckrakers tended to blame bad men for what was wrong with American society, and Tarbell was no exception.

Rockefeller was not the sole architect of Standard Oil, and the kind of individualism Tarbell championed was obsolete for the oil industry. The only way the independent producers and refiners could have defeated Rockefeller would have been with a combination of their own. With its vastly superior organization, Standard defeated the independents primarily because they were independent and unable to unite. Like most Progressives, Tarbell failed to appreciate the organizational revolution while exposing the enormous power and ruthless capacity of the Standard Oil group. But she convinced most Americans that Standard Oil had to be curbed even if it meant utilizing the Federal government.

Lincoln Steffens's articles on Pittsburgh and Philadelphia appearing in *McClure's Magazine* in 1903 also strengthened Progressive forces in Pennsylvania. Like Tarbell, Steffens tended to exaggerate. He pictured Quay, for instance, as more powerful than he really was. But despite the inescapable, everlasting boss, there was an undercurrent of hope in Steffens' articles. He wanted to shock citizens into reform, and he cheered the good fight made by Pittsburgh's Oliver McClintock and Philadelphia's Rudolph Blankenburg. Steffens gradually abandoned the notion that the boss caused political corruption for the idea that the business system prompted it, and in changing his mind he cooled on reformers. Although Steffens praised McClintock in his *Autobiography,* Philadelphia's Boss Israel W. Durham had by then grown to heroic proportions, for he was not only honest and frank about graft and corruption but also helped clarify Steffens' thinking. Under Durham's tutelage, Steffens concluded that "the ethics and the morals of politics are higher than those of business." "In a country where business is dominant," Steffens reasoned, "business men must and will corrupt a government which can pass laws to hinder or help business."

REFORMING PHILADELPHIA AND PITTSBURGH

"We are an inventive people," Steffens maintained, "and we all think that we shall devise some day a legal machine that will turn out good government automatically. The Philadelphians have treasured this belief longer than the rest of us and have tried it more often." The reform Committee of 100 successfully backed the Bullitt Charter, which concentrated power in the mayor, but after it went into effect in 1887 it failed to end municipal corruption because "back of this charter and working with and through it, there were the same old boss, ring, and machine." Indeed Quay allowed the charter to pass the Legislature to check the power of his enemy Boss James McManes, but David Martin (also obnoxious to Quay) succeeded McManes and ultimately Israel W. Durham replaced Martin. "The Bullitt Charter," reflected Durham, "was a great thing for us. It was the best, last throw of the reformers, and when we took that charter and went right on with our business, we took the heart out of our reform forever."

Durham was right in thinking that the reform Bullitt Charter would not hinder machine politics but wrong in supposing that reform was dead. In 1905 Philadelphia reformers—many of whom had been on the Committee of 100—formed the Committee of Seventy and organized the City party to obtain both honest elections and officials just in time to prevent the giveaway of their gas franchise. From the 1840s Philadelphia had a municipally owned gasworks, but in 1897 the city leased its works for thirty years to the United Gas Improvement Company retaining the right to determine the price and quality of gas and to terminate the lease in 1907. United Gas proposed and the city councils accepted a modification of the lease in 1905 that would extend it until 1980, would fix rates until 1980 and deny the city the right to lower them, and would replace annual payments with a lump sum of $25 million to be paid in three installments in 1905, 1906, and 1907. Irate that their councilmen had given away transportation and other franchises and had allowed entrepreneurs to steal the city blind, stung by Steffens's description of Philadelphia as "corrupt and contented," and inspired by the recent election of Theodore Roosevelt on a progressive platform, aroused citizens held mass meetings. The pressure was too great. Mayor John Weaver broke with the Republican machine and vetoed the gas steal, which the councils dared not pass over his veto. Indeed not only was the gas steal stymied but the City party defeated the Republican organization in the November 1905 election. Steffens also remarked that "reform with us is usually revolt, not government, and is soon over." Philadelphians relaxed after defeating the gas steal; the organization elected its mayor in 1907 and in time a ribald trio of "vote racketeers"—the brothers George Vare, Edwin Vare, and William Vare—controlled Philadelphia politics and were powerful enough to ignore reformers and to challenge Penrose.

Both reformers and Penrose attacked the Vare machine, whose main strength was in south Philadelphia, in the 1911 mayoralty campaign. Rudolph Blankenburg, who since 1880 had fought for reform, ran on the nonpartisan Keystone party ticket and was supported by the pitifully weak Democratic party, while in the savage Republican primary the Penrose candidate, George H. Earle, Jr. (whose son later became governor), defeated William S. Vare. Already hurt by scandals, Republicans narrowly lost the ensuing election to Blankenburg.

Mayor from 1912 to 1916, Blankenburg became known as "Old Dutch Cleanser." Nonpartisanship, honesty, and efficiency characterized his approach to the civil service, to engineering difficulties, to the city's expansion problems, and to contracts. He appointed superb subordinates—particularly Morris L. Cooke as director of public works—who introduced scientific management concepts, fired incompetents, forced utilities to lower rates and improve service, awarded contracts after open bidding, eliminated grade crossings, planned and began to build the Market Street Subway, and eliminated much of the politics from the police and fire departments. Blankenburg's accomplishments were largely administrative since the GOP-controlled city councils would not vote additional taxes and balked at a sharp rise in the municipal debt necessary to carry out ambitious programs. Though Philadelphia had but 15 miles of subway and elevated lines, only a token start was made on the Market Street Subway, which was not completed until 1928. Despite Blankenburg's superb record, independent Republicans were swamped in the 1915 mayoralty campaign by Penrose's man, and by 1916 most independents—Blankenburg was a conspicuous exception—returned to the Republican party. Penrose shrewdly welcomed them and promised municipal reform through the regular organization.

Penrose did help reformers clip the Vare brothers' power in 1919 by obtaining a new charter for Philadelphia. Since 1854 Philadelphia had been burdened with a double-chambered legislature of 146 unpaid members, making it one of the largest and most cumbersome bodies of its kind in the world. Its unwieldiness made organization or boss control almost inevitable. After much agitation the city obtained from the state Legislature in 1919 a new charter providing for a small council of twenty-one members who would each receive an annual salary of $5,000. Councilmen would be elected every four years from the eight districts of Philadelphia. The new charter prohibited dual officeholding, as well as political activity and contributions by both policemen and firemen, and placed 15,000 municipal positions on a classified civil service list. The charter also paved the way for the elimination of private garbage contractors (a most lucrative source of revenue for the Philadelphia machine), streamlined administration, shortened the ballot, created a purchasing agent, and provided for a city architect. The same Legislature enacted a series of electoral reform measures designed to prevent fraud and ballot-box stuffing.

Hailed as the triumph of a generation's effort, the new charter would never have passed without Penrose's strong support. Penrose realized that his state organization would profit by a smoother-running municipal government. The new charter would cut the Vares down to size and make them more respectable, thus inhibiting bad publicity, while his support of the charter would gain support for the state organization.

Less spectacular than a new charter and perhaps more significant in long-term results was the work of the Philadelphia Bureau of Municipal Research. It revealed another facet of progressivism, a facet concerned with administration and techniques of government. Though initially suspect, the bureau established a working relationship with many public officials, and its reports led to concrete improvements. It helped the Board of Education reorganize its Bureau of Compulsory Education into an effective branch, issued a manual of accounting and spurred the controller to install a modern system in his office, and persuaded city officials to use budget procedures. It also compiled a manual for policemen, a digest of all laws and ordinances pertaining to public health, and a better system for keeping case records.

Pittsburgh also responded to the progressive impulse. Having disposed of the remnants of the Magee-Flinn machine, Pittsburghers by 1903 had a new boss in Tom Bigelow. Bigelow headed the initially reformist Citizens party and worked to capture and combine with the old Magee-Flinn organization. "All we have to do," remarked undaunted reformers, "is to begin all over again." Along with young reformers, Oliver McClintock organized the Voters' League, and by 1906 their resolution bore fruit. In that year Mayor George W. Guthrie began his reform administration. Despite the Pittsburgh councils' hostility to reform, Guthrie closed 334 brothels, shut down gambling houses and pool rooms, enforced the liquor law, checked bunco games in hotels, stopped systematic grafting by police, and deprived pickpockets and other petty criminals of official protection. Pittsburgh rarely had had either a physician or a sanitarian as superintendent of the Bureau of Health, but Guthrie appointed Dr. James F. Edwards, who worked diligently to improve sanitary conditions in a number of areas including housing and milk supply.

The most spectacular manifestation of the reform spirit began in 1908 after a loose-tongued Pittsburgh reporter remarked to a councilman as he fingered $250, "Well, they have divided the bank swag—here's mine!" The councilman was part of the small minority who had bitterly contested the bank-ordinance bill just passed over Mayor Guthrie's veto. The ordinance had named six banks as four-year depositories for municipal funds amounting to approximately $10 million annually even though these banks offered but 2 percent interest when five other banks would have paid 2½ percent.

With the help of a few prominent Pittsburghers—particularly A. Leo Weil, president of the Voters' League—the handful of honest councilmen set about proving that their colleagues had been bribed. They called in Robert Wilson, a fearless itinerant preacher who as head of the Municipal League helped reform Scranton. Posing as a wood-block paving magnate, Wilson soon had three councilmen—John Klein, William Brand, and Joseph C. Wasson—accepting a bribe in his hotel room, which he had previously converted into a whispering gallery by boring small holes in doors to adjacent rooms and fitting megaphones into some of them. For ease in anticipated deals, a stakeholder was suggested. Klein named William W. Ramsey, president of the German National Bank of Pittsburgh, and volunteered that Ramsey was trustworthy because he had been tied up in the bank-ordinance deal. While stenographers wrote furiously in adjoining rooms, Klein proudly told how $25,000 had been collected from the favored banks and how councilmen and others had "*waited for the angel of charity to walk*—and I was the angel of charity." To further the investigation, Weil journeyed to Washington and persuaded President Theodore Roosevelt to send a special inspector to check the books of the German National Bank. When the examiner found the evidence, the bank's president and cashier readily confessed their guilt but insisted that other directors of their bank were not implicated.

Not content to have only three councilmen and two bankers convicted when many others were involved, reformers worked on Klein, who was now behind bars. At last in 1910 he broke down and to the delight of reformers gave "the day, date, place, hour, the smallest detail of every transaction and the words of every conversation." Klein's confession supplemented by that of other councilmen, who joined the confession stampede to keep out of prison, resulted in 186 indictments involving 116 persons and the jailing of four bankers and a score of councilmen.

Gathering momentum, the Voters' League demanded a new charter. A 1910 mass meeting authorized a committee representing seventeen civic organizations to draw up a charter. Pittsburghers backed that charter with enthusiastic meetings, and 15,000 petitioned the Legislature to pass it unchanged. The Penrose state organization cooperated with reformers since Guthrie's successor Mayor William A. Magee (Chris Magee's nephew) and William Flinn (who had repaired his fortunes), adroit manipulators of the local Republican machine, were getting too independent. By 1911 Pittsburgh had a nine-man council representing the whole city, in place of its unwieldly and easily corrupted councils with members representing various wards.

Who were these municipal reformers who rescued Pittsburgh from its corrupt councilmen, and what motivated their action? These questions can be answered, for Samuel P. Hays has made a study of the 745 members of Pittsburgh's two principal reform organizations during the Progressive era, the Civic Club and the Voters' League. Hays's findings question—at least on the municipal level—the assumption that Progressive reforms were designed to achieve democratic ends. Members of these reform organizations were primarily from the upper class and most of their wealth had been created after 1870 in the iron, steel, electrical equipment, and other industries. They tended to live in the newer fashionable areas. Fifty-two percent of Pittsburgh reformers were businessmen or their wives, and the other 48 percent were professional people. Hays observes that these reformers—all involved in rationalizing and systematizing modern life—condemned a municipal government dominated by local and particularistic interests. They were aware that the decentralized "ward system of government especially gave representation in city affairs to lower- and middle-class groups" concerned primarily with their local area of the city rather than with problems facing the whole city. While reformers "proclaimed an ideology of popular upheaval against a selfish few," municipal reform in Pittsburgh "involved not a broader distribution of political power but its concentration, not confidence in the political wisdom of the 'people' but a fear of it and an attempt to supplant it with a more centralized formal decision-making process more responsive to concentrated informal political power." In 1907 school boards were dominated by middle- and lower-class occupational groups with only 27 percent in the upper occupational group, and upper occupational levels were even lower on the city councils. After 1911, with the new Board of Education appointed by the judges of the courts of common pleas rather than elected, 93 percent came from upper occupational levels, and citywide elections for the new council produced the same dramatic social upheaval among Pittsburgh's decision makers.

REFORMING STATE POLITICS

Scandal produced reform on the state as well as on the municipal level. An aroused people ended the ancient and dishonorable practices of state treasurers, such as William H. Kemble, Robert W. Mackey, and Matthew S. Quay, of depositing state funds in friendly banks, of sometimes using that money for private speculation, and of accepting political contributions of 2 to 3 percent from these favored banks. The funds at the disposal of the state treasurer amounting to over $1 million in 1878 had grown by 1905 to $14 million, and pet banks paid no interest before 1897 and only 2 percent after that date. A series of treasury scandals came to a head in 1905 when William H. ("Bull") Andrews—former Standard Oil lobbyist, friend of Quay, and brother of the Republican State Committee chairman—invested state funds in a dubious New Mexico railroad scheme. The money had been deposited in small banks but particularly in the Enterprise National Bank in Allegheny City which had over $1 million (at least five times its capital stock) in state deposits. Already aroused by Philadelphia's revolt against the gas steal, Pennsylvanians took up the cry: "We want a new treasury deal." Democrats shrewdly nominated William H. Berry, a local Methodist preacher and Chester's reform mayor, for treasurer; and Independent Republicans (the Lincoln party), Prohibitionists, and Philadelphia's City party also supported him. In quick succession three weeks before the 1905 election, the cashier of the Enterprise National Bank (claiming "Andrews has worked my ruin") committed suicide and the bank failed. The slogan "Remember the Enterprise" swept Berry and the Democratic party to its only statewide victory from 1893 to 1931.

Republicans recognized that reform was imperative. Governor Samuel W. Pennypacker

(1903–1907) appropriately called a special legislative session in January 1906 to reform treasury practices, and state Treasurer William L. Mathues began removing the $4 million sinking fund (distinct from the $10 million in the general fund) from various banks to buy up 4 percent state bonds. It was appropriate for Pennypacker to call for reform since his cousin Quay astutely had chosen him—an admirable Philadelphia judge with no backing—to run for governor in 1902 because he would project a respectable image. Pennypacker had to overcome the sins of both Quay and Governor William A. Stone (1899–1903) as well as the popularity of the Democratic warhorse Pattison, who was running for a third term. Pennypacker proved to be an excellent administrator who appointed good men and fearlessly executed laws. He sent home from factories thousands of illegally employed children, forced the Corn Products Refining Company to withdraw glucose bleached with sulphur dioxide from the market, vetoed many loosely drawn bills, and established departments of mines and mineral industries, highways, fisheries, health, and state police as well as numerous bureaus. Paradoxically, Pennypacker attempted through the Libel Act of 1903 (repealed in 1907) "to muzzle the press" and prevent it from calling the mayor of Philadelphia a "traitor," a United States senator a "yokel with a sodden brain," and the governor of the commonwealth an "ugly little dwarf." This legislation along with Pennypacker's approval in 1905 of two out of four ripper bills transferring some of the mayor's power to the councils tarnished Pennypacker's reform reputation.

Berry's victory and the Philadelphia gas-steal uprising goaded Pennypacker into further reform action. The special legislative session began on January 15, 1906, and in one month Pennypacker had pushed through an excellent set of laws. No other state, Theodore Roosevelt remarked, had passed so many reform and progressive laws so quickly. Pennypacker not only protected state funds deposited in banks but also, despite Republican misgivings, rammed through a reapportionment act. In addition Pennypacker and the special session of 1906 created Greater Pittsburgh (permitting Pittsburgh and Allegheny City to unite), required personal voter registration, curbed corrupt practices at elections, improved primary election laws, regulated nomination and election expenses and required accounts to be publicly filed, prohibited employees of the city of Philadelphia from actively participating in politics and elections, established a civil service system for Philadelphia, and abolished fees in the offices of the secretary of the commonwealth and the Insurance Commission.

Pennypacker and his special legislative session, however, had not deprived Berry of all opportunity to reform. Taking office in May 1906, Berry promised that strict accounting and publicity would be his policy. He was true to his word. As soon as he brought his predecessor's books up to date, Berry exposed the capitol scandal. On February 2, 1897, the state capitol had burned, and in 1901 the Legislature had appropriated $4 million and appointed a commission headed by Governor Stone to build a new capitol by January 1, 1907. Acting under expert advice, the commission approved the plans of Joseph M. Huston of Philadelphia, and the building was completed on schedule and within the $4 million appropriation. The Board of Public Grounds and Buildings, consisting of Governor Pennypacker, the auditor general, and the state treasurer, in consultation with Huston furnished the capitol for $876,000; however, the board further decorated the capitol for the additional unappropriated cost of $7.7 million replacing in more elaborate fashion work already contracted for by the commission. The board and commission were independent of each other even though Auditor General William P. Snyder served on both and Architect Huston worked for both. Apart from Snyder, members of the commission apparently were unaware that the

The State Capitol at Harrisburg (1906), John H. Huston, architect. It is flanked on the left by the William Penn Memorial Museum and Archives. (Pennsylvania Historical and Museum Commission)

Board of Public Grounds and Buildings was replacing work they had contracted for. Ironically Pennsylvanians rejoiced in August 1906 over the announcement that their beautiful capitol had been completed for less than $4 million.

The rejoicing soon ended. Berry discovered and announced that the capitol had actually cost closer to $13 million thanks to its decoration and furnishing. After Berry heard that fifteen men had performed the impossible feat of laying $90,000 worth of parquet flooring in two weeks, he became suspicious and sought independent estimates for decorations in his office. His ceiling, estimated at $550, actually had cost $5,500, and oak wainscoting worth $1,800 had cost $15,500. Furthermore, Contractor John H. Sanderson of Philadelphia had sold the state chairs and chandeliers by the foot or pound. For example, he had offered to supply a chandelier for $193.50 but had billed it at the $4.85-per-pound rate for odds and ends, making the actual cost $2,500. The state, Berry estimated, had paid $5 million more for its capitol than it should have paid. Sure of Pennypacker's own honesty, the public blamed him only for lack of judgment.

Not even the capitol graft scandal, breaking as it did during a gubernatorial campaign, could overturn the Penrose machine. Recognizing that graft was bad politics, Republicans once again nominated a thoroughly respectable man, Edwin S. Stuart. A Philadelphia bookseller and a former mayor of the city, Stuart pledged that if elected he would thoroughly investigate the capitol scandal. Although the Democratic nominee Lewis Emery, Jr., cut Stuart's majority to 50,000, the Republican machine again triumphed.

A few days after it met in January, 1907, the Legislature appointed a commission to investigate the scandal. That commission, one of whose members was future Governor John S. Fisher, corroborated Berry's accusations and called for prosecutions. Stuart's attorney general, Moses Hampton Todd, prepared thirty indictments for conspiracy and seven others for false pretense and in 1908 obtained the convictions of Architect Huston, Contractor Sanderson, former State Treasurer Mathues, and former Auditor General Snyder. The defendents delayed sentencing by appeals to the state Supreme Court, and finally in 1910 the state dropped the case following restitution by the accused of $1.1 million.

The Stuart administration (1907–1911) accomplished little beyond investigating the capitol graft scandal. Confirmation of the fraud hurt Republican popularity and presented Democrats with the opportunity to recapture power in the 1910 campaign. But instead of nominating the hero of the capitol graft scandal, William H. Berry, Democrats named Webster Grim, who was virtually unknown. After the Penrose machine nominated John K. Tener, discontented Democrats and antimachine Republicans nominated Berry on a third-party (Keystone) ticket. Tener squeaked through with a minority of the votes cast, Berry ran a very strong second, and Grim a poor third. By splitting the opposition, the Keystone-Berry movement played into Penrose's hands.

Two years later, Penrose was not so successful. Dissident Republicans (a mixture of Progressives and frustrated machine politicos) led by Boss William Flinn and Alexander P. Moore of Pittsburgh, Edwin Van Valkenburg of the Philadelphia newspaper *North American,* and Gifford Pinchot of Milford gained control of the Republican State Convention and sent delegates to the 1912 Republican National Convention pledged to Theodore Roosevelt. After the William Howard Taft steamroller flattened the Progressives, insurgents from Pennsylvania and other states nominated Roosevelt on the Progressive party ticket. Progressives (called the Washington party in Pennsylvania) led by Boss Flinn concentrated their attack on the pro-Taft Penrose machine and carried the state by 50,000 votes, although Democrat Woodrow Wilson won the Presidency. It is true that Roosevelt was immensely popular in Pennsylvania, but he and other Progressives recognized that Flinn's well-organized campaign had brought them success.

Ironically Penrose, who had been hurt by the Progressive victory, had fostered progressivism. He chose both Governor Stuart, who prosecuted the capitol grafters, and Governor Tener, whose administration (1911–1915) passed a statewide direct primary for nominating state officials, the Sproul Road Act of 1911 which created a highway system maintained exclusively by the state, and a comprehensive 1911 revision of the school code, as well as established the Public Service Commission, the Pennsylvania Historical Commission, and the Department of Labor and Industry. Nevertheless in 1914 Gifford Pinchot, an ardent disciple of Roosevelt, challenged Penrose for his Senate seat. Penrose realized that with support from the Vares—the only politicians he hated and feared—Pinchot would win. Consequently Penrose swallowed his pride, accepted the Vares's gubernatorial candidate Martin G. Brumbaugh, and tacitly acknowledged the Vares's power in Philadelphia to save his senatorial seat. Penrose and Brumbaugh both triumphed at the polls. Governor Brumbaugh (1915–1919) had little sympathy with the idea of legislating progressivism, vetoed many reform bills, and as an ally of the Vares successfully opposed the new Philadelphia charter. Yet Brumbaugh—who had been president of Juniata College and superintendent of the Philadelphia Public Schools—encouraged vocational education, signed the child labor and workmen's compensation laws and the direct inheritance tax, and enlarged state forest lands. By 1918 Penrose was once more in firm control, and his last governor, William C. Sproul, proved far more progressive than Brumbaugh. Although no Progressive, Penrose was shrewd enough to make concessions and to avoid direct confrontations. Though progressive programs on the state level might threaten local pickpocket politicians, they were not a threat to Penrose, and the costs of social programs hit marginal producers harder than Penrose's special constituents, the gigantic and more efficient corporations.

SOCIAL LEGISLATION

Social reform paralleled political reform during the Progressive era. Concern for the less fortunate blossomed. In the private sector, settlement houses modeled on Jane Addams' Hull House sprang up. At houses such as Kingsley House in Pittsburgh and College Settlement in Philadelphia young idealists lived and researched among the poor. College Settlement, for example, arranged for the University of Pennsylvania to sponsor W. E. B. DuBois and helped him in other important ways while he studied the Philadelphia Negro. Unlike the organized charities of the day which blamed poverty on individual failings, these reformers stressed that social and economic conditions created poverty. Backed by extensive research and experience, their solution was to improve the community environment rather than to practice individual philanthropy.

The same spirit that propelled young idealists into slum settlement houses produced the pioneering and unique *Pittsburgh Survey*. A small group of Pittsburgh business, professional, and welfare leaders collaborating with the Charities Publication Committee of New York (later Survey Associates) engineered the *Survey*. There was no widespread local demand for criticism and reform; indeed the *Survey* humiliated and angered many Pittsburghers. Paul U. Kellogg, the director of the *Survey,* and his distinguished fellow workers emphasized that they selected Pittsburgh because: "It is the capital of a district representative of untrammeled industrial development, but of a district which, for richer, for poorer, in sickness and in health, for vigor, waste and optimism, is rampantly American."

An outstanding field staff made the actual survey during 1907 and 1908 with some supplementary studies in 1909 and 1910. The results were exhibited at the Carnegie Institute in November 1908 and subsequently published in *Charities and the Commons* and again in the six-volume *Pittsburgh Survey*. The *Survey* explored and related social, industrial, and civic issues; focused on wage earners; described social conditions in terms of actual household experiences; evaluated institutions in terms of their effect on people; and synthesized the statistics of the census report with the journalist's personalized reporting. The surveyors were activists and interpreted their findings to stimulate local reform efforts through luncheon meetings and addresses, newspaper and magazine articles, pamphlets, and exhibits.

The surveyors found an utter neglect of human resources since jobs could always be filled by new immigrants with low standards of living willing to work for abnormally low wages. "An altogether incredible amount of overwork by everybody" destroyed family life. This condition reached its extreme in the seven-day, 12-hour shift in the steel mills and railroad switchyards. The great majority of men employed in the mills received low wages, and women received only "one-half as much as unorganized men in the same shops and one-third as much as the men in the union." Considerably more than a thousand Pittsburgh homes were shattered each year by deaths caused by preventable typhoid fever and unnecessary industrial accidents. Neglect of life and health came about because centralized and coordinated business leadership, without any significant countervailing power, shaped the life of the region.

Progressives attacked social evils exposed by muckrakers, social workers, and the *Pittsburgh Survey*. They worked for Federal, state, and local laws to protect men, women, and children at work; for playgrounds and for tenement-house codes to ensure minimal living standards; for pure water, milk codes, sewage systems, and public garbage removal to preserve health. Though the laws they got passed helped alleviate many problems, they were more successful in some areas than in others. Regulatory legislation, for example, did not solve the housing problem. The Pennsylvania Tenement House Act of 1895 contained some helpful provisions, and the Housing Act of 1903 applying to second-class cities was also helpful, but three factors prevented these acts from realizing the hopes of their authors. Most slum houses in Philadelphia and Pittsburgh were one- and two-family dwellings and were not covered by laws applying to tenement houses; neither major city provided an adequate inspection force; and, most important, neither possessed a surplus of good, low-cost housing, with the result that standards could only be enforced to eliminate the worst houses. Effectively enforced housing codes actually reduced the net supply of low-income housing by raising construction costs and discouraging builders and by condemning unfit dwellings.

The struggle for child-labor laws, however, was reasonably successful. Legislation was considerably broadened and laws were better enforced. Although an 1868 law simply suggested the 8-hour day as a standard, and legislation in 1879 merely prohibited children under twelve from working inside mines, an 1885 law spelled things out in considerable detail. It prohibited females from working in or outside coal mines and boys under fourteen from working inside and boys under twelve from working outside anthracite mines with ten or more employees. It also prohibited boys under twelve from working inside and those under ten from working outside bituminous mines of the same size. The Legislature took one step backward and one forward in 1887 when it lowered the minimum age to twelve but extended the coverage to mills, factories, and mines. Two years later children under twelve were prohibited from working in mercantile establishments and a 60-hour work week was the maximum allowed. Daily hours were still unregulated, however, and some children worked 15 to 18 hours a day. The 1893 Factory Act widened coverage, established a thirteen-year minimum age, and limited hours to 12 daily and 60 weekly.

During the Progressive era, Pennsylvania led the nation in the number of working children. Coal mines, textile mills, and glass factories employed them in large numbers. Glass factories were particularly harmful since they exposed boys to high temperatures, to high tensions (rushing hot glassware from one work area to another), and to weekly alternating night shifts. Bad as the glassworks were, the horrors experienced by breaker boys were worse. As needy parents lied about their children's ages, underage children (even as young as nine) were often employed in anthracite regions. In 1906 child-labor reformer John Spargo described them:

> Crouched over the chutes, the boys sit hour after hour, picking out the pieces of slate and other refuse from the coal as it rushes past to the washers. From the cramped position they have to assume, most of them become . . . bent-backed like old men. . . . The coal is hard, and accidents to the hands,

Photo study by Lewis W. Hine, *A group of the youngest breaker boys in a Pennsylvania coal breaker. South Pittston, Pa. January, 1911.* (Lewis W. Hine Collection, Local History and Genealogy Division, New York Public Library, Astor, Lenox and Tilden Foundations)

such as cut, broken, or crushed fingers, are common among the boys. Sometimes there is a worse accident: a terrified shriek is heard, and a boy is mangled and torn in the machinery, or disappears in the chute to be picked out later smothered and dead. Clouds of dust fill the breakers and are inhaled by the boys, laying the foundations for asthma and miners' consumption.

Advocating child-labor legislation from 1904 to 1915, Progressives ran into serious opposition. Such "radical" legislation, Pennsylvania manufacturers argued, would hurt business ("We cannot compete with less hampered states"), working children ("conditions in the mills are far superior to many of the children's homes—certainly better than running the street"), and parents ("wages of these children are needed at home"). Nevertheless, reformers prevailed, and steps were taken to rescue thousands of previously neglected boys and girls. Aroused citizens established the Pennsylvania Child Labor Committee in 1904 as a side effect of the Anthracite Coal Strike Commission hearings the year before in Scranton. Testimony there told how miners' children as young as ten and eleven were working 12-hour night shifts in local silk mills. Indeed, when an organizer journeyed to Scranton to unionize the silk mills he found an audience of little girls. "I did not come here to organize children!" he exclaimed. "For God's sake, go home!" The Child Labor Committee conducted a six-month

Photo study by Lewis W. Hine, *Irish Stogie-maker,* Pittsburgh—1909.
(Lewis W. Hine Collection, Local History and Genealogy Division, New
York Public Library, Astor, Lenox and Tilden Foundations)

investigation in 1904 and helped shape and pass the Child Labor Act of 1905, which Governor Pennypacker signed into law. That law raised the minimum age for factory and mine workers to fourteen, prohibited night work for children except in continuous industries (glass factories and foundries), and, though the courts later declared the provision unconstitutional, attempted to eliminate false certificates of age.

Continued pressure by the Child Labor Association produced the 1909 law which lowered children's labor to 10 hours a day and 58 hours a week, again sought to eliminate false certificates of age by having school authorities issue the certificates, and tried to protect children from dangerous machines and occupations. In 1913, under a Women's Labor Law, maximum weekly hours of girls were lowered to 54. Finally in 1915 the Legislature made fourteen the minimum age in all establishments, abolished night work for children, established a 9-hour day and a 51-hour week, lengthened the list of dangerous occupations, and required completion of the sixth grade for fourteen- and fifteen-year-old working children. The act was signed by Governor Brumbaugh, who also approved the Workmen's Compensation Law. The next significant change for Pennsylvania's laboring children occurred during the Great Depression in 1935 when the Legislature raised the minimum working age to sixteen, established an 8-hour day and a 44-hour week for those under eighteen, and increased the number of prohibited occupations.

WORLD WAR I

The impact of progressivism was not limited to domestic political and social reforms. Its influence extended beyond the borders of the United States affecting the conduct of foreign relations. Although many Progressives were isolationists, the same Progressive paternalism that fought for tenement-house codes and child-labor laws at home also found expression in Theodore Roosevelt's and Woodrow Wilson's attempts to uplift downtrodden peoples and nations. This spirit culminated in American participation in World War I. Ironically, that war was rooted in the crass self-interest, intense nationalism, imperialistic rivalries, armaments races, and alliance systems of Great Britain, France, and Russia on the one hand and of Germany and Austria-Hungary on the other. Nevertheless most Americans were convinced that Britain and its allies were fighting for liberty and democracy, and though the Wilson administration ultimately went to war to preserve neutral rights on the high seas from attacks by German submarines as well as to keep the balance of power tipped in Britain's favor, the American people—as good Progressives—supported the war "to make the world safe for democracy" and "to end all wars."

Since men at war both utilize traditional and innovate new methods of warfare, any major war is both the first modern war and the last old-style war. In retrospect World War I with its George M. Cohan tunes, the Red Baron, and some military units organized along local and state lines has a quaint, archaic quality. Its machine guns, tanks, submarines, airplanes, and poison gas, however, were anything but quaint. They were modern advances in military technology that brought death and destruction not only to soldiers and sailors but to noncombatant men, women, and children. Furthermore in organizing the war effort the Federal government assumed enormous powers, which individualistic Americans heretofore had resisted, over all phases of American life. Growing Federal power reflected increasing bureaucratic capacity and efficiency.

The Federal government had little difficulty regimenting Pennsylvania even though it was a bastion of economic individualism (particularly hostile to Federal regulation of business), of personal individualism (as witnessed in resistance to the Civil War draft), and at the start of World War I of pro-German sentiment. On January 28, 1915, German-American members of the American Neutrality League of Philadelphia packed the Academy of Music. An overflow meeting kept up its spirit by singing "Die Wacht am Rhein" and "Deutschland über Alles," while, inside, Governor Brumbaugh presided and three congressmen made "bitter anti-British speeches." But once the United States entered the war Pennsylvania officials took steps to stifle opposition. When a Philadelphia mob attacked thirty socialists who were distributing antidraft handbills, authorities arrested thirteen socialists but no "patriots." A raid made a few nights later on the Young People's Socialistic Society captured some forty-nine "slackers and anti-draft agitators." In late August police blocked the doors of the Arch Street Theater when the Philadelphia Conscientious Objectors to War planned a meeting there. As the crowd dispersed, sailors attacked it and a riot ensued. Shortly thereafter the chief postal inspector raided Socialist headquarters on Arch Street, arresting the secretary and confiscating antidraft leaflets. Philadelphia gave Godspeed to its first World War I draftees with a spectacular parade on September 1, 1917. Soldiers, sailors, and marines combined with city organizations to form an escort for these first few thousand boys. Bombs were exploded on the roof of City Hall, planes flew overhead dropping messages from the mayor to friends and relatives of the drafted men, the Baldwin Locomotive Works exhibited a locomotive built for the French with the tag "Our Energies Are Concentrated to Help Win the War," and the Eddystone Corporation boasted that its shells would "clear the way for the United States boys when they go over the top."

Almost 371,000 Pennsylvanians served in the armed forces. Though only a fraction of these men served in the Twenty-eighth Division, it has come to symbolize the commonwealth's military contribution to the war. Organized in August 1917 from the Pennsylvania National Guard, the Twenty-eighth Division landed in France in May 1918. The German high command in the spring of 1918 had launched with telling effect a series of massive offensives against British and French lines. Weakened and wearied by four years of slaughter, the Allied line was in danger of cracking, but the timely appearance in June of fresh American troops (among them part of the Twenty-eighth Division) at Chateau-Thierry bolstered it. Elements of the Twenty-eighth along with other American units again strengthened French divisions at the second Battle of the Marne and tipped the balance in favor of the Allies. The Twenty-eighth participated in the Aisne-Marne counteroffensive, then in late September and early October became part of the American First Army and fought in the Meuse-Argonne offensive. The Twenty-eighth ended the war in the Thiancourt sector and returned in May 1919. Its casualties were heavy. The division fluctuated between 21,000 and 25,000 men and suffered just short of 14,000 casualties, almost 2,000 of whom died.

Pennsylvania's industrial contribution to the war effort was even more significant than that of its soldiers and sailors. The Emergency Fleet Corporation (headed by Charles M. Schwab of Bethlehem Steel) constructed the world's largest shipyard at Hog Island near Philadelphia. Fifty shipways and seven 1,000-foot piers with berths for twenty-eight vessels stretched 2½ miles where ten months before a wooded tract had stood. In one of the great organizational feats of the war, Hog Island assembled the first prefabricated vessel from parts produced in forty to fifty scattered steel-rolling and fabricating mills. Despite the expenditure of enormous energy, Hog Island did not deliver its first vessel to the government until the war was over. Existing, not new facilities, were most important in meeting the ship shortage.

Though Philadelphia and other manufacturing cities made tremendous contributions, steel production made the Pittsburgh district the "arsenal of the world." "Pittsburgh steel," a British general remarked, "was everywhere along the battle front." The struggle between Pittsburgh and the Ruhr was as significant as that between opposing armies. In early 1915 the Westinghouse Electric and Manufacturing Company began producing large quantities of munitions, forgings, railroad cars, and equipment for the Allies. By the time the United States entered the war Pittsburgh was partially geared to war production, and the district quickly converted to full war production. It had 250 war plants employing over 500,000 men and women and operating around the clock six or seven days a week. Pittsburgh mills furnished 80 percent of the munition steel used by the United States Army, and mines of the area furnished 75 percent of the coal used by munition makers. Indeed the Pittsburgh district mined 20 million more tons of coal in 1918 than it had in 1917. The Allied victory owed much to industrial supremacy and the role of Pittsburgh and indeed of all Pennsylvania in creating that supremacy was crucial.

THE STEEL STRIKE OF 1919

The war with its manpower needs created a favorable climate for organized labor. The Wilson administration set up the National War Labor Board (NWLB) to mediate disputes and the War Labor Policies Board (WLPB) to standardize labor policies among industries receiving government contracts. When the war ended, real wages had increased only slightly, but the work week had been shortened, and in five years the AFL had grown half again as large. After the war, however, organized labor fell back when deprived of governmental support.

Postwar Pennsylvania management reverted to its traditionally hostile attitude toward organized labor. The dominant attitude of the political establishment during the Progressive era was antiunion, antistrike, and antipicketing. During the anthracite strike in the spring of 1906 Governor Pennypacker proclaimed that while all men had the right to strike, the law protects the property rights of all men, and that the striker has "no right to interfere with another man who may want to labor." A few days later, Pennypacker recalled:

> There was rioting at Mount Carmel and the mob took possession of the town. The constabulary [state police] were sent there and the mob defied them. Then they rode through the town. The mob assailed them and they shot about eighty men, establishing a reputation which has gone all over the country and has been retained in many trying occasions since, with the result that the labor difficulties in the anthracite coal region entirely disappeared. It was in every way a most wholesome lesson.

Both George F. Baer of the Reading Railroad and Penrose congratulated Pennypacker on his stand.

Although Pennsylvania labor achieved shorter hours, higher wages, and better working conditions during the Progressive era and World War I, organized labor remained weak despite its wartime growth. The Great Steel Strike of 1919 exposed these weaknesses. Vast changes had occurred in the steel industry since Henry Clay Frick dealt the Amalgamated Association of Iron, Steel and Tin Workers a smashing defeat in the 1892 Homestead Strike. The extreme cutthroat competition that characterized the 1890s gave way, after J. P. Morgan organized United States Steel in 1901, to an era of cooperation and "fair competition" among steel manufacturers. Morgan and his particular representatives in U.S. Steel—Judge Elbert H. Gary and George W. Perkins—wanted to stabilize wages and labor relations as well as prices and the market. To improve working conditions, they backed safety devices, accident insurance, pensions, plant sanitation, stock options, and community improvement; and at the birth of U.S. Steel they were not particularly hostile to organized labor. The Amalgamated Association, however, badly bungled its opportunity. It struck the giant infant U.S. Steel in 1901, failed to accept a favorable offer, lost the strike, and alienated J. P. Morgan. Realizing that trade unionism ran counter to their plans, Morgan, Gary, and Perkins resolved by 1909 on the open shop in steel.

While the steel industry had been revolutionized, organized labor had undergone few changes. The Amalgamated Association—indeed the AFL as a whole—failed to adjust to mass production. It was obvious that the best approach to organizing steel or any mass-production industry was industrial unionism including all production workers, but the Amalgamated continued to limit its membership to skilled, English-speaking workers.

While the Amalgamated was reluctant to organize the unskilled and the immigrant steelworker, management effectively opposed any organizing activity. Though by 1910 most steel companies rarely required the yellow-dog contract (a promise not to join a union) and claimed they did not care if the men were unionized, union men in fact were shabbily treated. A U.S. Steel employee, urging the secretary of labor to work for the abolition of the 12-hour day, complained, "We dare not say anything about it or we [lose] our jobs." Bethlehem Steel in 1918 used Pinkerton detectives to spy on union activities and blacklisted ninety-one activists under the heading: "These Men Are Undesirable and Should Not Be Employed." Companies frequently controlled the mill towns and violated the first amendment to the Constitution by preventing union meetings. In April 1918 the police chief of Bethlehem refused to permit a union meeting, and the mayor (a vice-president of Bethlehem Steel) upheld the decision. Union organizers were ordered out of towns, and those who ignored the order were frequently jailed or mobbed. Most ministers, editors, professional men, and merchants were hostile to organized labor. In addition U.S. Steel wooed many skilled workers away from unions by offering low-interest housing loans, stock-purchase plans, and bonuses for workers who "showed a proper interest in its welfare and progress." By 1914 unionization of the steel industry seemed hopeless; the Amalgamated was weak, workers were fractured by ethnic differences, and companies were actively hostile.

World War I made unionization a distinct possibility. By 1915 steel mills faced a serious labor shortage. Black migrants from the South could not fill the void when the war shut off the foreign-born labor supply. Steel companies were earning record amounts but as late as January 1916 had passed little on to their workers. In April 1916 Pittsburgh district steelworkers, shouting "8 hours" joined striking Westinghouse employees. On May 2 a bloody riot occurred at the U.S. Steel works at Braddock, and a general strike threatened the Pittsburgh district. The general strike did not materialize, and a series of seven pay boosts, raising the common labor rate from 20 to 42 cents an hour by August 1, 1918, prevented further serious disturbances during the war. The labor shortage enabled unions to expand since management could no longer threaten to fire union members. The AFL sent organizers wherever trouble threatened and even the Amalgamated grew, but by the summer of 1918 no plants were organized and steel companies did not recognize unions for collective bargaining.

More important than the labor shortage to the growth of unionization was the positive support of the Wilson administration, which was eager to avoid wartime labor trouble. For the first time the nation's workingmen could organize without fear of penalty. The NWLB proved to be a powerful body; it made Eugene G. Grace of Bethlehem Steel raise wages, prohibit future discrimination against unions, and permit the election of shop committees. Shortly thereafter Felix Frankfurter, a future justice of the Supreme Court, then a Harvard law professor serving as secretary to the WLPB, forced Gary to accept as of October 1, 1918, the basic 8-hour day in steel. The decision amounted to a pay boost since the steelworkers continued the 12-hour day but received time and a half for overtime. With a friendly, powerful Federal administration, the time was ripe for organizing steel.

Prodded by William Z. Foster and Gompers, the AFL in August 1918 set up a National Committee for Organizing Iron and Steel Workers with Foster as its secretary treasurer. Twenty-four unions participated in the organizing committee, and though they managed to settle their jurisdictional disputes, their parsimonious financing of the committee proved fatal. The strategy of simultaneously organizing the entire industry had to be dropped, and the committee limited its opening campaign to the Chicago district. Chicago steelworkers, particularly unskilled immigrants, signed up in droves, and on October 1, 1918, the National Committee moved its headquarters to Pittsburgh. In a month and a half the war ended, the NWLB ceased to function effectively, and the hitherto friendly Wilson administration abandoned labor. Wilson did nothing when President Grace of Bethlehem Steel refused to give workers the back pay awarded them by the NWLB and fired shop committee members.

Steel companies combated organization with both hard and soft lines. Gary and Perkins successfully urged that there be no wage cuts after the war and unsuccessfully urged that Sunday work be eliminated. A number of little steel companies (as distinct from big U.S.

Steel) organized company unions, and companies sporadically discriminated against union men. These efforts were not effective. Rather than be grateful for no wage cuts, workmen were bitter over the 12-hour day and seven-day week, which many of them were still saddled with. An Italian laborer, coming off a 24-hour shift at an open-hearth furnace, hearing an observer's remark that he was making pretty good money, replied, "To hell with the money! No can live." Workmen knew company unions were jokes when the Midvale Steel union met in Atlantic City at company expense and resolved against "a shorter day's work and an increased wage."

With the help of local authorities, steel companies attempted to keep out organizers and to prevent union meetings. Mayor George H. Lysle of McKeesport refused to permit union meetings, and borough police allowed company thugs to beat up union organizers. Though McKeesport denied organizers their fundamental right of free speech, neither the Wilson administration nor Governor Brumbaugh went beyond faint disapproval. By the spring of 1919 the National Committee decided to unionize the mill towns surrounding Pittsburgh by using a flying squadron of seven or eight organizers including the legendary Mary Harris ("Mother") Jones, a fiery, white-haired lady who claimed to be eighty-nine. The Homestead police jailed Mother Jones, but her audience followed her and dispersed only when she came out and told them to go home.

Spurred by police interference, the drive was successful, but organizers had two major problems. Ultimate union success depended on the companies recognizing the union as the workers' bargaining agent, and steelworkers' impatience with their wages and hours made them eager to strike before perfecting their organization or collecting an adequate strike fund. The National Committee called a conference in Pittsburgh on May 25, 1919, to "pacify the restless spirits," but "far from damping the unrest," that conference "crystallized the sentiment for action." With Gary and the heads of other companies refusing to recognize the union or to communicate with its leaders and with mounting rank-and-file pressure, the National Committee reluctantly took a strike vote rather than let the situation "degenerate into an unorganized uprising." The vote was 98 percent in favor of striking for higher wages, shorter hours, and better working conditions.

Last-minute efforts to get the companies to the bargaining table failed. Foster and two committee members tried to see Gary who refused to talk with them; Gompers saw a sympathetic Wilson, and his emissary Bernard Baruch tried unsuccessfully on two occasions to get Gary to the conference table. Preoccupied with the fight for the League of Nations, Wilson took Gary's rebuff without castigating the steel industry. The National Committee set the strike date for September 22, Wilson requested a three-week postponement, and Gompers—realizing that a strike at that point would be a disaster—urged the committee to accept Wilson's proposal. The National Committee knew the union could not beat steel, but it felt that a postponement would discredit the AFL. When the strike began on September 22, the steel companies led by Gary welcomed the showdown and the business community backed the fight against organized labor. The strike affected more workers than anticipated; twice as many men struck as had joined the union. At its height 250,000 men, or about half the nation's steel workers, refused to work.

The timing of the strike was bad. Not only was the union unprepared, but the Red Scare was on. The Bolshevist triumph in Russia coupled with the Seattle general strike, the Boston police strike, bomb plots, and May Day riots had already aroused the American people. Newspapers propagated and the public believed the steel industry's charges that the strike was a radical conspiracy by Bolshevists and aliens. Unfortunately for the union, Foster had belonged to the Industrial Workers of the World (IWW) eight years previously. During his IWW days he had written a revolutionary pamphlet called *Syndicalism.* Printing extracts from this pamphlet, newspapers successfully identified the strikers' aspirations with Foster's earlier dreams. When Foster, appearing before a Senate committee investigating the strike, refused to repudiate his pamphlet, the radical label was firmly fixed on the strike.

With help from neither the Wilson administration nor public opinion and with local authorities cold or hostile, the strike was doomed. Though local officials in Johnstown, where labor united behind the strike, moved with restraint, in Allegheny County, where native Americans tended to stay on the job while unskilled immigrants struck, authorities with the help of 5,000 deputized coal and iron police (selected, paid, and armed by the steel companies) prohibited union meetings. Indeed, because of their antiunion activities, mounted state troopers became known among immigrant strikers as Cossacks. Nevertheless the strikers were tenacious. Thanks to steady work during the war years and immigrant frugality, they were not easily forced back to work. Furthermore the National Committee distributed food among needy strikers.

The strategy of the steel companies, however, paid off. Equating radicalism and bolshevism with foreigners, they drove a wedge between native and immigrant strikers. Furthermore, the companies undermined strikers' morale by employing at least 500 undercover agents, some of whom penetrated the National Committee and spread defeatism. With meetings of workers all but prohibited, newspapers further destroyed morale by exaggerating the number of men returning to work. The Johnstown *Leader* proclaimed "The Strike Is Broken" although Midvale Steel's Cambria plant attracted only one-tenth its work force and failed to reopen successfully. The men at Johnstown knew the truth, but newspapers gave strikers elsewhere the impression that Johnstown workers had gone back. With most unions excluding or segregating blacks, the steel companies exploited racism by recruiting 30,000 black strikebreakers. Untrained men could not produce steel unless aided by more experienced workers, but when in November these workers began drifting back, production in the Pittsburgh area returned to normal.

Lack of effective organization also weakened the strike. While the National Committee was nominally in charge, power actually lay in the twenty-four national unions with jurisdiction in steel. This splintering of authority and responsibility hurt the strike. National unions also tended to consider their own interests first. Indeed the Amalgamated betrayed its new members and the strike by ordering back to work 5,000 of its men who were covered by contracts in independent finishing mills. Though the National Committee could coordinate the twenty-four unions, it could not coerce them. A more effective method had to be found to organize mass-production industries.

Though 100,000 men were still on strike in December, they had no hope. The strike ended on January 8, 1920, and six months later the National Committee disbanded. Yet labor gained something from the strike. With steelmen back at work on company terms, the Interchurch World Movement published a report that convinced the public that steelworkers actually did work 12 hours a day and that many of them worked seven days a week. Public opinion and personal appeals by President Warren G. Harding moved the steel industry to institute an 8-hour day in the summer of 1923 with a compensating 25 percent wage increase. Though the steel strike had ultimately led to their receiving the 8-hour day, throughout the 1920s and into the 1930s steelworkers had not achieved the main hope of their 1919 strike—collective bargaining through their independent unions.

BIBLIOGRAPHY

On Penrose, see Walter Davenport: *Power and Glory: The Life of Penrose* (1931); Robert Douglas Bowden: *Boies Penrose: Symbol of an Era* (1937); Talcott Williams; "After Penrose, What?" *Century Magazine,* vol. 105 (1922), pp. 49–55.

For information on Progressives, see Richard Hofstadter's perceptive *The Age of Reform: From Bryan to F.D.R.* (1960), pp. 131-271. On George see Henry George: *Progress and Poverty,* which is available in many editions; Charles A. Barker: *Henry George* (1955); Daniel Aaron: *Men of Good Hope* (1961), pp. 55-91; Steven Cord: "Henry George and Urban Renewal in Pennsylvania" (paper read at the Pennsylvania Historical Association Convention, Oct. 20, 1967, at Beaver Falls). For a sampling of two muckrakers, see Lincoln Steffens: *The Shame of the Cities* (1957), and *Autobiography* (1931); Ida M. Tarbell: *The History of the Standard Oil Company,* edited by David M. Chalmers (1966). Some other contemporary accounts of reform in Philadelphia and Pittsburgh, in addition to Steffens, are useful; among them are B. O. Flower: "Philadelphia's Civic Awakening," *Arena,* vol. 34 (1905), pp. 196–199; Franklin S. Edmonds: "The Significance of the Recent Reform Movement in Philadelphia," *Annals of the American Academy of Political and Social Science,* vol. 27 (1906), pp. 180–190; Clinton Rogers Woodruff: "Municipal Progress: 1904–1905," *Annals of the American Academy of Political and Social Science,* vol. 27 (1906), pp. 192–193, and "Progress in Philadelphia," *American Journal of Sociology,* vol. 26 (1920–1921), pp. 315–332; Delos F. Wilcox: *Municipal Franchises . . .,* 2 vols. (1910–1911), vol. 1, pp. 566–572; vols. 5 and 6 of *Pittsburgh Survey,* particularly articles by Allen T. Burns, Robert A. Woods, and James Forbes; Samuel Hopkins Adams: "Pittsburgh's Foregone Asset, the Public Health: A Running Summary of the Present Administrative Situation," *Charities and the Commons,* vol. 21 (1909), pp. 940–950; Albert Jay Nock: "What a Few Men Did in Pittsburgh: A True Detective Story of To-day," *American Magazine,* vol. 70 (1910), pp. 808–818. Four relevant modern studies of municipal reform are Samuel P. Hays: "The Politics of Reform in Municipal Government in the Progressive Era," *Pacific Northwest Quarterly,* vol. 55 (1964), pp. 157–169, and "Historical Social Research in the Process of Urbanization: The Case of Pittsburgh" (paper read at the Pennsylvania Historical Association Convention, Oct. 20, 1967, at Beaver Falls); Bonnie R. Fox: "The Philadelphia Progressive: A Test of the Hofstadter-Hays Thesis," *Pennsylvania History,* vol. 34 (1967), pp. 372–394; Donald W. Disbrow: "Reform in Philadelphia under Mayor Blankenburg, 1912–1916," *Pennsylvania History,* vol. 27 (1960), 379–396. Also see Lucretia L. Blankenburg: *The Blankenburgs of Philadelphia* (1928). On the state level, see Isaac F. Marcosson: "The Fall of the House of Quay," *World's Work,* vol. 11 (1906), pp. 7119–7124; Clinton Rogers Woodruff: "The Paradox of Governor Pennypacker," *Yale Review,* vol. 16 (1907), pp. 172–193; Hampton L. Carson: "The Life and Services of Samuel Whitaker Pennypacker," *Pennsylvania Magazine of History and Biography,* vol. 41 (1917), pp. 1–125; Harold J. Howland: "A Costly Triumph," *Outlook,* vol. 85 (1907), pp. 192–210; Samuel W. Pennypacker: *The Desecration and Profanation of the Pennsylvania Capitol* (1911). The six-volume *Pittsburgh Survey* is also a superb source on social conditions. See in particular Edward T. Devine's article in vol. 5 and Florence Kelley's article in vol. 6. In addition, see Florence L. Sanville: "Social Legislation in the Keystone State: Daybreak for Pennsylvania's Working Children," *Survey,* vol. 33 (1915), pp. 481–486; John Spargo: *The Bitter Cry of the Children* (1906); Helen Marot: "Progress in Pennsylvania," *Charities,* vol. 14 (1905), pp. 834–836; J. Lynn Barnard: *Factory Legislation in Pennsylvania: Its History and Administration* (1907); Pennsylvania Bureau of Women and Children: *A History of Child Labor Legislation in Pennsylvania* (1928); Pennsylvania Bureau of Women and Children: *Child Workers in Pennsylvania: Analysis of Industrial Accidents to Minors 1934–1939* (1940). Two recent informative works are Allen F. Davis: *Spearheads for Reform:*

The Social Settlements and the Progressive Movement, 1890–1914 (1967); Roy Lubove: *Twentieth Century Pittsburgh: Government, Business and Environmental Change* (1968).

William E. Leuchtenburg succinctly discusses America's part in World War I in *The Perils of Prosperity, 1914–32* (1958); for a more elaborate and less critical view, see John Bach McMaster: *The United States in the World War,* 2 vols. (1918–1920). On the Twenty-eighth Division, see United States, American Battle Monuments Commission: *28th Division: Summary of Operations in the World War* (1944). For Pennsylvania's part in war production, see Grosvenor B. Clarkson: *Industrial America in the World War: The Strategy behind the Line, 1917–1918* (1923); and Frank R. Murdock, "Some Aspects of Pittsburgh's Industrial Contribution to the World War," *Western Pennsylvania Historical Magazine,* vol. 4 (1921), pp. 214–223.

For his attitude toward organized labor, see Samuel Whitaker Pennypacker: *The Autobiography of a Pennsylvanian* (1918). On the steel strike, see David Brody: *Labor in Crisis: The Steel Strike of 1919* (1965); William Z. Foster: *The Great Steel Strike and Its Lessons* (1920).

CHAPTER TWENTY-FOUR

Pinchot, Depression, and the Little New Deal

On the surface the United States in the 1920s enjoyed unprecedented prosperity, progressive reform suffered a severe setback, and a revolution occurred in manners and morals. The 1920s, however, are deceptive and in many ways forecast the 1930s. Prosperity was not universal; there were pockets of poverty and several major industries were depressed. Progressivism, furthermore, was not dead either on the national or the state level, and though profound changes did take place, it is easy to exaggerate the numbers involved in and the depth of the revolution in manners and morals.

The Great Depression brought changes to Pennsylvania and to the whole nation. Laissez-faire and small-government attitudes were discredited; big government—particularly big national government—was here to stay. For the disastrous 1930s, people blamed businessmen, the heroes of the prosperous 1920s; while the government sought formerly ignored professors to solve problems growing out of the Depression. With support from the Federal government, big labor—the American Federation of Labor and particularly the Congress of Industrial Organizations—emerged from the Depression strong enough to challenge industry. But the Depression's greatest impact was on politics. It made the Democratic party the nation's majority party for the next generation and once again a power in Pennsylvania politics.

BOOM FOR SOME

Immediately after the armistice on November 11, 1918, the United States rapidly demobilized without concern for the effect on its economy. The Federal government quickly canceled contracts, ended price controls, and discharged soldiers. A short, sharp depression reached its trough in early 1919, but by late 1919 a postwar speculative boom was underway. Pennsylvania's share in the boom was small. While the nation's iron and steel production grew steadily, Pennsylvania's proportion of that production, though impressive, had declined and continued to decline further. In 1900 Pennsylvania produced over 60 percent of the nation's steel; by 1916 Pennsylvania's output was no longer greater than the rest of the country combined. During World War II it supplied 30 percent of the nation's steel; in 1960 it supplied 24 percent. Located primarily in Michigan, the new automotive industry (on which so much of the boom in the 1920s depended) benefited Pennsylvania only in a secondary fashion. Despite the presence of steel mills, of skilled laborers (many of whom were experienced carriage makers), and of Charles Duryea, builder with his brother of the first successful American automobile, who produced three-cylinder cars at Reading until 1914, the automobile industry never flourished in Pennsylvania. The dominent transportation industry in the state remained the railroad and the predominant company the Pennsylvania Railroad, and unfortunately for the state's economy the automotive industry—beginning in the 1920s—seriously and increasingly challenged rail transportation. Nevertheless Pennsylvania remained the second manufacturing state throughout the 1920s and the Philadelphia and Pittsburgh districts remained the nation's third and sixth industrial areas, but Pennsylvania's annual rate of growth in value added by manufacture during these years was only one-tenth of 1 percent, placing it twenty-third among the twenty-five industrial states.

Coal, textiles, and agriculture—all conspicuously sick industries in the 1920s—were basic to the state's economy. In these industries competition ruled and change was made difficult by custom. Despite large corporations, the markets of these industries were too extensive to control. Coal production remained at a fairly high level, but the industry was beginning to decline. Pennsylvania produced a record 100 million tons of anthracite in 1917 and employed a record 180,000 anthracite miners in 1914. By 1929 there were 151,500 anthracite miners who produced 74 million tons. For the bituminous coal industry 1918, with 177 million tons, was the peak production year, while the top year for employment was 1923, with 200,500 miners. By 1929 bituminous coal miners numbered 135,000 and produced 144 million tons. Declining prices matched sinking production and employment figures. Bituminous coal prices fell from $3.75 a ton in 1920 to $1.78 in 1929, and total wages of all bituminous miners sank during the same period from 2.6 percent of the national total to 1.2 percent, marking a sharp decline in their importance to the national economy. Bankruptcies were frequent and most miners lived poorly during this decade and suffered from a high incidence of both accidents and disease. Increased mechanical cutting and loading eliminated labor, and management expanded in nonunionized West Virginia and Alabama rather than in largely unionized Pennsylvania, Ohio, and Illinois. Unemployment in mining areas usually entailed fewer working days rather than a complete discharge, which kept miners from looking for jobs elsewhere.

In textiles, wool and cotton manufacturers suffered more than silk and rayon manufacturers. In search of cheap labor to counteract fallen prices, cotton manufacturers migrated to the South where wages were from 25 to 60 percent lower. Since textiles employed more labor than any other manufacture and since cotton was its largest component, labor's depressed earnings in textiles considerably decreased popular purchasing power.

Fortunately for Pennsylvania the agricultural picture was not as bleak as coal or textiles. For much of the twentieth century one-third of the nation's population has been within overnight trucking range of Pennsylvania farms. Accessible markets led to diversification, and diversification stabilized income. Furthermore, dairy farming, Pennsylvania's most important branch of agriculture, was considerably more profitable than dirt farming in the 1920s. Nevertheless, while corn and wheat prices during the decade fell to roughly half of what they had been at its beginning, wholesale milk prices dropped about one quarter. Falling prices reduced the purchasing power of Pennsylvania farmers and hurt the economy of both the state and the nation.

After years of dynamic growth, the Pittsburgh district achieved economic maturity in 1910 and began a relative decline. Existing large plants and overspecialization in a limited range of heavy industries inhibited Pittsburgh's adaptation to twentieth-century economic trends. Pittsburgh was and is basically a coal, iron, and steel town; downward trends in these sectors were not offset by favorable growth rates in glass, electrical equipment, and aluminum; and no new major industries appeared. Unemployment persisted in Pittsburgh throughout the 1920s and in 1929 stood at 5 to 10 percent of the labor force. Population growth reflected economic growth: Pittsburgh's population was 156,389 in 1880, 553,905 in 1910, and 671,659 by midcentury.

During the 1920s Philadelphia manufactures maintained a slow rate of growth. Philadelphia differed from Pittsburgh in that its factories were smaller, its manufacturing interests were highly diversified, and its period of relative decline had begun in 1890. Several broad changes in the economy after World War I—particularly the migration of durable goods industries westward and textile mills southward—hurt Philadelphia. Furthermore, reflecting the community as a whole, Philadelphia business was conservative and stable and tended to adhere to traditional methods of production longer than was wise. The labor force and population in the 1920s expanded at a slow rate reflecting an overall economic sluggishness abetted by technological innovations. Clearly the prosperity of the 1920s was not universal; Pennsylvania did little more than hold its own throughout that decade.

The revolution in communication that was so much a part of the 1920s boom wrought vast changes in the behavior of Pennsylvanians and other Americans. Urbanization and the automobile, motion pictures and the radio (which came into its own when Pittsburgh's station KDKA broadcast election returns on November 2, 1920) altered life-styles. Whether uprooted from the farm or village in the United States or abroad, rural migrants had lives centered about the family, church, and a small circle of friends and neighbors. In the anonymity of the city, however, it was easy to escape these influences, and the automobile made it possible for rural Americans on a moment's notice to flee their surroundings for a distant town or city where, as strangers, they behaved as they wished. People no longer found entertainment in family singing around the piano or at religious meetings but found it on the radio or at the movies. Reflecting the outlook of New York and Hollywood, the radio and the movies challenged the traditional role of parents and ministers in setting patterns and standards of behavior. The automobile, the radio, and the movies also tended to standardize American life, to nationalize patterns and habits, to obliterate unique communities, and to weaken local and even state ties.

Perhaps the most striking development in the 1920s was the progress women made in their fight for equality. World War I created a labor shortage which enabled more women to hold jobs they had never held before, many of which they kept after the war. Women not only gained some economic independence but also in 1920 gained the vote. Though moralists deplored the rising divorce rate and women smoking and drinking in public, these developments emphasized that women in the 1920s had more freedom than their mothers to unmake a miserable alliance or to act as they pleased.

PINCHOT

More than any other person, Gifford Pinchot dominated Pennsylvania in the 1920s and early 1930s. Serving as governor from 1923 to 1927 and from 1931 to 1935, Pinchot gave Pennsylvania a progressive administration during the reactionary 1920s. Pinchot was born in Connecticut, but his family came from Milford, where his grandfather had settled and prospered. His father made a fortune as a New York merchant, married the daughter of millionaire New Yorker Amos R. Eno, and built the family mansion Grey Towers just outside Milford. Pinchot was committed to public service. "My own money," he remarked in 1914, "came from unearned increment on land in New York held by my grandfather, who willed the money, not the land, to me. Having got my wages in advance in that way, I am now trying to work them out." Graduating from Yale in 1889, Pinchot made forestry his career. After studying in Europe, he returned to the United States as its first trained forester. He was convinced that trees were a crop, that forestry was "the art of using the forest without destroying it," that scientific harvesting enabling forests to reseed themselves would pay commercially, and that such scientific management required governmental control of private cutting.

In 1897 Pinchot became a special forest agent for the Department of the Interior and in 1898 became head of the Department of Agriculture's Division of Forestry, which he developed into the U.S. Forest Service. His close friendship with Theodore Roosevelt was an asset, but people were not ambivalent about Pinchot—they either loved or hated him. Self-confident, self-important, aggressive, and outspoken, Pinchot had difficulty in working with superiors and equals unless they agreed with him.

In 1910 after a publicized rupture with Secretary of the Interior Richard A. Ballinger, Pinchot left the Forest Service with a yen for political office. His controversy with Ballinger had made him a progressive hero, a national figure, and a formidable candidate for office. He was an insurgent during his early years in Pennsylvania politics. In 1912 he played a prominent role in nominating Roosevelt as a Progressive and in carrying Pennsylvania for him. Two years later Pinchot ran for the Senate against Boies Penrose on the Progressive Washington ticket and was attacked as a "rank outsider" and a "whimsical, erratic, misguided enthusiast." With 520,000 votes, Penrose swamped both Pinchot (269,000) and the Democratic nominee A. Mitchell Palmer (266,000), but Pinchot emerged from the campaign with a wealthy and beautiful wife. She was Cornelia Bryce, the witty champion of the workingwoman and woman suffrage, who was "equally at home on a picket line with striking workers or as a lovely and gracious hostess at a formal reception." After 1916 Pinchot decided that as a "practicable method of getting action" he and the Progressives should no longer remain outside a major party.

After 1916, more eager than ever for office, Pinchot not only returned to the Republican fold but began to act like a candidate. He joined the Grange, vigorously championed the farmer, and increased his rural supporters by advocating prohibition. With Mrs. Pinchot, he cultivated organized labor and energetically entertained both at Milford and at Washington, D.C. He hoped anti-Penrose Republicans would support him for the gubernatorial nomination in 1918, but they passed him over saying he had "been too much absent" from Pennsylvania. Setting his sights on the senatorial race of 1920, Pinchot spent the 1918–1919 winter in Philadelphia, stumped the state the following spring and summer, and attacked Penrose in a public letter. When Penrose candidates won overwhelmingly in 1919, Pinchot wisely chose the governorship in 1922 as his new target. His ambitions had made him less of a political maverick. Though still thoroughly progressive, he went along with his party. He opposed Penrose's man William C. Sproul in the gubernatorial primary, but supported him in the regular 1918 election after he had championed two Progressive issues close to Pinchot's heart—woman suffrage and prohibition. Two years later Pinchot laid aside his misgivings and supported Penrose's choice for the Presidency, Warren G. Harding.

In 1920 Pinchot began to enjoy political success. Sproul appointed him state forestry commissioner that year, and soon Pinchot was reliving his earlier career. He refused to consider politics in making appointments and allowed no one in his department to be removed for political reasons. His great opportunity came with the death of Penrose on the last day of 1921. Five factions sought to dominate the Republican party, but none fell heir to Penrose's power. There were the Mellons, particularly Secretary of the Treasury Andrew Mellon with strength in Pittsburgh, the Federal government, and financial circles; the Vare brothers, renowned for stuffing ballot boxes in south Philadelphia; W. W. Atterbury, president of the state's most powerful corporation, the Pennsylvania Railroad; Joseph R. Grundy, president of the Pennsylvania Manufacturers Association and a diehard opponent of social and labor legislation, who was supported largely by legislators whose campaigns he had financed; and Gifford Pinchot. When these factions compromised on George Wharton Pepper as Penrose's successor in the Senate, Pinchot concentrated on obtaining the 1922 Republican gubernatorial nomination.

Pinchot ran a brilliant campaign for the nomination. He projected the image of the honest amateur who knew little about practical politics. He won wide acclaim when he ordered his Forestry Department subordinates not to use their positions to support his candidacy and demanded a "genuine open primary" with no "deals and set-ups." Pinchot successfully wooed the recently enfranchised women voters, disassociated himself from his earlier radical stance and reassured conservatives by campaigning for governmental efficiency rather than governmental controls, and won the support of progressives, labor unions, farmers, and—by managing to exploit a rift among party leaders—Grundy's Pennsylvania Manufacturers Association. In addition Pinchot and his wife contributed $112,000 of the $118,000 collected for his campaign. Pinchot built a viable coalition; and when he attacked Pennsylvania state government inefficiency he exploited a vote-getting issue. State employees were usually appointed, exploited, and removed for political reasons; the governor's authority over agencies varied and the functions of the agencies overlapped; and there was no state budget system.

Regular Republicans felt that Pinchot's attack on Governor William C. Sproul's progressive administration (1919–1923), of which Pinchot had been a part, was both disloyal and misleading. Sproul signed the Edmonds Act of 1921 (embodying the ideas of Dr. Thomas E. Finegan), which consolidated schools; increased state aid to education; standardized curriculum, teachers' qualifications, and salaries; and generally improved education in Pennsylvania. His administration developed a state highway system through an intelligent program of road building, making Sproul renowned as the "father of good roads." The Sproul regime also updated state administration. It created the Department of Public Welfare (which Pinchot's chief supporter Grundy spectacularly opposed), and it reorganized the Banking and Insurance departments, the National Guard, and the governor's staff. Pinchot, however, was a reformer; and reform is achieved by stressing shortcomings rather than accomplishments. "My opponents," he exclaimed, "are protesting against washing the State's dirty linen

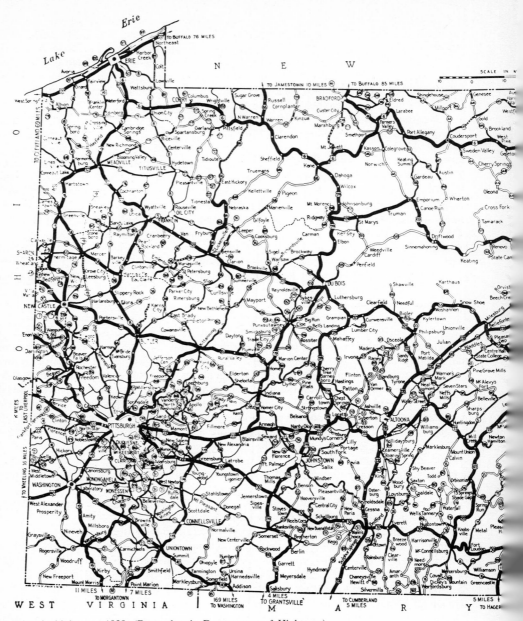

Pennsylvania highways, 1929. (Pennsylvania Department of Highways)

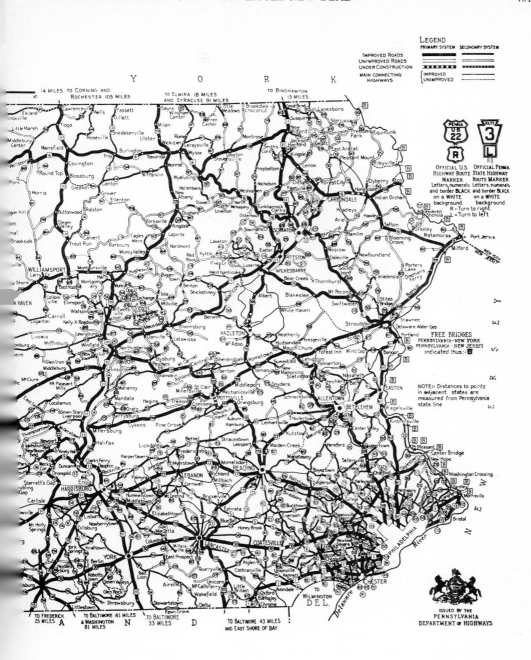

Gifford Pinchot, Republican governor. (Historical Society of Pennsylvania)

in public. It seems to me far better to wash than to wear it." Just ten days before the primary a report by the state's auditor general apparently confirmed Pinchot's attacks on the financial "mess in Harrisburg." Although Philadelphia and Pittsburgh reported thumping anti-Pinchot returns, Pinchot gained huge rural majorities and won the nomination by a scant 9,000 votes.

Despite the inevitability of his victory in November since he had won the nomination in a one-party state, Pinchot campaigned vigorously. He insisted that the Republican State Committee not collect the customary 3 percent assessment from state civil servants, and lest regular Republicans sabotage his campaign, he retained his own organizations throughout the state. With aspirants for office exceeding the number of offices, Pinchot forestalled disappointment by promising no appointments until after the election. He also personally saw all Republican candidates for the Legislature and sought their support for his program to reorganize the structure and finances of the state government and to ban the saloon, and locally publicized their stands, so that candidates later found it difficult to renege on their commitments. With the support of the Republican machine, Pinchot won a smashing victory.

Modeling himself on his hero Theodore Roosevelt, Pinchot sought to be chief legislator as well as chief executive during his first administration (1923–1927), and the Legislature fulfilled most of his demands. The administrative code, adopted in 1923, was Pinchot's most important legislation. Designed primarily by Clyde L. King, an expert on public finance from the Wharton School of the University of Pennsylvania, the new code provided for a budget system (governors before Pinchot did not submit budgets); grouped the existing 139 agencies into fifteen departments (headed by responsible cabinet officers) and three appointed commissions; and standardized state purchases, salaries, and positions. The reorganization centralized fiscal responsibility but decentralized administration. "I never knew what our appropriation was," remarked the chairman of a state board, "and I never inquired at any time what my unexpended balance was. My relations were with the governor. I simply told him what I wanted." Under Pinchot's code each board retained its power to administer its special function, but its budget had to be approved by both the cabinet member it was responsible to and the governor. Not only did the code make state purchasing policies more rational, but it also secured equality in pay and position for state civil servants working at similar tasks. The standardization of positions and salaries also made possible a fair system of promotion and improved morale and service.

Reorganization provoked little opposition. Progressives and conservatives, farmers and laborers, businessmen and merchants all cheered increased efficiency and economy but divided when Pinchot vigorously attacked utilities and booze. Pinchot hated electric utility companies and their "greedy unreasoning selfishness" that made their rates high and kept them from extending their lines into less lucrative rural areas. The Pinchot administration called for giant power—a state-controlled monopoly to replace unregulated monopoly—but utility lobbyists killed in committee nineteen bills designed to coordinate the production of power, electrify rural areas, and limit profits to a fair return. Pinchot also attacked the Public Service Commission (which regulated utilities) as "the catspaw of the corporations" after it allowed the Philadelphia Rapid Transit Company to raise its fare from 5 to 7 and then 8 cents, but the state Supreme Court prevented Pinchot from removing members of the commission.

"No governor of any state," observes M. Nelson McGeary, "ever tried harder to keep a pledge" than did Pinchot in his almost fanatic attempts to enforce prohibition. Though prohibition had been in force since January 1920, Pennsylvania had not supplemented inadequate enforcement by the U.S. Treasury Department under Mellon. Violations were flagrant and common. Accordingly the Pinchot administration in 1923 backed three enforcement bills, but with a maximum of effort and the barest of majorities succeeded only in getting one bill passed. When the Legislature refused to appropriate the $250,000 needed to enforce prohibition, Pinchot used the $150,000 raised by the Women's Christian Temperance Union (WCTU). He not only utilized state police to enforce prohibition but also insisted his appointees be "absolutely right on the dry question." Pinchot strained every nerve to make prohibition work, and the appreciative Law Enforcement League of Philadelphia "praised God for such a Governor."

Pinchot also pleased anthracite miners and their leader John L. Lewis. When in 1923 the miners struck for an 8-hour day, a closed shop, and a 20 percent wage increase, Pinchot mediated between the miners and the operators. After the strike lasted a week, he achieved a settlement including the 8-hour day and a 10 percent pay hike. In 1925 when that settlement expired, miners again struck, but this deadlock lasted six months and caused many coal consumers to change to oil heat. Again Pinchot offered to mediate; grateful miners agreed but suspicious operators refused.

Pinchot, however, could not repeat his stunning legislative success of 1923. Though he called for giant power and the regulation of breweries and distilleries in 1925, the Legislature refused to act. Not easily rebuffed, Pinchot called for a special legislative session, proposed thirty-six bills under eight headings including "clean elections," "regulation of anthracite," "poison drink," and "giant power." After a five-week battle, only four bills were ready for Pinchot's signature.

After the special session rejected his program, Pinchot in 1926 sought the nomination to the United States Senate. In the ensuing three-way primary campaign, Pinchot needed more than a program. As soon as he challenged the Republican incumbent and his fellow dry, George Wharton Pepper (who was supported by both Mellon and Grundy), William Vare—whom Pinchot described as "a wet gangster who represents everything that is bad in Pennsylvania"—jumped into the race. Thanks to his control of Philadelphia and the division of the dry vote, Vare won the primary while the unaligned Pinchot ran a poor third. When Vare triumphed in November, Pinchot refused to certify him as "duly chosen." Using the wording "appears to have been chosen," Pinchot informed the United States Senate that he was convinced Vare's nomination was "partly bought and partly stolen." Agreeing with Pinchot, the Senate refused to seat Vare because of his excessive primary campaign expenditures. Vare, however, had spent less than his unsuccessful opponent, Senator Pepper.

With his gubernatorial term over in January 1927, Pinchot left office with his "head up" and his "tail over the dashboard." He had earned the right to be proud. His administration (1923–1927) was probably the most outstanding up to that time in Pennsylvania history. Pinchot's achievement stemmed not only from reorganizing the state's government, improving election laws, and settling an anthracite strike, but also from his ability as an administrator. "The Governor is a very active man," remarked a staff member, "and is always stepping and it keeps us stepping too." Pinchot developed great esprit de corps among his staff, and it filtered down through the civil service. Not content with generalities, Pinchot, as he left office, condemned the Vare-Mitten machine of Philadelphia (the Mittens controlled Philadelphia Rapid Transit) and the Mellon machine of Pittsburgh; he also rebuked the "great monied interests" that ran Pennsylvania. Though it is sometimes questioned whether individual administrators can affect a bureaucracy, Pinchot's style made a difference. "Pinchot is no longer governor," remarked a dairyman to a local health officer. "It isn't necessary to be so strict now."

FISHER

Pinchot's successor, John S. Fisher (1927–1931), had a very different style. Amiable and well liked, Fisher gradually worked his way to the top in Pennsylvania politics and managed to be considered a friend not only of corporations and railroads but also, for a while, of labor. As a state senator, he was a disciple first of Quay and then of Penrose, and he backed legislation permitting railroads to merge and to hire police, as well as legislation prohibiting child labor. Renowned as "honest to the core," Fisher sponsored the direct primary election law of 1906 and successfully chaired the committee investigating the capitol graft scandal in 1907, thus insuring his political future. Business and politics mixed beautifully for Fisher, who entered both simultaneously and ultimately became not only governor but also a railroad president, a coal company vice-president, and a director of both an electric power company and a bank. Prior to his election as governor, Fisher was allied with Joseph R. Grundy and worked effectively for Pinchot's nomination in 1922. Four years later, supported by both Grundy and the Mellons, Fisher won the nomination in a close primary fight with the Vare candidate, former Lieutenant Governor Edward Beidleman. In the ensuing campaign, Fisher swamped the demoralized Democrats by a 3–1 majority.

The Fisher administration made solid contributions. Initially Fisher backed four election reform bills designed to strengthen registration procedures and to eliminate fraud, but in face of concerted Vare and Mellon opposition Fisher accepted amendments weakening his legislation. Nevertheless, the new legislation made frauds more difficult to perpetrate, and later Fisher supported legislation permitting voting machines. The Fisher administration also increased workmen's compensation benefits, and though it rejected William S. Vare's idea of a state social security pension of $1 a day for all persons, it approved a $50 million bond issue for welfare institutions. Perhaps its most progressive and far-reaching legislation created a Department of Revenue, reorganized the Department of Internal Affairs, and made innumerable constructive administrative adjustments. While Fisher was governor, Pennsylvania also acquired Cook's Forest and converted two-year state normal schools into four-year state teachers colleges.

During his term $235 million were spent on highways, $39 million on buildings, and $5 million on land, earning him the epitaph "Fisher, the Builder." The relative prosperity during most of his administration provided tax receipts to meet the commonwealth's needs for new roads and buildings in place of inadequate, overcrowded, antiquated facilities. Fisher's experience with the capitol graft scandal stood both him and the commonwealth in good stead. He placed all building operations of $10,000 or more under the newly created Bureau of Engineering and Construction "to insure careful planning, favorable contracts, . . . and close supervision in the performance of all contracts." New state office buildings, the Farm Show Building, state college buildings, and mental institutions were put up efficiently and without scandal. Furthermore the building program—particularly highway construction—provided a measure of work relief after the financial crash of 1929.

Nevertheless despite some support of progressive legislation, Fisher was not a progressive reformer and in many respects personified the stereotype conservative, myopic, business-oriented Republican politician of the 1920s. When the United States Senate refused to seat William S. Vare, Fisher quite naturally selected his long-time supporter Joseph R. Grundy. He also was instrumental in killing several Pinchot-initiated amendments to the Pennsylvania constitution authorizing bond issues for a greater building program. Furthermore, Fisher pledged himself to veto any modification of the 1794 Blue Laws even though they were so inhibiting that the Pittsburgh Symphony could not play on Sunday in its hometown.

Fisher's attitude toward labor illustrated his fundamental conservatism. AFL President William Green's prediction that if Fisher were elected "the laboring people of Pennsylvania will never have a better governor" proved wrong. Fisher in the past had sponsored humane legislation, but as governor he was inactive during the long bituminous coal strike of 1927 to 1928 and chose the weaker of two 1929 bills regulating coal and iron police. Falling bituminous coal prices led many operators to break the 1924 Jacksonville contract with the United Mine Workers (UMW) and to cut wages. The Mellon-owned Pittsburgh Coal Company reduced wages 33 percent for its 19,000 miners in 1925 and an additional 20 percent in 1927. On March 31, 1927, at the expiration of their contract, all union bituminous miners struck. Operators retaliated by using scab labor, by evicting the families of many strikers from company houses (some operators were content merely to shut off the water in strikers' homes), and by employing coal and iron police to combat the union. Despite pleas from such diverse sources as the UMW, New Kensington merchants, and the governor of Ohio that Fisher intervene and end the violence and the strike, he remained aloof.

Fisher's inaction led John L. Lewis to suggest that his connection with the Clearfield Bituminous Coal Corporation motivated him to permit "coal and iron police and deputy sheriffs to run amuck in coal mining regions." Fisher indignantly insisted he had divested himself of business interests upon becoming governor, and belatedly ordered his attorney general to investigate the appointment and duties of coal and iron police. No significant investigation occurred because the attorney general narrowly construed the law as giving the governor power only to issue and reject commissions, and Fisher accepted that construction.

The strike dragged on despite investigations by Congress that condemned the "squalor, suffering, misery, and distress" in the Pittsburgh coal regions as "a blotch on American civilization." Finally in March 1928, with the strike almost a year old, Fisher called for a conference of operators, labor representatives, and public officials, but his plea was ignored. In May a report by the Federal Council of Churches argued that nothing could be accomplished until "the fundamental ills of the industry" were treated, and condemned the operators for combining the roles of employer and landlord (specifically for evicting miners) and for employing coal and iron police to beat strikers and suppress unions. Investigations, calls for conferences, and reports were of little help to John L. Lewis and the miners, who finally capitulated in July 1928. In the prosperous 1920s these bituminous miners suffered a drastic pay loss, and the governor whom they had helped elect did nothing to help them.

Although during the strike the coal and iron police had earned the undying emnity of thousands, it took an outrage several months after the strike to unleash that hatred: On February 10, 1929, three Pittsburgh Coal Corporation police beat to death John Barkoski. Even Governor Fisher denounced the surrender of police power to private hands. State Representative Michael A. Musmanno, a former coal miner and steelworker and the chief counsel of the accused in the famous Sacco and Vanzetti case, and Senator William D. Mansfield of Pittsburgh agreed to sponsor identical bills drawn by Attorney General Cyrus Woods to curb the coal and iron police. The House strengthened the Musmanno bill to restrict industrial police further. Though Fisher had advocated greater restrictions, he signed the milder Mansfield bill in April 1929 but vetoed the Musmanno bill bringing on a storm of protest. Spurred by this public outcry, Fisher by executive action required that industrial police wear uniforms, that their jurisdiction be restricted to the actual protection of property (one of the important Musmanno bill amendments), and that they be prohibited from "undue violence in making arrests," unnecessary display or use of weapons, and profanity.

When he left office in 1931, Fisher was still a popular man, but his ideas and style were becoming obsolete. He later opposed the New Deal as "destructive to old fashioned business" and lamented that "death, migration, money, and birth control had killed the old fashioned Scotch-Irish, Pennsylvania-Dutch strains" that resisted change. He failed to realize that the Great Depression made inaction on both state and national levels not only inappropriate but impossible.

BUST FOR ALL

The Great Depression began in 1929 with the Great Crash of the stock market. The New York *Times* list of industrials gradually tended downward from 449 on August 31, plummeted disastrously from October 19 to 29, and slid sickeningly to 58 on July 8, 1932. Although President Herbert Hoover, Charles M. Schwab, the elder statesman of Pennsylvania industry, Samuel Vauclain, chairman of Philadelphia's Baldwin Locomotive Works, and other prominent individuals announced that the economy was fundamentally sound, the economy in fact was fundamentally unsound and could not shake off the effects of the crash. Income was badly distributed, with 5 percent of the people getting one-third of the personal income; weak corporate structure emphasized dividends rather than adequate investment in productive facilities; and the correspondingly weak banking system did not enable healthy banks to aid sick banks. High tariff rates not only curtailed imports but also—and most regrettably—curtailed American exports. Finally the traditional regard for a balanced budget prevented the government from expenditures that would create purchasing power and relieve distress. The government remained on the gold standard and feared inflation during the worst deflation the nation ever experienced.

By 1929 the United States had long since evolved from a local to a national economy. The shock waves of the Wall Street crash were felt throughout the nation; and Pennsylvania, which did not share heavily in the prosperity of the 1920s, shared fully in the poverty of the 1930s. In 1932 industrial production in Pennsylvania withered to less than half its 1929 level. The value of Pennsylvania's mineral products dropped from $872 million in 1929 to $405 million in 1933. Bituminous coal production fell from 144 million tons in 1929 to 75 million tons in 1932. During those same years Pennsylvania's production of pig iron fell from 14 million tons to 2 million tons, and production of open-hearth steel ingots and castings fell from 17½ million tons to 3½ million. The value of textiles produced in Pennsylvania fell 60 percent; wages paid in the metals industries fell from $808 million to $260 million, while wages paid textile employees dropped from $326 million to $173 million. By March 1933 unemployment peaked at the incredibly high figure of 1,379,351, or 37.1 percent of the state's working population. Per capita personal income in Pennsylvania plummeted from $775 in 1929 to $421 in 1933, painfully worked its way up to $648 in 1940, and with preparations for World War II, jumped back to $771 in 1941.

The unemployed were miserable, and with lowered wages many employed individuals were nearly destitute. In Pittsburgh many of the unemployed lived in squalid packing boxes and established a shantytown. Some sold apples on street corners for 5 cents each. The Depression also slashed the earnings of many employed individuals. To preserve profits or to minimize losses businessmen cut wages. Although they were not typical, some sawmills and tile plants paid their workers only 5 or 6 cents an hour. Sweatshops sprang up and child labor increased. Half the women in the Pennsylvania textile and clothing industries earned less than $6.58 a week and 20 percent got less than $5. Agricultural areas also suffered. Farm prices throughout the nation dropped more than 50 percent. Pennsylvania corn, which in the boom year of 1919 sold at $1.69 a bushel, brought 99 cents in 1929 and fell to 43 cents in 1931. The Depression slashed total cash receipts of Pennsylvania farmers from $324 million in 1929 to $175 million in 1932.

Local systems of public and private relief collapsed with the Depression. Chaos prevailed throughout the state with 920 directors of 425 local poor boards administering public relief. These local boards had the power to tax and raised taxes 50 percent between 1928 and 1932, but with twenty times more people on relief, payments fell to 20 percent of what they had been ten years earlier. Every Pennsylvania county had a relief problem, and private charity proved an inadequate supplement to local poor relief. In 1931 Pittsburghers gave almost $2 million for charity (approximately $12 each for the 150,000 unemployed). In Philadelphia Karl de Schweinitz, secretary of the Philadelphia Committee for Unemployment Relief, stated that private funds were exhausted and that many had nothing but dandelions to eat and were begging for food scraps. In addition Philadelphia hospitals had "definite cases of starvation." By 1931 the state Department of Health reported an increase in malnutrition, communicable diseases, and death.

PINCHOT AGAIN

The Depression produced profound changes in politics and government. Citizens found themselves dealing more and more with the Federal government. Efforts to restore prosperity centralized authority and forced the Federal government to formulate policies and programs and to implement decisions. In Pennsylvania politics the Depression spelled deep trouble for the Republican party in general and its conservative old guard in particular. Pinchot believed the stock market crash "had taken a good deal of the paint off" Andrew Mellon and the regular Republicans and thought he could "smell the beginnings of a new Progressive movement." He predicted that if hard times followed "the haughtiness of the old Gang was going to be quite considerably mitigated in the next few years." Anxious to regain lost power, Pinchot again maneuvered for the Republican gubernatorial nomination. "I don't want to make a fool of myself," he mused in February 1930, but "on the other hand, I don't want to miss a chance of having a real pulpit again for four years." The continuing Republican split between the followers of Grundy and Boss William S. Vare of Philadelphia gave Pinchot a chance similar to the one he enjoyed in 1922. Grundy was strongest in the smaller cities and towns and was allied with Pittsburgh's Mellon interests, while W. W. Atterbury, president of the Pennsylvania Railroad, and other Philadelphia industrial and banking interests supported Vare. When Pinchot announced on March 10 that he would run, Grundy backed Pinchot. Mellon, however, was unable to stomach Pinchot and supported Vare's man, a respected Philadelphia lawyer, former state Attorney General Francis Shunk Brown. Fortunately for Pinchot, a wet—Thomas W. Phillips—also ran.

"The primary battle," McGeary remarks, "was fought with bare knuckles." Pinchot attacked the utilities and the Pennsylvania Railroad, but heeding his advisers did not emphasize prohibition. Labor supported Brown, although Pinchot was still friendly to it. Labor's interest in Pinchot had cooled during his first term when he had given prohibition and the organization of administration the lion's share of his attention. The attacks on Vare by the well-heeled Grundy forces helped Pinchot, as did his slogan: "One good term deserves another," but Pinchot's primary victory by 20,000 votes was possible only because Phillips won 281,000 votes and kept the moderate Brown from winning. The Vare machine did its best: a recount of 550 ballot boxes in seven Philadelphia wards uncovered 122,889 errors and cost Brown over 10,000 votes.

Pinchot faced a tough fight in November 1930. He and Grundy attempted and failed to dump the conservative Republican state chairman, General Edward Martin, who would later serve as both governor and senator. Martin, however, proved more loyal to the Republican party than to conservative principles and fought intelligently and hard for Pinchot. Nevertheless, many Republicans—particularly followers of Vare, businessmen connected with utilities and the Pennsylvania Railroad, and wets—revolted and created the Liberal party with the Democratic gubernatorial nominee John M. Hemphill on its ticket. To prevent further erosion of Republican support, Martin claimed that there was nothing in Pinchot's policies objectionable to any fair public utility, and Grundy's *Pennsylvania Man-*

ufacturers' Journal asserted that "the manufacturer, the mine owner, the store-keeper, were all in the end benefited by Pinchot's efforts" during his first term. In addition Pittsburgh's Mellon machine supported Pinchot. Backing by Martin, Mellon, and Grundy combined with Pinchot's slashing attacks on utilities, his denunciation of the Vare machine, and his promise to "get the farmers out of the mud" brought victory. Though Pinchot's triumph can be considered part of the national dissatisfaction that would bring in Franklin Roosevelt's New Deal, it probably resulted more from Pinchot's own appeal and Pennsylvania's unsettled political climate.

Four subjects dominated Pinchot's mind as he embarked on his second administration (1931–1935): first, public utilities and, as he supposed, their control of the Public Service Commission; second, the Depression; third, rural roads; and fourth, the 1932 presidential nomination. In an attempt to keep Hoover from running again, some progressive Republicans, such as Senator George M. Norris and Harold L. Ickes, backed Pinchot for the nomination. When Ickes circulated among representative Republicans a letter boosting Pinchot's nomination (which Pinchot had himself written), it brought disappointing results and Pinchot gave up his ambition to become president.

Pinchot's bitter war against the public utilities—particularly the electric power companies—confirmed his enemies, alienated some of his friends, and accomplished little. Telling senators that their investigation of utilities was "worse than useless" earned Pinchot the prolonged applause of the galleries but did not convince the senators to pass his three bills designed to replace the Public Service Commission with a powerful fair-rate board. Indeed, though the House passed the bills, the Senate killed them in committee. Defeat only spurred Pinchot to attack more vigorously and even led him to hint that he might become an advocate of public ownership. "When public utilities," he informed the Senate in 1932, "are willing to . . . call off their lobbyists, quit their bribery, cease their extortion, . . . and generally act the part of decent and cooperative members of the Commonwealth . . . then the threat of public ownership which they so greatly fear will disappear."

Unable to secure his fair-rate board, Pinchot managed to gain control of the existing Public Service Commission. By 1932 he had not only appointed the majority of the commission but also its chairman Clyde L. King, who had been one of Pinchot's chief advisers and had contributed more than anyone to his success. Unfortunately King and Pinchot soon quarreled. King considered the commission semi-independent and did not take as gospel all Pinchot's allegations, while Pinchot wished to dominate the commission. Pinchot finally got rid of King, and less than four months from the end of his term the Senate belatedly confirmed his appointees. Though Pinchot rejoiced, his victory was empty; the incoming Democratic administration abolished the Public Service Commission.

Despite his preoccupation with utilities, Pinchot was keenly aware of the devastating impact of the Depression and led the nation's governors in efforts to combat its effects. Even before his election in 1930, Pinchot organized a committee on unemployment with King at its head and appointed as secretary the distinguished economist and future Senator from Illinois, Paul H. Douglas. The desperate straits of many Pennsylvanians convinced Pinchot that vigorous action by the state and Federal government was necessary. In August 1931 Pinchot told of little children in Pennsylvania who had "not tasted milk for many months" and concluded that "the only power strong enough, and able to act in time, to meet the new problem of the coming winter is the Government of the United States." To provide direct relief, Pinchot called a special session of the General Assembly in November

1931, but influenced by the conservative Martin (who was both state treasurer and Republican state chairman), it rejected both additional taxes and Pinchot's scheme of providing $35 million relief through the sale of property bonds. Rather than mortgage the future, the Assembly appropriated $10 million for distribution by local poor districts.

Since local poor boards wasted much of this original appropriation, the Assembly later created a State Emergency Relief Board (SERB) to help administer state and Federal relief. Spurred by the crisis, the SERB, with Pinchot at its head and organization Republicans—including Edward Martin—making up most of its body, avoided feuds, cooperated, and functioned effectively The leading spirit of the SERB was Eric Biddle, a young Ardmore businessman who, despite his inexperience in relief and social work, made that agency one of the most effective in the nation. By coupling action with careful record keeping and accounting, the SERB commended itself to Pennsylvania legislators who a few years later used it as a base for the permanent Department of Public Assistance.

During the remainder of his term, Pinchot alternately begged Washington and the Assembly for relief funds. "No governor," observes McGeary, "pounded more consistently or vigorously on Washington's door to obtain the various kinds of relief which the federal government made available." To provide relief money, Pinchot from 1932 to 1934 called three special sessions of the Assembly, but these and the regular session of 1933 produced battles but little money. By mid-1934 the Federal government, thanks to President Franklin Roosevelt's New Deal, was paying for most of Pennsylvania's unemployment relief. When Washington threatened to stop unless the state shared the burden, the Assembly came through with a $20 million appropriation.

Pinchot's concern embraced all whom the commonwealth had tended to ignore. Farmers, laborers, and minority groups benefited from his regime. To fulfill his promise to get the farmers out of the mud, Pinchot induced the state to take over from townships 20,000 miles of roads and embarked on an ambitious rural road-building program. Pinchot opted for "more miles of good road rather than fewer miles of faultless boulevards." The narrow, inexpensive Pinchot roads—costing only $7,000 per mile as compared with the usual $30,000 to $35,000—followed the contours of the land and consisted of a layer or two of stone covered by bituminous macadam. Though inadequate for the size and speed of later cars and trucks, Pinchot roads brought the farmer closer to market and farm children closer to school, and helped integrate the farmer into the mainstream of Pennsylvanian and American society. To furnish work relief throughout the state, Pinchot and the Department of Highways designed the road-building program to utilize a minimum of machinery and a maximum of manual labor.

Despite the coolness of labor leaders when he ran for his second term, Pinchot proved a warm friend to labor. In 1933 he urged old-age pensions, compulsory unemployment insurance, minimum wages for women and minors, maximum working hours, and prohibition of child labor. Initially the General Assembly under the sway of Martin even cut back funds for the Department of Labor and Industry. Pinchot received support from Frances Perkins, Roosevelt's secretary of labor, who called for state legislation to buttress New Deal measures, but Martin's plea not to enter "new fields of governmental activity" proved more persuasive. In a special session the Assembly passed an old-age assistance program and pensions for the blind, but more vital and far-reaching legislation on wages and hours died in the Senate.

The desperate plight of coal miners attracted Pinchot's attention. When a bituminous strike occurred in 1931, he emphasized human as well as property rights. After the 1931 strike, conditions grew worse. Coal prices continued to fall and companies cut the already low pay; by late 1932 there were miners whose payroll deductions for rent, blasting powder, and insurance erased every cent of their earnings. By 1933 Pinchot reported to President Franklin Roosevelt that conditions in the soft-coal areas were horrible and that miners working six and seven days a week earned so little they had to go on relief.

The New Deal presaged a better day for miners. The National Industrial Recovery Act (1933) required collective bargaining between labor unions and management in industries covered by National Recovery Administration codes. The bituminous coal industry (led by U.S. Steel's "captive" Frick Company mines) resisted recognizing John L. Lewis's UMW as labor's representative. In the ensuing strike, violence occurred in Fayette County, where thousands of miners armed with "pool cues, baseball bats, lead pipe, and some firearms" confronted a band of deputy sheriffs. When the sheriff called for state police, Pinchot told him to first send his deputies home. When he refused, Pinchot sent the National Guard, counseling it to be strictly neutral. Uneasy order with intermittent violence prevailed, while pressure by Pinchot and Roosevelt finally led U.S. Steel to capitulate. Above all Pinchot insisted on nonviolence. "Whatever else you do," he warned miners, "keep the peace. . . . I am your friend. . . . If you resort to violence then I am against you."

Pinchot also opposed discrimination. Women and Negroes, Catholics and Jews received from Pinchot a higher proportion of appointments than they had in the past. In addition, Pinchot defended the politically unpopular. When the University of Pittsburgh fired a professor allegedly for his liberal political activities, Pinchot lectured its chancellor that "academic freedom is a necessary condition for obtaining State aid. . . . If the Mellons want a school to teach their ideas, then let them support it." Pinchot was consistent. He opposed removing an alleged Nazi propagandist from the University of Pennsylvania's faculty, remarking "if academic liberty has been destroyed in Germany it is not for us to destroy it here." For supporting strikers and free speech, Pinchot was frequently called a Communist and accused of seeking "to make this country into a dependency of Russia."

By 1934 with the end of his term near, Pinchot for the third time set his sights on the United States Senate. Attacking the Republican incumbent David A. Reed as an "errand-boy of the Mellons" and the steel industry, Pinchot took his "stand beside President Roosevelt in his fight for the forgotten man." In the primary battle, however, Pinchot was on his own; the Republican organization opposed him, and Grundy, without whose support Pinchot never won an election, backed Reed. Although he ran well in the primary, Pinchot lost, leaving Grundy the master of the Republican party. Grundy's candidates also beat the Vare machine in Philadelphia. William S. Vare died a few months later, and since Pinchot carried Pittsburgh despite the Mellons, their power diminished. In June 1934 the Republican State Committee met and chose Grundy's man, M. Harvey Taylor, as state chairman.

Grundy, it turned out, had captured the Republican party only to lose the election. After Democrats nominated George H. Earle of Philadelphia for governor and Joseph F. Guffey from the Pittsburgh area for senator, Pinchot angled to replace Guffey on the Democratic ticket. Pinchot probably could have had the Democratic senatorial nomination in 1934 had he not changed his mind and vetoed as unconstitutional the 1933 bill to prevent party raiding. If enacted, the bill would have prevented majority-party candidates, other than judges, from also securing the minority party's nomination, a practice which had nearly eliminated the Democratic party from Republican areas. Having unsuccessfully begged

Joseph R. Grundy, Republican senator, boss, and president of the Pennsylvania Manufacturers Association. (Library of Congress)

Pinchot to sign the bill, Guffey resolved to support a loyal Democrat, namely himself, for the Senate. Pinchot, who had done all he could to stave off a Republican defeat, found himself and his party out of power. "The Republican Party," he lamented, "must go progressive or stay bust . . . the American people are sick of the Old Deal."

THE LITTLE NEW DEAL

Considerable rebuilding of the Democratic party preceded its 1934 victory. When Guffey abandoned Al Smith for Franklin Roosevelt in 1931 and gave Roosevelt the largest block of delegates at the 1932 convention, he became the undisputed master of the Pennsylvania Democratic party. That party was no longer the joke it had been when Lawrence H. Rupp, the 1930 Democratic gubernatorial nominee, withdrew from the campaign to concentrate on becoming the Grand Exalted Ruler of the Elks (a shrewd move since from 1893 to 1931 Democrats lost ninety-five out of ninety-six statewide elections) and when Republican Boss William S. Vare not only controlled the Democratic party in Philadelphia headed by John O'Donnell but also paid the rent on its headquarters. The Depression changed the Democratic party from a laughingstock to a vital organization. Guffey had an able lieutenant in David L. Lawrence, Allegheny County chairman since 1920, who was instrumental in strengthening the party. In 1933 Philadelphia Democrats, led by John B. Kelly (son of an

From left to right: Joseph F. Guffey, Democratic senator, and George H. Earle and David L. Lawrence, Democratic governors. (Historical Society of Pennsylvania)

Irish immigrant, bricklayer, wealthy contractor, world sculling champion, and father of the child who later became Princess Grace of Monaco) and Matthew H. McCloskey, Jr., smashed O'Donnell's and Vare's power over the Philadelphia Democratic party.

The Depression, and particularly Roosevelt's New Deal efforts to combat it, won laborers, immigrants, and blacks to the Democratic party. In the 1920s Democratic strength had been conspicuous in some agricultural areas and in a few mining counties, but the outstanding industrialized sections were solidly Republican.

In 1932, however, Robert Vann, distinguished black lawyer, editor and publisher of the widely read *Pittsburgh Courier,* and later an assistant attorney general under Roosevelt, told Negro audiences to "go home and turn Lincoln's picture to the wall. The debt has been paid in full." By 1934 black voters in Philadelphia emulated their brethren in Pittsburgh and began moving to the Democratic party. Philadelphia Italian-Americans shifted from 22.6 percent Democratic in 1932 to 52.2 percent two years later, and in 1936 Democrats carried virtually every ward with a foreign-born majority.

Guffey capitalized on the Democratic groundswell in his choice of candidates in 1934. For governor he selected an independent Republican, George H. Earle III, who had contributed heavily to Franklin Roosevelt's 1932 campaign. Wealthy, young, prominent, vigorous, and concerned, Earle would attract independent, liberal, and black Republican voters as well as help finance his own campaign. The Democratic master stroke was to slate Thomas Kennedy, secretary-treasurer of the United Mine Workers, for lieutenant governor. Kennedy's nomination coupled with the prolabor Democratic platform marked the beginning of a long alliance between the Pennsylvania Democratic party and organized labor.

Pledged to support Roosevelt, Guffey completed the Democratic ticket by running himself for the Senate.

Republicans fought a bitter campaign in a losing cause. While all Democrats ran on the New Deal—all other issues, David Lawrence exclaimed, were bunk—leading Republicans claimed they were not fighting Roosevelt but "the unsound policies the professors are reading into his administration." Not only did Earle and Guffey triumph, becoming Pennsylvania's first Democratic governor in the twentieth century and its first Democratic senator since the 1870s, but Democrats won 23 seats in the United States House of Representatives and gained control of the state House of Representatives with 116 Democratic members to 90 Republicans. Since only half of the state Senate had been up for election, Republicans continued to dominate that body (31 to 19). Democrats were under no illusions about why they won. Earle spoke for them all when he declared, "I literally rode into office on the coat-tails of President Roosevelt, and I have no hesitation in saying so."

"My fundamental conviction," Governor Earle (1935–1939) declared in his inaugural address, "is that life must be made secure for those millions who, by accident of birth, are left at the mercy of economic forces." Earle took the New Deal as a model, but the Republican Senate blocked his proposed legislation just as in the past it had blocked liberal Pinchot measures. The majority in 1935 changed the Senate rules to strengthen its position by requiring a majority vote of the membership (26) rather than a majority of members present to discharge a bill from committee. This maneuver enabled Republicans to kill legislation without bringing it to the floor of the Senate and was utilized on most of Earle's labor and reform measures designed to fulfill Democratic platform and campaign promises.

Seeking to end "the oppression of labor," Earle asked the Assembly to raise from fourteen to sixteen years the minimum age of working minors, to set minimum wages for women and minors and to reduce their work week to 40 hours, to eliminate coal and iron police and nonpublic compensation of deputy sheriffs, to regulate industrial work performed in the home (where some women earned as little as 5 cents an hour), to penalize employers who did not pay wages, to register industrial establishments annually, to increase workmen's compensation for injuries, and to enact for Pennsylvania the collective bargaining provisions of the National Industrial Recovery Act. The Democratic House approved all but one of the administration's measures, but the appropriate Senate committee either smothered or emasculated most of them. Pennsylvania desperately needed much of this legislation. For example, it was the second richest state in the Union, but was thirty-third in workmen's compensation, thirty-fourth in the length of the waiting period before compensation, fortieth in compensation for widows, and forty-fourth in medical provisions for injured workmen. While Pennsylvania limited medical benefits for serious injuries to a maximum of thirty days and $100, neighboring states neither limited the days nor were so parsimonious. The administration's measure would have doubled benefits, extended coverage, paid all medical expenses, and provided a lifetime income for permanently injured workmen. In its place the Senate committee on labor and industry offered a bill that added merely $1 a week to payments and extended medical coverage to two months and $200. The Assembly, however, eliminated the coal and iron police, and its stringent 1935 Child Labor Law prohibited the full-time employment of adolescents until sixteen years of age, regulated their hours until eighteen, and barred them from dangerous occupations until twenty-one.

The 1935 biennial session was more productive in other areas. Legislation prevented milk distributors from exploiting dairy farmers by giving Earle more control over State

Milk Control Board members and giving them power to fix prices, license dealers, and regulate the industry. Earle reported in September 1935 that thanks to this legislation farmers were getting half again as much for milk as they received the previous year. The 1935 session also revised the 1794 Blue Law to allow local option on Sunday sports events and the showing of motion pictures. More significantly a bipartisan majority passed the Equal Rights Act preventing racial discrimination in hotels, restaurants, and places of amusement. Predicting the bill would result in "rioting, bloodshed, and murder," the Pennsylvania Hotel Association persuaded the House to recall the bill, but the resolution came moments too late. Governor Earle, the descendent of prominent abolitionists, had signed the measure into law. The Earle administration also enacted the party-raiding bill, which Pinchot had earlier vetoed. The bill now received bipartisan support since Republicans recognized that Democrats were powerful enough to raid them.

Pennsylvania's most pressing problem was not reform but relief for the unemployed. Once again Republican legislators proved uncooperative. Pennsylvania could have gained about $250 million in Federal relief and public works money if the Assembly had passed the necessary legislation. The Earle administration prepared bills enabling state and local agencies to utilize these Federal funds, but the Senate passed only three bills and completely ignored one bill enabling Pennsylvania to participate in unemployment insurance under the Federal Social Security Act. The basic problem was that relief meant increased taxation. In early 1935 about 836,000 persons (22.5 percent of the state's laboring force) were out of work, and state relief funds were exhausted. During the next three months the Federal government assumed the entire cost of relief in Pennsylvania ($68 million). Harry Hopkins, the Federal emergency relief administrator, warned, however, that Pennsylvania must provide $5 million a month or be cut off from Federal funds. To meet this and other needs, Earle asked the Legislature for $203 million in new taxes and planned that the burden would fall not on the homeowner but on individuals and businesses better able to carry the weight. Republican State Chairman M. Harvey Taylor called Earle's tax program "a sock on the jaw for business," and Republican legislators, denying the need for Pennsylvania to put up so much money, demanded and got a meeting with Hopkins. When Hopkins did not budge, eight Republican senators, representing primarily mining and industrial areas, called for a one-year enactment of Earle's proposals. Republican leaders then relented, conferred with Earle, and agreed to compromise.

Genuine tax reform, however, demanded a new constitution. "We cannot," Earle declared, "have completely efficient and economical government until we have revision." For example, to bypass the constitutional ceiling on state indebtedness, the Earle administration created the General State Authority. Under this expedient but devious arrangement, the authority could borrow money to build facilities, which it then leased to the state. Republicans strongly opposed constitutional revision, accused the Guffey-Earle machine of planning to set up a dictatorship, and equated revision with socialism. Earle perceived that "constitutions are established and changed in times of unrest, and only in times of unrest" and predicted that "revision will destroy the privileges and immunities of a small and selfish group of men and big corporate interests which they represent." Earle's arguments had little effect. In September 1935 Pennsylvanians overwhelmingly rejected a constitutional convention. A low vote, effective Republican organization, basic rural conservatism, and a whispering campaign that revision would enable Roman Catholics to obtain state aid for their schools contributed to defeat.

Despite this setback, the Democrats were in the ascendancy. In 1936 Roosevelt became the first Democratic presidential candidate to carry Pennsylvania since 1856, and Democrats won a smashing two-thirds majority in the Pennsylvania Senate. When the new Legislature assembled in 1937 for its biennial session, there was no stopping the Little New Deal. Earle reminded the Assembly that liberal forces controlled both the executive and legislative branches of the state government for the first time in ninety-one years. "It is now our duty," he admonished, "to translate that liberalism into positive effective action." Indeed the new Legislature had already saved Pennsylvania $22 million in social security taxes by rushing through an unemployment compensation law to comply with the December 31 deadline in the Federal Social Security Act.

In 1937 Earle and the Assembly enacted the most sweeping reform program in Pennsylvania history. The new legislation benefited laboring men. It created a more efficient and professionalized state Department of Public Assistance, improved workmen's compensation, abolished privately paid deputy sheriffs, prohibited the importation of strikebreakers, and eliminated the sweatshop by establishing minimum wages and maximum hours and by regulating industrial work which employees could perform in their homes. It also restricted the issuance of labor injunctions and created (through the Little Wagner Act) the three-man state Labor Relations Board appointed by the governor to adjust labor disputes and carry out the provisions of the act. The Little Wagner Act also protected labor's right to organize and bargain collectively, outlawed company unions, and prohibited unfair labor practices, such as infiltrating unions with labor spies or circulating lists of troublesome workers. The act also denied recognition of unions that barred would-be members because of race, creed, or color.

The Little New Deal benefited other segments of the population through significant legislation. It continued to shift the tax burden from real estate to corporations, which had previously avoided the kind of taxation imposed in most states. The state now taxed the majority stockholdings of Pennsylvania corporations in out-of-state companies and moved to prevent individuals from avoiding taxes by shifting personal property across state lines. It created the Pennsylvania Turnpike Commission to build through the Alleghenies from Middlesex to Irwin a four-lane, toll highway, which with its maximum 3 percent grade and seven tunnels initiated a new era in road construction. The Federal government financed the $70 million turnpike—which opened in 1940—by advancing the money and allowing the commission to amortize the debt through tolls. The Federal government also financed, through various work-relief agencies, an enormous building program of highways, bridges, playgrounds, schools, courthouses, post offices, dams, and parks. The Little New Deal achieved more effective regulation of utilities by substituting the more powerful Public Utilities Commission for the Public Service Commission. Utilities had to prove the necessity for higher rates and could not challenge in the courts the reasonableness of the rates set by the Public Utilities Commission. The Earle administration supplemented the Federal Agricultural Adjustment Act (AAA) and aided farmers with the Little AAA, designed to promote reforestation and to conserve soil through contour plowing and the construction of small dams to prevent gullying and flooding. This session also placed milk control on a permanent basis (with Pennsylvania the first state to do so) by setting up a milk control commission with powers to fix prices and to regulate the industry. Rural Pennsylvania benefited from the Flood Control and Pure Streams Act (which began the struggle against polluted streams) and a further revision of the state's Blue Law to permit

Sunday fishing. Finally the state's first Teacher Tenure Law gave teachers security and a measure of immunity from attack for unconventional ideas. A leading Republican called these Little New Deal laws "vicious . . . unsound, unhealthy, and unwarranted class legislation," but David Lawrence proudly labeled them "the most constructive, liberal, and humane in generations."

The Little New Deal not only left a rich heritage of progressive legislation but also marked a fundamental change in governing Pennsylvania. It gave previously neglected groups more power and easier access to those who governed. Once started, that trend could not be reversed. The New Deal also left Pittsburgh with a flourishing Democratic machine and Philadelphia with a thriving Democratic opposition that would eventually triumph. The rise of the Pittsburgh Democratic machine led by David Lawrence runs counter to the widely accepted theory that New Deal welfare programs destroyed the hold of urban bosses over their constituents and presumably their machine. The New Deal won great numbers to the Democratic party, but its organization and its functions were not fundamentally changed. The Democratic precinct captains, ward chairmen, county leaders, and state chairman continued to offer—and were better able to deliver—services and favors. Always strongest among the neediest constituents, party organizations expanded their influence with the Great Depression. Never in the history of the United States were voters more aware of their dependence on government and on those who operated the government.

From the inception of the Civil Works Administration in 1933, politics and relief were inseparable in Pittsburgh and indeed in all of Pennsylvania. "Our chief trouble in Pennsylvania," Lorena Hickok reported to her boss Harry Hopkins, "is due to politics. From township to Harrisburg, the state is honeycombed with politicians all fighting for the privilege of distributing patronage." Since relief was locally administered and since Republicans controlled the state until 1935, the squabbling politicians during the early New Deal days were usually Republicans. The advent of the Works Progress Administration (WPA), which administered work-relief projects, made little difference; local political leadership, whether Republican as in Fayette County or Democratic as in Pittsburgh, dominated the WPA.

Patronage was important in building a political machine, and the enormous Federal patronage—created by agencies such as the WPA—strengthened local politicians. Party committeemen with patronage jobs worked harder for the party than those without appointments. By 1936 Lawrence reported to Roosevelt that registered Democrats in Pittsburgh outnumbered Republicans for the first time since the Civil War. In 1937 the Lawrence organization utilizing the WPA survived a serious challenge in the mayoralty primary, reunited the party, and running on the New Deal smashed Republicans in the general election.

Success, however, bred factionalism, and the 1938 primary campaign all but destroyed the Democrats. Liberal reformers, the CIO, and the Guffey-dominated WPA leadership supported Tom Kennedy for governor, while practical politicians (Lawrence, Kelly, and McCloskey) and the AFL backed a relatively unknown Pittsburgh lawyer Charles Alvin Jones. During the campaign a third candidate, Charles Margiotti—whom Earle fired as attorney general—accused Lawrence and other prominent Democrats of accepting bribes to pass legislation and provoked a grand jury investigation of the Earle administration. Chairman Lawrence complained that the state organization was being "beaten to a pulp" by the Guffey-dominated WPA. Lawrence exaggerated because Guffey's control of the WPA leadership in Pennsylvania did not mean that he controlled it on the local level, where voters were influenced. Jones and Earle, who wished to be senator, won the primary despite

WPA opposition. But using the ultimate weapon of the WPA on fellow Democrats "exacerbated" the quarrel and demoralized the party, while Margiotti's charges (which produced no convictions) lost the Democrats many recent converts from Republicanism. In November Democrats lost the state, but Jones and Earle won Pittsburgh. There the machine, nourished by the WPA, was firmly rooted.

THE ORGANIZATION OF INDUSTRIAL LABOR

The Great Depression not only led to a revived Democratic party and political upheaval but also to social upheaval and industrial labor unions. Unlike the union-destroying industrial depressions in the 1870s and 1890s, the Great Depression strengthened industrial unions. Positive support from the New Deal—supplemented in Pennsylvania by the Little New Deal—made phenomenal growth possible. Before the New Deal, unions—dependent on workers' dues—were devastated by and powerless to prevent widespread unemployment, long hours, and inadequate wages. The Amalgamated Association of Iron, Steel and Tin Workers declined from 31,500 members in 1920 to 8,605 in 1929. By 1933 there were only 4,944 members, and most of them were hanging on primarily so their heirs could collect death benefits.

Two major Federal laws, the National Industrial Recovery Act (NIRA, 1933) and the National Labor Relations or Wagner Act (1935), touched off and sustained the drive to organize labor in the 1930s. Section 7a of the NIRA ensured labor the right to organize and bargain collectively, and two months after the United States Supreme Court invalidated the NIRA the Wagner Act salvaged and bolstered the provisions of section 7a. It set up the powerful National Labor Relations Board (NLRB) to determine whether a trade, a company, or a shop constituted a bargaining unit; to hold elections to select the union which would represent workers; and to prevent unfair labor practices. Applying only to industries involved in interstate commerce, the Wagner Act left out large groups of workers. Pennsylvania's Little Wagner Act of 1937, however, covered more employees and guaranteed their right to organize and bargain collectively.

The impact of these laws can be seen in the organization of steelworkers, who formed Pennsylvania's most conspicuous group of unorganized labor. The key man in the organization of steel was John L. Lewis. Born in Iowa of Welsh immigrant parents, Lewis began working in coal mines at fifteen and in 1920 when he was forty became president of the United Mine Workers (UMW) of the AFL. Though he strengthened that union during the 1920s, the Depression broke membership down to about 100,000. Recognizing the need for Federal support, Lewis was largely responsible for including section 7a in the NIRA. With UMW organizers telling miners "the President wants you to join the union," membership quadrupled in two years. The AFL, however, was dominated by craft unions that cut across industrial lines, and its leaders were slow to organize semiskilled and unskilled industrial workers under section 7a. The 1934 AFL convention agreed to charter several industrial unions and to mount a new drive to organize steel, but the old-guard leaders did nothing.

Their inaction infuriated Lewis. If the UMW had a future, steel (with its very important "captive" bituminous mines) had to be organized, but in 1935 the AFL Executive Council "did not deem it advisable to launch an organizing drive for the steel industry." That year at the AFL convention Lewis passionately denounced the old guard. "Organize the unorganized," he pleaded, "and in so doing you make the American Federation of Labor the greatest instrumentality that has ever been forged in the history of modern civilization to befriend the cause of humanity and champion human rights." Despite his pleas, the convention rejected the minority report in favor of industrial unionism. Lewis and seven other industrial union leaders soon formed the Committee for Industrial Organization and requested industrial charters for steel, automobile, rubber, and radio workers. The AFL Executive Council refused, ordered the committee to disband, and by August 1936 suspended the participating unions. Undaunted, the Committee for Industrial Organization soon became the Congress of Industrial Organizations (CIO).

After an initial victory in rubber, the CIO in June 1936 ambitiously tackled steel in its first big organizing drive. The Steel Workers Organizing Committee (SWOC), superbly led by Chairman Philip Murray, a UMW vice-president, and Secretary-Treasurer David J. McDonald, discredited the companies' Employee Representative Plans (ERP)—basically company unions riddled with company agents and spies—and captured their machinery and personnel. By encouraging company union officials to be more independent the SWOC soon provoked many company unions to revolt and to join it. The SWOC also sent flying squadrons of organizers into mill towns to attract workers with the slogan "Be Wise, Organize!" By the end of 1936, with 125,000 steelworkers members of SWOC, management's rule of America's most basic industry was threatened.

Economic, social, and political factors made the SWOC a formidable antagonist for the steel industry. During the Depression profits had been slim or nonexistent, and U.S. Steel had actually lost money from 1931 to 1934. By early 1937, however, business was better and management realized that a shutdown during a period of recovery would hurt it more than during the depths of a depression. Myron C. Taylor, chairman of the board of U.S. Steel, later remarked, "The cost of a strike—to the Corporation, to the public and to the men—would have been incalculable." Society itself had changed since the Great Steel Strike of 1919. Immigration restriction reduced ethnic tensions which management had earlier exploited. Labor by 1937 also had political power. New Deal labor legislation forbade discrimination against workers belonging to unions, and CIO organizers were able to operate in the Pittsburgh district mill towns. Powerful political figures cooperated with the CIO. When Tom Kennedy, lieutenant governor of Pennsylvania and secretary-treasurer of the UMW, addressed a SWOC rally and memorial for 1892 strikers at Homestead (the first labor meeting permitted in that town since 1919), he was escorted to the platform by state troopers and he promised workers protection and state relief in case of a strike. The contrast between the political climate of 1936 and that of 1919 or 1892 was sharply driven home.

As they had proved in the past, steel companies were also formidable antagonists. Combining concessions to all workers, coercion for union men, and propaganda for the public, the companies sought to discredit the CIO. Management hastily formed the ERP company unions, after section 7a of the NIRA became law in 1933, and granted a 10 percent pay hike after the SWOC got under way; but management reacted harshly to SWOC organizers. After SWOC representative Joseph J. Timko arrived in June 1936 to organize Jones and Laughlin's Aliquippa plant, fourteen of the eighteen men who attended his first meeting were fired, dozens of union members were arrested on charges of drunkenness and disorderly conduct, and the local paper equated organizers with Communists and advocated treating them as mad dogs.

The steel companies were still powerful and were better able than labor to stand a long strike, but Myron C. Taylor of U.S. Steel recognized that unions and collective bargaining were here to stay. His foresight proved correct; the Supreme Court in April 1937 sustained the Wagner Act. Taylor was also aware that fighting unions could be more costly than recognizing them. On Saturday, January 9, 1937, John L. Lewis was lunching with Senator Guffey at Washington's Mayflower Hotel when Taylor and his wife chanced to enter the dining room. After lunch, Lewis joined the Taylors for 20 minutes' conversation and agreed to talk informally with Taylor the next day. A series of secret meetings followed during the next seven weeks.

Lewis and Taylor got along amiably. The public knew Lewis as a bellicose and theatrical man, but privately even those with whom he disagreed admitted that he was witty, courtly, and conciliatory. Furthermore, despite his seventh-grade education, Lewis was well read. Consequently it was in character for Lewis to charm the Taylors while exploring the possibility of Big Steel recognizing the SWOC. It was also in character for the flexible, forward-looking Taylor to offer Lewis on February 25 a formula recognizing the SWOC as the bargaining agent for its members (not for all U.S. Steel employees). Three days later Lewis accepted, and on March 1 the nation was shocked by the "surrender" of U.S. Steel. By May, after a NLRB election brought Jones and Laughlin into its camp, the SWOC had signed over a hundred contracts and had 300,000 members.

The Frick-Gary tradition was dead in Big Steel, but not in Little Steel. Bethlehem, Republic, Inland, and Youngstown Sheet and Tube—dominated by practical steelmen and led in particular by Republic's Tom Girdler and Bethlehem's Eugene Grace—fought on. "I won't have a contract, verbal or written, with an irresponsible, racketeering, violent, communistic body like the CIO," exclaimed Girdler, "and until they pass a law making me do it, I am not going to do it." The SWOC struck Little Steel, but the strike was not successful, its plants remained outside the union, and the men returned to work.

Girdler, however, had merely won a battle, not the war. By mid-1941 it was the law—specifically the Wagner Act—that made Little Steel recognize and bargain with the SWOC after elections demonstrated that a majority of its employees belonged to the CIO. A year of collective bargaining, however, produced no contract until in the middle of World War II the Federal government forced a settlement on management. With the industry organized, the temporary SWOC gave way in 1942 to the permanent United Steelworkers of America, a powerful organization that would consolidate and make permanent the social upheaval of the 1930s and enable labor to determine in large measure its share of the wealth produced by the steel industry. As John L. Lewis said, Myron C. Taylor possessed "the far-seeing vision of industrial statesmanship."

BIBLIOGRAPHY

Economic developments in the 1920s are covered in George Soule: *Prosperity Decade, from War to Depression: 1919–1929* (1968); Glenn E. McLaughlin: *Growth of American Manufacturing Areas: A Comparative Analysis with Special Emphasis on Trends in the Pittsburgh District* (1938); Gladys L. Palmer: *Philadelphia Workers in a Changing Economy* (1956); and Roy Lubove: *Twentieth Century Pittsburgh: Government, Business and Environmental Change* (1969). Much information on the revolution in manners and morals may be found in Edmund Wilson: *The American Earthquake: A Documentary of the Twenties and Thirties* (1958); Frederick Lewis Allen: *Only Yesterday: An*

Informal History of the Nineteen-twenties (1952); and William E. Leuchtenburg: *The Perils of Prosperity, 1914–32* (1958). On Pinchot, see M. Nelson McGeary: *Gifford Pinchot: Forester, Politician* (1960); Clyde L. King: "Fiscal and Administrative Reorganization in Pennsylvania," *The American Political Science Review,* vol. 17 (1923), pp. 597–608; and Gifford Pinchot: *The Extra Session: A Report to the People* (1926). A friendly portrayal of Fisher is William Ainsworth Cornell: "The Political Career of John S. Fisher: Governor of Pennsylvania, 1927–1931" (master's thesis, University of Pittsburgh, 1949).

On Wall Street's collapse, see John Kenneth Galbraith: *The Great Crash: 1929* (1954); and on the Depression, see Broadus Mitchell: *Depression Decade: From New Era through New Deal, 1929–1941* (1947). See also Arthur M. Schlesinger, Jr.: *The Age of Roosevelt,* 3 vols., (1957–1960); and Frederick Lewis Allen: *Since Yesterday: The Nineteen-thirties in America, September 3, 1929–September 3, 1939* (1961). Statistics that reveal the impact of the Depression on Pennsylvania may be found in Pennsylvania Department of Labor and Industry: *Pennsylvania Labor and Industry in the Depression . . . , 1931–1934 . . .* (1934); John J. Schanz, Jr.: *Historical Statistics of Pennsylvania's Mineral Industries, 1759–1955* (1957); E. L. Gasteiger and D. O. Boster: *Pennsylvania Agricultural Statistics, 1866–1950* (1954). The following three dissertations are valuable not only for their main focus but also for what they say about the Depression in general: Samuel John Astorino: "The Decline of the Republican Dynasty in Pennsylvania, 1929–1934" (University of Pittsburgh, 1962); Bruce M. Stave: "The New Deal and Building of an Urban Political Machine: Pittsburgh, A Case Study" (University of Pittsburgh, 1966); Richard C. Keller: "Pennsylvania's Little New Deal" (Columbia University, 1960). See also Richard C. Keller: "Pennsylvania's Little New Deal," *Pennsylvania History,* vol. 29 (1962); pp. 391–406; John L. Shover: "The Emergence of a Two-Party System in Republican Philadelphia: 1924–1936" (paper read at the American Historical Association Convention, December 29, 1971, at New York); and Walter Dean Burnham: *Critical Elections and the Mainsprings of American Politics* (1970). Joseph F. Guffey: *Seventy Years on the Red-fire Wagon: From Tilden to Truman, through New Freedom and New Deal* (1952), though biased and sketchy, is useful. On the rise of the CIO in general and the United Steelworkers in particular, see Joseph G. Rayback: *A History of American Labor* (1959); Foster Rhea Dulles: *Labor in America: A History* (1949); *C.I.O.: 1935–1955, Industrial Democracy in Action* (1955); Robert R. R. Brooks: *As Steel Goes, . . . Unionism in a Basic Industry* (1940); David Brody: *Labor in Crisis: The Steel Strike of 1919* (1965); Alden Whitman: "A Fighting Leader [John L. Lewis]," *New York Times* (June 12, 1969).

CHAPTER TWENTY-FIVE

The Republicans Return

The brief Little New Deal interlude was ended, but a fundamentally changed Pennsylvania had returned to its traditional Republican mooring. That party's massive electoral base had been severely, but not fatally, cut. The newly found Democratic strength—centering among city dwellers, organized laborers, Catholics, Jews, Negroes, and the poor—was not sufficient to overcome strong Republican support in Philadelphia and among the Protestant, native-stock elements in rural, small town, and suburban areas. Staunch Republicans included wealthy and better-educated citizens as well as traditionalists who wished to preserve their social and religious values. The four Republican administrations that succeeded the Earle regime professed in varying degrees to hate the New Deal, government controls, growing bureaucracies, large budgets, and high taxes. Yet these administrations not only failed to destroy Little New Deal legislation but ultimately espoused and even enlarged upon much of Earle's program. Despite their professions, Republican administrations regulated industry, improved education, and provided a variety of social services, all of which caused the state bureaucracy, budget, and taxes to increase while the functions of local governments decreased. The Republican party had moved a long way, but by 1954 voters judged that it had moved neither far enough nor fast enough to arrest postwar Pennsylvania's fundamental problem of relative economic decline.

THE END OF THE LITTLE NEW DEAL

Governor Arthur Horace James (1939–1943) began his career as a breaker boy, but he neither remained one long nor identified with his former colliery associates. Supported by industrial interests, James, an ardent foe of the Big and Little New Deals, defeated Pinchot in the 1938 Republican primary. During his gubernatorial campaign, James threatened to "make a bonfire of all the laws passed by the 1937 legislature" and promised to reduce "confiscatory" taxes, to "bring business back to Pennsylvania," and to provide "a job for every man who wants one." Democratic factionalism, small businessmen's and white collar workers' opposition to New Deal tax and labor policies, and the serious 1938 recession combined to give James the governorship and to give the Republican party control of the Legislature.

James had difficulty fulfilling his campaign threats and promises. Although his administration searched during a two-week recess of the Legislature for ways to reduce taxes, it had to reenact the old "confiscatory" taxes. The James administration established the Department of Commerce to attract new industry, and James claimed after a year to have induced $32 million worth of industrial expansion, but $25 million of that expansion had actually occurred under the Earle administration. James's attempt to combat unemployment by launching a "give-a-job" movement among employers was not very successful. Despite the growing defense boom in coal and steel, there were in 1940 about a million unemployed Pennsylvanians, only one-third of whom were on direct or work relief.

Retrenchment curtailed relief, reform, and public works. Rather than increase taxes, the Legislature appropriated only half of what was being spent for relief ($120 million for two years when the state was spending $10 million a month) and attempted to cut down relief rolls with the "Work to Eat" Act that required all recipients of relief to work for their money. In addition, earlier legislatures had come to the aid of property owners unable to pay their taxes, but by 1939 the Legislature required that all properties delinquent as of 1934 be sold at sheriffs' sales by August 1, 1940. Although the Earle administration had catapulted Pennsylvania to fourth place among the states in compensation paid for injured and killed workmen, a new workmen's compensation law placed Pennsylvania "with the most backward of the so-called backward states." The new law judged that sixty days and $150 were sufficient to heal any injury and that a broken back was entitled to no more medical care than a broken finger. To save money (at the obvious cost of more industrial accidents), James cut the number of factory inspectors from 100 to 59, quarry inspectors from 13 to 7, and elevator inspectors from 21 to 19. James also cut the budget of the Public Utility Commission by one-third, abolished some 2,000 state jobs, and postponed the construction of various state facilities.

The James administration was hostile to organized labor and strikes. It emasculated the Little Wagner Act by increasing the employer's power and giving the state secretary of labor a veto over the State Labor Relations Board's decisions. The Legislature also eased the restrictions placed on employers by the 1937 Anti-Injunction Act. In March 1941, over vigorous protests of the SWOC and under James's orders, state troopers intervened after a day of violence in a Bethlehem Steel strike (at Bethlehem), broke a picket line, and cleared a path to the main gate. Later in November during a strike in the captive coal mines, James pledged his support to any course Roosevelt "may determine upon to break the deadlock in defense production caused by short-sighted labor leaders" and did not intervene after fourteen pickets had been wounded by gunfire at the Edenborn Frick Company mine and the Fayette County sheriff had asked for state police aid.

The Legislature passed two significant laws affecting public servants. The first modified the Earle administration's teacher tenure law to include a two-year probationary period and to permit school boards to dismiss flagrantly immoral teachers. The second law established a Civil Service Commission to appoint and promote persons of character and ability according to their merit and fitness.

The 1940 election set Republicans back. Roosevelt carried Pennsylvania, Guffey returned to the Senate, and Democrats regained control of the state House of Representatives although Republicans retained the state Senate. Even though the 193-day session of the divided 1941 Legislature proved to be the longest in ninety-nine years, it accomplished little beyond introducing a statewide parole system administered by a five-man parole board and designed to eliminate political influence. Although it passed a bill to eliminate 104,000 phantom voters from the Philadelphia registration lists, the Legislature killed three charter reform bills for Philadelphia and the Senate reduced the Philadelphia Registration Commission to a one-man body by refusing to confirm three James appointees. The Legislature also deadlocked and failed to pass a congressional reapportionment plan necessitating a special session in early 1942 to enact a compromise. Only defense measures to meet the threat of World War II were readily agreed upon by both parties.

WORLD WAR II

The anticipation of war affected the economy as early as 1937. But economic recovery really accompanied the outbreak of war in 1939 and the fall of France in 1940 when the United States expended large sums on its own defense and on aid to Great Britain. With the Roosevelt admininstration in 1941 placing the nation on a wartime footing, business revived and unemployment dropped. The Japanese attack at Pearl Harbor plunged the nation directly into a war in which it was already deeply involved.

Befitting a populous state with an enormous industrial capacity, Pennsylvania contributed greatly to the Allied victory over German nazism and Japanese militarism. Nearly 1¼ million Pennsylvanians served in the armed forces, and 33,000 of them died in their country's service. Thirty-two members of the armed forces from Pennsylvania, more than from any other state, won the nation's highest award for valor, the Congressional Medal of Honor. Pennsylvania also provided an unusual number of outstanding leaders in the armed services. America's number one soldier, General of the Army George C. Marshall, was born and bred in Uniontown. Chief of staff of the army and chief architect of the triumph over the Axis powers, Marshall earned President Harry Truman's lavish praise: "To him as much as to any individual, the United States owes its future. He takes his place at the head of the great commanders of history." General of the Army Henry Harley ("Hap") Arnold of Gladwyne commanded the Army Air Force, and his second in command was General Carl ("Tooey") Spaatz of Boyertown. General Jacob L. Devers of York commanded the Sixth Army Group, forming Eisenhower's right wing during the final push on Germany; his subordinate was Lieutenant General Alexander M. Patch of Lebanon who commanded the Seventh Army. Other Pennsylvanians were Lieutenant General Lewis H. Brereton of Pittsburgh, who two months after D-day was named commander of the newly formed Allied Airborne Army; Major General Lyman L. Lemnitzer of Honesdale; and the youngest major general in the army, James M. ("Slim Jim") Gavin. Lemnitzer carried out incredible secret missions in North Africa and Italy, while Gavin—who once sold newspapers in Mount Carmel, enlisted in the army without finishing high school, and entered West Point from the ranks—jumped with his Eighty-second Airborne Division on battlefields from Sicily to Berlin. Admiral Harold R. Stark of

Wilkes-Barre was chief of Naval Operations and later commanded United States naval forces in European waters; Admiral Richard S. Edwards, a Philadelphian, was second in command of the navy throughout the war; Admiral Thomas C. Kinkaid, also of Philadelphia, commanded the Seventh Fleet in the Pacific; and Vice-Admiral Alan G. Kirk, another Philadelphian, commanded amphibious forces at landings in Sicily, Italy, and Normandy.

Though Pennsylvanians were in all services in all campaigns in all theaters of war, the experience of the Twenty-eighth Division—the Pennsylvania National Guard—illustrates the heroism and suffering of World War II servicemen. The Twenty-eighth Division under Major General Edward Martin was inducted into the army on February 17, 1941, at Indiantown Gap and went overseas on October 8, 1943. Though it saw no action until July 22, 1944, 1½ months after D-day, the Twenty-eighth soon had its fill. During a month's bitter fighting in Normandy, the Germans called it the "Bloody Bucket" Division (for its red keystone). The Twenty-eighth entered Paris on August 29, swept north into Belgium and Luxembourg, and on September 11 became the first division to enter Germany in force. There during November in the Huertgen Forest the Twenty-eighth suffered heavy casualties and in December was rewarded with a quiet section of the front. The reward was virtually a death warrant, for the Twenty-eighth sustained the full force of the surprise German Bulge offensive on December 16. Five German divisions, reinforced by four more, smashed the stubborn Twenty-eighth. Following the Bulge offensive, the Twenty-eighth was reconstituted, joined Patch's Seventh Army, captured Colmar, and crossed the Rhine before the Germans surrendered. It returned to Indiantown Gap in August 1945, was deactivated in December, and in 1946 was reactivated as part of the Pennsylvania National Guard.

Pennsylvania also provided numerous materials of war. The army and navy located significant installations throughout the state. The Philadelphia Navy Yard, employing nearly 70,000 people, built fifty war vessels including three battleships, two cruisers, and an aircraft carrier; fitted out an additional 480 vessels launched elsewhere; and repaired disabled, worn ships, making a grand total of 1,210 vessels worked on during the war. Recognizing Philadelphia's preeminence in textiles, the army made the Philadelphia Quartermaster Depot the central procurement agency for uniforms. The Frankford Arsenal not only manufactured small-arms ammunition but planned and trained workers for new ammunition plants. The Pennsylvania Ordnance Works near Williamsport and the Keystone Ordnance Works near Meadville produced large quantities of TNT. The navy maintained a huge supply depot at Mechanicsburg while the enormous Letterkenny Ordnance Depot near Chambersburg stored and handled 3 million tons of bombs, shells, and ordnance.

In finished war goods Pennsylvania made particularly important contributions in ships where it ranked fourth and in ordnance where it ranked third. The shipyards of Philadelphia and Chester on the Delaware, of Pittsburgh and Ambridge on the Ohio, and of Erie produced a variety of war vessels, many of which were designed to unload men, tanks, trucks, artillery, and supplies on beachheads. The yards of Sun Ship at Chester designed and built one-third of the nation's 525 T2 tankers. Ordnance—guns, ammunition, and vehicles—composed over one-third of Pennsylvania's war contracts. Perhaps the most significant Pennsylvania contribution to the Allied arsenal was the wakeless electrically powered torpedo—developed at Westinghouse's Sharon plant—which did not leave the telltale trail of bubbles that characterized conventional compressed-air-powered torpedoes. The Philadelphia Radio Corporation helped develop radar, and the Hershey Company produced that foxhole favorite, the D-ration bar. The Bantam Car Company of Butler developed the famous jeep,

Mack Truck Company of Allentown and Autocar of Ardmore produced heavy trucks and half-tracks, American Car and Foundry at Berwick made light tanks, and Baldwin Locomotive Works in Philadelphia made medium and heavy tanks as well as locomotives. From 1939 to 1944 Pennsylvania production jumped from $5 billion to $15.1 billion. The fact that Pennsylvania ranked low in the production of both vehicles and aircraft, however, was a bad omen for future industrial development.

The war effort required an enormous labor force at the very time that over a million men and women went to war. The rise in nonagricultural employment, from 2,700,600 in 1939 to 3,512,200 in 1943, coupled with the demands of the armed services, ended unemployment and pressed new groups into industry. One-fourth of all war workers were women as were nearly half of all other workers. The handicapped filled a small number of war jobs, and, with the help of the Fair Employment Practices Committee and the War Production Training Program of the Pennsylvania Department of Public Instruction, many black laborers moved into skilled jobs previously denied them.

Spectacular war production, business prosperity, and high employment figures, as State Historian S. K. Stevens perceived in 1944, concealed the fact that in relation to other industrial areas Pennsylvania was declining. The K. C. Stokes report of the U.S. Department of Commerce noted that the "center of gravity of American economic life has shifted markedly Westward and Southward during the war," and the shift was accelerated by all sections receiving numerous war contracts. Although Pennsylvania was still the second manufacturing state, it ranked seventh in war contracts awarded from June 1, 1940, to May 31, 1945. The war hastened the relative decline of Pennsylvania industry, which had begun with the twentieth century, but a few industries, primarily steel (producing 31 percent of the nation's supply in 1945), managed temporarily to reverse the trend. During the war, absolute gains over the productivity of the recent past in heavy and durable-goods industries were substantial, but gains in light industries were modest. A foundation had not been laid for rapid economic expansion. Indeed, Pennsylvania's share of the national income was 1 percent less in 1943 than it had been in 1939 and that percentage point was worth $1 billion. Considering that factories employed approximately one-third of working Pennsylvanians, failure to maintain a healthy growth in manufacturing could only bring serious consequences. S. K. Stevens prophesied the need to meet the challenge of shifting national industrial patterns, to attract new industries, to adopt new processes and products for old industries, to conserve present resources, to discover new resources, and above all to engage in "rational long-range planning" to "avert many dangers which may now impend." As Pennsylvania emerged from the war, it was still a rich state with vast diversified manufactures, splendid natural resources, and a skilled labor force, but to meet the challenge of the postwar world it needed imaginative and dedicated leadership.

MARTIN AND POSTWAR READJUSTMENT

Pennsylvania's new leader was General Edward Martin (1943-1947), former commander of the Twenty-eighth Division and a long-time stalwart in the Republican organization. Supported by Governor James, Joseph N. Pew, Jr., of Sun Oil Company, and Joseph R. Grundy, and clearly the choice of the Philadelphia and state organizations, Martin triumphed handily in the 1942 primary over Senator James J. Davis, who received independent Republican support. The Democratic state organization also triumphed. It rejected Roosevelt's suggestion that Attorney General William C. Bullitt run, and in a lively primary fight Lawrence's man, Auditor General F. Clair Ross, defeated the candidate of his erstwhile friend but current archenemy Senator Joseph F. Guffey, despite the fact that organized labor supported Guffey's man. Lawrence may have tightened his hold on the state party, but Martin and the Republicans swept the state in the November election. In his campaign Martin had called for lower state taxes, vowed to continue the policies and principles of Governor James, pledged support to the war effort, and condemned the New Deal for its "un-American domestic policies."

Martin wished to restrict the role of state and Federal government. Conceiving of bureaucracy and waste as interchangeable, he grew apoplectic at the thought of the 2½ million wartime civilian employees of the Federal government. "At a time when every dollar is needed for war, our social experiments go on and on," he complained. His ideal government balanced the budget and was thrifty, small, simple, and decentralized, assuring agriculture, labor, and management "equality of opportunity and freedom of action with a minimum of interference by government."

Despite his commitment to parsimonious government, Martin submitted to the 1945 Legislature a record biennial budget of two-thirds of a billion dollars and nearly $200 million in postwar construction and improvement plans. In addition, the Martin administration launched an ambitious $345 million five-year highway program. Thanks to war prosperity, Pennsylvania actually had a $171 million surplus, but Martin asked the Legislature to resist the temptation to lower taxes. Any tax reduction, he warned, would have to be offset by reduced expenditures. Hating public debt, Martin used $48 million of the surplus to retire General State Authority Bonds. In an effort to ease postwar adjustment, the 1945 Legislature appropriated $1 million for the Post War Planning Commission (created by the 1943 Legislature) to assist local government public works projects, while the state Department of Welfare planned $44 million in construction.

The Martin administration also passed significant legislation conserving Pennsylvania's natural and historical heritage. The 1945 Legislature created the Pennsylvania Historical and Museum Commission, and voted to extend Harrisburg's Capitol Park and to erect a memorial building there to William Penn, while Martin announced plans for a great plaza adjacent to Independence Hall. The Legislature also passed the Brunner anti-stream-pollution bill, appropriated $5 million to begin desilting the Schuylkill River, and overcame industrial lobbyists to approve interstate pacts to clean up the Delaware and Potomac rivers. The Legislature increased workmen's compensation, death, and occupational disease benefits by about 17 percent, increased maximum unemployment benefits to $20 for twenty weeks, and widened unemployment coverage. The Legislature caught up to the Little New Deal in providing compensation for second injuries that permanently disabled workers. Governor Earle had signed a similar law in 1937, but in 1939 the state Supreme Court had declared it unconstitutional. School appropriations and teachers' salaries were increased for the 1945 to 1947 biennium. Finally, the Martin administration made a significant contribution to public health and education when the 1945 Legislature appropriated $4 million to provide a complete medical and dental examination for the state's 1,550,000 school children and 60,000 school employees.

Martin wished to minimize Federal government activities and even the state government's role during the difficult period of adjusting to a peacetime economy. Warning against federalizing the unemployment insurance system and claiming that Pennsylvania's $20 a week unemployment benefit was sufficient, Martin opposed Federal legislation that would supplement state unemployment insurance payments to the level of $25 a week for 26 weeks, and boasted of the $600 million reserve in the state unemployment compensation trust fund and of the surplus in the state fund. Not only did Martin reject Federal aid, he also refused a Democratic request on August 31, 1945, for a special legislative session to deal with reconversion problems. "Pennsylvania has all the laws it needs," he observed. In the face of a severe housing shortage, skyrocketing rents, and emergency freezing of rents by numerous governors, Martin merely asked businessmen and landlords "to police" themselves so "that no injustice will be done to those who are unable to protect themselves."

By the end of 1946 Pennsylvania was industrially demobilized. Fortunately the demand for consumer goods unavailable during the war eased reconversion to a peacetime economy and kept employment high. In 1939, before the war, 965,000 worked in Pennsylvania factories; in November 1943 factory employment peaked at 1,594,000; and by the end of 1946 it had leveled off at 1,316,000. War production had brought shifts in Pennsylvania factory employment. There were significant expansion in machinery and heartening gains in metal products, but paralyzingly slow growth in textiles and clothing and an absolute decline in leather products, all of which had absorbed 29 percent of the prewar factory force.

Produced by and adding to inflation during the immediate postwar years, strikes irritated most Americans. On the national level, strikes provoked the Taft-Hartley Act reducing some of the advantages labor had won through the Wagner National Labor Relations Act. The shift in public opinion put Martin—never a friend of organized labor—right in step. During the 1944 campaign, he called the CIO Political Action Committee an ally of the Communist party, and in early 1946 when workers struck against General Electric in Philadelphia and Westinghouse in Pittsburgh, Philip Murray, head of the CIO, accused Martin of trying to "destroy trade unions" and warned that "brute force and writs of injunction don't settle labor disputes." Violence occurred in both cities when police sought to prevent mass picketing, prohibited by the courts. In Philadelphia police arrested seventeen and injured a score of strikers, provoking 10,000 to demonstrate at City Hall against police brutality, while the strikers' brutal tactic of tossing marbles under the hooves of police horses infuriated police. In Pittsburgh violence provoked Martin to order the opening of picket lines by state troopers. Strikers, however, did not resist Martin's order, and the troopers merely stood by while the picket lines opened.

During the 1946 campaign, Martin ran for the seat of Joseph F. Guffey, the New Deal, prolabor senator, while Martin's progressive attorney general, James H. Duff, ran for governor against Colonel John S. Rice of Gettysburg. The Republican platform repudiated communism and fascism, called for a hard-line foreign policy against the Soviet Union, supported the rights of the individual citizen against a bureaucratically planned economy, and favored a bonus as well as preference in housing materials for veterans. To win back the Negro vote that had been lost to the New Deal, the platform called for fair employment practices legislation, modifying Martin's earlier position. While opposed to discrimination in employment, Martin characteristically had favored reform through education rather than legislation. The election seemingly reduced Pennsylvania Democrats to their pre-New Deal status. Frustrated by strikes, shortages, and high prices, Philadelphians, farmers, and a substantial number of laborers voted Republican. Martin smashed Guffey by a 600,000-vote margin and emerged from the campaign a possible 1948 Republican presidential candidate despite his sixty-seven years. Duff's 550,000 majority over Rice was scarcely less impressive. "The people evidently wanted a change," reflected Guffey, "and they got it," but State Republican Chairman M. Harvey Taylor claimed the election was "a victory for Americanism over Communism."

DUFF AND PROGRESSIVE REPUBLICANISM

Twenty days before his term expired, Martin resigned and went off to Washington, and Lieutenant Governor John C. Bell, Jr., served as Pennsylvania's thirty-third governor until the inauguration of James H. Duff (1947–1951). Noting the "plague of industrial unrest" in his inaugural address, Duff called for "right" and "sincere" dealing among labor, management, and the public.

Some of Duff's ideas were enacted by the 1947 legislative session and represented a mix of mild progressivism and mild conservatism. The Duff administration restricted organized labor's capacity to strike and shaved away advantages it had won. The Legislature banned strikes not only by government employees but also by electric, gas, water, and steam-heat utilities employees, and required that their disputes with management be mediated and ultimately arbitrated. Duff approved a second law making it an unfair labor practice for nonemployees to picket a struck plant. The Legislature and Duff furthermore made strikers ineligible for unemployment compensation; declared secondary boycotts and jurisdictional strikes unfair labor practices; and allowed women to work a six-day, 48-hour week and 10-hour shifts either day or night; and lowered to eighteen the minimum age of women working night shifts. On the other hand, the Assembly increased minimum salaries for public school teachers (from $1,440 to $1,950 except in Philadelphia and Pittsburgh where they were increased to $2,175 a year) and local officials; codified much local legislation requiring in particular that all meetings of municipal agencies be open to the public and press except executive sessions, where no legislation could be enacted; appropriated nearly $90 million to expand overcrowded state mental hospitals and other welfare institutions; and broadened both the state and local tax base.

Perhaps the Pittsburgh package, permitting Pittsburgh and Allegheny County to reform and improve themselves, was the most significant legislation enacted by the 1947 session. Passed by a bipartisan majority and endorsed by Governor Duff, the Pittsburgh package permitted Allegheny County to attack its most serious problem, air pollution, by regulating railroads and building incinerators for its 129 municipalities; to improve its transportation through a transit and traffic commission; and to avoid future mistakes by giving the County Planning Commission control of subdivision plans in sprawling suburbs. The Legislature gave Pittsburgh a Parks and Recreation Department, permitted it to establish a Public Parking Authority, and broadened the tax base beyond real estate. "Permitted" is the key word in the Pittsburgh package; state authorities provided neither leadership nor money. Although the state built Point Park and partially financed the highway program through the gasoline tax, and although the Federal government both contributed heavily to highway construction and assumed full responsibility for flood control in the upper Ohio Valley, Pittsburgh and Allegheny County paid for most of their renaissance.

James H. Duff, Republican governor. (Historical
Society of Pennsylvania)

Duff hoped that the Pittsburgh package would be but the beginning of a revitalization
of local government, but his plan ran counter to the experience of both Republican and
Democratic administrations in the twentieth century, when the state acquired many of the
functions previously controlled by local government. By 1950 rural self-government had
disappeared with the state administering highways, police, health, recreation, and conservation. The second-class township essentially had been reduced to a road-maintenance unit
under the watchful eye of the state Department of Highways, and the county had lost
many of its responsibilities in the area of highways and law enforcement. In 1902 the state
budget was about $17 million, in 1919 it was $50 million for 2,710 officers and employees,
and in 1950 it was $500 million for 59,000 employees in twenty departments, ten indepen-
dent boards and commissions, and half a dozen other administrative agencies. Indeed the
state civil service had virtually doubled during the tenure of those haters of bureaucracy:
James, Martin, and Duff.

During 1948 Duff stressed his progressive brand of Republicanism. In February he
backed the European Recovery Plan (better known as the Marshall Plan) giving economic
aid to make Europe prosperous and to contain communism; and ten days later in a "hard-
hitting" address to Joseph R. Grundy's Pennsylvania Manufacturers Association (PMA)
he demanded that business—enjoying unprecedented profits—head off the inflationary
price-wage spiral by voluntarily rolling back prices. Deploring the recent unexpected steel
price rise, Duff pleaded with business to meet the inflationary crisis with "the same concerted
action" it showed "in prying off the price-control lid."

By June Duff disagreed with the Grundy–Martin–G. Mason Owlett–PMA wing of the party over who should be nominated at the Republican National Convention held in Philadelphia. Chaired by Duff, the seventy-three delegates planned to cast favorite-son ballots for Martin but disagreed on whom to support next. After conversations with Thomas E. Dewey, Martin decided not to stand as a favorite son, but both to nominate Dewey and to virtually assure his nomination by throwing him the forty-one votes that Martin personally controlled. Duff denounced Martin's "double cross," swore he would defeat the Grundy faction, and worked to head off the Dewey movement. Duff lost round one; the Republican convention nominated Dewey, who compensated the Grundy faction by allowing it to name Representative Hugh Scott, Jr., as Republican national chairman. In the ensuing campaign Duff, Martin, and Scott harmonized to seek a Republican victory. They carried Pennsylvania for Dewey, but Harry S. Truman—promising Federal action to attack economic and social problems—carried the nation, scoring the political upset of the century. Dewey's defeat dismayed Grundy Republicans (Scott was forced out as national chairman), but strengthened Duff who had conspicuously opposed Dewey's nomination.

By 1949 Duff's own administration belied his earlier hope to revitalize government at the local level. Conceiving the role of government as doing "the best for the most people," he fashioned his Pennsylvania Plan which involved much greater state participation than in the past in such areas as controlling stream pollution and managing public health, education, public housing, and welfare. The short 1949 General Assembly (only fifty-four legislative days) worked with dispatch, and Republican leaders in both houses cooperated with Governor Duff to get his program through. Despite its strength, the Democratic opposition in the House acted with becoming restraint since much of Duff's program elaborated legislation earlier introduced by the Democratic Little New Deal.

To bypass the constitutional limit on borrowing, the 1949 Legislature established authorities. The General State Authority (modeled on the 1935 authority of the same name) was empowered to borrow $175 million (by selling tax-exempt bonds) to construct, acquire, equip, and maintain a variety of public works including buildings, highways, and dams. The state would lease these facilities and pay for them in rentals; while the authority bonds were backed by state rentals, they were not secured by the full faith and credit of the commonwealth but by the nearest thing to it that Duff and the Legislature could devise. In addition, the Legislature created a state highway and bridge authority and enabled it to borrow up to $50 million for constructing and purchasing toll bridges.

The Legislature also authorized the further extension of the immensely successful Pennsylvania Turnpike. In 1940 the Legislature approved the extension from Harrisburg to Philadelphia and in 1941 the extension from Pittsburgh to Ohio, but work did not begin on these until 1948 and 1949, respectively, during the Duff administration. In 1949 the state authorized an extension from Pittsburgh to Erie and the Northeastern Extension to Scranton. After a bitter struggle, the Legislature refused to increase wear on the turnpike by raising the load limit of tractor-trailers from 45,000 to 60,000 pounds. Infuriated truckers staged a parkdown on the Pennsylvania Turnpike. Undaunted, Duff called for a crackdown on overloaded and speeding trucks "hitting at the group who are determined to defy the law and make the public like it."

The Legislature also recognized to a greater extent than in the past its social responsibilities. It increased unemployment, sickness, and death benefits under workmen's compensation, enabled the Department of Welfare to provide out-patient and clinical services for the mentally ill, established a camp for underprivileged children at Indiantown Gap (with 2,500 boys attending in 1949), and after some controversy passed Governor Duff's modest $15 million housing program to subsidize low-rental housing and to clear slums and renew urban areas. Finally the Legislature recognized more fully its obligation to education. Forty percent of the budget was earmarked for education, and approximately two-thirds of that sum ($200 million) subsidized teachers' salaries. The Legislature at last brought the state's 600,000 teachers under a uniform mandated salary schedule and ensured that all teachers would receive at least a $200 raise.

Progressive legislation, however modest, costs money, and Duff's ideas on taxation were less progressive than his laws. In late 1948 a special tax study committee created by the 1947 Legislature suggested a drastic revision of Pennsylvania's business tax structure, but Duff merely pushed a rise in the soft-drink and gasoline tax to finance his program.

Duff's mild progressivism did not revitalize Pennsylvania economy, although there were encouraging signs. The Department of Commerce surveyed 1,411 companies—all of whom employed over 100 persons—and conservatively estimated that in the three years 1946, 1947, and 1948 about $2 billion was spent on new plant expansion in Pennsylvania. The state industrial output valued at $18.6 billion in 1948 topped the previous high of $16.5 billion in 1947, while industrial employment rose 29,112 to 1,808,817 in 1948. By August 1949, however, Pennsylvania's leading industrial areas averaged a significant 13 percent drop in business activity from August 1948. And in a few years Pennsylvania would slip from its traditional second place among the industrial states of the Union.

At the close of 1949 Duff—easily the most popular Republican in Pennsylvania—announced his candidacy for the United States Senate seat held by Democrat Francis J. Myers. But Grundy, Martin, and Owlett had already declared for Representative John C. Kunkel of Harrisburg. Duff was in no mood to compromise. For more than thirty years the eighty-seven-year-old Grundy and the PMA, which he had founded, had been a power in the Republican party. Although the PMA was strong in rural county organizations, by late January 1950 Duff had gained the support of fifty-nine of the sixty-seven Republican county leaders. The Grundy leaders were willing to concede the senatorial nomination to Duff if he would give them the gubernatorial nomination, but Duff felt strong enough to make no concessions. Having achieved both national prominence and prestige in Pennsylvania as the leader of progressive Republican governors who wished to change their party from a party "of privilege" to a party "of service," Duff called for better public health but no socialized medicine; just farm income; care for the needy, aged, unemployed, and ill; affirmative world leadership; and conservation of natural resources. When Truman jestingly invited Duff to join the Democrats—and Duff's Republican enemies vehemently agreed he should show his true colors—Duff lashed out at the punitive taxation, deficit spending, and socialistic leanings of the Democratic party. He saved his choicest words, however, for the "selfish, baleful and unscrupulous" Grundy-Owlett faction. "In my opinion," Duff charged, "Grundy-Owlettism means government by a few, for the benefit of a few, at the expense of the public." Duff easily won the primary, while his gubernatorial selection, John S. Fine—the political dictator of Luzerne County for over twenty years—triumphed less impressively over Jay Cooke, a Philadelphia banker (as befitting the name) whom the Grundy faction supported. In his triumph Duff revenged his setback at the 1948 Republican convention and looked forward to controlling the Pennsylvania delegation at the 1952 convention.

Democrats were delighted at the flow of Republican blood. By selecting Senator Myers to succeed himself and by selecting the young, crusading Philadelphia city treasurer, Richardson Dilworth, for governor, Democrats were in an excellent position to capitalize on the Republican split. A marine hero in both World Wars and a great political campaigner, Dilworth led the 1949 revolution which upset the entrenched, corrupt Philadelphia Republican machine and attracted thousands of independent Republicans to the Democratic banner. Nevertheless the size of Duff's primary vote gave Democrats pause. Republican professionals furthermore closed ranks, supported the ticket, and ran a shrewd campaign. Duff coupled his progressive record as governor with attacks on the Truman administration for confusion, bungling, and social experimentation. Without Duff's blessing, Fine made peace with Cooke and the Grundy faction. They were capable of raising large political contributions, and Fine could ill afford to be without their help. Democrats carried Philadelphia and Pittsburgh for Myers and Dilworth (the first time a Democratic gubernatorial candidate had carried Philadelphia since the Civil War), but their margin was not enough to offset Republican strength in rural and small-town Pennsylvania.

FINE AND REPUBLICANS AT MIDCENTURY

Though he had been allied with both Pinchot and Duff, John S. Fine (1951–1955) was not renowned for progressivism. The son of an anthracite miner, he made no bones about being a politician's politician. "I like to give good government where I can, build up my organization, keep the confidence of the people, keep down the gripes, and refresh the organization with new blood." In many ways, however, Fine carried on Duff's progressive liberal Republicanism. The Legislature increased workmen's compensation liability payments 20 percent in 1951 and made further additions during the 1953 session. It also raised maximum weekly unemployment benefits from $25 to $30. When he failed to get a fair employment practices commission bill through the Legislature, Fine established the Governor's Industrial Race Relations Commission, composed of religious, business, labor, and civic leaders, which worked with local communities to eliminate discrimination. Fine also opened the state police to Negroes and ended segregation in the Pennsylvania National Guard. Expending almost 50 percent of its budget for public education, the Fine administration raised teachers' salaries about 20 percent, increased and equalized state aid to local school districts, and virtually doubled the appropriation to the Pennsylvania State University. It also granted state employees two 10 percent raises and a 40-hour week.

Rehabilitation was an important theme of Fine's administration. With his blessing, the General State Authority earmarked $2,120,000 to build a rehabilitation center to retrain injured workmen unable to return to their old jobs. His administration expanded the services of community mental health clinics, and during his tenure forty-eight buildings totaling almost 10,000 beds were added to the state mental hospital system. To rehabilitate alcoholics, he persuaded the 1953 Legislature to appropriate $500,000, a sum easily afforded since the Liquor Control Board yearly brought the state close to $90 million in profits and taxes. The spread of prison riots into Pennsylvania provoked Fine to appoint a commission of penologists headed by General Jacob L. Devers to suggest a system to end prison revolts. Eleven acts came out of the Devers Commission report, and prison administration was shifted from the Department of Welfare to the newly founded Bureau of Correction in the

Department of Justice. In addition to administrative reorganization, Fine's appointees to the Bureau of Correction were committed to the speedy rehabilitation of convicts.

The Fine administration was particularly active in public health. In 1948 the American Public Health Association ranked Pennsylvania among the lowest states in public health. During the campaign of 1950, Fine pledged Pennsylvanians the "finest health program of the Nation," affirmed his unalterable opposition to socialized medicine, and promised a new health code including a decentralized system that would bring health services closer to the public. Bipartisan majorities in the 1951 Legislature enacted nine public health laws embodying Fine's platform promises. State public health offices (90 percent of which had been filled by patronage appointments) were placed under civil service rules, a state advisory health board appointed by the governor offered guidance to the department's personnel, and scattered bureaus were consolidated. The cornerstone of Fine's reforms was the act establishing home rule in public health. This act, however, also established local option on public health since it gave a county or group of counties the authority to establish departments of health but did not insist that every county have one. Though containing genuine reforms, this legislation tended to avoid the commonwealth's responsibility for the health of all its citizens. In effect minimum standards required by state legislation were universally enforced, while some communities through their local ordinances and their boards of health enforced rigorous standards.

Like Martin and Duff, Fine emphasized public works. He eliminated almost all state dirt roads by surfacing and improving over 6,000 miles of road during his administration. Bridges, tunnels, parkways, and expressways for Philadelphia and Pittsburgh were built; and extension of the Pennsylvania Turnpike was continued.

Unlike his predecessors—James, Martin, and Duff—Fine pushed for a constitutional convention, for reapportionment, and for a new broad-based tax, all of which were necessary but unpopular. Fearing the worst in the changes a new constitution might entail, Pennsylvanians preferred not to tinker with the 1873 constitution. Influenced by their hostility to a graduated income tax, and by the opposition of the state Grange and other adamant groups, they rejected a 1953 referendum for a constitutional convention. At Fine's insistence, the Legislature reluctantly reapportioned districts of state representatives to take population shifts into account but left senatorial districts untouched. The Legislature (particularly the Democratic opposition) also refused to vote a mild, ungraded one-half of 1 percent income tax even though $100 million to $150 million additional revenue was needed to meet the rising cost of state government. Finally in December 1951, it passed an inadequate, "odorous" patchwork tax package. "I have been saying for ten months," Fine exclaimed, "and now repeat that 1953 must bring, no matter how unwelcome to all of us, an income, sales or mercantile tax, or any combination of them. It is inevitable. We cannot continue to compromise our tax difficulties at the expense of business." Indeed, to run the government, the state had to borrow $60 million.

When Fine in 1953 submitted a record biennial budget of $1,428,777,543, he also called for $157,202,397 in new taxes. Mindful of the recent fate of his income tax idea, Fine did not propose any specific tax but offered to cooperate with the Legislature in molding "the fairest possible tax program." The Legislature enacted a 1 percent sales tax for education, which enabled Fine to balance the budget but placed the onus of increasing taxes on Republicans. To offset the political disadvantage of the new tax, Fine boasted that the Pennsylvania budget, and therefore taxes, was only half that of New York and California, states with comparable populations. But bargains in public finance are as illusory as in private finance. Fine failed to mention that New Yorkers and Californians received proportionately more and better services from their governments, and that California by taxing and spending heavily for education had developed what was considered one of the greatest school systems and universities in the world.

With the nation involved in the cold war and in the hot Korean War (1950–1953), Fine shared Duff's fear of communism and the Soviet Union. In his farewell address in 1951, Duff had predicted war with Russia and dwelt on the possibility of a surprise atomic attack. He had insisted, however, that civilian defense was primarily a community responsibility. In his inaugural address, Fine promised to put Pennsylvania on a war footing, pledged thrifty government, and called for belt tightening and sacrifices. During this era of McCarthyism, the Legislature required all state and local government employees to take loyalty oaths, outlawed the Communist party, and enabled Pennsylvania to enter mutual military aid pacts with New York and New Jersey. Though he denied censorship was his objective, Fine added to the repressive atmosphere by ordering all state news releases, except routine ones, to be cleared through his office. Indeed, unlike Duff, Fine even supported Senator Joseph McCarthy in a speech to the Veterans of Foreign Wars.

Republican feuds continued. By the time of his election, Fine was reconciled with the Grundy group and alienated from Duff. When Duff left Harrisburg, Owlett and the PMA forces moved in. Fine needed both their money and support to get his program enacted. In August 1951, Owlett said Fine would chair the seventy-member Pennsylvania delegation to the 1952 Republican National Convention, but Duff, who had given up his own presidential aspirations, prepared to give the Grundy-Owlett group another "knock-down and drag-out" fight. While the Grundy forces leaned toward Harold E. Stassen, former Minnesota governor and president of the University of Pennsylvania, or Senator Robert A. Taft of Ohio, Duff was an early and leading supporter of General Dwight D. Eisenhower. In early 1952, however, observers agreed that Governor Fine, not Senator Duff, was the most powerful man in the Pennsylvania Republican party, and Fine's favorite presidential candidate was General Douglas MacArthur. Duff discovered that power in Pennsylvania depended more on control of county organizations than on popularity, which he had in abundance, or on being United States senator. Two fundamental changes had occurred since Cameron, Quay, and Penrose had run the state from the Senate. First, governors had relatively more and senators relatively less patronage with which to secure local political organizations. To serve society's needs, numerous state and Federal offices had been created, but the merit system had eliminated patronage faster in the Federal than in the state sector. Second, as local government atrophied, the state played a much larger role in local affairs than formerly, and the governor's capacity to formulate policies affecting local areas (and local parties) was enhanced.

As the Republican National Convention approached, front runners Eisenhower and Taft courted Fine, who controlled at least thirty-two delegates and made the cover of *Time* magazine as a possible president maker. Having extracted all the attention possible, Fine declared for Eisenhower; fifty-three delegates supported him while fifteen Grundy men remained loyal to Taft and two supported MacArthur. When the roll call was completed and Eisenhower lacked nine votes, Fine tried desperately to attract Chairman Joseph Martin's attention so that he could switch Pennsylvania's Taft and MacArthur votes to put Eisenhower over the top. But Martin gazed beyond the Pennsylvania delegation and gave the honor to an obscure Stassen leader from St. Paul named Warren Earl Burger. In the ensuing campaign, Eisenhower triumphed over Democratic nominee Adlai E. Stevenson, and Pennsylvania returned Edward Martin to the Senate. Portentous for the future, however, was the fact that Stevenson carried Philadelphia by 160,000 votes and that the rural vote saved Pennsylvania for the GOP. With the election over, a three-way Republican split became apparent. The Grundy-Owlett-PMA group hated Duff, who was supported by M. Harvey Taylor. Disliked by the extremes, Fine occupied a middle position. Rumors that Duff, chaffing in his relatively powerless roll as a freshman senator, planned with Eisenhower's blessing to run again for governor irritated his enemies. With Democrats increasing in Pittsburgh and Philadelphia, Republicans could ill afford factionalism. When the opening guns of the 1954 gubernatorial campaign sounded, their party was in trouble.

BIBLIOGRAPHY

On Arthur H. James, see the critical Burtt Evans and Samuel Botsford: "Pennsylvania after the New Deal," *New Republic* (May 6, 1940), pp. 599–601. Pennsylvania's contribution to World War II is covered in *Pennsylvania at War: 1941–1945* (1946); and in S. K. Stevens: "The Impact of the War on the Pennsylvania Economy," *Pennsylvania History,* vol.11 (1944), pp. 118–127.

Studies of the Martin, Duff, and Fine administrations are rare and have to be supplemented with newspaper accounts and with the following articles appearing in *Commonwealth: The Magazine for Pennsylvania:* Evan B. Alderfer: "Jobs in Pennsylvania Industries: Employment Returns to a Peacetime Pattern" (January 1947), pp. 8–9; "Employment in Pennsylvania" (August 1948), p. 22; H. F. Alderfer and Elizabeth Smedley: "The Legislative Harvest: A Record of the New State Laws—With Some Thoughts on Our Legislative Heritage" (July 1947), pp. 24–30, 32; "Mighty Pittsburgh Streamlines: City of Smog and Steel Maps Out a New Design for Living" (September 1947), pp. 2–6, 25–26, 28; M. Louise Rutherford: "Municipalities and the Labor Laws . . . " (October 1947), pp. 28–29; H. F. Alderfer and M. Nelson McGeary: "Pennsylvania Government: The Shape of Things Today and the Shape of Things to Come" (Summer 1950), pp. 20–21, 23; and "1949 Legislative Crop" (June 1949), pp. 26–28. Other useful articles are Robert Bendiner: "Outlook for November: Anything Goes in Pennsylvania," *Nation,* (Oct. 28, 1950), pp. 385–388; "Pennsylvania on the Band Wagon," *American Journal of Public Health* (March 1951), pp. 336–337; William S. White: "Senator Duff of the Eisenhower Team," *New York Times Magazine* (Nov. 11, 1951), pp. 17, 70–71; "Pennsylvania . . . Bosses, Not the People, Pick the Candidate," *Newsweek* (Apr. 21, 1952), pp. 28–29; "Two Men Can Determine the G.O.P. Nomination," *New Republic* (June 30, 1952), pp. 6, 17; "President Maker?" *Time* (June 30, 1952), pp. 18–21; and "Sweetheart Is Not the Name," *Time* (Oct. 26, 1953), p. 26. Two biased but useful pamphlets are *A Record of Achievement 1943–1945* (1946); and *A Record: Accomplishments of the Fine Administration* (1954). Also very useful is J. Roffe Wike: *The Pennsylvania Manufacturers' Association* (1960).

On the electoral base of both parties, see Walter Dean Burnham, *Critical Elections and the Mainsprings of American Politics* (1970).

CHAPTER TWENTY-SIX

Society in an Urban Age

Pennsylvania in the twentieth century has a remarkably diverse society. Though the growth of cities has dominated Pennsylvania society, and its citizens (whether dwelling in town or country) have adopted urban life styles, many Pennsylvanians do not conform to the behavioral patterns celebrated by television, press, radio, and motion pictures. The communications revolution has produced great conformity, but it has not homogenized all Pennsylvanians. Indeed not only have major groups such as the Amish and Negroes retained their singular identity, but the communications media have publicized and popularized the dress and behavior of nonconforming groups.

LIFE ON THE FARM

Twentieth-century Pennsylvania agriculture has been characterized by declining numbers of farmers, farms, and acres of improved cropland on one hand and by increased overall production on the other. In 1880 Pennsylvania had over 200,000 farms, totaling almost 20 million acres with over thirteen million improved acres, but by 1970 its farms had declined to 73,000 and its farmland to 10,585,000 acres with only 4,330,200 acres in improved cropland. Reflecting the declining number of farms, farm population has dropped from over one million in 1900 to 303,000 in 1970. The average Pennsylvania farm shrank from 117 acres in 1850 to 81 acres in 1925. But in recent years agriculture has undergone a profound revolution, which by 1970 had enlarged the average farm to 145 acres with 59 acres cultivated, while the total number of Pennsylvania farms continued to decline.

The apparent contradiction between shrinking farms and increasing production and investment is explained by a tremendous rise in output per unit, particularly during the post-World War II years. In the twentieth century, disease control and improved breeding, feeding, and management more than doubled the average yearly milk production per cow. Potato production shows the same sharp rise. From 1866 to 1870 the yield per acre was 86.6 bushels, from 1926 to 1930 it was 109.2 bushels, but from 1946 to 1950 it jumped to 213 bushels, and from 1965 to 1969 it rose to 340 bushels per acre. Wheat production follows the same pattern, but the growth in corn production while substantial has not been so striking. Utilizing intensive agriculture, Pennsylvania has risen above the national average for value of production per acre.

Through the 1960s Pennsylvania remained a productive agricultural state. Though it was thirty-second in size, in 1963 it ranked eighteenth in the value of farm products, and its investment in agriculture had grown to $4 billion. It possessed some of the most productive farmland in the nation. Lancaster, Chester, York, Bucks, and Berks counties were in 1949 among the country's 100 leading counties in value of farm products sold. In 1969 Pennsylvania led the nation in producing mushrooms; was third in sour cherries, maple syrup, and cut flowers; fourth in peaches; fifth in milk, eggs, apples, and grapes; seventh in tobacco; eighth in pears and sweet cherries; and tenth in hay and turkeys.

Pennsylvania farmers derived three times more income from animals than from crops. In 1968 livestock and livestock products accounted for 72 percent of Pennsylvania farmers' cash receipts ($689 million), while crops accounted for only 26 percent ($244 million). Government payments of $24 million (2 percent) brought Pennsylvania farm income to $957 million. Dairying produced 43 percent of the state's cash income from marketing in 1968, meat animals 15 percent, poultry products 15 percent, greenhouse and nursery products 10 percent, field crops 7 percent, and fruit and vegetables each 4 percent.

Farmers have increased their yield per unit by utilizing both technology and science. During and after World War I, Pennsylvania farmers replaced many horses with gasoline tractors, and the motor truck and the automobile eliminated more. By 1951 there were only one-fifth as many horses and mules in the state as there had been in 1915. Twentieth-century Pennsylvanians equipped with tractors have made wide use of grain combines, corn pickers, and other machines at a tremendous saving in man-hours. One man using the mechanical corn sheller, for instance, could accomplish a task that formerly required 100 men. Rivaling the coming of the tractor in importance was the tremendous increase in the use of electricity on farms made possible by the New Deal's Rural Electrification Administration. In 1920 only 30,669 Pennsylvania farm houses had electricity; 133,919 were equipped with it by 1950, enabling farmers to employ milking machines, chick brooders, refrigerators, pumps, tools, and lighting.

Science proved as useful to the farmer as technology, and state agencies, aided by the Federal government, played a crucial role in disseminating scientific information. After 1907 when the Pennsylvania State University's agricultural extension program was unified under a director, agriculture and rural living improved. In 1912 the university named Pennsylvania's first county agents; sixty counties had agents by 1920. The program was financed by Federal, state, and county governments. With the 1914 Smith-Lever Act, the Federal government established the Agricultural and Home Economics Extension Service on a national basis and provided funds that states could match. In addition the Pennsylvania Legislature in 1913 allowed a county to contribute to its extension program. Pennsylvania has been particularly fortunate in that its county agents, appointed as young men, have tended to make extension work their career. Floyd S. ("Dutch") Bucher, Lancaster County's first agent, served from 1913 to 1949, and Extension's second director, M. S. McDowell, served from 1912 to 1942. The recommendations of Agricultural Extension have increased crops, counteracted soil erosion, and helped farmers plan efficient farm buildings. One of the most impressive accomplishments of Agricultural Extension has been its 4-H Club program, which has helped answer the farmers' plaintive question, "How can we keep our boys and girls on the farm?" Beginning about 1914 these clubs have encouraged young people to appreciate farming as a career and have instructed them in agricultural techniques, homemaking skills, and health habits.

Fairs (particularly the State Farm Show) also instructed farmers in technological and scientific developments. The Pennsylvania Department of Agriculture, Pennsylvania State University, and state farm organizations sponsored the first State Farm Show in 1917, and it soon became a yearly institution. Governor John S. Fisher dedicated permanent grounds and buildings at Harrisburg during the 1931 show, which 146,000 attended. The Pennsylvania Farm Show, the largest and most representative in the country, has remained educational, and farm children participate in exhibitions, contests, and entertainment.

Many state and local regulations—though initially resisted by farmers—have improved the quality of milk produced and have been beneficial to Pennsylvania dairymen. Vigorous enforcement by the Pennsylvania Department of Agriculture of the 1909 Milk Adulteration Law and subsequent legislation eliminated much adulteration, but it was not until the 1930s that the consumer could be certain he was drinking pure milk. Pasteurized milk first came into favor about 1905 and was commonly used by 1925. By heating milk, tuberculosis, typhoid, undulant fever, dysentary, and diptheria germs are destroyed as well as 90 percent of the harmless bacteria. Victory over bovine tuberculosis came in 1936 when only one-half of 1 percent of Pennsylvania's 1,500,000 cattle reacted to the tuberculin test. Many farmers fearful that their herds might be infected, had opposed the tuberculin test. The most bitter opposition was in Lancaster and adjacent counties, where farmers formed the Protective Association in 1926 to contest a Lancaster ordinance demanding that its milk come from tuberculin-tested, disease-free herds. The Pennsylvania Supreme Court upheld the ordinance in 1927 and established the right of a municipality to set a standard for milk sold within its boundary. The *Pennsylvania Farmer* reported in 1929 that in Lancaster "there has been a noticeable decrease in the deaths of children under two years of age, due to tuberculosis."

Besides regulating the production and marketing of milk to ensure that the consumer purchases an unadulterated, disease-free product, the government has also regulated milk prices. Because milk production fluctuates (40 percent more milk is produced in June than in November), its price if not regulated would also fluctuate. Pennsylvanians tolerated these price changes until the Great Depression of the 1930s when both Federal and state governments experimented with price fixing. In 1933 the Federal Agricultural Adjustment Administration began setting minimum milk prices for both producers and consumers, and the Pinchot administration created the temporary Milk Control Board empowered to fix minimum wholesale and retail prices. With both the AAA and the Milk Control Board regulating milk prices and production, and with farmers and distributors hostile to regulation by either agency, conflict and chaos were inevitable. Confusion continued in Pennsylvania after the United States Supreme Court declared the AAA unconstitutional in January 1936. Finally on April 28, 1937, the Earle administration created the permanent, effective Milk

Control Commission and gave it jurisdiction over the production and marketing of milk. Though dubbed socialization and opposed by individual producers and by Pennsylvania's largest farm organization, the state Grange, control received support from large producer cooperatives and consumers. In time, however, small dairy farmers complained that both their interests and those of the consumer were forgotten while large-scale producers dominated the Milk Control Commission.

Although science and technology increased production and improved the quality of farm life, adequate medical care for rural Pennsylvanians has been a persistent problem. The ratio of country doctors to rural population decreased 20 percent in the first quarter of the twentieth century. In 1917 a joint committee of the American Medical Association and the National Council on Education reported: "Country school children are from three to fourteen percent more unhealthy than city children. In every health item, as lungs, heart, anemia, and nutrition, the country child is more defective than the child raised in the city." Thirty years later a survey of representative districts of rural Pennsylvania concluded: "Rural people are ill to about the same extent as urban people, but their proportion of illnesses not attended by a physician is about twice that of urban people. . . . They use a hospital about two-thirds as often. . . . The school health examinations found defects more frequent in rural children, and a smaller per cent of these defects had been corrected." Inadequate, monotonous diets, lack of sewage-disposal systems, contaminated water supplies, few doctors, and fewer medical facilities accounted for the poorer health of farm people. Throughout the nation in the midtwentieth century, metropolitan counties had twice the number of doctors per 100,000 residents as rural counties, and the child born in a metropolitan county had a better chance of survival than the child born in a rural county. To compound the problem, machines make farming a dangerous occupation; 22 percent more work accidents occur in United States farm areas than in cities. Improved roads, however, have made urban medical facilities more accessible to farmers.

Better roads in the twentieth century also have made possible improved, consolidated rural schools. Farmers, however, resisted consolidation (dubbed "Fineganizing" in reference to its chief advocate Thomas E. Finegan, an energetic superintendent of the State Department of Public Instruction from 1919 to 1923). Few districts provided adequate transportation until after 1920; and farmers, valuing home rule in school administration more than improved education through consolidation, clung to the little red schoolhouse throughout the next decade. By 1939 Pennsylvania had combined 4,000 one-room schools into 675 consolidated schools, but in counties where Pennsylvania German farmers—particularly sectarians—predominated, consolidation lagged. By midcentury, however, the one-room schoolhouse was largely eliminated. Better schools are an example of how the standard of living of the average farmer has improved through the years, of how improvements in transportation and communications have integrated him into a predominantly urban society.

On the other hand, carrying a bit of yesterday into today and tomorrow, the Amish continue living as their fathers and grandfathers lived before them. Near Lancaster, the Old Order Amish and the Old Order Mennonites formed what was probably the largest core of extremely orthodox sectarians in the United States. Largely displacing other farmers in the area, these sectarians proved that noncompromising factions are more stable than groups willing to yield old disciplines.

The Amish are distinguished from the Mennonites by their strict enforcement of the

Meidung, or shunning of excommunicated members. The command to shun an excommunicated member, even though he might be husband or child, has kept Amish groups resistant to change, but it has led to the splintering of already splintered groups until in some instances all that remains is a sliver made up of two families. The most splintered Amish community lies between Jacks and Stone mountains in the Kishacoquillas Valley in Mifflin County. In the 1960s this 30-mile-long valley contained five Amish groups and five additional Mennonite-related groups, all of which originated from an Amish group from southeastern Pennsylvania which settled in the valley in 1791. These groups ranked themselves according to their assimilation into the American culture on a low- to high-church scale, with the low church retaining traditions while the high church was more subject to change.

With farms bordering the Pennsylvania Turnpike, the Penn Central Railroad, and the Lincoln Highway, House Amish manage to live in a bygone era, spurning modern communications, pumping their water with waterwheels, lighting their homes with kerosene lamps, and using for farm chores nothing more modern than multipurpose, one-cylinder gasoline engines. Even though they think and talk religion a great deal, most Amish worship only every other Sunday because that is what their forebears did. House Amish take turns being host to the congregation. Benches are moved from home to home, and houses are constructed so that by opening partitions the downstairs becomes one huge room. After a morning of preaching in High German and hymn singing in "Dutch," dinner is served to the entire congregation. Small-farm-minded and largely self-sufficient in their food supply, the Amish are known for their good food and hearty appetites.

Although the Amish do not seek converts and make it almost impossible for outsiders to join them, their ranks have been steadily enlarged by natural increase. Despite a high rate of infant mortality, similar to that experienced in rural areas in the nineteenth century, Amish families recently averaged from seven to nine children, and at their death some Amish patriarchs have had as many as 400 living descendents. Like their parents and grandparents before them, most Amish children will not break the traditions that bind them to their way of life. But no society, not even that of the Amish, can remain static. Their world is changing, but changing so slowly that for many generations to come the Amish will be emulating nineteenth-century farm life in the midst of modern, urban Pennsylvania.

THE MEGALOPOLIS

Although Philadelphia and Pittsburgh grew rapidly until 1920, their subsequent relatively static population can be misleading. Cities, towns, and villages surrounding these cities have grown tremendously, creating metropolitan districts of vastly greater areas and populations than the city limits of either would indicate. Philadelphia in 1970 had a population of 1,949,000, while Greater Philadelphia numbered 4,818,000; Pittsburgh had 520,000, while Greater Pittsburgh had 2,401,000. Other important urban localities include the Scranton and Wilkes-Barre area, the Allentown-Bethlehem area, and the outgrowths of Erie, Harrisburg, and Reading.

To migrants from abroad and from rural areas, the twentieth-century metropolis has remained every bit as attractive as the nineteenth-century city. The economic, social, and cultural opportunities of rural Pennsylvania cannot compete with the offerings of twentieth-century urban areas. Metropolitan areas boast a variety of interesting, well-paying jobs,

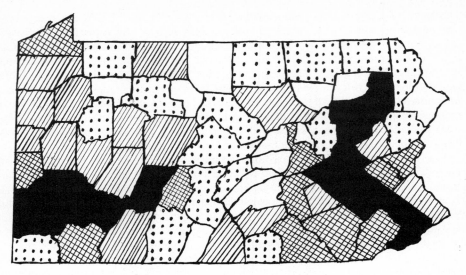

Population by county, 1930.

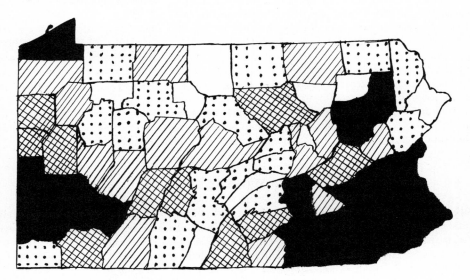

Population by county, 1970.

 Less than 25,000
25,000 to 50,000
50,000 to 100,000
100,000 to 200,000
More than 200,000

wide opportunities for fellowship with people of similar background or outlook, world-renowned institutions dedicated to scholarship, music, and the fine arts, and recreational pur-
suits different from and more interesting to many people than those offered by rural areas.
For example, Pennsylvania cities have had great major-league baseball. The Pittsburgh
Pirates sparked by their incomparable shortstop John ("Honus") Wagner won the National
League pennant in 1901, 1902, and 1903; and Connie Mack's Philadelphia Athletics had
incredible pitching in Eddie Plank (the pride of Gettysburg College) and the eccentric
George ("Rube") Waddell whose blazing fast ball and big curve enabled him to hold the
strikeout record for forty-two years. From 1911 to 1917 Philadelphians could see Grover
Cleveland Alexander pitch for the Phillies, and from 1929 to 1931 they could watch Mack's
Athletics win pennants with one of baseball's greatest teams. In the 1950s and 1960s the
Phillies had a great pitcher in Robin Roberts, while the Pirates had a superb outfielder in
Roberto Clemente, who led them to World Series victories in 1960 and 1971.

Just as the attractions of the city remained basically the same from late-nineteenth to
late-twentieth century, its functions and its problems did not appreciably alter. It continued
to feed, clothe, and house its residents, while it manufactured and marketed goods and
provided professional services for those living in its trading area. Pennsylvania cities in the
twentieth century improved housing, plumbing, drinking water, sewage systems, garbage
collection, police and fire protection, and transportation facilities and provided more parks,
playgrounds, and paved streets. Increases in population, however, offset many of these gains,
leaving the metropolis of the 1970s with chronic problems in most of these areas.

Housing remained the city's most pressing problem. Inflation following World War I
ended the speculative building of low-income housing. That factor, when coupled with the
deterioration of existing housing, produced a crisis in the 1920s that was still acute in the
1970s. Pittsburgh is a case in point. A real property inventory of Allegheny County in 1934
showed that out of 310,000 dwelling units, 45,000 (15 percent) were in buildings needing
major repairs and 10,000 (3 percent) were in structures unfit for use. By 1960 census data
revealed that of 503,006 Allegheny County dwelling units 67,809 (13.5 percent) were dete-
riorating, 17,444 (3 percent) were dilapidated, and 27,065 (5 percent) were sound but without
plumbing. With an existing shortage, however, mass housing could not be bettered by enforcing strict housing codes and demolishing unfit dwellings.

The Great Depression convinced some of Pittsburgh's business and professional leaders
that government would have to abandon its negative, regulatory role and intervene to provide adequate housing. The Buhl Foundation created Chatham Village to prove that if the
building industry would reorganize and mass-produce an entire neighborhood, rather than
scattered houses, costs would be cut and the environment improved. Chatham Village,
housing white-collar workers for a modest rent, was an architectural and economic success,
but it failed to spark major changes in the building industry. Aware by 1937 that more than
good examples were necessary, Pittsburgh established a housing authority, and by 1944
Federal funds had built eight housing projects, designed for low-income families and war
workers, and had established a precedent for government involvement in Pittsburgh's
renaissance.

While transforming the Golden Triangle, Pittsburgh's renaissance accentuated its housing
problem. The renaissance was in effect a reverse welfare state with public power promoting
private economic ends. Consequently Roy Lubove found that the major impact of urban
renewal in Pittsburgh was to "solidify its position as one of the nation's three leading ad-

ministrative centers of corporate headquarters" and to stabilize the city's supply of high-level jobs. During Pittsburgh's renaissance, urban renewal replaced thousands of low-income housing units primarily with commercial, industrial, and civic structures and high-rent apartments.

Hardships imposed by relocation spurred Pittsburgh in 1957 to establish the Allegheny Council to Improve Our Neighborhoods-Housing (ACTION-Housing). A business-oriented, voluntary, nonprofit agency, ACTION-Housing wished to utilize managerial and professional experts, to mobilize private capital, and to obtain available government aid to help solve the housing problem. In 1959 it set up the revolving Pittsburgh Development Fund (paying 4 percent dividends) to which foundations, corporations, and banks subscribed over $1.5 million by 1961. Utilizing the Development Fund and Federal Housing Authority mortgage insurance, ACTION-Housing sponsored during its first decade over $13 million (1,001 units) in new, moderate-cost housing. By experimenting with cluster housing in East Hills Park, ACTION-Housing achieved superior design while cutting costs 40 percent.

By the late 1960s ACTION-Housing had shifted its emphasis to rehabilitation. This change reflected a new concern with social as well as physical objectives. Utilizing the Economic Opportunity Act of 1964, ACTION-Housing developed a self-help, home-improvement program for low-income families on Wooster and Linton streets in the Hill District. This program was extended to other neighborhoods in 1966. Under the 1965 Housing Act (providing 3 percent interest mortgage money for nonprofit, FHA-approved housing rehabilitation), ACTION-Housing through the Development Fund rehabilitated a block on Cora Street in Homewood-Brushton. These successes led Pittsburgh's business leaders to establish in 1968 the Allegheny Housing Rehabilitation Corporation (AHRCO), and the growing concern with preserving neighborhood integrity led them to specify that six of nineteen executive committee members were to represent the community interest. ACTION-Housing also sought to infuse a sense of community and involvement.

The twentieth-century urban transportation problem is no closer to solution than the housing problem. Subway and elevated lines were built in Philadelphia, but they were basically rapid-transit links in a system of street surface transit. Despite the growth of Greater Philadelphia during the last few decades, the number of daily passengers using its public transportation has remained relatively constant. Pittsburgh's mass-transit system, consisting entirely of street surface lines, was not consolidated until the 1960s. The 1949 *Mass Transportation Report,* sponsored by the prime movers of the renaissance, condemned inept private transit management in Pittsburgh that led to "duplication of routes, competition, and a multiplicity of types, sizes and ages of equipment." The report recommended that buses be substituted for streetcars and that ownership and management be consolidated. By 1964 the Port Authority Transit owned the transit system and in 1967 it began replacing trolley cars with buses.

In the middle twentieth century, Americans prefer the automobile to public transportation. Carrying few passengers and requiring much space, automobiles have proved to be inefficient, and they accentuate many urban problems. Nevertheless in post-World War II years, with the building of Philadelphia's Schuylkill Expressway, Pittsburgh's Penn-Lincoln Parkway, and other major arteries, many commuters have abandoned public transportation for private automobiles. Endangering the life, character, and essence of cities with superhighways, congested streets, parking lots, and polluted air, automobiles not only fail to provide adequate urban transportation but threaten to destroy the cities themselves.

The Delaware River Port Authority, however, introduced an attractive alternative to the automobile in 1969 when it opened its high-speed transit line between Lindenwold, New Jersey, and downtown Philadelphia. Its clean, efficient trains made the 14.4 mile run in 22 minutes, one-third the normal driving time, and induced thousands to take the train for 60 cents and leave their cars at home. Unlike existing railroads which were saddled with labor "manning" union contracts, this first new suburban commuter line in fifteen years was able to utilize automated equipment to eliminate labor and cut costs. The authority further-more imaginatively financed construction of the $94 million system by doubling tolls on the Benjamin Franklin and Walt Whitman bridges. Clearly technology, if implemented on a grand scale, can help solve the transportation problem, but the question remains whether society will follow this pioneering effort and opt for high-speed transit systems.

While the functions and problems of cities show continuity from the nineteenth to the twentieth century, a comparative study of Philadelphia in 1774, 1860, and 1930 by Sam Bass Warner, Jr., reveals some changes. The percentage of Philadelphians working in manufactur-ing and mechanical industries declined from 54.9 percent in 1860 to 45.3 percent in 1930, and there was a corresponding rise in the percentage working in professions, government, commerce, and services.

Residential patterns sharply changed from 1860 to 1930. In 1860 the poor tended to settle in the outskirts where land was cheap, rather than at the core of the city, but by 1930 old, cheap housing at the core had reversed that pattern, and the poverty-stricken recent immi-grants — Italians, Poles, Russians, and Negroes — were ringed by older-stock homeowners and middle-income renters. "By the twentieth century," Warner observes, "income, ethnic, and racial segregation had become . . . characteristic of the giant industrial metropolis." Furthermore, late-nineteenth-century improvements in transportation no longer required people to cluster near their work and reorganized the residential patterns of twentieth-century Philadelphia not by industry but according to class, race, or ethnic background. In 1930 most well-paid, skilled workers lived throughout the city, while semiskilled and unskilled laborers, mostly Negroes and recent immigrants, lived in low-rent districts in the city's core.

Industrialism also increased the number of persons employed in an average establishment. In 1860 the figure was 15.6, while in 1930 it was 52.6 with three-quarters of Philadelphia's workers laboring in groups of fiteen or more. The importance of the work group in the life of the worker can scarcely be exaggerated. It influences his social, political, and cultural attitudes, and its development, Warner argues, explains in part "the rise and decline of unions and strikes, epidemics of street violence, and the development of an isolated mill-town culture in one quarter of Philadelphia as opposed to the suburban-downtown white-collar culture of another quarter." By 1930 northeast Philadelphia, the city's workshop, with its factories surrounded by workers' homes, fostered an organized, disciplined, group-struc-tured way of life. Its residents found jobs and recreation and acquired social and political attitudes through their craft unions, benefit associations, fraternal orders, ethnic organi-zations, athletic clubs, and local taverns. South Philadelphia, however, the refuge of recent immigrants, Negroes, and the poor, was more parochial and was divided into ghettos or neighborhoods, where unskilled workers depended on churches and ethnic societies but in particular on relatives and friendships formed in the gang, street, and saloon. In contrast, west and northwest Philadelphia residents commuted to the downtown area to shop and to work in corporation offices or in businesses or professions servicing the metropolitan area.

With friends scattered throughout suburbia, the commuter was more free and more isolated than the mill-town dweller, and he developed a more intense, private family life.

The lot of the average urban dweller improved in the twentieth century with technological innovations more often proving a blessing than a curse. An intensive interdisciplinary study of Norristown from 1900 to 1950 revealed that technological change did not seriously disorganize social life. New machinery in local plants did not cause unemployment, and although the migration of industries (cigar making in the twenties, textiles in the fifties) threw men out of work, good jobs in other industries were available. These new jobs, in growing iron and steel, metal-fabricating, stone and clay, plastics and rubber industries, made workers more loyal to their community than to their occupation. Through legislation and unions, technology made urban dwellers more secure. It eliminated child labor, cut the work week from 60 hours in 1900 to 40 hours in the 1930s, doubled real wages from 1899 to 1950, and by midcentury provided numerous fringe benefits.

BLACK URBANITES

During the twentieth century relatively few Negroes moved from the ghetto at the core of the city to its more affluent suburban ring. The vast majority of blacks were confronted by a cycle of economic, social, and cultural privation. The never-ending round of unemployment, low income, slum housing, high crime rate, bad health, and poor education made hopelessness dominant. Despair was rooted in facts, not misconceptions, in reality, not illusions. Change and progress had been offset by the growing complexity of racial problems. The influx of Southern migrants, particularly during World War I and the 1920s, actually increased segregation in Philadelphia schools, restaurants, theaters, and churches, causing established Negro residents to resent the newcomers who complicated life by arousing latent white hostility. In 1890 blacks lived in the center city in an area less segregated than the ghettos of the 1970s. Even in the Seventh Ward, blacks composed less than 30 percent of the people, but in the 1970s almost exclusively black areas existed in north, west, and south Philadelphia. Although some whites, tired of commuting and sick of suburban living, had returned to the inner city, displacing older Negro residents including many in the Seventh Ward, the black population of Philadelphia continued to grow. Blacks accounted for 26 percent of Philadelphia's population in 1960 and 34 percent (653,791) in 1970, while Pittsburgh in 1970 was 22 percent black (104,904). By 1970, however, significant numbers of Negroes, particularly in the twenty to thirty age range, did move into suburban towns, with the ironic result that the city's segregational patterns reappeared in the suburbs.

Negroes in Pennsylvania cities have consistently lived in inferior housing. The Pittsburgh Survey in 1907 and 1908 discovered that the "interiors of very many of the houses in which Negroes live were out of repair—paper torn off, plastering coming down, and windows broken." A 1934 study of 4,245 black Pittsburgh families revealed that "lodgers complicated the situation in one third of the homes. . . . Frequently six or more persons shared a bedroom; occasionally they shared the same bed. In fact, almost one half of all persons seen shared their room with two or more people." It was usual for two or three families to share toilet and water facilities, but instances were known "where nine families used the same toilet, and where fourteen families secured their water from a single tap in the backyard." Two percent of the families had an outside water supply and 15 percent had outdoor toilets,

40 percent were without bathing facilities, 55 percent shared their water supply, and 65 percent shared their toilet. In 1934 one-third of the Hill District dwellings were without hot water and 83 percent had no furnace-type heating. In 1940 approximately 84 percent of Pittsburgh's Negroes lived in substandard housing, and in 1968, after two decades of unprecedented prosperity for the larger society, that figure was still two-thirds for all non-white families living in center cities in the United States.

Few doors in Pittsburgh were open to Negroes. Although more than twice as many blacks as whites died of tuberculosis in 1928, the Tuberculosis League of the Pittsburgh Hospital rarely admitted Negroes and "never had more than one at a time." Affected Negroes were treated in a dispensary and their children were helped in the Open Air School. Negro physicians could not practice in the city's thirty-five hospitals in 1930, and only three out of nearly fifty eligible blacks had won that privilege by 1938. Of thirteen Hill District elementary schools in 1928, only two were rated physically adequate by the Pittsburgh Board of Education. Black students were not highly motivated, for diligence made few of their dreams come true. Virtually all aspired to be professional, white-collar, or skilled workers, but the mathematical chance of realizing their aspirations was small. A 1928 study of 274 black high school girls shows that 20 percent wanted to be stenographers and 20 percent teachers, but of 282 employed black high school girls 36 percent were doing general housework and 20 percent were maids. As late as 1938 teaching and medical careers were virtually closed to black Pittsburghers. No Allegheny County hospital accepted Negro interns or nurses for training. From 1915 to 1938 the University of Pittsburgh Medical School, which received substantial state support, did not graduate a single Negro physician. By 1940 Negroes held only five permanent, fourteen substitute, and twenty-three evening positions in the Pittsburgh school system.

Ironically the corrupt and inefficient spoils system integrated society more than did the pure and efficient merit system. Although black political power became significant in the twentieth century, the heritage of reform placed many civil service jobs beyond the grasp of poorly educated blacks and cut off an important avenue of social mobility. If twentieth-century police forces had been as heavily inundated with Negroes as nineteenth-century police departments were with Irish, a significant source of racial friction might have been removed.

The Horatio Alger story has been a meaningless myth for the black migrant. He has found higher wages than he earned down South, but neither he nor his children have progressed much beyond this initial advance. Black men have been chiefly employed as unskilled laborers in the iron and steel, mining and construction industries and as porters, janitors, and messengers; and black women have been primarily employed as domestics.

Genuine breakthroughs began in the 1940s. The Federal Fair Employment Practices Committee forbade discrimination in World War II defense industries. During the 1950s the percentage of Philadelphia blacks in white-collar employment rose sharply, with a 59 percent increase for men and a 222 percent increase for women. In the professions the rise was 46 percent for males and 91 percent for females, and in sales work, 31 percent for men and 88 percent for women. Percentage rates of increase, however, are misleading when the base figures are small. Negro impatience for skilled, higher-paying jobs came to a head in Pittsburgh during the summer of 1969 when nearly a thousand demonstrating blacks clashed with white construction workers and subsequently won an agreement to have more blacks employed in the building trades. In September 1969, the Nixon administration instituted the

"Philadelphia plan" setting minority hiring guidelines for six skilled construction crafts on federally assisted projects in that city. In July 1970, Harrisburg along with seventy-two other cities was ordered to hire more black construction workers or be confronted with a federally imposed quota system. When by July 1970 neither the voluntary Pittsburgh agreement nor the imposed Philadelphia plan had put additional blacks on construction jobs, Nixon's Department of Labor moved to sue contractors.

Despite progress since the 1890s, racial problems had multiplied by the 1970s. Though residential patterns had changed, Philadelphia's Negro population was more segregated, de facto school segregation was the rule, housing and living conditions had remained deplorable, and the ghetto milieu encouraged crime rather than scholarship. DuBois had noted that society's failure to advance the educated or hard-working Negro created an environment of "excuse and listless despair"; that mood still prevailed. The economic dreams of the average black were similar to those of the average white and far outran the twentieth-century reality of slums, unskilled labor, unemployment, and inferior schools. Though advances had been made in Pennsylvania, black unemployment was consistently higher than that of whites (7.3 percent as compared to 4.2 percent in 1970); and though black businesses in Philadelphia had grown from 300 in 1896 to 4,000 in 1964, they remained small and marginal.

The reasons for the riot of Philadelphia Negroes in August 1964, emphasize America's failure to solve its most pressing problem. With little hope for the future, the ghetto Negro felt despair, frustration, and anger. The riot began at an intersection in north Philadelphia's "Jungle" (where almost two thousand persons lived on each block and where the city's greatest occurrence of crime, disease, unemployment, and poverty was located) when an intoxicated, quarreling couple impeded traffic by refusing to allow police to move their stalled car. The riot killed 2 people, wounded 339, and destroyed $3 million in property. Most observers agreed with Andrew Freeman, executive director of the Philadelphia Urban League, who blamed the riot on deep economic injustices. In addition there were the dislocations caused by urban renewal, or as many blacks called it "Negro removal." Under the Urban Renewal Act of 1949, displaced persons were to be relocated, but in north Philadelphia one middle-class housing development alone displaced more than twenty thousand residents (three-quarters of whom were poor Negroes), and fourteen thousand of them moved into homes as inadequate as those they had been forced to vacate. Urban renewal had the effect of suddenly crowding and degrading the adjacent area. After a study of the 1964 Philadelphia riot, Lenora E. Berson concluded that only a massive five-point Federal, state, and local program for better education, greater employment, better housing, and improvement in both merchant-consumer and police-community relations could prevent future riots.

By the late 1960s militant blacks passionately represented America's urban Negroes. Among these was William ("Bouie") Hayden who told Pittsburgh's civic leaders in 1968:

> I have spoken to you a lot of times in hatred and anger, and you have not heard me. Well, you had better hear me today. . . . [I'm] from Nigger Hell and I know what's happening. If you won't listen to me when I make an appeal for the Negroes, because you have no concern for the Negro, listen to me when I make an appeal for America. You claim you love America. Well, we love America. But you're driving us back and you're making a Samson out of us, and we are going to pull down the pillars. . . . And then you think we have no right to ask for something. Is it too much to ask you to grant us human dignity? Should we be put down and shot to death for this request? If so, you can aim your gun. What the hell do you think we care about dying if you gonna deny us the right to live?

BIBLIOGRAPHY

For Pennsylvania agricultural statistics, see E. L. Gasteiger and D. O. Boster: *Pennsylvania Agricultural Statistics, 1866–1950* (1954); and Pennsylvania Department of Agriculture Crop Reporting Service: *Pennsylvania Crop and Livestock Annual Summary, 1969* (1970). The major source on Pennsylvania rural life and agriculture is Stevenson Whitcomb Fletcher: *Pennsylvania Agriculture and Country Life, 1840–1940* (1955). See also Norman M. Eberly: "Two Score Years of Extension," *Pennsylvania Farmer* (Jan. 10, 1948), pp. 10, 12, 14, 55. A valuable volume compiling articles on various phases of rural life is *A Place to Live: The Yearbook of Agriculture, 1963* (1963).

Especially useful on the Amish is John A. Hostetler: *Amish Society* (1963). Also useful are William I. Schreiber: *Our Amish Neighbors* (1962); Charles S. Rice and Rollin C. Steinmetz: *The Amish Year* (1956); and Walter M. Kollmorgen: "The Agricultural Stability of the Old Order Amish and Old Order Mennonites of Lancaster County, Pennsylvania," *American Journal of Sociology,* vol. 49 (1943), pp. 233–241.

For urban developments, see Roy Lubove: *Twentieth Century Pittsburgh: Government, Business, and Environmental Change* (1969); E. Digby Baltzell: *Philadelphia Gentlemen: The Making of a National Upper Class* (1958); Sam Bass Warner, Jr.: *The Private City: Philadelphia in Three Periods of Its Growth* (1968), and "If All the World Were Philadelphia: A Scaffolding for Urban History, 1774–1930," *American Historical Review,* vol. 74 (1968), pp. 26–43; Sidney Goldstein: *The Norristown Study: An Experiment in Interdisciplinary Research Training* (1961).

On Pittsburgh Negroes, see Paul U. Kellogg (ed.): *The Pittsburgh Survey,* 6 vols. (1909–1914); Abraham Epstein: *The Negro Migrant in Pittsburgh* (1918); Ira D. Reid: *Social Conditions of the Negro in the Hill District of Pittsburgh* (1930); Philip Klein: *A Social Study of Pittsburgh: Community Problems and Social Services of Allegheny County* (1938); Elsie Witchen: *Tuberculosis and the Negro in Pittsburgh* (1934); and Miriam Rosenbloom: "An Outline of the History of the Negro in the Pittsburgh Area" (master's thesis, University of Pittsburgh, 1945).

On Philadelphia Negroes, see W. E. B. DuBois: *The Philadelphia Negro: A Social Study,* with an introduction by E. Digby Baltzell (1967); John A. Saunders: *100 Years after Emancipation (History of the Philadelphia Negro, 1787–1963)* (1963); Roger D. Abrahams: *Deep Down in the Jungle . . . : Negro Narrative Folklore from the Streets of Philadelphia* (1964); and Federal Works Progress Administration for Pennsylvania: *Report of Philadelphia Real Property Survey 1934: Colored Housing,* vol. 1 (Project 4744). For information on the 1964 riot, see Lenora E. Berson: *Case Study of a Riot: The Philadelphia Story* (1966); and *Report of the National Advisory Commission on Civil Disorders* (1968).

CHAPTER TWENTY-SEVEN

A Two-party State

The relative economic decline of Pennsylvania during the post-World War II years formed the overshadowing, ominous background for the emergence of a two-party system. Though Pennsylvania remained the second manufacturing state as late as 1947, it slipped to third place in 1954 and fifth place in 1958. With sick and dying major industries creating high unemployment rates and with the Philadelphia machine refusing to mend its ways, many Republicans abandoned their party. Unhampered by laissez-faire and states'-rights notions, Democrats not only utilized the state government but also urged the Federal government with its great fiscal power to help solve Pennsylvania's economic and social problems. When the Republicans returned, they continued the use of state and Federal power in economic and social sectors.

Primarily because industry begets industry, Pennsylvania's economic ills could be alleviated by judicious Federal and state aid. Not only are factories and machinery available in an industrial area but also markets, transportation, banking facilities, and most important, a pool of skilled labor. In this way, the momentum initially derived from coal could be sustained by newer industries, even those unconnected with coal. Furthermore industries that migrate to a source of raw materials or to a pool of cheap, unskilled labor frequently are those that add little value to the commodity, while those attracted by skilled labor and elaborate technology enhance the value of the end product. State and Federal prodding enabled industry in midtwentieth-century Pennsylvania to coast to a remarkable degree on the momentum of its late nineteenth-century surge.

The two-party stance helped Pennsylvania secure Federal favors, since the national leaders of both parties sought to win its important block of electoral votes, and made its politicians more powerful. Governor Scranton contended for the 1964 presidential nomination; Nixon considered Governor Shafer as his 1968 running mate; Senator Clark was a national leader in advocating arms control, congressional reorganization, foreign aid, and jobs for the jobless; and Senator Scott in 1969 became the leader of Senate Republicans.

DEMOCRATIC UPHEAVAL

The key to the Democratic resurgence in Pennsylvania was the Philadelphia political revolution, which transformed a Republican stronghold into a Democratic citadel. Although after 1934 Democrats ran well in Catholic, working-class (particularly manufacturing or mining), urban areas, Philadelphia, which had gone Democratic during the New Deal period, returned to Republicanism during the postwar years. Even with this reprieve, the local Republican organization failed to save itself. In 1947 Richardson Dilworth ran for mayor. After making general charges of corruption, Dilworth specifically accused 128 city officials, ward leaders, and magistrates. He lost the election, but in 1948 four suicides among city employees touched off a series of city, state, and Federal investigations that confirmed Dilworth's accusations. In 1949 Dilworth and his running mate Joseph S. Clark, supported by independent Republicans including the Philadelphia *Inquirer,* swept into the city treasurer and controller offices with 120,000 votes to spare. By September 1950, a special grand jury, which since 1948 had been investigating corruption in city offices, presented an interim report that resulted in eight arrests. By April 1951, the grand jury named twenty-nine city officials as takers of graft and three Republican ward leaders as the principal violators. "Political influence," the grand jury declared, "has been exerted from all levels—committeemen, ward leaders and councilmen—their will in many cases being the determining factor." The Republican party looked even worse when the three deputy attorneys general who were directing the investigation resigned, charging that state Attorney General Robert E. Woodside (a Fine appointee) was blocking their work. In June 1951 the sixth suicide among city employees since the beginning of the investigation further undermined confidence in the Republican government of Philadelphia.

In an effort to achieve respectability, Republicans named for mayor the Reverend Dr. Daniel A. Poling, a Baptist clergyman, editor of the *Christian Herald,* and the newly elected president of the Military Chaplains Association. For mayor Democrats named Joseph S. Clark, city controller and the local leader of Americans for Democratic Action (ADA), and for district attorney Richardson Dilworth, city treasurer and an unsuccessful candidate both for mayor in 1947 and for governor in 1950. The Republican *Inquirer* again endorsed Clark and Dilworth—the first time in its 123-year history that it had supported a Democrat for mayor—urging independent Republicans to "place the welfare of their community above mere politics" and denouncing both "Republican boss rule that befouled City Hall" and the "stooge ticket headed by Daniel A. Poling." Using a broom as a symbol, Clark and Dilworth attacked "Republican misrule which has spawned shocking disclosers of graft, embezzlement, waste of public funds and incompetence in local government" and again triumphed by 120,000 votes, winning Philadelphia's City Hall for Democrats for the first time in the twentieth century.

Clark took office at a most fortuitous time. Philadelphia had recently adopted a boldly experimental home-rule charter eliminating the Legislature's control over the city's govern-

Joseph S. Clark, Democratic senator and mayor of Philadelphia.

ment and giving its mayor extensive administrative, investigative, and legislative powers including freedom to choose his subordinates with only minor restraints. The charter also provided for new officers including a finance director and a managing director, which was Philadelphia's version of a city manager. Ignoring pressure both from Democratic leaders and from organized labor, Clark refused to place labor's man on the Civil Service Commission and virtually eliminated patronage considerations in his appointments. He filled important posts with those he found best qualified even if they were Republican or from other states. Convinced that "good government is the best politics," he relied heavily on his ADA associates for his City Hall associates, calling them "the hard core of decency in Philadelphia politics."

By 1955 Clark boasted without contradiction that municipal government had been restored to the people, the spoils system abolished, and the corrupt triple alliance among politicians, police, and organized crime broken. Furthermore the Clark administration increased services, redeveloped blighted areas, erected a $15 million airport terminal building, improved and increased port facilities and business, expanded recreational opportunities, and altered traffic and parking regulations to improve the flow of traffic. Clark also instituted a classified civil service system that prohibited political activities by city employees, pegged salaries and raises at competitive figures, and adopted a 40-hour week for 26,000 municipal employees. Clark found revenue for these programs in a 1 percent real estate transfer tax and a 3-mill mercantile tax on gross business, in this way making business in general and corporations in particular pay their share of city taxes.

So dramatic was Philadelphia's progress that New York and Detroit studied how Philadelphia kept traffic moving on narrow streets, Chicago and Newark studied the new home-rule charter, and New Haven studied Philadelphia's urban renewal projects. Proud of their city's image, Philadelphians remained loyal to the Democratic party, and with both major cities in Democratic control, Pennsylvania was no longer a one-party state. Democrats now had an excellent chance to capture the governorship in 1954.

Realizing they were in trouble, Republican leaders shrewdly avoided a damaging primary fight while frustrating the ambitions of James H. Duff, who was eager to run again for governor. Hoping to leave the door open for himself, Duff had told party leaders that the only man he would support was his good friend Lieutenant Governor Lloyd H. Wood, a Montgomery County turkey farmer and an unlikely choice. Governor John S. Fine, Senator Edward Martin, and National Committeeman G. Mason Owlett met in January, cleverly pretended to take Duff at his word, and named Wood their gubernatorial candidate.

The overwhelming choice of Democrats was Richardson Dilworth, who had run in 1950, but Dilworth and Clark were battling a bipartisan move to wreck the new Philadelphia charter. Democratic city chairman William J. Green, Jr., and Republican city chairman Robert C. Duffy, Jr., wished to strip the charter of antipolitical activity provisions. Green and Duffy were maneuvering to ram through these changes at a primary election when political machines were most effective. Dilworth remained as district attorney and helped defeat the attempt to amend the charter. With Dilworth unavailable, the Democratic State Policy Committee turned for its 1954 gubernatorial candidate to George M. Leader, a York County chicken farmer who as state senator introduced fair employment practices legislation and courageously opposed the loyalty oath law as a "malevolent instrument of discrimination against educational and religious minorities."

As Fine's lieutenant governor, Wood stood on the record of his administration, but Leader attacked it as a "long playing record—one of record taxes, record spending and record debt." Proving himself an apt and appealing candidate, Leader also denounced the 1 percent sales tax instituted by the Fine administration as a "soak the poor tax." As the campaign grew hotter, fifteen Republican state officials including a member of Fine's cabinet were indicted by a Pittsburgh grand jury for macing state employees (requiring them to contribute a percentage of their salaries for party support). But above all Leader exploited the distressed economic condition of Pennsylvania, with 410,400 unemployed (particularly among hard-coal miners), and the discontent among farmers. Leader attacked national farm policies and promised to rid Pennsylvania of the "outlandish milk control policies that have placed the farmer behind the eight ball," accused the Republican national and state administrations of ignoring the anthracite industry, and pledged his administration to find new markets for hard coal, to develop new industry in the anthracite region, and to increase social services without taxes that would "sock the people." Leader won by 280,000 votes with pluralities of 112,000 in Philadelphia and 87,000 in Allegheny County. He would have won, however, without urban pluralities, for traditionally Republican rural areas went Democratic. A sincere, personable chicken farmer who promised relief had worked this miracle.

Leader The major contribution of the Leader administration (1955–1959) was administrative reform; and Leader's major problems centered about taxation, patronage, and pardons. The problems were compounded by a politically divided Legislature; Democrats controlled the House, but Republicans still ruled the Senate. Before taking office Leader had appointed

George M. Leader, Democratic governor.
(Fabian Bachrach)

an advisory committee of nineteen professors (mostly from institutes of state and local government at the Universities of Pennsylvania and Pittsburgh and at Pennsylvania State University) and had asked each member to report on a specific department. These reports underscored the need for reform. Though bills stemming from these reports passed the Democratic House, they were bottled up in the Republican Senate. The most important of Leader's measures proposed a state industrial development authority that would spend $75.5 million over five years to attract industry to Pennsylvania by building plants in distressed areas (particularly coal mining districts) and leasing them to "companies of good credit standing and high employment potential."

Leader's health, education, welfare, and economic development programs were costly and required new taxes. In addition Leader charged he had inherited a fiscal crisis that made his administration a receiver in bankruptcy. Needing to raise an additional $456 million over the next two years to meet existing obligations and to implement his program, Leader proposed a classified income tax, determined by the source rather than the size of income, which would tend to fall more heavily on those better able to pay. Utilizing political pressure, Leader rammed his tax measure through the House, but the Republican Senate rejected both it and the program it was to finance.

The fiscal crisis became worse after August 31 when the 1 percent sales tax expired. Republican strategists proposed a 2 percent sales tax, but apart from Leader's hatred of the sales-tax principle such a tax would not meet the obligations incurred by Duff and Fine, let alone finance the program proposed by Leader. With the commonwealth on the verge of bankruptcy, Leader and Senate Republicans finally agreed in March 1956 on a temporary 3 percent selective sales tax and on a 1 percent hike in the corporate income tax.

With the fiscal issue settled, the Legislature in May established a less ambitious Pennsylvania Industrial Development Authority to get the state's economy moving forward. The act appropriated $5 million to build factories in high-unemployment areas and permitted the authority to make second-mortgage loans (up to 30 percent of the cost of a new project) to nonprofit community industrial development corporations, which in turn had to raise 20 percent of the cost. For a first mortgage, banks would provide the remainder of the cost. The act provided that additional loans be made out of loan repayments and interest. Modest though the act was compared to Leader's original plans, the Federal Department of Commerce lauded it the best in the nation.

Before the seventeen-month 1955 session adjourned, it enacted much of Leader's program. Leader boasted that this longest session on record "saw more bills passed for the benefit of Pennsylvania's people than any other meeting of the Assembly." This legislation passed because Republican leaders, with their majority of two in the Senate, basically supported Leader's proposals. The Legislature appropriated $26.5 million to hire more skilled personnel to treat the mentally ill and $47 million for facilities for mentally retarded children, set up a public school program for physically and mentally handicapped children, and established the Mental Health Foundation to utilize private research funds in state hospitals. Culminating an eleven-year struggle, the Legislature established the Fair Employment Practices Commission and increased the amount and duration of both workmen's compensation and unemployment compensation benefits. Legislation also extended assistance for the disabled, blind, aged, and infirm, made $30 million available for slum clearance, and legislated on the problem of juvenile delinquency. Legislators also set aside $500 million for the largest school-building program in the state's history, increased state aid to universities by $14.5 million, provided $12.5 million for building at Pennsylvania State University, and twice as much for state teachers colleges. Funds for coal research and mine drainage supplemented the Industrial Development Authority in rehabilitating the anthracite region. Finally the Legislature financed the largest highway-construction program in the state's history and expanded flood control, recreation programs, and state parks.

The 1956 election spelled trouble for Leader and his party. The only bright spot for Democrats was Joseph S. Clark's defeat of James Duff, the incumbent United States Senator. President Eisenhower carried Pennsylvania, and Republicans gained firm control of its Legislature. When it met on January 1, 1957, Leader used a conciliatory tack stressing the problems involved in increased services without discussing the taxes necessary to pay for them. "If good is to be accomplished," he admonished, "we must learn to work together in these next months." A month later Leader submitted his record-breaking $1.6 billion biennial budget and stressed the need for a bipartisan approach to taxation. To make Pennsylvania more attractive to industry and to balance the budget, he advocated replacing three business taxes yielding $49 million with new taxes yielding $158 million.

The conciliatory approach made little headway. Vowing "to hold the line," the Republican 1957 Legislature slashed $70 million from the budget, eliminated one business tax, and reduced the gasoline tax, but made the 3 percent sales tax permanent. It smashed Leader's ambitious plans to develop industry, to expand health and welfare services, to clear slums, to provide up to 20,000 scholarships for college students and to establish junior colleges throughout the state, and cut in half Leader's proposed $100 million expansion of the General State Authority.

Controversies over patronage proved almost as great a curse to Leader as controversies over taxation. In 1955 the Pennsylvania governor controlled more patronage than any other governor and more offices (though less prestigious ones) than the President of the United States. Only 20 percent of the state's 65,000 employees were protected by civil service rules. While New York and California only had 7,000 non-merit-system employees, many of whom the governor did not appoint, Pennsylvania had 53,000, virtually all governor-appointed. Even though in effect the governor controlled jobs at Harrisburg and the county chairman controlled field jobs—including many Highway Department, state hospital, state college, and state prison employees—all appointments were cleared through Robert H. ("Pop") Jones, Leader's patronage secretary and a former football coach. Furthermore, Leader personally appointed in consultation with party leaders twenty-two department heads, members of boards and commissions, deputy secretaries in each department, and even some bureau chiefs.

Although Leader generally allowed county chairmen to make most of his field appointments, he deviated often enough to infuriate party leaders. He engaged in no wholesale dismissal of Republicans and frequently offended Democratic politicians with his appointments. He emphatically stated and believed, "No program can be effectively carried out unless we have first rate people in jobs which call for special training or special skills." He increased employees covered by civil service rules from 13,640 in July 1954 to 22,747 four years later, bringing patronage employees down to 46,000. He planned his most striking increase, which involved placing the top people of the state mental health program under civil service rules, to help achieve his goal to transform Pennsylvania from one of the most backward to one of the most progressive states in fighting mental illness.

The Philadelphia *Inquirer* fabricated Leader's third large-scale problem by accusing him of abusing the pardoning power. What impelled the *Inquirer* can only be conjectured, but Reed Smith suggests that perhaps editor Walter H. Annenberg avenged the earlier Democratic refusal to pardon his father, Moses L. Annenberg, by attacking Leader for his pardons. Whatever their inspiration, the *Inquirer's* attacks avoided the fact that a Pennsylvania governor cannot give pardons without the recommendation of the Board of Pardons, which is reported to the General Assembly and printed in the *Legislative Journal.* Furthermore, Leader and his board granted fewer pardons both in absolute numbers and in percentages than any of his recent predecessors. Indeed, 1956 when Leader granted only 12 percent of the petitions was the lowest year since 1915. Repeated lies, however, gain currency, and the pardon controversy hurt Leader in 1958 when he ran for the United States Senate.

Leader's achievement in administrative reform was rooted in the Fine administration. Aware of the need for reform, Fine had established the State Government Survey Committee (known as the Francis J. Chesterman Committee) which in 1953 had called for more centralized administration and accounting procedures. Although Fine had not acted on these recommendations, he had asked the Pennsylvania Economy League to use them in formulating a reorganization of the governor's office. When the plan arrived too late to use in his administration, Fine gave it to Leader, who was delighted with it both because it recognized the division between a governor's political and ceremonial functions and his administrative duties and because its Republican origin made it bipartisan. Adopting the

Economy League's plan, Leader not only attracted highly qualified personnel who infused new life into the state service, but he also overhauled central staff services and introduced new structures into the governor's office.

The reorganized governor's office had a secretary who supervised political and ceremonial activities, including relations with legislators, politicians, the press, and the public. In these functions he was aided by the legislative secretary, the public relations secretary, the personnel secretary, and the chief clerk. Again following the Economy League Plan, Leader created in 1955 the other wing of the governor's office, the Office of Administration, which was designed to relieve the governor of management details so he would have time for policy matters and state leadership. To help the governor supervise the 160-odd departments, boards, commissions, offices, and authorities, Leader created six bureaus within the Office of Administration including a bureau of budget, a bureau of management methods, a bureau of accounts, a bureau of personnel, a bureau of program evaluation (which was Leader's own brainchild and his most original contribution), and finally in 1956 a bureau of capital expenditures.

A large number of administrative reforms originated from these bureaus, which strengthened the governor's ability to lead and control his administration. The Bureau of Budget and the Bureau of Program Evaluation developed a program-type budget presenting each agency's plans and activities. The Bureau of Capital Expenditures developed the commonwealth's first capital budget—released during the succeeding administration—which enumerated each agency's projected capital expenditures over the next five or six years, giving officials an inkling of future fiscal needs. Through the Bureau of Management Methods, Leader revolutionized Harrisburg administration by improving inventory control, records management, and the use of floor space. Room for thirty new offices was found by sorting through "tons of rubbish" including outdated records, printed forms, stationery, old furniture, and filing cabinets.

The Bureau of Accounts initiated changes in the state's obsolete procedures. Pennsylvania had accounted for its biennial expenditures of $2.5 billion by a single-entry system of bookkeeping on a cash basis. As Leader justly complained, "No one was able to figure out the exact financial status of the Commonwealth. We found . . . a system of bookkeeping which did not disclose liabilities running into millions of dollars." Nor did it give any assurance that all taxes owed the commonwealth were collected. Within a year the Leader administration adopted a double-entry accrual system of disbursement accounting and modernized the accounts receivable bookkeeping system of the Department of Revenue. The Leader administration accelerated the trend toward punch-card machine accounting already begun by Governor Fine, mechanized the payroll system, installed a Univac electronic data processing center, and centralized the accounting system by making departmental controllers responsible to the secretary of administration.

Leader made other fiscal reforms. The funds which various departments had deposited in numerous accounts were combined and invested in short-term government securities, annually earning $100,000 in interest. Purchasing policies were consolidated to take advantage of the state's little-used system of central purchasing, instituted in 1923 with the establishment of the Department of Property and Supplies. Prior to 1955 the governor's office had not purchased insurance, supplies, and leases from and had not given contracts to the lowest bidder, but had used them as patronage to benefit the party in power. Insurance practices had been costly, with 4,000 out of 9,000 state automobiles carrying individual rather than fleet accident insurance. Adoption of a fleet automobile purchase plan enabling the state to sell year-old automobiles for as much as or more than they had originally cost saved Pennsylvania $4 million to $5 million per biennium.

Leader's most useful bureau was probably the Bureau of Program Evaluation. Headed by political science and history professors, the bureau improved the biennial reports of departments and the collection of statistics; evaluated publications; spearheaded governmental reorganization; appraised programs, such as milk control, education, migrant labor, and recreation; investigated proposals, including that of establishing community colleges; and finally coordinated interdepartmental and intergovernmental matters by smoothing the introduction of program and capital budgeting and by attempting to increase Federal grants to Pennsylvania, which ranked forty-seventh in grants per capita. Leader's administrative prowess was enhanced by a pragmatic idealism that demanded results, and the combination made him Pennsylvania's best governor since Gifford Pinchot.

Lawrence Leader wished to have Philadelphia's Mayor Richardson Dilworth succeed him, but other Democratic leaders and organized labor preferred Pittsburgh's Mayor David L. Lawrence. Lawrence and Leader, who was running for retiring Republican Senator Edward Martin's seat, easily won the primary.

Harold Stassen, Eisenhower's special assistant on disarmament, sought the Republican gubernatorial nomination, but party leaders opposed his candidacy. Republican State Chairman George I. Bloom, of the Pennsylvania Manufacturers Association, decided upon Arthur T. McGonigle, a self-made Reading pretzel manufacturer without political experience, as their candidate for governor and picked Hugh Scott to run for the Senate. Following a dull primary campaign both McGonigle and Scott triumphed.

Lawrence's program to rebuild Pittsburgh's deteriorated Golden Triangle made him a formidable candidate, but Leader proved as vulnerable as Lawrence proved strong. Galled by Leader's attempt to get a graduated wage tax, many voters echoed Republican charges of lenient pardons, payroll padding, and excessive and wasteful spending. Still chafing under his patronage policies, many Democratic professional politicians refused to give Leader's campaign their full devotion. Although analysts predicted victory for both Democrats, Leader failed to keep pace with Lawrence's huge pluralities in the party's Philadelphia and Pittsburgh strongholds and lost to Scott.

With more than fifty years' experience in politics, Lawrence combined the talents of an old-fashioned urban political boss with the progressive policies of a New and Fair Dealer. An early and consistent supporter of Franklin Roosevelt, Harry Truman, and Adlai Stevenson, Lawrence had directed Earle's successful gubernatorial campaign, had gotten Little New Deal laws through the Legislature, and had pushed Leader's candidacy in the preceding gubernatorial campaign. With help from Franklin Roosevelt, Lawrence had transformed Pittsburgh from a Republican to a Democratic city during the Great Depression, and as mayor of Pittsburgh during the post-World War II years he had cooperated with the Mellons to spur a remarkable urban renaissance. Lawrence had enforced the smoke law and had begun work on a sewage-disposal system to eliminate air and water pollution. With Pittsburgh plagued by strikes, he had become an outstanding mediator who lost the confidence of neither labor nor management. He also had pushed through a local fair employment practices ordinance in 1953 and had diligently protected minority rights. A politician's politician, Lawrence had suffered his share of adversity. In the late 1930s he was accused of conspiracy, blackmail, violating the election laws, and macing; although he was acquitted of these charges, his political career had suffered. As Lawrence took office, it was clear that neither social legislation nor the Democratic party would suffer but that administrative innovations would end.

Lawrence began his term (1959–1963) with an inaugural address calling for bipartisan cooperation in solving Pennsylvania's difficult fiscal problems and for political good feeling to promote industrial growth and combat unemployment. With Republicans controlling the Senate, Lawrence had reason to be conciliatory. His Tax Study Commission recommended $425 million in new taxes to cover an expected $90 million deficit and balance the new $1.9 billion 1959–1961 budget. Lawrence's proposals provoked a predictably vehement public response. Like their predecessors, Lawrence and state legislators were pressed to increase the state's social services by citizens who refused to pay the price. It is no small tribute to Lawrence's political skill that the politically divided Legislature agreed to increase the sales tax to 3½ percent by mid-April and to 4 percent in August, and to increase the cigarette tax by early May. The Legislature finally passed a $1.5 billion general appropriations bill in November that was short of Lawrence's original goal.

With his Pittsburgh mayoral experience, Lawrence was keenly aware of Pennsylvania's social problems. To solve or alleviate them, he sought massive Federal aid. He fought hard for a Federal Department of Urban Affairs and called for Federal solution of the metropolitan commuter crisis. Shortly after taking office, he urged that the Senate Banking Committee approve a $6 billion slum-removal, urban-renewal program proposed by Senator Joseph S. Clark, and two months later in March 1959 Lawrence urged the House Banking Committee to funnel $385 million into chronically depressed areas. Pennsylvania, he observed, "faces no greater problem than finding a cure" for unemployment with 500,000 workers or 11 percent of its work force jobless. Lawrence also urged Congress to improve "the grossly inhumane conditions" of migrant farm workers.

Lawrence did not rely entirely on Federal help to solve Pennsylvania's problems. In 1959 he asked for a law banning racial discrimination in private and public housing. Such legislation seemed necessary because the Borough Council of Rutledge, an all-white suburb of Philadelphia, had passed an ordinance at an unannounced meeting condemning a house and lot purchased by an Afro-American couple. Two days earlier the council had denied the couple's request for a permit to repair damage that had been done by fire to their new home the day before they planned to move in. Although the black couple pressed charges of racial discrimination and Rutledge officials settled out of court, allowing them to repair their house, proponents of housing equality were convinced that legislation was necessary. It was not until February 1961, however, that Lawrence got his fair-housing law that banned discrimination except in single homes that were owner-occupied or duplex housing in which one unit was owner-occupied.

In 1959 the state also moved to help lower-income families buy houses by setting up the Pennsylvania Housing Authority (PHA). Tight money and high interest rates had discouraged poorer people from buying homes. The first of its kind in any state, the PHA was designed to make mortgages available at interest rates 1 percent lower than the Federal Housing Authority maximum.

The basic element in solving Pennsylvania's problems was a healthy economy. With a sluggish economy, Pennsylvania in early 1959 led the nation both in areas of surplus labor and in the rate of unemployment. For example, the coal industry, coupling falling demand with automation, employed fewer and fewer men. Continuous mining machines that sliced into a coal seam and threw cut coal to the car or conveyor belt eliminated much drilling, blasting, and unskilled manual labor. Giant augers, boring holes three feet in diameter, mined more than 30 tons of coal a day, and roof bolts eliminated laborious and expensive timbering. From 1870 to 1930 annual anthracite production averaged less than 500 tons per miner, but in 1960 each man produced nearly 1,000 tons. A bituminous miner produced almost 3 tons a day in 1890, 4 tons in 1915, 5 tons in 1943, 6 tons in 1951, and 10.68 tons in 1960. There were 179,679 anthracite miners in 1914 and only 19,051 in 1960; 194,981 bituminous miners in 1923 and 32,651 in 1960.

To get jobs for these and other laid-off workers, the Lawrence administration launched an advertising campaign to attract industry to "Climate-Right Pennsylvania." In addition to abundant natural resources, Lawrence stressed a "new spirit of cooperation between men and communities, business and industry, and every branch of government." In the spring of 1959, even before the advertising campaign got under way, reassuring signs of recovery appeared in the near-capacity operations of the steel industry and the vigorous growth of the construction industry. But the economic picture was spotty. Although Harrisburg and Lancaster prospered, the anthracite region remained depressed, despite some improvement.

In contrast to coal, the steel industry was healthy and optimistic. Despite some losses to aluminum and plastic, steel in 10,000 shapes, sizes, and varieties (frequently combining steel with new materials) fought to retain old markets and to gain new ones. In 1956 Benjamin Fairless of United States Steel predicted that steel mills of the future would use revolutionary new machines, would abandon a batch-type process for continuous casting, and would move "beyond automation into 'atomation'" by using atomic energy to reduce iron ore directly into steel. In fulfilling Fairless's prophesy the industry expended billions of dollars on capital improvements. In the late 1950s and the early 1960s the gigantic rollers of the continuous strip mill (rolling red-hot steel into sheets at the rate of 2,000 feet a minute) and the continuous cold reduction mill (rolling cold sheet steel into thinner gauges while improving its quality and finish) provided steel for automobiles, cans, and a host of other products. Though the bulk of American steel production was still by the open-hearth method, electric furnaces—because they could be regulated with precision—were producing great quantities of the harder, tougher, rust-, heat-, and corrosion-resistant alloy steels. To control steelmaking as well as business details, the industry installed computers, and to produce better steel faster and cheaper, it emphasized oxygen steelmaking, vacuum degassing, and continuous casting. By 1964 more steel was made by the oxygen process than by electric furnaces. The advantage of the oxygen furnace was speed. It made high-quality steel four to five times faster than the open-hearth furnace, saving approximately $5 a ton. Immediately casting the oxygen furnace "heat" into basic shapes known as slabs, billets, and bars saved an additional $5 per ton. Since continuous casting required a higher grade of molten steel than traditional methods produced, the vacuum degassing device (removing a high percentage of gasses and other impurities) was necessary. By 1959 growing efficiency, automation, and the ultimate promise of "atomation" gratified steel management but not steelworkers who feared technological unemployment.

Negotiations for a new contract proved fruitless; the old one expired on June 30 and the United Steelworkers of America struck on July 15. By demanding more control over local work rules and by offering pay raises in exchange for increased plant efficiency, management unwittingly made the strike popular. That exchange proposal, one Local president said,

Oxygen furnace at Bethlehem. (Bethlehem Steel Corporation)

"put the fellows 100 per cent behind the union." The strike continued through summer and into autumn. On October 9 Eisenhower invoked the Taft-Hartley Law and following a fact-finding investigation got an eighty-day back-to-work cooling-off injunction, which the Supreme Court upheld on November 7, ending the 116-day strike. Wearing black armbands and filled with resentment, workers returned to the mills. Negotiations continued but remained deadlocked. On New Year's Eve, Vice President Richard M. Nixon and Secretary of Labor James P. Mitchell began working for a settlement, which materialized on January 4.

A victory for the United Steelworkers of America, the settlement gained stature for Nixon as a mediator. He gave the steel company heads a realistic picture of the political alternatives to a settlement in a presidential election year. Ironically, Nixon, usually regarded as a friend of business, had been urged by the United Steelworkers' president, David J. McDonald, to enter negotiations, and the generous settlement Nixon secured for the workers went far beyond the companies' last offer. Not only did Nixon help steelworkers win higher wages but he also won for them the guarantee that the companies would pay the employee's share of insurance costs. But Nixon profited more than did steelworkers from the settlement; he had demonstrated his political skill and his ability to master difficult detail, and he became an even bigger man in the Republican party.

Being at the center of the steel strike, Pennsylvania bore the brunt of its cost, estimated at $6 billion in wages and production. With almost 200,000 additional Pennsylvanians out of work, economic recovery halted; relief expenditures were up and tax receipts down. After the settlement in January 1960, the future brightened; Pennsylvania could look forward to thirty months of uninterrupted employment in its basic industry.

The year 1960 brought peace in steel but renewed the quadrennial war over the Presidency. Richard Nixon secured the Republican nomination with ease, while John F. Kennedy, the young, attractive Massachusetts Senator, overcame diehard liberal supporters of Adlai E. Stevenson to head the Democratic ticket. No longer a safe Republican state, Pennsylvania was wooed by both parties. Though both candidates campaigned extensively in Pennsylvania, Kennedy proved more successful, particularly in the northeastern industrial and mining areas. Estimating on one occasion that more than 500,000 people had turned out to see Kennedy, Lawrence reminded reporters, "this is one of the most depressed economic areas in the nation. And these people look to this fellow as a messiah who will lead them out." Kennedy carried the state with landslide pluralities in both Philadelphia (an astonishing 325,000) and Pittsburgh and went on to win the Presidency. In addition, Democrats narrowly won the lower house of the state Legislature, while the Senate was evenly divided between the two parties.

Both Lawrence and Kennedy were sympathetic to the plight of the underdog, but neither came to the aid of the Seneca Indians. The proposed, federally financed Kinzua Dam (on the Allegheny River just south of the New York border) was designed primarily to protect Pittsburgh from floods and to provide water storage for its industries. When built, the dam would flood the Senecas's best land (given them by a 1794 treaty signed by George Washington) and would destroy reservation life. Federal courts—including the Supreme Court— ruled that despite the old treaty Seneca lands were subject to the public right of eminent domain just as were the lands of other Americans. Kennedy refused to halt the Kinzua project because the need for flood protection was "real and immediate." The Federal government ignored Washington's treaty, completed the dam in 1965, appropriated $15 million to relocate the Senecas, and flooded their lands. Both Lawrence and Kennedy were more attuned to the demands of an urban area such as Pittsburgh than to the needs of a rural Indian tribe.

With Kennedy in the White House, Lawrence continued to demand Federal help in solving economic and social problems facing Pennsylvania. He commended Kennedy for giving top priority to the proposals of a task force on unemployment and prepared to take immediate advantage of Federal action. At the beginning of 1961, Pennsylvania needed all the help it could get. The steel strike and a business slump had exhausted public assistance funds and the state had had to borrow to continue its relief payments of $18 million a month to 400,000 of its citizens. Lawrence enthusiastically backed a $394 million depressed-areas bill, which Kennedy signed a few months after taking office. The bill authorized loans and grants to rural and industrial areas suffering from chronically heavy unemployment to build new plants and facilities to service the plants. Convinced that the answer to Pennsylvania's economic ills lay in Washington, Lawrence urged Congress to appropriate $600 million for a public works program to combat unemployment, and he also urged it to cut the Federal income tax in the low- and middle-income brackets to stimulate business, employment, and the economy.

Lawrence also looked to Washington for help in solving giant social problems. He urged Congress to pass a $50 million Federal aid program to improve state and local efforts to curb juvenile delinquency. Stating that broken homes and blighted neighborhoods nurtured hostilities in young people that made them "society's time bombs," Lawrence urged society to make "certain that the fuse is never lighted."

The oldest man ever to become governor of Pennsylvania, Lawrence was particularly aware of problems of the aged. Observing that private insurance "simply has not met the need," he urged the Federal government to provide medical care for the aged through the social security program.

Benefits of state partnership with the Federal government are illustrated by the interstate-Federal Delaware River Basin Pact of 1961. The compact set up a five-member commission, consisting of the governors of Pennsylvania, New York, New Jersey, and Delaware and a presidential appointee, to control and develop the water resources of the Delaware River. This compact—the culmination of three decades of maneuvering—was unusual in that the Federal government was made a full member. Plans based on a three-year study by army engineers called for the construction over the next fifty years of eleven reservoirs in addition to flood control and recreational projects costing about $591 million. The Federal government was to assume 48.6 percent of the cost, and states and municipalities were to divide the remaining costs in proportion to benefits derived.

Tourism which the Delaware River project would encourage, had become one of the state's leading and fastest-growing industries. Lawrence and the 1962 Legislature gave tourism its most vigorous boost by enacting Project 70 to acquire park and recreation lands and to develop tourist facilities by 1970. Arguing that "lands essential for future public use will never be as abundant or as reasonable in price as they are today," Lawrence proposed a $70 million bond issue (which required voter endorsement) to finance the program. Of these funds $20 million was to be available on a matching basis to local communities for parks and recreation and conservation programs, $10 million to the Fish and Game Commission for purchasing hunting and fishing areas threatened by developers, and $40 million (which would also qualify for 30 percent Federal grants) to the Department of Forests and Waters to acquire lands suitable for reservoirs and parks to serve metropolitan areas. Lawrence stressed the fact that ringing metropolitan areas with recreational facilities was urgent since suitable areas were disappearing, and Pennsylvanians heeded his warning and voted for the bond issue. Their foresight was rewarded; in 1969 tourism grossed $4.2 billion, topping agriculture and bituminous and anthracite coal mining.

The Legislature promoted both tourism and education in 1959 by allocating funds for the William Penn Memorial Museum and Archives Building in Harrisburg. The vision of a memorial to Penn, a repository for state records with facilities for historical research, and a museum to preserve and display the artifacts of Pennsylvania's past experience belonged to Governor Edward Martin, who in 1945 secured legislation authorizing such a building. Since funds were not appropriated, serious planning did not begin until 1957. Money was secured in 1959, and in January 1962 Lawrence broke ground for the $9 million structure, which was opened in October 1964. An appropriate memorial to Pennsylvania's founder, the Museum and Archives Building is both a major tourist attraction and an installation where Pennsylvanians can become aware of their historical heritage.

Legislators proved less willing to better their schools than to promote tourism. In April 1961 Lawrence's special Committee on Education called for a ten-year program of sweeping changes in school organization that would place Pennsylvania "in the front line of America's educational revolution." To finance this program the committee suggested a variety of taxes. Reflecting the values of their constituents, legislators increased both the gasoline tax and the state highway budget, but killed Lawrence's proposed $23 million in new taxes (specifically a 2 percent tax on royalties, dividends, and capital gains) that would effect the committee's preliminary suggestions. The 1961 Legislature, on the other hand, did approve the Fair Education Opportunities Act. The act forbade any school—except religious and denominational institutions—from accepting students on the basis of racial, ethnic, or religious quotas.

REPUBLICAN REVIVAL

Intraparty struggles in 1962 wracked Pennsylvania. Up for reelection, Senator Joseph S. Clark backed Philadelphia's Mayor Richardson Dilworth for the Democratic gubernatorial nomination, but Representative William J. Green, Jr., their old enemy who headed the Philadelphia Democratic organization, opposed Dilworth. Lawrence, however, who combined reform policies with machine tactics, convinced Green to accept Dilworth, and the seventy-two-member Democratic State Policy Committee unanimously ratified the slate of Dilworth for governor and Clark for senator. A severe factional fight between the old guard and the followers of Hugh Scott rocked the Republican party. Led by George I. Bloom, Republican state chairman, the old guard wanted Robert E. Woodside, a superior court judge, to run for governor and Representative James E. Van Zandt to oppose Clark in the senatorial race. Scott bitterly opposed Woodside as the candidate of "a few hungry men," reluctantly entered the gubernatorial race, and refused to withdraw unless the party leaders named Representative William W. Scranton for governor. Scott prevailed; the Republican State Committee and county chairmen ended months of feuding by naming the Scranton–Van Zandt harmony ticket and backing state Senator Raymond P. Shafer of Meadville for lieutenant governor.

In the May 1962 primary both parties endorsed the selections of their leaders, but there were ill omens for the Democrats. Sixty-two thousand more Republicans voted in the primary than Democrats; in the Republican primary Scranton with one rival polled 93,000 more votes than Dilworth who had two rivals in the Democratic primary.

The gubernatorial candidates had much in common. Both were articulate, independently wealthy graduates of Yale Law School who had interrupted their studies to serve in the armed services. Both had entered politics in their forties and had attractive, energetic wives. Both were identified with liberal and reform elements within their parties and had come from distinguished Pennsylvania families. Dilworth's great-grandfather had pioneered in Pittsburgh, while the city of Scranton was named for Scranton's great-grandfather George Whitefield Scranton.

The campaign was one of the bitterest in Pennsylvania history. Both parties rolled out their heaviest artillery. President Kennedy campaigned for Dilworth and Clark, while former President Eisenhower helped the Republican cause by speaking in Scranton and Pittsburgh. Scranton's clever needling—in an understated steely manner—and Dilworth's overheated responses obscured the virtues of both candidates, the issues, and the importance of the election. Dilworth was a distinguished mayor of Philadelphia whose programs of urban renewal, industrial development, and imaginative government were rescuing that city from

decay. Scranton had been a State Department aide under Eisenhower and was not reactionary. "I'm apt," he said, "to be quite liberal on civil rights, conservative on fiscal policy and
generally a middle-of-the roader." Shrewdly avoiding specific issues, Scranton proved to be
an effective sidewalk campaigner. On the other hand, Dilworth, a seasoned politician,
cut up Scranton in two public debates, but his concrete program to promote industrial
development, tourism, school district consolidation, and community colleges hurt him,
particularly when he forthrightly admitted that if necessary he would call for new taxes.
More important, many voters thought that after eight years of Democratic rule it was time
for a change and many of the 363,700 unemployed had lost faith in the Democratic party.
Finally, Dilworth's hot temper and the cold reaction of the Philadelphia and Pittsburgh
machines also cost him votes. Scranton swamped Dilworth by more than 470,000 votes, but
an enormous number of split ballots enabled Clark to triumph over Van Zandt by 100,000
votes.

Scranton Though his stunning victory in an important state made him a contender for the
Republican presidential nomination, Scranton privately derided himself as White House
material and put his attention to his immediate and difficult task as governor. He faced a
sluggish economy with major industries sick and dying, he faced unemployment, and like
his predecessors Leader and Lawrence, he needed increased state revenues to deal with these
problems. Scranton's first job, however, was to rebuild the Pennsylvania Republican party.
He announced that he would dismiss "thousands of political hacks and free-loaders" and
thereby increase the unemployment rate among Democrats. With 50,000 out of 84,000 state

William W. Scranton, Republican governor.

employees unprotected by civil service rules, Republicans planned to dismiss "Democratic hacks," replace them with Republicans, and then extend civil service rules to freeze these newly appointed Republicans in office. Scranton hoped to rebuild Philadelphia and Pittsburgh GOP machines with state offices in time to make a good showing in the 1964 presidential election.

Upon assuming his term of office (1963–1967), Scranton called for unity in solving the state's chronic economic problems and in bringing about "a new era in Pennsylvania progress." His inaugural address resembled a coach's talk at a pep rally. "Don't tell me that Pennsylvania can't lick its problems, because I know it can," he declared. Scranton, however, realized that spirit alone could not end unemployment caused by the decline of coal, steel, and railroads and the general failure of Pennsylvania industry to rise to the technological challenges of the 1960s. "We know," he told the Chicago Executives Club, "that a certain amount of regulation of business by government is tolerable and necessary—necessary for the nation as a whole, and for business as well." Pennsylvania Republicans had traveled a long way since the days of Joseph Grundy. A week after assuming office Scranton presented the Legislature with a sweeping program including a proposed referendum on the need for a constitutional convention. The subject closest to Scranton's heart, however, was industrial development to spur the economy. His program called for extending the lending capacity of the Pennsylvania Industrial Development Authority, for tax revisions that would include greater depreciation allowances for new plants, for highway construction designed to promote industry, for development of new markets and uses for coal, for more research at Pennsylvania's schools and universities that would attract space age industries, for a citizens group of 100,000 Pennsylvanians to "sell Pennsylvania," and for increased advertising to promote industrial development and tourism.

Scranton's enthusiasm caught on. Businessmen liked his program, and Democrats could not oppose it since it resembled their platform. With a bare Republican majority in both houses, the Legislature enacted much of Scranton's program. Some of his more impressive victories, besides his industrial development program, included stronger controls on anthracite strip mines, a $35 million increase in school subsidies, the first pay raise to state teachers in seven years, a legislative reapportionment act (declared unconstitutional in 1964 for violating the one-man, one-vote principle), and most notably a civil service reform bill extending the merit system to 17,000 additional state employees.

Programs cost money, and Scranton in 1963 had to fight for higher taxes to balance his proposed $1.12 billion budget. Over Democratic opposition Scranton succeeded in raising the sales tax from 4 to 5 percent and secured increases in the cigarette and liquor tax. Though the 5 percent rate was the highest in the nation, the exemption of food and clothing from the sales tax and the absence of an income tax meant that compared to other big states Pennsylvania was still in a low tax bracket.

Scranton conceded that government must play an important role in the economy and society, but he was reluctant to embrace that concept wholeheartedly as did Lawrence. Scranton showed his distrust of Keynesian economists when he attacked deficit spending and unbalanced budgets. His cool reception to the Kennedy administration's plan for massive joint Federal-state aid to the ten-state Appalachian area which included parts of Pennsylvania contrasted sharply with the attitude of Lawrence toward Federal aid. Scranton talked politics with New York's Governor Nelson Rockefeller while state Secretary of Commerce John K. Tabor consulted with Franklin D. Roosevelt, Jr., head of the Appalachian Regional

Commission, and bluntly questioned whether Pennsylvania "with its strong economic base" had "a truly common interest" with the other states involved.

But Scranton soon called as loudly as anyone for Federal help. In April 1964 he suggested that Lyndon B. Johnson, who had become President after Kennedy's assassination, add $10 million to his $228 million Appalachian region emergency program. The added funds Scranton would earmark to promote new uses for coal, to improve mining techniques, and to restore land scarred by open-pit mines. By July Scranton urged that the Republican platform recognize that Federal funds and programs were necessary to end chronic poverty but that these funds should be administered by state and local governments. Later in his administration, Scranton enthusiastically supported Johnson's 1965 bill which provided for joint Federal and state financing of highways, water and land resources development, colleges, vocational schools, health clinics, and sewage treatment plants for Appalachia. By the last year of his term, Scranton sounded like Lawrence when he urged that the Federal government build urban rapid-transit systems (instead of "gargantuan highways") by assuming 90 percent of the cost, as it did with the interstate highway system. Clearly Scranton wanted a maximum of Federal dollars and planning expertise, but a minimum of Federal control.

Scranton's defiance of organized labor sharply differentiated him from his immediate predecessors. In early 1964 he argued that the almost bankrupt unemployment compensation fund deterred new industry from moving into Pennsylvania and thereby compounded the unemployment problem. He requested a $35 million increase in payroll taxes, an increase in benefits, and more rigid eligibility rules to eliminate loopholes, such as the ones enabling some unemployed persons to receive a second round of benefits for a total of sixty weeks. Scranton's courageous proposals were designed to reduce total annual payments of $28.5 million. In addition Scranton risked his political future by attacking the AFL-CIO leadership as "Demagogues" who used "the big lie and the half-truth" and completely disregarded "the future of Pennsylvania and its people." Scranton encountered immediate opposition from both organized labor and the National Association for the Advancement of Colored People (NAACP). The executive council of the AFL-CIO claimed that Scranton would deprive 90,000 unemployed—particularly workers in seasonal and low-paying industries—of benefits and acidly observed that "instead of attacking unemployment, he attacks the unemployed." After a bitter 21-hour debate the Republican Senate overcame Democratic opposition, approved Scranton's bill, and sent it to the House. Though 15,000 men and women marched and chanted against the bill in Harrisburg, it passed the House with one vote to spare.

Despite the NAACP's disappointment with his stand on unemployment compensation, Scranton was an ardent advocate of civil rights legislation. He conspicuously supported Kennedy's proposed civil rights bill with its public accomodations provision, which in 1964 became law under Johnson. On the state level, Scranton in early 1964 urged the Legislature to double the staff of the Human Relations Commission. "All Pennsylvanians," he urged, "should be seeking for greater justice, greater charity, greater equality in relationships between the races." Although the Congress of Racial Equality (CORE) and other civil rights groups held Scranton responsible for alleged Pennsylvania state police brutality during the April 1964 civil rights demonstrations at Chester, Scranton ordered the public hearings by the Human Relations Commission that disclosed that the Chester School District did "commit unlawful discriminatory practices." The commission ordered the school board to eliminate its all-Negro schools served by all-Negro teachers and staff and housed in inferior buildings.

Scranton's commitment to civil rights led him to seek the 1964 Republican presidential nomination. Specifically, opposition to the Civil Rights Act by Senator Barry Goldwater, the front-running candidate, compelled Scranton to run as a more legitimate successor to the mantle of Abraham Lincoln. Appalled by Goldwater's hostility to antipoverty measures and his "cruel misunderstanding" of how the economy worked, Scranton feared for the future of the Republican party. Candidates for lesser offices also begged Scranton to run lest Goldwater, renowned for reactionary domestic and quick-trigger foreign policies, drag them to defeat. With only a month left before the convention, Scranton vigorously campaigned for delegates, but despite his efforts Goldwater swamped him 883 to 214. In the ensuing election President Johnson overwhelmed Goldwater in the nation as well as in Pennsylvania, and many Republican candidates felt that if Scranton had won the nomination they would not have been defeated. In Pennsylvania Republicans lost the state offices of auditor general and treasurer, two superior court judgeships, two seats in the United States House of Representatives, and control of the state House of Representatives.

Despite Johnson's overwhelming victory in Pennsylvania, some Republican candidates did well. Not only was the vote more anti-Goldwater than anti-Republican, but a Democratic split contributed to Republican successes. The Democratic organization as well as David Lawrence and Richardson Dilworth had backed state Supreme Court Justice Michael A. Musmanno (a champion of mine laborers, a prominent Italian-American, and a judge at the Nuremburg war crime trials) to run against Hugh Scott for the United States Senate,

Hugh Scott, Republican senator.

while Senator Joseph S. Clark and Mayor James H. J. Tate of Philadelphia had supported state Secretary of Internal Affairs Genevieve Blatt. Not only had Clark insisted that Blatt would "get more votes and be a better Senator," but he also had maintained that her nomination would prevent the new boss of Philadelphia, Francis R. Smith, "from taking over the state organization." The bitter primary battle was not decided until mid-August when after protracted counting and litigation Blatt emerged the victor by 491 votes. Blatt, however, never fully recovered from the internecine struggle, while Scott shrewdly maintained that he supported the entire Republican ticket but managed not to appear with Goldwater in Pennsylvania. Although Goldwater lost Pennsylvania by almost 1.4 million votes, Scott carried the state by 50,000.

Scranton opened the 1965 session with an appeal to the divided Legislature to continue the new era, but Democrats, boasting it was the Legislature's day, permitted neither radio nor television to cover the event. Scranton proudly reported that the state's unemployment rate had dropped from 9.6 to 4.3 percent during his administration and that 1964 had been "the first year in the history of record-keeping that Pennsylvania's unemployment rate figured lower than the rest of the nation." To continue the march "toward greatness," Scranton called for reapportionment along lines of the Supreme Court's one-man, one-vote ruling, revision of the 1873 constitution, a 5 percent pay raise for state employees, a 32 percent increase in state expenditures for eduction, state-supported school buses for private and parochial schools, expansion of the Fair Employment Practices Act to include all employers, and increased expenditures for mental health, law enforcement, unemployment compensation, and industrial retraining. Scranton's budget to implement his ideas during the 1965–1966 fiscal year was $1.26 billion, more than half of which was designated for education. Because of a budget surplus (which proved to be a record $102.7 million), he estimated no new taxes were necessary.

Democrats seemed intent on thwarting and frustrating Scranton and eliminating him as a potential 1968 presidential candidate. By June the Republican Senate had passed most of Scranton's program. Democrats labeled the program the Great Society, Jr., and complained that Scranton was out-Johnsoning Johnson. The Democratic House, however, refused to enact either Scranton's program or a program of its own. When Scranton shrewdly attacked House Demoncrats as obstructionists, they privately admitted, "He has not only beaten us to the punch, he has beaten us to a pulp." By the end of June Democrats had changed their strategy. They labeled Scranton's program inadequate and suggested a larger budget. After persuading Republicans to pass the Democratic budget, Scranton cleverly reduced it by vetoing specific appropriation items as allowed by the Pennsylvania constitution of 1873.

Despite their differences, the Legislature and the Governor combined to give Pennsylvania some needed legislation. The General Assembly increased pay for its members to $7,200 a year and their expense allowance to $4,800, making them the third-highest-paid state legislators in the nation. An act of major importance was a new, tough clean-streams law, passed over strong opposition by the coal industry. The act forbade discharge of mine acids—"the major cause of stream pollution in Pennsylvania"—into streams and waterways after January 1, 1966. Scranton enthusiastically pledged "all the resources of this administration" to advance a "great new era of conservation." The Legislature also created a new state department of community affairs.

Though there was some accord, contentiousness was the salient characteristic of the year-long 1965 session. Since the Legislature could not agree on a reapportionment of the General Assembly in accordance with the United States Supreme Court's one-man, one-vote ruling, the Pennsylvania Supreme Court assumed this task and completed it by February 1966. Furthermore for most of the year the Senate's Democratic minority prevented the confirmation of 850 appointments, though it finally cleared all but 63 of them. By remaining in session until the 1966 Legislature convened, the Democratic House blocked an appointment to the Turnpike Commission that would have given Republicans a majority and control of 1,500 patronage jobs, and in an effort to acquire political capital for the 1966 campaign, it passed thirty-eight bills on January 4, 1966, that could not become law because the Senate had already adjourned.

Confining itself largely to fiscal and constitutional matters, the 1966 legislative session was also contentious. Scranton's $1.4 billion budget proposed increases for education and mental health but thanks to increased revenue returns from a booming economy did not require new taxes. Nevertheless this budget produced a three-month stalemate until the Democratic House and the Republican Senate agreed to an even higher $1.5 billion budget.

Although Democrats refused to believe it, Scranton's main objective as Governor was not the White House but the industrial development of Pennsylvania. In this chosen field he did well. The Scranton years coincided with four years of uninterrupted economic growth for Pennsylvania. By September 1966 the Pennsylvania unemployment rate was only 2.8 percent as compared to the national average of 3.8 percent, while from 1950 to 1962 Pennsylvania's unemployment rate was 50 percent higher than the national average and after West Virginia the highest in the nation. "I never thought I'd live to see the day when Pennsylvania would have a labor shortage, but that's what we've got," Scranton exclaimed in March 1966. The 2,400 plants built and expanded under the state's development program during the first three years of Scranton's administration created at least 100,000 jobs. Indeed the Bureau of Industrial Development attracted and located new businesses, which in turn could obtain 100 percent financing of plants through the Pennsylvania Industrial Development Authority and local agencies. The Bureau of Business Service actually helped businessmen get state aid and advice while the Bureau of Travel Development promoted tourism, which as the commonwealth's fastest-growing industry rose 20 percent in 1965. Clearly Pennsylvania turned an important corner in 1964 when its unemployment rate fell below the national average. Though nationwide prosperity engendered by Vietnam war spending coupled with policies originated by the Leader and Lawrence administrations helped Pennsylvania turn that corner, the triumph was largely Scranton's. It was his single-minded devotion to industrial development and to creating jobs, his willingness to utilize Federal and state funds and agencies to those ends, and his ability to engender enthusiasm that halted Pennsylvania's sickening decline.

Shafer Republicans had little trouble picking Scranton's successor. Scranton, Scott, and the Republican Executive Committee agreed that Lieutenant Governor Raymond P. Shafer and state Attorney General Walter E. Alessandroni should run for governor and lieutenant governor, respectively. Harold E. Stassen, compaigning for peace in Vietnam, opposed Shafer but was swamped in the primary. Although Alessandroni died in an air crash nine days before the primary, Republicans confirmed his nomination. With the backing of the Republican State Committee, Shafer then chose as his running mate the Philadelphia Republican leader Raymond J. Broderick.

The Penn Central's Conway Yard, 22 miles west of Pittsburgh. It is the biggest and busiest push-button freight classification yard in the world. In a single day it has received, reclassified, and dispatched more than 50 freight trains totaling more than 5,000 cars. (Penn Central Transportation Company)

Democrats failed to match Republican harmony. The Democratic primary turned into a row when Leader refused to run again for governor. The Policy Committee unenthusiastically recommended state Senator Robert P. Casey of Scranton, an attractive, young, progressive Roman Catholic. A millionaire Philadelphia electronics manufacturer, Milton E. Shapp, challenged Casey for the nomination. Shapp waged a vigorous and costly campaign attacking Casey as the creature of the Democratic organization and selling himself as "the man against the machine." When Democratic leaders charged Shapp with trying to buy the nomination, he freely admitted, "It does cost money." He filled the airwaves with thousands of radio and television spots and thirty-four half-hour telecasts at prime time. He also sent a large pamphlet to 1.6 million homes and issued a series of position papers on issues ranging from milk control to crime control. Casey's campaign was hampered by lack of funds and by bickering in Philadelphia between Mayor James H. J. Tate and the city Democratic leader Francis R. Smith. Despite Shapp's howls, the 1966 Democratic machine was ineffectual. With Casey running poorly in Philadelphia and Pittsburgh, Shapp won the primary and demonstrated that advertising can beat a lethargic and divided organization.

Shapp, however, had to face the healthy Republican organization with the machine he had just defeated. A self-made man who started work at 22 cents an hour, Shapp had established a scholarship fund to place Negro and Puerto Rican youth in college, and he claimed to have suggested the Peace Corps idea to John F. Kennedy. Both the ADA and the Pennsylvania AFL-CIO (which had named him 1963 man of the year) supported Shapp, who proved to be an attractive candidate.

Shapp continued to utilize the same advertising techniques that won him the primary. He occupied an advanced liberal position on virtually all issues, but his major and most breathtaking proposal was to establish a Pennsylvania human resources authority which would sell $5.5 billion in bonds to provide among other things "a free college education for all Pennsylvanians." Better-educated Pennsylvanians, Shapp argued, would earn more and increase tax revenues sufficiently to redeem the bonds. Shapp also wished to replace the sales tax with a state income tax. Finally, he tried to identify Republicans with "fat cats" and "trusts"—attacking in particular railroads and utilities.

Shapp called the campaign's tune. To counteract his proposals, the Republican platform was unusually liberal, but Republicans focused their campaign more on Shapp's heavy expenditures than on exploiting the four-year Scranton record or Shafer's liberal stance. Despite his advertising blitz, Shapp, who was hurt by an anti-Semitic undercurrent, lost by over 200,000 votes to a well-organized foe. His majorities in Philadelphia and Pittsburgh, where he apparently suffered from white backlash, were not large enough to carry the state, and in addition Shafer captured roughly a third of the black vote, which Shapp had counted on. Republicans also won all statewide offices and retained a thin majority in both houses of the Legislature.

The main thrust of the Shafer administration (1967-1971) was for constitutional reform. "Pennsylvania spoke to the nation in Benjamin Franklin's day," Shafer announced in his inaugural address. "It is high time we speak again. It is high time we reassert the concept of the republic which was fashioned in Philadelphia in 1787—strong states, united in strong partnership with the national government." But if Pennsylvania were to "lead the nation" in restoring "balance and meaning to our Federal system of government," it would have to modernize its 1873 constitution. Having invoked the blessing of the founding fathers upon constitutional revision, Shafer was off to a good start. On March 15 in Congress Hall, next door to Independence Hall, flanked by former Governors Leader and Scranton, Shafer signed a bill calling for a May 16 referendum on the question of a constitutional convention. The convention would be charged not with writing a new constitution but merely with considering changes in crucial areas of reapportionment, the judiciary, local government, and state finances.

As co-chairmen of the Citizens Committee for Constitutional Revision, Leader and Scranton faced a serious challenge. Six previous attempts to alter the 1873 constitution had failed because of apathy, the graduated income tax scare, rural opposition (particularly from the Grange), and the hostility of minor officeholders whose jobs were guaranteed by the constitution. In 1967, for example, the 6,000 justices of the peace, who tended to be powerful local figures, were against altering the constitution, which required no legal qualifications for their jobs, permitted them to be elected rather than appointed, and allowed them to be compensated by the archaic system of fees which they themselves collected. There was also general, widespread fear of change and particular fear of tampering with the uniformity clause (which as interpreted by the state Supreme Court prohibited a graduated state income tax) despite Shafer's assurance that the uniformity clause would not be touched. Having made constitutional revision the main goal of his administration, Shafer campaigned hard for "a 20th century document." With Leader and Scranton, Senators Clark and Scott, the Pennsylvania Manufacturers Association, the Pennsylvania Chamber of Commerce, the Pennsylvania AFL-CIO, and most members of the bar favoring a constitutional convention, revision triumphed by a 240,000-vote majority.

In addition, the electorate approved on May 16 a series of important constitutional amendments designed to achieve specific reforms. These amendments, embodying as much constitutional reform as the Scranton administration could get through the Legislature, limited future governors to two consecutive terms rather than one, made the General Assembly a continuing body that could consider a bill over a two-year period rather than being limited to one session, and converted the secretary of internal affairs into an appointive position. The constitutional convention, however, was necessary because several reform proposals could not clear the Legislature.

The convention of eighty-eight Republicans and seventy-five Democratic delegates met in Harrisburg on December 1, 1967, and had its proposed articles written by February 29, 1968. Those amendments somewhat disappointed Shafer, Leader, and Scranton. "In some ways," an academic consultant remarked, "this draft is probably the most progressive in the country, but in others it is a terrible failure." Perhaps most disappointing, the delegates rejected proposals for a smaller Legislature and froze the size of the House at 203 and the Senate at 50. On the other hand, the proposal creating constitutional machinery for federated municipal government—"metro governments composed of two or more jurisdictions in one urban area"—was unique and would serve as a model for other states with large urban sprawls. Furthermore all units of local government were permitted to choose a home-rule charter, and the one-man, one-vote apportionment principle was required in municipalities. The proposals on state finance, raising the ceiling on state borrowing to 1¾ times the average tax collected over a five-year period, promised to save the state thousands of dollars, since the commonwealth can borrow at a lower interest rate than can its authorities.

Finally, the Judiciary Article unified the judicial system under the Supreme Court of Pennsylvania, enabled voters in any judicial district to replace justices of the peace with a community court, limited the number of justices of the peace, replaced their fee system with salaries, and made their training mandatory. The Judiciary Article also permitted voters to determine in the 1969 primary whether statewide judges would continue to be elected or would be appointed by the governor from a list selected by a judicial qualifications commission. The people of Pennsylvania in May 1969 chose to elect judges. Despite their shortcomings, the new articles received strong support and were adopted April 24, 1968.

As progressive as its predecessors, the Shafer administration increased efforts to provide social services and to rehabilitate the economy. To balance his record $1.8 billion budget for the 1968 fiscal year, Shafer asked for $266.6 million in new taxes. The Legislature responded with increases in the cigarette, liquor, inheritance, and various business taxes; and in December 1967, enacted a temporary 6 percent sales tax. Although Shafer did not ask the 1968 General Assembly for any new taxes since it was an election year, he warned, "Pennsylvania has a continuing financial crisis that will not end until we clearly establish spending priorities and provide the revenue structure to pay for them."

By 1969 Pennsylvania had not resolved its financial crisis. Shafer's proposed $2.5 billion budget for the 1970 fiscal year (which represented a 25 percent rise in spending) necessitated $493 million in new taxes. Following the advice of his tax study commission, Shafer espoused an income tax and suggested eight plans (five of which would reduce the 6 percent sales tax) with rates varying from 1.5 to 3 percent. In addition, Shafer called for six corporate tax increases. These changes would continue the tax ratio of collecting from consumers 70 percent and from business 30 percent of Pennsylvania revenue.

Shafer faced a difficult fight. Democrats, who won control of the House in 1968, insisted Shafer "prove . . . that an income tax is justified." To rally support for his budget and tax proposals, Shafer began stumping the state in April, when weary citizens struggling with their Federal income tax returns were in no mood to contemplate more forms and more taxes, and he failed to convince the public or the Legislature. Though the Assembly agreed to make the 6 percent sales tax permanent, it deadlocked thirteen months before it finally balanced the 1970 budget.

The Shafer administration needed additional revenue because it continued the progressive Scranton tradition. Shortly after taking office Shafer joined the governors of New York and New Jersey to announce plans for the Mid Atlantic States Air Pollution Control Commission to attack the problem on a regional basis. Shafer also lauded the Delaware River Basin Commission's plan to spend $245 million over a twenty-year period to clean up the Delaware River. Shafer continued to promote business expansion and, like Scranton, was blessed with business prosperity. By 1967 even the anthracite region of northeastern Pennsylvania, despite its dying major industry, had undergone an industrial transformation. From 1958 to 1967, thanks largely to the Pennsylvania Industrial Development Authority, 547 new industries located in that nine-county area and created 40,000 jobs, while many existing industries expanded. During those years unemployment in the anthracite region dropped from 17 percent of the work force to 4 percent, and after 1963 people no longer fled the area.

The Republican party prospered less in Pennsylvania than did the economy. In 1967, however, it once again became the state's majority party, and in 1968 Congressman Richard S. Schweiker successfully challenged Joseph S. Clark for his Senate seat. An outstanding liberal and an outspoken critic of the Vietnam War, Clark had angered Italian-Americans by supporting Genevieve Blatt rather than Musmanno (who rekindled their anger by appropriately dying on Columbus Day before the election); sportsmen by supporting strong gun-control legislation; and organization Democrats, such as Mayors James H. J. Tate and Joseph M. Barr of Philadelphia and Pittsburgh, respectively, by supporting Senator George S. McGovern of South Dakota for the 1968 presidential nomination, rather than Hubert Humphrey. Despite Schweiker's impressive victory by 250,000 votes, Pennsylvania Republicans suffered a setback in 1968. Nixon trailed Humphrey in the state by 230,000 votes, Republicans lost both the state auditor general and the treasurer, lost control of the state Supreme Court as well as the state House of Representatives, and elected a minority of the Pennsylvania delegation to the House of Representatives (13 out of 27). Furthermore,

Shafer's 1967 sales-tax increase and particularly his 1969 state income-tax proposal severely damaged the Republican party, jeopardizing both Scott's Senate seat and the governor's chair in 1970. Finally—and ominous for both parties—the 8 percent vote Pennsylvanians gave conservative, American Independent candidate George C. Wallace in 1968 indicated that bipartisan efforts to achieve civil rights for blacks had alienated enough voters to pose a third party threat.

SHAPP

The campaign of 1970 seemed but a rerun of the 1966 contest. The disorganized Democratic state organization again chose Auditor General Robert P. Casey to run for governor, and in the primary he was once again defeated by Milton Shapp, whom both Tate and Mayor Peter F. Flaherty of Pittsburgh as well as the Americans for Democratic Action (ADA) supported. Although Casey took a liberal stance, Shapp, who wished to substitute a graduated income tax for the 6 percent sales tax, who wanted state legislation to prevent Pennsylvanians from serving in undeclared wars, and who favored a liberal abortion reform went considerably beyond him. Again, Republicans were united. Their gubernatorial nominee Lieutenant Governor Raymond J. Broderick and Senator Hugh Scott were unopposed in the primary. Scott's Democratic challenger was state Senator William G. Sesler, a forty-two-year-old Erie lawyer who attacked Scott for his age and for his support of Nixon's decision to send troops into Cambodia but who himself had vacillated on the Vietnam war issue. With his enormous prestige Scott had little difficulty with Sesler, but Broderick had little but trouble. He inherited the hostility engendered by Shafer's proposed income tax and the fiscal crisis caused by failure to enact Shafer's proposed income tax. Broderick repudiated the income tax solution and promised he could balance the budget by firing state employees and eliminating waste. Neither Shafer nor a host of other Pennsylvanians were convinced that Broderick could save enough to offset the half-billion-dollar deficit predicted by mid-1971. Running as a responsible businessman, Shapp took Shafer's old position and called for an income tax combined with a reduction in the 6 percent sales tax. Unlike his effort four years earlier, Shapp ran a conservative campaign. Despite a last-minute attempt by Broderick to portray him as an opponent of law and order and a leader of stone-throwing revolutionaries, Shapp piled up the largest majority (half a million votes) ever won by a Democratic governor. For the first time since 1936, the landslide gave the Democrats firm control of both the governorship and the Legislature.

Shapp moved quickly to avert fiscal disaster. His initial proposal of a 5 percent income tax was shaved to 3.5 percent when it passed in March 1971 by a strict party vote. A system of "vanishing credits" reduced or completely eliminated the tax for low-income families, and a companion measure exempted most common household necessities from the 6 percent sales tax. Shapp's proposed $3.3 billion budget coupled with the new income tax assured Pennsylvanians that the services of the state, ranging from police protection through education to drug clinics, would be continued and enlarged. In late June, however, the Pennsylvania Supreme Court declared (5–2) that the income tax was unconstitutional because its graduated feature (vanishing credits) violated the requirement that "all taxes shall be uniform on the same class of subjects." That feature of the 1873 constitution had not been altered by the recent constitutional convention. Again facing financial disaster,

Milton E. Shapp, Democratic governor.

the Shapp administration asked for a flat 2.5 percent emergency income tax, under which 80 percent of the state's taxpayers would pay more than under the measure which had been declared unconstitutional. The Legislature—particularly Democrats associated with Mayor Tate of Philadelphia—balked, and during early August in the absence of emergency legislation Pennsylvania was without spending power and 29,000 state employees were without pay. Finally in late August, Shapp's compromise (a flat 2.3 percent income tax coupled with a reduction of business taxes) attracted enough Republican votes to make up for Democratic defections, and Pennsylvania's fiscal crisis was over.

Solving the budget problem helped Shapp project the image of a responsible businessman at the head of a "business-like administration." He appointed Republican Walter G. Arader secretary of commerce, actively recruited other businessmen, and continued his predecessors' efforts to attract industry to Pennsylvania. More important, Shapp eliminated 17,500 blue-collar highway workers from the spoils system by signing, in November 1971, a collective bargaining contract with the American Federation of State, County, and Municipal Employees. The eighteen-month contract—negotiated under the Pennsylvania Public Employees Relations Act of 1970—prohibited discrimination on account of race, religion, or politics, prevented dismissals on political grounds, and forbade mandatory political contributions and party work. With 65,000 of the 110,000 state employees protected by civil service regulations, this labor contract effectively reduced state patronage jobs to 27,500. Further patronage reductions were slated to follow with more collective bargaining agreements. Although patronage appeared on the way out, unions of public service employees were becoming strong political forces in their own right.

By the end of 1971 the divisive race relations issue appeared to be causing the first substantial realignment of major party supporters since the 1930s. The 8 percent Wallace vote in Pennsylvania in 1968 indicated widespread alienation from both major parties over the race issue, and the 1971 Philadelphia mayoralty campaign proved that this issue could force both political leaders and rank-and-file members to bolt their party. The commitment of both major parties to integration was reflected in the June 1971 Pennsylvania Human Relations Commission's order that racial imbalance in the public schools be eliminated by 1974. Racial imbalance, defined as occuring when over 79 percent of one race make up a school, was found in 92 of 115 Pittsburgh schools and in 228 of 281 Philadelphia schools.

Liberal Philadelphia Democrats and Shapp, however, suffered a setback when their candidate, Representative William J. Green, lost the Democratic nomination for mayor to "the toughest cop in America," Police Commissioner Frank L. Rizzo. A high school drop-out (after his mother's death) from south Philadelphia's Little Italy who worked his way up through the ranks to become a volatile and charismatic leader, Rizzo contrasted sharply with the Princeton educated, moderately liberal Republican nominee, Thacher Longstreth. Rizzo's attitude toward blacks was the campaign's main issue, and Philadelphians knew that his shrewd slogan "Rizzo means business" referred to race relations rather than the economy. Campaigning primarily in white, working-class areas, Rizzo promised to end permissiveness, to emphasize the three R's in the public schools, and not to raise taxes. Liberal Democrats, including local luminaries such as Joseph S. Clark and Richardson Dilworth and national figures such as Ramsey Clark and Eugene McCarthy, supported Republican Longstreth as did blacks, whose attitude was summed up by a woman who told him, "You ain't much, baby, but you're all we got." Despite mass desertions by blacks and liberal Democrats, Rizzo won. His support came primarily from white, blue-collar workers, many of whom deserted the Republican party.

Rizzo confirmed liberal hostility when he passed over seventeen higher-ranking firemen to appoint his brother fire commissioner and when he fired—as he had promised he would— innovative Superintendent of Schools Mark R. Shedd who had worked closely with School Board President Richardson Dilworth to transform Philadelphia schools. Having in the primary campaign accused Rizzo of police brutality, Shapp moved two weeks after Rizzo's election to investigate alleged corruption in the Philadelphia Police Department. Democratic party convulsions continued into 1972. The immediate prospects of uniting a racially polarized city and political party appeared dim, whereas a fundamental realignment of major party constituents appeared possible.

As summer 1972 approached, the Shapp administration laid plans for Pennsylvania's role in the Democratic presidential nominating convention. But politics came to an abrupt halt during the week of June 18 when the most devastating flood in the nation's history struck the eastern seaboard with Pennsylvania at its center. A week of torrential rains bred by hurricane Agnes raised river levels at some points to 15 feet above any flood crests known before. The entire state suffered, but towns along the North Branch of the Susquehanna from Wilkes-Barre to Sunbury were all but wiped out. In Wilkes-Barre, the business district was engulfed and most residents had to be evacuated. In Kingston, scarcely a dozen homes remained undamaged. Danville and Bloomsburg were submerged.

Along the West Branch, Lock Haven and Williamsport were inundated and isolated, and all river towns along the Susquehanna appeared from the air as rooftops protruding from the swirling flood. Harrisburg suffered a major disaster as raging waters ravaged the city and rose to the second floor of the new governor's mansion. Pittsburgh's riverside industries and the Goldern Triangle were flooded, and water lapped into Three Rivers Stadium. Each small stream wrought its local ruin with tiny rivulets becoming rushing torrents and tearing away houses, roads, bridges, railways, power and communications facilities, sewage plants, and public water systems. After an air tour of the region, President Nixon declared the commonwealth a disaster area and called in Federal relief agencies.

Miraculously the death toll remained below fifty, but the direct property loss was well over a billion dollars. As after the Johnstown Flood, people who had been spared rushed to aid those of the stricken areas, and dozens of organized and hastily assembled volunteer groups participated in rescue and rehabilitation efforts. But during the weeks of cleanup it became apparent that many of the old Pennsylvania landmarks had been destroyed and that lives, businesses, and cities would have to be built anew. With the approach of the bicentennial of the nation and the tricentennial of Pennsylvania, it seemed clear that these observances would not so much commemorate the old as they would signal the building of a new commonwealth.

BIBLIOGRAPHY

On the Democratic triumph in Philadelphia, see Roger Butterfield: "Revolt in Philadelphia," *Saturday Evening Post* (Nov. 8, 1952), pp. 19–21, 106–107; (Nov. 15, 1952), pp. 40–41, 65, 67–68, 70;(Nov. 22, 1952), pp. 36, 164–166. Also see William G. Weart: "New Era Dawns for Philadelphia," *New York Times* (Mar. 20, 1955); and James Reichley: "Clean-cut Reformers of Philadelphia," *New Republic* (Oct. 24, 1955), pp. 7–9, and *The Art of Government: Reform and Organization Politics in Philadelphia* (1959).

On Leader, see Reed M. Smith: *State Government in Transition: Reforms of the Leader Administration, 1955–1959* (1961); James Higgins: "The Issues that Counted: Pennsylvania," *Nation* (Nov. 13, 1954), pp. 416–417; "Voter's Farmer," *Time* (Nov. 15, 1954), pp. 27–28, 30, 32; "Pennsylvania's Leader," *Nation* (Feb. 19, 1955), p. 151; James Higgins: "Two Obstructive Votes in the Keystone State," *Nation* (Nov. 5, 1955), p. 408.

On patronage, see Frank J. Sorauf, "State Patronage in a Rural County," *American Political Science Review,* vol. 50 (1956), pp. 1046–1056; "Reform Makes a Deal in Pennsylvania," *New Republic* (Feb. 13, 1956), pp. 8–9; and Samuel Shaffer, "The Senate Race: How Pennsylvania Tilts," *Newsweek* (Oct. 15, 1956), pp. 47–48.

On Lawrence, see Frank Hawkins: "Lawrence of Pittsburgh: Boss of the Mellon Patch," *Harper's Magazine* (August 1956), pp. 55–61; and "As Recession Ebbs, Pennsylvania Wonders about Steel Strike, " *Business Week* (May 30, 1959), pp. 54–55. On Lawrence's educational plans, see Natalie Jaffe: "Pennsylvania Reform Plan," *New York Times* (April 9, 1961).

On Scranton, see James Welsh: "Portrait of a Not-so-dark Horse," *New York Times Magazine* (Jan. 12, 1964); on both Scranton and Shafer, see Paul B. Beers: *The Republican Years* (1971). For an analysis of presidential elections, see Walter Dean Burnham and John Sprague: "Additive and Multiplicative Models of the Voting Universe: The Case of Pennsylvania: 1960–1968," *American Political Science Review,* vol. 64 (1970), pp. 471–490. Finally, newspapers and news magazines must be relied upon for recent events. Though most newspaper accounts lack perspective, the thoughtful dispatches to the *New York Times* by William G. Weart, Leo Egan, Joseph A. Loftus, Homer Bigart, Ben A. Franklin, and Donald Janson succeed in capsuling and analyzing much significant and recent Pennsylvania history.

CHAPTER TWENTY-EIGHT

Culture in an Urban Age

The wealth and productivity of industrial Pennsylvania enabled its citizens to cultivate the mind and the spirit. The machine provided the leisure for virtually all to pursue knowledge, for many to patronize the arts, and for a few to create original works. Mass education through the schools and the press led to widespread appreciation for scholarship, literature, theater, music, art, and architecture. This appreciation helped Pennsylvania both to attract and to produce men and women with national and international reputations for their intellectual and artistic pursuits, and made both Philadelphia and Pittsburgh major cultural centers.

EDUCATION AND SCHOLARSHIP

Education in twentieth-century Pennsylvania not only responded to society's need but improved tremendously. The consolidation of one-room primary schools into larger units promoted better teaching by enabling instructors to concentrate on one grade. Primary school curriculums were enlarged to include more social and natural science and more vocational, health, and physical education. Methodology, furthermore, was revolutionized by John Dewey's ideas. Teachers gradually abandoned efforts to break students' spirits, stopped beating their bodies, deemphasized learning by rote, and tried to make learning both meaningful and pleasant. High schools grew as public-supported secondary education ceased to be a privilege enjoyed by a few city children and became the right of all children. Secondary school curriculums were also widened to include vocational and physical education, other social studies in addition to history, greater emphasis on mathematics, science, and languages (particularly in the space age), and even driver and sex education. With increasing numbers of young people graduating from high schools, colleges expanded to provide higher education for an increasing number of Pennsylvanians.

Expansion, consolidation, and centralization have characterized Pennsylvania education in the twentieth century. The number of high schools grew rapidly after 1901 when the Legislature offered state support. In 1911 the Legislature codified and clarified existing educational legislation, classified school districts and high schools, specified qualifications for various teaching certificates and the minimum salaries their holders should receive, and established a board of education to supervise and equalize the state school system. World War I brought an emphasis on vocational education with the Federal government providing funds through the 1917 Smith-Hughes Act.

More significant changes occurred after Governor Sproul in 1919 appointed Dr. Thomas E. Finegan superintendent of public instruction. Finegan reorganized the Department of Public Instruction and centralized control of the state's school system. The omnibus Edmonds Act (1921) consisting of seventy-two laws embodied the Finegan program. It replaced the Board of Education with the State Council of Education which was empowered to issue new statewide teaching certificates. Raising standards, salaries, and state subsidies, the act also defined primary and secondary educational systems, made the junior high school a part of the system, and gave the State Council power to prescribe high school curriculum. "Czar" Finegan was damned—particularly by the Grange—for raising salaries and limiting local control, but no one has subsequently equaled Finegan's impact on education in Pennsylvania.

Although the educational system's main problem was survival during the Great Depression and World War II, the postwar era was one of expansion. School districts desperately needed more state money for more schools, more teachers, better equipment, and better salaries. In 1945 the Legislature devised the Hare-Lee-Sollenberger Act to supplement educational programs in poorer districts and to provide for a new single salary schedule for teachers. In 1947 and in 1951 the state utilized the authority device to help school districts build new schools. Initial legislation in 1947 to consolidate school districts was unsuccessful, but when the state offered subsidies for reorganization in 1951, districts began to consolidate; by 1968 reorganization had compressed 2,056 school districts into 742. Although the Lawrence administration passed a sweeping school reorganization bill in 1961, the Scranton administration replaced it in 1963 with a less sweeping but effective measure, which among other things created a new state board of education. In 1965 the Legislature completely revised the school subsidy program to provide larger subsidies for virtually all school districts and to subsidize transportation for parochial elementary and secondary school pupils.

Despite the great strides Pennsylvania's schools made in the twentieth century, they lagged behind the schools of most other wealthy states. Good education is an expensive investment; and until the 1960s Pennsylvania did not support its schools sufficiently. Since educational expenditures dominated local and state budgets, Pennsylvania's jerry-built tax structure (particularly before the advent of the sales tax in 1953) was to blame for inadequate educational support. In 1959 the total per capita tax collected by state and local governments in Pennsylvania was $158.27, placing it thirty-sixth among the states. Expenditures in the state's schools per pupil in average daily attendance in 1958–1959 was $370 (seventeenth among the states) as compared to the national average of $340. Since teachers' salaries are the largest part of a school's budget, low cost per pupil meant low pay for teachers, which in turn meant that the best-qualified individuals were not attracted to teaching. In the early 1930s on tests of general culture given by the Carnegie Foundation for the Advancement of Teaching prospective teachers scored below prospective nonteachers in nearly every subject. During the 1960s Pennsylvanians and other Americans began to realize that there was no substitute for a good teacher in a well-equipped classroom with a moderate number of students, and that those items and conditions were expensive. By 1969–1970 yearly expenditures per pupil had jumped to $876 (ninth place) as compared to the national average of $766. Pennsylvania teachers' salaries, however, lagged behind the national average ($7,858 compared to $7,908) as well as behind neighboring New York ($9,000), New Jersey ($8,425), Delaware ($8,360), and Maryland ($8,815). Higher salaries paid by neighboring states meant that Pennsylvania had difficulty both keeping teachers it had and attracting those trained in other states. Out of 986 Pennsylvania teachers sampled in the late 1960s, 90 percent had attended high school in the state and 53 percent were teaching in their home districts.

By the late 1960s growing centralization and expenditures had improved primary and secondary education and had introduced some exciting new services and programs. With seven educational television stations reaching 97 percent of the state's population in 1968, students could view interesting programs, produced by the Department of Public Instruction, highlighting a variety of school subjects. The department also developed new courses in fine arts and in the religious literature of the Western world. Using Federal funds made available by the Elementary and Secondary Education Act of 1965, Pennsylvania established seventeen Educational Development Centers to introduce schools to promising educational practices and to evaluate the quality of education in Pennsylvania.

Perhaps the most exciting educational development in Pennsylvania—indeed in the United States—was the opening in January 1969 of Philadelphia's Parkway Program financed primarily by a $100,000 Ford Foundation grant. The "high school without walls" allowed students to choose their own subjects (such as adolescent psychology, game theory, computer programming, and even an encounter group) and to attend classes, often conducted by specialists, in the civic, cultural, and business buildings of the city. More conventional classes were conducted by certified teachers. Stressing freedom, responsibility, and equality, the Parkway Program allowed a wide variety of courses to meet basic requirements such as English and social studies, eliminated marks except for "pass" and "fail," and placed students and faculty on an informal first-name basis. Designed to educate students who found the curriculum and discipline of conventional schools confining and dull, the Parkway Program received 10,000 applicants for 500 openings. Though virtually all students and most parents thought the program successful, many parents wondered whether their children were mature enough to pick their options wisely.

Pennsylvania colleges and universities also grew rapidly in the twentieth century, but made fewer fundamental changes than did elementary and secondary schools. In 1938 the Carnegie Foundation for the Advancement of Teaching published a report based on examinations of general culture and intelligence, administered to Pennsylvania high school and college students in 1928, 1930, and 1932. The report found that an alarming number of superior high school graduates did not go to college, that state subsidies and private endowments were frequently spent on mediocre students, and that colleges differed radically in their capacity to instruct. Evaluating these tests in Pennsylvania, the Carnegie report suggested that college curriculum, instruction, and facilities be geared to self-education. It called for replacing the old, rigid four-year prescribed-course system with a fluid, individually geared curriculum. Suggesting more communication between professors and students and fewer formal lectures, it warned that college administrations must be in close contact with students. Finally, the report called for replacing the conventional marking system with occasional elaborate objective tests coupled with oral and written comprehensive examinations which would be given after students had participated in seminars and discussion groups.

Colleges paid scant heed to the advice of the Carnegie Foundation. Had they listened, they might have been spared much campus unrest a generation later. Instead of major changes they merely expanded course offerings and existing facilities and enlarged classes to make room for the World War II veterans enabled to attend college by the GI Bill of Rights. Unprecedented affluence and increased public support of higher education combined in the 1950s, 1960s, and 1970s to further increase college attendance, but the cost of educating students on an individual basis grew far more rapidly than income from tuition, endowments, and appropriations. Classes consequently became larger, and the lecture often displaced the discussion as a pedagogical technique. In large universities and even in many small colleges hundreds of students filed into auditoriums where professors utilizing microphones addressed them, and machines or graduate students graded their papers. In many classes closed-circuit television replaced the teacher.

Although Pennsylvania with its many privately endowed colleges had a weak tradition of public higher education, public funds assumed a larger share of the costs of providing young Pennsylvanians with a college education. In 1959 the fourteen state teachers colleges became liberal arts colleges, and during the 1960s and 1970s the state expanded both their plants and their offerings with one of these colleges becoming in 1965 Indiana University of Pennsylvania. The Legislature authorized the establishment of a community college system in 1963, and by 1968 twelve community colleges, whose expenditures had already exceeded $29 million, were operating on fourteen campuses. Recognizing rising costs, the 1963 Legislature set up the Pennsylvania Higher Education Assistance Agency to offer state-guaranteed loans to students. Furthermore the state combined Temple University (1965) and the University of Pittsburgh (1966) with the Pennsylvania State University to form a triumvirate of state-related commonwealth universities, half of whose swelling budgets it supplied. The University of Pennsylvania and Drexel Institute of Technology were also given increased aid. Finally in 1967 the Shafer administration created the Pennsylvania Higher Education Facilities Authority to help the building programs of private colleges and universities. From 1958 to 1968 Pennsylvania multiplied its grants of $30 million to state and private institutions of higher learning (excluding state colleges) almost five times ($148 million). Rising costs and swelling enrollments, however, soaked up the vast increases, leaving colleges more impersonal in the 1970s than they were in the 1950s.

The student unrest, riots, and revolts of this period were rooted in the impersonality of colleges and in their slowness to change. Why had colleges changed so little in a period of unprecedented change in society and unprecedented public spending for higher education? Professors who did not hesitate to reconstitute society but adamantly refused to change established patterns on their own campuses were part of the answer, but the higher cost of a more personalized system was a more important factor.

While higher education expanded and individual instruction in colleges and universities languished, research flourished. Indeed, the undergraduates' complaint that scholarship, research, and particularly graduate education were at their expense was in many instances true. Scholars in the twentieth century have almost invariably held academic positions. Distinguished research scholars tended to congregate in the state's largest institutions, but they were found on nearly every campus. The largest concentration of Pennsylvania scholars is located in Philadelphia and is centered at the University of Pennsylvania. Throughout the twentieth century, when scholars have ranked American institutions, the University of Pennsylvania has either just made or just missed the top ten list. With strength in the biological and social sciences and the humanities, the University of Pennsylvania in 1964 was ranked by the American Council on Education as the state's outstanding multiversity with the University of Pittsburgh and Pennsylvania State University tieing for second place. Bryn Mawr College also received mention for strength in the humanities, and both Carnegie Institute of Technology (now Carnegie-Mellon University) and Lehigh University were listed as having strong engineering departments.

JOURNALISM

In the twentieth century, major city newspapers became bigger and less dependent on the whims of individual advertisers. These newspapers forsook the personalized journalism of an earlier era, and became links in chains. For example, in 1902 Adolph S. Ochs of the *New York Times* purchased the *Philadelphia Public Ledger* from the Drexel estate for $2,250,000, and a few weeks later merged it with the *Philadelphia Times* (established by A. K. McClure), and in 1923 Pittsburgh dailies combined to buy and destroy the *Pittsburgh Dispatch* and *Leader.* By 1940 Pittsburgh along with many other cities had but one morning paper. In 1923 the Scripps-Howard chain bought the *Pittsburgh Press,* and in 1927 William Randolph Hearst acquired four Pittsburgh papers—the *Sun,* the *Chronicle Telegraph,* the *Post,* and the *Gazette Times.* The last two, nominally owned by Paul Block, were consolidated as the *Pittsburgh Post Gazette.* Consolidations, chains, and extensive use of wire services cut the number of editorial opinions and nationalized the outlook of many local papers. Although local editors of chain newpapers were usually free to deal with local issues, editorial policies were generally set by the central office.

Philadelphia journalism illustrates the trend toward larger and fewer newspapers. One of the giants was William L. McLean's *Evening Bulletin,* which was Philadelphia's strongest, steadiest, most conservative, and most profitable paper during the first half of the twentieth century. Despite its size, the *Bulletin* was like a small-town paper. McLean's successful formula—"the more names the better"—is still used by many Pennsylvania papers.

The trend toward fewer papers was hastened by Cyrus H. K. Curtis, the successful magazine publisher who entered the newspaper field, lost several million dollars, and killed four historic Philadelphia papers. In 1913 Curtis bought the conservative *Public Ledger* from Adolph S. Ochs and for the next fifteen years attempted to make it the greatest American daily. Curtis developed a remarkable, widely syndicated foreign news service, featuring men like William C. Bullitt; celebrities, including former President William Howard Taft, contributed columns; and its Wall Street, trade, and commerce section was admirable. Curtis started an evening version of the *Public Ledger,* a shortlived tabloid named the *Sun,* and built a $15 million plant for his newspapers on Independence Square. In 1918, to acquire an Associated Press franchise and to eliminate a competitor, he bought and killed the *Evening Telegraph*. He purchased the *Press,* which John W. Forney had made famous, two years later and the *North American* in 1925, and merged them with the *Public Ledger*. The *Ledger* began making money in the middle 1920s, but with the Depression, circulation tumbled and profits disappeared.

Though he successfully pioneered new styles in magazines, Curtis floundered as a newspaperman. "Vacillating and contradictory, with undefined aims," the *Ledger's* editorial page reflected his lack of objectives. According to seasoned newspaperman Oswald Garrison Villard, the *Ledger* also failed to understand the hidden motives in Philadelphia and Pennsylvania politics the way its sophisticated rival the *North American* had understood them. Although the *Ledger* supported both reform Mayor Rudolph Blankenburg and reform Governor Gifford Pinchot, it was antilabor and either played down or refused to print news detrimental to important advertisers. During the 1919 Amalgamated Clothing Workers strike, the *Ledger* ran a series of antiunion ads but refused to accept prostrike ones. After the crash in 1929 Curtis expanded despite the fact that both the *Ledger* and his *New York Evening Post* were losing money. In 1930 he acquired the Philadelphia *Inquirer* for $18 million and conducted it as a separate and competing newspaper. In 1934, shortly after Curtis died, the *Inquirer* absorbed the *Public Ledger* and was again controlled by its pre-1930 owner. The evening *Public Ledger* lasted until January 1942.

J. David Stern was a different breed of newspaper publisher than Curtis. Stern had served as a cub reporter on the *Public Ledger* under George W. Ochs and in 1919 purchased the Camden *Courier* and returned to the Philadelphia area. In 1926 he acquired the competing Camden *Post-Telegram,* and in 1928 he bought the dying *Philadelphia Record* from the Rodman Wanamaker estate. Shortly after acquiring the *Record* Stern heard of plans for a secret Sunday morning meeting to refinance the transit system by persuading the city to pay $250 million for subways and surface lines worth about $75 million. Since the meeting was scheduled for the office of W. W. Atterbury, president of the Pennsylvania Railroad, Stern ordered reporters and photographers to surround the Broad Street Station. In vain Stern's managing editor protested, "this sort of thing just isn't done in Philadelphia. . . . I don't think you realize how powerful the railroad is and how dangerous such a story might be." Stern did know. Twenty years earlier the *Public Ledger* had fired him for insulting the Pennsy. To escape the reporters whom they had earlier barred from their meeting, bankers and city and transit officials left by a freight elevator, only to be met by an alert press photographer. The resulting picture with some of the notables covering their faces to avoid recognition launched the *Record's* seven-year battle which pared the transit-system capitalization down to $87 million, saving Philadelphia millions of dollars. More popular was Stern's crusade against Pennsylvania's Sunday blue laws, which forbade movies, professional sports, or any entertainment that charged admission on Sunday. To prove Stern's contention that 80 percent of Pennsylvanians opposed the blue laws, the *Record* sent out reply postcards to a million registered voters. Ninety percent of the responses favored a liberal Sunday; these replies gave legislators courage to permit local option. Utilizing the "upchuck method" of increasing circulation by horrifying readers, Stern ran a series on the overcrowded tuberculosis pavilion at the Philadelphia General Hospital that provoked the city council to appropriate $3 million for a new pavilion. Finding the *Record's* traditional Democratic stance congenial, Stern supported Al Smith and Franklin Roosevelt for president and George Earle for governor.

The *Record* and Stern faced tough competition when another fascinating newspaperman, Moses L. Annenberg, bought the *Inquirer* in 1936. Having in 1922 obtained the *Daily Racing Form* and later the *New York Morning Telegraph,* a theater and turf paper, Annenberg also secured wire services connecting twenty-nine race tracks to thousands of bookies in 223 cities located in thirty-nine states, and earned $2 million a year from them.

Boasting "I can lose five dollars to make Dave Stern lose one," Annenberg vowed to put the *Record* out of business. Annenberg had greater assets than mere money. He was a courageous, resourceful, able executive "with an uncanny knack for picking the right man for every job in his many legitimate enterprises." He spent millions on circulation promotion, increased the *Inquirer's* news coverage, and added many features. Nevertheless, though Stern's profits were reduced, he proved stronger because he was less vulnerable. When Annenberg attempted to control a Wilmington, Delaware, newspaper-distributing agency which would enable him to cut the *Record's* circulation overnight, Stern obtained a preliminary injunction. Anticipating that Annenberg would intimidate Philadelphia newsstand dealers, Stern called the White House for the FBI, Governor Earle for the state police, and Mayor S. Davis Wilson for city detectives to guard newsstands. Whatever Stern feared, or pretended to fear, Annenberg did not use strong-arm methods to destroy the *Record's* circulation. Stern himself admitted that Annenberg "bought the Inquirer to cover himself with a cloak of respectability. A circulation war would have torn that cloak to tatters." The FBI thoroughly investigated Annenberg's past, particularly after his scandal sheet, Baltimore *Brevities,* ran a "scurrilous" story about J. Edgar Hoover. In 1939 a Federal grand jury indicted Annenberg for income tax evasion, running lotteries, and attempted bribery. Hoover's agents had collected such overwhelming evidence that Annenberg pleaded guilty to income-tax evasion, paid $8 million in back taxes plus $1.5 million in interest, and got a three-year prison term. Two years later illness led to his parole; and he died a month later of a brain tumor. His name lives on in the M. L. Annenberg School of Communication at the University of Pennsylvania which his son Walter—later Nixon's ambassador to Britain—endowed as a memorial to him.

As indicated earlier, Cyrus H. K. Curtis matched his failure in newspapers with success in magazines. Although New York had become America's magazine capital long before 1900, Curtis pioneered modern, low-priced, mass-circulated magazines from Philadelphia and proved that with a large circulation a publisher could sell magazines for less than cost and become wealthy on the advertising. The modern magazine was born in early October 1897 when Curtis, publisher of the popular *Ladies Home Journal,* purchased for $1,000 the expiring *Saturday Evening Post.* With a mere 2,000 subscribers, the *Post* had only age to recommend it. The oldest literary and family magazine in the United States, it had been established in 1821, but Curtis claimed for it an even earlier and more distinguished beginning by capitalizing on an error in J. Thomas Scharf and Thompson Wescott's *History of Philadelphia* which listed it as an incarnation of Benjamin Franklin's *Pennsylvania Gazette.* To make the *Post* worthy of Franklin, Curtis improved its fiction and illustrations and launched a vigorous circulation drive which increased subscriptions to 250,000 by 1899, the year he made George Horace Lorimer editor.

Lorimer aimed the *Post* at "ambitious young men of the great middle-class American public." His formula emphasized success in business, public affairs, and romance but also noted sports, humor, science, photography, the theater, literature, and foreign affairs. *Post* articles particularly stressed the romantic and personal aspects of making a fortune. Incorporating the nineteenth-century ideals of Horatio Alger as well as the eighteenth-cen-

Cyrus H. K. Curtis, publisher. (Curtis Publishing
Company)

tury pragmatism of Franklin, Lorimer made the *Post* the prophet of twentieth-century
business success. Along with and sometimes contributing to this theme were stories and
novels by excellent authors, such as Rudyard Kipling, Stephen Crane, Joel Chandler Harris, Charles Egbert Craddock, and Frank Norris. Circulation topped a million in December 1908 and reached and remained at about 2.5 million throughout the 1920s, when 200-
page issues, more than half devoted to advertising, became common. Having anticipated
the twentieth-century stress on production and distribution of consumer goods which led
to increased advertising, Curtis in 1924 was one of four men in the United States whose
personal income exceeded $5 million; in 1925 the Curtis Publishing Company earned $16
million, and in 1927 the *Post*'s advertising revenue topped $50 million.

Although its circulation and gross advertising revenues in later years would exceed
those figures, the *Post* had its heyday in the 1920s. The 1929 crash dated the business-
success theme and made it a hollow mockery. The nation had changed with the Depression,
but Lorimer and the *Post* had remained the same. Bitterly hostile to the New Deal, Lorimer
resigned shortly after Roosevelt's smashing victory in 1936. Even though circulation held its
own during the Depression, advertising revenue plummeted as radio and other publications
offered stiff competition. Lorimer's successors further damaged the *Post*'s prestige with
an unpopular isolationist stand while the nation prepared for war with Hitler. After Pearl
Harbor advertising fell off 20 percent. In 1942 a shakeup in the *Post*'s offices brought in a
new editor, Ben Hibbs, who revitalized the *Post*. Removing Franklin's picture from the
cover, Hibbs modernized the typography and layout; increased, shortened, and lightened the

subjects of nonfiction articles; and ran more cartoons; but he continued the *Post*'s ardent Republican politics, which during the Eisenhower years were again in style. It was "as American as the public school, the big department store, the television network program, the hot dog and the ice cream cone." By 1955 the *Post* circulated 4.6 million copies and grossed $83.7 million, but the high cost of paper and labor cut profits. Despite a circulation of 6.8 million in the 1960s, the *Post* lost both advertisers and money. Slim profits soon became severe losses, and the *Post* died in 1969, only to be resurrected as a large quarterly in 1971.

LITERATURE

Pennsylvania's literary reputation improved in the twentieth century when several of its writers, among them John O'Hara of Pottsville, James A. Michener of Doylestown, and John Updike of Shillington won wide critical acclaim. O'Hara's and Updike's novels and stories are frequently set in Pennsylvania; Michener's stories are often set abroad.

John O'Hara (1905–1970) spent the first twenty-two years of his life in and about Pottsville, and much of his best work is set in "O'Hara Country," a rough triangle with Philadelphia at its eastern extremity, Harrisburg (Fort Penn) at its western end, and Pottsville (Gibbsville), Tamaqua, and Lykens (Lyons) forming its northern apex. O'Hara's father, a successful Irish Catholic surgeon, died in 1925, plunging his wife and eight children into genteel poverty. John, the eldest child, could not afford to attend Yale, where he had been accepted, but continued his work as a newspaper reporter and soon moved to New York, where by early 1928 he began publishing short stories and sketches. His first novel, *Appointment in Samarra,* published in 1934, was well received. Until the mid-1940s O'Hara worked on films and explored Hollywood and New York themes in works such as *Butterfield 8* (1935) and *Pal Joey* (1940). Settling in Princeton in 1949, O'Hara returned to the Pennsylvania milieu in his stories. Among his many books are *A Rage to Live* (1949), *The Farmer's Hotel* (1951), *Ten North Frederick* (1955), *A Family Party* (1956), *From the Terrace* (1958), *Ourselves to Know* (1960), and *Elizabeth Appleton* (1963).

O'Hara's virtues as a writer were many. His unsurpassed eye for detail and ear for dialogue have been described as phonophotographic, and hostile critics have contended that he was merely a superb reporter. The details, however, are meaningful, for he caught "the insignia of social station, . . . the objects which fill or clutter our lives, and . . . the clothes, cars, houses, which comprise the surface and much of the texture of American life." He was keenly aware of social stratification, perhaps because he had access to most but not all levels of Pottsville society. He skillfully depicted the relationships, particularly the tensions, among parents and children, husbands and wives, and lovers, friends, and enemies. He recognized that the class distinctions he perceived so well frequently caused the private hell endured by the rich as well as the poor. His long line of tragic heroes illustrated, as Wolcott Gibbs observes, "the sadness of potentially valuable lives failing, but not without some dignity, because they were not born quite strong enough for the circumstances they had to meet." They behaved compulsively, and only love and compassion could save them, but at the moment of crisis they were bereft of both and were lost. As befits a disciple of Ernest Hemingway and F. Scott Fitzgerald, O'Hara wrote prose that is terse, clear, precise, and deft. "I try," he said, "to make every word count." Writing about himself, O'Hara accurately evaluated

John O'Hara; much of his work is set in a rough triangle with Philadelphia at its eastern extremity, Harrisburg at its western end, and Pottsville, Tamaqua, and Lykens forming its northern apex. (Random House)

his achievement: "Better than anyone else he told the truth about his time, the first half of the twentieth century. He was a professional. He wrote honestly and well."

James A. Michener (b. 1907?) is another professional who writes well and tells the truth about his time. Exotic Pacific islands frequently provide the setting for Michener's work, but his grand and recurring theme—the stupidity of racial prejudice and class bias—is appropriate for all of the world. Indeed, much of his love of humanity and of democracy stems from his early life in Pennsylvania. Michener never had a birth certificate, nor does he know who his parents were, or where or when he was born. His widowed, Quaker foster mother Mabel Michener, who raised five waifs beside her own son, earned a precarious living embroidering buttonholes on women's shirtwaists, which Michener picked up and delivered in Philadelphia. When times were particularly hard, young Michener lived in the Bucks County poorhouse near Doylestown, where destitute inmates kindly shared hoarded delicacies, such as margarine, with him. After being graduated from Doylestown grammar school at fourteen, Michener bummed around the country, and the fifty-odd families that fed and housed him confirmed his optimistic view of human nature. Experience taught him that virtue had no connection with ancestors, wealth, or status, that worthy individuals could be found everywhere in all conditions. Attending Doylestown High School while holding a variety of jobs, Michener excelled in both sports and studies and earned a scholarship to

James A. Michener; his recurring theme is the
stupidity of racial prejudice and class bias.
(Ellen Levine)

Swarthmore College. A few months before the stock market crash, he graduated *summa cum
laude,* having majored in English and history, and began his teaching career at Hill School,
Pottstown. After teaching at George School near Doylestown, Colorado State College at
Greeley, and Harvard University's School of Education, Michener became high school textbook editor for the Macmillan Company.

When World War II came Michener joined the navy. He served in the South Pacific,
where he visited about fifty islands and atolls. While writing reports and histories for the
navy, he was also gathering material for his Pulitzer Prize–winning first novel, *Tales of
the South Pacific* (1947). When Richard Rodgers and Oscar Hammerstein based their hit
musical *South Pacific* on Michener's book, they generously made him part owner of the
play. These royalties and returns freed him to write whatever he wished.

Experimenting with many forms, Michener has been versatile and prolific. His second
book *The Fires of Spring* (1949) was a sentimental and contrived autobiographical novel,
while his next, *Return to Paradise* (1951)—called "a Gunther with a dash or two of Dr.
Kinsey"—brilliantly combined factual essays on nine regions with stories illustrating their
salient characteristics. Michener based *The Voice of Asia* (1951) on 120 lengthy interviews
from which he constructed fifty-three vignettes supplemented by knowledgeable observations ranging from Japan through Pakistan. Among Michener's other books are his passionate report on the Hungarian revolution, *The Bridge at Andau* (1957); *Hawaii* (1959), in which
he tells the story of Hawaii from its geological beginnings through the mingling of the

Polynesian, American, Chinese, and Japanese peoples in the state; *Report of the County Chairman* (1961), recounting his participation in the 1960 campaign and revealing a slice of Pennsylvania politics on the local level; *Caravans* (1963), a novel on Afganistan; *The Source* (1965), a novel on archaeology in Israel; *Iberia: Spanish Travels and Reflections* (1968); and *Presidential Lottery: The Reckless Gamble in Our Electoral System* (1969). In 1971 Michener focused with tolerance and understanding but not enthusiasm on the new life-styles of disaffected young Americans in *Kent State,* a detailed report of the 1970 shooting at Kent State University, and in a novel *The Drifters.*

Michener is a man with a message. Moralistic and optimistic, he believes that man is a rational being who can improve himself, that mankind can progress. He is neither a realist nor a naturalist but a latter-day muckraking, crusading novelist in the tradition of Jack London or Upton Sinclair. In book after book he teaches and preaches his Quaker version of the brotherhood of man. This message sometimes gets in the way of characterization, as does his fascination with history. Unlike O'Hara, Michener revels in adjectives and adverbs, metaphors and similes; but although his imagery is occasionally strained, his writing is vivid. Like O'Hara he is a historian and a reporter, and his history and reports from Israel to Hawaii, from Hungary to Bucks County, are informative and engrossing. But it is Michener's skill as a novelist, utilizing his ability to report and to recount history, that will make his work endure.

More than a generation separates John Updike (b. 1932) from O'Hara and Michener. As a

John Updike, a superb stylist who examines the meaning of life. (Michael Chikiris)

boy in Shillington, as an adolescent on a nearby farm, as a student in the high school where his father taught, at Harvard, and at Oxford, and as a young man of thirty acclaimed the "most talented writer of his age in America," Updike suffered neither from the poverty that plagued Michener nor from the lack of social status that nagged O'Hara. His background did not compel him to write about individual failures and class differences or about social and political problems but freed him to transcend these themes to explore in parables the meaning of life itself.

A superb stylist whose stories are frequently set in Pennsylvania, Updike has struggled to keep his verbal brilliance from overpowering his serious insight. He began to examine the meaning of life and death in *The Poorhouse Fair* (1958) and continued examining it in *Rabbit, Run* (1960), an existentialist novel in which the hero Rabbit both flees the responsibilities of adulthood and searches for meaning in his seemingly meaningless existence. Ten years later in *Rabbit, Redux* (1971), the hero is an older, serene "inversion from his mobile, restless earlier self," but the banality and boredom of middle-class life remains. Updike amplifies his existentialist view in *Pigeon Feathers* (1962) and *The Centaur* (1963). The fear and threat of death and the poignance of life are the themes of these works. Although the oblivion that awaits us "gives death its terror and life its poignance," Updike offers hope by arguing that oblivion need not be complete. Even though the details of our lives are irrevocably lost, our values can be transmitted to our children from generation to generation. Furthermore, ceremonies, particularly of a religious nature, can help man cope with ultimate nothingness.

Updike has shunned political themes but helps us understand contemporary society. "I am convinced," he remarked, "that the life of a nation is reflected, or distorted, by private people and their minute concerns." While Updike's writings take a dim view of contemporary social and cultural development, he believes individuals capable of achieving nobility of character. Life means what one chooses it to mean, man determines his own destiny. In short, "right and wrong aren't dropped from the sky. We. We make them."

THE DANCE

Theatrical activity in twentieth-century Philadelphia has been "largely confined to Broadway tryouts," but Philadelphia has continued to excel in ballet. America's three greatest dancers in the nineteenth century—Augusta Maywood, Mary Ann Lee, and George Washington Smith—were all Philadelphians. In the 1930s Catherine and Dorothie Littlefield formed the Littlefield Ballet, which as the Philadelphia Ballet survived until 1942. It was the first native American company, it produced Tchaikovsky's complete *Sleeping Beauty* in 1935, and in 1937 it became the first American company to tour Europe. The ballet returned to Philadelphia in the summer of 1963 with the debut of the Pennsylvania Ballet. With courage and skill its director Barbara Weisberger built an exciting ensemble and repertory. Aided by the New York City Ballet—particularly its director George Balanchine—and by the Ford Foundation, Miss Weisberger developed a remarkably promising company in a very short time. Her repertory was international in scope, balancing modern classics with new works and reflecting the honest quality of the company. Although she initially invited guest artists, Miss Weisberger soon resolved to give the Pennsylvania Ballet a character and personality of its own. By 1968 it had invaded Broadway and was acclaimed for "the blissful exuberance, the unblasé brilliance, that sometimes young companies do possess, and which makes up for almost any amount of the finer points of choreographic grooming."

MUSIC

Throughout most of the twentieth century Philadelphia and Pittsburgh have claimed two of the nation's finest symphony orchestras. The Pittsburgh Symphony was founded in 1896, attained eminence and toured under Victor Herbert but unfortunately broke up in 1910. It was revived in 1927, became a world-renowned orchestra under its Hungarian-born director Fritz Reiner, and its international reputation was sustained in the 1960s by Reiner's successor William Steinberg. In music Pittsburgh became and remained one of the nation's most polished cities.

The Philadelphia Orchestra was established in 1900 on a base of nineteenth-century professional and amateur organizations. It was even more fortunate than the Pittsburgh Symphony in its leaders, including its first director Fritz Scheel. Leopold Stokowski—a successor to Scheel—modestly declared: "The man who really made the Philadelphia Orchestra from a musical standpoint, is Fritz Scheel. . . . He must have had very high musical ideals. They are evident in everything he did. Also he must have had a wonderful

William Steinberg, director of the Pittsburgh Symphony Orchestra. (Pittsburgh Symphony Society)

Eugene Ormandy and Leopold Stokowski of the Philadelphia Orchestra. (Adrian Siegel)

faculty for choosing the highest type of artists for the orchestra. . . . It was Scheel's vision that laid such a wonderful foundation for this orchestra. . . ."

Despite his praise of Scheel, Leopold Stokowski, who took over the Philadelphia Orchestra in 1912, brought it worldwide recognition. Stokowski scolded Philadelphians for their hats and their noise and for their indifference to contemporary and unusual music, which he successfully sold them by mingling it with the familiar on his programs. In this way he retained and educated old friends while making new friends, and in time achieved his aim "to make the spectacular the usual." Most notable was Stokowski's successful production of Gustav Mahler's Eighth Symphony which required a chorus of nearly a thousand voices to sing with the orchestra, but the Philadelphia Orchestra under Stokowski gave the American premiers of many other composers, including Strauss, Rachmaninoff, Stravinsky, Debussy, Sibelius, Bartok, Schoenberg, Prokofieff, and Shostakovitch. Stokowski also began developing and perfecting the "Philadelphia sound" which has become the orchestra's hallmark.

The Philadelphia Orchestra maintained its superb reputation under Eugene Ormandy, who in 1938 was musical director and co-conductor with Stokowski. Although Ormandy boasted with some justification, "The Philadelphia sound, it's me," other factors also contribute to the sound and to the technical virtuosity of the orchestra. Important among these factors are that in sixty years the orchestra has had only two regular conductors, that its players have much pride and esprit de corps, that its stringed instruments are priceless, and that it is linked with the Curtis Institute of Music, from which more than half its members have been graduated. Founded and endowed in 1924 by Mrs. Edward Bok, the Curtis Institute has always had as teachers the first-desk players of the Philadelphia Orchestra. The close association of these two institutions has helped them achieve and maintain greatness and has made Philadelphia a leading center for musicians and music lovers. It is no wonder that the Philadelphia Orchestra is renowned as America's greatest orchestra.

ART

Although in his prime Eakins seemed to have had little influence on his contemporaries either in Philadelphia or elsewhere, time proved his influence on American art to be monumental. Through his disciple Thomas Pollock Anshutz (1851–1912), Eakin's strong, realist tradition influenced many younger artists and made Philadelphia "the cradle of artistic realism." The catalyzing agent in this school of realism was Robert Henri (1865–1929) who came to Philadelphia at twenty-one to study with Anshutz at the Pennsylvania Academy of Fine Arts. Henri later went on the first of his many sojourns to Paris, where he was dissatisfied with the way painting was taught and supplemented his studies with viewing old masters. He became especially fond of Frans Hals, Velasquez, Rembrandt, Goya, and Manet. He abandoned the sentimental landscapes and period costumes that were the hallmarks of contemporary art and worked to get his sitters' personalities on canvas in warm-blooded, realistic portraits.

Like Eakins and Anshutz, Henri was a superb teacher as well as a gifted artist. His one-man show in 1907 at the Pennsylvania Academy showed him to be an outstanding American artist. Called the greatest single influence in American art, Henri's personal magnetism caused pupils and disciples to cluster about him first in Philadelphia and later in New York, where his influence extended to most of the best young artists painting there during his lifetime. To Henri art was a medium with which to express life, and the distinguishing mark of all great men was their humanity. Making pictures from life was his great message, and an ethical concept of justice was basic to his character. Henri's radical teaching put truth above tradition and expounded Whitman's ideal of a brotherhood of free individuals. Although Henri was voted one of the three most important living American artists in 1929, he was a greater teacher than a painter. His art fell short of his ideal. Influenced by his radical reputation and his belief in the new, contemporary critics emphasized his break with the past, but his work now is placed in the older tradition of Sargent, Chase, and Duveneck.

Foremost in Henri's Philadelphia circle was a group of young newspaper artists most of whom worked for the Philadelphia *Press* as well as for other publications, illustrating stories and news accounts in the 1890s. Members of this group, who would later with Henri become the Philadelphia Five, important in the realist movement as the builders of the Ash Can school, were John Sloan (1871–1951), William James Glackens (1870–1938), George Benjamin Luks (1867–1933), and Everett Shinn (1876–1953). These newspaper artists had all studied at the Pennsylvania Academy, but probably would not have become serious painters without the influence of Henri. He urged them to paint the life familiar to them as newspapermen and helped form their philosophies of life during the Thursday evenings they spent together in his studio at 806 Walnut Street. In their evenings together they learned from Henri the principles on which the Ash Can school was founded: truth above beauty, life before art, and the real rather than the artificial.

Etching by John Sloan, *Memory* (1906). Left to right: Robert and Linda Henri, Dolly and John Sloan. (Philadelphia Museum of Art)

With magazines leaving Philadelphia for New York and the Sunday newspaper supplement also originating there, work became scarce in Philadelphia, and one by one members of the group gravitated to New York. John Sloan, who had been born in Lock Haven and had moved to Philadelphia when he was six, was the last to go. Many of Sloan's early-twentieth-century pictures record simple acts of living glimpsed from the back window of his studio, at McSorley's bar, or along the street, and are rich in truth and gentle pathos. A superb recorder of both atmosphere and character, Sloan had technical skill to match his warmth as an individual and was probably the most outstanding painter of the Ash Can school.

Born in Philadelphia, where his ancestors had lived for many years, William Glackens was a realist more because he had been a reporter than because of social beliefs. Called by Sloan "the greatest draughtsman . . . this side of the ocean," Glackens easily remembered details for his illustrations, such as those of the drills, girders, and cranes of the Baldwin Locomotive Works in Philadelphia, even when he knew nothing of their function. Covering the Spanish-American War in Cuba for *McClure's Magazine,* he produced drawings that are now valued as historical documents. Possessing a lively sense of the comic, he sometimes painted New York slum dwellers because they appeared uninhibited and seemed to be having a good time, but he also painted elegant scenes. By the time of the 1913 Armory Show, Glackens painted in hot reds and purples and had more in common with Renoir than did any other American.

The most colorful founder of the Ash Can school was George Luks, the son of a Williamsport physician. Boastful, talented, proud, and vigorous, "Lusty Luks" was a born storyteller who identified with the lower classes and through his knowledge of coal mining and wrestling fabricated a past for himself. Admiring and usually painting people of the slums, Luks found in them an exuberance to match his own. Haunting New York's East Side for subjects, he became a well-known figure in his broad-brimmed black hat. An uneven painter sometimes unable to plan or to sustain his efforts, Luks also lacked critical ability, but like Frans Hals with whom he is frequently compared, he had spontaneity and he had vigor. These qualities gave many of Luks's paintings a life of their own and placed him with the best of his American contemporaries.

The youngest of the Philadelphia Five, Everett Shinn came to Philadelphia from New Jersey more interested in engineering than in art. First a mechanical drafter, he became a newspaper illustrator and studied five years at the Pennsylvania Academy. Always primarily interested in the theater, Shinn soon moved from the orbit of Manet to that of Degas. He painted many of his era's leading theatrical figures, decorated their homes, and wrote numerous plays. In his work as a decorator, Shinn forsook realism and developed a version of French Rococo. But his realistic paintings, rendered early in the century, make him a worthy member of the Philadelphia Five. In 1911 Shinn returned to realism briefly when he broke with tradition and painted murals for the Trenton City Hall commemorating "not past glories but present ones." In his old age when the Ash Can school had become historically important and of the Five only he and Sloan were living, Shinn painted and readily sold vaudeville scenes reminiscent of his early paintings.

The Armory Show, which introduced Americans to modern art in 1913, influenced both the reputations and paintings of the Five. By placing Henri and his followers next to French Cubists, this show partially sheared these Americans of their radical reputation and led some of them away from realism. Even so Henri paid lip service to the new, as was his habit. He urged artists "to pierce to the core of the modern movement and not to be confused by its sensational exterior." The Armory Show had shifted the position of Philadelphia's giants in art. Looking beyond Henri and his group for the roots of realism, the Armory Show had discovered Thomas Eakins and three years before his death had enshrined him as one of the great figures of American art.

It was no accident that all five of the early founders of the Ash Can school had studied at the Pennsylvania Academy of Art. Its position in art was comparable to the position in music held by the Curtis Institute or the Julliard School. In the decades both before and after 1776 Philadelphia was unsurpassed as an art center. It was logical that the academy should be founded there in 1805. Stressing fundamentals rather than fads and amassing an excellent collection of American art, the academy became the nation's most important art school, and its Annual Exhibition of American Painting became a prestigious affair. As the nineteenth century ended and the twentieth century began, its position in American art was colossal. In recent decades it had produced Thomas Eakins, Mary Cassatt, and Henry Tanner; and more recently it had schooled Robert Henri and his four associates who had changed the direction of American art. But as the twentieth century wore on, it became apparent that the nation's most venerable art institution was out of touch and living on past glory. The academy bestirred itself, however, after 1962. No longer content to rest on past achievements, it inspired Philadelphians to give it some financial aid as well as veneration. With support and planning, it should be able to approach its reputation of the past.

The most-appreciated American artist of the midtwentieth century, Andrew Wyeth lives in Chadds Ford, where he was born in 1917. Wyeth comes from a family of painters; his father N. C. Wyeth was the most famous illustrator of his generation, Wyeth's sisters are artists, and his son James while still in his youth produced an incredibly lifelike portrait

Tempera by Andrew Wyeth, *Ground Hog Day*
(1959). (Philadelphia Museum of Art)

of President John F. Kennedy. Wyeth's first one-man show, held when he was twenty and stocked with brilliant water colors, was an immediate success. Now an unexcelled painter in tempera who prefers subdued colors, Wyeth has not let success stunt his talent. He has continued to grow in both depth and technical skill.

Like Thomas Eakins, Wyeth has his own brand of realism, and like Eakins he is content to live in the area of his birth and childhood, maintaining a close relationship with his family and the landscape and objects familiar to his youth. Also like Eakins, Wyeth paints portraits in uncompromising detail, yet is not content to be a human camera. In their pictures, both artists create a mood which envelops the viewer and if he is in the least perceptive takes him beyond the familiar views and the faces of ordinary people. Despite his realism, there is an abstract undercurrent in Wyeth's work; he judges his paintings by how forcefully this undercurrent makes itself felt.

"If I have anything to offer," Wyeth says, "it is my emotional contact with the place where I live and the people I do." His paintings have made his vast audience aware of the subtle, changing beauty of the Pennsylvania countryside. "I paint these hills here," Wyeth explains, "not because they're better than other hills. It's that I was born here. And I can do an awful lot of thinking and dreaming about the past and future—the timelessness of these rocks and these hills—about all the people who have existed here."

Unlike Eakins's contemporaries who refused to accept his realism, Wyeth's contemporaries applaud his portrayals and flock to see his paintings. Wyeth's roots in the rural past seem deep enough to steady his viewers, as well as himself, amid the many changes of time. His pictures help dwellers in an urban world remember and interpret their almost forgotten past. They appreciate Wyeth for taking time to discover what Richard Meryman has termed, "the richness, the dignity, and sadness unnoticed behind the menial and the strange" and for picturing with splendid technical skill that which their subconscious only dimly remembers or realizes.

ARCHITECTURE

The modern skyscraper, utilizing structural steel and the elevator, had evolved by the turn of the century. Its chief exponent was Daniel Hudson Burnham (1846–1912), a practical Chicago architect, to whom Pennsylvanians turned because he knew how to make a commercial building a paying enterprise. Burnham designed the John Wanamaker store (1902–1910) in Philadelphia, the Frick Building (1902) in Pittsburgh, and the Union or Pennsylvania Railroad Station (1900–1903), also in Pittsburgh, with its large, pleasing rotunda, which is considered one of the finest architectural spaces in Pittsburgh. A twenty-storied, column-like tower, the Frick Building, like the Wanamaker store, has the traditional three-part

Ceiling of the rotunda of the Pennsylvania Railroad Station (1900–1903), Daniel H. Burnham, architect. The profligately detailed ceiling of this wide, low dome forms a stunning circle in a square. (Pittsburgh History & Landmarks Foundation)

division of classical antiquity: a templelike base, a relatively plain midsection, and a boldly projecting cornice top. Built a section at a time so business could continue during construction, the Wanamaker store reconciled Renaissance design with modern construction and functionalism. Its 45 acres of floor space made it the world's largest building devoted to retail merchandising. Like the Pittsburgh railroad station rotunda, its great covered court is a pleasing and well-executed architectural space.

In the twenties and thirties the earlier tradition of Creative Eclecticism was carried on by a number of competent architects. The most influential and best known of these was Paul Philippe Cret (1876–1945) of the University of Pennsylvania. Cret left his native France in 1903 after students and alumni of the University of Pennsylvania department of architecture collected the money to induce him to come. Cret decisively influenced architecture in this country both through his own designs and through those of three generations of students. In World War I Cret lost his hearing, and later cancer of the throat caused total loss of speech. Writing "I would rather be deaf and dumb than blind," he continued to teach and work at his drawing board designing numerous buildings, bridges, and monuments. Besides many important works outside of Pennsylvania and buildings and bridges in Philadelphia, Cret designed the Market Street Bridge in Harrisburg, the Valley Forge Arch, and the Peace Memorial at Gettysburg. Carefully planned with good proportions, Cret's buildings expressed his individuality. The Rodin Museum (1929) on the Benjamin Franklin Parkway shows his tasteful handling of the classical tradition, but his talent is especially apparent in his design for the Federal Reserve Bank of Philadelphia (1932–1936). Although the general organization of the design is Greek, as is the sparse ornamental detail, only the classic spirit remains in Cret's free adaptation, which carefully takes into account modern technology and structural methods.

Cret's interest in new technical developments led him to design streamlined passenger railroad cars for Philadelphia's Edward G. Budd Manufacturing Company and even a locomotive for the Reading Railroad. His technical side and love of utilitarian beauty also made him a superb bridge designer. Cret and his architectural firm working with the engineering firm of Modjeski and Masters are responsible for all three Philadelphia bridges that cross the Delaware River—the Benjamin Franklin Bridge (1926; at first called simply the Delaware River Bridge), the Tacony-Palmyra Bridge (1929), and the Walt Whitman Bridge

Architect's drawing by Paul P. Cret of the Delaware River Bridge (later renamed the Benjamin F. Franklin Bridge). It conveys the image of a majestic waterbird in flight. (Delaware River Port Authority of Pennsylvania and New Jersey)

(1958), designed by Cret's partners, Harbeson, Hough, Livingston, and Larson, who continued his firm under their own names. Cret also helped with initial designs for the Benjamin Franklin Parkway and selected the site for the Philadelphia Museum of Art. In 1931 Philadelphia presented him with the Bok Prize for distinguished public service, and in 1938 he received the Gold Medal, the highest award of the American Institute of Architects.

George Howe (1886–1955), who like Cret used the forms of the past with taste and professional success, shocked Philadelphia when in 1928 he left the firm of Mellor, Meigs & Howe to practice the "modern system of design." A well-to-do and well-connected Philadelphian who in his old firm had practiced as an individual, Howe took with him an important corporate client, the president and board of the Philadelphia Saving Fund Society (PSFS), for whom he had designed several branch offices. In 1929 they decided to construct a building which would provide an income from office rental as well as banking space. Howe and his new partner, William Lescaze (1896–1969), presented their design for the building. Refusing to accept the plan, members of the board of the Philadelphia Saving Fund Society complained that it looked like a loft and requested more vertical exterior lines. Howe tactfully explained that the horizontal look was both natural and necessary since the supports in a skyscraper's steel frame are "the continuous horizontal brackets" at each floor. In the end Howe's tact, his reputation, and the fact that he was an established Philadelphian made modern architecture not only acceptable to the bank's board but respectable in Philadelphia fifteen years before it was generally accepted in America. The 27-foot neon

PSFS Building (1930–1932), George Howe and William Lescaze, architects. (Historical Society of Pennsylvania)

The Alfred Newton Richards Medical Research
Building (1959–1960), Louis I. Kahn, architect.
Its functional design creates a powerful and
original abstract pattern. (University of Pennsylvania)

sign which tops the building has made the letters PSFS known to every Philadelphian. Called
at the time of Howe's death the finest skyscraper in America, the PSFS Building (1930–1932)
was the first large commercial building in America to exploit new materials and methods
fully, without obscuring them with historic styles and details.

Howe also designed Square Shadows (1934) built in Whitemarsh and usually listed as the
first large modern-designed house in the East. The first house to have a central air-con-
ditioning system, Square Shadows coupled the International style with the use of local
materials, but it stands out in its surroundings rather than blending with them as does
Falling Water (1936), the western Pennsylvania summer retreat on Bear Run (Fayette
County) designed by Frank Lloyd Wright (1869-1959) for Edgar Kaufmann. Called "a match-
less fusion of fantasy and engineering," Falling Water is built over a waterfall and anchored
in nearby stone. A splendid example of Wright's genius, this vacation home, now open to the
public, is "permeated with the vigor of an organic growth." Wright ranks with foremost
American figures in the creative arts, and Pennsylvania is fortunate in having within its
boundaries this famous creation of his.

With the Lankenau Hospital and Health Center (1953–1959) at Overbrook and the
Alfred Newton Richards Medical Research Building (1959–1960) at the University of
Pennsylvania, Philadelphia maintained the leadership in medical buildings which was begun

more than two centuries before with the Pennsylvania Hospital. Designed by Vincent G. Kling (b.1916) and built of warm salmon-colored Roman brick, the Lankenau Hospital exploits the different levels of its site by varying the height and position of its buildings, located atop a former golf course. Planned by Louis I. Kahn (b.1901) as a monument to functionalism, the Newton Richards Medical Research Building generated admiration even before it was completed and was tagged by many as the greatest building of the decade or even of the century.

In midtwentieth century both Philadelphia and Pittsburgh participated in gigantic urban renewal programs. In 1948 the Federal government began work on the area east of Independence Hall. Many important early buildings such as Blodgett's Bank, the Second Bank of the United States, and the Philadelphia Exchange were restored and preserved, but other important buildings including the Jayne Building were demolished because they were built after the cutoff period—the Greek Revival stage in American architecture. Many citizens, who have criticized the scheme as one to embalm Georgian structures in an attempt to make Philadelphia another Williamsburg, have preferred their city's own approach in the restoration of Society Hill. Here buildings out of place in a residential area have been removed, and garden areas and footpaths have been built, as have multistory apartment buildings, such as the one designed by I. M. Pei & Associates in 1958, which mingle with historical buildings of various vintages. The area has become a living and lived-in medley of past and present.

In Pittsburgh, before the point of the Golden Triangle (where the Allegheny and Monongahela rivers meet) could be renewed, both smoke and flood control had to be promised

The Golden Triangle in 1971. (United States Steel)

would-be investors. In a gigantic effort to prevent an exodus from their city, Mayor David Lawrence, Richard Mellon, and other Democrats and Republicans worked together in numerous agencies of which the most important was the Allegheny Conference on Community Development(ACCD). For decades there had been plans to refurbish the point of the Golden Triangle, but these plans were stymied by clashes between those insisting that Fort Pitt be restored in its entirety and those insisting that existing traffic routes and bridges be preserved. The deadlock was broken when the ACCD, through the Point Park Committee under Arthur Van Buskirk, began coordinating the project and persuaded the Equitable Life Assurance Society to invest in it. As was later noted, "The whole program was put together before a single shovel of earth was turned." Construction on Gateway Center, "the catalyst of the downtown building revival," which bordered on Point State Park, started in 1950 and between then and the mid-1960s twelve new buildings were built in the immediate area, and more than 25 percent of the whole 330-acre Golden Triangle was rebuilt.

But scant attention was given to architectural planning. The Regional Planning Association complained that the strong areas of the renewed section—Point State Park, Gateway Center, Mellon Square (a block-size parklet topping an underground garage given to the city by three Mellon foundations), and the Civic Auditorium—were related neither to each other nor to their surroundings. The association proposed a series of parks, squares, and walkways as well as extensive landscaping. In 1967 a group of Pittsburgh architects and artists joined the protest by vowing that they would no longer silently watch "our City being defaced by thoughtless buildings and projects." To these protests were added the angry voices of blacks who were no longer willing to be uprooted by urban renewal, which by 1966 had displaced 5,400 families and only provided 1,719 new housing units, few of which were for low-income families. These pressures brought promise of change; the ACCD revised its priorities in the late 1960s and emerged newly committed to a social renaissance.

BIBLIOGRAPHY

On primary and secondary education, see "Education in Pennsylvania," in *The Pennsylvania Manual 1968–1969* (1969); Maurice J. Thomas: *The Educational Challenge, It Can Be Met: An Appraisal and Some Considerations of Educational Needs in Pennsylvania* (c. 1960); and National Education Association: *Rankings of the States: 1970* (1970).

On higher education, see William S. Learned and Ben D. Wood: *The Student and His Knowledge: A Report to the Carnegie Foundation on the Results of the High School and College Examinations of 1928, 1930, and 1932* (1938), and a pamphlet based on that study, *How Good Are Our Colleges?* (1938); and the excellent *Critique of a College* [Swarthmore] (1967). Other useful studies of individual institutions are Richard H. Shryock: *The University of Pennsylvania Faculty: A Study in American Higher Education* (1959); George W. Corner: *Two Centuries of Medicine: A History of the School of Medicine, University of Pennsylvania* (1965); Wayland Fuller Dunaway: *History of the Pennsylvania State College* (1946); and Cornelia Meigs: *What Makes a College? A History of Bryn Mawr* (1956). For comparisons among universities and colleges, see Allan M. Cartter: *An Assessment of Quality in Graduate Education* (1966).

On Philadelphia newspapers, see Frank Luther Mott: *American Journalism, A History: 1690–1960* (1962); Oswald Garrison Villard: *The Disappearing Daily: Chapters in American Newspaper Evolution* (1944); and J. David Stern: *Memoirs of a Maverick Publisher* (1962). For the rise and fall of the *Saturday Evening Post*, see Theodore Peterson: *Magazines in the Twentieth Century* (1956); Frank Luther Mott:

A History of American Magazines: 1885–1905 (1957); Otto Friedrich: *Decline and Fall* (1970); and Robert E. Bedingfield and Israel Shenker: "Saturday Evening Post Comes to End Today," *New York Times* (Jan. 10, 1969).

On O'Hara, Sheldon Norman Grebstein: *John O'Hara* (1966) is particularly useful, but also see Edward Russell Carson, *The Fiction of John O'Hara* (1961); Alden Whitman: "O'Hara, in Rare Interview, Calls Literary Landscape Fairly Bleak," *New York Times* (Nov. 13, 1967); and Don A. Schanche: "John O'Hara Is Alive and Well in the First Half of the Twentieth Century," *Esquire* (August 1969), pp. 84–86, 142, 146–149. On Michener, A. Grove Day: *James A. Michener* (1964) is particularly useful since Day collaborated with Michener on *Rascals in Paradise*. On Updike, see the very useful Howard M. Harper, Jr.: *A Study of Bellow, Salinger, Mailer, Baldwin and Updike* (1967) as well as David D. Galloway: *The Absurd Hero in American Fiction: Updike, Styron, Bellow, Salinger* (1966); Alice Hamilton and Kenneth Hamilton: *The Elements of John Updike* (1970); Arthur Mizener: "Behind the Dazzle Is a Knowing Eye," *New York Times Book Review,* (Mar. 8, 1962); and Henry Raymont: "John Updike Completes a Sequel to 'Rabbit, Run,'" *New York Times* (July 27, 1971).

On the Pennsylvania Ballet, see three articles by Clive Barnes: *New York Times* (Jan. 28, Jan. 30, and Feb. 3, 1968). On music, see George Naugle: "Downbeat at 8:30," *Commonwealth: The Magazine for Pennsylvania* (July 1947), pp. 15–16; James R. Hayes: "Pittsburgh Finds Its Soul," *Commonwealth* (March 1948), pp. 17–18; Robert A. Gerson: *Music in Philadelphia: A History of Philadelphia Music, A Summary of Its Current State, and a Comprehensive Index Dictionary* (1940); and Herbert Kupferberg: *Those Fabulous Philadelphians: The Life and Times of a Great Orchestra* (1969).

On art and architecture in general, see Oliver W. Larkin: *Art and Life in America* (1949). For information on the Ash Can school and its position in American art, see Milton W. Brown: *American Painting from the Armory Show to the Depression* (1955); Van Wyck Brooks: *John Sloan: A Painter's Life* (1955); and John Sloan: *Gist of Art* (1939). For pictures by these artists, see *Catalogue of a Memorial Exhibition of the Work of Robert Henri* (1931); and the following volumes in the American Artists Series of the Whitney Museum of American Art: Helen Appleton Read: *Robert Henri* (1931); Guy Pène Du Bois: *John Sloan* (1931), and *William J. Glackens* (1931); and Elizabeth L. Gary: *George Luks* (1931). The best book on Wyeth, his art, and his world is Richard Meryman: *Andrew Wyeth* (1968).

On Pennsylvania architecture, see Harold E. Dickson: *One Hundred Pennsylvania Buildings* (1954); and Irwin Richman: *Pennsylvania's Architecture* (1969). The best book on Philadelphia architecture is George B. Tatum: *Penn's Great Town* (1961). For additional information on Cret, see Homer T. Rosenberger: "Paul Philippe Cret (1876–1945)," *Cosmos Club Bulletin* (June 1961), pp. 2–5. For information on the Pittsburgh renaissance, see Roy Lubove: *Twentieth Century Pittsburgh: Government, Business and Environmental Change* (1969).

APPENDICES

Chief Executives of the Commonwealth of Pennsylvania

UNDER THE CONSTITUTION OF 1776
PRESIDENTS OF THE SUPREME EXECUTIVE COUNCIL

	Term began
Thomas Wharton, Jr.	1777
George Bryan, Acting President	May–Dec. 1778
Joseph Reed	1778
William Moore	1781
John Dickinson	1782
Benjamin Franklin	1785
Thomas Mifflin	1788

UNDER THE CONSTITUTION OF 1790
GOVERNORS OF THE COMMONWEALTH

Thomas Mifflin (No party)	
Thomas McKean (Jeffersonian)	1790
Simon Snyder (Jeffersonian, New School)	1799
William Findlay (Jeffersonian, New School)	1808
Joseph Hiester (Jeffersonian, Old School)	1817
John A. Schulze (Jeffersonian, Adams)	1820
George Wolf (Jacksonian Democrat)	1823
Joseph Ritner (Anti-Mason)	1829
	1835

UNDER THE CONSTITUTION OF 1838

David R. Porter (Jacksonian Democrat)	1839
Francis R. Shunk (Jacksonian Democrat)	1845
William F. Johnston (Whig)	1848
William Bigler (Democrat)	1852
James Pollock (Whig–Know-Nothing)	1855
William F. Packer (Democrat)	1858
Andrew G. Curtin (Republican-People's)	1861
John W. Geary (Republican)	1867
John F. Hartranft (Republican)	1873

UNDER THE CONSTITUTION OF 1873

John F. Hartranft (Republican)	1876
Henry M. Hoyt (Republican)	1879
Robert E. Pattison (Democrat)	1883
James A. Beaver (Republican)	1887
Robert E. Pattison (Democrat)	1891
Daniel H. Hastings (Republican)	1895
William A. Stone (Republican)	1899
Samuel W. Pennypacker (Republican)	1903
Edwin S. Stuart (Republican)	1907
John K. Tener (Republican)	1911
Martin G. Brumbaugh (Republican)	1915
William C. Sproul (Republican)	1919
Gifford Pinchot (Republican)	1923
John S. Fisher (Republican)	1927
Gifford Pinchot (Republican)	1931
George H. Earle (Democrat)	1935
Arthur H. James (Republican)	1939
Edward Martin (Republican)	1943
John C. Bell, Jr. (Republican)	1947
James H. Duff (Republican)	1947
John S. Fine (Republican)	1951
George M. Leader (Democrat)	1955
David L. Lawrence (Democrat)	1959
William W. Scranton (Republican)	1963
Raymond P. Shafer (Republican)	1967
Milton E. Shapp (Democrat)	1971

Several discrepancies in the length of terms of office arose from the following circumstances: Thomas Wharton, Jr., died in office, 1778; Francis Shunk resigned in 1848 before his term expired; John C. Bell, Jr., served briefly in 1947 when Governor Edward Martin resigned to enter the U.S. Senate.

Organization of Counties by Order of Creation and Date

1. 1682 Bucks
2. 1682 Chester
3. 1682 Philadelphia
4. 1729 Lancaster
5. 1749 York
6. 1750 Cumberland
7. 1752 Berks
8. 1752 Northampton
9. 1771 Bedford
10. 1772 Northumberland
11. 1773 Westmoreland
12. 1781 Washington
13. 1783 Fayette
14. 1784 Franklin
15. 1784 Montgomery
16. 1785 Dauphin
17. 1786 Luzerne
18. 1787 Huntingdon
19. 1788 Allegheny
20. 1789 Delaware
21. 1789 Mifflin
22. 1795 Somerset
23. 1795 Lycoming
24. 1796 Greene
25. 1798 Wayne
26. 1800 Armstrong
27. 1800 Adams
28. 1800 Butler
29. 1800 Beaver
30. 1800 Centre
31. 1800 Crawford
32. 1800 Erie
33. 1800 Mercer
34. 1800 Venango
35. 1800 Warren
36. 1803 Indiana
37. 1804 Jefferson
38. 1804 McKean
39. 1804 Potter
40. 1804 Tioga
41. 1804 Cambria
42. 1804 Clearfield
43. 1810 Bradford
44. 1810 Susquehanna
45. 1811 Schuylkill
46. 1812 Lehigh
47. 1813 Lebanon
48. 1813 Columbia
49. 1813 Union
50. 1814 Pike
51. 1820 Perry
52. 1831 Juniata
53. 1836 Monroe
54. 1839 Clarion
55. 1839 Clinton
56. 1842 Wyoming
57. 1843 Carbon
58. 1843 Elk
59. 1846 Blair
60. 1847 Sullivan
61. 1848 Forest
62. 1849 Lawrence
63. 1850 Fulton
64. 1850 Montour
65. 1855 Snyder
66. 1860 Cameron
67. 1878 Lackawanna

COUNTY MAP

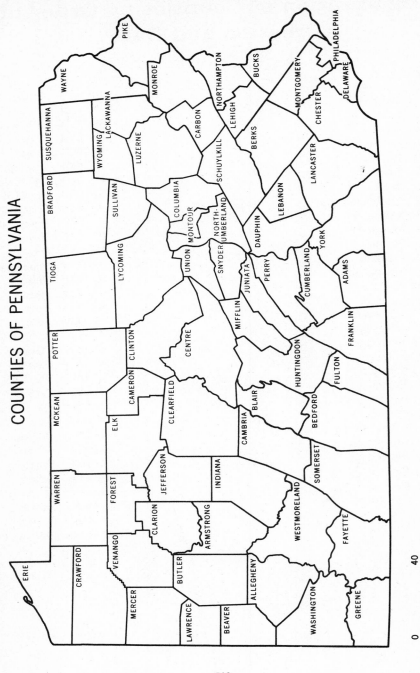

COUNTIES OF PENNSYLVANIA

508

Index

75744